Spillmon

Exam 70-536: *Microsoft .NET Framework—Application Development Foundation, Second Edition*

Objective	Location in Book
Developing applications that use system types and collections	
Manage data in a .NET Framework application by using .NET Framework system types.	Chapter 1, Lessons 1, 2, and 4
Manage a group of associated data in a .NET Framework application by using collections.	Chapter 4, Lesson 1
Improve type safety and application performance in a .NET Framework application by using generic collections.	Chapter 4, Lesson 2
Manage data in a .NET Framework application by using specialized collections.	Chapter 4, Lesson 1
Implement .NET Framework interfaces to cause components to comply with standard contracts.	Chapter 1, Lesson 3
Control interactions between .NET Framework application components by using events and delegates.	Chapter 1, Lesson 3
Implementing service processes, threading, and application domains in a .NET Framework application	
Implement, install, and control a service.	Chapter 8, Lesson 3
Develop multithreaded .NET applications.	Chapter 7, Lessons 1 and 2
Create a unit of isolation for common language runtime within a .NET Framework application by using application domains.	Chapter 8, Lessons 1 and 2
Embedding configuration, diagnostic, management, and installation features into a .NET Framework application	
Embed configuration management functionality into a .NET Framework application.	Chapter 9, Lessons 1 and 2
Create a custom Microsoft Windows Installer for .NET components by using the System.Configuration.Install namespace, and configure .NET Framework applications by using configuration files, environment variables, and the .NET Framework Configuration tool (Mscorcfg.msc).	Chapter 9, Lesson 3
Manage an event log by using the System.Diagnostics namespace.	Chapter 10, Lesson 1
Manage system processes and monitor the performance of a .NET application by using the diagnostics functionality of the .NET Framework 2.0.	Chapter 10, Lessons 2 and 3
Debug and trace a .NET Framework application by using the System.Diagnostics namespace.	Chapter 10, Lesson 1
Embed management information and events into a .NET Framework application.	Chapter 10, Lesson 3
Implementing serialization and input/output functionality in a .NET Framework application	
Serialize or deserialize an object or an object graph by using runtime serialization techniques.	Chapter 5, Lesson 1
Control the serialization of an object into XML format by using the System.Xml.Serialization namespace.	Chapter 5, Lesson 2

Objective	Location in Book
Implement custom serialization formatting by using the Serialization Formatter classes.	Chapter 5, Lesson 3
Access files and folders by using the File System classes.	Chapter 2, Lesson 1
Manage byte streams by using Stream classes.	Chapter 2, Lesson 2
Manage .NET Framework application data by using Reader and Writer classes.	Chapter 2, Lesson 2
Compress or decompress stream information in a .NET Framework application, and improve the security of application data by using isolated storage.	Chapter 2, Lesson 2
Improving the security of .NET Framework applications by using the .NET Framework security features	
Implement code access security to improve the security of a .NET Framework application.	Chapter 11, Lesson 1
Implement access control by using the *System.Security.AccessControl* classes.	Chapter 12, Lesson 2
Implement a custom authentication scheme by using the *System.Security.Authentication* classes.	Chapter 12, Lesson 190
Encrypt, decrypt, and hash data by using the *System.Security.Cryptography* classes.	Chapter 12, Lesson 3
Control permissions for resources by using the *System.Security.Permission* classes.	Chapter 11, Lessons 1, 2, and 3
Control code privileges by using the *System.Security.Policy* classes.	Chapter 11, Lessons 1, 2, and 3
Access and modify identity information by using the *System.Security.Principal* classes.	Chapter 12, Lesson 1
Implementing interoperability, reflection, and mailing functionality in a .NET Framework application	
Expose COM components to the .NET Framework and .NET Framework components to COM.	Chapter 13, Lessons 1 and 2
Call unmanaged DLL functions within a .NET Framework application, and control the marshalling of data in a .NET Framework application.	Chapter 13, Lessons 1 and 2
Implement reflection functionality in a .NET Framework application, and create metadata, Microsoft intermediate language (MSIL), and a PE file by using the System.Reflection.Emit namespace.	Chapter 14, Lesson 1
Send electronic mail to a Simple Mail Transfer Protocol (SMTP) server for delivery from a .NET Framework application.	Chapter 15, Lessons 1 and 2
Implementing globalization, drawing, and text manipulation functionality in a .NET Framework application	
Format data based on culture information.	Chapter 16, Lesson 1
Enhance the user interface of a .NET Framework application by using the System.Drawing namespace.	Chapter 6, Lessons 1, 2, and 3
Enhance the text handling capabilities of a .NET Framework application, and search, modify, and control text within a .NET Framework application by using regular expressions.	Chapter 3, Lessons 1 and 2

NOTE Exam objectives

The exam objectives listed here are current as of this book's publication date. Exam objectives are subject to change at any time without prior notice and at Microsoft's sole discretion. Please visit the Microsoft Learning Web site for the most current listing of exam objectives: *http://www.microsoft.com/learning/en/us/exams/70-536.mspx.*

Microsoft

MCTS Self-Paced Training Kit (Exam 70-536): Microsoft® .NET Framework—Application Development Foundation, Second Edition

Tony Northrup

PUBLISHED BY
Microsoft Press
A Division of Microsoft Corporation
One Microsoft Way
Redmond, Washington 98052-6399

Library of Congress Control Number: 2008935429

Printed and bound in the United States of America.

4 5 6 7 8 9 WCT 3 2 1 0

Distributed in Canada by H.B. Fenn and Company Ltd.

A CIP catalogue record for this book is available from the British Library.

Microsoft Press books are available through booksellers and distributors worldwide. For further information about international editions, contact your local Microsoft Corporation office or contact Microsoft Press International directly at fax (425) 936-7329. Visit our Web site at www.microsoft.com/mspress. Send comments to tkinput@microsoft.com.

Microsoft, Microsoft Press, Active Directory, Internet Explorer, MS, MSDN, MS-DOS, OpenType, Outlook, SQL Server, Visual Basic, Visual C#, Visual C++, Visual Studio, Win32, Windows, Windows NT, Windows Server, and Windows Vista are either registered trademarks or trademarks of the Microsoft group of companies. Other product and company names mentioned herein may be the trademarks of their respective owners.

The example companies, organizations, products, domain names, e-mail addresses, logos, people, places, and events depicted herein are fictitious. No association with any real company, organization, product, domain name, e-mail address, logo, person, place, or event is intended or should be inferred.

This book expresses the author's views and opinions. The information contained in this book is provided without any express, statutory, or implied warranties. Neither the authors, Microsoft Corporation, nor its resellers, or distributors will be held liable for any damages caused or alleged to be caused either directly or indirectly by this book.

Acquisitions Editor: Ken Jones
Developmental Editor: Laura Sackerman
Project Editor: Carol Vu
Editorial Production: S4Carlisle Publishing Services
Technical Reviewer: Kurt Meyer; Technical Review services provided by Content Master, a member of CM Group, Ltd.
Cover: Tom Draper Design

Body Part No. X15-12470

In loving memory of Chelsea Knowles

About the Author

Tony Northrup

In the mid-1980s, Tony Northrup, MCTS, MCSE, CISPP, and MVP, learned to program in BASIC on a ZX-81 personal computer built from a kit. Later, he mastered 68000 assembly and ANSI C on the Motorola VERSAdos operating system before beginning to write code for MS-DOS. After a brief time with the NEXTSTEP operating system, Tony returned to a Microsoft platform because he was impressed by the beta version of Microsoft Windows NT 3.1. Although he has dabbled in other operating systems, Tony has since focused on Windows development in Microsoft Visual C++,  Microsoft Visual Basic, C#, and Perl (for automation projects). Tony now develops almost exclusively for the .NET Framework.

Tony started writing in 1997 and has since published more than a dozen technology books on the topics of development and networking. In addition, Tony has written dozens of articles at *http://www.microsoft.com,* covering topics ranging from securing ASP.NET applications to designing firewalls to protect networks and computers. Tony spends his spare time hiking through the woods near his Phillipston, Massachusetts, home. He's rarely without his camera, and in the past six years has created what might be the largest and most popular publicly accessible database of nature and wildlife photographs on the Internet. Tony lives with his dog, Sandi, and his cat, Sam. For more information about Tony, visit *http://www.northrup.org.*

Contents at Glance

Table of Contents

What do you think of this book? We want to hear from you!

Microsoft is interested in hearing your feedback so we can continually improve our books and learning resources for you. To participate in a brief online survey, please visit:

www.microsoft.com/learning/booksurvey/

What do you think of this book? We want to hear from you!

Microsoft is interested in hearing your feedback so we can continually improve our books and learning resources for you. To participate in a brief online survey, please visit:

www.microsoft.com/learning/booksurvey/

Acknowledgments

The author's name appears on the cover of a book, but I am only one member of a much larger team. First of all, thanks to Ken Jones at Microsoft for allowing me to update the first edition of this book. During the writing process, I worked most closely with Carol Vu, Laura Sackerman, and Susan McClung. Carol, Laura, and Sue, thanks for your patience with me, and for making this a great book. Kurt Meyer was my technical reviewer, and he was far more committed to the project than any reviewer I've worked with in the past. Each of my editors contributed significantly to this book and I hope to work with them all in the future.

Many other people helped with this book, albeit a bit more indirectly, by keeping me sane throughout the writing process. Lori Hendrickson introduced me to Cacique in Costa Rica. Nisha Rajasekaran helped me buy clothes. Tara Banks, Eric Parucki, and Stephanie Wunderlich improved my vocabulary by repeatedly beating me at Scrabble. Chris and Diane Geggis trusted me with Remy. Jennie Lozier drank my Chardonnay. Eric and Alyssa Faulkner, with the help of Amy Gilvary, threw an Independence Day party (at my house, oddly). Finally, Diane and Franklin Glenn made some incredible chocolate cake. Thanks, guys.

Introduction

This training kit is designed for developers who plan to take Microsoft Certified Technical Specialist (MCTS) exam 70-536, as well as for developers who need to know how to develop applications using the Microsoft .NET Framework. Before you begin using this kit, you should have a working knowledge of Microsoft Windows and Microsoft Visual Basic or C#.

By using this training kit, you'll learn how to do the following:

- Develop applications that use system types and collections
- Implement service processes, threading, and application domains to enable application isolation and multithreading
- Create and deploy manageable applications
- Create classes that can be serialized to enable them to be easily stored and transferred
- Create hardened applications that are resistant to attacks and restrict access based on user and group roles
- Use interoperability and reflection to leverage legacy code and communicate with other applications
- Write applications that send e-mail messages
- Create applications that can be used in different regions with different languages and cultural conventions
- Draw charts and create images, and either display them as part of your application or save them to files

Hardware Requirements

The following hardware is required to complete the practice exercises:

- A computer with a 1.6 GHz or faster processor (2.2 GHz recommended)
- 512 megabytes (MB) of RAM or more (1 GB recommended)
- 2 gigabytes (GB) of available hard disk space
- A DVD-ROM drive

- 1,024 x 768 or higher resolution display with 256 or higher colors (1280 x 1024 recommended)

- A keyboard and Microsoft mouse, or compatible pointing device

Software Requirements

The following software is required to complete the practice exercises:

- One of the following operating systems, using either a 32-bit or 64-bit architecture:
  - ❑ Windows XP
  - ❑ Windows Server 2003
  - ❑ Windows Vista

- Visual Studio 2008 (A 90-day evaluation edition of Visual Studio 2008 Professional Edition is included on DVD with this book.)

Using the CD and DVD

A companion CD and an evaluation software DVD are included with this training kit. The companion CD contains the following:

- **Practice tests**   You can reinforce your understanding of how to create .NET Framework applications by using electronic practice tests you customize to meet your needs from the pool of Lesson Review questions in this book. Or you can practice for the 70-536 certification exam by using tests created from a pool of 200 realistic exam questions, which is enough to give you many different practice exams to ensure that you're prepared.

- **Code**   Each chapter in this book includes sample files associated with the lab exercises at the end of every lesson. For most exercises, you will be instructed to open a project prior to starting the exercise. For other exercises, you will create a project on your own and be able to reference a completed project on the CD in the event you experience a problem following the exercise. A few exercises do not involve sample files. To install the sample files on your hard disk, run Setup.exe in the Code folder on the companion CD. The default installation folder is \Documents\Microsoft Press\MCTS Self-Paced Training Kit Exam 70-536_2E.

- **An eBook**   An electronic version (eBook) of this book is included for times when you don't want to carry the printed book with you. The eBook is in Portable Document Format (PDF), and you can view it by using Adobe Acrobat or Adobe Reader.

The evaluation software DVD contains a 90-day evaluation edition of Visual Studio 2008 Professional Edition, in case you want to use it with this book.

> **Digital Content for Digital Book Readers:** If you bought a digital-only edition of this book, you can enjoy select content from the print edition's companion CD.
> Visit *http://go.microsoft.com/fwlink/?LinkId=128438* to get your downloadable content. This content is always up-to-date and available to all readers.

How to Install the Practice Tests

To install the practice test software from the companion CD to your hard disk, do the following:

1. Insert the companion CD into your CD drive, and accept the license agreement. A CD menu appears.

   NOTE   If the CD Menu Doesn't Appear

   If the CD menu or the license agreement doesn't appear, AutoRun might be disabled on your computer. Refer to the Readme.txt file on the CD-ROM for alternate installation instructions.

2. On the CD menu click the Practice Tests item, and follow the instructions on the screen.

How to Use the Practice Tests

To start the practice test software, follow these steps:

1. Click Start, select All Programs, and then select Microsoft Press Training Kit Exam Prep. A window appears that shows all the Microsoft Press training kit exam prep suites installed on your computer.

2. Double-click the lesson review or practice test you want to use.

   NOTE   Lesson Reviews vs. Practice Tests

   Select the (70-536) Microsoft .NET Framework—Application Development Foundation Lesson Review to use the questions from the "Lesson Review" sections of this book. Select the (70-536) Microsoft .NET Framework—Application Development Foundation *practice test* to use a pool of questions similar to those in the 70-536 certification exam.

Lesson Review Options

When you start a lesson review, the Custom Mode dialog box appears so that you can configure your test. You can click OK to accept the defaults, or you can customize the number of questions you want, how the practice test software works, which exam objectives you want the questions to relate to, and whether you want your lesson review to be timed. If you're retaking a test, you can select whether you want to see all the questions again or only those questions you missed or didn't answer.

After you click OK, your lesson review starts, as follows:

- To take the test, answer the questions and use the Next, Previous, and Go To buttons to move from question to question.

- After you answer an individual question, if you want to see which answers are correct–along with an explanation of each correct answer–click Explanation.

- If you'd rather wait until the end of the test to see how you did, answer all the questions and then click Score Test. You'll see a summary of the exam objectives you chose and the percentage of questions you got right overall and per objective. You can print a copy of your test, review your answers, or retake the test.

Practice Test Options

When you start a practice test, you choose whether to take the test in Certification Mode, Study Mode, or Custom Mode, as follows:

- **Certification Mode**   Closely resembles the experience of taking a certification exam. The test has a set number of questions, it's timed, and you can't pause and restart the timer.

- **Study Mode**   Creates an untimed test in which you can review the correct answers and the explanations after you answer each question.

- **Custom Mode**   Gives you full control over the test options so that you can customize them as you like.

In all modes, the user interface you see when taking the test is basically the same, but with different options enabled or disabled depending on the mode. The main options are discussed in the previous section, "Lesson Review Options."

When you review your answer to an individual practice test question, a "References" section is provided that lists where in the training kit you can find the information that relates to that question and provides links to other sources of information. After you click Test Results to score your entire practice test, you can click the Learning Plan tab to see a list of references for every objective.

How to Uninstall the Practice Tests

To uninstall the practice test software for a training kit, use the Add Or Remove Programs option in the Control Panel.

Microsoft Certified Professional Program

The Microsoft certifications provide the best method to prove your command of current Microsoft products and technologies. The exams and corresponding certifications are developed to validate your mastery of critical competencies as you design and develop, or implement and support, solutions with Microsoft products and technologies. Computer professionals who become Microsoft-certified are recognized as experts and are sought after industry-wide. Certification brings a variety of benefits to the individual and to employers and organizations.

MORE INFO   All the Microsoft Certifications

For a full list of Microsoft certifications, go to *www.microsoft.com/learning/mcp/default.asp*.

Technical Support

Every effort has been made to ensure the accuracy of this book and the contents of the companion CD. If you have comments, questions, or ideas regarding this book or the companion CD, please send them to Microsoft Press by using either of the following methods:

E-mail: *tkinput@microsoft.com*

Postal Mail:

Microsoft Press
Attn: *MCTS Self-Paced Training Kit (Exam 70-536): Microsoft .NET Framework–Application Development Foundation, Second Edition* Editor
One Microsoft Way
Redmond, WA 98052–6399

For additional support information regarding this book and the CD-ROM (including answers to commonly asked questions about installation and use), visit the Microsoft Press Technical Support Web site at *www.microsoft.com/learning/support/books/*. To connect directly to the Microsoft Knowledge Base and enter a query, visit *support.microsoft.com/search/*. For support information regarding Microsoft software, please connect to *support.microsoft.com*.

Evaluation Edition Software Support

The 90-day evaluation edition provided with this training kit is not the full retail product and is provided only for the purposes of training and evaluation. Microsoft and Microsoft Technical Support do not support this evaluation edition.

Information about any issues relating to the use of this evaluation edition with this training kit is posted to the Support section of the Microsoft Press Web site (*www.microsoft.com/learning/support/books/*). For information about ordering the full version of any Microsoft software, please call Microsoft Sales at (800) 426-9400 or visit *www.microsoft.com*.

Chapter 1
Framework Fundamentals

The .NET Framework is an integral Microsoft Windows component designed to support next-generation applications and services.This chapter provides an overview of .NET Framework programming, including knowledge required for every other chapter in this book.

Exam objectives in this chapter:

- Manage data in a .NET Framework application by using the .NET Framework system types.
- Implement .NET Framework interfaces to cause components to comply with standard contracts.
- Control interactions between .NET Framework application components by using events and delegates.

Lessons in this chapter:

Before You Begin

This book assumes that you have at least two to three years of experience developing Web-based, Windows-based, or distributed applications by using the .NET Framework. Candidates should have a working knowledge of Microsoft Visual Studio. Before you begin, you should be familiar with Microsoft Visual Basic or C# and be comfortable with the following tasks:

- Creating Console, Windows Forms, and Windows Presentation Foundation (WPF) applications in Visual Studio using Visual Basic or C#
- Adding namespaces and system class library references to a project
- Running a project in Visual Studio, setting breakpoints, stepping through code, and watching the values of variables

Lesson 1: Using Value Types

The simplest types in the .NET Framework, primarily numeric and boolean types, are value types. *Value types* are variables that contain their data directly instead of containing a reference to the data stored elsewhere in memory. Instances of value types are stored in an area of memory called the *stack*, where the runtime can create, read, update, and remove them quickly with minimal overhead.

MORE INFO   Reference types

For more information about reference types, refer to Lesson 2, "Using Common Reference Types."

There are three general value types:

- Built-in types
- User-defined types
- Enumerations

Each of these types is derived from the *System.ValueType* base type. The following sections show how to use these different types.

After this lesson, you will be able to:

- Choose the most efficient built-in value type
- Declare value types
- Create your own types
- Use enumerations

Estimated lesson time: 30 minutes

Built-in Value Types

Built-in value types are base types provided with the .NET Framework, with which other types are built. All built-in numeric types are value types. You choose a numeric type based on the size of the values you expect to work with and the level of precision you require. Table 1-1 lists the most common numeric types by size, from smallest to largest. The first six types are used for whole number values and the last three represent real numbers in order of increasing precision.

Table 1-1   Built-in Value Types

Type (Visual Basic/ C# alias)	Bytes	Range	Use for
System.SByte (*SByte/sbyte*)	1	−128 to 127	Signed byte values
System.Byte (*Byte/byte*)	1	0 to 255	Unsigned bytes
System.Int16 (*Short/short*)	2	−32768 to 32767	Interoperation and other specialized uses
System.Int32 (*Integer/int*)	4	−2147483648 to 2147483647	Whole numbers and counters
System.UInt32 (*UInteger/uint*)	4	0 to 4294967295	Positive whole numbers and counters
System.Int64 (*Long/long*)	8	−9223372036854775808 to 9223372036854775807	Large whole numbers
System.Single (*Single/float*)	4	−3.402823E+38 to 3.402823E+38	Floating point numbers
System.Double (*Double/ double*)	8	−1.79769313486232E+308 to 1.79769313486232E+308	Precise or large floating point numbers
System.Decimal (*Decimal/ decimal*)	16	−79228162514264337593543950335 to 79228162514264337593543950335	Financial and scientific calculations requiring great precision

NOTE Optimizing performance with built-in types

The runtime optimizes the performance of 32-bit integer types (*Int32* and *UInt32*), so use those types for counters and other frequently accessed integral variables. For floating-point operations, *Double* is the most efficient type because those operations are optimized by hardware.

Numeric types are used so frequently that Visual Basic and C# define aliases for them. Using the alias is equivalent to using the full type name, so most programmers use the shorter aliases. In addition to the numeric types, the non-numeric data types listed in Table 1-2 are also value types.

Table 1-2 Other Value Types

Type (Visual Basic/ C# alias)	Bytes	Range	Use for
System.Char (*Char/char*)	2	N/A	Single Unicode characters
System.Boolean (*Boolean/bool*)	1	N/A	*True/False* values
System.IntPtr (none)	Platform-dependent	N/A	Pointer to a memory address
System.DateTime (*Date/date*)	8	1/1/0001 12:00:00 AM to 12/31/9999 11:59:59 PM	Moments in time

There are nearly 300 more value types in the .NET Framework, but the types shown here cover most needs. When you assign between value-type variables, the data is copied from one variable to the other and stored in two different locations on the stack. This behavior is different from that of reference types, which are discussed in Lesson 2.

Even though value types often represent simple values, they still function as objects. In other words, you can call methods on them. In fact, it is common to use the *ToString* method when displaying values as text. *ToString* is overridden from the fundamental *System.Object* type.

NOTE The *Object* base class

In the .NET Framework, all types are derived from *System.Object*. That relationship helps establish the common type system used throughout the .NET Framework.

How to Declare a Value Type Variable

To use a type, you must first declare a symbol as an instance of that type. Value types have an implicit constructor, so declaring them instantiates the type automatically; you don't have to include the *New* keyword as you do with classes. The constructor assigns a default value (usually *null* or *0*) to the new instance, but you should always explicitly initialize the variable within the declaration, as shown in the following code block:

```
' VB
Dim b As Boolean = False
```

```
// C#
bool b = false;
```

NOTE   Keyword differences in Visual Basic and C#

One of the cosmetic differences between Visual Basic and C# is that Visual Basic capitalizes keywords, whereas C# uses lowercase keywords. In the text of this book, Visual Basic keywords always are capitalized for readability. Code samples always include separate examples for Visual Basic and C#.

NOTE   Variable capitalizations in Visual Basic and C#

C# is case sensitive, but Visual Basic is not case sensitive. Traditionally, variable names begin with a lowercase letter in C# and are capitalized in Visual Basic. For consistency between the languages, this book will use lowercase variable names for most Visual Basic examples. Feel free to capitalize Visual Basic variables in your own code—it does not affect how the runtime processes your code.

Declare a variable as *nullable* if you want to be able to determine whether a value has been assigned. For example, if you are storing data from a yes/no question on a form and the user did not answer the question, you should store a *null* value. The following code declares a boolean variable that can be *true*, *false*, or *null*:

```
' VB
Dim b As Nullable(Of Boolean) = Nothing
```

```
// C#
Nullable<bool> b = null;
```

```
// Shorthand notation, only for C#
bool? b = null;
```

Declaring a variable as *nullable* enables the *HasValue* and *Value* members. Use *HasValue* to detect whether a value has been set as follows:

```
' VB
If b.HasValue Then Console.WriteLine("b is {0}.", b.Value) _
  Else Console.WriteLine("b is not set.")
```

```
// C#
if (b.HasValue) Console.WriteLine("b is {0}.", b.Value);
  else Console.WriteLine("b is not set.");
```

How to Create User-Defined Types

User-defined types are also called *structures* (or simply *structs*, after the language keyword used to create them). As with other value types, instances of user-defined types are stored on the stack and they contain their data directly. In most other ways, structures behave nearly identically to classes.

Structures are a composite of other types that makes it easier to work with the related data represented by those other types. The simplest example of this is *System.Drawing.Point*, which contains *X* and *Y* integer properties that define the horizontal and vertical coordinates of a point. The *Point* structure simplifies working with coordinates by providing the constructor and members demonstrated here:

```
' VB - Requires reference to System.Drawing
' Create point
Dim p As New System.Drawing.Point(20, 30)

' Move point diagonally
p.Offset(-1, -1)
Console.WriteLine("Point X {0}, Y {1}", p.X, p.Y)

// C# - Requires reference to System.Drawing
// Create point
System.Drawing.Point p = new System.Drawing.Point(20, 30);

// Move point diagonally
p.Offset(-1, -1);
Console.WriteLine("Point X {0}, Y {1}", p.X, p.Y);
```

You define your own structures by using the *Structure* keyword in Visual Basic or the *struct* keyword in C#. For example, the following code creates a type that cycles through a set of integers between the minimum and maximum values set by the constructor. Notice that it implements the *Value* property and the addition and subtraction operators:

```
' VB
Structure Cycle
    ' Private fields
    Dim _val, _min, _max As Integer

    ' Constructor
    Public Sub New(ByVal min As Integer, ByVal max As Integer)
        _val = min : _min = min : _max = max
    End Sub
```

```vb
    ' Public members
    Public Property Value() As Integer
        Get
            Return _val
        End Get
        Set(ByVal value As Integer)
            ' Ensure new setting is between _min and _max.
            If value > _max Then Me.Value = value - _max + _min - 1 _
              Else If value < _min Then Me.Value = _min - value + _max - 1 _
              Else _val = value
        End Set
    End Property

    Public Overrides Function ToString() As String
        Return Value.ToString
    End Function

    Public Function ToInteger() As Integer
        Return Value
    End Function

    Public Shared Operator +(ByVal arg1 As Cycle, _
      ByVal arg2 As Integer) As Cycle
        arg1.Value += arg2
        Return arg1
    End Operator

    Public Shared Operator -(ByVal arg1 As Cycle, _
      ByVal arg2 As Integer) As Cycle
        arg1.Value -= arg2
        Return arg1
    End Operator
End Structure
```

```csharp
// C#
struct Cycle
{
    // Private fields
    int _val, _min, _max;

    // Constructor
    public Cycle(int min, int max)
    {
        _val = min;
        _min = min;
        _max = max;
    }

    public int Value
    {
        get { return _val; }
        set
        {
            if (value > _max)
                this.Value = value - _max + _min - 1;
```

```
        else
        {
            if (value < _min)
                this.Value = _min - value + _max - 1;
            else
                _val = value;
        }
    }
}

public override string ToString()
{
    return Value.ToString();
}

public int ToInteger()
{
    return Value;
}

public static Cycle operator +(Cycle arg1, int arg2)
{
    arg1.Value += arg2;
    return arg1;
}

public static Cycle operator -(Cycle arg1, int arg2)
{
    arg1.Value -= arg2;
    return arg1;
}
}
```

You can use this structure to represent items that repeat over a fixed range, such as degrees of rotation or quarters of a football game, as shown here:

```
' VB
Dim degrees As New Cycle(0, 359), quarters As New Cycle(1, 4)
For i As Integer = 0 To 8
    degrees += 90 : quarters += 1
    Console.WriteLine("degrees = {0}, quarters = {1}", degrees, quarters)
Next
```

```
// C#
Cycle degrees = new Cycle(0, 359);
Cycle quarters = new Cycle(1, 4);
for (int i = 0; i <= 8; i++)
{
    degrees += 90; quarters += 1;
    Console.WriteLine("degrees = {0}, quarters = {1}", degrees, quarters);
}
```

The *Cycle* structure can be easily converted from a value type to a reference type by changing the *Structure/struct* keywords to *Class.* If you make that change, instances of the *Cycle* class would be allocated on the managed heap rather than as 12 bytes on the stack (4 bytes for each private integer field) and assignment between two *Cycle* variables results in both variables pointing to the same instance.

While the functionality is similar, structures are usually more efficient than classes. You should define a structure, rather than a class, if the type will perform better as a value type than a reference type. Specifically, structure types should meet all of these criteria:

- Represents a single value logically.

- Has an instance size that is less than 16 bytes.

- Is not frequently changed after creation.

- Is not cast to a reference type. (*Casting* is the process of converting between types.)

How to Create Enumerations

Enumerations are related symbols that have fixed values. Use enumerations to provide a list of choices for developers using your class. For example, the following enumeration contains a set of titles:

```
' VB
Enum Titles
    Mr
    Ms
    Mrs
    Dr
End Enum
```

```
// C#
enum Titles { Mr, Ms, Mrs, Dr };
```

If you create an instance of the *Titles* type, Visual Studio displays a list of the available values when you assign a value to the variable. Although the value of the variable is an integer, it is easy to output the name of the symbol rather than its value, as shown here:

```
' VB
Dim t As Titles = Titles.Dr
Console.WriteLine("{0}.", t) ' Displays "Dr."
```

```
// C#
Titles t = Titles.Dr;
Console.WriteLine("{0}.", t); // Displays "Dr."
```

The purpose of enumerations is to simplify coding, avoid programming errors, and improve code readability by enabling you to use meaningful symbols instead of simple numeric values. Use enumerations when developers consuming your types must choose from a limited set of choices for a value.

Lab: Declaring and Using Value Types

The following exercises demonstrate how to create and use a structure and how to create an enumeration. If you encounter a problem completing an exercise, the completed projects are available along with the sample files.

Exercise 1: Create a Structure

In this exercise, you create a simple structure with several public members.

1. Using Visual Studio, create a new Console Application project. Name the project CreateStruct.

2. Create a new structure named *Person*, as the following code demonstrates:

    ```
    ' VB
    Structure Person
    End Structure
    ```

    ```
    // C#
    struct Person
    {
    }
    ```

3. Within the *Person* structure, define three public members:

    firstName (a string)

    lastName (a string)

    age (an integer)

    The following code demonstrates this:

    ```
    ' VB
    Public firstName As String
    Public lastName As String
    Public age As Integer
    ```

    ```
    // C#
    public string firstName;
    public string lastName;
    public int age;
    ```

4. Create a constructor that initializes all three member variables, as the following code demonstrates:

```
' VB
Public Sub New(ByVal _firstName As String, ByVal _lastName As String, _
    ByVal _age As Integer)
    firstName = _firstName
    lastName = _lastName
    age = _age
End Sub
```

```
// C#
public Person(string _firstName, string _lastName, int _age)
{
    firstName = _firstName;
    lastName = _lastName;
    age = _age;
}
```

5. Override the *ToString* method to display the person's first name, last name, and age. The following code demonstrates this:

```
' VB
Public Overrides Function ToString() As String
    Return firstName + " " + lastName + ", age " + age.ToString
End Function
```

```
// C#
public override string ToString()
{
    return firstName + " " + lastName + ", age " + age;
}
```

6. Within the *Main* method of the console application, write code to create an instance of the structure and pass the instance to the *Console.WriteLine* method, as the following code demonstrates:

```
' VB
Dim p As Person = New Person("Tony", "Allen", 32)
Console.WriteLine(p)
```

```
// C#
Person p = new Person("Tony", "Allen", 32);
Console.WriteLine(p);
```

7. Run the application to verify that it works correctly.

NOTE When running a Console application from the debugger, it might automatically close the console window when the application ends, preventing you from seeing the output. To cause the console application to wait until you press a key, call the *Console.ReadKey* method at the end of the *Main* method.

Exercise 2: Add an Enumeration to a Structure

In this exercise, you extend the structure you created in Exercise 1 by adding an enumeration.

1. Open the project you created in Exercise 1.

2. Declare a new enumeration in the *Person* structure. Name the enumeration *Genders*, and specify two possible values: *Male* and *Female*. The following code sample demonstrates this:

```
' VB
Enum Genders
    Male
    Female
End Enum
```

```
// C#
public enum Genders { Male, Female };
```

3. Add a public member of type *Genders*, and modify the *Person* constructor to accept a *Gender* enumeration value. The following code shows the changes in bold:

```
' VB
Public firstName As String
Public lastName As String
Public age As Integer
Public gender As Genders

Public Sub New(ByVal _firstName As String, ByVal _lastName As String, _
    ByVal _age As Integer, ByVal _gender As Genders)
    firstName = _firstName
    lastName = _lastName
    age = _age
    gender = _gender
End Sub
```

```
// C#
public string firstName;
public string lastName;
public int age;
public Genders gender;

public Person(string _firstName, string _lastName, int _age, Genders _gender)
{
    firstName = _firstName;
    lastName = _lastName;
    age = _age;
    gender = _gender;
}
```

4. Modify the *Person.ToString* method to also display the gender, as the following code sample demonstrates:

```
' VB
Public Overrides Function ToString() As String
    Return firstName + " " + lastName + " (" + gender.ToString() + "), age " + age.ToString
End Function
```

```
// C#
public override string ToString()
{
    return firstName + " " + lastName + " (" + gender + "), age " + age;
}
```

5. Modify your *Main* code to properly construct an instance of the *Person* structure, as the following code sample demonstrates:

```
' VB
Sub Main()
    Dim p As Person = New Person("Tony", "Allen", 32, Person.Genders.Male)
    Console.WriteLine(p)
End Sub
```

```
// C#
static void Main(string[] args)
{
    Person p = new Person("Tony", "Allen", 32, Person.Genders.Male);
    Console.WriteLine(p.ToString());
}
```

6. Run the application to verify that it works correctly.

Lesson Summary

-   The .NET Framework includes a large number of built-in types that you can use directly or use to build your own custom types.

-   Value types directly contain their data, offering excellent performance. However, value types are limited to types that store very small pieces of data. In the .NET Framework, all value types are 16 bytes or shorter.

-   You can create user-defined types that store multiple values and have methods. In object-oriented applications, a large portion of your application logic is coded within user-defined types.

-   Enumerations improve code readability by providing symbols for a set of values.

Lesson Review

You can use the following questions to test your knowledge of the information in Lesson 1, "Using Value Types." The questions are also available on the companion CD if you prefer to review them in electronic form.

Answers   Answers to these questions and explanations of why each answer choice is right or wrong are located in the "Answers" section at the end of the book.

---

1. Which of the following are value types? (Choose all that apply.)

    A. *Decimal*

    B. *String*

    C. *System.Drawing.Point*

    D. *Integer*

2. Which is the correct declaration for a nullable integer?

    A.
    ```vb
    ' VB
    Dim i As Nullable<Of Integer> = Nothing
    ```
    ```csharp
    // C#
    Nullable(int) i = null;
    ```
    B.
    ```vb
    ' VB
    Dim i As Nullable(Of Integer) = Nothing
    ```
    ```csharp
    // C#
    Nullable<int> i = null;
    ```
    C.
    ```vb
    ' VB
    Dim i As Integer = Nothing
    ```
    ```csharp
    // C#
    int i = null;
    ```
    D.
    ```vb
    ' VB
    Dim i As Integer(Nullable) = Nothing
    ```
    ```csharp
    // C#
    int<Nullable> i = null;
    ```

Lesson 2: Using Common Reference Types

Most types in the .NET Framework are reference types. Reference types provide a great deal of flexibility, and they offer excellent performance when passing them to methods. The following sections introduce reference types by discussing common built-in classes. Lesson 4, "Converting Between Types," covers creating classes, interfaces, and delegates.

After this lesson, you will be able to:

- Explain the difference between value types and reference types
- Describe how value types and reference types differ when assigning values
- List some built-in reference types
- Describe when you should use the *StringBuilder* type
- Create and sort arrays
- Open, read, write, and close files
- Detect when exceptions occur and respond to the exception

Estimated lesson time: 40 minutes

What Is a Reference Type?

Reference types store the address of their data, also known as a *pointer*, on the stack. The actual data to which that address refers is stored in an area of memory called the *heap*. The runtime manages the memory used by the heap through a process called *garbage collection*. Garbage collection recovers memory periodically, as needed, by disposing of items that are no longer referenced.

NOTE   Garbage Collection

Garbage collection occurs only when needed or when triggered by a call to *GC.Collect*. Automatic garbage collection in the Common Language Runtime (CLR) is optimized for applications where most instances are short-lived, except for those allocated at the beginning of the application. Following that design pattern results in the best performance.

Comparing the Behavior of Reference and Value Types

Because reference types directly store the address of data rather than the data itself, assigning one reference variable to another doesn't copy the data. Instead, assigning a reference variable to another instance merely creates a second copy of the reference, which refers to the same memory location on the heap as the original variable.

Consider the following simple structure declaration:

```vb
' VB
Structure Numbers
    Public val As Integer

    Public Sub New(ByVal _val As Integer)
        val = _val
    End Sub

    Public Overrides Function ToString() As String
        Return val.ToString
    End Function
End Structure
```

```csharp
// C#
struct Numbers
{
    public int val;

    public Numbers(int _val)
    { val = _val; }

    public override string ToString()
    { return val.ToString(); }
}
```

Now consider the following code, which creates an instance of the *Numbers* structure, assigns that structure to a second instance, modifies both instances, and displays the results:

```vb
' VB
Dim n1 As Numbers = New Numbers(0)
Dim n2 As Numbers = n1
n1.val += 1
n2.val += 2
Console.WriteLine("n1 = {0}, n2 = {1}", n1, n2)
```

```csharp
// C#
Numbers n1 = new Numbers(0);
Numbers n2 = n1;
n1.val += 1;
n2.val += 2;
Console.WriteLine("n1 = {0}, n2 = {1}", n1, n2);
```

This code would display "n1 = 1, n2 = 2" because a structure is a value type, and assigning a value type results in two distinct values. However, if you change the *Numbers* type declaration from a structure to a class, the same application would display "n1 = 3, n2 = 3". Changing *Numbers* from a structure to a class causes it to be a reference type rather than a value type. When you modify a reference type variable, you modify the data pointed to by the reference. All references point to that data and then refer to the updated value.

Built-in Reference Types

There are about 2,500 built-in reference types in the .NET Framework. Everything not derived from *System.ValueType* is a reference type, including these 2,500 or so built-in reference types. Table 1-3 lists the most commonly used types, from which many other reference types are derived.

Table 1-3   Common Reference Types

Type	Use for
System.Object	The *Object* type is the most general type in the .NET Framework. You can convert any type to *System.Object*, and you can rely on any type having *ToString*, *GetType*, and *Equals* members inherited from this type.
System.String	Text data.
System.Text.StringBuilder	Dynamic text data.
System.Array	Arrays of data. This is the base class for all arrays. Array declarations use language-specific array syntax.
System.IO.Stream	Buffer for file, device, and network input/output (I/O). This is an abstract base class; task-specific classes are derived from *System.IO.Stream*.
System.Exception	Handling system and application-defined exceptions. Task-specific exceptions inherit from this type.

Strings and String Builders

Types are more than just containers for data; they also provide the means to manipulate that data through their members. *System.String* provides a set of members for working with text. For example, the following code does a quick search and replace:

```
' VB
Dim s As String = "this is some text to search"
s = s.Replace("search", "replace")
Console.WriteLine(s)
```

```
// C#
string s = "this is some text to search";
s = s.Replace("search", "replace");
Console.WriteLine(s);
```

Strings of type *System.String* are immutable in the .NET Framework. That means any change to a string causes the runtime to create a new string and abandon the old one. That happens invisibly, and many programmers might be surprised to learn that the following code allocates four new strings in memory:

```
' VB
Dim s As String

s = "wombat"            ' "wombat"
s += " kangaroo"        ' "wombat kangaroo"
s += " wallaby"         ' "wombat kangaroo wallaby"
s += " koala"           ' "wombat kangaroo wallaby koala"
Console.WriteLine(s)
```

```
// C#
string s;

s = "wombat";           // "wombat"
s += " kangaroo";       // "wombat kangaroo"
s += " wallaby";        // "wombat kangaroo wallaby"
s += " koala";          // "wombat kangaroo wallaby koala"
Console.WriteLine(s);
```

After running this code, only the last string has a reference; the other three are disposed of during garbage collection. Avoiding these types of temporary strings helps avoid unnecessary garbage collection, which improves performance. There are several ways to avoid temporary strings:

- Use the *Concat*, *Join*, or *Format* methods of the *String* class to join multiple items in a single statement.
- Use the *StringBuilder* class to create dynamic (mutable) strings.

The *StringBuilder* solution is the most flexible because it can span multiple statements. The default constructor creates a 16-byte buffer that grows as needed. You can specify an initial size and a maximum size if you like. The following code demonstrates using *StringBuilder*:

```
' VB
Dim sb As New System.Text.StringBuilder(30)
sb.Append("wombat")       ' Build string.
sb.Append(" kangaroo")
sb.Append(" wallaby")
sb.Append(" koala")
Dim s as String = sb.ToString          ' Copy result to string.
Console.WriteLine(s)
```

```
// C#
System.Text.StringBuilder sb = new System.Text.StringBuilder(30);
sb.Append("wombat");      // Build string.
sb.Append(" kangaroo");
sb.Append(" wallaby");
sb.Append(" koala");
string s = sb.ToString();      // Copy result to string.
Console.WriteLine(s);
```

Another subtle but important feature of the *String* class is that it overloads operators from *System.Object*. Table 1-4 lists the operators the *String* class overrides.

Table 1-4 String Operators

Operator	Visual Basic	C#	Action on *System.String*
Addition	+ or &	+	Joins two strings to create a new string.
Equality	=	==	Returns *True* if two strings have the same contents, and *False* if they are different.
Inequality	<>	!=	The inverse of the *Equality* operator.
Assignment	=	=	Copies the contents of one string into a new one. This causes strings to behave like value types, even though they are implemented as reference types. This operator is called implicitly when you pass parameters by value.

How to Create and Sort Arrays

Arrays are declared using parentheses (in Visual Basic) or square braces (in C#) as part of a variable declaration. As with the *String* type, *System.Array* provides members for working with its contained data. The following code declares an array with some initial data and then sorts the array:

```
' VB
' Declare and initialize an array.
Dim ar() As Integer = { 3, 1, 2 }

' Call a shared/static array method.
Array.Sort(ar)
```

```
' Display the result.
Console.WriteLine("{0}, {1}, {2}", ar(0), ar(1), ar(2))

// C#
// Declare and initialize an array.
int[] ar = { 3, 1, 2 };

// Call a shared/static array method.
Array.Sort(ar);

// Display the result.
Console.WriteLine("{0}, {1}, {2}", ar[0], ar[1], ar[2]);
```

How to Use Streams

Streams are another very common type because they are the means for reading from and writing to the disk and communicating across the network. The *System.IO.Stream* type is the base type for all task-specific stream types. Table 1-5 shows some of the most commonly used stream types. In addition, network streams are found in the *System.Network.Sockets* namespace, and encrypted streams are found in the *System.Security.Cryptography* namespace.

Table 1-5   Common Stream Types

System.IO Type	Use to
FileStream	Create a base stream used to write to or read from a file
MemoryStream	Create a base stream used to write to or read from memory
StreamReader	Read data from a text file
StreamWriter	Write data to a text file

The simplest stream classes are *StreamReader* and *StreamWriter*, which enable you to read and write text files. You can pass a filename as part of the constructor, enabling you to open a file with a single line of code. After you have processed a file, call the *Close* method so that the file does not remain locked. The following code, which requires the *System.IO* namespace, demonstrates how to write to and read from a text file:

```
' VB
' Create and write to a text file
Dim sw As StreamWriter = New StreamWriter("text.txt")
sw.WriteLine("Hello, World!")
sw.Close
```

```
' Read and display a text file
Dim sr As StreamReader = New StreamReader("text.txt")
Console.WriteLine(sr.ReadToEnd)
sr.Close
```

```
// C#
// Create and write to a text file
StreamWriter sw = new StreamWriter("text.txt");
sw.WriteLine("Hello, World!");
sw.Close();

// Read and display a text file
StreamReader sr = new StreamReader("text.txt");
Console.WriteLine(sr.ReadToEnd());
sr.Close();
```

MORE INFO   Streams

For more information about streams, refer to Chapter 2, "Input/Output."

How to Throw and Catch Exceptions

Exceptions are unexpected events that interrupt the normal execution of an assembly. For example, if your assembly is reading a large text file from a removable disk and the user removes the disk, the runtime throws an exception. This makes sense because your assembly could not possibly continue running under those circumstances.

Exceptions should never cause your assembly to fail completely. Instead, you should plan that exceptions will occur, and that you will catch them and respond to the events. In the preceding example, you could notify the user that the file was not available and then wait for the user to respond. The following snippet of code, which requires the *System.IO* namespace, demonstrates this action:

```
' VB
Try
    Dim sr As StreamReader = New StreamReader("C:\boot.ini")
    Console.WriteLine(sr.ReadToEnd)
Catch ex As Exception
    ' If there are any problems reading the file, display an error message
    Console.WriteLine("Error reading file: " + ex.Message)
End Try
```

```
// C#
try
{
    StreamReader sr = new StreamReader(@"C:\boot.ini");
    Console.WriteLine(sr.ReadToEnd());
}
```

```
catch (Exception ex)
{
    // If there are any problems reading the file, display an error message
    Console.WriteLine("Error reading file: " + ex.Message);
}
```

In the preceding example, if any type of error occurs—including a "File not found" error, "Insufficient privileges" error, or an error during the reading of the file—processing continues within the *catch* block. If no problems occur, the runtime skips the *catch* block.

The base *Exception* class is very useful. It contains an error message and other application data. In addition to the base *Exception* class, the .NET Framework defines hundreds of exception classes to describe different types of events, all derived from *System.SystemException*. In addition, when you need to describe an event in more detail than the standard exception classes allow, you can define your own exceptions by deriving from *System.ApplicationException*.

Having multiple exception classes allows you to respond differently to different types of errors. The runtime executes only the first *catch* block with a matching exception type, however, so order *catch* blocks from most specific to least specific. This process is sometimes called *filtering exceptions*. The following code sample displays different error messages for a "File not found" error, an "Insufficient privileges" error, and any other type of error that might occur:

```
' VB
Try
    Dim sr As StreamReader = New StreamReader("text.txt")
    Console.WriteLine(sr.ReadToEnd)
Catch ex As System.IO.FileNotFoundException
    Console.WriteLine("The file could not be found.")
Catch ex As System.UnauthorizedAccessException
    Console.WriteLine("You do not have sufficient permissions.")
Catch ex As Exception
    Console.WriteLine("Error reading file: " + ex.Message)
End Try

// C#
try
{
    StreamReader sr = new StreamReader("text.txt");
    Console.WriteLine(sr.ReadToEnd());
}
catch (System.IO.FileNotFoundException ex)
{
    Console.WriteLine("The file could not be found.");
}
```

```
catch (System.UnauthorizedAccessException ex)
{
    Console.WriteLine("You do not have sufficient permissions.");
}
catch (Exception ex)
{
    Console.WriteLine("Error reading file: " + ex.Message);
}
```

Exception handling also supports a *finally* block. The *finally* block runs after the *try* block and any *catch* blocks have finished executing, whether or not an exception was thrown. Therefore, you should use a *finally* block to close any streams or clean up any other objects that might be left open if an exception occurs. The following code sample closes the *StreamReader* object whether or not an exception occurs:

```
' VB
Dim sr As StreamReader = New StreamReader("text.txt")
Try
    Console.WriteLine(sr.ReadToEnd)
Catch ex As Exception
    ' If there are any problems reading the file, display an error message
    Console.WriteLine("Error reading file: " + ex.Message)
Finally
    ' Close the StreamReader, whether or not an exception occurred
    sr.Close
End Try
```

```
// C#
StreamReader sr = new StreamReader("text.txt");
try
{
    Console.WriteLine(sr.ReadToEnd());
}
catch (Exception ex)
{
    // If there are any problems reading the file, display an error message
    Console.WriteLine("Error reading file: " + ex.Message);
}
finally
{
    // Close the StreamReader, whether or not an exception occurred
    sr.Close();
}
```

Notice that the *StreamReader* declaration was moved outside the *try* block in the preceding example. This is necessary because the *finally* block cannot access variables that are declared within the *try* block, which makes sense because depending on where an exception occurred, variable declarations within the *try* block might not yet have been executed. To catch exceptions that occur both during and after the *StreamReader* declaration, use nested *try/catch/finally* blocks. Typically, all code except for simple variable declarations should occur within *try* blocks. Exceptions that occur outside of *try* blocks, or exceptions that occur within a *try* block but do not have a *catch* block that matches their type, are passed up to the code that called the current method. If no higher-level code catches the exception, the exception is considered unhandled, and the CLR stops running the application.

The *Exception.Message* property provides a text message that describes the exception. For example, if you attempt to open a file that does not exist, the .NET Framework throws an exception with the message, "Could not find file '*filename*'." While many users can interpret the exception messages (many of which are more complex than the example message here), you should strive to provide robust error handling and custom error messages for common scenarios.

The *Exception.StackTrace* property is useful for debugging because it includes the specific file and line number that initiated the exception. While you should never show *Exception.StackTrace* to a user, you should log the data in an event log if you might need to troubleshoot the exception outside the debugging environment. The following shows a *StackTrace* generated when a file could not be found:

```
at System.IO.__Error.WinIOError(Int32 errorCode, String maybeFullPath)
   at System.IO.FileStream.Init(String path, FileMode mode, FileAccess access, Int32 rights,
Boolean useRights, FileShare share, Int32 bufferSize, FileOptions options, SECURITY_ATTRIBUTES
secAttrs, String msgPath, Boolean bFromProxy)
   at System.IO.FileStream..ctor(String path, FileMode mode, FileAccess access, FileShare
share, Int32 bufferSize, FileOptions options)
   at System.IO.StreamReader..ctor(String path, Encoding encoding, Boolean
detectEncodingFromByteOrderMarks, Int32 bufferSize)
   at System.IO.StreamReader..ctor(String path)
   at ConsoleApplication2cs.Program.Main(String[] args) in C:\apps\MyApps\Program.cs:line 16
```

NOTE

Robust error handling improves the user experience when problems occur and greatly simplifies debugging. However, exception handling does incur a slight performance penalty. To conserve space and focus on specific topics, sample code within this book typically will not include exception handling.

Lab: Working with Reference Types

The following exercises reinforce knowledge of reference types, strings, and exceptions. If you encounter a problem completing an exercise, the completed projects are available along with the sample files.

Exercise 1: Identify Types as Value or Reference

In this exercise, you write a Console application that displays whether objects are value or reference types.

1. Using Visual Studio, create a new Console Application project. Name the project List-Value-Types.

2. In the *Main* method, create and initialize instances of the following classes:

   ❑ *SByte*

   ❑ *Byte*

   ❑ *Int16*

   ❑ *Int32*

   ❑ *Int64*

   ❑ *String*

   ❑ *Exception*

   The following code demonstrates this:

   ```vb
   ' VB
   Dim a As SByte = 0
   Dim b As Byte = 0
   Dim c As Int16 = 0
   Dim d As Int32 = 0
   Dim e As Int64 = 0
   Dim s As String = ""
   Dim ex As Exception = New Exception
   ```

   ```csharp
   // C#
   SByte a = 0;
   Byte b = 0;
   Int16 c = 0;
   Int32 d = 0;
   Int64 e = 0;
   string s = "";
   Exception ex = new Exception();
   ```

3. Add each of the instances to a new object array, as the following code demonstrates:

   ```vb
   ' VB
   Dim types As Object() = { a, b, c, d, e, s, ex }
   ```

   ```csharp
   // C#
   Object[] types = { a, b, c, d, e, s, ex };
   ```

4. Within a *foreach* loop, check the *Object.GetType().IsValueType* property to determine whether the type is a value type. Display each type name and whether it is a value type or a reference type, as the following code demonstrates:

```
' VB
For Each o As Object In types
    Dim type As String
    If o.GetType.IsValueType Then
        type = "Value type"
    Else
        type = "Reference Type"
    End If
    Console.WriteLine("{0}: {1}", o.GetType, type)
Next
```

```
// C#
foreach ( object o in types )
{
    string type;
    if (o.GetType().IsValueType)
        type = "Value type";
    else
        type = "Reference Type";

    Console.WriteLine("{0}: {1}", o.GetType(), type );
}
```

5. Run the application and verify that each type matches your understanding.

Exercise 2: Work with Strings and Arrays

In this exercise, you write a function to sort a string.

1. Using Visual Studio, create a new Console Application project. Name the project SortString.

2. Define a string. Then use the *String.Split* method to separate the string into an array of words. The following code demonstrates this:

```
' VB
Dim s As String = "Microsoft .NET Framework Application Development Foundation"
Dim sa As String() = s.Split(" ")
```

```
// C#
string s = "Microsoft .NET Framework Application Development Foundation";
string[] sa = s.Split(' ');
```

3. Call the *Array.Sort* method to sort the array of words, as the following code demonstrates:

```
' VB
Array.Sort(sa)
```

```
// C#
Array.Sort(sa);
```

4. Call the *String.Join* method to convert the array of words back into a single string, and then write the string to the console. The following code sample demonstrates this:

```
' VB
s = String.Join(" ", sa)
Console.WriteLine(s)
```

```
// C#
s = string.Join(" ", sa);
Console.WriteLine(s);
```

5. Run the application and verify that it works correctly.

Exercise 3: Work with Streams and Exceptions

Consider a scenario in which a coworker has written a simple Windows Forms application to view text files. However, users complain that it is very temperamental. If the user mistypes the filename or if the file is not available for any reason, the application fails with an unhandled exception error. In this exercise, you add exception handling to the application to display friendly error messages to users if a file is not available.

1. Navigate to the \<*InstallHome*>\Chapter01\Lesson1\Exercise1\Partial folder and open either the C# version or the Visual Basic .NET version of the ViewFile project.

2. Exceptions occur when users attempt to view a file. Therefore, edit the code that runs for the *showButton.Click* event. Add code to catch any type of exception that occurs and display the error in a dialog box to the user. After the *TextReader* object is initialized, you should close it whether or not an exception occurs. You will need two nested *try* blocks: one to catch exceptions during the *TextReader* initialization and a second one to catch exceptions when the file is read. The following code sample demonstrates this:

```
' VB
Try
    Dim tr As TextReader = New StreamReader(locationTextBox.Text)
    Try
        displayTextBox.Text = tr.ReadToEnd
    Catch ex As Exception
        MessageBox.Show(ex.Message)
    Finally
        tr.Close()
    End Try
Catch ex As Exception
    MessageBox.Show(ex.Message)
End Try
```

```
// C#
try
{
    TextReader tr = new StreamReader(locationTextBox.Text);
    try
    { displayTextBox.Text = tr.ReadToEnd(); }
    catch (Exception ex)
    { MessageBox.Show(ex.Message); }
    finally
    { tr.Close(); }
}
catch (Exception ex)
{ MessageBox.Show(ex.Message); }
```

3. Run your application. First, verify that it can successfully display a text file. Then provide an invalid filename and verify that a message box appears when you provide an invalid filename.

4. Add overloaded exception handling to catch a *System.IO.FileNotFoundException* and *System.UnauthorizedAccessException*. The following code sample shows the changes in bold:

```
' VB
Try
    Dim tr As TextReader = New StreamReader(locationTextBox.Text)
    Try
        displayTextBox.Text = tr.ReadToEnd
    Catch ex As Exception
        MessageBox.Show(ex.Message)
    Finally
        tr.Close()
    End Try
Catch ex As System.IO.FileNotFoundException
    MessageBox.Show("Sorry, the file does not exist.")
Catch ex As System.UnauthorizedAccessException
    MessageBox.Show("Sorry, you lack sufficient privileges.")
Catch ex As Exception
    MessageBox.Show(ex.Message)
End Try

// C#
try
{
    TextReader tr = new StreamReader(locationTextBox.Text);
    try
    { displayTextBox.Text = tr.ReadToEnd(); }
    catch (Exception ex)
    { MessageBox.Show(ex.Message); }
```

```
        finally
        { tr.Close(); }
}
catch (System.IO.FileNotFoundException ex)
{ MessageBox.Show("Sorry, the file does not exist."); }
catch (System.UnauthorizedAccessException ex)
{ MessageBox.Show("Sorry, you lack sufficient privileges."); }
catch (Exception ex)
{ MessageBox.Show(ex.Message); }
```

5. Run your application again and verify that it displays your new error message when you provide an invalid filename.

Lesson Summary

- Reference types directly contain the address of data rather than the actual data.

- When you assign an instance of a value type, a second copy of the value is created. When you assign an instance of a reference type, only the pointer is copied. Therefore, if you assign an instance of a reference type and then modify the data, the data referenced by both the original variable and the second variable are changed.

- The .NET Framework includes a large number of built-in reference types that you can use directly or use to build your own custom types.

- Strings are immutable; use the *StringBuilder* class to create a dynamic string.

- Use streams to read from and write to files, memory, and the network.

- Use the *catch* clause within *try* blocks to filter exceptions by type. Close and dispose of nonmemory resources in the *finally* clause of a *try* block.

Lesson Review

You can use the following questions to test your knowledge of the information in Lesson 2, "Using Common Reference Types." The questions are also available on the companion CD if you prefer to review them in electronic form.

NOTE Answers

Answers to these questions and explanations of why each answer choice is right or wrong are located in the "Answers" section at the end of the book.

---

1. Which of the following are reference types? (Choose all that apply.)

    A. Types declared *Nullable*

    B. *String*

    C. *Exception*

    D. All types derived from *System.Object*

2. What is the correct order for *catch* clauses when handling different exception types?

    A. Most general to most specific

    B. Most likely to occur to least likely to occur

    C. Most specific to most general

    D. Least likely to occur to most likely to occur

3. Of the following scenarios, which would be a good reason to use the *String-Builder* class instead of the *String* class?

    A. When building a string from shorter strings

    B. When working with text data longer than 256 bytes

    C. When you want to search and replace the contents of a string

    D. When a string is a value type

4. Why should you close and dispose of resources in a *finally* block instead of a *catch* block?

    A. It keeps you from having to repeat the operation in each *catch*.

    B. A *finally* block runs whether or not an exception occurs.

    C. The compiler throws an error if resources are not disposed of in the *finally* block.

    D. You cannot dispose of resources in a *catch* block.

5. You create an application with built-in exception handling. For some types of exceptions, you want to add an event to the Event Log that specifies the line of code that initiated the exception. Which *Exception* property should you use?

    A. *Message*

    B. *StackTrace*

    C. *Source*

    D. *Data*

6. You pass a value-type variable into a procedure as an argument. The procedure changes the variable; however, when the procedure returns, the variable has not changed. What happened? (Choose one.)

    A. The variable was not initialized before it was passed in.

    B. Passing a value type into a procedure creates a copy of the data.

    C. The variable was redeclared within the procedure level.

    D. The procedure handled the variable as a reference.

Lesson 3: Constructing Classes

In object-oriented languages, the bulk of the work should be performed within objects. All but the simplest applications require constructing one or more custom classes, each with multiple properties and methods used to perform tasks related to that object. This lesson discusses how to create custom classes.

After this lesson, you will be able to:
- Describe and use inheritance
- Describe and use interfaces
- Describe and use partial classes
- Create a generic type and use the built-in generic types
- Respond to and raise events
- Add attributes to describe assemblies and methods
- Move a type from one class library to another using type forwarding

Estimated lesson time: 40 minutes

What Is Inheritance?

The .NET Framework has thousands of classes, and each class has many different methods and properties. Keeping track of all these classes and members would be impossible if the .NET Framework were not implemented extremely consistently. For example, every class has a *ToString* method that performs exactly the same task—converting an instance of the class into a string. Similarly, most classes support certain operators, such as the comparison operator that compares two instances of a class for equality.

This consistency is possible because of *inheritance* and *interfaces* (described in the section "What Is an Interface?" later in this chapter). Use inheritance to create new classes from existing ones. For example, you will learn in Chapter 6, "Graphics," that the *Bitmap* class inherits from the *Image* class and extends it by adding functionality. Therefore, you can use an instance of the *Bitmap* class in the same way that you would use an instance of the *Image* class. However, the *Bitmap* class provides additional methods that enable you to do more with pictures.

You can easily create a custom exception class by inheriting from *System .ApplicationException*, as shown here:

```vb
' VB
Class DerivedException
    Inherits System.ApplicationException
```

```
    Public Overrides ReadOnly Property Message() As String
        Get
            Return "An error occurred in the application."
        End Get
    End Property
End Class
```

```
// C#
class DerivedException : System.ApplicationException
{
    public override string Message
    {
        get { return "An error occurred in the application."; }
    }
}
```

You can throw and catch the new exception because the custom class inherits the behavior of its base class, as shown here:

```
' VB
Try
    Throw New DerivedException
Catch ex As DerivedException
    Console.WriteLine("Source: {0}, Error: {1}", ex.Source, ex.Message)
End Try
```

```
// C#
try
{
    throw new DerivedException();
}
catch (DerivedException ex)
{
    Console.WriteLine("Source: {0}, Error: {1}", ex.Source, ex.Message);
}
```

Notice that the custom exception not only supports the throw/catch behavior, but it also includes a *Source* member (as well as others) inherited from *System.ApplicationException*.

Another benefit of inheritance is the ability to use derived classes interchangeably, a concept called polymorphism. For example, there are five classes that inherit from the *System.Drawing.Brush* base class: *HatchBrush, LinearGradientBrush, PathGradientBrush, SolidBrush*, and *TextureBrush*. The *Graphics.DrawRectangle* method requires a *Brush* object as one of its parameters; however, you never pass an object of the base *Brush* class to *Graphics.DrawRectangle*. Instead, you pass an object of one of the derived classes. Because they are each derived from the *Brush* class, the *Graphics.DrawRectangle* method can accept any of them. Similarly, if you were to create a custom class derived from the *Brush* class, you could also pass an object of that class to *Graphics.DrawRectangle*.

What Is an Interface?

Interfaces, also known as *contracts*, define a common set of members that all classes that implement the interface must provide. For example, the *IComparable* interface defines the *CompareTo* method, which enables two instances of a class to be compared for equality. All classes that implement the *IComparable* interface, whether custom-created or built in the .NET Framework, can be compared for equality.

IDisposable is an interface that provides a single method, *Dispose,* to enable assemblies that create an instance of your class to free up any resources the instance has consumed. To create a class that implements the *IDisposable* interface using Visual Studio, follow these steps:

1. Create the class declaration. For example:

   ```
   ' VB
   Class BigClass
   End Class
   ```

   ```
   // C#
   class BigClass
   {
   }
   ```

2. Add the interface declaration, as shown in bold here:

   ```
   ' VB
   Class BigClass
       Implements IDisposable
   End Class
   ```

   ```
   // C#
   class BigClass : IDisposable
   {
   }
   ```

3. If you are using Visual Basic, Visual Studio should generate method declarations automatically for each of the required methods after you press Enter at the end of the *Implements* command. If it does not, delete the *Implements* command and try again; Visual Studio may still be starting up. If you are using C#, right-click the *Interface* declaration, click Implement Interface, and then click Implement Interface again, as shown in Figure 1-1.

4. Write code for each of the interface's methods. In this example, you would write code in the *Dispose* method to deallocate any resources you had allocated.

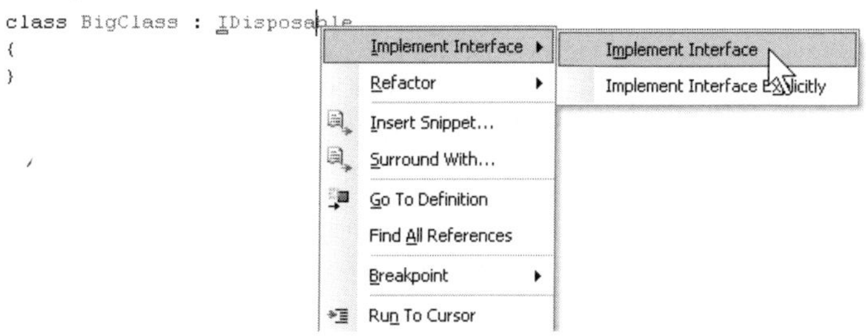

Figure 1-1 Visual Studio simplifies implementing an interface

Table 1-6 lists the most commonly used interfaces in the .NET Framework.

Table 1-6 Commonly Used Interfaces

Interface	Description
IComparable	Implemented by types whose values can be ordered; for example, the numeric and string classes. *IComparable* is required for sorting.
IDisposable	Defines methods for disposing of an object manually. This interface is important for large objects that consume considerable resources, or objects such as databases that lock access to resources.
IConvertible	Enables a class to be converted to a base type such as *Boolean*, *Byte*, *Double*, or *String*.
ICloneable	Supports copying an object.
IEquatable	Allows you to compare instances of a class for equality. For example, if you implement this interface, you could say *if (a == b)*.
IFormattable	Enables you to convert the value of an object into a specially formatted string. This provides greater flexibility than the base *ToString* method.

You can create your own interfaces, too. This is useful if you need to create multiple custom classes that behave similarly and can be used interchangeably. For example, the following code defines an interface containing three members:

```
' VB
Interface IMessage
    Function Send() As Boolean
    Property Message() As String
    Property Address() As String
End Interface
```

```
// C#
interface IMessage
{
    bool Send();
    string Message { get; set; }
    string Address { get;  set; }
}
```

If you implement that interface in a new class, Visual Studio generates the following template for the interface members:

```
' VB
Class EmailMessage
    Implements IMessage

    Public Property Address() As String Implements IMessage.Address
        Get
        End Get
        Set(ByVal value As String)
        End Set
    End Property

    Public Property Message() As String Implements IMessage.Message
        Get
        End Get
        Set(ByVal value As String)
        End Set
    End Property

    Public Function Send() As Boolean Implements IMessage.Send
    End Function
End Class
```

```
// C#
class EmailMessage : IMessage
{
    public bool Send()
    {
    throw new Exception("The method or operation is not implemented.");
    }

    public string Message
    {
        get
        {
        throw new Exception("The method or operation is not implemented.");
        }
        set
        {
        throw new Exception("The method or operation is not implemented.");
        }
    }
```

```
    public string Address
    {
        get
        {
        throw new Exception("The method or operation is not implemented.");
        }
        set
        {
        throw new Exception("The method or operation is not implemented.");
        }
    }
}
```

If you create a custom class and later decide that it would be useful to have multiple classes with the same members, Visual Studio has a shortcut to extract an interface from a custom class. Simply follow these steps:

1. Right-click the class in Visual Studio.

2. Click Refactor and then click Extract Interface.

3. Specify the interface name, select the public members that should form the interface, and then click OK.

Classes can implement multiple interfaces. For example, a class could implement both the *IComparable* and *IDisposable* interfaces.

What Are Partial Classes?

Partial classes allow you to split a class definition across multiple source files. The benefit of this approach is that it hides details of the class definition so that developers can focus on more significant portions.

The *Windows Form* class is an example of a built-in partial class. In Visual Studio 2003 and earlier, form classes included code generated by the form designer. Now that code is hidden in a partial class stored in files named *form.Designer.vb* or *form.Designer.cs*.

In Visual Basic, you must select the Show All Files toolbar button in Solution Explorer to see the partial class files. In C#, that view is enabled by default.

Exam Tip   Partial classes aren't part of the exam objectives, but you need to know about them so that you can find the Form Designer code when you create a new Windows Form.

What Are Generics?

Generics are part of the type system of the CLR that allow you to define a type while leaving some details unspecified. Instead of specifying the types of certain parameters or members, you can allow code that uses your generic class to specify those types. This allows consumer code to tailor your class to meet specific needs of the consumer code.

Exam Tip   Generic types are a complex concept, and you will probably see a significant number of questions about generics on the exam.

The .NET Framework includes several generic classes in the *System.Collections.Generic* namespace, including *Dictionary*, *Queue*, *SortedDictionary*, and *SortedList*. These classes work similarly to their nongeneric counterparts in *System.Collections*, but they offer improved performance and type safety.

MORE INFO   Generic Collections

The .NET Framework includes the *System.Collections.Generic* namespace, which provides built-in collections that offer improved performance over standard collections. For more information, refer to Chapter 4, "Collections and Generics."

Why Use Generics?

Generics offer two significant advantages over using the *object* class:

- **Reduced run-time errors**   The compiler cannot detect type errors when you cast to and from the *Object* class. For example, if you cast a string to an *Object* class and then attempt to cast that *Object* to an integer, the compiler does not catch the error. Instead, the application throws an exception at run time. Using generics allows the compiler to catch this type of bug before your program runs. In addition, you can specify constraints to limit the classes used in a generic, enabling the compiler to detect an incompatible type being called for by consumer code.

- **Improved performance**   Casting requires boxing and unboxing (explained later in Lesson 4), which steals processor time and slows performance. Using generics doesn't require casting or boxing, so run-time performance improves.

> ### Real World
>
> *Tony Northrup*
>
> I haven't been able to reproduce the performance benefits of generics; however, according to Microsoft, generics are faster than using casting. In practice, casting proved to be several times faster than using a generic. However, you probably won't notice performance differences in your applications. (My tests over 100,000 iterations took only a few seconds.) Regardless, you should use generics because they are type-safe.

How to Create a Generic Type

First, examine the following classes. Classes *Obj* and *Gen* perform exactly the same tasks, but *Obj* uses the *Object* class to enable any type to be stored in its field, while *Gen* uses generics:

```vb
' VB
Class Obj
    Public V1 As Object
    Public V2 As Object

    Public Sub New(ByVal _V1 As Object, ByVal _V2 As Object)
        V1 = _V1
        V2 = _V2
    End Sub
End Class

Class Gen(Of T, U)
    Public V1 As T
    Public V2 As U

    Public Sub New(ByVal _V1 As T, ByVal _V2 As U)
        V1 = _V1
        V2 = _V2
    End Sub
End Class
```

```csharp
// C#
class Obj
{
    public Object t;
    public Object u;

    public Obj(Object _t, Object _u)
    {
        t = _t;
```

```
        u = _u;
    }
}

class Gen<T, U>
{
    public T t;
    public U u;

    public Gen(T _t, U _u)
    {
        t = _t;
        u = _u;
    }
}
```

As you can see, the *Obj* class has two members of type *Object*. The *Gen* class has two field members of type *T* and *U*. The consuming code determines the types for *T* and *U*. Depending on how the consuming code uses the *Gen* class, *T* and *U* could be a *string*, an *int*, a custom class, or any combination thereof.

There is a significant limitation to creating a generic class (without constraints, as discussed in the section "How to Use Constraints," later in this chapter): Generic code is valid only if it compiles for every possible constructed instance of the generic, whether an *Int*, a *string*, or any other class. Essentially, you are limited to the capabilities of the base *Object* class when writing generic code. Therefore, you could call the *ToString* or *GetHashCode* method within your class, but you could not use the + operator or the > operator. These same restrictions do not apply to the consuming code because the consuming code declares a specific type for the generic.

How to Consume a Generic Type

When you consume a generic type, you must specify the types for any generics used. Consider the following Console application code, which uses the *Gen* and *Obj* classes:

```
' VB
' Add two Strings using the Obj class
Dim oa As Obj = New Obj("Hello, ", "World!")
Console.WriteLine(CType(oa.V1, String) + CType(oa.V2, String))

' Add two Strings using the Gen class
Dim ga As New Gen(Of String, String)("Hello, ", "World!")
Console.WriteLine(ga.V1 + ga.V2)

' Add a Double and an Integer using the Obj class
Dim ob As Obj = New Obj(10.125, 2005)
Console.WriteLine(CType(ob.V1, Double) + CType(ob.V2, Integer))
```

```
' Add a Double and an Integer using the Gen class
Dim gb As New Gen(Of Double, Integer)(10.125, 2005)
Console.WriteLine(gb.V1 + gb.V2)
```

```
// C#
// Add two strings using the Obj class
Obj oa = new Obj("Hello, ", "World!");
Console.WriteLine((string)oa.t + (string)oa.u);
```

```
// Add two strings using the Gen class
Gen<string, string> ga = new Gen<string, string>("Hello, ", "World!");
Console.WriteLine(ga.t + ga.u);
```

```
// Add a double and an int using the Obj class
Obj ob = new Obj(10.125, 2005);
Console.WriteLine((double)ob.t + (int)ob.u);
```

```
// Add a double and an int using the Gen class
Gen<double, int> gb = new Gen<double, int>(10.125, 2005);
Console.WriteLine(gb.t + gb.u);
```

If you run that code in a Console application, the *Obj* and *Gen* classes produce exactly the same results. However, the code that uses the *Gen* class actually works faster because it does not require boxing and unboxing to and from the *Object* class. (Boxing and unboxing are discussed in the section "What Are Boxing and Unboxing?" later in this chapter.) In addition, developers would have a much easier time using the *Gen* class. First, developers would not have to cast manually from the *Object* class to the appropriate types. Second, type errors would be caught at compile time rather than at run time. To demonstrate that benefit, consider the following code, which contains an error (shown in bold):

```
' VB
' Add a Double and an Integer using the Gen class
Dim gb As New Gen(Of Double, Integer)(10.125, 2005)
Console.WriteLine(gb.V1 + gb.V2)
```

```
' Add a Double and an Integer using the Obj class
Dim ob As Obj = New Obj(10.125, 2005)
Console.WriteLine(CType(ob.V1, Integer) + CType(ob.V2, Integer))
```

```
// C#
// Add a double and an int using the Gen class
Gen<double, int> gc = new Gen<double, int>(10.125, 2005);
Console.WriteLine(gc.t + gc.u);
```

```
// Add a double and an int using the Obj class
Obj oc = new Obj(10.125, 2005);
Console.WriteLine((int)oc.t + (int)oc.u);
```

The last line in that code sample contains an error—the *oc.V1* value (*oc.t* in C#) is cast to an *int* instead of to a *double*. Unfortunately, the compiler won't catch the mistake. Instead, in C#, a run-time exception is thrown when the runtime attempts to cast a *double* to an *int* value. In Visual Basic, which allows narrowing conversions by default, the result is even worse—a miscalculation occurs. It's much easier to fix a bug that the compiler catches and much harder to detect and fix a run-time error, so the generic class provides a clear benefit.

How to Use Constraints

Generics would be extremely limited if you could only write code that would compile for any class, because you would be limited to the capabilities of the base *Object* class. To overcome this limitation, use constraints to place requirements on the types that consuming code can substitute for your generic parameter.

Generics support four types of constraints:

- **Interface**   Allows only types that implement specific interfaces to be used as a generic type argument

- **Base class**   Allows only types that match or inherit from a specific base class to be used as a generic type argument

- **Constructor**   Requires types that are used as the type argument for your generic to implement a parameterless constructor

- **Reference or value type**   Requires types that are used as the type argument for your generic to be either a reference or a value type

Use the *As* clause in Visual Basic or the *where* clause in C# to apply a constraint to a generic. For example, the following generic class could be used only by types that implement the *IComparable* interface:

```
' VB
Class CompGen(Of T As IComparable)
    Public t1 As T
    Public t2 As T

    Public Sub New(ByVal _t1 As T, ByVal _t2 As T)
        t1 = _t1
        t2 = _t2
    End Sub

    Public Function Max() As T
        If t2.CompareTo(t1) < 0 Then
            Return t1
```

```
        Else
            Return t2
        End If
    End Function
End Class

// C#
class CompGen<T>
    where T : IComparable
{
    public T t1;
    public T t2;

    public CompGen(T _t1, T _t2)
    {
        t1 = _t1;
        t2 = _t2;
    }

    public T Max()
    {
        if (t2.CompareTo(t1) < 0)
            return t1;
        else
            return t2;
    }
}
```

The preceding class compiles correctly. However, if you remove the *As/where* clause, the compiler returns an error indicating that generic type *T* does not contain a definition for *CompareTo*. By constraining the generic to classes that implement *IComparable*, you guarantee that the *CompareTo* method will always be available.

Events

Most projects are nonlinear. In Windows Presentation Foundation (WPF) applications, you might have to wait for a user to click a button or press a key and then respond to that event. In server applications, you might have to wait for an incoming network request. These capabilities are provided by events in the .NET Framework, as described in the following sections.

What Is an Event?

Objects, known as *event senders*, trigger *events* when an action takes place, such as the user clicking a button, a method completing a calculation, or a network communication being received. *Event receivers* can handle these events but running a method, known as an event handler, when the event occurs. Because the event sender doesn't know which method will handle an event, you must create a *delegate* to act as a pointer to the event handler.

What Is a Delegate?

A *delegate* is a reference to a method that itself does not contain code. The signature for a delegate must match the signature of the event handler. The following code sample demonstrates a delegate in its entirety:

```
' VB
Public Delegate Sub myEventHandler(sender As Object, e As EventArgs)
```

```
// C#
public delegate void myEventHandler(object sender, EventArgs e);
```

Like this example, most delegates have no return value, accept an *Object* as the first parameter, and a class derived from *EventArgs* as the second parameter. The *Object* contains information that the event handler might need. For example, if you created a method that returned the results of a calculation using an event handler, you would store the results in the *Object* parameter. Then, in your event handler, you would cast the *Object* to the correct type.

To associate the event with the method that handles the event, add an instance of the delegate to the event, as shown in the next section. The event handler is called whenever the event occurs unless you remove the delegate.

How to Respond to an Event

You must do two things to respond to an event:

- Create a method to respond to the event. The method must match the *delegate* signature. Typically, this means it must return *void* and accept two parameters: an *object* and an *EventArgs* (or a derived class). The following code demonstrates such a method:

```
' VB
Public Sub Button1_Click(sender As Object, e As EventArgs)
    ' Method code
End Sub
```

```
// C#
private void button1_Click(object sender, EventArgs e)
{
    // Method code
}
```

■ Add the event handler to indicate which method should receive events, as the following code demonstrates:

```
' VB
AddHandler Me.Button1.Click, AddressOf Me.Button1_Click
```

```
// C#
this.button1.Click += new System.EventHandler(this.button1_Click);
```

When the event occurs, the method you specified runs.

How to Raise an Event

You must do at least three things to raise an event:

■ Create a delegate, as follows:

```
' VB
Public Delegate Sub MyEventHandler(ByVal sender As Object, ByVal e As EventArgs)
```

```
// C#
public delegate void MyEventHandler(object sender, EventArgs e);
```

■ Create an event object, as follows:

```
' VB
Public Event MyEvent As MyEventHandler
```

```
// C#
public event MyEventHandler MyEvent;
```

■ Invoke the delegate within a method when you need to raise the event, as the following code demonstrates:

```
' VB
Dim e As EventArgs = New EventArgs
RaiseEvent MyEvent(Me, e)
```

```
// C#
EventArgs e = new EventArgs();

if (MyEvent != null)
{
    // Invokes the delegates.
    MyEvent(this, e);
}
// Note that C# requires a check to determine whether handler is null.
// This is not necessary in Visual Basic.
```

In addition, you can derive a custom class from *EventArgs* if you need to pass information to the event handler.

NOTE   Differences Between Raising Events in Visual Basic and in C#

Visual Basic and C# differ when raising events. In C#, you must check whether the event object is *null* before calling it. In Visual Basic, you can omit that check.

What Are Attributes?

Attributes describe a type, method, or property in a way that can be queried programmatically using a technique called *reflection*. Some common uses for attributes are the following:

- To specify which security privileges a class requires
- To specify security privileges to refuse in order to reduce security risk
- To declare capabilities, such as supporting serialization
- To describe the assembly by providing a title, description, and copyright notice

Attribute types derive from the *System.Attribute* base class and are specified using <> notation (in Visual Basic) or *[]* notation (in C#). The following code sample, which requires the *System.Reflection* namespace, demonstrates how to add assembly attributes:

```vb
' VB - AssemblyInfo.vb
<Assembly: AssemblyTitle("ch01vb")>
<Assembly: AssemblyDescription("Chapter 1 Samples")>
<Assembly: AssemblyCompany("Microsoft Learning")>
<Assembly: AssemblyProduct("ch01vb")>
<Assembly: AssemblyCopyright("Copyright © 2008")>
<Assembly: AssemblyTrademark("")>
```

```csharp
// C# - AssemblyInfo.cs
[assembly: AssemblyTitle("ch01cs")]
[assembly: AssemblyDescription("Chapter 1 Samples")]
[assembly: AssemblyConfiguration("")]
[assembly: AssemblyCompany("Microsoft Learning")]
[assembly: AssemblyProduct("ch01cs")]
[assembly: AssemblyCopyright("Copyright © 2008")]
[assembly: AssemblyTrademark("")]
```

Visual Studio automatically creates some standard attributes for your assembly when you create a project, including a title, description, company, globally unique identifier (GUID), and version. You should edit these attributes for every project you create because the defaults do not include important information such as the description.

Attributes do more than describe an assembly to other developers. They can also declare requirements or capabilities. For example, to enable a class to be serialized, you must add the *Serializable* attribute, as the following code demonstrates:

```vb
' VB
<Serializable()> Class ShoppingCartItem
End Class
```

```csharp
// C#
[Serializable]
class ShoppingCartItem
{
}
```

Without the *Serializable* attribute, a class is not serializable. Similarly, the following code uses attributes to declare that it needs to read the C:\Boot.ini file. Because of this attribute, the runtime throws an exception prior to execution if the application lacks the specified privilege:

```vb
' VB
Imports System.Security.Permissions

<Assembly: FileIOPermissionAttribute(SecurityAction.RequestMinimum, _
Read := "C:\boot.ini")>
Module Module1
    Sub Main()
        Console.WriteLine("Hello, World!")
    End Sub
End Module
```

```csharp
// C#
using System.Security.Permissions;

[assembly:FileIOPermissionAttribute(SecurityAction.RequestMinimum,
    Read=@"C:\boot.ini")]
namespace DeclarativeExample
{
    class Program
    {
        static void Main(string[] args)
        {
            Console.WriteLine("Hello, World!");
        }
    }
}
```

What Is Type Forwarding?

Type forwarding allows you to move a type from one assembly (assembly A) into another (assembly B), and to do so in such a way that it is not necessary to recompile clients that consume assembly A. You use the *TypeForwardedTo* attribute to implement type forwarding. After a component (assembly) ships and is being used by client applications, you can use type forwarding to move a type from the component (that is, the assembly) into another assembly and ship the updated component (and any additional assemblies required), and the client applications still work without being recompiled. Type forwarding works only for components referenced by existing applications. When you rebuild an application, there must be appropriate assembly references for any types used in the application.

To move a type from one class library to another, follow these steps:

1. Add a *TypeForwardedTo* attribute to the source class library assembly.
2. Cut the type definition from the source class library.
3. Paste the type definition into the destination class library.
4. Rebuild both libraries.

The following code shows the attribute declaration used to move *TypeA* to the *DestLib* class library:

```
' VB
Imports System.Runtime.CompilerServices
<Assembly:TypeForwardedTo(GetType(DestLib.TypeA))>
```

```
// C#
using System.Runtime.CompilerServices;
[assembly:TypeForwardedTo(typeof(DestLib.TypeA))]
```

Lab: Create a Derived Class with Delegates

The following exercises demonstrate inheritance and events. If you encounter a problem completing an exercise, the completed projects are available along with the sample files.

Exercise 1: Derive a New Class from an Existing Class

In this exercise, you derive a new class from the *Person* class you created in Lesson 1.

1. Navigate to the \<*InstallHome*>\Chapter01\Lesson1\Exercise1\Partial folder and open either the C# version or the Visual Basic version of the CreateStruct project.
2. Change the *Person* structure to a class.

3. Create a new class definition named *Manager* that inherits from the base *Person* class, as this code demonstrates:

```
' VB
Class Manager
    Inherits Person
End Class
```

```
// C#
class Manager : Person
{
}
```

4. Add two new public member fields as strings: *phoneNumber* and *officeLocation*.

5. Overload the constructor to accept a phone number and office location to define the new members. To do this, you need to call the base class's constructor, as shown in the following code sample:

```
' VB
Public Sub New(ByVal _firstName As String, ByVal _lastName As String, _
    ByVal _age As Integer, ByVal _gender As Genders, _
    ByVal _phoneNumber As String, _ ByVal _officeLocation As String)
    MyBase.New(_firstName, _lastName, _age, _gender)
    phoneNumber = _phoneNumber
    officeLocation = _officeLocation
End Sub
```

```
// C#
public Manager(string _firstName, string _lastName, int _age,
    Genders _gender, string _phoneNumber, string _officeLocation)
    : base (_firstName, _lastName, _age, _gender)
{
    phoneNumber = _phoneNumber;
    officeLocation = _officeLocation;
}
```

6. Override the *ToString* method to add the phone number and office location, as shown in the following sample:

```
' VB
Public Overrides Function ToString() As String
    Return MyBase.ToString + ", " + phoneNumber + ", " + officeLocation
End Function
```

```
// C#
public override string ToString()
{
    return base.ToString() + ", " + phoneNumber + ", " + officeLocation;
}
```

7. Modify the *Main* method to create a *Manager* object instead of a *Person* object and pass a phone number and location into the constructor. Then run your application to verify that it works correctly.

Exercise 2: Respond to an Event

In this exercise, you create a class that responds to a timer event.

1. Using Visual Studio, create a new Windows Forms Application project. Name the project TimerEvents.

2. Add a *ProgressBar* control to the form, as shown in Figure 1-2.

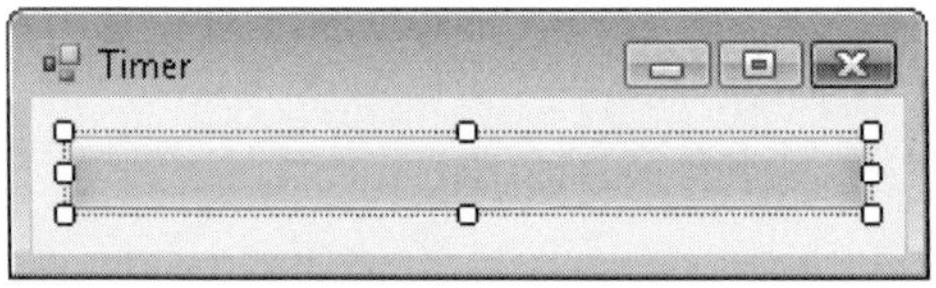

Figure 1-2   You will control this progress bar by responding to timer events

3. Within the form class declaration, declare an instance of a *System.Windows .Forms.Timer* object. *Timer* objects can be used to throw events after a specified number of milliseconds. The following code sample shows how to declare a *Timer* object:

```
' VB
Dim t As System.Windows.Forms.Timer
```

```
// C#
System.Windows.Forms.Timer t;
```

4. In the designer, view the properties for the form. Then view the list of events. Double-click the *Load* event to automatically create an event handler that runs the first time the form is initialized. Within the method, initialize the *Timer* object, set the interval to 1 second, create an event handler for the *Tick* event, and start the timer. The following code sample demonstrates this:

```
' VB
Private Sub Form1_Load(ByVal sender As System.Object, _
    ByVal e As System.EventArgs) _
    Handles MyBase.Shown
    t = New System.Windows.Forms.Timer
    t.Interval = 1000
    AddHandler t.Tick, AddressOf Me.t_Tick
    t.Start()
End Sub
```

```
// C#
private void Form1_Load(object sender, EventArgs e)
{
    t = new System.Windows.Forms.Timer();
    t.Interval = 1000;
    t.Tick += new EventHandler(t_Tick);
    t.Start();
}
```

5. Implement the method that responds to the *Timer.Tick* event. When the event occurs, add 10 to the *ProgressBar.Value* property. Then stop the timer if the *ProgressBar.Value* property has reached 100. The following code sample demonstrates this:

```
' VB
Private Sub t_Tick(ByVal sender As Object, ByVal e As EventArgs)
    ProgressBar1.Value += 10

    If ProgressBar1.Value >= 100 Then
        t.Stop()
    End If
End Sub
```

```
// C#
void t_Tick(object sender, EventArgs e)
{
    progressBar1.Value += 10;

    if (progressBar1.Value >= 100)
        t.Stop();
}
```

6. Run the application to verify that it responds to the *Timer* event every second.

Lesson Summary

- Use inheritance to create new types based on existing ones.
- Use interfaces to define a common set of members that must be implemented by related types.
- Partial classes split a class definition across multiple source files.
- Events allow you to run a specified method when something occurs in a different section of code.
- Use attributes to describe assemblies, types, and members.
- Use the *TypeForwardedTo* attribute to move a type from one class library to another.

Lesson Review

You can use the following questions to test your knowledge of the information in Lesson 3, "Constructing Classes." The questions are also available on the companion CD if you prefer to review them in electronic form.

NOTE   Answers

Answers to these questions and explanations of why each answer choice is right or wrong are located in the "Answers" section at the end of the book.

---

1. Which of the following statements are true? (Choose all that apply.)

   A. Inheritance defines a contract between types.

   B. Interfaces define a contract between types.

   C. Inheritance derives a type from a base type.

   D. Interfaces derive a type from a base type.

2. Which of the following are examples of built-in generic types? (Choose all that apply.)

   A. *Nullable*

   B. *Boolean*

   C. *EventHandler*

   D. *System.Drawing.Point*

3. You create a generic class in which you store field members whose type is generic. What do you do to dispose of the objects stored in the fields?

   A. Call the *Object.Dispose* method.

   B. Implement the *IDisposable* interface.

   C. Derive the generic class from the *IDisposable* class.

   D. Use constraints to require the generic type to implement the *IDisposable* interface.

4. You've implemented an event delegate from a class, but when you try to attach an event procedure you get a compiler error that there is no overload that matches the delegate. What happened?

   A. The signature of the event procedure doesn't match that defined by the delegate.

   B. The event procedure is declared *Shared/static*, but it should be an instance member instead.

    C. You mistyped the event procedure name when attaching it to the delegate.

    D. The class was created in a different language.

5. You are creating a class that needs to be sorted when in a collection. Which interface should you implement?

    A. *IEquatable*

    B. *IFormattable*

    C. *IDisposable*

    D. *IComparable*

Lesson 4: Converting Between Types

Often, you need to convert between two different types. For example, you might need to determine whether an *int* is greater or less than a *double*, pass a *double* to a method that requires an *int* as a parameter, or display a number as text.

This lesson describes how to convert between types in both Visual Basic and C#. Type conversion is one of the few areas where Visual Basic and C# differ considerably.

After this lesson, you will be able to:

- Convert between types
- Explain boxing and why it should be avoided
- Implement conversion operators

Estimated lesson time: 20 minutes

Conversion in Visual Basic and C#

By default, Visual Basic allows implicit conversions between types, while C# prohibits implicit conversions that lose precision. To turn off implicit conversions in Visual Basic, add *Option Strict On* to the top of each code file, or (in Visual Studio) select Project, choose Properties, select Compile, and select Option Strict On for the entire project.

Both Visual Basic and C# allow implicit conversion if the destination type can accommodate all possible values from the source type. That is called a *widening conversion*, and it is illustrated by the following example:

```
' VB
Dim i As Integer = 1
Dim d As Double = 1.0001
d = i          ' Conversion allowed
```

```
// C#
int i = 1;
double d = 1.0001;
d = i;   // Conversion allowed.
```

If the range or precision of the source type exceeds that of the destination type, the operation is called a *narrowing conversion*, which usually requires explicit conversion. Table 1-7 lists the ways to perform explicit conversions.

Table 1-7   Methods for Explicit Conversion

System Type	Visual Basic	C#	Converts
System.Convert			Between types that implement the *System.IConvertible* interface.
	CType	(*type*) cast operator	Between types that define conversion operators.
type.*ToString*, type.*Parse*			Between string and base types; throws an exception if the conversion is not possible.
type.*TryParse*, type.*TryParseExact*			From string to a base type; returns false if the conversion is not possible.
	CBool, CInt, CStr, etc.		Between base Visual Basic types; compiled inline for better performance. (Visual Basic only.)
	DirectCast, TryCast		Between types. *DirectCast* throws an exception if the types are not related through inheritance or if they do not share a common interface; *TryCast* returns *Nothing* in those situations. (Visual Basic only.)

Narrowing conversions may return an incorrect result if the source value exceeds the destination type's range. If a conversion between the types is not defined, you receive a compile-time error.

What Are Boxing and Unboxing?

Boxing converts a value type to a reference type, and *unboxing* converts a reference type to a value type. The following example demonstrates boxing by converting an *int* (a value type) to an *object* (a reference type):

```
' VB
Dim i As Integer = 123
Dim o As Object = CType(i, Object)
```

```
// C#
int i = 123;
object o = (object)i;
```

Unboxing occurs if you assign a reference *object* to a value type variable. The following example demonstrates unboxing:

```
' VB
Dim o As Object = 123
Dim i As Integer = CType(o, Integer)
```

```
// C#
object o = 123;
int i = (int)o;
```

Boxing Tips

Boxing and unboxing incur overhead, so you should avoid them when programming intensely repetitive tasks. Boxing also occurs when you call virtual methods that a structure or any value type inherits from *System.Object*, such as *ToString*. Follow these tips to avoid unnecessary boxing:

- Implement type-specific versions (overloads) for a procedure that must be able to accept various value types. It is better to create several overloaded procedures than one procedure that accepts an *Object* argument.
- Use generics whenever possible instead of coding arguments of the *object* type.
- Override the *ToString*, *Equals*, and *GetHash* virtual members when defining structures.

How to Implement Conversion in Custom Types

You can define conversions for your own types in several ways. Which technique you choose depends on the type of conversion you want to perform, as follows:

- Define conversion operators to simplify narrowing and widening conversions between numeric types.

- Override *ToString* to provide conversion to strings, and override *Parse* to provide conversion from strings.

- Implement *System.IConvertible* to enable conversion through *System.Convert*. Use this technique to enable culture-specific conversions.

- Implement a *TypeConverter* class to enable design-time conversion for use in the Properties window of Visual Studio. Design-time conversion is outside the scope of the exam, and the *TypeConverter* class is not covered in this book.

MORE INFO   Design-Time Conversion

For more information about design-time conversion, read "Extending Design-Time Support" at *http://msdn.microsoft.com/en-us/library/37899azc.aspx*.

Defining conversion operators allows you to assign from a value type directly to your custom type. Use the *Widening/implicit* keyword for conversions that don't lose precision; use the *Narrowing/explicit* keyword for conversions that could lose precision. For example, the following structure defines operators that allow assignment to and from integer values (note the bold keywords):

```vb
' VB
Structure TypeA
    Public Value As Integer

    ' Allows implicit conversion from an integer.
    Public Shared Widening Operator CType(ByVal arg As Integer) As TypeA
        Dim res As New TypeA
        res.Value = arg
        Return res
    End Operator

    ' Allows explicit conversion to an integer.
    Public Shared Narrowing Operator CType(ByVal arg As TypeA) As Integer
        Return arg.Value
    End Operator

    ' Provides string conversion (avoids boxing).
    Public Overrides Function ToString() As String
        Return Me.Value.ToString
    End Function

End Structure
```

```csharp
// C#
struct TypeA
{
    public int Value;
```

```
    // Allows implicit conversion from an integer.
    public static implicit operator TypeA(int arg)
    {
        TypeA res = new TypeA();
        res.Value = arg;
        return res;
    }

    // Allows explicit conversion to an integer.
    public static explicit operator int(TypeA arg)
    {
        return arg.Value;
    }

    // Provides string conversion (avoids boxing).
    public override string ToString()
    {
        return this.Value.ToString();
    }
}
```

The preceding type also overrides *ToString* to perform the string conversion without boxing. Now you can assign integers to a variable of this type directly, as shown here:

```
' VB
Dim a As TypeA, i As Integer
' Widening conversion is OK implicit.
a = 42   ' Rather than a.Value = 42
' Narrowing conversion in VB does not need to be explicit.
i = a
' Narrowing conversion can be explicit.
i = CInt(a) ' Rather than i = a.Value
' This syntax is OK, too.
i = CType(a, Integer)
Console.WriteLine("a = {0}, i = {1}", a.ToString, i.ToString)
```

```
// C#
TypeA a; int i;
// Widening conversion is OK implicit.
a = 42;  // Rather than a.Value = 42
// Narrowing conversion must be explicit in C#.
i = (int)a; // Rather than i = a.Value
Console.WriteLine("a = {0}, i = {1}", a.ToString(), i.ToString());
```

To implement the *System.IConvertible* interface, add the *IConvertible* interface to the type definition. Then use Visual Studio to implement the interface automatically. Visual Studio inserts member declarations for 17 methods, including *GetTypeCode*, *ChangeType*, and *ToType* methods for each base type. You don't have to implement every method, and some—such as *ToDateTime*—probably are invalid. For invalid methods, simply throw an exception—in C#, Visual Studio automatically adds code to throw an exception for any conversion methods you don't implement.

After you implement *IConvertible*, the custom type can be converted using the standard *System.Convert* class, as shown here:

```
' VB
Dim a As TypeA, b As Boolean
a = 42
' Convert using ToBoolean.
b = Convert.ToBoolean(a)
Console.WriteLine("a = {0}, b = {1}", a.ToString, b.ToString)
```

```
// C#
TypeA a; bool b;
a = 42;
// Convert using ToBoolean.
b = Convert.ToBoolean(a);
Console.WriteLine("a = {0}, b = {1}", a.ToString(), b.ToString());
```

If you do not implement a conversion, throw an *InvalidCastException*.

Lab: Safely Performing Conversions

The following exercises show how to avoid problems with implicit conversions so that your programs function predictably. Navigate to the \<*InstallHome*>\Chapter01\ Lesson1\Exercise1\Partial folder.

Exercise 1: Examine Implicit Conversion

In this exercise, you examine conversion to determine which number types allow implicit conversion.

1. Create a new Console Application project in Visual Studio.

2. Declare instances of three value types: *Int16*, *Int32*, and *double*. The following code sample demonstrates this:

    ```
    ' VB
    Dim i16 As Int16 = 1
    Dim i32 As Int32 = 1
    Dim db As Double = 1
    ```

    ```
    // C#
    Int16 i16 = 1;
    Int32 i32 = 1;
    double db = 1;
    ```

3. Attempt to assign each variable to all the others, as the following code sample demonstrates:

    ```
    ' VB
    i16 = i32
    i16 = db
    ```

```
i32 = i16
i32 = db

db = i16
db = i32

// C#
i16 = i32;
i16 = db;

i32 = i16;
i32 = db;

db = i16;
db = i32;
```

4. Attempt to build your project. Which implicit conversions did the compiler allow, and why?

Exercise 2: Enable Option Strict (Visual Basic Only)

In this exercise, which is only for developers using Visual Basic, you modify the compiler's options and then rebuild the project you created in Exercise 1.

1. In Visual Studio, open the project you created in Exercise 1.

2. From the Project menu choose <ProjectName> Properties.

3. Select the Compile tab. In the Condition list, find the Implicit Conversion item and change the Notification type to Error.

4. Attempt to build your project. Which implicit conversions did the compiler allow, and why?

Lesson Summary

- The .NET Framework can convert between built-in types automatically. Widening conversions occur implicitly in both Visual Basic and C#. Narrowing conversions require explicit conversion in C#, while Visual Basic allows narrowing conversions by default.

- Boxing allows any type to be treated as a reference type.

- You must specifically implement conversion operators to enable conversion in custom types.

Lesson Review

You can use the following questions to test your knowledge of the information in Lesson 4, "Converting Between Types." The questions are also available on the companion CD if you prefer to review them in electronic form.

NOTE **Answers**

Answers to these questions and explanations of why each answer choice is right or wrong are located in the "Answers" section at the end of the book.

1. Why should boxing be avoided?

   A. It adds overhead.

   B. Users must have administrative privileges to run the application.

   C. It makes code less readable.

2. Structures inherit *ToString* from *System.Object*. Why would someone override that method within a structure? (Choose all that apply.)

   A. To avoid boxing

   B. To return something other than the type name

   C. The compiler requires structures to override the *ToString* method

   D. To avoid run-time errors caused by invalid string conversions

3. If there is no valid conversion between two types, what should you do when implementing the *IConvertible* interface?

   A. Delete the *ToType* member that performs the conversion.

   B. Throw an *InvalidCastException*.

   C. Throw a new custom exception reporting the error.

   D. Leave the member body empty.

4. With strict conversions enabled, which of the following would allow an implicit conversion? (Choose all that apply.)

   A. *Int16* to *Int32*

   B. *Int32* to *Int16*

   C. *Int16* to *double*

   D. A *double* to *Int16*

Chapter Review

To practice and reinforce the skills you learned in this chapter further, you can perform any or all of the following tasks:

- Review the chapter summary.
- Review the list of key terms introduced in this chapter.
- Complete the case scenario. The scenario sets up a real-world situation involving the topics of this chapter and asks you to create a solution.
- Complete the suggested practices.
- Take a practice test.

Chapter Summary

- Instances of value types are small variables that store data directly rather than storing a pointer to a second memory location that contains the data. Assignment between value types copies the data from one variable to the other, creating a separate instance of the data. You can make value types nullable using the *Nullable* generic type, and you can create structures that combine multiple value types.

- Reference types directly contain the address of data rather than the actual data. The .NET Framework includes thousands of reference types to perform many common tasks you might require. The most commonly used reference type is the *String* class. Because the string stored in a *String* object is immutable, it behaves differently from other reference types. When you assign instances of most reference classes, only the pointer is copied, which means changes made to the data pointed to by one instance are also reflected in the other instance.

- When an unexpected event occurs, the .NET Framework throws an exception. You can handle these exceptions by creating *try/catch* blocks in your code.

- Classes in .NET Framework languages are custom types that can include value type fields, reference type fields, methods, attributes, and properties, among others. To enable consistency between classes, you can use inheritance (where you derive a new class from an existing class) or interfaces (where you are required to implement members specified by an interface). Generics enable you to create a single class or method that works with a variety of types. To enable applications to respond to planned events, you can raise and respond to events.

■ Conversion enables you to compare and copy values between different types. Implicit conversion happens automatically and behaves differently in Visual Basic and C#. C# allows implicit conversion only for widening conversions, where no information could be lost. Visual Basic by default allows implicit conversion for both narrowing and widening conversions. When values are converted from a value type to a reference type, it is called boxing, and incurs potentially significant overhead. Unboxing occurs if you assign a reference type object to a value type object.

Key Terms

Do you know what these key terms mean? You can check your answers by looking up the terms in the glossary at the end of the book.

■ Boxing
■ Cast
■ Constraint
■ Contract
■ Exception
■ Filtering exceptions
■ Garbage collection
■ Generic type
■ Heap
■ Interface
■ Narrowing
■ Nullable type
■ Signature
■ Stack
■ Structure
■ Unboxing
■ Widening

Case Scenario

In the following case scenario, you apply what you've learned about types. You can find answers to these questions in the "Answers" section at the end of this book.

Case Scenario: Designing an Application

You have recently accepted a job as an internal application developer in the information technology department of an enterprise healthcare company. Your first task is to design an internal application that employees will use to manage information about customers (whom everyone calls "subscribers"), their current plans, medications, and doctors. Answer your manager's questions about your design choices.

1. We need to manage information about both subscribers and doctors. How will you do this? Will you have one class for both, two distinct classes, or something else?

2. Our employees need to search for groups of subscribers or doctors. For example, if a doctor retires, we need to contact all that doctor's subscribers and assist them in finding a new physician. Similarly, we contact doctors annually to renew their contracts. How can you store a group of subscribers or doctors in your application?

3. One of the tasks your application will perform is generating mailing labels for groups of subscribers or doctors. Is there any way that you can write a single method that will handle addresses for both subscribers and doctors? How will you implement this?

4. The privacy of our information is extremely important to us. Our database developer is going to restrict permissions on the database to prevent unauthorized users from gaining access. If user privileges are rejected, I'd like you to instruct users to contact their manager to gain access. How will you handle it if a database query is rejected for insufficient privileges?

Suggested Practices

To help you successfully master the exam objectives presented in this chapter, complete the following tasks.

Manage Data in a .NET Framework Application by Using .NET Framework System Types

For this task, you should complete at least Practices 1 and 2. If you want a better understanding of how generics perform in the real world, complete Practice 3 as well.

- **Practice 1**   Open the last project you created and add exception handling to your code. Unless performance is a higher priority than reliability, all code outside of value type variable declarations should be in a *try* block.

- **Practice 2**   Create a linked-list generic class that enables you to create a chain of objects of different types.

- **Practice 3**   Create two classes with identical functionality. Use generics for the first class and use the *Object* types for the second class. Create a *for* loop that uses the class over thousands of iterations. Time the performance of both the generic class and the *Object*-based class to determine which performs better. You can use *DateTime.Now.Ticks* to measure the time.

Implement .NET Framework Interfaces to Cause Components to Comply with Standard Contracts

For this task, you should complete all three practices to gain experience implementing common interfaces with real-world classes.

- **Practice 1**   Create a custom class that implements the necessary interfaces to allow an array of objects of that class to be sorted.

- **Practice 2**   Create a custom class that can be converted to common value types.

- **Practice 3**   Create a custom class that can be disposed of using the *IDisposable* .Dispose method.

Control Interactions Between .NET Framework Application Components by Using Events and Delegates

For this task, you should complete both Practices 1 and 2.

- **Practice 1**   Open the last Windows Forms application you created and examine the code that Visual Studio automatically generated to respond to user interface events.

■ **Practice 2** Create a class that raises an event and derives a custom class based on *EventArgs*. Then create an assembly that responds to the event.

Take a Practice Test

The practice tests on this book's companion CD offer many options. For example, you can test yourself on just one exam objective or you can test yourself on all the 70-536 certification exam content. You can set up the test so that it closely simulates the experience of taking a certification exam or you can set it up in study mode so that you can look at the correct answers and explanations after you answer each question.

MORE INFO Practice tests

For details about all the practice test options available, see the section "How to Use the Practice Tests," in the Introduction of this book.

Chapter 2

Input/Output

Applications often need to store data to the disk in order to save data between sessions, log data for troubleshooting or auditing, or communicate with other applications. This chapter describes how to examine and manage the file system and read and write files.

Exam objectives in this chapter:
- Access files and folders by using the File System classes.
- Manage byte streams by using *Stream* classes.
- Manage .NET Framework application data by using *Reader* and *Writer* classes.
- Compress or decompress stream information in a .NET Framework application and improve the security of application data by using isolated storage.

Lessons in this chapter:

Before You Begin

This book assumes that you have at least two to three years of experience developing Web-based, Microsoft Windows–based, or distributed applications using the .NET Framework. Candidates should have a working knowledge of Microsoft Visual Studio. Before you begin, you should be familiar with Microsoft Visual Basic or C# and be comfortable with the following tasks:

- Creating console, Windows Forms, and Windows Presentation Foundation (WPF) applications in Visual Studio using Visual Basic or C#
- Adding namespaces and system class library references to a project
- Running a project in Visual Studio, setting breakpoints, stepping through code, and watching the values of variables

Lesson 1: Working with the File System

The .NET Framework includes classes for performing basic file management tasks, including browsing drives, managing files and folders, and responding to changes to the file system. This lesson describes the most useful classes for managing the file system.

> **After this lesson, you will be able to:**
> - Generate a list of drives attached to the computer
> - Browse, copy, move, and delete files and folders
> - Respond to new or changed files and folders
>
> **Estimated lesson time: 30 minutes**

Enumerating Drives

To list all the drives connected to a computer, use the static *DriveInfo.GetDrives* method (in the *System.IO* namespace) to retrieve a collection of *DriveInfo* objects. For example, the following loop outputs a list of all drives to the console:

```vb
' VB
For Each di As DriveInfo In DriveInfo.GetDrives()
    Console.WriteLine("  {0} ({1})", di.Name, di.DriveType)
Next
```

```csharp
// C#
foreach (DriveInfo di in DriveInfo.GetDrives())
    Console.WriteLine("  {0} ({1})", di.Name, di.DriveType);
```

DriveInfo has the following properties:

- *AvailableFreeSpace*   Indicates the amount of available free space on a drive
- *DriveFormat*   Gets the name of the file system, such as NTFS or FAT32
- *DriveType*   Gets the drive type
- *IsReady*   Indicates whether a drive is ready
- *Name*   Gets the name of a drive
- *RootDirectory*   Gets the root directory of a drive
- *TotalFreeSpace*   Gets the total amount of free space available on a drive
- *TotalSize*   Gets the total size of storage space on a drive
- *VolumeLabel*   Gets or sets the volume label of a drive

Managing Files and Folders

The .NET Framework provides classes that you can use to browse files and folders, create new folders, and manage files. The following sections describe how to use these classes.

Browsing Folders

You can use the *DirectoryInfo* class to browse folders and files. First, create an instance of *DirectoryInfo* by specifying the folder to browse. Then, call the *DirectoryInfo.Get-Directories* or *DirectoryInfo.GetFiles* method.

The following example displays the files and folders in the C:\Windows\folder.

```vb
' VB
Dim dir As New DirectoryInfo("C:\Windows")

Console.WriteLine("Folders:")
For Each dirInfo As DirectoryInfo In dir.GetDirectories()
    Console.WriteLine(dirInfo.Name)
Next

Console.WriteLine("Files:")
For Each fi As FileInfo In dir.GetFiles()
    Console.WriteLine(fi.Name)
Next
```

```csharp
// C#
DirectoryInfo dir = new DirectoryInfo(@"C:\Windows");

Console.WriteLine("Folders:");
foreach (DirectoryInfo dirInfo in dir.GetDirectories())
    Console.WriteLine(dirInfo.Name);
Console.WriteLine("\nFiles:");
foreach (FileInfo fi in dir.GetFiles())
    Console.WriteLine(fi.Name);
```

Creating Folders

To create folders, create an instance of *DirectoryInfo* and then call the *DirectoryInfo.Create* method. You can check the boolean *DirectoryInfo.Exists* property to determine if a folder already exists. The following sample checks for the existence of a folder and creates it if it doesn't already exist, although the Common Language Runtime (CLR) does not throw an exception if you attempt to create a folder that already exists.

```vb
' VB
Dim newDir As New DirectoryInfo("C:\deleteme")
If newDir.Exists Then
    Console.WriteLine("The folder already exists")
Else
    newDir.Create()
End If
```

```
// C#
DirectoryInfo newDir = new DirectoryInfo(@"C:\deleteme");
if (newDir.Exists)
    Console.WriteLine("The folder already exists");
else
    newDir.Create();
```

Creating, Copying, Moving, and Deleting Files

To create, copy, move, and delete files, you can use the static *File.Create*, *File.CreateText*, *File.Copy*, *File.Move*, and *File.Delete* methods. The following sample creates a file, copies it, and then moves/renames it:

```
' VB
File.CreateText("mynewfile.txt")
File.Copy("mynewfile.txt", "newfile2.txt")
File.Move("newfile2.txt", "newfile3.txt")
```

```
// C#
File.CreateText("mynewfile.txt");
File.Copy("mynewfile.txt", "newfile2.txt");
File.Move("newfile2.txt", "newfile3.txt");
```

Alternatively, you can create an instance of the *FileInfo* class representing the file and call the *Create*, *CreateText*, *CopyTo*, *MoveTo*, and *Delete* methods. The following code performs the same functions as the previous sample:

```
' VB
Dim fi As New FileInfo("mynewfile.txt")
fi.CreateText()
fi.CopyTo("newfile2.txt")

Dim fi2 As New FileInfo("newfile2.txt")
fi2.MoveTo("newfile3.txt")
```

```
// C#
FileInfo fi = new FileInfo("mynewfile.txt");
fi.CreateText();
fi.CopyTo("newfile2.txt");

FileInfo fi2 = new FileInfo("newfile2.txt");
fi2.MoveTo("newfile3.txt");
```

To delete a file, create an instance of the *FileInfo* class and then call *FileInfo.Delete*.

Monitoring the File System

You can use the *FileSystemWatcher* class (part of the *System.IO* namespace) to respond to updated files, new files, renamed files, and other updates to the file system. First, create an instance of *FileSystemWatcher* by providing the path to be monitored. Then, configure properties of the *FileSystemWatcher* instance to control whether to monitor subdirectories and which types of changes to monitor. Next, add a method as an event handler. Finally, set the *FileSystemWatcher.EnableRaisingEvent* property to *true*. The following code sample demonstrates a basic usage (creating the method to handle the *Changed* events is discussed next):

```
' VB
' Create an instance of FileSystemWatcher
Dim fsw As New _
    FileSystemWatcher(Environment.GetEnvironmentVariable("USERPROFILE"))

' Set the FileSystemWatcher properties
fsw.IncludeSubdirectories = True
fsw.NotifyFilter = NotifyFilters.FileName Or NotifyFilters.LastWrite

' Add the Changed event handler
AddHandler fsw.Changed, AddressOf fsw_Changed

' Start monitoring events
fsw.EnableRaisingEvents = True

// C#
// Create an instance of FileSystemWatcher
FileSystemWatcher fsw = new
    FileSystemWatcher(Environment.GetEnvironmentVariable("USERPROFILE"));

// Set the FileSystemWatcher properties
fsw.IncludeSubdirectories = true;
fsw.NotifyFilter = NotifyFilters.FileName | NotifyFilters.LastWrite;

// Add the Changed event handler
fsw.Changed += new FileSystemEventHandler(fsw_Changed);

// Start monitoring events
fsw.EnableRaisingEvents = true;
```

Handling *FileSystemWatcher* Events   When a file is changed that meets the criteria you specify, the CLR calls the *FileSystemWatcher.Changed* event handler for all changes, creations, and deletions. For files and folders that are renamed, the CLR calls the *FileSystemWatcher.Renamed* event handler. The previous code sample added the *fsw_Changed* method to handle the *Changed* event. The following code sample shows a simple way to handle the event:

```
' VB
Sub fsw_Changed(ByVal sender As Object, ByVal e As FileSystemEventArgs)
    ' Write the path of a changed file to the console
    Console.WriteLine(e.ChangeType + ": " + e.FullPath)
End Sub
```

```
// C#
static void fsw_Changed(object sender, FileSystemEventArgs e)
{
    // Write the path of a changed file to the console
    Console.WriteLine(e.ChangeType + ": " + e.FullPath);
}
```

You can use a single event handler for the *Changed*, *Created*, and *Deleted* events, as demonstrated by Exercise 2, later in this lesson. The *FileSystemEventArgs* parameter provides the path to the updated file and the type of change that occurred.

If you need to respond to files that are renamed, you need to create an event handler that accepts a *RenamedEventArgs* parameter instead of a *FileSystemEventArgs* parameter, as the following code sample demonstrates:

```
' VB
Sub fsw_Renamed(ByVal sender As Object, ByVal e As RenamedEventArgs)
    ' Write the path of a changed file to the console
    Console.WriteLine(e.ChangeType + " from " + e.OldFullPath + _
        " to " + e.Name)
End Sub
```

```
// C#
static void fsw_Renamed(object sender, RenamedEventArgs e)
{
    // Write the path of a changed file to the console
    Console.WriteLine(e.ChangeType + " from " + e.OldFullPath +
        " to " + e.Name);
}
```

Configuring *FileSystemWatcher* Properties   You can configure the following properties of the *FileSystemWatcher* class to control which types of updates cause the CLR to throw the *Changed* event:

- **Filter**   Used to configure the filenames that trigger events. To watch for changes in all files, set the *Filter* property to an empty string ("") or use wildcards ("*.*"). To watch a specific file, set the *Filter* property to the filename. For example, to watch for changes in the file MyDoc.txt, set the *Filter* property to "MyDoc.txt". You can also watch for changes in a certain type of file. For example, to watch for changes in text files, set the *Filter* property to "*.txt".

- **NotifyFilter**   Configure the types of changes for which to throw events by setting *NotifyFilter* to one or more of these values:
  - *FileName*
  - *DirectoryName*
  - *Attributes*

- ❑ *Size*
- ❑ *LastWrite*
- ❑ *LastAccess*
- ❑ *CreationTime*
- ❑ *Security*

- ■ **Path** Used to define the folder to be monitored. You can define the path using the *FileSystemWatcher* constructor.

You can watch for the renaming, deletion, or creation of files or directories. For example, to watch for the renaming of text files, set the *Filter* property to "*.txt" and call the *WaitForChanged* method with a *Renamed* value specified for its parameter.

Real World

Tony Northrup

In the real world, the operating system and applications make so many changes that if you're not very specific when configuring filters on your *FileSystemWatcher* properties, you will notice background processes making many updates to the file system that you probably aren't interested in monitoring. This is especially true if you simply monitor all events for a directory tree (especially a commonly used directory tree such as the user Documents folder or the System folder). In addition, some file system changes result in multiple different events being thrown. For example, moving a file between folders throws separate events for changing the file, creating the new file, and deleting the old file.

On earlier versions of Windows (such as Windows XP without any service packs, or Windows 2000 SP2 or earlier), if multiple *FileSystemWatcher* objects are watching the same Universal Naming Convention (UNC) path, then only one of the objects raises an event. On machines running Windows XP SP1 and later, Windows 2000 SP3 or later, Windows Server 2003, Windows Vista, or Windows Server 2008, all *FileSystemWatcher* objects raise the appropriate events.

Lab: Working with the File System

In this lab, you will write a console application to browse the file system and then write a second console application to respond to changes to the file system.

Exercise 1: Browse the File System

In this exercise, you will create a Console application that lists the volumes connected to the computer and then displays the files and folders in the root of the volume.

1. Using Visual Studio, create a new Console Application project. Name the project BrowseFileSystem.

2. Add the *System.IO* namespace.

3. Write code to display a list of all volumes attached to the computer. For example:

```
' VB
Console.WriteLine("Drives:")
For Each di As DriveInfo In DriveInfo.GetDrives()
    Console.WriteLine("  {0} ({1})", di.Name, di.DriveType)
Next
```

```
// C#
Console.WriteLine("Drives:");
foreach (DriveInfo di in DriveInfo.GetDrives())
    Console.WriteLine("  {0} ({1})", di.Name, di.DriveType);
```

4. Next, add code to prompt the user to select a volume to browse and use that input to create a *DirectoryInfo* instance. For example, the following code prompts the user to type the drive letter associated with the volume:

```
' VB
Console.WriteLine()
Console.WriteLine("Press a drive letter to view files and folders")
Dim drive As ConsoleKeyInfo = Console.ReadKey(True)
Dim dir As New DirectoryInfo(drive.Key.ToString() + ":\")
```

```
// C#
Console.WriteLine("\nPress a drive letter to view files and folders");
ConsoleKeyInfo drive = Console.ReadKey(true);
DirectoryInfo dir = new DirectoryInfo(drive.Key.ToString() + @":\");
```

5. Add code to display the folders contained in the root of the selected volume as follows:

```
' VB
Console.WriteLine()
Console.WriteLine("Folders:")
For Each dirInfo As DirectoryInfo In dir.GetDirectories()
    Console.WriteLine("  " + dirInfo.Name)
Next
```

```
// C#
Console.WriteLine("\nFolders:");
foreach (DirectoryInfo dirInfo in dir.GetDirectories())
    Console.WriteLine("  " + dirInfo.Name);
```

6. Finally, add code to display the files contained in the root of the selected volume as follows:

```vb
' VB
Console.WriteLine()
Console.WriteLine("Files:")
For Each fi As FileInfo In dir.GetFiles()
    Console.WriteLine("  " + fi.Name)
Next
```

```csharp
// C#
Console.WriteLine("\nFiles:");
foreach (FileInfo fi in dir.GetFiles())
    Console.WriteLine("  " + fi.Name);
```

7. Build and run your application and verify that you can list volumes, folders, and files.

Exercise 2: Respond to File System Changes

In this exercise, you create a Console application that lists changes to the file system.

1. Using Visual Studio, create a new Console Application project. Name the project WatchFileSystem.

2. Add the *System.IO* namespace.

3. First, write code to create an instance of *FileSystemWatcher* as follows:

```vb
' VB
Dim fsw As New _
    FileSystemWatcher(Environment.GetEnvironmentVariable("USERPROFILE"))
```

```csharp
// C#
FileSystemWatcher fsw = new
    FileSystemWatcher(Environment.GetEnvironmentVariable("USERPROFILE"));
```

4. Next, configure the properties of your *FileSystemWatcher* instance to include sub-directories and notify you only if a file is renamed or updated as follows:

```vb
' VB
fsw.IncludeSubdirectories = True
fsw.NotifyFilter = NotifyFilters.FileName Or NotifyFilters.LastWrite
```

```csharp
// C#
fsw.IncludeSubdirectories = true;
fsw.NotifyFilter = NotifyFilters.FileName | NotifyFilters.LastWrite;
```

5. Add a method to handle the *FileSystemWatcher.Changed* event and that writes the type of change and the path of the changed file to the console as follows:

```vb
' VB
Sub fsw_Changed(ByVal sender As Object, ByVal e As FileSystemEventArgs)
    Console.WriteLine(e.ChangeType.ToString + ": " + e.FullPath)
End Sub
```

```
// C#
static void fsw_Changed(object sender, FileSystemEventArgs e)
{
    Console.WriteLine(e.ChangeType + ": " + e.FullPath);
}
```

6. Add a method to handle the *FileSystemWatcher.Renamed* event and write the type of change and the path of the renamed file before and after the change to the console as follows:

```
' VB
Sub fsw_Renamed(ByVal sender As Object, ByVal e As RenamedEventArgs)
    ' Write the path of a changed file to the console
    Console.WriteLine(e.ChangeType.ToString + " from " + e.OldFullPath + _
        " to " + e.Name)
End Sub
```

```
// C#
static void fsw_Renamed(object sender, RenamedEventArgs e)
{
    Console.WriteLine(e.ChangeType + " from " + e.OldFullPath +
        " to " + e.Name);
}
```

7. Next, in your *Main* method, add event handlers for each of the four *FileSystem-Watcher* event types as follows:

```
' VB
AddHandler fsw.Changed, AddressOf fsw_Changed
AddHandler fsw.Created, AddressOf fsw_Changed
AddHandler fsw.Deleted, AddressOf fsw_Changed
AddHandler fsw.Renamed, AddressOf fsw_Renamed
```

```
// C#
fsw.Changed += new FileSystemEventHandler(fsw_Changed);
fsw.Created += new FileSystemEventHandler(fsw_Changed);
fsw.Deleted += new FileSystemEventHandler(fsw_Changed);
fsw.Renamed += new RenamedEventHandler(fsw_Renamed);
```

8. Finally, set the *FileSystemWatcher.EnableRaisingEvents* property to *true* and wait for user input before terminating the program as follows:

```
' VB
fsw.EnableRaisingEvents = True

' Wait for user input before ending
Console.WriteLine("Press a key to end the program.")
Console.ReadKey()
```

```
// C#
fsw.EnableRaisingEvents = true;

Console.WriteLine("Press a key to end the program.");
Console.ReadKey();
```

9. Run the program. Then, open Windows Explorer and add a file to your Documents folder. Notice that the creation of the file, as well as any changes to it, are displayed in the console. Rename the file; you will notice that the change also appears. Finally, delete the file.

Lesson Summary

- Use the *DriveInfo.GetDrives* static method to retrieve an array of *DriveInfo* objects that describe the drives attached to the computer.

- The *File* class provides static methods for copying, moving, and deleting folders and files. You can also create instances of the *FileInfo* and *DirectoryInfo* classes.

- Use the *FileSystemWatcher* class to respond to changes in the file system, such as new or changed files.

Lesson Review

You can use the following questions to test your knowledge of the information in Lesson 1, "Working with the File System." The questions are also available on the companion CD if you prefer to review them in electronic form.

NOTE Answers

Answers to these questions and explanations of why each answer choice is right or wrong are located in the "Answers" section at the end of the book.

1. You need to retrieve a list of subdirectories. Which class should you use?

    A. *FileInfo*

    B. *DriveInfo*

    C. *FileSystemWatcher*

    D. *DirectoryInfo*

2. Which of the following types of changes CANNOT be detected by an instance of *FileSystemWatcher*?

    A. A text file that is appended

    B. A USB flash drive connected to the computer

    C. A directory added to the root of the C:\ drive

    D. A file that is renamed

3. You want to copy an existing file, File1.txt, to File2.txt. Which code samples do this correctly? (Choose two. Each answer forms a complete solution.)

A.

```vb
' VB
Dim fi as new File()
fi.Copy("file1.txt", "file2.txt")
```

```csharp
// C#
File fi = new File();
fi.Copy("file1.txt", "file2.txt");
```

B.

```vb
' VB
File.Copy("file1.txt", "file2.txt")
```

```csharp
// C#
File.Copy("file1.txt", "file2.txt");
```

C.

```vb
' VB
Dim fi As New FileInfo("file1.txt")
fi.CreateText()
fi.CopyTo("file2.txt")
```

```csharp
// C#
FileInfo fi = new FileInfo("file1.txt");
fi.CreateText();
fi.CopyTo("file2.txt");
```

D.

```vb
' VB
Dim fi As New FileInfo("file1.txt")
fi.CopyTo("file2.txt")
```

```csharp
// C#
FileInfo fi = new FileInfo("file1.txt");
fi.CopyTo("file2.txt");
```

Lesson 2: Reading and Writing Files and Streams

You can use different *Stream* classes to read and write files. The .NET Framework provides different classes for text files and binary files, and specialized classes to allow you to compress data or store data in memory. You can also use streams to store files in isolated storage, a private file system managed by the .NET Framework.

After this lesson, you will be able to:

- ■ Read and write text files, binary files, and strings
- ■ Write to a stream stored in memory
- ■ Compress a file when writing it
- ■ Use isolated storage to improve the privacy of data you store

Estimated lesson time: 45 minutes

Reading and Writing Text Files

To read a text file, create an instance of *TextReader* or *StreamReader*. Then, call one of the class's methods to read as much or as little of the file as you want. For example, the following sample code displays a text file to the console:

```
' VB
Dim tr As TextReader = File.OpenText("C:\windows\win.ini")
Console.Write(tr.ReadToEnd())
tr.Close()
```

```
// C#
TextReader tr = File.OpenText(@"C:\windows\win.ini");
Console.Write(tr.ReadToEnd());
tr.Close();
```

The previous example uses the *TextReader* class, but it works equally well with the *StreamReader* class (which counterintuitively derives from *TextReader*). When using *TextReader*, you typically create an instance using the static *File.OpenText* method (as demonstrated in the previous example). When using *StreamReader*, you can use *File.OpenText* or the *StreamReader* constructor. The following example displays the same text file using an instance of *StreamReader* and a *while* loop:

```
' VB
Dim sr As New StreamReader("C:\windows\win.ini")
Dim input As String
Do
    input = sr.ReadLine()
    Console.WriteLine(input)
Loop Until input Is Nothing
sr.Close()
```

```
// C#
StreamReader sr = new StreamReader(@"C:\windows\win.ini");
string input;
while ((input = sr.ReadLine()) != null )
    Console.WriteLine(input);
sr.Close();
```

When reading text files, you typically use the self-explanatory *ReadLine* or *ReadToEnd* methods.

To write a text file, create an instance of *TextWriter* or *StreamWriter*. After creating an instance of the class, writing to the file is no more complex than writing to the console (although you need to call the *Close* method after you finish writing to the file, a task that should typically be handled in a *Finally* block). See the following code example:

```
' VB
Dim tw As TextWriter = File.CreateText("output.txt")
tw.WriteLine("Hello, world!")
tw.Close()
```

```
// C#
TextWriter tw = File.CreateText("output.txt");
tw.WriteLine("Hello, world!");
tw.Close();
```

If you want to ensure that data is written to the disk without closing the file, call the *Flush* method. Otherwise, it might be stored in a buffer, and changes would be lost if the computer were suddenly shut down.

Reading and Writing Binary Files

You can use binary files and the *BinaryWriter* and *BinaryReader* classes to store and retrieve non-text values. The following shows how to read and write a series of integers:

```
' VB
' Write ten integers
Dim fs As New FileStream("data.bin", FileMode.Create)
Dim w As New BinaryWriter(fs)
For i As Integer = 0 To 10
    w.Write(CInt(i))
Next
w.Close()
fs.Close()

' Read the data
fs = New FileStream("data.bin", FileMode.Open, FileAccess.Read)
```

```
Dim r As New BinaryReader(fs)
For i As Integer = 0 To 10
    Console.WriteLine(r.ReadInt32())
Next
r.Close()
fs.Close()

// C#
// Write ten integers
FileStream fs = new FileStream("data.bin", FileMode.Create);
BinaryWriter w = new BinaryWriter(fs);
for (int i = 0; i < 11; i++)
    w.Write((int)i);
w.Close();
fs.Close();

// Read the data
fs = new FileStream("data.bin", FileMode.Open, FileAccess.Read);
BinaryReader r = new BinaryReader(fs);
for (int i = 0; i < 11; i++)
    Console.WriteLine(r.ReadInt32());
r.Close();
fs.Close();
```

Generally, serialization is a more efficient way of storing objects. For more information, refer to Chapter 5, "Serialization."

Reading and Writing Strings

You can use *StringWriter* to write to *StringBuilder* instances like a stream and *String-
Reader* to read from strings. The following example demonstrates this:

```
' VB
Dim sb As New StringBuilder()
Dim sw As New StringWriter(sb)
sw.Write("Hello, ")
sw.Write("World!")
sw.Close()

Dim sr As New StringReader(sb.ToString())
Console.WriteLine(sr.ReadToEnd())
sr.Close()

// C#
StringBuilder sb = new StringBuilder();
StringWriter sw = new StringWriter(sb);

sw.Write("Hello, ");
sw.Write("World!");
sw.Close();
```

```
StringReader sr = new StringReader(sb.ToString());
Console.WriteLine(sr.ReadToEnd());
sr.Close();
```

Typically, you use *StringWriter* and *StringBuilder* only if you have a specific reason to use streams instead of accessing the strings directly. For example, you might use *StringWriter* if you had a method that required a stream object but you did not want to create a file.

Using a *MemoryStream*

The most common use of a *MemoryStream* is to store temporarily data that will be written to a file eventually. Using a *MemoryStream*, you can take your time to create the stream in memory, add data to it, and then write it all to disk at once—minimizing the time the file needs to be locked open. In multi-user environments where a file might need to be accessed by other processes, this minimizes the potential for conflict.

The following code sample demonstrates how to write data to a temporary *MemoryStream* and then write the data to a text file. As you can see, it also uses the *StreamWriter* class to make it easier to write a string to the *MemoryStream*. Without *StreamWriter*, *MemoryStream* instances can only read and write bytes and byte arrays using the *WriteByte* method (for writing a single byte), *Write* method (for writing an array of bytes), *ReadByte* method (for reading a single byte), and *Read* method (for reading an array of bytes).

```vb
' VB
' Create a MemoryStream object
Dim ms As New MemoryStream()

' Create a StreamWriter object to allow
' writing strings to the MemoryStream
Dim sw As New StreamWriter(ms)

' Write to the StreamWriter and MemoryStream
sw.WriteLine("Hello, World!")

' Flush the contents of the StreamWriter so it can be written to disk
sw.Flush()

' Write the contents of the MemoryStream to a file
ms.WriteTo(File.Create("memory.txt"))

' Close the file and MemoryStream
sw.Close()
ms.Close()

// C#
// Create a MemoryStream object
MemoryStream ms = new MemoryStream();
```

```
// Create a StreamWriter object to allow
// writing strings to the MemoryStream
StreamWriter sw = new StreamWriter(ms);

// Write to the StreamWriter and MemoryStream
sw.WriteLine("Hello, World!");

// Flush the contents of the StreamWriter so it can be written to disk
sw.Flush();

// Write the contents of the MemoryStream to a file
ms.WriteTo(File.Create("memory.txt"));

// Close the file and MemoryStream
sw.Close();
ms.Close();
```

Using a *BufferedStream*

You don't need to use a *BufferedStream* with a *FileStream* object. *FileStream* objects contain the exact same buffering logic as the *BufferedStream* class, so a second layer of buffering would be redundant and inefficient. In fact, *BufferedStream* is primarily intended for use with custom stream implementations because the stream classes built into the .NET Framework already include built-in buffering capabilities.

The *BufferedStream* class can be used exactly like the *MemoryStream* class. Like the *MemoryStream* class, the *BufferedStream* class natively supports writing only bytes and byte arrays.

Using Compressed Streams

You can use the .NET Framework to write compressed streams, which can consume less storage space. Generally, text files can be highly compressed, binary files benefit slightly from compression, and data that is already compressed (like most music or image files) does not benefit from further compression. Like the *MemoryStream* class, you can read and write only individual bytes and byte arrays using the *GZipStream* class. Therefore, if you are storing something other than bytes, you should use *StreamWriter* and *StreamReader* to write strings to a compressed stream.

The following sample code demonstrates writing and reading text data using the *GZipStream* class:

```
' VB
' Create a compressed stream using a new file
Dim gzOut As New GZipStream(File.Create("data.zip"), _
    CompressionMode.Compress)

' Create a StreamWriter object to allow
' writing strings to the GZipStream
```

```
Dim sw As New StreamWriter(gzOut)
For i As Integer = 1 To 999
    sw.Write("Hello, World! ")
Next

' Write data to the compressed stream, and then close it

' Close the stream objects
sw.Close()
gzOut.Close()

' Open the file containing the compressed data
Dim gzIn As New GZipStream(File.OpenRead("data.zip"), _
    CompressionMode.Decompress)

' Read and display the compressed data
Dim sr As New StreamReader(gzIn)
Console.WriteLine(sr.ReadToEnd())

' Close the stream objects
sr.Close()
gzIn.Close()

// C#
// Create a compressed stream using a new file
GZipStream gzOut = new GZipStream(File.Create("data.zip"),
    CompressionMode.Compress);

// Create a StreamWriter object to allow
// writing strings to the GZipStream
StreamWriter sw = new StreamWriter(gzOut);

// Write data to the compressed stream, and then close it
for (int i = 1; i < 1000; i++)
    sw.Write("Hello, World! ");

// Close the stream objects
sw.Close();
gzOut.Close();

// Open the file containing the compressed data
GZipStream gzIn = new GZipStream(File.OpenRead("data.zip"),
    CompressionMode.Decompress);

// Read and display the compressed data
StreamReader sr = new StreamReader(gzIn);
Console.WriteLine(sr.ReadToEnd());

// Close the stream objects
sr.Close();
gzIn.Close();
```

The compressed file produced by the previous code sample consumes only 289 bytes of disk space. If you used *FileStream* objects instead of *GZipStream* objects, the same file would consume 13,986 bytes.

As the code sample demonstrates, you must provide two parameters when creating an instance of *GZipStream*: another stream object (such as a file) and the *CompressionMode* enumeration. *CompressionMode* simply indicates whether the *GZipStream* instance compresses or decompresses data.

You can also use *DeflateStream*, a class that provides similar functionality using the Deflate data format, exactly as you would use *GZipStream*, which uses the GZip data format.

Using Isolated Storage

Isolated storage is a private file system managed by the .NET Framework. Like the standard file system, you can use familiar techniques (such as *StreamReader* and *StreamWriter*) to read and write files. However, writing to isolated storage requires fewer privileges than writing directly to the file system, making it useful for implementing least privilege.

In addition, isolated storage is private, and isolated by user, domain, and assembly. While this provides some additional protection not offered by the file system, isolated storage should not be used to store high-value secrets, such as unencrypted keys or passwords, because isolated storage is not protected from highly trusted code, unmanaged code, or trusted users of the computer.

Types of Isolated Storage

Access to a file in isolated storage is always restricted to the user who created it. In addition to isolation by user, access to isolated storage is generally restricted to a specific assembly. In other words, AssemblyB cannot access files located in an isolated store created by AssemblyA.

In addition to isolating storage by user and assembly, you can isolate assemblies in one additional, optional way: by the application domain. If a store is isolated by application domain, the same assembly running in different application domains cannot access a single store.

IMPORTANT   Always isolate storage by application domain unless you specifically need to share data between instances of the application. For example, if you create a shared assembly that will be called from multiple external assemblies, and you plan to use isolated storage to allow the external assemblies to share data, you must not isolate storage by application domain.

Classes for Working with Isolated Storage

The *System.IO.IsolatedStorage* namespace has three classes that are useful for interacting with isolated storage:

- **IsolatedStorageFile**   Provides management of isolated storage stores. Individual stores are separate isolated storage systems that are implemented as a single file in the file system.

- **IsolatedStorageFileStream**   Provides access to read and write isolated storage files within stores. Isolated storage files behave exactly like conventional files stored directly on a file system; however, they exist within an isolated storage store.

- **IsolatedStorageException**   A class for exceptions relating to isolated storage.

IsolatedStorageFile is used to access the individual stores, whereas *IsolatedStorageFileStream* manages individual files within a store.

How to Access Isolated Storage

Working with isolated storage is very similar to working with standard files. The primary differences are that you must do the following:

- Use or import the *System.IO.IsolatedStorage* namespace, in addition to the *System.IO* namespace.

- Optionally, declare an *IsolatedStorageFile* object to specify the type of isolation.

- Construct file system objects, *StreamWriters*, *StreamReaders*, and other *System.IO* objects by using objects in the *System.IO.IsolatedStorage* namespace.

The following code gets a user store isolated by assembly, creates a file named Myfile.txt, creates a new *StreamWriter* object using the isolated storage file, writes a line of text to the file, and then closes the isolated storage file. To use the store isolated by the application domain, simply change the *IsolatedStorageFile.GetUserStoreForAssembly* method call to *IsolatedStorageFile.GetUserStoreForDomain*.

```
' VB
' Get the store isolated by the assembly
Dim isoStore As IsolatedStorageFile = _
    IsolatedStorageFile.GetUserStoreForAssembly()

' Create the isolated storage file in the assembly we just grabbed
Dim isoFile As IsolatedStorageFileStream = New _
    IsolatedStorageFileStream("myfile.txt",FileMode.Create,isoStore)

' Create a StreamWriter using the isolated storage file
Dim sw As StreamWriter = New StreamWriter(isoFile)
```

```
' Write a line of text to the file
sw.WriteLine("This text is written to a isolated storage file.")

' Close the file
sw.Close()
```

```
// C#
// Get the store isolated by the assembly
IsolatedStorageFile isoStore =
    IsolatedStorageFile.GetUserStoreForAssembly();

// Create the isolated storage file in the assembly we just grabbed
IsolatedStorageFileStream isoFile = new
    IsolatedStorageFileStream("myfile.txt", FileMode.Create, isoStore);

// Create a StreamWriter using the isolated storage file
StreamWriter sw = new StreamWriter(isoFile);

// Write a line of text to the file
sw.WriteLine("This text is written to a isolated storage file.");

// Close the file
sw.Close();
```

Similarly, the following code would read the contents of the isolated storage file created in the previous example:

```
' VB
' Get the store isolated by the assembly
Dim isoStore As IsolatedStorageFile = _
    IsolatedStorageFile.GetUserStoreForAssembly()

' Open the isolated storage file in the assembly we just grabbed
Dim isoFile As IsolatedStorageFileStream =  New _
    IsolatedStorageFileStream("myfile.txt",FileMode.Open,isoStore)

' Create a StreamReader using the isolated storage file
Dim sr As StreamReader =  New StreamReader(isoFile)

' Read a line of text from the file
Dim fileContents As String =  sr.ReadLine()

' Close the file
sr.Close()
```

```
// C#
// Get the store isolated by the assembly
IsolatedStorageFile isoStore =
    IsolatedStorageFile.GetUserStoreForAssembly();

// Open the isolated storage file in the assembly we just grabbed
IsolatedStorageFileStream isoFile = new
    IsolatedStorageFileStream("myfile.txt", FileMode.Open, isoStore);
```

```
// Create a StreamReader using the isolated storage file
StreamReader sr = new StreamReader(isoFile);

// Read a line of text from the file
string fileContents = sr.ReadLine();

// Close the file
sr.Close();
```

If the *IsolatedStorageFile.GetUserStoreForAssembly* and *IsolatedStorageFile.GetUserStore-ForDomain* are not specific enough to specify the specific store you need to access, you can use the *IsolatedStorageFile.GetStore* method instead. To create or access isolated storage, code must be granted *IsolatedStorageFilePermission*.

Lab: Using Streams

In this lab, you will create a simple word processor that writes user input to a text file and then displays it to the screen. First, you will create a text file on the standard file system. Then you update the application to use isolated storage.

Exercise 1: Read and Write a Standard Text File

In this exercise, you accept user input, save the data to a *MemoryStream*, and then write the entire *MemoryStream* to a file. Then, you read the file and display it to the console.

1. Using Visual Studio, create a new Console Application project. Name the project WriteText.

2. Add the *System.IO* namespace.

3. Create an instance of *MemoryStream* and then create an instance of *StreamWriter* to allow you to write strings to the *MemoryStream*. The following code demonstrates this:

```
' VB
' Create a MemoryStream object
Dim ms As New MemoryStream()

' Create a StreamWriter object to allow
' writing strings to the MemoryStream
Dim sw As New StreamWriter(ms)

// C#
// Create a MemoryStream object
MemoryStream ms = new MemoryStream();

// Create a StreamWriter object to allow
// writing strings to the MemoryStream
StreamWriter sw = new StreamWriter(ms);
```

4. Next, create a loop that allows the user to type until he or she enters the word
    quit. Add each line of user input to the *StreamWriter* object (and thus to the
    underlying *MemoryStream* object). The following code demonstrates this:

```vb
' VB
Console.WriteLine("Enter 'quit' on a blank line to exit.")
While True
    Dim input As String = Console.ReadLine()
    If input = "quit" Then
        Exit While
    End If
    sw.WriteLine(input)
End While
```

```csharp
// C#
Console.WriteLine("Enter 'quit' on a blank line to exit.");
while (true)
{
    string input = Console.ReadLine();
    if (input == "quit")
        break;
    sw.WriteLine(input);
}
```

5. Next, flush the *StreamWriter* object, write the contents of the *MemoryStream*
    object to a file, and close all resources. The following code demonstrates this:

```vb
' VB
' Flush the contents of the StreamWriter so it can be written to disk
sw.Flush()

' Write the contents of the MemoryStream to a file
Dim fs As FileStream = File.Create("output.txt")
ms.WriteTo(fs)

' Close the file and MemoryStream
sw.Close()
ms.Close()
fs.Close()
```

```csharp
// C#
// Flush the contents of the StreamWriter so it can be written to disk
sw.Flush();

// Write the contents of the MemoryStream to a file
FileStream fs = File.Create("output.txt");
ms.WriteTo(fs);

// Close the file and MemoryStream
sw.Close();
ms.Close();
fs.Close();
```

6. Finally, read the text file and display it to the console to verify that it was saved correctly, as follows:

```vb
' VB
' Display the file to the console
Dim tr As TextReader = File.OpenText("output.txt")
Console.Write(tr.ReadToEnd())
tr.Close()
```

```csharp
// C#
// Display the file to the console
TextReader tr = File.OpenText("output.txt");
Console.Write(tr.ReadToEnd());
tr.Close();
```

7. Build and run the console application. Type in several lines of text and verify that they are correctly written to the text file.

Streams are one of the most commonly used classes, so you will receive additional practice using streams in other chapters of this book.

Exercise 2: Use Isolated Storage

In this exercise, you will update the application you created in Exercise 1 to use isolated storage in a user store isolated by assembly.

1. Continue working from the WriteText project that you created in Exercise 1.

2. Add the *System.IO.IsolatedStorage* namespace.

3. Replace the code that creates the *FileStream* object with code that creates an *IsolatedStorageFileStream* object. First, you need to create an *IsolatedStorageFile* object for the user store. The following code sample demonstrates this:

```vb
' VB
' Get the store isolated by the assembly
Dim isoStore As IsolatedStorageFile = _
    IsolatedStorageFile.GetUserStoreForAssembly()

' Create the isolated storage file in the assembly we just grabbed
Dim isoFile As New IsolatedStorageFileStream("output.txt", _
    FileMode.Create, isoStore)
```

```csharp
// C#
// Get the store isolated by the assembly
IsolatedStorageFile isoStore =
    IsolatedStorageFile.GetUserStoreForAssembly();

// Create the isolated storage file in the assembly we just grabbed
IsolatedStorageFileStream isoFile = new
    IsolatedStorageFileStream("output.txt", FileMode.Create, isoStore);
```

4. Change the *MemoryStream.WriteTo* method call to write to the *IsolatedStorage-FileStream* object instead of the *FileStream* object. Also, change the code that closes the *FileStream* object to close the *IsolatedStorageFileStream* object after you have written to it instead.

5. Update the code that reads the file to read it from isolated storage. The following code sample demonstrates this:

```
' VB
' Display the file to the console
Dim readIsoFile As New IsolatedStorageFileStream("output.txt", _
    FileMode.Open, isoStore)
Dim tr As TextReader = New StreamReader(readIsoFile)
Console.Write(tr.ReadToEnd())
tr.Close()
```

```
// C#
IsolatedStorageFileStream readIsoFile = new
    IsolatedStorageFileStream("output.txt", FileMode.Open, isoStore);
TextReader tr = new StreamReader(readIsoFile);
Console.Write(tr.ReadToEnd());
tr.Close();
```

6. Run the application and verify that it functions exactly the same. This time, the file is stored in isolated storage, rather than directly on the file system.

Lesson Summary

- Use the *TextReader* and *TextWriter*, *BinaryReader* and *BinaryWriter*, and *StringReader* and *StringWriter* classes to read and write text files, binary files, and strings (respectively) as streams.

- Use the *MemoryStream* class to store a stream in memory. You can then call *MemoryStream.WriteTo* to save the stream to a file on the disk.

- Use the *GZipStream* and *DeflateStream* classes to read and write compressed data.

- Isolated storage, implemented in the *System.IO.IsolatedStorage* namespace, allows you to save files in a part of the file system that is managed by the .NET Framework.

Lesson Review

You can use the following questions to test your knowledge of the information in Lesson 2, "Reading and Writing Files and Streams." The questions are also available on the companion CD if you prefer to review them in electronic form.

NOTE Answers

Answers to these questions and explanations of why each answer choice is right or wrong are located in the "Answers" section at the end of the book.

---

1. You want to create a stream that you can use to store a file temporarily while your application processes data. After all data processing is complete, you want to write it to the file system. It's important that you minimize the time that the file is locked. Which class should you use?

   A. *MemoryStream*

   B. *BufferedStream*

   C. *GZipStream*

   D. *FileStream*

2. You want to read a standard text file and process the data as strings. Which classes can you use? (Choose two. Each answer forms a complete solution.)

   A. *GZipStream*

   B. *TextReader*

   C. *StreamReader*

   D. *BinaryReader*

3. You need to store data to isolated storage in such a way that other applications that are run by the same user and other users running the same application cannot access the data directly. Which method should you call to create the *IsolatedStorageFile* object?

   A. *IsolatedStorageFile.GetUserStoreForAssembly()*

   B. *IsolatedStorageFile.GetMachineStoreForAssembly()*

   C. *IsolatedStorageFile.GetUserStoreForDomain()*

   D. *IsolatedStorageFile.GetMachineStoreForDomain()*

Chapter Review

To practice and reinforce the skills you learned in this chapter further, you can perform any or all of the following:

- Review the chapter summary.
- Review the list of key terms introduced in this chapter.
- Complete the case scenarios. These scenarios set up real-word situations involving the topics of this chapter and ask you to create a solution.
- Complete the suggested practices
- Take a practice test.

Chapter Summary

- The *System.IO* namespace provides classes for enumerating drives, managing files and folders, and responding to changes in the file system.
- Streams provide a flexible way to store data to files or memory. Using different types of streams, you can compress data or store it to isolated storage.

Key Terms

Do you know what these key terms mean? You can check your answers by looking up the terms in the glossary at the end of the book.

- Deflate
- GZip
- Isolated storage

Case Scenarios

In the following case scenarios, you will apply what you've learned about how to work with the file system and streams. You can find answers to these questions in the "Answers" section at the end of this book.

Case Scenario 1: Creating a Log File

You are an application developer for Contoso, Inc. To meet regulatory requirements, the financial application you developed must generate text-based log files for all transactions.

A new file must be generated every day, and a copy of each file must be stored on a shared folder. Systems administrators from your accounting department need to have direct access to both the original and copy of each log file.

Questions

Answer the following questions for your manager.

1. Which class should you use to create the text log file?

2. How can you copy the log file to the shared folder?

3. Should you use isolated storage?

Case Scenario 2: Compressing Files

You are an application developer working for Humongous Insurance. Your application records detailed transaction logs to the local file system. The transaction logs are accessed only from within your application.

The size of the transaction logs can exceed more than 1 gigabyte (GB) per day. To reduce storage requirements, you would like to compress the transaction logs. Currently, you write to the transaction logs using the *BinaryWriter* class.

Questions

Answer the following questions for your manager.

1. How can you compress the transaction logs?

2. Can you open the compressed transaction logs in other applications?

3. Can you write the compressed transaction logs to isolated storage?

Suggested Practices

To master the exam objectives covered in this chapter, complete the following tasks.

Access Files and Folders by Using the FileSystem Classes

For this task, you should complete all three practices.

- **Practice 1** Create a WPF application and populate a *TreeView* control with the local computer's drives, folders, and files.

- **Practice 2**   Create an application that lists the folders containing files that consume the most disk space.

- **Practice 3**   Create an application that detects new files written to your Documents folder (and subfolders) and copies the file to a backup folder.

Manage the .NET Framework Application Data by Using *Reader* and *Writer* Classes

For this task, you should complete both practices to gain experience using the *Reader* and *Writer* classes.

- **Practice 1**   Expand the last real-world application that you wrote to log all user actions to a text file.

- **Practice 2**   Using the last real-world application you wrote, store user settings and data in a binary file by using the *BinaryWriter* class.

Compress or Decompress Stream Information in a .NET Framework Application and Improve the Security of Application Data by Using Isolated Storage

For this task, you should complete at least Practices 1 and 3. If you want in-depth knowledge of compression efficiency, complete Practice 2 as well.

- **Practice 1**   Create an application that produces a 1-megabyte (MB) text file by repeating the same phrase over and over. Then, update the application to write the file using both the *GZipStream* and *DeflateStream* classes. Compare the file sizes produced by each of the techniques.

- **Practice 2**   Using the same approach as Practice 1, store binary data (such as an assembly) to an uncompressed file and two compressed files using *GZipStream* and *DeflateStream*.

- **Practice 3**   Using the last application you wrote that stores files to the file system, update it to save data to isolated storage instead.

Take a Practice Test

The practice tests on this book's companion CD offer many options. For example, you can test yourself on just the content covered in this chapter, or you can test yourself on all the 70-536 certification exam content. You can set up the test so that it closely simulates the experience of taking a certification exam, or you can set it up in study mode so that you can look at the correct answers and explanations after you answer each question.

MORE INFO **Practice tests**

For details about all the practice test options available, see the section "How to Use the Practice Tests," in the Introduction of this book.

Chapter 3

Searching, Modifying, and Encoding Text

Processing text is one of the most common programming tasks. User input is typically in text format, and it might need to be validated, sanitized, and reformatted. Often, developers need to process text files generated from a legacy system to extract important data. These systems often use nonstandard encoding techniques. In addition, developers might need to output text files in specific formats to input data into a legacy system.

This chapter describes how to use regular expressions to validate input, reformat text, and extract data. In addition, this chapter describes different encoding types used by text files.

Exam objectives in this chapter:
- Enhance the text handling capabilities of a .NET Framework application and search, modify, and control text in a .NET Framework application by using regular expressions.

Lessons in this chapter:

Before You Begin

To complete the lessons in this chapter, you should be familiar with Microsoft Visual Basic or C# and be comfortable performing the following tasks:

- Creating a console application in Microsoft Visual Studio using Visual Basic or C#
- Adding system class library references to a project
- Reading and writing to files and streams

Lesson 1: Forming Regular Expressions

Developers frequently need to process text. For example, you might need to process input from a user to remove or replace special characters. Or you might need to process text that has been output from a legacy application to integrate your application with an existing system. For decades, UNIX and Perl developers have used a complex but efficient technique for processing text: regular expressions.

A *regular expression* is a set of characters that can be compared to a string to determine whether the string meets specified format requirements. You can also use regular expressions to extract portions of the text or to replace text. To make decisions based on text, you can create regular expressions that match strings consisting entirely of integers, strings that contain only lowercase letters, or strings that match hexadecimal input. You can also extract key portions of a block of text (to extract the state from a user's address or image links from a Hypertext Markup Language (HTML) page, for example). Finally, you can update text using regular expressions to change the format of text or remove invalid characters.

After this lesson, you will be able to:

- Use regular expressions to determine whether a string matches a specific pattern
- Use regular expressions to extract data from a text file
- Use regular expressions to reformat text data

Estimated lesson time: 45 minutes

How to Use Regular Expressions for Pattern Matching

To test regular expressions, create a Console application named TestRegExp that accepts two strings as input and determines whether the first string (a regular expression) matches the second string. The following code, which uses the *System.Text .RegularExpressions* namespace, performs this check using the static *System.Text .RegularExpressions.Regex.IsMatch* method and displays the results to the console:

```
' VB
Console.Write("Enter regular expression: ")
Dim regularExpression As String = Console.ReadLine()

Console.Write("Enter input for comparison: ")
Dim input As String = Console.ReadLine()
```

```
If Regex.IsMatch(input, regularExpression) Then
    Console.WriteLine("Input matches regular expression.")
Else
    Console.WriteLine("Input DOES NOT match regular expression.")
End If

// C#
Console.Write("Enter regular expression: ");
string regularExpression = Console.ReadLine();

Console.Write("Enter input for comparison: ");
string input = Console.ReadLine();

if (Regex.IsMatch(input, regularExpression))
    Console.WriteLine("Input matches regular expression.");
else
    Console.WriteLine("Input DOES NOT match regular expression.");
```

Next, run the application to determine whether the regular expression ^\d{5}$ matches the string *12345* or *1234*. The regular expression won't make sense now, but it will by the end of the lesson. Your output should resemble the following:

```
C:\>TestRegExp
Enter regular expression: ^\d{5}$
Enter input for comparison: 1234
InputDOESNOTmatchregularexpression.

C:\>TestRegExp
Enter regular expression: ^\d{5}$
Enter input for comparison: 12345
Inputmatchesregularexpression.
```

As this code demonstrates, the *Regex.IsMatch* method compares a regular expression to a string and returns *true* if the string matches the regular expression. In this example, ^\d{5}$ means that the string must be exactly five numeric digits. As shown in Figure 3-1, the caret (^) represents the start of the string, \d means numeric digits, {5} indicates five sequential numeric digits, and $ represents the end of the string.

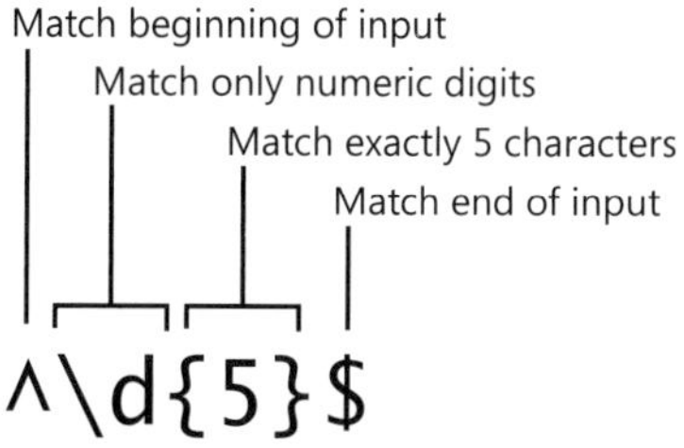

Match beginning of input
    Match only numeric digits
        Match exactly 5 characters
            Match end of input

$$^\backslash d\{5\}\$$$

Figure 3-1 Analysis of a regular expression

If you remove the first character from the regular expression, you drastically change the meaning of the pattern. The regular expression \d{5}$ still matches valid five-digit numbers, such as *12345*. However, it also matches the input string *abcd12345* or *drop table customers – 12345*. In fact, the modified regular expression will match any input string that ends in any five-digit number.

IMPORTANT Include the Leading Caret

When validating input, forgetting the leading caret can expose a security vulnerability. Use peer code reviews to limit the risk of human error.

When validating input, always begin regular expressions with a caret (^) and end them with a dollar sign ($). This system ensures that the entire input exactly matches the specified regular expression and does not merely *contain* a matching input string.

Regular expressions can be used to match complex input patterns, too. The following regular expression (shown on two lines to fit on the printed page) matches e-mail addresses:

```
^([\w-\.]+)@((\[[0-9]{1,3}\.[0-9]{1,3}\.[0-9]{1,3}\.)|(([\w-]+\.)+))
([a-zA-Z]{2,4}|[0-9]{1,3})(\]?)$
```

Regular expressions are an extremely efficient way to check user input; however, using regular expressions has the following limitations:

- **Regular expressions are difficult to create unless you are extremely familiar with the format.** If you have years of Perl programming experience, you won't have any problem using regular expressions. However, if you have a background in more structured programming languages (including Visual Basic and C#), the cryptic format of regular expressions will initially seem completely illogical.

- **Creating regular expressions might be confusing sometimes, but reading regular expressions definitely is.** There is a good chance that other programmers will overlook errors in regular expressions when performing a peer code review. The more complex the regular expression, the greater the chance that the structure of the expression contains an error that will be overlooked.

The following sections describe these and other aspects of regular expression pattern matching in more detail. As you read through these sections, experiment with different types of regular expressions using the TestRegExp application.

MORE INFO Regular Expressions

Entire books have been written about regular expressions, and this lesson can only scratch the surface of this topic. The information provided in this lesson should be sufficient for the exam. However, if you would like to learn more about the advanced features of regular expressions, read "Regular Expression Language Elements" in the .NET Framework General Reference at *http://msdn.microsoft.com/en-us/library/az24scfc.aspx*.

How to Match Simple Text

The simplest use of regular expressions is to determine whether a string matches a pattern. For example, the regular expression *abc* matches the strings *abc*, *abcde*, or *yzabc* because each of the strings contains those letters. No wildcards are necessary.

How to Match Text in Specific Locations

If you want to match text beginning at the first character of a string, start the regular expression with a caret (^) symbol. For example, the regular expression *^abc* matches the strings *abc* and *abcde*, but it does not match *yzabc*. To match text that ends at the last character of a string, place a $ symbol at the end of the regular expression. For example, the regular expression *abc$* matches *abc* and *yzabc*, but it does not match *abcde*. To exactly match a string, include both ^ and $. For example, *^abc$* only matches *abc* and does not match *abcde* or *yzabc*.

When searching for words, use the metacharacter \b to match a word boundary. For example, *car\b* matches *car* or *tocar* but not *carburetor*. Similarly, \B matches a nonword boundary and can be used to ensure that a character appears in the middle of a word. For example, *car\B* matches *carburetor* but not *tocar*.

NOTE Confused?

If regular expressions seem cryptic, that's because they are. Unlike almost everything else in the .NET Framework, regular expressions rely heavily on special characters with meanings that no human being could ever decipher on his or her own. The reason for this is simple: Regular expressions originated in the UNIX world during a time when memory and storage were extremely limited and developers had to make every single character count. Because of this, you should always comment regular expressions. As hard as they can be to create, interpreting another developer's regular expressions is almost impossible.

Table 3-1 lists characters that you can use to cause your regular expression to match a specific location in a string. Of these, the most important to know are ^ and $.

Table 3-1   Metacharacters That Match Location in Strings

Metacharacter	Description
^	Specifies that the match must begin at either the first character of the string or the first character of the line. By default if you are analyzing multiline input, the ^ matches the beginning of any line.
$	Specifies that the match must end at either the last character of the string, the last character before a carriage return at the end of the string, or the last character at the end of the line. By default, if you are analyzing multiline input, the $ matches the end of any line.
\A	Specifies that the match must begin at the first character of the string (and ignores multiple lines).
\Z	Specifies that the match must end at either the last character of the string or the last character before \n at the end of the string (and ignores multiple lines).
\z	Specifies that the match must end at the last character of the string (and ignores multiple lines).
\G	Specifies that the match must occur at the point where the previous match ended. When used with *Match.NextMatch*, this arrangement ensures that matches are all contiguous.
\b	Specifies that the match must occur on a boundary between \w (alphanumeric) and \W (nonalphanumeric) characters. The match must occur on word boundaries, which are the first or last characters in words separated by any nonalphanumeric characters.
\B	Specifies that the match must not occur on a \b boundary.

Notice that regular expression metacharacters are case-sensitive, even in Visual Basic. Often, capitalized characters have the opposite meaning of lowercase characters.

Many regular expression codes begin with a backslash. When developing in C#, you should begin every regular expression with an @ so that backslashes are treated literally. Do this even if your regular expression does not contain a backslash, because it reduces the risk of adding a bug that will be very difficult to find if you edit the regular expression later. For example:

```
// C#
Regex.IsMatch("pattern",@"\Apattern\Z")
```

Exam Tip   Don't even try to memorize every regular expression. Sure, it would impress the UNIX crowd at the office, but for the exam, you need to know only the most commonly used codes, which this book calls out in examples.

How to Match Special Characters

You can match special characters in regular expressions. For example, \t represents a tab, and \n represents a new line. The special characters shown in Table 3-2 might not appear in user input or the average text file; however, they might appear if you are processing output from a legacy or UNIX system.

Table 3-2   Metacharacter Escapes Used in Regular Expressions

Metacharacter	Description
\a	Matches a bell (alarm). The same as \u0007.
\b	In a regular expression, \b denotes a word boundary (between the \w and \W characters).
\t	Matches a tab. The same as \u0009.
\r	Matches a carriage return. The same as \u000D.
\v	Matches a vertical tab. The same as \u000B.
\f	Matches a form feed. The same as \u000C.
\n	Matches a new line. The same as \u000A.
\e	Matches an escape. The same as \u001B.
\040	Matches an ASCII character as octal, up to three digits. (\040 represents a space and is provided as an example; any three digits will work.)

Table 3-2   Metacharacter Escapes Used in Regular Expressions

Metacharacter	Description
\x20	Matches an ASCII character using hexadecimal representation (exactly two digits). (\x20 is provided as an example; any two digits will work.)
\cC	Matches an ASCII control character—for example, \cC is Ctrl-C. (\cC is provided as an example; any character will work.)
\u0020	Matches a Unicode character using hexadecimal representation (exactly four digits). (\u0020 is provided as an example; any four digits will work.)
\	When followed by a character that is not recognized as an escaped character, matches that character. For example, * represents an asterisk (rather than matching repeating characters), and \\ represents a single backslash.

How to Match Text Using Wildcards

You can also use regular expressions to match repeated characters. The * symbol matches the preceding character zero or more times. For example, *to*n* matches *ton, tooon,* or *tn.* The + symbol works similarly, but it must match one or more times. For example, *to+n* matches *ton* or *tooon,* but not *tn.*

To match a specific number of repeated characters, use {n}, where n is a digit. For example, *to{3}n* matches *tooon* but not *ton* or *tn.* To match a range of repeated characters, use {min,max}. For example, *to{1,3}n* matches *ton* or *tooon* but not *tn* or *toooon.* To specify only a minimum, leave the second number blank. For example, *to{3,}n* requires three or more consecutive *o* characters.

To make a character optional, use the ? symbol. For example, *to?n* matches *ton* or *tn,* but not *tooon.* To match any single character, use the period (.). For example, *to.n* matches *totn* or *tojn* but not *ton* or *tn.*

To match one of several characters, use brackets. For example, *to[ro]n* would match *toon* or *torn* but not *ton* or *toron.* You can also match a range of characters. For example, *to[o-r]n* matches *toon, topn, toqn,* or *torn,* but it would not match *toan* or *toyn.*

Table 3-3 summarizes the regular expression characters used to match multiple characters or a range of characters.

Table 3-3   Wildcard and Metacharacter Ranges Used in Regular Expressions

Metacharacter	Description
*	Matches the preceding character or subexpression zero or more times. For example, *zo** matches *z* and *zoo*. The * character is equivalent to *{0,}*. Subexpressions are discussed later in this chapter.
+	Matches the preceding character or subexpression one or more times. For example, *zo+* matches *zo* and *zoo*, but not *z*. The + character is equivalent to *{1,}*.
?	Matches the preceding character or subexpression zero or one time. For example, *do(es)?* matches *do* or *does*. The ? character is equivalent to *{0,1}*.
{n}	The *n* is a non-negative integer. Matches the preceding character or subexpression exactly *n* times. For example, *o{2}* does not match the *o* in *Bob*, but it does match the two *o*'s in *food*.
{n,}	The *n* is a non-negative integer. Matches the preceding character or subexpression at least *n* times. For example, *o{2,}* does not match the *o* in *Bob* and does match all the *o*'s in *foooood*. The sequence *o{1,}* is equivalent to *o+*. The sequence *o{0,}* is equivalent to *o**.
{n,m}	The *m* and *n* are non-negative integers, where *n <= m*. Matches the preceding character or subexpression at least *n* and at most *m* times. For example, *o{1,3}* matches the first three *o*'s in *foooooood*, and *o{0,1}* is equivalent to "*o?*". Note that you cannot put a space between the comma and the numbers.
?	When this character immediately follows any of the other quantifiers [*, +, ?, {n}, {n,}, {n,m}], the matching pattern is nongreedy. A nongreedy pattern matches as little of the searched string as possible, whereas the default greedy pattern matches as much of the searched string as possible. For example, in the string *oooo*, *o+?* matches a single *o*, whereas *o+* matches all *o*'s.

Table 3-3   Wildcard and Metacharacter Ranges Used in Regular Expressions

Metacharacter	Description
.	Matches any single character except \n. To match any character including the \n, use a pattern such as [\s\S].
x|y	Matches either x or y. For example, z|food matches z or food, and (z|f)ood matches zood or food.
[xyz]	A character set. Matches any one of the enclosed characters. For example, [abc] matches the a in plain.
[a-z]	A range of characters. Matches any character in the specified range. For example, [a-z] matches any lowercase alphabetic character in the range a through z.

Regular expressions also provide special characters to represent common character ranges. You could use [0-9] to match any numeric digit, or you can use \d. Similarly, \D matches any non-numeric character. Use \s to match any white-space character, and use \S to match any non-white-space character. Table 3-4 summarizes these symbols.

Table 3-4   Symbols Used in Regular Expressions

Metacharacter	Description
\d	Matches a digit character. Equivalent to [0-9].
\D	Matches a nondigit character. Equivalent to [^0-9].
\s	Matches any white-space character, including Space, Tab, and form-feed. Equivalent to [\f\n\r\t\v].
\S	Matches any non-white-space character. Equivalent to [^\f\n\r\t\v].
\w	Matches any word character, including underscore. Equivalent to [A-Za-z0-9_].
\W	Matches any nonword character. Equivalent to [^A-Za-z0-9_].

To match a group of characters, surround the characters with parentheses. For example, foo(loo){1,3}hoo would match fooloohoo and fooloolooloohoo but not foohoo or foololohoo. Similarly, foo(loo|roo)hoo would match either fooloohoo or fooroohoo. You can apply any wildcard or other special character to a group of characters.

You can also name a group so that later you can retrieve the data that matched the group. To name a group, use the format (?<name>pattern). For example, the regular expression *foo(?<mid>loo|roo)hoo* would match *fooloohoo*. Later, you could reference the group *mid* to retrieve *loo*. If you used the same regular expression to match *fooroohoo, mid* would contain *roo*.

How to Match Using Backreferences

Backreferencing uses either named groups and the \k metacharacter or a backslash followed by a one-digit number to allow you to search for other instances of characters that match a wildcard. Backreferences provide a convenient way to find repeating groups of characters. They can be thought of as a shorthand instruction to match the same string again.

For example, the regular expression (?<char>\w)\k<char>, using named groups and backreferencing, searches for adjacent paired characters. When applied to the string *I'll have a small coffee,* it finds matches in the words *I'll, small,* and *coffee.* The metacharacter \w finds any single-word character. The grouping construct (?<char>) encloses the metacharacter to force the regular expression engine to remember a subexpression match (which, in this case, is any single character) and save it under the name *char.* The backreference construct \k<char> causes the engine to compare the current character to the previously matched character stored under *char.* The entire regular expression successfully finds a match wherever a single character is the same as the preceding character.

To find repeating whole words, you can modify the grouping subexpression to search for any group of characters preceded by a space instead of simply searching for any single character. You can substitute the subexpression \w+, which matches any group of characters, for the metacharacter \w and use the metacharacter \s to match a space preceding the character group. This yields the regular expression (?<char>\s\w+)\k<char>, which finds any repeating whole words such as *the the* but also matches other repetitions of the specified string, as in the phrase *the theory.* This technique never matches the first character of a string, however, because it must be preceeded by white space.

To verify that the second match is on a word boundary, add the metacharacter \b after the repeat match. The resulting regular expression, (?<char>\s\w+)\k<char>\b, finds only repeating whole words that are embedded in white space.

A backreference refers to the most recent definition of a group (the definition most immediately to the left when matching left to right). Specifically, when a group makes multiple captures, a backreference (such as \1 in the following example) refers to the group captures, numbered from left to right. For example, (?<first>a)(?<second>\1b)* matches *aababb,* with the capturing pattern (a)(ab)(abb). The \1 metacharacter refers to the first group, \2 refers to the second group, and so on.

Table 3-5 lists optional parameters that add backreference modifiers to a regular expression.

Table 3-5   Backreference Parameters

Backreference Construct	Definition
\number	Backreference. For example, (\w)\1 finds doubled characters.
\k<name>	Named backreference. For example, (?<char>\w)\k<char> finds doubled words. The expression (?<43>\w)\43 does the same. You can use single quotes instead of angle brackets—for example, \k'char'.

How to Specify Regular Expression Options

You can modify a regular expression pattern with options that affect matching behavior. Regular expression options can be set in one of two basic ways: they can be specified in the *options* parameter in the *Regex(pattern, options)* constructor, where *options* is a bit-wise OR combination of *RegexOptions* enumerated values, or they can be set within the regular expression pattern using the inline *(?imnsx-imnsx:)* grouping construct or *(?imnsx-imnsx)* miscellaneous construct.

In inline option constructs, a minus sign (−) before an option or set of options turns off those options. For example, the inline construct *(?ix−ms)* turns on the *IgnoreCase* and *IgnorePatternWhitespace* options and turns off the *Multiline* and *Singleline* options. All regular expression options are turned off by default.

Table 3-6 lists the members of the *RegexOptions* enumeration and the equivalent inline option characters.

NOTE   The options *RightToLeft* and *Compiled* apply only to an expression as a whole and are not allowed inline. (They can be specified only in the options parameter to the *Regex* constructor.) The options *None* and *ECMAScript* are not allowed inline.

Table 3-6   Regular Expression Options

RegexOption Member	Inline Character	Description
None	N/A	Specifies that all options are turned off.
IgnoreCase	*i*	Specifies case-insensitive matching.
Multiline	*m*	Specifies multiline mode. Changes the meaning of ^ and $ so that they perform matching at the beginning and end, respectively, of any line, not just at the beginning and end of the whole string.
ExplicitCapture	*n*	Specifies that the only valid captures are explicitly named or numbered groups of the form (?<*name*>...). This allows parentheses to act as noncapturing groups.
Compiled	N/A	Specifies that the regular expression will be compiled to an assembly. Generates Microsoft Intermediate Language (MSIL) code for the regular expression; yields faster execution at the expense of start-up time.
Singleline	*s*	Specifies single-line mode. Changes the meaning of the period character (.) so that it matches every character (instead of every character except *n*).
IgnorePattern-Whitespace	*x*	Specifies that unescaped white space is excluded from the pattern, and enables comments following a number sign (#).
RightToLeft	N/A	Specifies that the search moves from right to left instead of from left to right. A regular expression with this option moves to the left of the starting position instead of to the right. (Therefore, the starting position should be specified as the end of the string instead of the beginning.) This option cannot be specified in midstream, which is a limitation designed to prevent the possibility of crafting regular expressions with infinite loops. *RightToLeft* changes only the search direction. It does not reverse the substring that is searched for.

Table 3-6 Regular Expression Options

RegexOption Member	Inline Character	Description
ECMAScript	N/A	Specifies that ECMAScript-compliant behavior is enabled for the expression. This option can be used only in conjunction with the *IgnoreCase* and *Multiline* flags. Use of *ECMAScript* with any other flags results in an exception.
CultureInvariant	N/A	Specifies that cultural differences in language are ignored.

Consider the following three-line text file:

```
abc
def
ghi
```

If this text file is read into a string named *s*, the following method call returns *false* because *def* is not at both the beginning and end of the string:

```
Regex.IsMatch(s,"^def$")
```

But the following method call returns *true* because the *RegexOptions.Multiline* option enables the ^ symbol to match the beginning of a line (rather than the entire string), and also enables the $ symbol to match the end of a line:

```
Regex.IsMatch(s,"^def$",RegexOptions.Multiline)
```

How to Extract Matched Data

Besides simply determining whether a string matches a pattern, you can extract information from a string. For example, if you are processing a text file that contains *Company Name: Contoso, Inc.*, you could extract just the name of the company using a regular expression.

To match a pattern and capture the match, follow these steps:

1. Create a regular expression and enclose in parentheses the pattern to be matched.

2. Create an instance of the *System.Text.RegularExpressions.Match* class using the static *Regex.Match* method.

3. Retrieve the matched data by accessing the elements of the *Match.Groups* array.

For example, the following code sample extracts the company name from the string named *input* and displays the name to the console:

```vb
' VB
Dim input As String = "Company Name: Contoso, Inc."
Dim m As Match = Regex.Match(input, "Company Name: (.*$)")
Console.WriteLine(m.Groups(1))
```

```csharp
// C#
string input = "Company Name: Contoso, Inc.";
Match m = Regex.Match(input, @"Company Name: (.*$)");
Console.WriteLine(m.Groups[1]);
```

Running this Console application (which requires the *System.Text.RegularExpressions* namespace) displays *Contoso, Inc.* This example demonstrates that with very little code, you can perform complex text extraction using regular expressions. Note that this example uses unnamed groups, which the runtime automatically numbers starting at 1.

The following example searches an input string and prints out all the *href="..."* values and their locations in the string. It does this by constructing a compiled *Regex* object and then using a *Match* object to iterate through all the matches in the string. In this example, the metacharacter \s matches any space character, and \S matches any nonspace character:

```vb
' VB
Sub DumpHrefs(inputString As String)
    Dim r As Regex
    Dim m As Match

    r = New Regex("href\s*=\s*(?:""(?<1>[^""]*)""|(?<1>\S+))", _
        RegexOptions.IgnoreCase Or RegexOptions.Compiled)

    m = r.Match(inputString)
    While m.Success
        Console.WriteLine("Found href " & m.Groups(1).Value _
            & " at " & m.Groups(1).Index.ToString())
        m = m.NextMatch()
    End While
End Sub
```

```
// C#
void DumpHrefs(String inputString)
{
    Regex r;
    Match m;

    r = new Regex(@"href\s*=\s*(?:""(?<1>[^""]*)""|(?<1>\S+))",
        RegexOptions.IgnoreCase|RegexOptions.Compiled);
    for (m = r.Match(inputString); m.Success; m = m.NextMatch())
    {
        Console.WriteLine("Found href " + m.Groups[1] + " at "
            + m.Groups[1].Index);
    }
}
```

You can also call the *Match.Result* method to retrieve and then reformat extracted substrings. The following code example uses *Match.Result* to extract a protocol and port number from a Uniform Resource Locator (URL). For example, passing the string *"http://www.contoso.com:8080/letters/readme.html"* to the *Extension* method results in a return value of *"http:8080"*:

```
' VB
Function Extension(url As String) As String
    Dim r As New Regex("^(?<proto>\w+)://[^/]+?(?<port>:\d+)?/", _
        RegexOptions.Compiled)
    Return r.Match(url).Result("${proto}${port}")
End Function
```

```
// C#
String Extension(String url)
{
    Regex r = new Regex(@"^(?<proto>\w+)://[^/]+?(?<port>:\d+)?/",
        RegexOptions.Compiled);
    return r.Match(url).Result("${proto}${port}");
}
```

How to Replace Substrings Using Regular Expressions

You can use regular expressions to perform replacements far more complex than is possible with the *String.Replace* method. The following code example uses the static *Regex.Replace* method to replace dates in *mm/dd/yy* format with dates in *dd-mm-yy* format:

```
' VB
Function MDYToDMY(input As String) As String
    Return Regex.Replace(input, _
        "\b(?<month>\d{1,2})/(?<day>\d{1,2})/(?<year>\d{2,4})\b", _
            "${day}-${month}-${year}")
End Function
```

```
// C#
String MDYToDMY(String input)
{
    return Regex.Replace(input,
        @"\b(?<month>\d{1,2})/(?<day>\d{1,2})/(?<year>\d{2,4})\b",
        "${day}-${month}-${year}");
}
```

This example demonstrates the use of named backreferences within the replacement pattern for *Regex.Replace*. Here, the replacement expression *${day}* inserts the substring captured by the group *(?<day>...)*.

The following code example uses the static *Regex.Replace* method to strip invalid characters from a string. You can use the *CleanInput* method defined here to strip potentially harmful characters that have been entered into a text field in a form that accepts user input. *CleanInput* returns a string after stripping out all nonalphanumeric characters except @, – (a dash), and . (a period):

```
' VB
Function CleanInput(strIn As String) As String
    ' Replace invalid characters with empty strings.
    Return Regex.Replace(strIn, "[^\w\.@-]", "")
End Function
```

```
// C#
String CleanInput(string strIn)
{
    // Replace invalid characters with empty strings.
    return Regex.Replace(strIn, @"[^\w\.@-]", "");
}
```

Substitutions denoted by the $ metacharacter and character escapes are the only special constructs recognized in a replacement pattern. All the syntactic constructs described in the previous sections are allowed only in regular expressions; they are not recognized in replacement patterns. For example, the replacement pattern *a*${txt}b* inserts the string *a** followed by the substring matched by the *txt* capturing group, if any, followed by the string *b*. The * character is not recognized as a metacharacter within a replacement pattern.

Similarly, $ patterns are not recognized within regular expression matching patterns. Within regular expressions, $ only designates the end of the string.

Table 3-7 shows how to define named and numbered replacement patterns.

Table 3-7   Metacharacter Escapes Used in Substitutions

Metacharacter	Description
$number	Substitutes the last substring matched by group number *number* (decimal)
${name}	Substitutes the last substring matched by a *(?<name>)* group
$$	Substitutes a single $ literal
$&	Substitutes a copy of the entire match itself
$`	Substitutes all the text of the input string before the match
$'	Substitutes all the text of the input string after the match
$+	Substitutes the last group captured
$_	Substitutes the entire input string

How to Use Regular Expressions to Constrain String Input

When building security into your application, regular expressions are the most efficient way to validate user input. If you build an application that accepts a five-digit number from a user, you can use a regular expression to ensure that the input is exactly five characters long and that each character is a number from 0 through 9. Similarly, when prompting a user for her first and last name, you can check her input with a regular expression and throw an exception when the input contains numbers, delimiters, or any other nonalphabetic character.

Unfortunately, not all input is as easy to describe as numbers and e-mail addresses. Names and street addresses are particularly difficult to validate because they can contain a wide variety of characters from international alphabets that are unfamiliar to you. For example, O'Dell, Varkey Chudukatil, Skjønaa, Craciun, and McAskill-White are all legitimate last names. Programmatically filtering these examples of valid input from malicious input such as *1' DROP TABLE PRODUCTS–*(a SQL injection attack) is difficult.

One common approach is to instruct users to replace characters in their own names. For example, users who normally enter an apostrophe or a hyphen in their names could omit those characters. Users with letters that are not part of the standard Roman alphabet could replace letters with the closest similar Roman character. Although this system allows you to validate input more rigorously, it requires users to sacrifice the accurate spelling of their names—something many people take very personally.

As an alternative, you can perform as much filtering as possible on the input and then clean the input of any potentially malicious content. Most input validation should be pessimistic and allow only input that consists entirely of approved characters. However, input validation of real names might need to be optimistic and cause an error only when specifically denied characters exist. For example, you could reject a user's name if it contains one of the following characters: *!, @, #, $, %, ^, *, (,), <, >.* All these characters are unlikely to appear in a name but are likely to be used in an attack. Visual Studio .NET provides the following regular expression to match valid names: *[a-zA-Z'`-Ãâå´\s]{1,40}.*

Real World

Tony Northrup

I'm often stubborn to a fault. For many years, I simply refused to learn regular expressions. Regular expressions were the UNIX way of doing things, and I was a Windows guy.

Recently, I reviewed some code I wrote several years ago when I was still being stubborn. I had written dozens of lines of code to check the validity of text data that could have been written with a singular regular expression. That doesn't bother me in itself, because sometimes writing more code improves readability. However, in this case, the text checking had gotten so complex that the text-checking code contained bugs.

I rewrote the code using regular expressions, and it not only fixed the bugs, but it simplified the code. So, for your own sake, don't ignore regular expressions just because they seem overly complex. Dive in, spend a few hours working with them, and you won't regret it.

Lab: Create a *Regex* Expression Evaluator

In this lab, you process an array of strings to distinguish valid phone numbers and ZIP codes. Then you reformat the phone numbers. If you encounter a problem completing an exercise, the completed projects are available along with the sample files.

Exercise 1: Distinguish Between a Phone Number and a ZIP Code

In this exercise, you will write code to distinguish between a phone number, a ZIP code, and invalid data.

1. Navigate to the \<*InstallHome*>\Chapter03\Lesson1\Exercise1\Partial folder and open either the C# version or the Visual Basic .NET version of the solution file.

2. Using one line of code, complete the *IsPhone* method so that it returns *true* if the parameter matches any of the following formats:

    ❑ (555)555-1212

    ❑ (555) 555-1212

    ❑ 555-555-1212

    ❑ 5555551212

    Although many different regular expressions would work, the *IsPhone* method you write could look like this:

    ```
    ' VB
    Function IsPhone(ByVal s As String) As Boolean
        Return Regex.IsMatch(s, "^\(?\d{3}\)?[\s\-]?\d{3}\-?\d{4}$")
    End Function
    ```

    ```
    // C#
    static bool IsPhone(string s)
    {
        return Regex.IsMatch(s, @"^\(?\d{3}\)?[\s\-]?\d{3}\-?\d{4}$");
    }
    ```

    Each component of this regular expression matches a required or optional part of a phone number:

    ❑ ^   Matches the beginning of the string.

    ❑ \(?   Optionally matches an opening parenthesis. The parenthesis is preceded with a backslash, because the parenthesis is a special character in regular expressions. The question mark that follows the parenthesis makes the parenthesis optional.

    ❑ \d{3}   Matches exactly three numeric digits.

    ❑ \)?   Optionally matches a closing parenthesis. The parenthesis is preceded with a backslash because the parenthesis is a special character in regular expressions. The question mark that follows the parenthesis makes the parenthesis optional.

- ❑ **[\s\-]?** Matches either a space (\s) or a hyphen (\-) separating the area code from the rest of the phone number. The question mark that follows the brackets makes the space or hyphen optional.

- ❑ **\d{3}** Matches exactly three numeric digits.

- ❑ **\-?** Optionally matches a hyphen.

- ❑ **\d{4}$** Requires that the string end with four numeric digits.

3. Using one line of code, complete the *IsZip* method so that it returns *true* if the parameter matches any of the following formats:

   - ❑ 01111

   - ❑ 01111-1111

   Although many different regular expressions would work, the *IsZip* method you write could look like this:

```
' VB
Function IsZip(ByVal s As String) As Boolean
    Return Regex.IsMatch(s, "^\d{5}(\-\d{4})?$")
End Function
```

```
// C#
static bool IsZip(string s)
{
    return Regex.IsMatch(s, @"^\d{5}(\-\d{4})?$");
}
```

   Each component of this regular expression matches a required or optional part of a ZIP code:

   - ❑ **^** Matches the beginning of the string.

   - ❑ **\d{5}** Matches exactly five numeric digits.

   - ❑ **(\-\d{4})?** Optionally matches a hyphen followed by exactly four numeric digits. Because the expression is surrounded by parentheses and followed by a question mark, the expression is considered optional.

   - ❑ **$** Matches the end of the string.

4. Build and run the project. The output should match the following:

```
(555)555-1212 is a phone number
(555) 555-1212 is a phone number
555-555-1212 is a phone number
5555551212 is a phone number
01111 is a zip code
```

```
01111-1111 is a zip code
47 is unknown
111-11-1111 is unknown
```

If the output you get does not match the output just shown, adjust your regular expressions as needed.

Exercise 2: Reformat a String

In this exercise, you must reformat phone numbers into a standard (###) ###-#### format.

1. Open the project that you created in Exercise 1.

2. Add a method named *ReformatPhone* that returns a string and accepts a single string as an argument. Using regular expressions, accept phone-number data provided in one of the formats used in Exercise 1, and reformat the data into the (###) ###-#### format.

   Although many different regular expressions would work, the *ReformatPhone* method you write could look like this:

```
' VB
Function ReformatPhone(ByVal s As String) As String
    Dim m As Match = Regex.Match(s, _
        "^\(?(\d{3})\)?[\s\-]?(\d{3})\-?(\d{4})$")
    Return String.Format("({0}) {1}-{2}", _
        m.Groups(1), m.Groups(2), m.Groups(3))
End Function
```

```
// C#
static string ReformatPhone(string s)
{
    Match m = Regex.Match(s,
        @"^\(?(\d{3})\)?[\s\-]?(\d{3})\-?(\d{4})$");
    return String.Format("({0}) {1}-{2}",
        m.Groups[1], m.Groups[2], m.Groups[3]);
}
```

   Notice that this regular expression almost exactly matches that used in the *IsPhone* method. The only difference is that each of the \d{n} expressions is surrounded by parentheses. This places each of the sets of numbers into a separate group that can be easily formatted using *String.Format*.

3. Change the *Main* method so that it writes *ReformatPhone(s)* in the *foreach* loop instead of simply writing s. The *foreach* loop should now look like this (the changes are shown in bold):

```
' VB
For Each s As String In input
    If IsPhone(s) Then
```

```
            Console.WriteLine(ReformatPhone(s) + " is a phone number")
        Else
            If IsZip(s) Then
                Console.WriteLine(s + " is a zip code")
            Else
                Console.WriteLine(s + " is unknown")
            End If
        End If
    Next

    // C#
    foreach (string s in input)
    {
        if (IsPhone(s)) Console.WriteLine(ReformatPhone(s) + " is a phone number");
        else if (IsZip(s)) Console.WriteLine(s + " is a zip code");
        else Console.WriteLine(s + " is unknown");
    }
```

4. Build and run the project. The output should match the following:

```
(555) 555-1212 is a phone number
(555) 555-1212 is a phone number
(555) 555-1212 is a phone number
(555) 555-1212 is a phone number
01111 is a zip code
01111-1111 is a zip code
47 is unknown
111-11-1111 is unknown
```

Notice that each of the phone numbers has been reformatted even though they were initially in four different formats. If your output does not match the output just shown, adjust your regular expressions as needed.

Lesson Summary

- Regular expressions enable you to determine whether text matches almost any type of format. Regular expressions support dozens of special characters and operators. The most commonly used are ^ to match the beginning of a string, $ to match the end of a string, ? to make a character optional, . to match any character, and * to match zero or more characters.

- To extract data using a regular expression, create a pattern using groups to specify the data you need to extract, call *Regex.Match* to create a *Match* object, and then examine each of the items in the *Match.Groups* array.

- To reformat text data using a regular expression, call the static *Regex.Replace* method.

Lesson Review

You can use the following questions to test your knowledge of the information in Lesson 1, "Forming Regular Expressions." The questions are also available on the companion CD if you prefer to review them in electronic form.

NOTE **Answers**

Answers to these questions and explanations of why each answer choice is right or wrong are located in the "Answers" section at the end of the book.

---

1. You are writing an application to update absolute hyperlinks in HTML files. You have loaded the HTML file into a string named *s*. Which of the following code samples best replaces *http://* with *https://*, regardless of whether the user types the URL in uppercase or lowercase?

   A.
   ```
   ' VB
   s = Regex.Replace(s, "http://", "https://")
   ```

   ```
   // C#
   s = Regex.Replace(s, "http://", "https://");
   ```
   B.
   ```
   ' VB
   s = Regex.Replace(s, "https://", "http://")
   ```

   ```
   // C#
   s = Regex.Replace(s, "https://", "http://");
   ```
   C.
   ```
   ' VB
   s = Regex.Replace(s, "http://", "https://", RegexOptions.IgnoreCase)
   ```

   ```
   // C#
   s = Regex.Replace(s, "http://", "https://", RegexOptions.IgnoreCase);
   ```
   D.
   ```
   ' VB
   s = Regex.Replace(s, "https://", "http://", RegexOptions.IgnoreCase)
   ```

   ```
   // C#
   s = Regex.Replace(s, "https://", "http://", RegexOptions.IgnoreCase);
   ```

2. You are writing an application to process data contained in a text form. Each file contains information about a single customer. The following is a sample form:

   ```
   First Name: Tom
   Last Name: Perham
   ```

```
Address: 123 Pine St.
City: Springfield
State: MA
Zip: 01332
```

You have read the form data into the *String* variable *s*. Which of the following code samples correctly stores the data portion of the form in the *fullName*, *address*, *city*, *state*, and *zip* variables?

A.

```vb
' VB
Dim p As String = "First Name: (?<firstName>.*$)\n" + _
    "Last Name: (?<lastName>.*$)\n" + _
    "Address: (?<address>.*$)\n" + _
    "City: (?<city>.*$)\n" + _
    "State: (?<state>.*$)\n" + _
    "Zip: (?<zip>.*$)"
Dim m As Match = Regex.Match(s, p, RegexOptions.Multiline)
Dim fullName As String = m.Groups("firstName").ToString + " " + _
    m.Groups("lastName").ToString
Dim address As String = m.Groups("address").ToString
Dim city As String = m.Groups("city").ToString
Dim state As String = m.Groups("state").ToString
Dim zip As String = m.Groups("zip").ToString
```

```csharp
// C#
string p = @"First Name: (?<firstName>.*$)\n" +
    @"Last Name: (?<lastName>.*$)\n" +
    @"Address: (?<address>.*$)\n" +
    @"City: (?<city>.*$)\n" +
    @"State: (?<state>.*$)\n" +
    @"Zip: (?<zip>.*$)";
Match m = Regex.Match(s, p, RegexOptions.Multiline);
string fullName = m.Groups["firstName"] + " " + m.Groups["lastName"];
string address = m.Groups["address"].ToString();
string city = m.Groups["city"].ToString();
string state = m.Groups["state"].ToString();
string zip = m.Groups["zip"].ToString();
```

B.

```vb
Dim p As String = "First Name: (?<firstName>.*$)\n" + _
    "Last Name: (?<lastName>.*$)\n" + _
    "Address: (?<address>.*$)\n" + _
    "City: (?<city>.*$)\n" + _
    "State: (?<state>.*$)\n" + _
    "Zip: (?<zip>.*$)"
Dim m As Match = Regex.Match(s, p)
Dim fullName As String = m.Groups("firstName").ToString + " " + _
    m.Groups("lastName").ToString
Dim address As String = m.Groups("address").ToString
Dim city As String = m.Groups("city").ToString
Dim state As String = m.Groups("state").ToString
Dim zip As String = m.Groups("zip").ToString
```

```csharp
// C#
string p = @"First Name: (?<firstName>.*$)\n" +
    @"Last Name: (?<lastName>.*$)\n" +
    @"Address: (?<address>.*$)\n" +
    @"City: (?<city>.*$)\n" +
    @"State: (?<state>.*$)\n" +
    @"Zip: (?<zip>.*$)";
Match m = Regex.Match(s, p);
string fullName = m.Groups["firstName"] + " " + m.Groups["lastName"];
string address = m.Groups["address"].ToString();
string city = m.Groups["city"].ToString();
string state = m.Groups["state"].ToString();
string zip = m.Groups["zip"].ToString();
```

C.

```vb
Dim p As String = "First Name: (?<firstName>.*$)\n" + _
    "Last Name: (?<lastName>.*$)\n" + _
    "Address: (?<address>.*$)\n" + _
    "City: (?<city>.*$)\n" + _
    "State: (?<state>.*$)\n" + _
    "Zip: (?<zip>.*$)"
Dim m As Match = Regex.Match(s, p, RegexOptions.Multiline)
Dim fullName As String = m.Groups("<firstName>").ToString + " " + _
    m.Groups("<lastName>").ToString
Dim address As String = m.Groups("<address>").ToString
Dim city As String = m.Groups("<city>").ToString
Dim state As String = m.Groups("<state>").ToString
Dim zip As String = m.Groups("<zip>").ToString
```

```csharp
// C#
string p = @"First Name: (?<firstName>.*$)\n" +
    @"Last Name: (?<lastName>.*$)\n" +
    @"Address: (?<address>.*$)\n" +
    @"City: (?<city>.*$)\n" +
    @"State: (?<state>.*$)\n" +
    @"Zip: (?<zip>.*$)";
Match m = Regex.Match(s, p, RegexOptions.Multiline);
string fullName = m.Groups["<firstName>"] + " " + m.Groups["<lastName>"];
string address = m.Groups["<address>"].ToString();
string city = m.Groups["<city>"].ToString();
string state = m.Groups["<state>"].ToString();
string zip = m.Groups["<zip>"].ToString();
```

D.

```vb
Dim p As String = "First Name: (?<firstName>.*$)\n" + _
    "Last Name: (?<lastName>.*$)\n" + _
    "Address: (?<address>.*$)\n" + _
    "City: (?<city>.*$)\n" + _
    "State: (?<state>.*$)\n" + _
    "Zip: (?<zip>.*$)"
Dim m As Match = Regex.Match(s, p)
Dim fullName As String = m.Groups("<firstName>").ToString + " " + _
    m.Groups("<lastName>").ToString
```

```
Dim address As String = m.Groups("<address>").ToString
Dim city As String = m.Groups("<city>").ToString
Dim state As String = m.Groups("<state>").ToString
Dim zip As String = m.Groups("<zip>").ToString
```

```csharp
// C#
string p = @"First Name: (?<firstName>.*$)\n" +
    @"Last Name: (?<lastName>.*$)\n" +
    @"Address: (?<address>.*$)\n" +
    @"City: (?<city>.*$)\n" +
    @"State: (?<state>.*$)\n" +
    @"Zip: (?<zip>.*$)";
Match m = Regex.Match(s, p);
string fullName = m.Groups["<firstName>"] + " " + m.Groups["<lastName>"];
string address = m.Groups["<address>"].ToString();
string city = m.Groups["<city>"].ToString();
string state = m.Groups["<state>"].ToString();
string zip = m.Groups["<zip>"].ToString();
```

3. Which of the following regular expressions matches the strings *zoot* and *zot*?

   A. *z(oo)+t*

   B. *zo*t$*

   C. *$zo*t*

   D. *^(zo)+t*

4. Which of the following strings match the regular expression *^a(mo)+t.*z$*? (Choose all that apply.)

   A. *amotz*

   B. *amomtrewz*

   C. *amotmoz*

   D. *atrewz*

   E. *amomomottothez*

Lesson 2: Encoding and Decoding

Every string and text file is encoded using one of many different encoding standards. Most of the time, the .NET Framework handles the encoding for you automatically. However, there are times when you might need to control encoding and decoding manually, such as during the following procedures:

- Interoperating with legacy or UNIX systems
- Reading or writing text files in other languages
- Creating HTML pages
- Generating e-mail messages

This lesson describes common encoding techniques and shows you how to use them in .NET Framework applications.

After this lesson, you will be able to:

- Describe the importance of encoding and list common encoding standards
- Use the *Encoding* class to specify encoding formats and convert between encoding standards
- Programmatically determine which code pages the .NET Framework supports
- Create files using a specific encoding format
- Read files using unusual encoding formats

Estimated lesson time: 30 minutes

Understanding Encoding

Although it was not the first encoding type, American Standard Code for Information Interchange (ASCII) is still the foundation for existing encoding types. ASCII assigned characters to 7-bit bytes using the numbers 0 through 127. These characters included English uppercase and lowercase letters, numbers, punctuation, and some special control characters. For example, 0x21 is !, 0x31 is 1, 0x43 is C, 0x63 is c, and 0x7D is }.

While ASCII was sufficient for most English-language communications, ASCII did not include characters used in non-English alphabets. To enable computers to be used in non-English-speaking locations, computer manufacturers used the remaining values—128 through 255—in an 8-bit byte. Over time, different locations assigned unique characters to values greater than 127. Because different locations might have different characters assigned to a single value, transferring documents between different languages created problems.

To help reduce these problems, the American National Standards Institute (ANSI) defined code pages that had standard ASCII characters for 0 through 127 and language-specific characters for 128 through 255. A *code page* is a list of selected character codes (characters represented as code points) in a certain order. Code pages are usually defined to support specific languages or groups of languages that share common writing systems. Windows code pages contain 256 code points and are zero-based.

If you've ever received an e-mail message or seen a Web page that seemed to have box characters or question marks where letters should appear, you have seen an encoding problem. Because people create Web pages and e-mails in many different languages, each must be tagged with an encoding type. For example, an e-mail might include one of the following headers:

```
Content-Type: text/plain; charset=ISO-8859-1
Content-Type: text/plain; charset="Windows-1251"
```

ISO-8859-1 corresponds to code page 28591, Western European (ISO). If it had specified *ISO-8859-7,* it could have contained characters from the Greek (ISO) code page, number 28597. Similarly, HTML Web pages typically include a meta tag such as one of the following:

```
<meta http-equiv="Content-Type" content="text/html; charset=iso-8859-1">
<meta http-equiv="Content-Type" content="text/html; charset=utf-8">
```

More and more, ASCII and ISO 8859 encoding types are being replaced by Unicode. *Unicode* is a massive code page with tens of thousands of characters that support most languages and scripts, including Latin, Greek, Cyrillic, Hebrew, Arabic, Chinese, and Japanese.

Unicode itself does not specify an encoding type; however, there are several standards for encoding Unicode. The .NET Framework uses Unicode UTF-16 (Unicode Transformation Format, 16-bit encoding form) to represent characters. In some cases, the .NET Framework uses UTF-8 internally. The *System.Text* namespace provides classes that allow you to encode and decode characters. *System.Text* encoding support includes the following encodings:

- **Unicode UTF-32 encoding** Unicode UTF-32 encoding represents Unicode characters as sequences of 32-bit integers. You can use the *UTF32Encoding* class to convert characters to and from UTF-32 encoding.

- **Unicode UTF-16 encoding** Unicode UTF-16 encoding represents Unicode characters as sequences of 16-bit integers. You can use the *UnicodeEncoding* class to convert characters to and from UTF-16 encoding.

■ **Unicode UTF-8 encoding**   Unicode UTF-8 uses 8-bit, 16-bit, 24-bit, and up to 48-bit encoding. Values 0 through 127 use 8-bit encoding and exactly match ASCII values, providing some degree of interoperability. Values from 128 through 2047 use 16-bit encoding and provide support for Latin, Greek, Cyrillic, Hebrew, and Arabic alphabets. Values 2048 through 65535 use 24-bit encoding for Chinese, Japanese, Korean, and other languages that require large numbers of values. You can use the *UTF8Encoding* class to convert characters to and from UTF-8 encoding.

■ **ASCII encoding**   ASCII encoding encodes the Latin alphabet as single 7-bit ASCII characters. Because this encoding supports only character values from \u0000 through \u007F, in most cases it is inadequate for internationalized applications. You can use the *ASCIIEncoding* class to convert characters to and from ASCII encoding.

■ **ANSI/ISO Encodings**   The *System.Text.Encoding* class provides support for a wide range of ANSI/ISO encodings.

MORE INFO   Unicode

For more information about Unicode, see the Unicode Standard at *http://www.unicode.org*.

Using the Encoding Class

You can use the *System.Text.Encoding.GetEncoding* method to return an encoding object for a specified encoding. You can use the *Encoding.GetBytes* method to convert a Unicode string to its byte representation in a specified encoding. The following code example uses the *Encoding.GetEncoding* method to create a target encoding object for the Korean code page. The code calls the *Encoding.GetBytes* method to convert a Unicode string to its byte representation in the Korean encoding. The code then displays the byte representations of the strings in the Korean code page:

```
' VB
' Get Korean encoding
Dim e As Encoding = Encoding.GetEncoding("Korean")

' Convert ASCII bytes to Korean encoding
Dim encoded As Byte()
encoded = e.GetBytes("Hello, World!")

' Display the byte codes
Dim i As Integer
```

```
For i = 0 To encoded.Length - 1
    Console.WriteLine("Byte {0}: {1}", i, encoded(i))
Next i
```

```
// C#
// Get Korean encoding
Encoding e = Encoding.GetEncoding("Korean");

// Convert ASCII bytes to Korean encoding
byte[] encoded;
encoded = e.GetBytes("Hello, World!");

// Display the byte codes
for (int i = 0; i < encoded.Length; i++)
    Console.WriteLine("Byte {0}: {1}", i, encoded[i]);
```

This code sample demonstrates how to convert text to a different code page; however, normally you would not convert an English-language phrase into a different code page. In most code pages, the code points 0 through 127 represent the same ASCII characters. This allows for continuity and for accommodating legacy code. The code points 128 through 255 differ significantly between code pages. Because the sample code translated the ASCII phrase, "Hello, World!" (which consists entirely of ASCII bytes falling in the range of code points from 0 through 127), the translated bytes in the Korean code page exactly match the original ASCII bytes.

MORE INFO Code Pages

For a list of all supported code pages, see the "Encoding Class" topic at *http://msdn.microsoft.com/en-us/library/system.text.encoding.aspx*.

How to Examine Supported Code Pages

To examine all supported code pages in the .NET Framework, call *Encoding.GetEncodings*. This method returns an array of *EncodingInfo* objects. The following code sample displays the number, official name, and friendly name of the .NET Framework code pages:

```
' VB
Dim ei As EncodingInfo() = Encoding.GetEncodings
For Each e As EncodingInfo In ei
    Console.WriteLine("{0}: {1}, {2}", e.CodePage, e.Name, e.DisplayName)
Next
```

```
// C#
EncodingInfo[] ei = Encoding.GetEncodings();
foreach (EncodingInfo e in ei)
    Console.WriteLine("{0}: {1}, {2}", e.CodePage, e.Name, e.DisplayName);
```

How to Specify the Encoding Type When Writing a File

To specify the encoding type when writing a file, use an overloaded *Stream* constructor that accepts an *Encoding* object. For example, the following code sample creates several files with different encoding types:

```vb
' VB
Dim swUtf7 As StreamWriter = New StreamWriter("utf7.txt", False, Encoding.UTF7)
swUtf7.WriteLine("Hello, World!")
swUtf7.Close

Dim swUtf8 As StreamWriter = New StreamWriter("utf8.txt", False, Encoding.UTF8)
swUtf8.WriteLine("Hello, World!")
swUtf8.Close

Dim swUtf16 As StreamWriter = New StreamWriter( _
    "utf16.txt", False, Encoding.Unicode)
swUtf16.WriteLine("Hello, World!")
swUtf16.Close

Dim swUtf32 As StreamWriter = New StreamWriter("utf32.txt", False, Encoding.UTF32)
swUtf32.WriteLine("Hello, World!")
swUtf32.Close
```

```csharp
// C#
StreamWriter swUtf7 = new StreamWriter("utf7.txt", false, Encoding.UTF7);
swUtf7.WriteLine("Hello, World!");
swUtf7.Close();

StreamWriter swUtf8 = new StreamWriter("utf8.txt", false, Encoding.UTF8);
swUtf8.WriteLine("Hello, World!");
swUtf8.Close();

StreamWriter swUtf16 = new StreamWriter("utf16.txt", false, Encoding.Unicode);
swUtf16.WriteLine("Hello, World!");
swUtf16.Close();

StreamWriter swUtf32 = new StreamWriter("utf32.txt", false, Encoding.UTF32);
swUtf32.WriteLine("Hello, World!");
swUtf32.Close();
```

If you run the previous code sample, you will notice that the four different files each have different file sizes: the UTF-7 file is 19 bytes, the UTF-8 file is 18 bytes, the UTF-16 file is 32 bytes, and the UTF-32 file is 64 bytes. If you open each of the files in Notepad, the UTF-8 and UTF-16 files display correctly. However, the UTF-7 and UTF-32 files display incorrectly. All the files were correctly encoded, but Notepad is not capable of reading UTF-7 and UTF-32 files correctly.

NOTE   Choosing an Encoding Type

If you are not sure which encoding type to use when creating a file, simply accept the default by not specifying an encoding type. The .NET Framework then chooses UTF-16.

How to Specify the Encoding Type When Reading a File

Typically, you do not need to specify an encoding type when reading a file. The .NET Framework automatically decodes most common encoding types. However, you can specify an encoding type using an overloaded *Stream* constructor, as the following sample shows:

```vb
' VB
Dim fn As String = "file.txt"
Dim sw As StreamWriter = New StreamWriter(fn, False, Encoding.UTF7)
sw.WriteLine("Hello, World!")
sw.Close

Dim sr As StreamReader = New StreamReader(fn, Encoding.UTF7)
Console.WriteLine(sr.ReadToEnd)
sr.Close
```

```csharp
// C#
string fn = "file.txt";
StreamWriter sw = new StreamWriter(fn, false, Encoding.UTF7);
sw.WriteLine("Hello, World!");
sw.Close();

StreamReader sr = new StreamReader(fn, Encoding.UTF7);
Console.WriteLine(sr.ReadToEnd());
sr.Close();
```

Unlike most Unicode encoding types, the unusual UTF-7 encoding type in the previous code sample requires you to declare it explicitly when reading a file. If you run the following code, which does not specify the UTF-7 encoding type when reading the file, it is read incorrectly and displays the wrong result:

```vb
' VB
Dim fn As String = "file.txt"
Dim sw As StreamWriter = New StreamWriter(fn, False, Encoding.UTF7)
sw.WriteLine("Hello, World!")
sw.Close

Dim sr As StreamReader = New StreamReader(fn)
Console.WriteLine(sr.ReadToEnd)
sr.Close
```

```
// C#
string fn = "file.txt";
StreamWriter sw = new StreamWriter(fn, false, Encoding.UTF7);
sw.WriteLine("Hello, World!");
sw.Close();

StreamReader sr = new StreamReader(fn);
Console.WriteLine(sr.ReadToEnd());
sr.Close();
```

Lab: Read and Write an Encoded File

In this lab, you will convert a text file from one encoding type to another. If you encounter a problem completing an exercise, the completed projects are available along with the sample files.

Exercise: Convert a Text File to a Different Encoding Type

In this exercise, you will convert a text file to UTF-7.

1. Use Visual Studio to create a new Console application.

2. Write code to read the C:\windows\win.ini file (or any text file), and then write it to a file named win-utf7.txt using the UTF-7 encoding type. For example, the following code (which requires the *System.IO* namespace) would work:

```
' VB
Dim sr As StreamReader = New StreamReader("C:\windows\win.ini")
Dim sw As StreamWriter = New StreamWriter("win-utf7.txt", False, Encoding.UTF7)
sw.WriteLine(sr.ReadToEnd)
sw.Close()
sr.Close()
```

```
// C#
StreamReader sr = new StreamReader(@"C:\windows\win.ini");
StreamWriter sw = new StreamWriter("win-utf7.txt", false, Encoding.UTF7);
sw.WriteLine(sr.ReadToEnd());
sw.Close();
sr.Close();
```

3. Run your application and open the win-utf7.txt file in Notepad. If the file was translated correctly, Notepad will display it with some invalid characters because Notepad does not support the UTF-7 encoding type.

Lesson Summary

- Encoding standards map byte values to characters. ASCII is one of the oldest, most widespread encoding standards; however, it provides very limited support for non-English languages. Today, various Unicode encoding standards provide multilingual support.

- The *System.Text.Encoding* class provides static methods for encoding and decoding text.

- Call *Encoding.GetEncodings* to retrieve a list of supported code pages.

- To specify the encoding type when writing a file, use an overloaded *Stream* constructor that accepts an *Encoding* object.

- You typically do not need to specify an encoding type when reading a file. However, you can specify an encoding type by using an overloaded *Stream* constructor that accepts an *Encoding* object.

Lesson Review

You can use the following questions to test your knowledge of the information in Lesson 2, "Encoding and Decoding." The questions are also available on the companion CD if you prefer to review them in electronic form.

NOTE Answers

Answers to these questions and explanations of why each answer choice is right or wrong are located in the "Answers" section at the end of the book.

---

1. Which of the following encoding types would yield the largest file size?

    A. UTF-32

    B. UTF-16

    C. UTF-8

    D. ASCII

2. Which of the following encoding types support Chinese? (Choose all that apply.)

    A. UTF-32

    B. UTF-16

    C. UTF-8

    D. ASCII

3. You need to decode a file encoded in ASCII. Which of the following decoding types would yield correct results? (Choose all that apply.)

    A. Encoding.UTF32

    B. Encoding.UTF16

    C. Encoding.UTF8

    D. Encoding.UTF7

4. You are writing an application that generates summary reports nightly. These reports will be viewed by executives in your Korea office and must contain Korean characters. Which of the following encoding types is the best one to use?

    A. iso-2022-kr

    B. x-EBCDIC-KoreanExtended

    C. x-mac-korean

    D. UTF-16

Chapter Review

To practice and reinforce the skills you learned in this chapter further, you can perform the following tasks:

- Review the chapter summary.
- Review the list of key terms introduced in this chapter.
- Complete the case scenarios. These scenarios set up real-world situations involving the topics of this chapter and ask you to create a solution.
- Complete the suggested practices.
- Take a practice test.

Chapter Summary

- Regular expressions have roots in UNIX and Perl, and they can seem complicated and unnatural to .NET Framework developers. However, regular expressions are extremely efficient and useful for validating text input, extracting text data, and reformatting data.
- In the past decade, the most commonly used encoding standard for text files has gradually shifted from ASCII to Unicode. Unicode itself supports several different encoding standards. While the .NET Framework uses the UTF-16 encoding standard by default, you can specify other encoding standards to meet interoperability requirements.

Key Terms

Do you know what these key terms mean? You can check your answers by looking up the terms in the glossary at the end of the book.

- Code page
- Regular expression
- Unicode

Case Scenarios

In the following case scenarios, you apply what you've learned about how to validate input using regular expressions and how to process text files with different encoding types. You can find answers to these questions in the "Answers" section at the end of this book.

Case Scenario 1: Validating Input

Your organization, Northwind Traders, is creating a Web-based application to allow customers to enter their own contact information into your database. As a new employee, you are assigned a simple task: create the front-end interface and prepare the user input to be stored in a database. You begin by interviewing several company personnel and reviewing the technical requirements.

Interviews

The following is a list of company personnel that you interviewed and their statements.

IT Manager "This is your first assignment, so I'm starting you out easy. Slap together a Web page that takes user input. That should take you, what, five minutes?"

Database Developer "Just drop the input into strings named *companyName*, *contactName*", and *phoneNumber*. It's going into a SQL back-end database, but I'll write that code after you're done. Oh, the *companyName* can't be longer than 40 characters, *contactName* is limited to 30 characters, and *phoneNumber* is limited to 24 characters."

Chief Security Officer "This is not as easy an assignment as it seems. This page is going to be available to the general public on the Internet, and there are lots of black hats out there. We've gotten some negative attention in the press recently for our international trade practices. Specifically, we've irritated a couple of groups with close ties to hacker organizations. Just do your best to clean up the input, because you're going to see some malicious junk thrown at you."

Technical Requirements

Create an ASP.NET application that accepts the following pieces of information from users and validates it rigorously:

- Company name
- Contact name
- Phone number

Questions

Answer the following questions for your manager:

1. How can you constrain the input before you write any code?
2. How can you constrain the input further by writing code?

Case Scenario 2: Processing Data from a Legacy Computer

You are an application developer working for Humongous Insurance. Recently, management decided to begin the process of migrating from a legacy system (nicknamed "Mainframe") to custom-built .NET Framework applications. As part of the kickoff meeting for the migration project, your manager asks you questions about how you will handle various challenges.

Questions

Answer the following questions for your manager:

1. "Mainframe" stores its data in a database; however, the raw data itself isn't accessible to us unless we can find a programmer who knows how to write code for that system. We can output the data we need in text-based reports, however. Is it possible to parse the text reports to extract just the data, without the labels and formatting? How would you do that, and which classes and methods would you use?

2. "Mainframe's" reports are in ASCII format. Can you handle that in ASCII? If so, how?

Suggested Practices

To help you master the exam objectives presented in this chapter, complete the following tasks.

Enhance the Text-Handling Capabilities of a .NET Framework Application, and Search, Modify, and Control Text Within a .NET Framework Application by Using Regular Expressions

For this task, you should complete at least Practices 1 through 4. If you want a better understanding of how to specify encoding types, complete Practice 5 as well.

- **Practice 1** Write a Console application that reads your C:\Boot.ini file and displays just the timeout.

- **Practice 2** Write a Console application that processes your %Windir%\WindowsUpdate.log file and displays the time, date, and exit code for any rows that list an exit code.

- **Practice 3** Write a Windows Forms application that accepts a name, address, and phone number from a user. Add a Submit button that uses regular expressions to validate the input.

■ **Practice 4** Write a Console application that reads the %Windir%\Windows-Update.log file, changes the date format to *mm-dd-yy*, and writes the output to a second file.

■ **Practice 5** Write a Console application with a method that reads the %windir%\WindowsUpdate.log file and writes the output to a second file using an encoding type provided in a parameter. Compare the file sizes of each encoding type.

Take a Practice Test

The practice tests on this book's companion CD offer many options. For example, you can test yourself on just one exam objective, or you can test yourself on all the 70-536 certification exam content. You can set up the test so that it closely simulates the experience of taking a certification exam, or you can set it up in study mode so that you can look at the correct answers and explanations after you answer each question.

MORE INFO Practice tests

For details about all the practice test options available, see the section "How to Use the Practice Tests" section in the Introduction of this book.

Chapter 4
Collections and Generics

Developers often need to store groups of related objects. For example, an e-mail inbox would contain a group of messages, a phone book would contain a group of phone numbers, and an audio player would contain a group of songs.

The .NET Framework provides the *System.Collections* namespace to allow developers to manage groups of objects. Different collections exist to provide performance benefits in different scenarios, flexible sorting capabilities, support for different types, and dictionaries that pair keys and values.

Exam objectives in this chapter:
- Manage a group of associated data in a .NET Framework application by using collections.
- Improve type safety and application performance in a .NET Framework application by using generic collections.
- Manage data in a .NET Framework application by using specialized collections.

Lessons in this chapter:

Before You Begin

This book assumes that you have at least two to three years of experience developing Web-based, Microsoft Windows–based, or distributed applications using the .NET Framework. Candidates should have a working knowledge of Microsoft Visual Studio. Before you begin, you should be familiar with Microsoft Visual Basic or C# and be comfortable with the following tasks:

- Creating console and Windows Presentation Foundation (WPF) applications in Visual Studio using Visual Basic or C#
- Adding namespaces and system class library references to a project
- Running a project in Visual Studio, setting breakpoints, stepping through code, and watching the values of variables

Lesson 1: Collections and Dictionaries

The *System.Collections* and *System.Collections.Specialized* namespaces contain a number of classes to meet varying requirements for storing groups of related objects. To use them most efficiently, you need to understand the benefits of each class. This lesson describes each collection and dictionary type and shows you how to use them.

After this lesson, you will be able to:

■ Use collections and choose the best collection class for different requirements

■ Use dictionaries and choose the best dictionary class for different requirements

Estimated lesson time: 30 minutes

Collections

A collection is any class that allows for gathering items into lists and for iterating through those items. The .NET Framework includes the following collection classes:

- **ArrayList** A simple collection that can store any type of object. *ArrayList* instances expand to any required capacity.

- **Queue** A first-in, first-out (FIFO) collection. You might use a *Queue* on a messaging server to store messages temporarily before processing or to track customer orders that need to be processed on a first-come, first-serve basis.

- **Stack** A last-in, first-out (LIFO) collection. You might use a *Stack* to track changes so that the most recent change can be undone.

- **StringCollection** Like *ArrayList*, except values are strongly typed as strings, and *StringCollection* does not support sorting.

- **BitArray** A collection of boolean values.

ArrayList

Use the *ArrayList* class (in the *System.Collections* namespace) to add objects that can be accessed directly using a zero-based index or accessed in a series using a *foreach* loop. The capacity of an *ArrayList* expands as required. The following example shows how to use the *ArrayList.Add* method to add different types of objects to a single array, and then access each object using a *foreach* loop:

```vb
' VB
Dim al As New ArrayList()
al.Add("Hello")
al.Add("World")
```

```
al.Add(5)
al.Add(New FileStream("delemete", FileMode.Create))

Console.WriteLine("The array has " + al.Count.ToString + " items:")

For Each s As Object In al
    Console.WriteLine(s.ToString())
Next

// C#
ArrayList al = new ArrayList();
al.Add("Hello");
al.Add("World");
al.Add(5);
al.Add(new FileStream("delemete", FileMode.Create));

Console.WriteLine("The array has " + al.Count + " items:");

foreach (object s in al)
    Console.WriteLine(s.ToString());
```

This console application displays the following:

```
The array has 4 items:
Hello
World
5
System.IO.FileStream
```

In practice, you generally add items of a single type to an *ArrayList*. This allows you to call the *Sort* method to sort the objects using their *IComparable* implementation. You can also use the *Remove* method to remove an object you previously added and use the *Insert* method to add an element at the specified location in the zero-based index. The following code sample demonstrates this:

```
' VB
Dim al As New ArrayList()
al.Add("Hello")
al.Add("World")
al.Add("this")
al.Add("is")
al.Add("a")
al.Add("test")

al.Remove("test")
al.Insert(4, "not")

al.Sort()

For Each s As Object In al
    Console.WriteLine(s.ToString())
Next
```

```
// C#
ArrayList al = new ArrayList();
al.Add("Hello");
al.Add("World");
al.Add("this");
al.Add("is");
al.Add("a");
al.Add("test");

al.Remove("test");
al.Insert(4, "not");

al.Sort();

foreach (object s in al)
    Console.WriteLine(s.ToString());
```

This code sample results in the following display. Notice that the items are sorted alphabetically (using the string *IComparable* implementation) and "test" has been removed:

```
A
Hello
is
not
this
World
```

IMPORTANT Using *StringCollection*

You could also use *StringCollection* in place of *ArrayList* in the previous example. However, *StringCollection* does not support sorting, described next. The primary advantage of *StringCollection* is that it's strongly typed for string values.

You can also create your own custom *IComparer* implementations to control sort order. While the *IComparable.CompareTo* method controls the default sort order for a class, *IComparer.Compare* can be used to provide custom sort orders. For example, consider the following simple class, which only implements *IComparer*:

```
' VB
Public Class reverseSort
    Implements IComparer
    Private Function Compare(ByVal x As Object, ByVal y As Object) _
        As Integer Implements IComparer.Compare
        Return ((New CaseInsensitiveComparer()).Compare(y, x))
    End Function
End Class
```

```
// C#
public class reverseSort : IComparer
{
    int IComparer.Compare(Object x, Object y)
    {
        return ((new CaseInsensitiveComparer()).Compare(y, x));
    }
}
```

Given that class, you could pass an instance of the class to the *ArrayList.Sort* method. The following code sample demonstrates this and also demonstrates using the *Array-List.AddRange* method, which adds each element of an array as a separate element to the instance of *ArrayList*:

```
' VB
Dim al As New ArrayList()
al.AddRange(New String() {"Hello", "world", "this", "is", "a", "test"})

al.Sort(New reverseSort())

For Each s As Object In al
    Console.WriteLine(s.ToString())
Next
```

```
// C#
ArrayList al = new ArrayList();
al.AddRange(new string[] {"Hello", "world", "this", "is", "a", "test"});

al.Sort(new reverseSort());

foreach (object s in al)
    Console.WriteLine(s.ToString());
```

This code displays the following:

```
world
this
test
is
Hello
A
```

You can also call the *ArrayList.Reverse* method to reverse the current order of items in the *ArrayList*.

To locate a specific element, call the *ArrayList.BinarySearch* method and pass an instance of the object you are searching for. *BinarySearch* returns the zero-based index of the item. For example, the following code sample displays 2 because the string "this" is in the third position, and the first position is 0:

```vb
' VB
Dim al As New ArrayList()
al.AddRange(New String() {"Hello", "world", "this", "is", "a", "test"})
Console.WriteLine(al.BinarySearch("this"))
```

```csharp
// C#
ArrayList al = new ArrayList();
al.AddRange(new string[] {"Hello", "world", "this", "is", "a", "test"});
Console.WriteLine(al.BinarySearch("this"));
```

Similarly, the *ArrayList.Contains* method returns *true* if the *ArrayList* instance contains the specified object and *false* if it does not contain the object.

Queue and *Stack*

The *Queue* and *Stack* classes (in the *System.Collections* namespace) store objects that can be retrieved and removed in a single step. *Queue* uses a FIFO sequence, while *Stack* uses a LIFO sequence. The *Queue* class uses the *Enqueue* and *Dequeue* methods to add and remove objects, while the *Stack* class uses *Push* and *Pop*. The following code demonstrates the differences between the two classes:

```vb
' VB
Dim q As New Queue()
q.Enqueue("Hello")
q.Enqueue("world")
q.Enqueue("just testing")

Console.WriteLine("Queue demonstration:")
For i As Integer = 1 To 3
    Console.WriteLine(q.Dequeue().ToString())
Next

Dim s As New Stack()
s.Push("Hello")
s.Push("world")
s.Push("just testing")

Console.WriteLine("Stack demonstration:")
For i As Integer = 1 To 3
    Console.WriteLine(s.Pop().ToString())
Next
```

```csharp
// C#
Queue q = new Queue();
q.Enqueue("Hello");
q.Enqueue("world");
q.Enqueue("just testing");
```

```
Console.WriteLine("Queue demonstration:");
for (int i = 1; i <= 3; i++)
    Console.WriteLine(q.Dequeue().ToString());

Stack s = new Stack();
s.Push("Hello");
s.Push("world");
s.Push("just testing");

Console.WriteLine("Stack demonstration:");
for (int i = 1; i <= 3; i++)
    Console.WriteLine(s.Pop().ToString());
```

The application produces the following output:

```
Queue demonstration:
Hello
world
just testing
Stack demonstration:
just testing
world
Hello
```

You can also use *Queue.Peek* and *Stack.Peek* to access an object without removing it from the stack. Use *Queue.Clear* and *Stack.Clear* to remove all objects from the stack.

BitArray and *BitVector32*

BitArray is an array of boolean values, where each item in the array is either true or false. While *BitArray* can grow to any size, *BitVector32* (a structure) is limited to exactly 32 bits. If you need to store boolean values, use *BitVector32* anytime you require 32 or fewer items, and use *BitArray* for anything larger.

Dictionaries

Dictionaries map keys to values. For example, you might map an employee ID number to the object that represents the employee, or you might map a product ID to the object that represents the product. The .NET Framework includes the following dictionary classes:

- *Hashtable* A dictionary of name/value pairs that can be retrieved by name or index

- *SortedList* A dictionary that is sorted automatically by the key

- *StringDictionary* A hashtable with name/value pairs implemented as strongly typed strings

- **ListDictionary**   A dictionary optimized for a small list of objects with fewer than 10 items

- **HybridDictionary**   A dictionary that uses a *ListDictionary* for storage when the number of items is small and automatically switches to a *Hashtable* as the list grows

- **NameValueCollection**   A dictionary of name/value pairs of strings that allows retrieval by name or index

SortedList (in the *System.Collections* namespace) is a dictionary that consists of key/value pairs. Both the key and the value can be any object. *SortedList* is sorted automatically by the key. For example, the following code sample creates a *SortedList* instance with three key/value pairs. It then displays the definitions for *Queue*, *SortedList*, and *Stack*, in that order:

```vb
' VB
Dim sl As New SortedList()
sl.Add("Stack", "Represents a LIFO collection of objects.")
sl.Add("Queue", "Represents a FIFO collection of objects.")
sl.Add("SortedList", "Represents a collection of key/value pairs.")

For Each de As DictionaryEntry In sl
    Console.WriteLine(de.Value)
Next
```

```csharp
// C#
SortedList sl = new SortedList();
sl.Add("Stack", "Represents a LIFO collection of objects.");
sl.Add("Queue", "Represents a FIFO collection of objects.");
sl.Add("SortedList", "Represents a collection of key/value pairs.");

foreach (DictionaryEntry de in sl)
    Console.WriteLine(de.Value);
```

Notice that *SortedList* is an array of *DictionaryEntry* objects. As the previous code sample demonstrates, you can access the objects you originally added to the *SortedList* using the *DictionaryEntry.Value* property. You can access the key using the *DictionaryEntry.Key* property.

You can also access values directly by accessing the *SortedList* as a collection. The following code sample (which builds upon the previous code sample) displays the definition for *Queue* twice. *Queue* is the first entry in the zero-based index because the *SortedList* instance automatically sorted the keys alphabetically:

```vb
' VB
Console.WriteLine(sl("Queue"))
Console.WriteLine(sl.GetByIndex(0))
```

```
// C#
Console.WriteLine(sl["Queue"]);
Console.WriteLine(sl.GetByIndex(0));
```

The *ListDictionary* class (in the *System.Collections.Specialized* namespace) also provides similar functionality, and is optimized to perform best with lists of fewer than 10 items. *HybridDictionary* (also in the *System.Collections.Specialized* namespace) provides the same performance as *ListDictionary* with small lists, but it scales better when the list is expanded.

While *SortedList* can take an object of any type as its value (but only strings as keys), the *StringDictionary* class (in the *System.Collections.Specialized* namespace) provides similar functionality, without the automatic sorting, and requires both the keys and the values to be strings.

NameValueCollection also provides similar functionality, but it allows you to use either a string or an integer index for the key. In addition, you can store multiple string values for a single key. The following code sample demonstrates this by displaying two definitions for the terms *stack* and *queue*:

```
' VB
Dim sl As New NameValueCollection()
sl.Add("Stack", "Represents a LIFO collection of objects.")
sl.Add("Stack", "A pile of pancakes.")
sl.Add("Queue", "Represents a FIFO collection of objects.")
sl.Add("Queue", "In England, a line.")
sl.Add("SortedList", "Represents a collection of key/value pairs.")

For Each s As String In sl.GetValues(0)
    Console.WriteLine(s)
Next

For Each s As String In sl.GetValues("Queue")
    Console.WriteLine(s)
Next
```

```
// C#
NameValueCollection sl = new NameValueCollection();
sl.Add("Stack", "Represents a LIFO collection of objects.");
sl.Add("Stack", "A pile of pancakes.");
sl.Add("Queue", "Represents a FIFO collection of objects.");
sl.Add("Queue", "In England, a line.");
sl.Add("SortedList", "Represents a collection of key/value pairs.");

foreach (string s in sl.GetValues(0))
    Console.WriteLine(s);

foreach (string s in sl.GetValues("Queue"))
    Console.WriteLine(s);
```

Lab: Creating a Shopping Cart

In this lab, you create a simple shopping cart that can be sorted by the price of the items.

Exercise: Using *ArrayList*

In this exercise, you use an *ArrayList* and a custom class to create a shopping cart with basic functionality.

1. Using Visual Studio, create a new Console Application project. Name the project ShoppingCart.

2. Add a simple class to represent a shopping cart item, containing properties for the item name and price. The following code sample shows one way to do this:

```vb
' VB
Public Class ShoppingCartItem
    Public itemName As String
    Public price As Double

    Public Sub New(ByVal _itemName As String, ByVal _price As Double)
        Me.itemName = _itemName
        Me.price = _price
    End Sub
End Class
```

```csharp
// C#
public class ShoppingCartItem
{
    public string itemName;
    public double price;

    public ShoppingCartItem(string _itemName, double _price)
    {
        this.itemName = _itemName;
        this.price = _price;
    }
}
```

3. Add the *System.Collections* namespace to your project.

4. In the *Main* method create an instance of *ArrayList*, and then add four shopping cart items with different names and prices. Display the items on the console using a *foreach* loop. The following code sample demonstrates this:

```vb
' VB
Dim shoppingCart As New ArrayList()
shoppingCart.Add(New ShoppingCartItem("Car", 5000))
shoppingCart.Add(New ShoppingCartItem("Book", 30))
```

```
shoppingCart.Add(New ShoppingCartItem("Phone", 80))
shoppingCart.Add(New ShoppingCartItem("Computer", 1000))

For Each sci As ShoppingCartItem In shoppingCart
    Console.WriteLine(sci.itemName + ": $" + sci.price.ToString())
Next

// C#
ArrayList shoppingCart = new ArrayList();
shoppingCart.Add(new ShoppingCartItem("Car", 5000));
shoppingCart.Add(new ShoppingCartItem("Book", 30));
shoppingCart.Add(new ShoppingCartItem("Phone", 80));
shoppingCart.Add(new ShoppingCartItem("Computer", 1000));

foreach (ShoppingCartItem sci in shoppingCart)
    Console.WriteLine(sci.itemName + ": $" + sci.price.ToString());
```

5. Build and run your application and verify that it works correctly.

6. Now, implement the *IComparable* interface for the *ShoppingCartItem* class to sort the items by price. The following code should replace the existing class definition for *ShoppingCartItem*:

```
' VB
Public Class ShoppingCartItem
    Implements IComparable
    Public itemName As String
    Public price As Double

    Public Sub New(ByVal _itemName As String, ByVal _price As Double)
        Me.itemName = _itemName
        Me.price = _price
    End Sub

    Public Function CompareTo(ByVal obj As Object) _
        As Integer Implements System.IComparable.CompareTo
        Dim otherItem As ShoppingCartItem = _
            DirectCast(obj, ShoppingCartItem)
        Return Me.price.CompareTo(otherItem.price)
    End Function
End Class

// C#
public class ShoppingCartItem : IComparable
{
    public string itemName;
    public double price;

    public ShoppingCartItem(string _itemName, double _price)
    {
        this.itemName = _itemName;
        this.price = _price;
    }
}
```

```
public int CompareTo(object obj)
{
    ShoppingCartItem otherItem = (ShoppingCartItem)obj;
    return this.price.CompareTo(otherItem.price);
}
}
```

7. Now, write code to sort the shopping cart collection from most to least expensive. The simplest way is to add two lines of code just before the *foreach* loop:

```
' VB
shoppingCart.Sort()
shoppingCart.Reverse()
```

```
// C#
shoppingCart.Sort();
shoppingCart.Reverse();
```

8. Build and run your application again and verify that the shopping cart is sorted from most to least expensive.

Lesson Summary

■ You can use the *ArrayList, Queue,* and *Stack* collection classes to create collections using any class. *ArrayList* allows you to iterate through items and sort them. *Queue* provides FIFO sequencing, while *Stack* provides LIFO sequencing. *BitArray* and *BitVector32* are useful for boolean values.

■ Dictionaries organize instances of objects in key/value pairs. The *HashTable* class can meet most of your requirements. If you want the dictionary to be sorted automatically by the key, use the *SortedDictionary* class. *ListDictionary* is designed to perform well with fewer than 10 items.

Lesson Review

You can use the following questions to test your knowledge of the information in Lesson 1, "Collections and Dictionaries." The questions are also available on the companion CD if you prefer to review them in electronic form.

NOTE Answers

Answers to these questions and explanations of why each answer choice is right or wrong are located in the "Answers" section at the end of the book.

1. You create an instance of the *Stack* class. After adding several integers to it, you need to remove all objects from the *Stack*. Which method should you call?

   A. *Stack.Pop*

   B. *Stack.Push*

   C. *Stack.Clear*

   D. *Stack.Peek*

2. You need to create a collection to act as a shopping cart. The collection will store multiple instances of your custom class, *ShoppingCartItem*. You need to be able to sort the items according to price and time added to the shopping cart (both properties of the *ShoppingCartItem*). Which class should you use for the shopping cart?

   A. *Queue*

   B. *ArrayList*

   C. *Stack*

   D. *StringCollection*

3. You create an *ArrayList* object and add 200 instances of your custom class, *Product*. When you call *ArrayList.Sort*, you receive an *InvalidOperationException*. How should you resolve the problem? (Choose two. Each answer forms part of the complete solution.)

   A. Implement the *IComparable* interface.

   B. Create a method named *CompareTo*.

   C. Implement the *IEnumerable* interface.

   D. Create a method named *GetEnumerator*.

Lesson 2: Generic Collections

Collections like *ArrayList*, *Queue*, and *Stack* use the *Object* base class to allow them to work with any type. However, accessing the collection usually requires you to cast from the base *Object* type to the correct type. Not only does this make development tedious and more error-prone, but it hurts performance.

Using generics, you can create strongly typed collections for any class, including custom classes. This simplifies development within the Visual Studio editor, helps ensure appropriate use of types, and can improve performance by reducing the need to cast.

After this lesson, you will be able to:

- Explain why you should use generic collections
- Use the *SortedList* generic collection
- Use generics with custom classes
- Use the *Queue* and *Stack* collection generically
- Use the generic *List* collection

Estimated lesson time: 30 minutes

Generics Overview

Many of the collections in the .NET Framework support adding objects of any type, such as *ArrayList*. Others, like *StringCollection*, are strongly typed. Strongly typed classes are easier to develop with because the Visual Studio designer can list and validate members automatically. In addition, you do not need to cast classes to more specific types, and you are protected from casting to an inappropriate type.

Generics provide many of the benefits of strongly typed collections, but they can work with any type that meets the requirements. In addition, using generics can improve performance by reducing the number of casting operations required. Table 4-1 lists the most useful generic collection classes and the corresponding nongeneric collection type.

Table 4-1   Generic Collection Classes

Generic Class	Comparable Nongeneric Classes
List<T>	*ArrayList, StringCollection*
Dictionary<T,U>	*Hashtable, ListDictionary, HybridDictionary, OrderedDictionary, NameValueCollection, StringDictionary*
Queue<T>	*Queue*

Table 4-1 Generic Collection Classes

Generic Class	Comparable Nongeneric Classes
Stack<T>	*Stack*
SortedList<T,U>	*SortedList*
Collection<T>	*CollectionBase*
ReadOnlyCollection<T>	*ReadOnlyCollectionBase*

Generic *SortedList<T,U>* Collection

The following code sample creates a generic *SortedList<T,U>* using strings as the keys and integers as the values. As you type this code into the Visual Studio editor, notice that it prompts you to enter string and integer parameters for the *SortedList.Add* method as if *SortedList.Add* were strongly typed:

```
' VB
Dim sl As New SortedList(Of String, Integer)()
sl.Add("One", 1)
sl.Add("Two", 2)
sl.Add("Three", 3)

For Each i As Integer In sl.Values
    Console.WriteLine(i.ToString())
Next
```

```
// C#
SortedList<string, int> sl = new SortedList<string,int>();
sl.Add("One", 1);
sl.Add("Two", 2);
sl.Add("Three", 3);

foreach (int i in sl.Values)
    Console.WriteLine(i.ToString());
```

In Visual Basic, specify the type arguments for the generic class using the constructor parameters by specifying the *Of* keyword. In C#, specify the type arguments using angle brackets before the constructor parameters.

Real World

Tony Northrup

You can get the job done by working with a collection that accepts objects, such as *ArrayList*. However, using generics to create strongly typed collections makes development easier in many ways. First, you won't ever forget to cast something, which will reduce the number of bugs in your code (and I've had some really odd bugs when working with the base *Object* class). Second, development is easier because the Visual Studio editor prompts you to provide the correct type as you type the code. Finally, you don't suffer the performance penalty incurred when casting.

Using Generics with Custom Classes

You can use generics with custom classes as well. Consider the following class declaration:

```vb
' VB
Public Class person
    Private firstName As String
    Private lastName As String

    Public Sub New(ByVal _firstName As String, ByVal _lastName As String)
        firstName = _firstName
        lastName = _lastName
    End Sub

    Public Overloads Overrides Function ToString() As String
        Return firstName + " " + lastName
    End Function
End Class
```

```csharp
// C#
public class person
{
    string firstName;
    string lastName;

    public person(string _firstName, string _lastName)
    {
        firstName = _firstName;
        lastName = _lastName;
    }

    override public string ToString()
    {
        return firstName + " " + lastName;
    }
}
```

You can use the *SortedList<T,U>* generic class with the custom class exactly as you would use it with an integer, as the following code sample demonstrates:

```vb
' VB
Dim sl As New SortedList(Of String, person)()
sl.Add("One", New person("Mark", "Hanson"))
```

```
sl.Add("Two", New person("Kim", "Akers"))
sl.Add("Three", New person("Zsolt", "Ambrus"))

For Each p As person In sl.Values
    Console.WriteLine(p.ToString())
Next


// C#
SortedList<string, person> sl = new SortedList<string,person>();
sl.Add("One", new person("Mark", "Hanson"));
sl.Add("Two", new person("Kim", "Akers"));
sl.Add("Three", new person("Zsolt", "Ambrus"));

foreach (person p in sl.Values)
    Console.WriteLine(p.ToString());
```

Generic *Queue<T>* and *Stack<T>* Collections

Similarly, the following code sample demonstrates using the generic versions of both *Queue* and *Stack* with the *person* class:

```
' VB
Dim q As New Queue(Of person)()
q.Enqueue(New person("Mark", "Hanson"))
q.Enqueue(New person("Kim", "Akers"))
q.Enqueue(New person("Zsolt", "Ambrus"))

Console.WriteLine("Queue demonstration:")
For i As Integer = 1 To 3
    Console.WriteLine(q.Dequeue().ToString())
Next

Dim s As New Stack(Of person)()
s.Push(New person("Mark", "Hanson"))
s.Push(New person("Kim", "Akers"))
s.Push(New person("Zsolt", "Ambrus"))

Console.WriteLine("Stack demonstration:")
For i As Integer = 1 To 3
    Console.WriteLine(s.Pop().ToString())
Next


// C#
Queue<person> q = new Queue<person>();
q.Enqueue(new person("Mark", "Hanson"));
q.Enqueue(new person("Kim", "Akers"));
q.Enqueue(new person("Zsolt", "Ambrus"));

Console.WriteLine("Queue demonstration:");
for (int i = 1; i <= 3; i++)
    Console.WriteLine(q.Dequeue().ToString());
```

```
Stack<person> s = new Stack<person>();
s.Push(new person("Mark", "Hanson"));
s.Push(new person("Kim", "Akers"));
s.Push(new person("Zsolt", "Ambrus"));

Console.WriteLine("Stack demonstration:");
for (int i = 1; i <= 3; i++)
    Console.WriteLine(s.Pop().ToString());
```

Generic *List<T>* Collection

Some aspects of generic collections might require specific interfaces to be implemented by the type you specify. For example, calling *List.Sort* without any parameters requires the type to support the *IComparable* interface. The following code sample expands the *person* class to support the *IComparable* interface and the required *CompareTo* method and allows it to be sorted in a *List<T>* generic collection using the person's first and last name:

```
' VB
Public Class person
    Implements IComparable
    Private firstName As String
    Private lastName As String

    Public Function CompareTo(ByVal obj As Object) _
        As Integer Implements System.IComparable.CompareTo
        Dim otherPerson As person = DirectCast(obj, person)
        If Me.lastName <> otherPerson.lastName Then
            Return Me.lastName.CompareTo(otherPerson.lastName)
        Else
            Return Me.firstName.CompareTo(otherPerson.firstName)
        End If
    End Function

    Public Sub New(ByVal _firstName As String, ByVal _lastName As String)
        firstName = _firstName
        lastName = _lastName
    End Sub

    Public Overrides Function ToString() As String
        Return firstName + " " + lastName
    End Function
End Class

// C#
public class person : IComparable
{
    string firstName;
    string lastName;
```

```
public int CompareTo(object obj)
{
    person otherPerson = (person)obj;
    if (this.lastName != otherPerson.lastName)
        return this.lastName.CompareTo(otherPerson.lastName);
    else
        return this.firstName.CompareTo(otherPerson.firstName);
}

public person(string _firstName, string _lastName)
{
    firstName = _firstName;
    lastName = _lastName;
}

override public string ToString()
{
    return firstName + " " + lastName;
}
}
```

After adding the *IComparable* interface to the *person* class, you now can sort it in a generic *List<T>*, as the following code sample demonstrates:

```
' VB
Dim l As New List(Of person)()
l.Add(New person("Mark", "Hanson"))
l.Add(New person("Kim", "Akers"))
l.Add(New person("Zsolt", "Ambrus"))

l.Sort()

For Each p As person In l
    Console.WriteLine(p.ToString())
Next
```

```
// C#
List<person> l = new List<person>();
l.Add(new person("Mark", "Hanson"));
l.Add(new person("Kim", "Akers"));
l.Add(new person("Zsolt", "Ambrus"));

l.Sort();

foreach (person p in l)
    Console.WriteLine(p.ToString());
```

With the *IComparable* interface implemented, you could also use the *person* class as the key in a generic *SortedList<T,U>* or *SortedDictionary<T,U>* class.

Lab: Creating a Shopping Cart with a Generic *List<T>*

In this lab, you update a simple WPF application to manage a shopping cart.

Exercise: Using *List<T>*

In this exercise, you update a pre-made user interface to display a list with multiple sorting options.

1. Navigate to the *<InstallHome>*\Chapter04\Lesson2\Exercise1\Partial folder from the companion CD to your hard disk, and open either the C# version or the Visual Basic .NET version of the solution file. Notice that a basic user interface for the WPF application already exists.

2. This application should allow the user to add shopping cart items to a shopping cart and display the items in the *ListBox* control. First, create a class declaration for *ShoppingCartItem* that includes name and price properties and override the *ToString* method to display both properties, as shown here:

```vb
' VB
Public Class ShoppingCartItem
    Public itemName As String
    Public price As Double

    Public Sub New(ByVal _itemName As String, ByVal _price As Double)
        Me.itemName = _itemName
        Me.price = _price
    End Sub

    Public Overrides Function ToString() As String
        Return Me.itemName + ": " + Me.price.ToString("C")
    End Function
End Class
```

```csharp
// C#
public class ShoppingCartItem
{
    public string itemName;
    public double price;

    public ShoppingCartItem(string _itemName, double _price)
    {
        this.itemName = _itemName;
        this.price = _price;
    }

    public override string ToString()
    {
        return this.itemName + ": " + this.price.ToString("C");
    }
}
```

3. Next, create an instance of a generic collection to act as the shopping cart. The shopping cart object should be strongly typed to allow only *ShoppingCartItem* instances. The following example shows how to do this with the *List<T>* class:

```vb
' VB
Dim shoppingCart As New List(Of ShoppingCartItem)()
```

```csharp
// C#
List<ShoppingCartItem> shoppingCart = new List<ShoppingCartItem>();
```

4. Bind the *shoppingCartList.ItemSource* property to the *shoppingCart*. While there are several ways to do this, the following code demonstrates how to do it from within the *Window_Loaded* event handler:

```vb
' VB
shoppingCartList.ItemsSource = shoppingCart
```

```csharp
// C#
shoppingCartList.ItemsSource = shoppingCart;
```

5. Now, add a handler for the *addButton.Click* event that reads the data that the user has typed into the *nameTextBox* and *priceTextBox*, creates a new *ShoppingCartItem*, adds it to the *shoppingCart*, and then refreshes the *shoppingCartList*:

```vb
' VB
Try
    shoppingCart.Add(New ShoppingCartItem(nameTextBox.Text, _
        Double.Parse(priceTextBox.Text)))
    shoppingCartList.Items.Refresh()
    nameTextBox.Clear()
    priceTextBox.Clear()
Catch ex As Exception
    MessageBox.Show("Please enter valid data: " + ex.Message)
End Try
```

```csharp
// C#
try
{
    shoppingCart.Add(new ShoppingCartItem(nameTextBox.Text,
        double.Parse(priceTextBox.Text)));
    shoppingCartList.Items.Refresh();
    nameTextBox.Clear();
    priceTextBox.Clear();
}
catch (Exception ex)
{
    MessageBox.Show("Please enter valid data: " + ex.Message);
}
```

6. Build and run your application. Verify that you can add items to the shopping cart and that they are displayed in the *ListBox*.

7. Now, add functionality to the *ShoppingCartItem* class so that you can sort the shopping cart by price or item name, as the following code sample demonstrates:

```vb
' VB
Public Shared Function SortByName(ByVal item1 As ShoppingCartItem, _
    ByVal item2 As ShoppingCartItem) As Integer
    Return item1.itemName.CompareTo(item2.itemName)
End Function

Public Shared Function SortByPrice(ByVal item1 As ShoppingCartItem, _
    ByVal item2 As ShoppingCartItem) As Integer
    Return item1.price.CompareTo(item2.price)
End Function
```

```csharp
// C#
public static int SortByName(ShoppingCartItem item1,
    ShoppingCartItem item2)
{
    return item1.itemName.CompareTo(item2.itemName);
}

public static int SortByPrice(ShoppingCartItem item1,
    ShoppingCartItem item2)
{
    return item1.price.CompareTo(item2.price);
}
```

8. After adding those two methods, update the *sortNameButton.Click* and *sortPriceButton.Click* event handlers to sort the *shoppingCart* and then refresh the *shoppingCartList* as follows:

```vb
' VB
Sub sortNameButton_Click(ByVal sender As Object, _
    ByVal e As RoutedEventArgs)
    shoppingCart.Sort(AddressOf ShoppingCartItem.SortByName)
    shoppingCartList.Items.Refresh()
End Sub

Sub sortPriceButton_Click(ByVal sender As Object, _
    ByVal e As RoutedEventArgs)
    shoppingCart.Sort(AddressOf ShoppingCartItem.SortByPrice)
    shoppingCartList.Items.Refresh()
End Sub
```

```csharp
// C#
private void sortNameButton_Click(object sender, RoutedEventArgs e)
{
    shoppingCart.Sort(ShoppingCartItem.SortByName);
    shoppingCartList.Items.Refresh();
}
```

```
private void sortPriceButton_Click(object sender, RoutedEventArgs e)
{
    shoppingCart.Sort(ShoppingCartItem.SortByPrice);
    shoppingCartList.Items.Refresh();
}
```

9. Build and run your application. Add several items to the shopping cart with different names and prices. Click each of the sorting buttons and verify that the shopping cart is re-sorted.

Lesson Summary

- Generic collections allow you to create strongly typed collections for any class.

- The *SortedList<T,U>* generic collection automatically sorts items.

- You can use generics with custom classes. However, to allow the collection to be sorted without providing a comparer, the custom class must implement the *IComparable* interface.

- The *Queue* and *Stack* collections have both generic and nongeneric implementations.

- The *List<T>* collection provides a generic version of *ArrayList*.

Lesson Review

You can use the following questions to test your knowledge of the information in Lesson 2, "Generic Collections." The questions are also available on the companion CD if you prefer to review them in electronic form.

NOTE   Answers

Answers to these questions and explanations of why each answer choice is right or wrong are located in the "Answers" section at the end of the book.

---

1. You are creating a collection that will act as a database transaction log. You need to be able to add instances of your custom class, *DBTransaction*, to the collection. If an error occurs, you need to be able to access the most recently added instance of *DBTransaction* and remove it from the collection. The collection must be strongly typed. Which class should you use?

   A. *HashTable*

   B. *SortedList*

   C. *Stack*

   D. *Queue*

2. You are creating a custom dictionary class. You want it to be type-safe, using a string for a key and your custom class *Product* as the value. Which class declaration meets your requirements?

    A.

```
' VB
Public Class Products2
    Inherits StringDictionary
End Class

// C#
public class Products2 : StringDictionary
{ }
```

    B.

```
' VB
Class Products
    Inherits Dictionary(Of String, Product)
End Class

// C#
class Products : Dictionary<string, Product>
{ }
```

    C.

```
' VB
Class Products
    Inherits StringDictionary(Of String, Product)
End Class

// C#
class Products : StringDictionary<string, Product>
{ }
```

    D.

```
' VB
Class Products
    Inherits Dictionary
End Class

// C#
class Products : Dictionary
{ }
```

3. You create an instance of the *SortedList* collection, as shown here:

```
' VB
Dim sl As New SortedList(Of Product, string)()

// C#
SortedList<Product, string> sl = new SortedList<Product, string>();
```

Which declaration of the *Product* class works correctly?

A.

```vb
' VB
Public Class Product
    Implements IComparable
    Public productName As String

    Public Sub New(ByVal _productName As String)
        Me.productName = _productName
    End Sub

    Public Function CompareTo(ByVal obj As Object) As Integer _
        Implements System.IComparable.CompareTo
        Dim otherProduct As Product = DirectCast(obj, Product)
        Return Me.productName.CompareTo(otherProduct.productName)
    End Function
End Class
```

```csharp
// C#
public class Product : IComparable
{
    public string productName;

    public Product(string _productName)
    {
        this.productName = _productName;
    }

    public int CompareTo(object obj)
    {
        Product otherProduct = (Product)obj;
        return this.productName.CompareTo(otherProduct.productName);
    }
}
```

B.

```vb
' VB
Public Class Product
    Public productName As String

    Public Sub New(ByVal _productName As String)
        Me.productName = _productName
    End Sub

    Public Function CompareTo(ByVal obj As Object) As Integer _
        Implements System.IComparable.CompareTo
        Dim otherProduct As Product = DirectCast(obj, Product)
        Return Me.productName.CompareTo(otherProduct.productName)
    End Function
End Class
```

```csharp
// C#
public class Product
{
    public string productName;

    public Product(string _productName)
    {
        this.productName = _productName;
    }

    public int CompareTo(object obj)
    {
        Product otherProduct = (Product)obj;
        return this.productName.CompareTo(otherProduct.productName);
    }
}
```

C.

```vb
' VB
Public Class Product
    Implements IEquatable
    Public productName As String

    Public Sub New(ByVal _productName As String)
        Me.productName = _productName
    End Sub

    Public Function Equals(ByVal obj As Object) As Integer _
        Implements System.IEquatable.Equals
        Dim otherProduct As Product = DirectCast(obj, Product)
        Return Me.productName.Equals(otherProduct.productName)
    End Function
End Class
```

```csharp
// C#
public class Product : IEquatable
{
    public string productName;

    public Product(string _productName)
    {
        this.productName = _productName;
    }

    public int Equals(object obj)
    {
        Product otherProduct = (Product)obj;
        return this.productName.Equals(otherProduct.productName);
    }
}
```

D.

```vb
' VB
Public Class Product
    Public productName As String

    Public Sub New(ByVal _productName As String)
        Me.productName = _productName
    End Sub

    Public Function Equals(ByVal obj As Object) As Integer
        Dim otherProduct As Product = DirectCast(obj, Product)
        Return Me.productName.Equals(otherProduct.productName)
    End Function
End Class
```

```csharp
// C#
public class Product
{
    public string productName;

    public Product(string _productName)
    {
        this.productName = _productName;
    }

    public int Equals(object obj)
    {
        Product otherProduct = (Product)obj;
        return this.productName.Equals(otherProduct.productName);
    }
}
```

Chapter Review

To practice and reinforce the skills you learned in this chapter further, you can do the following:

- Review the chapter summary.
- Review the list of key terms introduced in this chapter.
- Complete the case scenarios. These scenarios set up real-word situations involving the topics of this chapter and ask you to create a solution.
- Complete the suggested practices
- Take a practice test

Chapter Summary

- Collections store groups of related objects. *ArrayList* is a simple collection that can store any object and supports sorting. *Queue* is a FIFO collection, while *Stack* is a LIFO collection. Dictionaries provide key/value pairs for circumstances that require you to access items in an array using a key.
- Whenever possible, you should use generic collections over collections that use the *Object* base class. Generic collections are strongly typed and offer better performance.

Key Terms

Do you know what these key terms mean? You can check your answers by looking up the terms in the glossary at the end of the book.

- Collection
- Generic

Case Scenarios

In the following case scenarios you apply what you've learned about how to plan and use collections. You can find answers to these questions in the "Answers" section at the end of this book.

Case Scenario 1: Using Collections

You are an application developer for Contoso, Inc. You are creating a WPF application that correlates unsolved crimes with behaviors of known convicts. You create classes called *Crime*, *Evidence*, *Convict*, and *Behavior*.

Questions

Answer the following questions for your manager:

1. Each *Crime* will have multiple *Evidence* objects, and each *Convict* will have multiple *Behavior* objects. How can you enable this?

2. You need to be able to sort the *Evidence* and *Behavior* collections to allow investigators to identify the most relevant results. Investigators should be able to sort the collections using multiple methods. What type of collection should you use?

3. How can you provide different sorting algorithms?

Case Scenario 2: Using Collections for Transactions

You are an application developer working for Fabrikam, Inc., a financial services company. You are creating an application that will handle financial transactions.

Your application receives incoming transactions from a Web service and must process the transactions in the order they arrive. Each transaction can involve multiple debits and credits. For example, transferring money from account A to account B requires a debit from account A and a credit to account B. If any credit or debit involved in a transaction fails, all credits and debits must be rolled back, starting with the most recently completed transactions.

Questions

Answer the following questions for your manager:

1. Transactions might come in faster than you can process them. How can you store the transactions and ensure that you process them in the correct sequence?

2. How can you track the debits and credits you have performed so they can be rolled back if required?

3. Should you use generic classes?

Suggested Practices

To master the system types and collections exam objective, complete the following tasks.

Manage a Group of Associated Data in a .NET Framework Application by Using Collections

For this task, you should complete at least Practices 1 and 2 to gain experience using collections. For a better understanding of the performance implications of using the *BitArray* collection instead of the *BitVector32* structure, complete Practice 3 as well.

- **Practice 1**   Create an instance of *ArrayList* and add several instances of your own custom class to it. Next, sort the array in at least two different ways.

- **Practice 2**   Create a console application that creates instances of each of the different dictionary classes. Populate the dictionaries and access the items both directly and by iterating through them using a *foreach* loop.

- **Practice 3**   Write a simple console application that adds 20 boolean values to an instance of the *BitArray* class and then iterates through each of them using a *foreach* loop. Repeat the process 100,000 times using a *for* loop. Time how long the entire process takes by comparing *DateTime.Now* before and after the process. Next, perform the same test using *BitVector32*. Determine which is faster and whether the performance impact is significant.

Improve Type Safety and Application Performance in a .NET Framework Application by Using Generic Collections

For this task, you should complete at least Practices 1 and 2 to gain experience using generic collections. For a better understanding of the performance implications of using generic collections, complete Practice 3 as well.

- **Practice 1**   Write an application that creates an instance of each of the built-in generic collection classes, adds items to each of the collections, and then displays them using a *foreach* loop.

- **Practice 2**   Using a custom class that you created for real-world use, create a class that acts as a collection of your custom class objects and is derived from the generic *Dictionary<T,U>* class.

■ **Practice 3**   Write a simple console application that performs hundreds of thousands of *Push* and *Pop* operations with the nongeneric and generic versions of the *Stack* class. Time how long it takes for both the nongeneric and generic versions and determine whether the generic version is actually faster.

Manage Data in a .NET Framework Application by Using Specialized Collections

For this task, you should complete at least Practice 1. For a better understanding of the performance implications of using specialized collections, complete Practice 2 as well.

■ **Practice 1**   Write an application that creates an instance of each of the built-in specialized collection classes, adds items to each of the collections, and then displays them using a *foreach* loop.

■ **Practice 2**   Write a simple console application that adds hundreds of thousands of strings to an instance of the *StringCollection* class and then iterates through each of them using a *foreach* loop. Time how long the process takes by comparing *DateTime.Now* before and after it completes. Next, perform the same process using the generic version of *List<T>*, typed for the *string* class. Determine which is faster and whether the performance impact is significant.

Take a Practice Test

The practice tests on this book's companion CD offer many options. For example, you can test yourself on just the content covered in this chapter, or you can test yourself on all the 70-536 certification exam content. You can set up the test so that it closely simulates the experience of taking a certification exam, or you can set it up in study mode so that you can look at the correct answers and explanations after you answer each question.

MORE INFO   **Practice tests**

For details about all the practice test options available, see the section "How to Use the Practice Tests," in the Introduction of this book.

Chapter 5
Serialization

Many applications need to store or transfer objects. To make these tasks as simple as possible, the .NET Framework includes several serialization techniques. These techniques convert objects into binary, SOAP, or Extensible Markup Language (XML) documents that can be easily stored, transferred, and retrieved. This chapter discusses how to implement serialization using the tools built into the .NET Framework and how to implement serialization to meet custom requirements.

Exam objectives in this chapter:
- Serialize or deserialize an object or an object graph by using runtime serialization techniques. (Refer *System.Runtime.Serialization* namespace.)
- Control the serialization of an object into XML format by using the *System.Xml .Serialization* namespace.
- Implement custom serialization formatting by using the serialization formatter classes.

Lessons in this chapter:

Before You Begin

To complete the lessons in this chapter, you should be familiar with Microsoft Visual Basic or C# and be comfortable with the following tasks:

- Creating a console application in Microsoft Visual Studio using Visual Basic or C#
- Adding namespaces and system class library references to a project
- Writing to files and stream objects

Lesson 1: Serializing Objects

When you create an object in a .NET Framework application, you probably never think about how the data is stored in memory. You shouldn't have to–the .NET Framework takes care of that for you. However, if you want to store the contents of an object to a file, send an object to another process, or transmit an object across the network, you do have to think about how the object is represented because you will need to convert it to a different format. This conversion is called *serialization*.

After this lesson, you will be able to:

- Choose between binary, SOAP, XML, and custom serialization
- Serialize and deserialize objects using the standard libraries
- Create classes that can be serialized and deserialized
- Change the standard behavior of the serialization and deserialization process
- Implement custom serialization to take complete control of the serialization process

Estimated lesson time: 45 minutes

What Is Serialization?

Serialization, as implemented in the *System.Runtime.Serialization* namespace, is the process of serializing and deserializing objects so that they can be stored or transferred and then later re-created. *Serializing* is the process of converting an object into a linear sequence of bytes that can be stored or transferred. *Deserializing* is the process of converting a previously serialized sequence of bytes into an object.

Real World

Tony Northrup

Serialization can save a lot of development time. Before serialization was available, I had to write custom code just to store or transfer information. Of course, this code tended to break when I made changes elsewhere in the application. Nowadays, with the .NET Framework, I can store and transfer data with just a couple of lines of code. In fact, I rarely find the need to modify the default serialization behavior–it just works.

Basically, if you want to store an object (or multiple objects) in a file for later retrieval, you store the output of serialization. The next time you want to read the objects, you call the deserialization methods, and your object is re-created exactly as it previously had been. Similarly, if you want to send an object to an application running on another computer, you establish a network connection, serialize the object to the stream, and then deserialize the object on the remote application. Teleportation in science fiction is a good example of serialization (although teleportation is not currently supported by the .NET Framework).

NOTE Serialization Behind the Scenes

Microsoft Windows relies on serialization for many important tasks, including calling Web services, remoting, and copying items to the clipboard.

How to Serialize an Object

At a high level, the steps for serializing an object are as follows:

1. Create a stream object to hold the serialized output.

2. Create a *BinaryFormatter* object (located in *System.Runtime.Serialization.Formatters.Binary*).

3. Call the *BinaryFormatter.Serialize* method to serialize the object and output the result to the stream.

At the development level, serialization can be implemented with very little code. The following Console application—which requires the *System.IO* and *System.Runtime.Serialization.Formatters.Binary* namespaces—demonstrates this:

```
' VB
Dim data As String = "This must be stored in a file."

' Create file to save the data to
Dim fs As FileStream = New FileStream("SerializedString.Data", _
    FileMode.Create)

' Create a BinaryFormatter object to perform the serialization
Dim bf As BinaryFormatter = New BinaryFormatter

' Use the BinaryFormatter object to serialize the data to the file
bf.Serialize(fs, data)

' Close the file
fs.Close
```

```
// C#
string data = "This must be stored in a file.";

// Create file to save the data to
FileStream fs = new FileStream("SerializedString.Data", FileMode.Create);

// Create a BinaryFormatter object to perform the serialization
BinaryFormatter bf = new BinaryFormatter();

// Use the BinaryFormatter object to serialize the data to the file
bf.Serialize(fs, data);

// Close the file
fs.Close();
```

If you run the application and then open the SerializedString.Data file in Notepad, you'll see the contents of the string you stored surrounded by binary information (which appears as garbage in Notepad). The .NET Framework stores the string as ASCII text and then adds a few more binary bytes before and after the text to describe the data for the deserializer.

If you just needed to store a single string in a file, you wouldn't need to use serialization—you could simply write the string directly to a text file. Serialization becomes useful when storing more complex information, such as the current date and time. As the following code sample demonstrates, serializing complex objects is as simple as serializing a string:

```
' VB
' Create file to save the data to
Dim fs As FileStream = New FileStream("SerializedDate.Data", _
    FileMode.Create)

' Create a BinaryFormatter object to perform the serialization
Dim bf As BinaryFormatter = New BinaryFormatter

' Use the BinaryFormatter object to serialize the data to the file
bf.Serialize(fs, System.DateTime.Now)

' Close the file
fs.Close()

// C#
// Create file to save the data to
FileStream fs = new FileStream("SerializedDate.Data", FileMode.Create);

// Create a BinaryFormatter object to perform the serialization
BinaryFormatter bf = new BinaryFormatter();

// Use the BinaryFormatter object to serialize the data to the file
bf.Serialize(fs, System.DateTime.Now);

// Close the file
fs.Close();
```

How to Deserialize an Object

Deserializing an object allows you to create a new object based on stored data. Essentially, deserializing restores a saved object. At a high level, the steps for deserializing an object are as follows:

1. Create a stream object to read the serialized output.
2. Create a *BinaryFormatter* object.
3. Create a new object to store the deserialized data.
4. Call the *BinaryFormatter.Deserialize* method to deserialize the object, and cast it to the correct type.

At the code level, the steps for deserializing an object are easy to implement. The following Console application—which requires the *System.IO, System.Runtime.Serialization*, and *System.Runtime.Serialization.Formatters.Binary* namespaces—demonstrates how to read and display the serialized string data saved in an earlier example:

```
' VB
' Open file from which to read the data
Dim fs As FileStream = New FileStream("SerializedString.Data", FileMode.Open)

' Create a BinaryFormatter object to perform the deserialization
Dim bf As BinaryFormatter = New BinaryFormatter

' Create the object to store the deserialized data
Dim data As String = ""

' Use the BinaryFormatter object to deserialize the data from the file
data = DirectCast(bf.Deserialize(fs), String)

' Close the file
fs.Close

' Display the deserialized string
Console.WriteLine(data)
```

```
// C#
// Open file from which to read the data
FileStream fs = new FileStream("SerializedString.Data", FileMode.Open);

// Create a BinaryFormatter object to perform the deserialization
BinaryFormatter bf = new BinaryFormatter();

// Create the object to store the deserialized data
string data = "";

// Use the BinaryFormatter object to deserialize the data from the file
data = (string)bf.Deserialize(fs);
```

```
// Close the file
fs.Close();

// Display the deserialized string
Console.WriteLine(data);
```

Deserializing a more complex object, such as *DateTime*, works exactly the same. The following code sample displays the day of the week and the time stored by a previous code sample:

```
' VB
' Open file from which to read the data
Dim fs As FileStream = New FileStream("SerializedDate.Data", FileMode.Open)

' Create a BinaryFormatter object to perform the deserialization
Dim bf As BinaryFormatter = New BinaryFormatter

' Create the object to store the deserialized data
Dim previousTime As DateTime = New DateTime

' Use the BinaryFormatter object to deserialize the data from the file
previousTime = DirectCast(bf.Deserialize(fs), DateTime)

' Close the file
fs.Close

' Display the deserialized time
Console.WriteLine(("Day: " + (previousTime.DayOfWeek + (", Time: " _
    + previousTime.TimeOfDay.ToString))))
```

```
// C#
// Open file from which to read the data
FileStream fs = new FileStream("SerializedDate.Data", FileMode.Open);

// Create a BinaryFormatter object to perform the deserialization
BinaryFormatter bf = new BinaryFormatter();

// Create the object to store the deserialized data
DateTime previousTime = new DateTime();

// Use the BinaryFormatter object to deserialize the data from the file
previousTime = (DateTime) bf.Deserialize(fs);

// Close the file
fs.Close();

// Display the deserialized time
Console.WriteLine("Day: " + previousTime.DayOfWeek + ", Time: " +
    previousTime.TimeOfDay.ToString());
```

As these code samples demonstrate, storing and retrieving objects requires only a few lines of code, no matter how complex the object is (assuming the object supports serialization, as discussed later in this chapter).

NOTE   **The Inner Workings of Deserialization**

Within the runtime, deserialization can be a complex process. The runtime proceeds through the deserialization process sequentially, starting at the beginning and working its way through to the end. The process gets complicated if an object in the serialized stream refers to another object.

If an object references another object, the *Formatter* (discussed in more detail in Lesson 3 of this chapter, "Custom Serialization") queries the *ObjectManager* to determine whether the referenced object has already been deserialized (a backward reference), or whether it has not yet been deserialized (a forward reference). If it is a backward reference, the *Formatter* immediately completes the reference. However, if it is a forward reference, the *Formatter* registers a *fixup* with the *ObjectManager*. A *fixup* is the process of finalizing an object reference after the referenced object has been deserialized. Once the referenced object is deserialized, *ObjectManager* completes the reference.

How to Create Classes That Can Be Serialized

You can make custom classes serializable and deserializable by adding the *Serializable* attribute to the class. This is important because it allows you, or other developers using your class, to store or transfer instances of the class easily. Even if you do not immediately need serialization, it is good practice to enable it for future use.

If you are satisfied with the default handling of the serialization, no other code besides the *Serializable* attribute is necessary. When your class is serialized, the runtime serializes all members, including private members.

NOTE   **Security Concerns with Serialization**

Serialization can allow other code to see or modify object instance data that would be inaccessible otherwise. Therefore, code performing serialization requires the *SecurityPermission* attribute (from the *System.Security.Permissions* namespace) with the *SerializationFormatter* flag specified. Under default policy, this permission is not given to Internet-downloaded or intranet code; only code on the local computer is granted this permission. The *GetObjectData* method should be explicitly protected either by demanding the *SecurityPermission* attribute with the *SerializationFormatter* flag specified, as illustrated in the sample code in Lesson 3, or by demanding other permissions that specifically help protect private data. For more information about code security, refer to Chapter 12, "User and Data Security."

You can control serialization of your classes to improve the efficiency of your class or to meet custom requirements. The following sections discuss how to customize how your class behaves during serialization.

How to Disable Serialization of Specific Members

Some members of your class, such as temporary or calculated values, might not need to be stored. For example, consider the following class, *ShoppingCartItem*:

```vb
' VB
<Serializable()> Class ShoppingCartItem
    Public productId As Integer
    Public price As Decimal
    Public quantity As Integer
    Public total As Decimal

    Public Sub New(ByVal _productID As Integer, ByVal _price As Decimal, _
        ByVal _quantity As Integer)
        MyBase.New
        productId = _productID
        price = _price
        quantity = _quantity
        total = price * quantity
    End Sub
End Class
```

```csharp
// C#
[Serializable]
class ShoppingCartItem
{
    public int productId;
    public decimal price;
    public int quantity;
    public decimal total;

    public ShoppingCartItem(int _productID, decimal _price, int _quantity)
    {
        productId = _productID;
        price = _price;
        quantity = _quantity;
        total = price * quantity;
    }
}
```

The *ShoppingCartItem* includes three members that must be provided by the application when the object is created. The fourth member, *total*, is dynamically calculated by multiplying the price and quantity. If this class were serialized as-is, the total would be stored with the serialized object, wasting a small amount of storage. To reduce the size of the serialized object (and thus reduce storage requirements when writing the serialized object to a disk and bandwidth requirements when transmitting the serialized object across the network), add the *NonSerialized* attribute to the *total* member as follows:

```
' VB
<NonSerialized()> Public total As Decimal
```

```
// C#
[NonSerialized] public decimal total;
```

Now, when the object is serialized, the *total* member is omitted. Similarly, the *total* member is not initialized when the object is deserialized. However, the value for *total* must still be calculated before the deserialized object is used.

To enable your class to initialize a nonserialized member automatically, use the *IDeserializationCallback* interface and then implement *IDeserializationCallback.OnDeserialization*. Each time your class is deserialized, the runtime calls the *IDeserializationCallback.OnDeserialization* method after deserialization is complete. The following example shows the *ShoppingCartItem* class modified to not serialize the *total* value and to automatically calculate the value upon deserialization. The changes are shown in bold:

```
' VB
<Serializable()> Class ShoppingCartItem
    Implements IDeserializationCallback

    Public productId As Integer
    Public price As Decimal
    Public quantity As Integer
    <NonSerialized()> Public total As Decimal

    Public Sub New(ByVal _productID As Integer, ByVal _price As Decimal, _
        ByVal _quantity As Integer)
        MyBase.New
        productId = _productID
        price = _price
        quantity = _quantity
        total = price * quantity
    End Sub

    Sub IDeserializationCallback_OnDeserialization(ByVal sender As Object) _
        Implements IDeserializationCallback.OnDeserialization
        ' After deserialization, calculate the total
        total = price * quantity
    End Sub
End Class
```

```
// C#
[Serializable]
class ShoppingCartItem : IDeserializationCallback {
    public int productId;
    public decimal price;
    public int quantity;
    [NonSerialized] public decimal total;
    public ShoppingCartItem(int _productID, decimal _price, int _quantity)
    {
        productId = _productID;
        price = _price;
        quantity = _quantity;
        total = price * quantity;
    }
     void IDeserializationCallback.OnDeserialization(Object sender)
    {
        // After deserialization, calculate the total
        total = price * quantity;
    }
}
```

With *OnDeserialization* implemented, the *total* member is now properly initialized and available to applications after the object is deserialized.

How to Provide Version Compatibility

You might have version compatibility issues if you ever attempt to deserialize an object that has been serialized by an earlier version of your application. Specifically, if you add a member to a custom class and attempt to deserialize an object that lacks that member, the runtime throws an exception. In other words, if you add a member to a class in version 3.1 of your application, it will not be able to deserialize an object created by version 3.0 of your application.

To overcome this limitation, you have two choices:

■ Implement custom serialization, as described in Lesson 3, that is capable of importing earlier serialized objects.

■ Apply the *OptionalField* attribute to newly added members that might cause version compatibility problems.

The *OptionalField* attribute does not affect the serialization process. During deserialization, if the member was not serialized, the runtime leaves the member's value as *null* rather than throwing an exception. The following example shows in bold how to use the *OptionalField* attribute:

```
' VB
<Serializable()> Class ShoppingCartItem
    Implements IDeserializationCallback
```

```
    Public productId As Integer
    Public price As Decimal
    Public quantity As Integer
    <NonSerialized()> Public total As Decimal
    <OptionalField()> Public taxable As Boolean
```

```
// C#
[Serializable]
class ShoppingCartItem : IDeserializationCallback
{
    public int productId;
    public decimal price;
    public int quantity;
    [NonSerialized] public decimal total;
    [OptionalField] public bool taxable;
```

If you need to initialize optional members, either implement the *IDeserializationCallback* interface as described in the section "How to Disable Serialization of Specific Members," earlier in this lesson, or respond to serialization events as described in Lesson 3.

Best Practices for Version Compatibility

To ensure proper versioning behavior, follow these rules when modifying a custom class from version to version:

■ Never remove a serialized field.

■ Never apply the *NonSerialized* attribute to a field if the attribute was not applied to the field in a previous version.

■ Never change the name or type of a serialized field.

■ When adding a new serialized field, apply the *OptionalField* attribute.

■ When removing a *NonSerialized* attribute from a field that was not serializable in a previous version, apply the *OptionalField* attribute.

■ For all optional fields, set meaningful defaults using the serialization callbacks unless *0* or *null* are acceptable defaults.

Choosing a Serialization Format

The .NET Framework includes two classes for formatting serialized data in the *System .Runtime.Serialization* namespace, both of which implement the *IRemotingFormatter* interface:

■ **BinaryFormatter** Located in the *System.Runtime.Serialization.Formatters.Binary* namespace, this formatter is the most efficient way to serialize objects that will be read by only .NET Framework–based applications.

■ *SoapFormatter*   Located in the *System.Runtime.Serialization.Formatters.Soap* namespace, this XML-based formatter is the most reliable way to serialize objects that will be transmitted across a network or read by non–.NET Framework applications. Objects serialized with *SoapFormatter* are more likely to successfully traverse firewalls than *BinaryFormatter*.

In summary, you should choose *BinaryFormatter* only when you know that all clients opening the serialized data will be .NET Framework applications. Therefore, if you are writing objects to the disk to be read later by your application, *BinaryFormatter* is perfect. Use *SoapFormatter* when other applications might read your serialized data and when sending data across a network. *SoapFormatter* also works reliably in situations where you could choose *BinaryFormatter;* the drawback is that the serialized object can consume three to four times more space.

Although *SoapFormatter* formats data using XML, it is primarily intended to be used by SOAP Web services. If your goal is to store objects in an open, standards-based document that might be consumed by applications running on other platforms, the most flexible way to perform serialization is to choose XML serialization. Lesson 2 in this chapter, "XML Serialization," discusses XML serialization at length.

How to Use *SoapFormatter*

To use *SoapFormatter*, add a reference to the *System.Runtime.Serialization.Formatters .Soap.dll* assembly to your project. (Unlike *BinaryFormatter*, it is not included by default.) Then write code exactly as you would to use *BinaryFormatter*, but substitute the *SoapFormatter* class for the *BinaryFormatter* class.

Although writing code for *BinaryFormatter* and *SoapFormatter* is very similar, the serialized data is very different. The following example is a three-member object serialized with *SoapFormatter* that has been slightly edited for readability:

```
<SOAP-ENV:Envelope xmlns:xsi="http://www.w3.org/2001/XMLSchema-instance">
  <SOAP-ENV:Body>
    <a1:ShoppingCartItem id="ref-1">
      <productId>100</productId>
      <price>10.25</price>
      <quantity>2</quantity>
    </a1:ShoppingCartItem>
  </SOAP-ENV:Body>
</SOAP-ENV:Envelope>
```

How to Control SOAP Serialization

Binary serialization is intended for use only by .NET Framework–based applications. Therefore, you rarely need to modify the standard formatting. However, SOAP serialization is intended to be read by a variety of platforms. In addition, you might need to serialize an object to meet specific requirements, such as predefined SOAP attributes and element names.

You can control the formatting of a SOAP serialized document by using the attributes listed in Table 5-1.

Table 5-1   SOAP Serialization Attributes

Attribute	Applies to	Specifies
SoapAttribute	Public field, property, parameter, or return value	The class member will be serialized as an XML attribute.
SoapDefault-Value	Public properties and fields	The default value of an XML element or attribute.
SoapElement	Public field, property, parameter, or return value	The class will be serialized as an XML element.
SoapEnum	Public field that is an enumeration identifier	The element name of an enumeration member.
SoapIgnore	Public properties and fields	The property or field should be ignored when the containing class is serialized.
SoapType	Public class declarations	The schema for the XML that is generated when a class is serialized.

SOAP serialization attributes function similarly to XML serialization attributes. For more information about XML serialization attributes, refer to the section "How to Control XML Serialization," in Lesson 2 of this chapter.

Guidelines for Serialization

Keep the following guidelines in mind when using serialization:

■ When in doubt, mark a class as *Serializable*. Even if you do not need to serialize it now, you might need to do so later, or another developer might need to serialize a derived class or a class that includes your class as a member.

■ Mark calculated or temporary members as *NonSerialized*. For example, if you track the current thread ID in a member variable, the thread ID is likely to be invalid upon deserialization. Therefore, you should not store it.

■ Use *SoapFormatter* when you require portability. Use *BinaryFormatter* for greatest efficiency.

Lab: Serialize and Deserialize Objects

In this lab, you modify a class to enable efficient serialization and then update an application to perform serialization and deserialization of that class. If you encounter a problem completing an exercise, the completed projects are available along with the sample files.

Exercise 1: Make a Class Serializable

In this exercise, you will modify a custom class so that developers can easily store it to disk for later retrieval or transfer it across a network to another .NET Framework application.

1. Navigate to the \<*InstallHome*>\Chapter05\Lesson1\Exercise1\Partial folder and open either the C# version or the Visual Basic .NET version of the solution file.

2. Examine the *Person* class. To make the *Person* class serializable, you must add the *Serializable* attribute. To do so, first import the *System.Runtime.Serialization* namespace to the file.

3. Add the *Serializable* attribute to the *Person* class, and then build the project to ensure it compiles correctly.

Exercise 2: Serialize an Object

In this exercise, you will write code to store an object to disk using the most efficient method possible.

1. Open the project that you modified in Exercise 1.

2. Add the *System.IO*, *System.Runtime.Serialization* and *System.Runtime.Serialization .Formatters.Binary* namespaces to the file containing *Main*.

3. Add code to the *Serialize* method to serialize the *sp* object to a file in the current directory named Person.dat. Your code could look like the following:

```
' VB
Private Sub Serialize(ByVal sp As Person)
    ' Create file to save the data to
    Dim fs As FileStream = New FileStream("Person.Dat", FileMode.Create)

    ' Create a BinaryFormatter object to perform the serialization
    Dim bf As BinaryFormatter = New BinaryFormatter

    ' Use the BinaryFormatter object to serialize the data to the file
    bf.Serialize(fs, sp)

    ' Close the file
    fs.Close()
End Sub
```

```csharp
// C#
private static void Serialize(Person sp)
{
    // Create file to save the data to
    FileStream fs = new FileStream("Person.Dat", FileMode.Create);

    // Create a BinaryFormatter object to perform the serialization
    BinaryFormatter bf = new BinaryFormatter();

    // Use the BinaryFormatter object to serialize the data to the file
    bf.Serialize(fs, sp);

    // Close the file
    fs.Close();
}
```

4. Build the project and resolve any errors.

5. Open a command prompt to the build directory, and then test the application by running the following command:

```
Serialize-People Tony 1923 4 22
```

6. Examine the serialized data by opening the file that your application produced to verify that the name you entered was successfully captured. The date and age information are contained in the serialized data as well; however, they are more difficult to interpret in Notepad.

Exercise 3: Deserialize an Object

In this exercise, you must read an object from a disk that has been serialized by using *BinaryFormatter*.

1. Open the Serialize-People project that you modified in Exercises 1 and 2.

2. Add code to the *Deserialize* method in the main program to deserialize the *dsp* object from a file in the default directory named *Person.dat*. Your code could look like the following:

```vb
' VB
Private Function Deserialize() As Person
    Dim dsp As Person = New Person

    ' Open file to read the data from
    Dim fs As FileStream = New FileStream("Person.Dat", FileMode.Open)

    ' Create a BinaryFormatter object to perform the deserialization
    Dim bf As BinaryFormatter = New BinaryFormatter

    ' Use the BinaryFormatter object to deserialize the data from the file
    dsp = DirectCast(bf.Deserialize(fs), Person)
```

```
        ' Close the file
        fs.Close()

        Return dsp
    End Function

    // C#
    private static Person Deserialize()
    {
        Person dsp = new Person();

        // Open file to read the data from
        FileStream fs = new FileStream("Person.Dat", FileMode.Open);

        // Create a BinaryFormatter object to perform the deserialization
        BinaryFormatter bf = new BinaryFormatter();

        // Use the BinaryFormatter object to deserialize the data from the file
        dsp = (Person)bf.Deserialize(fs);

        // Close the file
        fs.Close();

        return dsp;
    }
```

3. Build the project and resolve any errors.

4. Open a command prompt to the build directory and then run the following command with no command-line parameters:

```
Serialize-People
```

Note that the *Serialize-People* command displays the name, date of birth, and age of the previously serialized *Person* object.

Exercise 4: Optimize a Class for Deserialization

In this exercise, you will modify a class to improve the efficiency of serialization.

1. Open the Serialize-People project that you modified in Exercises 1, 2, and 3.

2. Modify the *Person* class to prevent the age member from being serialized. To do this, add the *NonSerialized* attribute to the member, as the following code demonstrates:

```
' VB
<NonSerialized()> Public age As Integer

// C#
[NonSerialized] public int age;
```

3. Build and run the project with no command-line parameters. Note that the *Serialize-People* command displays the name and date of birth of the previously serialized *Person* object. However, the age is displayed as zero.

4. Modify the *Person* class to implement the *IDeserializationCallback* interface, as the following code snippet demonstrates:

```
' VB
<Serializable()> Public Class Person
    Implements IDeserializationCallback

// C#
namespace Serialize_People
{
    [Serializable]
    class Person : IDeserializationCallback
```

5. Add the *IDeserializationCallback.OnDeserialization* method to the *Person* class. Your code could look like the following:

```
' VB
Sub IDeserializationCallback_OnDeserialization(ByVal sender As Object) _
    Implements IDeserializationCallback.OnDeserialization
    ' After deserialization, calculate the age
    CalculateAge()
End Sub

// C#
void IDeserializationCallback.OnDeserialization(Object sender)
{
    // After deserialization, calculate the age
    CalculateAge();
}
```

6. Build and run the project with no command-line parameters. Note that the *Serialize-People* command displays the name, date of birth, and age of the previously serialized *Person* object. The age displays properly this time because it is calculated immediately after deserialization.

Lesson Summary

- Serialization is the process of converting information into a byte stream that can be stored or transferred.

- To serialize an object, first create a stream object. Then create a *BinaryFormatter* object and call the *BinaryFormatter.Serialize* method. To deserialize an object, follow the same steps but call the *BinaryFormatter.Deserialize* method.

- To create a class that can be serialized, add the *Serializable* attribute. You can also use attributes to disable serialization of specific members.

- *SoapFormatter* provides a less efficient, but more interoperable, alternative to the *BinaryFormatter* class.

- To use *SoapFormatter*, follow the same process as you would for *BinaryFormatter*, but use the *System.Runtime.Serialization.Formatters.Soap.SoapFormatter* class.

- You can control *SoapFormatter* serialization by using attributes to specify the names of serialized elements and to specify whether a member is serialized as an XML element or as an XML attribute.

- It is a good practice to make all classes serializable even if you do not immediately require serialization. You should disable serialization for calculated and temporary members.

Lesson Review

You can use the following questions to test your knowledge of the information in Lesson 1, "Serializing Objects." The questions are also available on the companion CD if you prefer to review them in electronic form.

NOTE Answers

Answers to these questions and explanations of why each answer choice is right or wrong are located in the "Answers" section at the end of the book.

1. Which of the following are required to serialize an object? (Choose all that apply.)

   A. An instance of *BinaryFormatter* or *SoapFormatter*

   B. File permissions to create temporary files

   C. Microsoft Internet Information Services (IIS)

   D. A stream object

2. Which of the following attributes should you add to a class to enable it to be serialized?

   A. *ISerializable*

   B. *Serializable*

   C. *SoapInclude*

   D. *OnDeserialization*

3. Which of the following attributes should you add to a member to prevent it from being serialized by *BinaryFormatter*?

   A. *NonSerialized*

   B. *Serializable*

   C. *SerializationException*

   D. *SoapIgnore*

4. Which of the following interfaces should you implement to enable you to run a method after an instance of your class is deserialized?

   A. *IFormatter*

   B. *ISerializable*

   C. *IDeserializationCallback*

   D. *IObjectReference*

Lesson 2: XML Serialization

XML is a standardized, text-based document format for storing application-readable information. Just as Hypertext Markup Language (HTML) provided a text-based standard for formatting human-readable documents, XML provides a standard that can be easily processed by computers. XML can be used to store any type of data, including documents, pictures, music, binary files, and database information. (The latest version of Microsoft Office stores documents using XML.)

The .NET Framework includes several libraries for reading and writing XML files, including the *System.Xml.Serialization* namespace. *System.Xml.Serialization* provides methods for converting objects, including those based on custom classes, to and from XML files. With XML serialization, you can write almost any object to a text file for later retrieval with only a few lines of code. Similarly, you can use XML serialization to transmit objects between computers through Web services—even if the remote computer is not using the .NET Framework.

***

After this lesson, you will be able to:

- Serialize and deserialize objects using XML serialization
- Customize serialization behavior of custom classes to meet specific requirements, such as an XML schema
- Serialize a data set

Estimated lesson time: 40 minutes

***

Why Use XML Serialization?

Use XML serialization when you need to exchange an object with an application that might not be based on the .NET Framework, and you do not need to serialize any private members. XML serialization provides the following benefits over standard serialization:

- **Greater interoperability**   XML is a text-based file standard, and all modern development environments include libraries for processing XML files. Therefore, an object that is serialized by using XML can be processed easily by an application written for a different operating system in a different development environment.

- **More administrator-friendly**   Objects serialized by using XML can be viewed and edited by using any text editor, including Notepad. If you are storing objects in files, this gives administrators the opportunity to view and edit the XML files. This can be useful for customizing your application, troubleshooting problems, and developing new applications that interoperate with your existing application.

■ **Better forward-compatibility** Objects serialized by using XML are self-describing and easily processed. Therefore, when the time comes to replace your application, the new application will have an easier time processing your serialized objects if you use XML.

In addition, you must use XML serialization anytime you need to conform to a specific XML schema or control how an object is encoded. XML cannot be used for every situation, however. Specifically, XML serialization has the following limitations:

■ XML serialization can serialize only public data. You cannot serialize private data.

■ You cannot serialize object graphs; you can use XML serialization only on objects.

How to Use XML to Serialize an Object

At a high level, the steps for serializing an object to XML are as follows:

1. Create a stream, *TextWriter*, or *XmlWriter* object to hold the serialized output.

2. Create an *XmlSerializer* object (in the *System.Xml.Serialization* namespace) by passing it the type of object you plan to serialize.

3. Call the *XmlSerializer.Serialize* method to serialize the object and output the results to the stream.

At the code level, these steps are similar to standard serialization. The following Console application—which requires the *System.IO* and *System.Xml.Serialization* namespaces—demonstrates the simplicity of XML serialization:

```
' VB
' Create file to save the data
Dim fs As FileStream = New FileStream("SerializedDate.XML", FileMode.Create)

' Create an XmlSerializer object to perform the serialization
Dim xs As XmlSerializer = New XmlSerializer(GetType(DateTime))

' Use the XmlSerializer object to serialize the data to the file
xs.Serialize(fs, System.DateTime.Now)

' Close the file
fs.Close

// C#
// Create file to save the data
FileStream fs = new FileStream("SerializedDate.XML", FileMode.Create);

// Create an XmlSerializer object to perform the serialization
XmlSerializer xs = new XmlSerializer(typeof(DateTime));
```

```
// Use the XmlSerializer object to serialize the data to the file
xs.Serialize(fs, System.DateTime.Now);

// Close the file
fs.Close();
```

When run, the application produces a text file similar to the following:

```
<?xml version="1.0" ?>
<dateTime>2008-06-05T16:28:11.0533408-05:00</dateTime>
```

Compared with the serialized *DateTime* object created in Lesson 1, XML serialization produces a very readable, easily edited file.

How to Use XML to Deserialize an Object

To deserialize an object, follow these steps:

1. Create a stream, *TextReader*, or *XmlReader* object to read the serialized input.

2. Create an *XmlSerializer* object (in the *System.Xml.Serialization* namespace) by passing it the type of object you plan to deserialize.

3. Call the *XmlSerializer.Deserialize* method to deserialize the object, and cast it to the correct type.

The following code sample deserializes an XML file containing a *DateTime* object and displays that object's day of the week and time:

```
' VB
' Open file from which to read the data
Dim fs As FileStream = New FileStream("SerializedDate.XML", FileMode.Open)

' Create an XmlSerializer object to perform the deserialization
Dim xs As XmlSerializer = New XmlSerializer(GetType(DateTime))

' Use the XmlSerializer object to deserialize the data from the file
Dim previousTime As DateTime = DirectCast(xs.Deserialize(fs), DateTime)

' Close the file
fs.Close

' Display the deserialized time
Console.WriteLine(("Day: " _
    & (previousTime.DayOfWeek & (", Time: " _
    & previousTime.TimeOfDay.ToString))))

// C#
// Open file from which to read the data
FileStream fs = new FileStream("SerializedDate.XML", FileMode.Open);
```

```
// Create an XmlSerializer object to perform the deserialization
XmlSerializer xs = new XmlSerializer(typeof(DateTime));

// Use the XmlSerializer object to deserialize the data from the file
DateTime previousTime = (DateTime)xs.Deserialize(fs);

// Close the file
fs.Close();

// Display the deserialized time
Console.WriteLine("Day: " + previousTime.DayOfWeek + ", Time: "
    + previousTime.TimeOfDay.ToString());
```

How to Create Classes That Can Be Serialized by Using XML Serialization

To create a class that can be serialized by using XML serialization, you must perform the following tasks:

- Specify the class as public.
- Specify all members that must be serialized as public.
- Create a parameterless constructor.

Unlike classes processed with standard serialization, classes do not have to have the *Serializable* attribute to be processed with XML serialization. If there are private or protected members, they are skipped during serialization.

How to Control XML Serialization

If you serialize a class that meets the requirements for XML serialization but does not have any XML serialization attributes, the runtime uses default settings that meet many people's requirements. The names of XML elements are based on class and member names, and each member is serialized as a separate XML element. For example, consider the following simple class:

```
' VB
Public Class ShoppingCartItem
    Public productId As Int32
    Public price As Decimal
    Public quantity As Int32
    Public total As Decimal

    Public Sub New()
        MyBase.New
    End Sub
End Class
```

```csharp
// C#
public class ShoppingCartItem
{
    public Int32 productId;
    public decimal price;
    public Int32 quantity;
    public decimal total;

    public ShoppingCartItem()
    {
    }
}
```

Serializing an instance of this class with sample values creates the following XML (which has been slightly simplified for readability):

```xml
<?xml version="1.0" ?>
<ShoppingCartItem>
    <productId>100</productId>
    <price>10.25</price>
    <total>20.50</total>
    <quantity>2</quantity>
</ShoppingCartItem>
```

If you are defining the XML schema, this might be sufficient. However, if you need to create XML documents that conform to specific standards, you might need to control how the serialization is structured. You can do this using the attributes listed in Table 5-2.

Table 5-2 XML Serialization Attributes

Attribute	Applies to	Specifies
XmlAnyAttribute	Public field, property, parameter, or return value that returns an array of *XmlAttribute* objects	When deserializing, the array is filled with *XmlAttribute* objects that represent all XML attributes unknown to the schema.
XmlAnyElement	Public field, property, parameter, or return value that returns an array of *XmlElement* objects	When deserializing, the array is filled with *XmlElement* objects that represent all XML elements unknown to the schema.
XmlArray	Public field, property, parameter, or return value that returns an array of complex objects	The members of the array are generated as members of an XML array.

Table 5-2   XML Serialization Attributes

Attribute	Applies to	Specifies
XmlArrayItem	Public field, property, parameter, or return value that returns an array of complex objects	The derived types can be inserted into an array. Usually applied in conjunction with the *XmlArray* attribute.
XmlAttribute	Public field, property, parameter, or return value	The member is serialized as an XML attribute.
XmlChoiceIdentifier	Public field, property, parameter, or return value	The member can be further disambiguated by using an enumeration.
XmlElement	Public field, property, parameter, or return value	The field or property is serialized as an XML element.
XmlEnum	Public field that is an enumeration identifier	The element name of an enumeration member.
XmlIgnore	Public properties and fields	The property or field should be ignored when the containing class is serialized. This functions similarly to the *NonSerialized* standard serialization attribute.
XmlInclude	Public-derived class declarations and return values of public methods for Web Services Description Language (WSDL) documents	The class should be included when generating schemas (to be recognized when serialized).
XmlRoot	Public class declarations	Controls XML serialization of the attribute target as an XML root element. Use the attribute to specify the namespace and element name.

Table 5-2   XML Serialization Attributes

Attribute	Applies to	Specifies
XmlText	Public properties and fields	The property or field should be serialized as XML text.
XmlType	Public class declarations	The name and namespace of the XML type.

You can use these attributes to make a serialized class conform to specific XML requirements. For example, consider the attributes required to make the following three changes to the serialized XML document for the *ShoppingCartItem* example:

- Change the *ShoppingCartItem* element name to *CartItem*.

- Make *productId* an XML attribute of *CartItem*, rather than a separate XML element.

- Do not include the total in the serialized document.

NOTE   XML Attributes and Elements

An XML element can contain other XML elements, much like an object can have members. XML elements can also have XML attributes, which describe the XML element, just as a property can describe an object in the .NET Framework. When examining an XML document, you can recognize XML attributes because they appear within an XML element's < > brackets. Examine the differences between the two XML examples in this section to understand the distinction. Don't confuse XML attributes with VB and C# attributes.

To make these changes, modify the class with attributes, as shown here in bold:

```vb
' VB
<XmlRoot("CartItem")> Public Class ShoppingCartItem
    <XmlAttribute()>  Public productId As Int32
    Public price As Decimal
    Public quantity As Int32
    <XmlIgnore()> Public total As Decimal

    Public Sub New()
        MyBase.New
    End Sub
End Class

// C#
[XmlRoot ("CartItem")]
public class ShoppingCartItem
{
    [XmlAttribute] public Int32 productId;
    public decimal price;
```

```
    public Int32 quantity;
    [XmlIgnore] public decimal total;

    public ShoppingCartItem()
    {
    }
}
```

This would result in the following XML file, which meets the specified requirements:

```
<?xml version="1.0" ?>
<CartItem productId="100">
    <price>10.25</price>
    <quantity>2</quantity>
</CartItem>
```

Although attributes enable you to meet most XML serialization requirements, you can take complete control over XML serialization by implementing the *IXmlSerializable* interface in your class. For example, you can separate data into bytes instead of buffering large data sets, and also avoid the inflation that occurs when the data is encoded using Base64 encoding. To control the serialization, implement the *ReadXml* and *WriteXml* methods to control the *XmlReader* and *XmlWriter* classes used to read and write the XML.

How to Conform to an XML Schema

Typically, when two different applications are going to exchange XML files, the developers work together to create an XML schema file. An XML schema defines the structure of an XML document. Many types of XML schemas already exist, and whenever possible, you should leverage an existing XML schema.

MORE INFO XML Schemas

For more information about XML schemas, visit *http://www.w3.org/XML/Schema.*

If you have an XML schema, you can run the XML Schema Definition tool (Xsd.exe) to produce a set of classes that are strongly typed to the schema and annotated with attributes. When an instance of such a class is serialized, the generated XML adheres to the XML schema. This is a simpler alternative to using other classes in the .NET Framework, such as the *XmlReader* and *XmlWriter* classes, to parse and write an XML stream.

To generate a class based on a schema, follow these steps:

1. Create or download the XML schema .xsd file on your computer.

2. Open a Visual Studio Command Prompt. You can start the command prompt from within the Microsoft Visual Studio\Visual Studio Tools folder on your Start menu.

3. From the command prompt, type **Xsd.exe schema.xsd /classes /language:[CS | VB]** and press Enter. For example, to create a new class based on a schema file named C:\Schema\Library.xsd, you would run the following command:

```
' VB
xsd C:\schema\library.xsd /classes /language:VB
```

```
// C#
xsd C:\schema\library.xsd /classes /language:CS
```

4. Open the newly created file (named Schema.cs or Schema.vb), and add the class to your application.

When you serialize the newly created class, it automatically conforms to the XML schema. This makes it simple to create applications that interoperate with standards-based Web services.

MORE INFO   **Conforming to the XML Schema**

For more information about conforming to the XML Schema, read "XML Schema Part 0: Primer" at *http://www.w3.org/TR/2001/REC-xmlschema-0-20010502/* and "Using Schema and Serialization to Leverage Business Logic" by Eric Schmidt at *http://msdn.microsoft.com/library/ms950771.aspx*.

How to Serialize a *DataSet*

In addition to serializing an instance of a public class, an instance of a *DataSet* object can be serialized, as shown in the following example:

```
' VB
Private Sub SerializeDataSet(filename As String)
    Dim ser As XmlSerializer = new XmlSerializer(GetType(DataSet))
    ' Creates a DataSet; adds a table, column, and ten rows.
    Dim ds As DataSet = new DataSet("myDataSet")
    Dim t As DataTable = new DataTable("table1")
    Dim c As DataColumn = new DataColumn("thing")
    t.Columns.Add(c)
    ds.Tables.Add(t)
    Dim r As DataRow
    Dim i As Integer
    for i = 0 to 10
        r = t.NewRow()
        r(0) = "Thing " & i
        t.Rows.Add(r)
    Next
    Dim writer As TextWriter = new StreamWriter(filename)
    ser.Serialize(writer, ds)
    writer.Close()
End Sub
```

```
// C#
private void SerializeDataSet(string filename){
    XmlSerializer ser = new XmlSerializer(typeof(DataSet));

    // Creates a DataSet; adds a table, column, and ten rows.
    DataSet ds = new DataSet("myDataSet");
    DataTable t = new DataTable("table1");
    DataColumn c = new DataColumn("thing");
    t.Columns.Add(c);
    ds.Tables.Add(t);
    DataRow r;
    for(int i = 0; i<10;i++){
        r = t.NewRow();
        r[0] = "Thing " + i;
        t.Rows.Add(r);
    }
    TextWriter writer = new StreamWriter(filename);
    ser.Serialize(writer, ds);
    writer.Close();
}
```

Similarly, you can serialize arrays, collections, and instances of an *XmlElement* or *Xml-Node* class. Although this is useful, it does not provide the same level of control that you would have if the data were stored in custom classes. Alternatively, you could use the *DataSet.WriteXml*, *DataSet.ReadXML*, and *DataSet.GetXml* methods.

Lab: Using XML Serialization

In this lab, you will update an application that currently uses *BinaryFormatter* serialization to instead use XML serialization. If you encounter a problem completing an exercise, the completed projects are available along with the sample files.

Exercise: Replacing Binary Serialization with XML Serialization

In this exercise, you will upgrade a project to support storing data using open standards-based XML serialization.

1. Navigate to the \<*InstallHome*>\Chapter05\Lesson2\Exercise1\Partial folder and open either the C# version or the Visual Basic .NET version of the solution file.

2. Add the *System.Xml.Serialization* namespace to the main program.

3. Rewrite the *Serialize* method to use XML serialization instead of binary serialization. Name the temporary file Person.xml. Your code could look like the following (the changes are shown in bold):

```
' VB
Private Sub Serialize(ByVal sp As Person)
    ' Create file to save the data to
    Dim fs As FileStream = New FileStream("Person.XML", FileMode.Create)
```

```
' Create an XmlSerializer object to perform the serialization
Dim xs As XmlSerializer = New XmlSerializer(GetType(Person))

' Use the XmlSerializer object to serialize the data to the file
xs.Serialize(fs, sp)

' Close the file
fs.Close
End Sub
```

```
// C#
private static void Serialize(Person sp)
{
    // Create file to save the data to
    FileStream fs = new FileStream("Person.XML", FileMode.Create);

    // Create an XmlSerializer object to perform the serialization
    XmlSerializer xs = new XmlSerializer(typeof(Person));

    // Use the XmlSerializer object to serialize the data to the file
    xs.Serialize(fs, sp);

    // Close the file
    fs.Close();
}
```

4. Rewrite the *Deserialize* method to use XML deserialization instead of binary
   deserialization. Your code could look like the following (the changes are shown
   in bold):

```
' VB
Private Function Deserialize() As Person
    Dim dsp As Person = New Person

    ' Create file to save the data to
    Dim fs As FileStream = New FileStream("Person.XML", FileMode.Open)

    ' Create an XmlSerializer object to perform the deserialization
    Dim xs As XmlSerializer = New XmlSerializer(GetType(Person))

    ' Use the XmlSerializer object to deserialize the data from the file
    dsp = DirectCast(xs.Deserialize(fs), Person)

    ' Close the file
    fs.Close()
    Return dsp
End Function
```

```
// C#
private static Person Deserialize()
{
    Person dsp = new Person();
```

```
// Create file to save the data to
FileStream fs = new FileStream("Person.XML", FileMode.Open);

// Create an XmlSerializer object to perform the deserialization
XmlSerializer xs = new XmlSerializer(typeof(Person));

// Use the XmlSerializer object to deserialize the data to the file
dsp = (Person)xs.Deserialize(fs);

// Close the file
fs.Close();
return dsp;
}
```

5. Build the project and resolve any errors.

6. Open a command prompt to the build directory, and then run the following command:

   ```
   Serialize-People Tony 1923 4 22
   ```

   What exception message do you receive, and why?

   You see the message "Invalid parameters. Serialize_People.Person is inaccessible due to its protection level. Only public types can be processed." The error occurs because the *Person* class is not marked as public.

7. Edit the *Person* class, and mark it as public. Then rebuild the project, and run the following command again:

   ```
   Serialize-People Tony 1923 4 22
   ```

8. Examine the serialized data to verify that the information you provided on the command line was successfully captured. Why does the age appear in the serialized file even though the age member has the *NonSerialized* attribute?

   The *NonSerialized* attribute applies to binary serialization, but it does not affect XML serialization.

9. Now run the command with no parameters to verify that deserialization works properly.

Lesson Summary

- XML serialization provides interoperability to communicate with different platforms and flexibility to conform to an XML schema.

- XML serialization cannot be used to serialize private data or object graphs.

- To serialize an object, first create a stream, *TextWriter*, or *XmlWriter*. Then create an *XmlSerializer* object and call the *XmlSerializer.Serialize* method. To deserialize an object, follow the same steps but call the *XmlSerializer.Deserialize* method.

- To create a class that can be serialized as XML, specify the class and all members as public and create a parameterless constructor.

- You can control XML serialization by using attributes. Attributes can change the names of elements, serialize members as XML attributes rather than as XML elements, and exclude members from serialization.

- Use the Xsd.exe tool to create a class that automatically conforms to an XML schema when serialized.

- Data sets, arrays, collections, and instances of an *XmlElement* or *XmlNode* class can all be serialized with *XmlSerializer*.

Lesson Review

You can use the following questions to test your knowledge of the information in Lesson 2, "XML Serialization." The questions are also available on the companion CD if you prefer to review them in electronic form.

NOTE Answers

Answers to these questions and explanations of why each answer choice is right or wrong are located in the "Answers" section at the end of the book.

1. Which of the following are requirements for a class to be serialized with XML serialization? (Choose all that apply.)

   A. The class must be public.

   B. The class must be private.

   C. The class must have a parameterless constructor.

   D. The class must have a constructor that accepts a *SerializationInfo* parameter.

2. Which of the following attributes would you use to cause a member to be serialized as an XML attribute, rather than as an XML element?

   A. *XmlAnyAttribute*

   B. *XmlType*

   C. *XmlElement*

   D. *XmlAttribute*

3. Which tool would you use to help you create a class that, when serialized, would produce an XML document that conformed to an XML schema?

    A. Xsd.exe

    B. Xdcmake.exe

    C. XPadsi90.exe

    D. Xcacls.exe

4. Which of the following attributes should you add to a member to prevent it from being serialized by XML serialization?

    A. *XmlType*

    B. *XmlIgnore*

    C. *XmlElement*

    D. *XmlAttribute*

Lesson 3: Custom Serialization

Custom serialization is the process of controlling the serialization and deserialization of a type. By controlling serialization, it is possible to ensure serialization compatibility, which is the ability to serialize and deserialize between versions of a type without breaking the core functionality of the type. For example, in the first version of a type, there might be only two fields. In the next version of a type, several more fields are added. Yet the second version of an application must be able to serialize and deserialize both types. This lesson describes how to control serialization by implementing your own serialization classes.

After this lesson, you will be able to:

- Implement the *ISerializable* interface to take control over how a class is serialized
- Respond to serialization events to run code at different stages of the serialization process
- Write code that adjusts serialization and deserialization according to the context
- Describe the role of *IFormatter*

Estimated lesson time: 30 minutes

How to Implement Custom Serialization

Serialization in the .NET Framework is very flexible and can be customized to meet most development requirements. In some circumstances, you might need complete control over the serialization process.

You can override the serialization built into the .NET Framework by implementing the *ISerializable* interface and applying the *Serializable* attribute to the class. This is particularly useful in cases where the value of a member variable is invalid after deserialization, but you need to provide the variable with a value to reconstruct the full state of the object. In addition, you should not use default serialization on a class that is marked with the *Serializable* attribute and has declarative or imperative security at the class level or on its constructors. Instead, these classes should always implement the *ISerializable* interface.

Implementing *ISerializable* involves implementing the *GetObjectData* method and a special constructor that is used when the object is deserialized. The runtime calls *GetObjectData* during serialization, and the serialization constructor during deserialization. The compiler warns you if you forget to implement *GetObjectData*, but if you forget to implement the special constructor, you won't notice a problem until runtime when you receive a serialization exception.

When the runtime calls *GetObjectData* during serialization, you are responsible for populating the *SerializationInfo* object that is provided with the method call. Simply add the variables to be serialized as name/value pairs using the *AddValue* method, which internally creates *SerializationEntry* structures to store the information. Any text can be used as the name. You have the freedom to decide which member variables are added to the *SerializationInfo* object, provided that sufficient data is serialized to restore the object during deserialization. When the runtime calls your serialization constructor, simply retrieve the values of the variables from *SerializationInfo* using the names used during serialization.

The following sample code, which uses the *System.Runtime.Serialization* and *System .Security.Permissions* namespaces, shows how to implement *ISerializable*, the serialization constructor, and the *GetObjectData* method:

```vb
' VB
<Serializable()> Class ShoppingCartItem
    Implements ISerializable

    Public productId As Int32
    Public price As Decimal
    Public quantity As Int32
    <NonSerialized()> Public total As Decimal

    ' The standard, non-serialization constructor
    Public Sub New(ByVal _productID As Integer, ByVal _price As Decimal, _
        ByVal _quantity As Integer)
        MyBase.New()
        productId = _productID
        price = _price
        quantity = _quantity
        total = price * quantity
    End Sub

    ' The following constructor is for deserialization
    Protected Sub New(ByVal info As SerializationInfo, _
        ByVal context As StreamingContext)
        MyBase.New()
        productId = info.GetInt32("Product ID")
        price = info.GetDecimal("Price")
        quantity = info.GetInt32("Quantity")
        total = price * quantity
    End Sub

    ' The following method is called during serialization
    <SecurityPermissionAttribute(SecurityAction.Demand, _
        SerializationFormatter:=True)> _
    Public Overridable Sub GetObjectData(ByVal info As SerializationInfo, _
        ByVal context As StreamingContext) _
        Implements System.Runtime.Serialization.ISerializable.GetObjectData
```

```
            info.AddValue("Product ID", productId)
            info.AddValue("Price", price)
            info.AddValue("Quantity", quantity)
        End Sub

        Public Overrides Function ToString() As String
            Return productId + ": " + price + " x " + quantity + " = " + total
        End Function
End Class
```

```
// C#
[Serializable]
class ShoppingCartItem : ISerializable
{
    public Int32 productId;
    public decimal price;
    public Int32 quantity;
    [NonSerialized]
    public decimal total;

    // The standard, non-serialization constructor
    public ShoppingCartItem(int _productID, decimal _price, int _quantity)
    {
        productId = _productID;
        price = _price;
        quantity = _quantity;
        total = price * quantity;
    }

    // The following constructor is for deserialization
    protected ShoppingCartItem(SerializationInfo info,
        StreamingContext context)
    {
        productId = info.GetInt32("Product ID");
        price = info.GetDecimal("Price");
        quantity = info.GetInt32("Quantity");
        total = price * quantity;
    }

    // The following method is called during serialization
    [SecurityPermissionAttribute(SecurityAction.Demand,
        SerializationFormatter=true)]
    public virtual void GetObjectData(SerializationInfo info,
        StreamingContext context)
    {
        info.AddValue("Product ID", productId);
        info.AddValue("Price", price);
        info.AddValue("Quantity", quantity);
    }

    public override string ToString()
    {
        return productId + ": " + price + " x " + quantity + " = " + total;
    }
}
```

In this example, *SerializationInfo* does much of the work of serialization and deserialization. The construction of a *SerializationInfo* object requires an object whose type implements the *IFormatterConverter* interface. *BinaryFormatter* and *SoapFormatter* always construct an instance of the *System.Runtime.Serialization.FormatterConverter* type, without giving you the opportunity to use a different *IFormatterConverter* type. *FormatterConverter* includes methods for converting values between core types, such as converting a *Decimal* to a *Double* or a signed integer to an unsigned integer.

IMPORTANT   Reducing Security Risks by Using Data Validation

You must perform data validation in your serialization constructor and throw a *SerializationException* if invalid data is provided. The risk is that an attacker could use your class but provide fake serialization information in an attempt to exploit a weakness. You should assume that any calls made to your serialization constructor are initiated by an attacker, and allow the construction only if all the data provided is valid and realistic. For more information about code security, refer to Chapter 12.

Responding to Serialization Events

The .NET Framework supports binary serialization events when using the *Binary-Formatter* class. Events are supported only for *BinaryFormatter* serialization. For *SoapFormatter* or custom serialization, you are limited to using the *IDeserialization-Callback* interface, as discussed in Lesson 1 of this chapter. These events call methods in your class when serialization and deserialization take place. There are four serialization events:

- **Serializing**   This event is raised just before serialization takes place. Apply the *OnSerializing* attribute to the method that should run in response to this event.

- **Serialized**   This event is raised just after serialization takes place. Apply the *OnSerialized* attribute to the method that should run in response to this event.

- **Deserializing**   This event is raised just before deserialization takes place. Apply the *OnDeserializing* attribute to the method that should run in response to this event.

- **Deserialized**   This event is raised just after deserialization takes place and after *IDeserializationCallback.OnDeserialization* has been called. You should use *IDeserializationCallback.OnDeserialization* instead when formatters other than *BinaryFormatter* might be used. Apply the *OnDeserialized* attribute to the method that should run in response to this event.

The sequence of these events is illustrated in Figure 5-1.

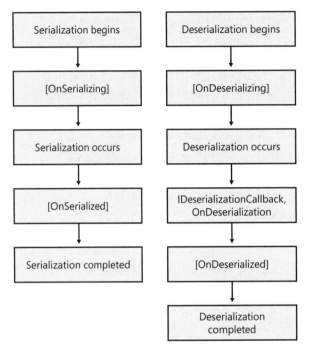

Figure 5-1   You can use serialization events to run methods during different phases of the serialization and deserialization process

Using these events is the best and easiest way to control the serialization process. The methods do not access the serialization stream but instead allow you to alter the object before and after serialization or before and after deserialization. The attributes can be applied at all levels of the type inheritance hierarchy, and each method is called in the hierarchy from the base to the most derived. This mechanism avoids the complexity and any resulting issues of implementing the *ISerializable* interface by giving the responsibility for serialization and deserialization to the most derived implementation.

For a method to respond to one of these events, the method must meet the following requirements:

- Accept a *StreamingContext* object as a parameter
- Return *void*
- Have the attribute that matches the event you want to intercept

The following example demonstrates how to create an object that responds to serialization events. In your own code, you can respond to as many or as few events as you want. In addition, you can apply the same serialization event to multiple methods or apply multiple events to a single method:

```vb
' VB
<Serializable()> Class ShoppingCartItem
    Public productId As Int32
    Public price As Decimal
    Public quantity As Int32
    Public total As Decimal

    <OnSerializing()> _
    Private Sub CalculateTotal(ByVal sc As StreamingContext)
        total = price * quantity
    End Sub

    <OnDeserialized()> _
    Private Sub CheckTotal(ByVal sc As StreamingContext)
        If (total = 0) Then
            CalculateTotal(sc)
        End If
    End Sub
End Class
```

```csharp
// C#
[Serializable]
class ShoppingCartItem
{
    public Int32 productId;
    public decimal price;
    public Int32 quantity;
    public decimal total;

    [OnSerializing]
    void CalculateTotal(StreamingContext sc)
    {
        total = price * quantity;
    }

    [OnDeserialized]
    void CheckTotal(StreamingContext sc)
    {
        if (total == 0) { CalculateTotal(sc); }
    }
}
```

How to Change Serialization Based on Context

Typically, when you serialize an object, the destination does not matter. In some circumstances, however, you might want to serialize and deserialize an object differently depending on the destination. For example, you typically should not serialize members that contain information about the current process because that information might be invalid when the object is deserialized. However, that information would be useful if the object is going to be deserialized by the same process. Alternatively, if the object is useful only if deserialized by the same process, you might choose to throw an exception if you knew the destination was a different process.

The *StreamingContext* structure can provide information about the destination of a serialized object to classes that implement the *ISerializable* interface. *StreamingContext* is passed to both *GetObjectData* and an object's serialization constructor. The *Streaming-Context* structure has two properties:

- **Context**   A reference to an object that contains any user-desired context information.

- **State**   A set of bit flags indicating the source or destination of the object being serialized/deserialized. The flags are the following:
    - *CrossProcess*   The source or destination is a different process on the same machine.
    - *CrossMachine*   The source or destination is on a different machine.
    - *File*   The source or destination is a file. Don't assume that the same process will deserialize the data.
    - *Persistence*   The source or destination is a store such as a database, file, or other. Don't assume that the same process will deserialize the data.
    - *Remoting*   The source or destination is remoting to an unknown location. The location might be on the same machine but might also be on another machine.
    - *Other*   The source or destination is unknown.
    - *Clone*   The object graph is being cloned. The serialization code might assume that the same process will deserialize the data and it is therefore safe to access handles or other unmanaged resources.
    - *CrossAppDomain*   The source or destination is a different *AppDomain*.
    - *All*   The source or destination might be any of the above contexts. This is the default context.

To make context decisions during serialization and deserialization, implement the *ISerializable* interface in your class. For serialization, inspect the *StreamingContext* structure passed to your object's *GetObjectData* method. For deserialization, inspect the *StreamingContext* structure passed to your object's serialization constructor.

If you are serializing or deserializing an object and want to provide context information, modify the *StreamingContext* object returned by the *IFormatter.Context* property before calling the formatter's *Serialize* or *Deserialize* methods. This property is implemented by both the *BinaryFormatter* and *SoapFormatter* classes. When you construct a formatter, the formatter automatically sets the *Context* property to *null* and the *State* property to *All*.

How to Create a Custom Formatter

To create a custom formatter, implement the *IFormatter* interface. Both *BinaryFormatter* and *SoapFormatter* implement the *IFormatter* interface. The *FormatterServices* class provides static methods (including *GetObjectData*) to aid with the implementation of a formatter.

MORE INFO   Custom Formatters

Very few people need to implement custom formatters. Therefore, this book covers them at a very high level. For detailed information about custom formatters, read "Format Your Way to Success with the .NET Framework Versions 1.1 and 2.0" at *http://msdn.microsoft.com/en-us/magazine/cc163902.aspx* and "Run-time Serialization" at *http://msdn.microsoft.com/en-us/library/cc301761.aspx* .Also, read "Writing Simple Custom Formatter" at *http://geekswithblogs.net/luskan/archive/2007/07/16/113956.aspx*.

Lab: Implement Custom Serialization

In this lab, you will modify a class to override the default serialization and take control over which members are serialized. If you encounter a problem completing an exercise, the completed projects are available along with the sample files.

Exercise: Update a Class to Use Custom Serialization

In this exercise, you will update a class to improve the efficiency of serialization while maintaining complete control over how data is stored and retrieved.

1. Navigate to the \<*InstallHome*>\Chapter05\Lesson3\Exercise1\Partial folder and open either the C# version or the Visual Basic .NET version of the solution file.

2. Add the *System.Runtime.Serialization* namespace to the *Person* class.

3. Add the *Serializable* attribute to the *Person* class, and then build the project to ensure it compiles correctly.

4. Modify the *Person* class so that it implements *ISerializable*.

5. Add the *GetObjectData* method, which accepts a *SerializationInfo* object and a *StreamingContext* object and adds items to be serialized to the *SerializationInfo* object. Add the *name* and *dateOfBirth* variables to the *SerializationInfo* object, but do not add the age variable. Your code could look like the following:

```vb
' VB
Public Overridable Sub GetObjectData(ByVal info As SerializationInfo, _
    ByVal context As StreamingContext) _
    Implements System.Runtime.Serialization.ISerializable.GetObjectData
    info.AddValue("Name", name)
    info.AddValue("DOB", dateOfBirth)
End Sub
```

```csharp
// C#
public virtual void GetObjectData(SerializationInfo info,
    StreamingContext context)
{
    info.AddValue("Name", name);
    info.AddValue("DOB", dateOfBirth);
}
```

6. Add the serialization constructor, which accepts a *SerializationInfo* object and a *StreamingContext* object and then initializes member variables using the contents of the *SerializationInfo* object. Use the same element names you used in the previous step. After you have deserialized all variables, call the *CalculateAge* method to initialize the age variable. Your code could look like the following:

```vb
' VB
Public Sub New(ByVal info As SerializationInfo, ByVal context As StreamingContext)
    name = info.GetString("Name")
    dateOfBirth = info.GetDateTime("DOB")
    CalculateAge
End Sub
```

```csharp
// C#
public Person(SerializationInfo info, StreamingContext context)
{
    name = info.GetString("Name");
    dateOfBirth = info.GetDateTime("DOB");
    CalculateAge();
}
```

7. Build the project and resolve any errors.

8. Open a command prompt to the build directory, and then run the following command:

```
Serialize-People Tony 1923 4 22
```

9. Now run the command with no parameters to verify that deserialization works properly.

Lesson Summary

- You can implement *ISerializable* to perform custom serialization.
- *BinaryFormatter* provides four events that you can use to control parts of the serialization process: *OnSerializing*, *OnSerialized*, *OnDeserializing*, and *OnDeserialized*.
- The *StreamingContext* class, an instance of which is provided to methods called during serialization events, gives you information about the origin or planned destination of the serialization process. The method performing serialization must specify this information for it to be useful.
- Although few developers require total control over serialization, you can implement the *IFormatter* interface to create custom formatters.

Lesson Review

You can use the following questions to test your knowledge of the information in Lesson 3, "Custom Serialization." The questions are also available on the companion CD if you prefer to review them in electronic form.

NOTE Answers

Answers to these questions and explanations of why each answer choice is right or wrong are located in the "Answers" section at the end of the book.

1. Which parameters must a constructor accept if the class implements *ISerializable*? (Choose all that apply.)

   A. *SerializationInfo*

   B. *Formatter*

   C. *StreamingContext*

   D. *ObjectManager*

2. Which event would you use to run a method immediately before deserialization occurs?

   A. *OnSerializing*

   B. *OnDeserializing*

   C. *OnSerialized*

   D. *OnDeserialized*

3. Which event would you use to run a method immediately after serialization occurs?

    A. *OnSerializing*

    B. *OnDeserializing*

    C. *OnSerialized*

    D. *OnDeserialized*

4. Which of the following are requirements for a method that is called in response to a serialization event? (Choose all that apply.)

    A. Accept a *StreamingContext* object as a parameter.

    B. Accept a *SerializationInfo* object as a parameter.

    C. Return *void.*

    D. Return a *StreamingContext* object.

Chapter Review

To practice and reinforce the skills you learned in this chapter further, you can do any of the following tasks:

- Review the chapter summary.
- Review the list of key terms introduced in this chapter.
- Complete the case scenarios. These scenarios set up real-world situations involving the topics of this chapter and ask you to create a solution.
- Complete the suggested practices.
- Take a practice test.

Chapter Summary

- Serialization outputs an object as a series of bytes, whereas deserialization reads a serialized object and defines the value of an object. Most custom classes can be serialized by simply adding the *Serializable* attribute. In some cases, you might be able to improve efficiency or provide for changes to the structure of classes by modifying your class to change the default serialization behavior.
- XML serialization provides a way to store and transfer objects using open standards. XML serialization can be customized to fit the exact requirements of an XML schema, making it simple to convert objects into XML documents and back into objects.
- Custom serialization is required in situations where classes contain complex information, significant changes have occurred to the structure of a class between different versions, or where you need complete control over how information is stored. You can perform custom serialization by implementing the *ISerializable* interface and by responding to serialization events.

Key Terms

Do you know what these key terms mean? You can check your answers by looking up the terms in the glossary at the end of the book.

- *BinaryFormatter*
- Extensible Markup Language (XML)
- Deserialization
- Serialization
- *SoapFormatter*

Case Scenarios

In the following case scenarios, you apply what you've learned about how to implement and apply serialization, as well as how to upgrade applications that make use of serialization. You can find answers to these questions in the "Answers" section at the end of this book.

Case Scenario 1: Choosing a Serialization Technique

You are an application developer for City Power & Light. For the last year, you and your team have been creating a distributed .NET Framework solution to replace the antiquated system that currently accounts for electrical usage and distributes bills to customers. You have created components for monitoring electrical usage, and you are at the stage of development when you need to transmit usage information to the billing system. Your manager asks you to interview key people and then answer some questions about your design choices.

Interviews

The following is a list of company personnel you interviewed and their statements:

- **Billing System Development Manager** "I've already got my guy working on this, and he has built methods with .NET that accept your *Usage* objects and add billing information to the database. So we just need you to create those objects and send them over the internal network to us."

- **Network Manager** "All the accounting and billing servers are on the same subnet, so you don't have to worry about your network traffic going through any firewalls. I would like you to try and minimize the bandwidth used—we have millions of accounts, and that subnet is close to being saturated already."

Questions

Answer the following questions for your manager:

1. Which serialization method will you use?
2. What changes will you need to make to your class to enable serialization?
3. About how many lines of code will you need to write to perform the serialization?

Case Scenario 2: Serializing Between Versions

You are an application developer working for Humongous Insurance. Recently, you have launched version 1.0 of Incident, an application based on an earlier version of the .NET Framework that tracks insurance events throughout their life cycle.

Subsequent to this successful launch, you have begun development of Incident 2.0. Incident 2.0 is based on the latest version of the .NET Framework. During a planning meeting, your manager asks you questions about how Incident 2.0 will handle the upgrade process during deployment.

Questions

Answer the following questions for your manager:

1. In Incident 1.0, I know you save some user preferences, such as window position, to a file by serializing your *Preferences* object using *BinaryFormatter*. Now that the application will be based on a newer version of the .NET framework, will you be able to deserialize those settings directly in Incident 2.0 if you don't make any changes to the *Preferences* class?

2. We have some feature requests that will require you to add more preferences. If you add more members to the *Preferences* class, will you still be able to deserialize settings stored from the previous version? If so, what special accommodations will you need to make?

3. The IT department has requested we switch to using XML-based configuration files so that they can edit them more easily. How could you deserialize the existing binary-formatted object, while serializing an XML object?

Suggested Practices

To help you successfully master the "Implementing serialization and input/output functionality in a .NET Framework application" exam objective, complete the following tasks.

Serialize or Deserialize an Object or an Object Graph by Using Runtime Serialization Techniques

For this task, you should complete at least Practices 1 and 2. If you want a better understanding of how serialization can be used in the real world and you have the resources needed to do Practice 3, complete it as well.

- **Practice 1**   Using the last custom class that you created as part of your job, modify it so that it can be serialized. Then write an application to serialize and deserialize it using *BinaryFormatter*. Examine the serialized data. Then modify the application to use *SoapFormatter*. Examine the serialized data.

- **Practice 2**   Examine the class that you used in Practice 1 and, if possible, identify a member that does not need to be serialized. Modify your class so that the member will not be serialized but will be defined automatically upon deserialization.

- **Practice 3**   Write a client/server application to transfer an object between two networked computers using serialization and deserialization.

Control the Serialization of an Object into XML Format by Using the *System.Xml.Serialization* Namespace

For this task, you should complete all three practices to gain experience using XML serialization with real-world classes and schema.

- **Practice 1**   Write an application that uses XML serialization to serialize and deserialize the last class that you created as part of your job.

- **Practice 2**   Examine the class that you used in Practice 1 and, if possible, identify a member that does not need to be serialized. Use an attribute to modify your class so that the member will not be serialized.

- **Practice 3**   Find an XML schema on the Internet and create a class that, when serialized, conforms to that XML schema. Create the class using two different techniques: manually and with Xsd.exe.

Implement Custom Serialization Formatting by Using the Serialization Formatter Classes

For this task, you should complete at least Practices 1 and 2. If you want in-depth knowledge of the serialization process, complete Practice 3 as well.

- **Practice 1**   Using the last custom class that you created as part of your job, modify it so that it implements *ISerializable* and can be successfully serialized and deserialized. Examine the members to determine whether you can optimize serialization by omitting calculated values.

- **Practice 2**   Create a class that provides methods for all four *BinaryFormatter* serialization events.

■ **Practice 3**   Implement the *IFormatter* interface to create a custom formatter. Use it during serialization and deserialization to understand the formatter's role in serialization.

Take a Practice Test

The practice tests on this book's companion CD offer many options. For example, you can test yourself on just one exam objective, or you can test yourself on all the 70-536 certification exam content. You can set up the test so that it closely simulates the experience of taking a certification exam, or you can set it up in study mode so that you can look at the correct answers and explanations after you answer each question.

MORE INFO   Practice tests

For details about all the practice test options available, see the section "How to Use the Practice Tests" in the Introduction of this book.

Chapter 6

Graphics

You can use graphics to enhance the user interface of your applications, generate graphical charts and reports, and edit or create images. The .NET Framework includes tools that allow you to draw lines, shapes, patterns, and text. This chapter discusses how to create graphics and images using the classes in the *System.Drawing* namespace.

NOTE WPF Graphics

.NET Framework versions 3.0 and later include Windows Presentation Foundation (WPF), which provides robust graphics capabilities beyond those provided by the *System.Drawing* namespace. However, the 70-536 certification exam covers only the *System.Drawing* namespace. Therefore, for the purpose of this exam, you should disregard the WPF graphics capabilities.

Exam objectives in this chapter:

- Enhance the user interface of a .NET Framework application by using the *Sysem.Drawing* namespace.

- Enhance the user interface of a .NET Framework application by using brushes, pens, colors, and fonts.

- Enhance the user interface of a .NET Framework application by using graphics, images, bitmaps, and icons.

- Enhance the user interface of a .NET Framework application by using shapes and sizes.

Lessons in this chapter:

Before You Begin

To complete the lessons in this chapter, you should be familiar with Microsoft Visual Basic or C# and be comfortable with the following tasks:

- Creating a Windows Forms or WPF application in Microsoft Visual Studio using Visual Basic or C#
- Adding namespaces and system class library references to a project
- Writing to files and streams

Lesson 1: Drawing Graphics

You can use the .NET Framework to enhance the user interface by drawing lines, circles, and other shapes. With just a couple of lines of code, you can display these graphics on a form or other Windows Forms control.

After this lesson, you will be able to:

- Describe the members of the *System.Drawing* namespace
- Control the location, size, and color of controls
- Draw lines, empty shapes, and solid shapes
- Customize pens and brushes to enhance graphics

Estimated lesson time: 60 minutes

The *System.Drawing* Namespace

The .NET Framework includes the *System.Drawing* namespace, which enables you to create graphics from scratch or modify existing images. With the *System.Drawing* namespace, you can do the following:

- Add circles, lines, and other shapes to the user interface dynamically.
- Create charts from scratch.
- Edit and resize pictures.
- Change the compression ratios of pictures saved to disk.
- Crop or zoom pictures.
- Add copyright logos or text to pictures.

This lesson focuses on drawing graphics. Lesson 2 covers working with images, and Lesson 3 describes how to format text.

Table 6-1 lists the most important classes in the *System.Drawing* namespace, which you can use to build objects used for creating and editing images.

Of these classes, you use *Graphics* the most because it provides methods for drawing to the display device. The *Pen* class is used to draw lines and curves, while classes derived from the abstract class *Brush* are used to fill the interiors of shapes. In addition, you should be familiar with the *PictureBox* class (in the *System.Windows.Forms* namespace), which you can use in Windows Forms applications to display an image as part of the user interface. The *System.Drawing* namespace includes the structures shown in Table 6-2.

Table 6-1 *System.Drawing* **Classes**

Class	Description
Bitmap	Encapsulates a GDI+ (Graphical Device Interface) bitmap, which consists of the pixel data for a graphics image and its attributes. A *Bitmap* object is an object used to work with images defined by pixel data. This is the class you use when you need to load or save images.
Brush	Classes derived from this abstract base class, described in the section "How to Fill Shapes," later in this lesson, define objects used to fill the interiors of graphical shapes such as rectangles, ellipses, pies, polygons, and paths.
Brushes	Provides brushes for all the standard colors. This class cannot be inherited. Use this class to avoid creating an instance of a *Brush* class.
ColorConverter	Converts colors from one data type to another. Access this class through the *TypeDescriptor*.
ColorTranslator	Translates colors to and from GDI+ *Color* structures. This class cannot be inherited.
Font	Defines a particular format for text, including font face, size, and style attributes. This class cannot be inherited.
FontConverter	Converts *Font* objects from one data type to another. Access the *FontConverter* class through the *TypeDescriptor* object.
FontFamily	Defines a group of type faces having a similar basic design and certain variations in styles. This class cannot be inherited.
Graphics	Encapsulates a GDI+ drawing surface. This class cannot be inherited. You use this class anytime you need to draw lines, draw shapes, or add graphical text to a control or image.
Icon	Represents a Microsoft Windows icon, which is a small bitmap image used to represent an object. Icons can be thought of as transparent bitmaps, although their size is determined by the system.

Table 6-1 *System.Drawing* Classes

Class	Description
IconConverter	Converts an *Icon* object from one data type to another. Access this class through the *TypeDescriptor* object.
Image	An abstract base class that provides functionality for the *Bitmap*- and *Metafile*-descended classes.
ImageAnimator	Animates an image that has time-based frames.
ImageConverter	Converts *Image* objects from one data type to another. Access this class through the *TypeDescriptor* object.
ImageFormat-Converter	Converts colors from one data type to another. Access this class through the *TypeDescriptor* object.
Pen	Defines an object used to draw lines, curves, and arrows. This class cannot be inherited.
Pens	Provides pens for all the standard colors. This class cannot be inherited. Use this class to avoid creating an instance of a *Pen* class.
PointConverter	Converts a *Point* object from one data type to another. Access this class through the *TypeDescriptor* object.
Rectangle-Converter	Converts rectangles from one data type to another. Access this class through the *TypeDescriptor* object.
Region	Describes the interior of a graphics shape composed of rectangles and paths. This class cannot be inherited.
SizeConverter	The *SizeConverter* class is used to convert from one data type to another. Access this class through the *TypeDescriptor* object.
SolidBrush	Defines a brush of a single color. Brushes are used to fill graphics shapes, such as rectangles, ellipses, pies, polygons, and paths. This class cannot be inherited.
StringFormat	Encapsulates text layout information (such as alignment and line spacing), display manipulations (such as ellipsis insertion and national digit substitution), and *OpenType* features. This class cannot be inherited.

Table 6-1   *System.Drawing* Classes

Class	Description
SystemBrushes	Each property of the *SystemBrushes* class is a *SolidBrush* object that is the color of a Windows display element.
SystemColors	Each property of the *SystemColors* class is a *Color* structure that is the color of a Windows display element.
SystemFonts	Specifies the fonts used to display text in Windows display elements.
SystemIcons	Each property of the *SystemIcons* class is an *Icon* object for Windows systemwide icons. This class cannot be inherited.
SystemPens	Each property of the *SystemPens* class is a *Pen* object that is the color of a Windows display element and that has a width of 1.
TextureBrush	Each property of the *TextureBrush* class is a *Brush* object that uses an image to fill the interior of a shape. This class cannot be inherited.
ToolboxBitmap-Attribute	You can apply a *ToolboxBitmapAttribute* to a control so that containers, such as the Form Designer in Visual Studio, can retrieve an icon that represents the control. The bitmap for the icon can be in a file by itself or embedded in the assembly that contains the control.
	The size of the bitmap that you embed in the control's assembly (or store in a separate file) should be 16 by 16. The *GetImage* method of a *ToolboxBitmapAttribute* object can return the small 16-by-16 image or a large 32-by-32 image that it creates by scaling the small image.

Table 6-2   *System.Drawing* Structures

Structure	Description
CharacterRange	Specifies a range of character positions within a string.
Color	Represents a color.
Point	Represents an ordered pair of integer *x* and *y* coordinates that defines a point in a two-dimensional plane.

Table 6-2 *System.Drawing* **Structures**

Structure	Description
PointF	Represents an ordered pair of floating-point *x* and *y* coordinates that defines a point in a two-dimensional plane.
Rectangle	Stores a set of four integers that represent the location and size of a rectangle. For more advanced region functions, use a *Region* object.
RectangleF	Stores a set of four floating-point numbers that represent the location and size of a rectangle. For more advanced region functions, use a *Region* object.
Size	Stores an ordered pair of integers, typically the width and height of a rectangle.
SizeF	Stores an ordered pair of floating-point numbers, typically the width and height of a rectangle.

The most important of these structures—the structures you use most often—are *Color*, *Point*, *Rectangle*, and *Size*.

How to Specify the Location and Size of Controls

One of the simplest and most common uses for the *System.Drawing* namespace is specifying the location of controls in a Windows Forms application. This process can be useful to create forms that dynamically adjust based on user input.

To specify a control's location, create a new *Point* structure by specifying the coordinates relative to the upper-left corner of the form, and use the *Point* to set the control's *Location* property. The related *PointF* structure accepts coordinates as floating points, rather than integers, but *PointF* cannot be used to specify the location of graphical user interface (GUI) controls. For example, to move a button to the upper-left corner of a form, exactly 10 pixels from the top and left sides, you would use the following code:

```
' VB
button1.Location = New Point(10, 10)
```

```
// C#
button1.Location = new Point(10, 10);
```

NOTE   Graphics Require a Windows Forms Application

Most of this book relies on Console applications for samples. However, this chapter uses Windows Forms applications to display graphics easily.

As an alternative to using *Point*, you could perform the same function using the *Left* and *Top* or *Right* and *Bottom* properties of a control. However, this requires two lines of code, as the following example illustrates:

```
' VB
button1.Left = 10
button1.Top = 10
```

```
// C#
button1.Left = 10;
button1.Top = 10;
```

You can specify the size of a control just as simply as you specify the location. The following code demonstrates how to specify the size using the *Size* class:

```
' VB
button1.Size = New Size(30, 30)
```

```
// C#
button1.Size = new Size(30, 30);
```

How to Specify the Color of Controls

You can specify a control's color using the *Color* structure. The simplest way to specify a color is to use one of the predefined properties located within *System.Drawing.Color*, as the following example demonstrates:

```
' VB
Button1.ForeColor = Color.Red
Button1.BackColor = Color.Blue
```

```
// C#
button1.ForeColor = Color.Red;
button1.BackColor = Color.Blue;
```

If you need to specify a custom color, use the static *Color.FromArgb* method. The method has several overloads, so you can specify the color by using a single byte, by specifying the red, green, and blue levels individually, or by using other information. The following example illustrates how to specify color by providing three integers, for red, green, and blue:

```
' VB
Button1.ForeColor = Color.FromArgb(10, 200, 200)
Button1.BackColor = Color.FromArgb(200, 5, 5)

// C#
button1.ForeColor = Color.FromArgb(10, 200, 200);
button1.BackColor = Color.FromArgb(200, 5, 5);
```

How to Draw Lines and Shapes

To draw on a form or control, follow these high-level steps:

1. Create a *Graphics* object by calling the *System.Windows.Forms.Control.Create-Graphics* method.

2. Create a *Pen* object.

3. Call a member of the *Graphics* class to draw on the form or control using the *Pen*.

Drawing begins with the *System.Drawing.Graphics* class. To create an instance of this class, you typically call a control's *CreateGraphics* method. Alternatively, as discussed in Lesson 2, you can create a *Graphics* object based on an *Image* object if you want to be able to save the picture as a file. Once you create the *Graphics* object, you can call many methods to perform the drawing, including the following:

- **Clear**   Clears the entire drawing surface and fills it with a specified color.

- **DrawEllipse**   Draws an ellipse or circle defined by a bounding rectangle specified by a pair of coordinates, a height, and a width. The ellipse touches the edges of the bounding rectangle.

- **DrawIcon** and **DrawIconUnstretched**   Draws the image represented by the specified icon at the specified coordinates, with or without scaling the icon.

- **DrawImage, DrawImageUnscaled,** and **DrawImageUnscaledAndClipped**   Draws the specified *Image* object at the specified location, with or without scaling or cropping the image.

- **DrawLine**   Draws a line connecting the two points specified by the coordinate pairs.

- **DrawLines**   Draws a series of line segments that connect an array of *Point* structures.

- **DrawPath**   Draws a series of connected lines and curves.

- **DrawPie** Draws a pie shape defined by an ellipse specified by a coordinate pair, a width, a height, and two radial lines. Note that the coordinates you supply with *DrawPie* specify the upper-left corner of an imaginary rectangle that would form the pie's boundaries; the coordinates do not specify the pie's center.

- **DrawPolygon** Draws a shape with three or more sides as defined by an array of *Point* structures.

- **DrawRectangle** Draws a rectangle or square specified by a coordinate pair, a width, and a height.

- **DrawRectangles** Draws a series of rectangles or squares specified by *Rectangle* structures.

- **DrawString** Draws the specified text string at the specified location with the specified *Brush* and *Font* objects.

To use any of these methods, you must provide an instance of the *Pen* class. Typically, you specify the color and width of the *Pen* class in pixels with the constructor. For example, the following code draws a red line 7 pixels wide from the upper-left corner (1, 1) to a point near the middle of the form (100, 100), as shown in Figure 6-1. To run this code, create a Windows Forms application and add the code to a method that runs in response to the form's *Paint* event:

```
' VB
' Create a graphics object from the form
Dim g As Graphics = Me.CreateGraphics

' Create a pen object with which to draw
Dim p As Pen = New Pen(Color.Red, 7)

' Draw the line
g.DrawLine(p, 1, 1, 100, 100)

// C#
// Create a graphics object from the form
Graphics g = this.CreateGraphics();

// Create a pen object with which to draw
Pen p = new Pen(Color.Red, 7);

// Draw the line
g.DrawLine(p, 1, 1, 100, 100);
```

Figure 6-1   Use *Graphics.DrawLine* to create straight lines

Similarly, the following code draws a blue pie shape with a 60-degree angle, as shown in Figure 6-2:

```
' VB
Dim g As Graphics = Me.CreateGraphics
Dim p As Pen = New Pen(Color.Blue, 3)

g.DrawPie(p, 1, 1, 100, 100, -30, 60)
```

```
// C#
Graphics g = this.CreateGraphics();
Pen p = new Pen(Color.Blue, 3);

g.DrawPie(p, 1, 1, 100, 100, -30, 60);
```

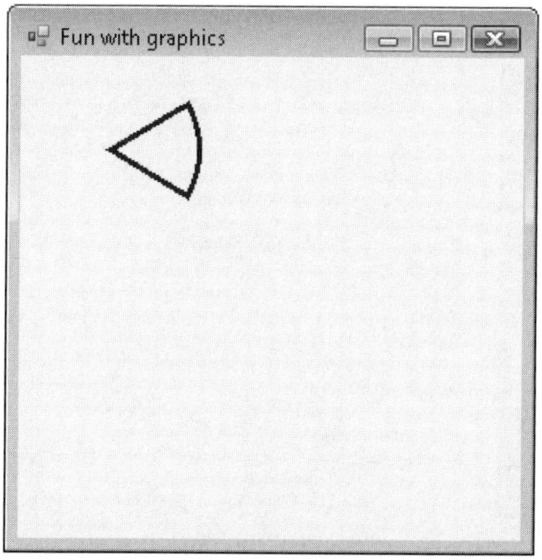

Figure 6-2   Use *Graphics.DrawPie* to create pie shapes

The *Graphics.DrawLines*, *Graphics.DrawPolygon*, and *Graphics.DrawRectangles* methods accept arrays as parameters to allow you to create more complex shapes. For example, the following code draws a purple, five-sided polygon, as shown in Figure 6-3:

```
' VB
Dim g As Graphics = Me.CreateGraphics
Dim p As Pen = New Pen(Color.MediumPurple, 2)

' Create an array of points
Dim points As Point() = New Point() {New Point(10, 10), _
    New Point(10, 100), _
    New Point(50, 65), _
    New Point(100, 100), _
    New Point(85, 40)}

' Draw a shape defined by the array of points
g.DrawPolygon(p, points)
```

```
// C#
Graphics g = this.CreateGraphics();
Pen p = new Pen(Color.MediumPurple, 2);

// Create an array of points
Point[] points = new Point[]
    {new Point(10, 10),
        new Point(10, 100),
        new Point(50, 65),
        new Point(100, 100),
        new Point(85, 40)};

// Draw a shape defined by the array of points
g.DrawPolygon(p, points);
```

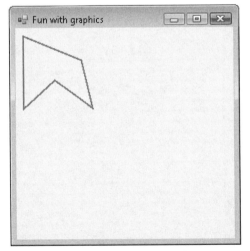

Figure 6-3   Use *Graphics.DrawPolygon* to create shapes made of multiple lines

NOTE Horizontal, Then Vertical

When you pass coordinates to any .NET Framework method, you pass the horizontal (*x*) coordinate first, and then the vertical (*y*) coordinate second. In a 100-by-100 pixel image, (0,0) is the upper-left corner, (100,0) is the upper-right corner, (0, 100) is the lower-left corner, and (100,100) is the lower-right corner.

How to Customize Pens

Besides controlling the color and size of a pen, which are specified in the *Pen* constructor, you can also control the pattern and endcaps. The endcaps are the ends of the line, and you can use them to create arrows and other special effects.

By default, pens draw solid lines. To draw a dotted line, create an instance of the *Pen* class, and then set the *Pen.DashStyle* property to one of these values: *DashStyle.Dash*, *DashStyle.DashDot*, *DashStyle.DashDotDot*, *DashStyle.Dot*, or *DashStyle.Solid*. The following code, which requires the *System.Drawing.Drawing2D* namespace, demonstrates each of these pen styles and creates the result shown in Figure 6-4:

```vb
' VB
Dim g As Graphics = Me.CreateGraphics
Dim p As Pen = New Pen(Color.Red, 7)

p.DashStyle = DashStyle.Dot
g.DrawLine(p, 50, 25, 400, 25)

p.DashStyle = DashStyle.Dash
g.DrawLine(p, 50, 50, 400, 50)

p.DashStyle = DashStyle.DashDot
g.DrawLine(p, 50, 75, 400, 75)

p.DashStyle = DashStyle.DashDotDot
g.DrawLine(p, 50, 100, 400, 100)

p.DashStyle = DashStyle.Solid
g.DrawLine(p, 50, 125, 400, 125)
```

```csharp
// C#
Graphics g = this.CreateGraphics();
Pen p = new Pen(Color.Red, 7);

p.DashStyle = DashStyle.Dot;
g.DrawLine(p, 50, 25, 400, 25);

p.DashStyle = DashStyle.Dash;
g.DrawLine(p, 50, 50, 400, 50);
```

```
p.DashStyle = DashStyle.DashDot;
g.DrawLine(p, 50, 75, 400, 75);

p.DashStyle = DashStyle.DashDotDot;
g.DrawLine(p, 50, 100, 400, 100);

p.DashStyle = DashStyle.Solid;
g.DrawLine(p, 50, 125, 400, 125);
```

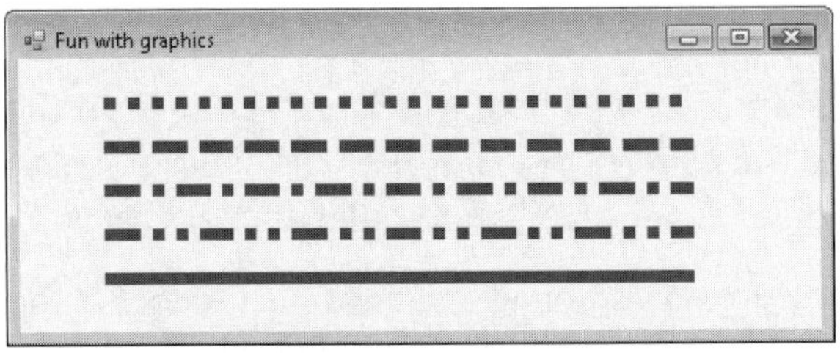

Figure 6-4 The *Pen* class provides several dash styles

You can also use the *Pen.DashOffset* and *Pen.DashPattern* properties to define a custom dash pattern.

To control the endcaps and create arrows or callouts, modify the *Pen.StartCap* and *Pen.EndCap* properties using the *LineCap* enumeration. The following code demonstrates most of the pen cap styles and creates the result shown in Figure 6-5:

```
' VB
Dim g As Graphics = Me.CreateGraphics
Dim p As Pen = New Pen(Color.Red, 10)

p.StartCap = LineCap.ArrowAnchor
p.EndCap = LineCap.DiamondAnchor
g.DrawLine(p, 50, 25, 400, 25)

p.StartCap = LineCap.SquareAnchor
p.EndCap = LineCap.Triangle
g.DrawLine(p, 50, 50, 400, 50)

p.StartCap = LineCap.Flat
p.EndCap = LineCap.Round
g.DrawLine(p, 50, 75, 400, 75)

p.StartCap = LineCap.RoundAnchor
p.EndCap = LineCap.Square
g.DrawLine(p, 50, 100, 400, 100)

// C#
Graphics g = this.CreateGraphics();
Pen p = new Pen(Color.Red, 10);
```

```
p.StartCap = LineCap.ArrowAnchor;
p.EndCap = LineCap.DiamondAnchor;
g.DrawLine(p, 50, 25, 400, 25);

p.StartCap = LineCap.SquareAnchor;
p.EndCap = LineCap.Triangle;
g.DrawLine(p, 50, 50, 400, 50);

p.StartCap = LineCap.Flat;
p.EndCap = LineCap.Round;
g.DrawLine(p, 50, 75, 400, 75);

p.StartCap = LineCap.RoundAnchor;
p.EndCap = LineCap.Square;
g.DrawLine(p, 50, 100, 400, 100);
```

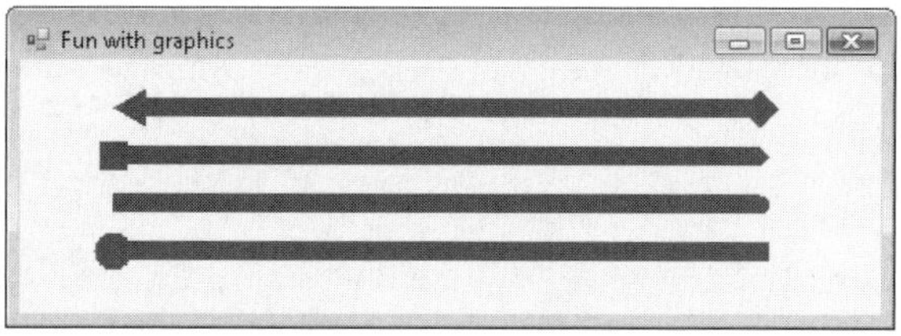

Figure 6-5   The *Pen* class provides options for startcaps and endcaps

How to Fill Shapes

For most of the *Draw* methods, the *Graphics* class also has *Fill* methods that draw a shape and fill in the contents. These methods work exactly like the *Draw* methods, except they require an instance of the *Brush* class instead of the *Pen* class. The *Brush* class is abstract, so you must instantiate one of the following child classes:

- *System.Drawing.Drawing2D.HatchBrush*   Defines a rectangular brush with a hatch style, a foreground color, and a background color

- *System.Drawing.Drawing2D.LinearGradientBrush*   Encapsulates a brush with a linear gradient that provides a visually appealing, professional-looking fill

- *System.Drawing.Drawing2D.PathGradientBrush*   Provides similar functionality to *LinearGradientBrush*; however, you can define a complex fill pattern that fades between multiple points

- *System.Drawing.SolidBrush*   Defines a brush of a single color

- *System.Drawing.TextureBrush*   Defines a brush made from an image that can be tiled across a shape, like a wallpaper design

For example, the following code draws a solid maroon, five-sided polygon, as shown in Figure 6-6:

```vb
' VB
Dim g As Graphics = Me.CreateGraphics
Dim b As Brush = New SolidBrush(Color.Maroon)
Dim points As Point() = New Point() {New Point(10, 10), _
    New Point(10, 100), _
    New Point(50, 65), _
    New Point(100, 100), _
    New Point(85, 40)}

g.FillPolygon(b, points)
```

```csharp
// C#
Graphics g = this.CreateGraphics();
Brush b = new SolidBrush(Color.Maroon);
Point[] points = new Point[]
    {new Point(10, 10),
        new Point(10, 100),
        new Point(50, 65),
        new Point(100, 100),
        new Point(85, 40)};

g.FillPolygon(b, points);
```

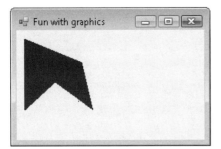

Figure 6-6 Use the *Brush* class with the various *Graphics.Fill* methods to draw solid objects

You can draw filled objects with an outline by first calling the *Graphics.Fill* method and then calling the *Graphics.Draw* method. For example, the following code draws a polygon with an outline and a linear gradient fill pattern, as shown in Figure 6-7:

```vb
' VB
Dim g As Graphics = Me.CreateGraphics
Dim p As Pen = New Pen(Color.Maroon, 2)
Dim b As Brush = New LinearGradientBrush(New Point(1, 1), New Point(100, 100), _
    Color.White, Color.Red)
Dim points As Point() = New Point() {New Point(10, 10), _
    New Point(10, 100), _
    New Point(50, 65), _
    New Point(100, 100), _
    New Point(85, 40)}
```

```
g.FillPolygon(b, points)
g.DrawPolygon(p, points)

// C#
Graphics g = this.CreateGraphics();
Pen p = new Pen(Color.Maroon, 2);
Brush b = new LinearGradientBrush(new Point(1,1), new Point(100,100),
    Color.White, Color.Red);
Point[] points = new Point[]
    {new Point(10, 10),
        new Point(10, 100),
        new Point(50, 65),
        new Point(100, 100),
        new Point(85, 40)};

g.FillPolygon(b, points);
g.DrawPolygon(p, points);
```

Figure 6-7 Combine *Graphics.Fill* and *Graphics.Draw* methods to create solid objects with outlines

You can use the same techniques to draw on controls, such as buttons or the instances of the *PictureBox* class. If you need to fill an entire *Graphics* object with a single color, call the *Graphics.Clear* method.

Lab: Create a Method to Draw a Pie Chart

In this lab, you will create a method to draw a pie chart, and then improve that method to make the pie chart more visually appealing. If you encounter a problem completing an exercise, the completed projects are available on the companion CD in the Code folder.

Exercise 1: Draw a Pie Chart

In this exercise, you will write a method that draws a pie chart given an array of data and a *Size* structure. At this point, simple black lines will suffice.

1. Navigate to the \<*InstallHome*>\Chapter06\Lesson1\Exercise1\Partial folder and open either the C# version or the Visual Basic .NET version of the solution file.

2. Examine the form. The form has a single *PictureBox* named *chart* that is bound to all four sides of the form. Notice that the *Paint* event calls the *Draw* method.

3. Examine the *Draw* method that takes no parameters. This method includes sample data that will be passed as parameters to the *drawPieChart* method you will complete. Notice that the *drawPieChart* method returns an *Image* object, which is used to define the chart *PictureBox*.

4. Examine the *PieChartElement* class. This simple class contains information to describe a single section of your pie chart.

5. Examine the *drawPieChart* method in the Form1 file. It receives two parameters: an *ArrayList* containing only *PieChartElement* objects, and a *Size* structure.

6. Complete the *drawPieChart* method. First, define a *Bitmap* object to be returned, create a *Graphics* object from the *Bitmap* object, and then return the *Bitmap* object. For example, the following code would work:

```
' VB
Dim bm As Bitmap = New Bitmap(s.Width, s.Height)
Dim g As Graphics = Graphics.FromImage(bm)

' TODO: Draw pie chart in g
Return bm

// C#
Bitmap bm = new Bitmap(s.Width, s.Height);
Graphics g = Graphics.FromImage(bm);

// TODO: Draw pie chart in g
return bm;
```

7. At this point, the project compiles, but if you run the application no pie chart is drawn. Before you can create a pie chart from the *PieChartElement* objects in the *ArrayList*, you must determine how many degrees each element uses. To do that, in the *drawPieChart* method you must calculate the total of the *value* properties of all the *PieChartElement* objects. For example, the following code would work:

```
' VB
' Calculate total value of all rows
Dim total As Single = 0

For Each e As PieChartElement In elements
    If e.value < 0 Then
        Throw New ArgumentException("All elements must have positive values")
    End If
    total += e.value
Next

// C#
// Calculate total value of all rows
float total = 0;
```

```
foreach (PieChartElement e in elements)
{
   if (e.value < 0)
   {
      throw new ArgumentException("All elements must have positive values");
   }
   total += e.value;
}
```

8. Now you should define the rectangle that the pie chart will consume based on the *Size* structure passed to the *drawPieChart* method as a parameter. The following code would work, and it provides a sufficient buffer on all sides of the image:

```
' VB
' Define the rectangle that the pie chart will use
Dim rect As Rectangle = New Rectangle(1, 1, s.Width - 2, s.Height - 2)
```

```
// C#
// Define the rectangle that the pie chart will use
Rectangle rect = new Rectangle(1, 1, s.Width - 2, s.Height - 2);
```

9. Next, define a *Pen* object with which to draw the pie chart. This can be a simple, black, one-pixel pen, defined with the following code:

```
' VB
Dim p As Pen = New Pen(Color.Black, 1)
```

```
// C#
Pen p = new Pen(Color.Black, 1);
```

10. Finally, create a *foreach* loop that calculates the degrees for each pie chart section, and draws the pie chart sections. There are many ways to do this, such as the following code:

```
' VB
' Draw the first section at 0 degrees
Dim startAngle As Single = 0

' Draw each of the pie shapes
For Each e As PieChartElement In elements
    ' Calculate the degrees that this section will consume
    ' based on the percentage of the total
    Dim sweepAngle As Single = (e.value / total) * 360

    ' Draw the pie shape
    g.DrawPie(p, rect, startAngle, sweepAngle)

    ' Calculate the angle for the next pie shape by adding
    ' the current shape's degrees to the previous total.
    startAngle += sweepAngle
Next
```

```
// C#
// Draw the first section at 0 degrees
float startAngle = 0;

// Draw each of the pie shapes
foreach (PieChartElement e in elements)
{
    // Calculate the degrees that this section will consume
    // based on the percentage of the total
    float sweepAngle = (e.value / total) * 360;

    // Draw the pie shape
    g.DrawPie(p, rect, startAngle, sweepAngle);

    // Calculate the angle for the next pie shape by adding
    // the current shape's degrees to the previous total.
    startAngle += sweepAngle;
}
```

11. Build the application and fix any errors; then run the application. Resize the form, and notice that the pie chart is automatically resized; the *Paint* event calls the *Draw* method when you resize the form.

Exercise 2: Improve the Appearance of the Pie Chart

In this exercise, you will improve the project presented in Exercise 1 to make the pie chart more visually appealing. Specifically, you fill in each section with a different color and enable anti-aliasing to smooth the lines.

1. Navigate to the \<*InstallHome*>\Chapter06\Lesson1\Exercise2\Partial folder, and open either the C# version or the Visual Basic version of the PieChart project. Alternatively, you can continue working from the project you created in Exercise 1.

2. First, at the beginning of the *drawPieChart* method, create an array containing the colors you want to use in your pie chart. You will assign the colors sequentially, so do not place similar colors after each other. For the sake of simplicity, throw an exception if the pie chart has more elements than you have colors in your array. For example:

```
' VB
Dim colors As Color() = {Color.Red, Color.Orange, Color.Yellow, Color.Green, _
    Color.Blue, Color.Indigo, Color.Violet, Color.DarkRed, Color.DarkOrange, _
    Color.DarkSalmon, Color.DarkGreen, Color.DarkBlue, Color.Lavender, _
    Color.LightBlue, Color.Coral}

If elements.Count > colors.Length Then
    Throw New ArgumentException("Pie chart must have " + _
        colors.Length.ToString() + " or fewer elements")
End If
```

```csharp
// C#
Color[] colors = { Color.Red, Color.Orange, Color.Yellow, Color.Green,
    Color.Blue, Color.Indigo, Color.Violet, Color.DarkRed,
    Color.DarkOrange, Color.DarkSalmon, Color.DarkGreen,
    Color.DarkBlue, Color.Lavender, Color.LightBlue, Color.Coral };

if (elements.Count > colors.Length)
{
    throw new ArgumentException("Pie chart must have " +
        colors.Length.ToString() + " or fewer elements");
}
```

NOTE Keeping It Simple

For the sake of keeping the exercise focused, some aspects of this project are not exactly as you would design them in the real world. For example, you typically would want to give the calling application the option of specifying colors for different sections, which could be done by adding a *Color* object to the *PieChartElement* class. In addition, elements of robust programming such as catching exceptions, validating input, and asserting are omitted from the examples.

---

3. You need to track the color in use. Before the *foreach* loop, initialize an integer to zero to act as a counter:

```vbnet
' VB
Dim colorNum As Integer = 0
```

```csharp
// C#
int colorNum = 0;
```

4. Within the *foreach* loop that calls *DrawPie*, add two lines: one to create a new *Brush* object, and a second to call the *Graphics.FillPie* method. Call *Graphics.FillPie* immediately before you call *Graphics.DrawPie* so that the outline is drawn over the filled pie. The following code uses the *LinearGradientBrush* class, which requires adding the *System.Drawing.Drawing2D* namespace to the project. Changes are shown in bold:

```vbnet
' VB
' Draw each of the pie shapes
For Each e As PieChartElement In elements
    ' Create a brush with a nice gradient
    Dim b As Brush = New LinearGradientBrush( _
        rect, colors(colorNum), Color.White, 45)
    colorNum += 1

    ' Calculate the degrees that this section will consume
    ' based on the percentage of the total
    Dim sweepAngle As Single = (e.value / total) * 360
```

```
' Draw the filled-in pie shapes
g.FillPie(b, rect, startAngle, sweepAngle)

' Draw the pie shape
g.DrawPie(p, rect, startAngle, sweepAngle)

' Calculate the angle for the next pie shape by adding
' the current shape's degrees to the previous total.
startAngle += sweepAngle
Next

// C#
// Draw each of the pie shapes
foreach (PieChartElement e in elements)
{
    // Create a brush with a nice gradient
    Brush b = new LinearGradientBrush(
        rect, colors[colorNum++], Color.White, (float)45);

    // Calculate the degrees that this section will consume
    // based on the percentage of the total
    float sweepAngle = (e.value / total) * 360;

    // Draw the filled-in pie shapes
    g.FillPie(b, rect, startAngle, sweepAngle);

    // Draw the pie shape outlines
    g.DrawPie(p, rect, startAngle, sweepAngle);

    // Calculate the angle for the next pie shape by adding
    // the current shape's degrees to the previous total.
    startAngle += sweepAngle;
}
```

5. Now, run the application. Experiment with different brush types to find the one that is most appealing. Notice that the lines appear a bit jagged; you can make the lines appear smoother by setting *Graphics.SmoothingMode*, as the following line demonstrates:

```
' VB
g.SmoothingMode = SmoothingMode.HighQuality

// C#
g.SmoothingMode = SmoothingMode.HighQuality;
```

Lesson Summary

- The *System.Drawing* namespace provides tools for drawing graphics and editing existing images. The most useful classes are *Graphics*, *Image*, and *Bitmap*.

- Use the *Point* and *Size* classes to specify the location and size of controls.

- The *System.Drawing.Color* structure provides predefined properties for common colors.

- To draw lines and shapes, create an instance of the *Graphics* class, create a *Pen* object, and then call one of the *Graphics* member methods to draw a line or a shape using the *Pen* instance.

- Pens can be customized by adding endcaps or changing the line pattern to various combinations of dots and dashes.

- To draw solid shapes, create an instance of the *Graphics* class, create a *Brush* object, and then call one of the *Graphics* member methods to draw the shape using the *Brush* instance.

Lesson Review

You can use the following questions to test your knowledge of the information in Lesson 1, "Drawing Graphics." The questions are also available on the companion CD if you prefer to review them in electronic form.

NOTE Answers

Answers to these questions and explanations of why each answer choice is right or wrong are located in the "Answers" section at the end of the book.

---

1. Which of the following methods is the best to use to draw a square with a solid color?

   A. *Graphics.DrawLines*

   B. *Graphics.DrawRectangle*

   C. *Graphics.DrawPolygon*

   D. *Graphics.DrawEllipse*

   E. *Graphics.FillRectangle*

   F. *Graphics.FillPolygon*

   G. *Graphics.FillEllipse*

2. Which of the following methods is the best to use to draw an empty triangle?

   A. *Graphics.DrawLines*

   B. *Graphics.DrawRectangle*

   C. *Graphics.DrawPolygon*

   D. *Graphics.DrawEllipse*

   E. *Graphics.FillRectangle*

   F. *Graphics.FillPolygon*

   G. *Graphics.FillEllipse*

3. Which of the following classes is required to draw an empty circle? (Choose all that apply.)

   A. *System.Drawing.Graphics*

   B. *System.Drawing.Pen*

   C. *System.Drawing.Brush*

   D. *System.Drawing.Bitmap*

4. Which of the following brush classes is the best to use to create a solid rectangle that is red at the top and gradually fades to white towards the bottom?

   A. *System.Drawing.Drawing2D.HatchBrush*

   B. *System.Drawing.Drawing2D.LinearGradientBrush*

   C. *System.Drawing.Drawing2D.PathGradientBrush*

   D. *System.Drawing.SolidBrush*

   E. *System.Drawing.TextureBrush*

5. What type of line would the following code sample draw?

```
' VB
Dim g As Graphics = Me.CreateGraphics
Dim p As Pen = New Pen(Color.Red, 10)

p.StartCap = LineCap.Flat
p.EndCap = LineCap.ArrowAnchor
g.DrawLine(p, 50, 50, 400, 50)

// C#
Graphics g = this.CreateGraphics();
Pen p = new Pen(Color.Red, 10);

p.StartCap = LineCap.Flat;
p.EndCap = LineCap.ArrowAnchor;
g.DrawLine(p, 50, 50, 400, 50);
```

   A. An arrow pointing up

   B. An arrow pointing down

   C. An arrow pointing left

   D. An arrow pointing right

Lesson 2: Working with Images

Often developers need to display, create, or modify images. The .NET Framework provides tools to work with a variety of image formats, enabling you to perform many common image-editing tasks.

After this lesson, you will be able to:

- Describe the purpose of the *Image* and *Bitmap* classes
- Display pictures in forms or *PictureBox* objects
- Create a new picture, add lines and shapes to the picture, and save it as a file

Estimated lesson time: 30 minutes

The *Image* and *Bitmap* Classes

The *System.Drawing.Image* abstract class gives you the ability to create, load, modify, and save images such as .bmp files, .jpg files, and .tif files. Some useful things you can do with the *Image* class include the following:

- Create a drawing or chart and save the results as an image file.

- Use text (as described in Lesson 3 later in this chapter) to add copyright information or a watermark to a picture.

- Resize JPEG images so that they consume less space and can be downloaded faster.

The *Image* class is abstract, but you can create instances of the class using the *Image.FromFile* method (which accepts a path to an image file as a parameter) and the *Image.FromStream* method (which accepts a *System.IO.Stream* object as a parameter). You can also use two classes that inherit *Image*: *System.Drawing.Bitmap* for still images, and *System.Drawing.Imaging.Metafile* for animated images.

Bitmap is the most commonly used class for working with new or existing images. The different constructors allow you to create a *Bitmap* from an existing *Image*, file, or stream, or to create a blank bitmap of a specified height and width. *Bitmap* contains two particularly useful methods that *Image* lacks:

- **GetPixel**   Returns a *Color* object describing a particular pixel in the image. A pixel is a single colored dot in the image that consists of a red, green, and blue component.

- **SetPixel**   Sets a pixel to a specified color.

However, more complex image editing requires you to create a *Graphics* object by calling *Graphics.FromImage*.

How to Display Pictures

To display in a form an image that is saved to the disk, load it with *Image.FromFile* and create a *PictureBox* control, and then use the *Image* to define *PictureBox.Background-Image*. The following sample code (which requires a form with an instance of *PictureBox* named *pictureBox1*) demonstrates this process. Change the filename to any valid image file:

```
' VB
Dim I As Image = Image.FromFile("picture.bmp")
PictureBox1.BackgroundImage = I
```

```
// C#
Image i = Image.FromFile(@"picture.bmp");
pictureBox1.BackgroundImage = i;
```

Similarly, the following code accomplishes the same thing using the *Bitmap* class:

```
' VB
Dim B As Bitmap = New Bitmap("picture.bmp")
PictureBox1.BackgroundImage = B
```

```
// C#
Bitmap b = new Bitmap(@"picture.bmp");
pictureBox1.BackgroundImage = b;
```

Alternatively, you can display an image as the background for a form or control by using the *Graphics.DrawImage* method. This method has 30 overloads, so you have a wide variety of options for how you specify the image location and size. The following code uses this method to set an image as the background for a form, no matter what the dimensions of the form are:

```
' VB
Dim Bm As Bitmap = New Bitmap("picture.jpg")
Dim G As Graphics = Me.CreateGraphics
G.DrawImage(Bm, 1, 1, Me.Width, Me.Height)
```

```
// C#
Bitmap bm = new Bitmap(@"picture.jpg");
Graphics g = this.CreateGraphics();
g.DrawImage(bm, 1, 1, this.Width, this.Height);
```

How to Create and Save Pictures

To create a new, blank picture, create an instance of the *Bitmap* class with one of the constructors that does not require an existing image. You can then edit it using the *Bitmap.SetPixel* method, or you can call *Graphics.FromImage* and edit the image using the *Graphics* drawing methods.

To save a picture, call *Bitmap.Save*. This method has several easy-to-understand over-loads. Two of the overloads accept a parameter of type *System.Drawing.Imaging.Image-Format*, for which you should provide one of the following properties to describe the file type: *Bmp, Emf, Exif, Gif, Icon, Jpeg, MemoryBmp, Png, Tiff,* or *Wmf. Jpeg* is the most common format for photographs, and *Gif* is the most common format for charts, screen shots, and drawings.

For example, the following code creates a blank 600-by-600 *Bitmap*, creates a *Graphics* object based on the *Bitmap*, uses the *Graphics.FillPolygon* and *Graphics.DrawPolygon* methods to draw a shape in the *Bitmap*, and then saves it to a file named Bm.jpg in the current directory. This code can run as a Console application (because it doesn't display any images), and it requires the *System.Drawing.Drawing2D* and *System.Drawing.Imaging* namespaces:

```vb
' VB
Dim Bm As Bitmap = New Bitmap(600, 600)
Dim G As Graphics = Graphics.FromImage(bm)

Dim B As Brush = New LinearGradientBrush( _
    New Point(1, 1), New Point (600, 600), _
    Color.White, Color.Red)
Dim Points As Point() = New Point() {New Point(10, 10), _
    New Point(77, 500), _
    New Point(590, 100), _
    New Point(250, 590), _
    New Point(300, 410)}

G.FillPolygon(B, Points)
Bm.Save("bm.jpg", ImageFormat.Jpeg)
```

```csharp
// C#
Bitmap bm = new Bitmap(600, 600);
Graphics g = Graphics.FromImage(bm);

Brush b = new LinearGradientBrush(
    new Point(1, 1), new Point(600, 600),
    Color.White, Color.Red);
Point[] points = new Point[]
    {new Point(10, 10),
        new Point(77, 500),
        new Point(590, 100),
        new Point(250, 590),
        new Point(300, 410)};

g.FillPolygon(b, points);
bm.Save("bm.jpg", ImageFormat.Jpeg);
```

To edit an existing image, simply change the *Bitmap* constructor in the previous example to load a picture.

How to Use Icons

Icons are transparent bitmaps of specific sizes that are used by Windows to convey status. The .NET Framework provides standard 40-by-40 system icons as properties of the *SystemIcons* class, including icons for exclamation, information, and question symbols.

The simplest way to add an icon to a form or image is to call the *Graphics.DrawIcon* or *Graphics.DrawIconUnstretched* methods. The following code produces the result shown in Figure 6-8:

```
' VB
Dim G As Graphics = Me.CreateGraphics
G.DrawIcon(SystemIcons.Question, 40, 40)
```

```
// C#
Graphics g = this.CreateGraphics();
g.DrawIcon(SystemIcons.Question, 40, 40);
```

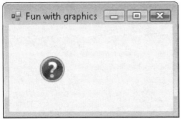

Figure 6-8 *SystemIcons* provides access to common icons that you can use to convey status

You can also edit system icons or load saved icons using the constructors built into the *Icon* class. Once you create an instance of the *Icon* class, call *Icon.ToBitmap* to create a *Bitmap* object that can be edited.

Lab: Save a Pie Chart as a Picture

In this lab, you write code to save a *Bitmap* object to the disk as a JPEG file. If you encounter a problem completing an exercise, the completed projects are available along with the sample files.

Exercise: Save a Pie Chart as a Picture

In this exercise, you add code to save a pie chart picture to the disk as a file.

1. Navigate to the \<*InstallHome*>\Chapter06\Lesson2\Exercise1\Partial folder and open either the C# version or the Visual Basic .NET version of the solution file.

2. Add code to the *saveButton_Click* method to prompt the user for a filename, and then write the pie chart to disk. For simplicity, always save the picture as a JPEG file. The following code, which requires the *System.Drawing.Imaging* namespace, is an example of how to do this:

```
' VB
' Display the Save dialog
Dim saveDialog As SaveFileDialog = New SaveFileDialog
saveDialog.DefaultExt = ".jpg"
saveDialog.Filter = "JPEG files (*.jpg)|*.jpg;*.jpeg|All files (*.*)|*.*"

If Not (saveDialog.ShowDialog = DialogResult.Cancel) Then
    ' Save the image to the specified file in JPEG format
    chart.Image.Save(saveDialog.FileName, ImageFormat.Jpeg)
End If

// C#
// Display the Save dialog
SaveFileDialog saveDialog = new SaveFileDialog();
saveDialog.DefaultExt = ".jpg";
saveDialog.Filter = "JPEG files (*.jpg)|*.jpg;*.jpeg|All files (*.*)|*.*";

if (saveDialog.ShowDialog() != DialogResult.Cancel)
{
    // Save the image to the specified file in JPEG format
    chart.Image.Save(saveDialog.FileName, ImageFormat.Jpeg);
}
```

3. Run and test the application to verify that it works properly and that you can view the saved file.

Lesson Summary

- The *Image* and *Bitmap* classes enable you to edit or create pictures and save the results as a file.

- To display a picture in a Windows Forms window, load the picture into an instance of the *Image* or *Bitmap* class, create an instance of the *PictureBox* control, and then use the *Image* or *Bitmap* object to define the *PictureBox.BackgroundImage* property.

- To create and save a picture, create a *Bitmap* object, edit it using a *Graphics* object, and then call the *Bitmap.Save* method.

- To display an icon, call the *Graphics.DrawIcon* or *Graphics.DrawIconUnstretched* methods using one of the properties of the *SystemIcons* class.

Lesson Review

You can use the following questions to test your knowledge of the information in Lesson 2, "Working with Images." The questions are also available on the companion CD if you prefer to review them in electronic form.

NOTE Answers

Answers to these questions and explanations of why each answer choice is right or wrong are located in the "Answers" section at the end of the book.

---

1. Which of the following classes could you use to display a JPEG image from an existing file in a form? (Choose all that apply.)

    A. *System.Drawing.Image*

    B. *System.Drawing.Bitmap*

    C. *System.Drawing.Imaging.Metafile*

    D. *System.Windows.Forms.PictureBox*

2. How can you draw a black border around a JPEG image that you have saved to disk and then save the updated image back to the disk?

    A. Create a *Graphics* object by loading the JPEG image from the disk. Draw the border by calling *Graphics.DrawRectangle*. Finally, save the updated image by calling *Graphics.Save*.

    B. Create a *Bitmap* object by loading the JPEG image from the disk. Draw the border by calling *Bitmap.DrawRectangle*. Finally, save the updated image by calling *Bitmap.Save*.

    C. Create a *Bitmap* object by loading the JPEG image from the disk. Create a *Graphics* object by calling *Graphics.FromImage*. Draw the border by calling *Graphics.DrawRectangle*. Finally, save the updated image by calling *Bitmap.Save*.

    D. Create a *Bitmap* object by loading the JPEG image from the disk. Create a *Graphics* object by calling *Bitmap.CreateGraphics*. Draw the border by calling *Graphics.DrawRectangle*. Finally, save the updated image by calling *Bitmap.Save*.

3. Which format is the best choice to use if you want to save a photograph that could be opened by a wide variety of applications?

    A. *ImageFormat.Bmp*

    B. *ImageFormat.Gif*

    C. *ImageFormat.Jpeg*

    D. *ImageFormat.Png*

4. Which format is the best choice to use if you want to save a pie chart that could be opened by a wide variety of applications?

    A. *ImageFormat.Bmp*

    B. *ImageFormat.Gif*

    C. *ImageFormat.Jpeg*

    D. *ImageFormat.Png*

Lesson 3: Formatting Text

Developers often add text to images to label objects or create reports. This lesson describes how to add formatted text to images.

> **After this lesson, you will be able to:**
> - Describe the process of creating the objects required to add text to images
> - Create *Font* objects to meet your requirements for type, size, and style
> - Use *Graphics.DrawString* to annotate images with text
> - Control the formatting of text
>
> **Estimated lesson time: 30 minutes**

How to Add Text to Graphics

You can add text to images by creating an instance of the *Graphics* class, in the same way that you add solid objects. At a high level, you follow these steps:

1. Create a *Graphics* object, as discussed in Lessons 1 and 2 earlier in this chapter.
2. Create a *Font* object.
3. Optionally, create a *Brush* object if none of the standard *Brush* objects meet your needs.
4. Call *Graphics.DrawString* and specify the location for the text.

How to Create a *Font* Object

The *Font* class offers 13 different constructors. The simplest way to create a *Font* object is to pass the font family name (as a string), font size (as an integer or float), and font style (a *System.Drawing.FontStyle* enumeration value). For example, the following constructor creates an Arial 12-point bold font:

```
' VB
Dim F As Font = New Font("Arial", 12, FontStyle.Bold)
```

```
// C#
Font f = new Font("Arial", 12, FontStyle.Bold);
```

You can also create a new *Font* object using a *FontFamily*, as the following code shows:

```
' VB
Dim Ff As FontFamily = New FontFamily("Arial")
Dim F As Font = New Font(Ff, 12)
```

```
// C#
FontFamily ff = new FontFamily("Arial");
Font f = new Font(ff, 12);
```

If you need to read the font type from a string, you can use the *FontConverter* class. This is not the preferred method, however, because using a string to describe a font is less reliable. (It's less reliable because the compiler cannot detect errors or typos.) Therefore, you won't discover an error in the font name until a run-time *Argument-Exception* is thrown. The following example creates an Arial 12-point font:

```
' VB
Dim Converter As FontConverter = New FontConverter
Dim F As Font = CType(converter.ConvertFromString("Arial, 12pt"), Font)
```

```
// C#
FontConverter converter = new FontConverter();
Font f = (Font)converter.ConvertFromString("Arial, 12pt");
```

How to Write Text

After you create a *Font* object, you need to create a *Brush* object (as described in Lesson 1) to define how the text will be filled. Alternatively, you can simply provide a *System.Drawing.Brushes* property to avoid creating a *Brush* object. To finally add the text to the image, call *Graphics.DrawString*. The following code draws text on the current form and produces the result shown in Figure 6-9:

```
' VB
Dim G As Graphics = Me.CreateGraphics
Dim F As Font = New Font("Arial", 40, FontStyle.Bold)
G.DrawString("Hello, World!", F, Brushes.Blue, 10, 10)
```

```
// C#
Graphics g = this.CreateGraphics();
Font f = new Font("Arial", 40, FontStyle.Bold);
g.DrawString("Hello, World!", f, Brushes.Blue, 10, 10);
```

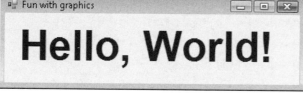

Figure 6-9   Call *Graphics.DrawString* to add text to a *Graphics* object

Of course, it's much easier to add text to a form using *Label* objects. However, *Graphics* *.DrawString* also enables you to add text to *Images* and *Bitmaps*. This is useful for adding visible copyright information to a picture, adding timestamps to images, and annotating charts.

> **Real World**
>
> *Tony Northrup*
>
> When I'm not coding, I'm taking pictures. I sell photos on the Web to cover the outrageous cost of my camera equipment. Unfortunately, while they have digital rights management (DRM) for music and video, nobody has really figured out DRM for pictures. So, until someone develops a good image DRM system, your best bet is to add obtrusive watermarks and visible copyright notifications to images published on the Web. This won't stop someone from copying your pictures and violating the copyright, but the copyright text does make the pictures more difficult to use.

How to Control the Formatting of Text

The .NET Framework gives you control over the alignment and direction of text using the *StringFormat* class. After creating and configuring a *StringFormat* object, you can provide it to the *Graphics.DrawString* method to control how text is formatted. The most important members of the *StringFormat* class are the following:

- **Alignment** Gets or sets horizontal text alignment. Possible options include:
  - ❏ **StringAlignment.Center** Horizontally centers text.
  - ❏ **StringAlignment.Near** Aligns text to the left.
  - ❏ **StringAlignment.Far** Aligns text to the right.
- **FormatFlags** Gets or sets a *StringFormatFlags* enumeration that contains formatting information. Possible options for *StringFormatFlags* include:
  - ❏ **DirectionRightToLeft** Text is displayed from right to left.
  - ❏ **DirectionVertical** Text is vertically aligned.
  - ❏ **DisplayFormatControl** Control characters, such as the left-to-right mark, are shown in the output with a representative glyph.
  - ❏ **FitBlackBox** Parts of characters are allowed to overhang the string's layout rectangle. By default, characters are repositioned to avoid any overhang.

❑ *LineLimit*   Only entire lines are laid out in the formatting rectangle. By default, layout continues until the end of the text or until no more lines are visible as a result of clipping, whichever comes first. Note that the default settings allow the last line to be partially obscured by a formatting rectangle that is not a whole multiple of the line height. To ensure that only whole lines are seen, specify this value and be careful to provide a formatting rectangle at least as tall as the height of one line.

❑ *MeasureTrailingSpaces*   Includes the trailing space at the end of each line. By default, the boundary rectangle returned by the *MeasureString* method excludes the space at the end of each line. Set this flag to include that space in measurement.

❑ *NoClip*   Overhanging parts of glyphs, and unwrapped text reaching outside the formatting rectangle are allowed to show. By default, all text and glyph parts reaching outside the formatting rectangle are clipped.

❑ *NoFontFallback*   Fallback to alternate fonts for characters not supported in the requested font is disabled. Any missing characters are displayed with the fonts-missing glyph, usually an open square.

❑ *NoWrap*   Text wrapping between lines when formatting within a rectangle is disabled. This flag is implied when a point is passed instead of a rectangle, or when the specified rectangle has a zero line length.

■ *LineAlignment*   Gets or sets vertical text alignment. Possible options include:

❑ *StringAlignment.Center*   Vertically centers text.

❑ *StringAlignment.Near*   Aligns text to the top.

❑ *StringAlignment.Far*   Aligns text to the bottom.

■ *Traimming*   Gets or sets the *StringTrimming* enumeration for this *StringFormat* object. Possible options include:

❑ *Character*   Specifies that the text is trimmed to the nearest character.

❑ *EllipsisCharacter*   Specifies that the text is trimmed to the nearest character, and an ellipsis is inserted at the end of a trimmed line.

❑ *EllipsisPath*   The center is removed from trimmed lines and replaced by an ellipsis. The algorithm keeps as much of the last slash-delimited segment of the line as possible.

❑ *EllipsisWord*   Specifies that text is trimmed to the nearest word, and an ellipsis is inserted at the end of a trimmed line.

❑ *None*   Specifies no trimming.

❑ *Word*   Specifies that text is trimmed to the nearest word.

The following code demonstrates the use of the *StringFormat* class and produces the output shown in Figure 6-10:

```vb
' VB
Dim G As Graphics = Me.CreateGraphics

' Construct a new Rectangle
Dim R As Rectangle = New Rectangle(New Point(40, 40), New Size(80, 80))

' Construct 2 new StringFormat objects
Dim F1 As StringFormat = New StringFormat(StringFormatFlags.NoClip)
Dim F2 As StringFormat = New StringFormat(f1)

' Set the LineAlignment and Alignment properties for
' both StringFormat objects to different values
F1.LineAlignment = StringAlignment.Near
f1.Alignment = StringAlignment.Center
f2.LineAlignment = StringAlignment.Center
f2.Alignment = StringAlignment.Far
f2.FormatFlags = StringFormatFlags.DirectionVertical

' Draw the bounding rectangle and a string for each
' StringFormat object
G.DrawRectangle(Pens.Black, R)
G.DrawString("Format1", Me.Font, Brushes.Red, CType(R, RectangleF), F1)
G.DrawString("Format2", Me.Font, Brushes.Red, CType(R, RectangleF), F2)
```

```csharp
// C#
Graphics g = this.CreateGraphics();

// Construct a new Rectangle.
Rectangle r = new Rectangle(new Point(40, 40), new Size(80, 80));

// Construct 2 new StringFormat objects
StringFormat f1 = new StringFormat(StringFormatFlags.NoClip);
StringFormat f2 = new StringFormat(f1);

// Set the LineAlignment and Alignment properties for
// both StringFormat objects to different values.
f1.LineAlignment = StringAlignment.Near;
f1.Alignment = StringAlignment.Center;
f2.LineAlignment = StringAlignment.Center;
f2.Alignment = StringAlignment.Far;
f2.FormatFlags = StringFormatFlags.DirectionVertical;

// Draw the bounding rectangle and a string for each
// StringFormat object.
g.DrawRectangle(Pens.Black, r);
g.DrawString("Format1", this.Font, Brushes.Red, (RectangleF)r, f1);
g.DrawString("Format2", this.Font, Brushes.Red, (RectangleF)r, f2);
```

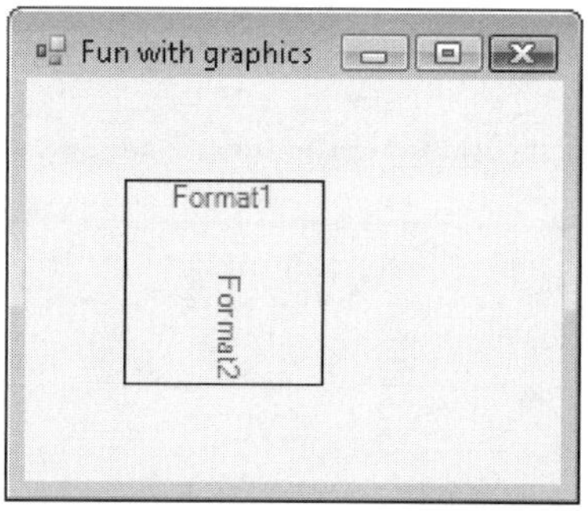

Figure 6-10   Use *StringFormat* to control the alignment and direction of text

Lab: Add Text to an Image

In this lab, you will add a copyright logo to a picture before writing it to disk, and you update a pie chart to display a legend. If you encounter a problem completing an exercise, the completed projects are available along with the sample files.

Exercise 1: Add a Copyright Notice to a Picture

  1. Navigate to the \<*InstallHome*>\Chapter06\Lesson3\Exercise1\Partial folder and open either the C# version or the Visual Basic .NET version of the solution file. Alternatively, you can continue working from the project you created in Lesson 2.

  2. Without modifying the chart *PictureBox*, modify the *saveButton_Click* method to add a copyright notice to the saved image. The notice should say "Copyright 2006, Contoso, Inc." and appear in the upper-left corner. The following code could replace the previous contents of the *if* statement:

```
' VB
If Not (saveDialog.ShowDialog = DialogResult.Cancel) Then
    ' Define the Bitmap, Graphics, Font, and Brush for copyright logo
    Dim bm As Bitmap = CType(chart.Image, Bitmap)
    Dim g As Graphics = Graphics.FromImage(bm)
    Dim f As Font = New Font("Arial", 12)
    Dim b As Brush = New SolidBrush(Color.White)

    ' Add the copyright text
    g.DrawString("Copyright 2006, Contoso, Inc.", f, b, 5, 5)

    ' Save the image to the specified file in JPEG format
    chart.Image.Save(saveDialog.FileName, ImageFormat.Jpeg)
End If
```

```
// C#
if (saveDialog.ShowDialog() != DialogResult.Cancel)
{
    // Define the Bitmap, Graphics, Font, and Brush for copyright logo
    Bitmap bm = (Bitmap)chart.Image;
    Graphics g = Graphics.FromImage(bm);
    Font f = new Font("Arial", 12);
    Brush b = new SolidBrush(Color.White);

    // Add the copyright text
    g.DrawString("Copyright 2006, Contoso, Inc.", f, b, 5, 5);

    // Save the image to the specified file in JPEG format
    bm.Save(saveDialog.FileName, ImageFormat.Jpeg);
}
```

3. Run the application and save a picture. Notice that the copyright notice is diffi-
    cult to read where it overlaps the picture. One way to resolve this is to draw text
    with a contrasting color behind the string, and offset by one pixel in each direc-
    tion. For example, the following code adds a black background to the white
    copyright text:

```
' VB
' Define the Bitmap, Graphics, Font, and Brush for copyright logo
Dim bm As Bitmap = CType(chart.Image, Bitmap)
Dim g As Graphics = Graphics.FromImage(bm)
Dim f As Font = New Font("Arial", 12)

' Create the foreground text brush
Dim b As Brush = New SolidBrush(Color.White)

' Create the background text brush
Dim bb As Brush = New SolidBrush(Color.Black)

' Add the copyright text background
Dim ct As String = "Copyright 2006, Contoso, Inc."
g.DrawString(ct, f, bb, 4, 4)
g.DrawString(ct, f, bb, 4, 6)
g.DrawString(ct, f, bb, 6, 4)
g.DrawString(ct, f, bb, 6, 6)

' Add the copyright text foreground
g.DrawString(ct, f, b, 5, 5)

' Save the image to the specified file in JPEG format
chart.Image.Save(saveDialog.FileName, ImageFormat.Jpeg)
```

```
// C#
// Define the Bitmap, Graphics, Font, and Brush for copyright logo
Bitmap bm = (Bitmap)chart.Image;
Graphics g = Graphics.FromImage(bm);
Font f = new Font("Arial", 12);
```

```
// Create the foreground text brush
Brush b = new SolidBrush(Color.White);

// Create the backround text brush
Brush bb = new SolidBrush(Color.Black);

// Add the copyright text background
string ct = "Copyright 2006, Contoso, Inc.";
g.DrawString(ct, f, bb, 4, 4);
g.DrawString(ct, f, bb, 4, 6);
g.DrawString(ct, f, bb, 6, 4);
g.DrawString(ct, f, bb, 6, 6);

// Add the copyright text foreground
g.DrawString(ct, f, b, 5, 5);

// Save the image to the specified file in JPEG format
bm.Save(saveDialog.FileName, ImageFormat.Jpeg);
```

4. Re-run the application and save the picture again. Notice that where the copyright text overlaps the pie chart, the text has a black background, which makes it easy to read.

Exercise 2: Add a Legend to the Pie Chart

In this exercise, you will modify the *drawPieChart* method created in previous exercises to split the image into two parts. The left half displays the pie chart, and the right half displays a legend showing the color of each pie chart segment, the name of that segment, and the value.

1. Navigate to the \<*InstallHome*>\Chapter06\Lesson3\Exercise2\Partial folder, and open either the C# version or the Visual Basic .NET version of the solution file. Alternatively, you can continue working from the project you created in Exercise 1 of this lesson.

2. First, modify the *drawPieChart* method so that the pie chart consumes only the left half of the image. The following modification accomplishes this:

```
' VB
' Define the rectangle that the pie chart will use
' Use only half the width to leave room for the legend
Dim rect As Rectangle = New Rectangle(1, 1, (s.Width/2) - 2, s.Height - 2)
```

```
// C#
// Define the rectangle that the pie chart will use
// Use only half the width to leave room for the legend
Rectangle rect = new Rectangle(1, 1, (s.Width/2) - 2, s.Height - 2);
```

3. Next, in the right half of the image, draw a black box with a white background. The following code shows one way to do this:

```vb
' VB
' Define the rectangle that the legend will use
Dim lRectCorner As Point = New Point((s.Width / 2) + 2, 1)
Dim lRectSize As Size = New Size(s.Width - (s.Width / 2) - 4, s.Height - 2)
Dim lRect As Rectangle = New Rectangle(lRectCorner, lRectSize)

' Draw a black box with a white background for the legend.
Dim lb As Brush = New SolidBrush(Color.White)
Dim lp As Pen = New Pen(Color.Black, 1)
g.FillRectangle(lb, lRect)
g.DrawRectangle(lp, lRect)
```

```csharp
// C#
// Define the rectangle that the legend will use
Point lRectCorner = new Point((s.Width / 2) + 2, 1);
Size lRectSize = new Size(s.Width - (s.Width / 2) - 4, s.Height - 2);
Rectangle lRect = new Rectangle(lRectCorner, lRectSize);

// Draw a black box with a white background for the legend.
Brush lb = new SolidBrush(Color.White);
Pen lp = new Pen(Color.Black, 1);
g.FillRectangle(lb, lRect);
g.DrawRectangle(lp, lRect);
```

4. Calculate values required to draw each legend item, including the following:

   ❑ The number of vertical pixels for each legend item

   ❑ The width of the legend box

   ❑ The height of the legend box

   ❑ The buffer space between legend elements

   ❑ The left border of the legend text

   ❑ The width of the legend text

The following code demonstrates one way to do this:

```vb
' VB
' Determine the number of vertical pixels for each legend item
Dim vert As Integer = (lRect.Height - 10) / elements.Count

' Calculate the width of the legend box as 20% of the total legend width
Dim legendWidth As Integer = lRect.Width / 5

' Calculate the height of the legend box as 75% of the legend item height
Dim legendHeight As Integer = CType((vert * 0.75), Integer)

' Calculate a buffer space between elements
Dim buffer As Integer = CType((vert - legendHeight), Integer) / 2
```

```
' Calculate the left border of the legend text
Dim textX As Integer = lRectCorner.X + legendWidth + buffer * 2

' Calculate the width of the legend text
Dim textWidth As Integer = lRect.Width - (lRect.Width / 5) - (buffer * 2)
```

```
// C#
// Determine the number of vertical pixels for each legend item
int vert = (lRect.Height - 10) / elements.Count;

// Calculate the width of the legend box as 20% of the total legend width
int legendWidth = lRect.Width / 5;

// Calculate the height of the legend box as 75% of the legend item height
int legendHeight = (int) (vert * 0.75);

// Calculate a buffer space between elements
int buffer = (int)(vert - legendHeight) / 2;

// Calculate the left border of the legend text
int textX = lRectCorner.X + legendWidth + buffer * 2;

// Calculate the width of the legend text
int textWidth = lRect.Width - (lRect.Width / 5) - (buffer * 2);
```

5. Finally, loop through the *PieChartElements* objects and draw each legend element. The following example shows a separate *foreach* loop for simplicity; however, for efficiency, this should be combined with the existing *foreach* loop:

```
' VB
' Start the legend five pixels from the top of the rectangle
Dim currentVert As Integer = 5
Dim legendColor As Integer = 0

For Each e As PieChartElement In elements
    ' Create a brush with a nice gradient
    Dim thisRect As Rectangle = New Rectangle(lRectCorner.X + buffer, _
        currentVert + buffer, legendWidth, legendHeight)
    Dim b As Brush = New LinearGradientBrush(thisRect, _
        colors(System.Math.Min( _
            System.Threading.Interlocked.Increment(legendColor), _
            legendColor - 1)), Color.White, CType(45, Single))

    ' Draw the legend box fill and border
    g.FillRectangle(b, thisRect)
    g.DrawRectangle(lp, thisRect)

    ' Define the rectangle for the text
    Dim textRect As RectangleF = New Rectangle(textX, currentVert + buffer, _
        textWidth, legendHeight)

    ' Define the font for the text
    Dim tf As Font = New Font("Arial", 12)
```

```vbnet
    ' Create the foreground text brush
    Dim tb As Brush = New SolidBrush(Color.Black)

    ' Define the vertical and horizontal alignment for the text
    Dim sf As StringFormat = New StringFormat
    sf.Alignment = StringAlignment.Near
    sf.LineAlignment = StringAlignment.Center

    ' Draw the text
    g.DrawString(e.name + ": " + e.value.ToString(), tf, tb, textRect, sf)

    ' Increment the current vertical location
    currentVert += vert
Next
```

```csharp
// C#
// Start the legend five pixels from the top of the rectangle
int currentVert = 5;
int legendColor = 0;

foreach (PieChartElement e in elements)
{
    // Create a brush with a nice gradient
    Rectangle thisRect = new Rectangle(lRectCorner.X + buffer,
        currentVert + buffer, legendWidth, legendHeight);
    Brush b = new LinearGradientBrush(thisRect, colors[legendColor++],
        Color.White, (float)45);

    // Draw the legend box fill and border
    g.FillRectangle(b, thisRect);
    g.DrawRectangle(lp, thisRect);

    // Define the rectangle for the text
    RectangleF textRect = new Rectangle(textX, currentVert + buffer,
        textWidth, legendHeight);

    // Define the font for the text
    Font tf = new Font("Arial", 12);

    // Create the foreground text brush
    Brush tb = new SolidBrush(Color.Black);

    // Define the vertical and horizontal alignment for the text
    StringFormat sf = new StringFormat();
    sf.Alignment = StringAlignment.Near;
    sf.LineAlignment = StringAlignment.Center;

    // Draw the text
    g.DrawString(e.name + ": " + e.value, tf, tb, textRect, sf);
```

```
        // Increment the current vertical location
        currentVert += vert;
    }
}
```

6. Run the application to verify that it works. With the legend added, more of the copyright text now overlaps with the pie chart, demonstrating the effectiveness of the black background.

Lesson Summary

- To add text to graphics, create a *Graphics* object, create a *Font* object, create a *Brush* object if you want, and then call the *Graphics.DrawString* method.

- To create a *Font* object, pass the font family name, font size, and font style to the constructor.

- Write text by calling the *Graphics.DrawString* method. The *DrawString* method requires a *Font* object, a *Brush* object that specifies the color of the text, and the location to draw the text.

- Use the *StringFormat* class to control the formatting of text. You can use this class to change the direction of the text, or to change the alignment of text.

Lesson Review

You can use the following questions to test your knowledge of the information in Lesson 3, "Formatting Text." The questions are also available on the companion CD if you prefer to review them in electronic form.

NOTE Answers

Answers to these questions and explanations of why each answer choice is right or wrong are located in the "Answers" section at the end of the book.

---

1. What are the steps for adding text to an image?

   A. Create a *Graphics* object and a *string* object. Then call *string.Draw*.

   B. Create a *Graphics* object, a *Font* object, and a *Brush* object. Then call *Graphics .DrawString*.

   C. Create a *Graphics* object, a *Font* object, and a *Pen* object. Then call *Graphics .DrawString*.

   D. Create a *Bitmap* object, a *Font* object, and a *Brush* object. Then call *Bitmap .DrawString*.

2. Which class would you need to create an instance of to specify that a string should be centered when drawn?

   A. *StringFormat*

   B. *StringAlignment*

   C. *FormatFlags*

   D. *LineAlignment*

3. Which of the following commands would cause a string to be flush left?

   A. *StringFormat.LineAlignment = Near*

   B. *StringFormat.LineAlignment = Far*

   C. *StringFormat.Alignment = Near*

   D. *StringFormat.Alignment = Far*

4. You are developing an application that will add text to JPEG, PNG, and GIF image files. Which class should you use to allow you to edit any of those image formats?

   A. *Metafile*

   B. *Icon*

   C. *Bitmap*

   D. *Image*

Chapter Review

To practice and reinforce the skills you learned in this chapter further, you can complete the following tasks:

- Review the chapter summary.
- Review the list of key terms introduced in this chapter.
- Complete the case scenarios. These scenarios set up real-world situations involving the topics of this chapter and ask you to create solutions.
- Complete the suggested practices.
- Take a practice test.

Chapter Summary

- To draw lines and curves, create two objects: a *Pen* object and a *Graphics* object. Use the *Pen* object to define the color and width of the drawing. The *Graphics* object exposes methods for drawing lines and shapes. To fill in shapes, use a *Brush* object with a *Graphics* object.
- To work with images, use the *Image* and *Bitmap* classes. To edit images, create a *Graphics* object based on the *Image* or *Bitmap* object.
- To add text to an image or graphic, create *Font* and *Brush* objects. Then call *Graphics.DrawString*. To format the text, use the *StringFormat* class.

Key Terms

Do you know what these key terms mean? You can check your answers by looking up the terms in the glossary at the end of the book.

- *Bitmap*
- *Brush*
- *Graphics*
- *Pen*

Case Scenarios

In the following case scenarios, you apply what you've learned in this chapter. You can find answers to these questions in the "Answers" section at the end of this book.

Case Scenario 1: Choosing Graphics Techniques

You are an internal application developer for Contoso, Inc. You and your team are responsible for an internal application that Contoso uses for order tracking and inventory management. Recently, a person in the Public Relations group asked your manager to discuss changes that are necessary to the look and feel of your internal applications. Your manager delegated the discussion to you.

Interviews

The following is a list of company personnel interviewed and their statements.

Public Relations Representative "We are in the process of re-inventing our corporate image. There are many elements to our new image, including pictures, the use of specific color and fonts, and logos. For consistent branding both internally and externally, everything we produce must conform to these standards. Specifically, on our internal application, I'd like to show a splash screen that displays a photo of our corporate headquarters with our logo in the upper-left corner. When the program loads, I'd like the logo to appear in the upper-left corner. In addition, all fonts in the application should be Arial 12. Oh, Legal is still in the process of approving our logo, so that's likely to change. I can provide you with the current logo and the picture of our headquarters in JPEG format."

IT Manager "These PR guys will change the logo and picture about a dozen times before they decide what they want to use, so I'd suggest storing the pictures as files in the installation directory and loading them dynamically with the application. I wouldn't take anything for granted, including the size of the images."

Questions

Answer the following questions for your manager:

1. The photo of the headquarters is 6 megapixels, and it's way too big for the splash screen. How can you resize it?

2. How can you display the corporate logo over the photo of the corporate headquarters?

3. If the size of the corporate logo changes, how can you ensure it doesn't cover the entire photo of the headquarters and consumes only the upper-left corner of the picture?

4. How can you change the fonts used throughout the application?

Case Scenario 2: Creating Simple Charts

You are a developer in the IT department of Fabrikam, Inc. Recently, you released version 1.0 of Sales, an internal application used by the sales team to track orders. Sales replaced their previous paper-based tracking methods, and everyone on the Sales team has been pleased with the application.

Now the vice president of Sales would like to discuss feature requests for the next version of your application.

Interviews

The following is a list of company personnel interviewed and their statements.

Vice President, Sales   "The sales-tracking application you wrote is great, and it has really improved the efficiency of our sales organization. Now that we have this data stored in a database, I'd like the ability to access it to provide more insight into how different sales teams are performing over time. I want to be able to see either a line graph or a bar chart showing sales performance for each quarter of the year, with each team's performance in a different color. I also need to be able to save the graph so I can add it to a presentation I have to give before the board of directors."

Questions

Answer the following questions for your manager:

1. What type of control will you use to display a chart in a Windows Forms application?

2. What method will you use to draw a line graph?

3. What method will you use to draw a bar graph?

4. How will you save the chart to a file?

Suggested Practices

To help you master the "Enhance the user interface of a .NET Framework application by using the *System.Drawing* namespace" exam objective, complete the following tasks.

Enhance the User Interface of a .NET Framework Application by Using Brushes, Pens, Colors, and Fonts

For this task, you should complete at least Practices 1 through 3 to gain experience using brushes, colors, and fonts. If you want in-depth knowledge of using pens, complete Practice 4 as well.

- **Practice 1** Create a Windows Forms application to demonstrate the different *Graphics.SmoothingMode* techniques available. Draw a circle and display the name of the current *SmoothingMode*. Every 5 seconds, redraw the circle, and display the new *SmoothingMode*. Examine the edges of the circle with the different *SmoothingMode* settings.

- **Practice 2** Draw a solid circle on a form and change the color every 2 seconds while displaying the name of the color at the bottom of the form.

- **Practice 3** Draw a solid circle on a form and change the brush every 5 seconds while displaying the name of the brush at the bottom of the form.

- **Practice 4** Create an application that uses the *Pen.DashOffset* and *Pen.DashPattern* properties to define a custom dash pattern.

Enhance the User Interface of a .NET Framework Application by Using Graphics, Images, Bitmaps, and Icons

For this task, you should complete all three practices to gain experience working with images in real-world scenarios.

- **Practice 1** Create a Windows Forms application to allow you to browse pictures saved on your computer.

- **Practice 2** Create an application that creates 80-by-80-pixel thumbnails for all images saved in a folder.

- **Practice 3** Create an application that reads images from one folder, adds a copyright logo to the picture, and saves the images in a second folder.

Enhance the User Interface of a .NET Framework Application by Using Shapes and Sizes

For this task, you should complete at least Practices 1 and 2. If you want in-depth knowledge of drawing shapes, complete Practice 3 as well.

- **Practice 1**   Create an application that allows you to draw polygons by clicking on a form. Each time the user clicks on the form, add a new point to the polygon at the location clicked.

- **Practice 2**   Add a series of randomly generated rectangles to an array, and then call *Graphics.DrawRectangles* to display them.

- **Practice 3**   Create a method to draw a bar graph that is similar in function to the *DrawPieChart* method used in this chapter.

Take a Practice Test

The practice tests on this book's companion CD offer many options. For example, you can test yourself on just one exam objective, or you can test yourself on all the 70-536 certification exam content. You can set up the test so that it closely simulates the experience of taking a certification exam, or you can set it up in study mode so that you can look at the correct answers and explanations after you answer each question.

MORE INFO   Practice tests

For details about all the practice test options available, see the section "How to Use the Practice Tests," in the Introduction to this book.

Chapter 7
Threading

Most developers begin their programming training by writing linear programs in which the computer executes a single line of code, waits for processing to complete, and continues to the next line of code. Such single-threaded programming has serious limitations, however. The program might be unresponsive to the user while processing a request. If the application is waiting for a network resource to respond, it cannot do anything else. If the computer has multiple processors, only one processor is used at a time, limiting performance.

You can improve the responsiveness and efficiency of your programs by using multiple threads. The .NET Framework provides tools to start a method in a background thread, allowing the method to run while your program continues processing. Multithreading can be complex, however. There's a chance that multiple threads will attempt to access a resource simultaneously. In addition, your application might need to start, pause, resume, or abort background threads. This chapter shows you how to create and control threads.

Exam objective in this chapter:
- Develop multithreaded .NET applications.

Lessons in this chapter:

Before You Begin

This book assumes that you have at least two to three years of experience developing Web-based, Microsoft Windows–based, or distributed applications using the .NET Framework. Candidates should have a working knowledge of Microsoft Visual Studio. Before you begin, you should be familiar with Microsoft Visual Basic or C# and be comfortable with the following tasks:

- Creating console applications in Visual Studio using Visual Basic or C#

- Adding namespaces and system class library references to a project

- Running a project in Visual Studio, setting breakpoints, stepping through code, and watching the values of variables

Lesson 1: Starting Multiple Threads

Though multithreading can be an incredibly complex topic, many uses are very simple. In fact, running a method in a background thread is as easy as adding the *System .Threading* namespace to your application and calling *ThreadPool.QueueUserWorkItem*. This lesson provides an overview of threading and shows you how to start methods in background threads.

After this lesson, you will be able to:

■ Describe threading

■ Use the *ThreadPool* class

■ Describe foreground and background threads

Estimated lesson time: 25 minutes

Threading Overview

Applications often need to perform tasks that take a long time, such as printing a document, downloading a file, or generating a report. If your main application thread were dedicated to this task, the application would stop responding to user input until the method completed.

To allow an application to perform a task and continue to respond to user input, or to perform multiple tasks simultaneously, you can start multiple threads. A *thread* is a unit of execution within a process. A single process can have multiple threads, in which case it is referred to as *multithreaded*. If a computer has multiple processors or multiple cores within a single processor, it can execute multiple threads simultaneously, even if they both require processing time.

Besides performing background processing, threading is a great way to improve the performance of processor-intensive tasks on computers with multiple processors or cores. Each thread can be executed on a different processor or core simultaneously. Therefore, adding multithreading to an application and running it on a computer with two cores could reduce the time it takes to complete a processor-intensive task by almost half.

> **Real World**
>
> *Tony Northrup*
>
> Threads have some level of overhead. Therefore, if a computer has multiple processors and you split processing into two threads, you won't see a 100 percent performance improvement. The actual performance improvement will be somewhat lower because of the processing time the operating system requires to manage the different threads.

The best reasons to use multithreading are to run code in the background and to improve performance on modern computers. There are drawbacks, however. First, writing multithreaded code is more complex, as you will learn in Lesson 2, "Managing Threads." Troubleshooting is complicated, too. Using multiple threads consumes more memory and requires some processor overhead, so performance can actually be reduced in some circumstances.

IMPORTANT The *BackgroundWorker* Component

The .NET Framework version 2.0 and later includes the *BackgroundWorker* component, which simplifies implementing multithreading. *BackgroundWorker* is particularly useful for creating background threads that interact with the user interface. The 70-536 certification exam and this chapter focus on the .NET Framework's core multithreading capabilities. For more information about *BackgroundWorker*, visit *http://msdn.microsoft.com/library/8xs8549b.aspx*.

Using the *ThreadPool* Class

You can use the *System.Threading.ThreadPool* class to run methods in background threads easily. The following Console application (which requires the *System.Threading* namespace) shows how to use the static *ThreadPool.QueueUserWorkItem* method to run a method using a new thread:

```
' VB
Sub Main()
    ' Queue the task.
    ThreadPool.QueueUserWorkItem(AddressOf ThreadProc)

    Console.WriteLine("Main thread does some work, then sleeps.")
    Thread.Sleep(1000)

    Console.WriteLine("Main thread exits.")
End Sub
```

```
' This thread procedure performs the task.
Sub ThreadProc(ByVal stateInfo As Object)
    Console.WriteLine("Hello from the thread pool.")
End Sub
```

```
// C#
static void Main(string[] args)
{
    // Queue the task.
    ThreadPool.QueueUserWorkItem(ThreadProc);

    Console.WriteLine("Main thread does some work, then sleeps.");
    Thread.Sleep(1000);

    Console.WriteLine("Main thread exits.");
}

// This thread procedure performs the task.
static void ThreadProc(Object stateInfo)
{
    Console.WriteLine("Hello from the thread pool.");
}
```

You can also use the overloaded *ThreadPool.QueueUserWorkItem* method to pass an object to the method that you want to run in the background. The following code expands the previous example to provide a *string* object to the *ThreadProc* sample method. You could provide an object of any class, however:

```
' VB
Sub Main()
    Dim state As String = "Hello, world!"
    ThreadPool.QueueUserWorkItem(AddressOf ThreadProc, state)

    Console.WriteLine("Main thread does some work, then sleeps.")
    Thread.Sleep(1000)

    Console.WriteLine("Main thread exits.")
End Sub

' Notice that Visual Basic automatically casts the object to a string
Sub ThreadProc(ByVal state As String)
    Console.WriteLine("Hello from the thread pool: " + state)
End Sub
```

```
// C#
static void Main(string[] args)
{
    string state = "Hello, world!";
    ThreadPool.QueueUserWorkItem(ThreadProc, state);

    Console.WriteLine("Main thread does some work, then sleeps.");
```

```
    Thread.Sleep(1000);

    Console.WriteLine("Main thread exits.");
}

// You must manually cast from the Object class in C#
static void ThreadProc(Object stateInfo)
{
    string state = (string)stateInfo;
    Console.WriteLine("Hello from the thread pool: " + state);
}
```

You can call *ThreadPool.QueueUserWorkItem* multiple times, even if the threads need to run simultaneously. For example, you could replace the single method call in the previous example with the following code:

```
' VB
ThreadPool.QueueUserWorkItem(AddressOf ThreadProc, "Thread 1")
ThreadPool.QueueUserWorkItem(AddressOf ThreadProc, "Thread 2")
ThreadPool.QueueUserWorkItem(AddressOf ThreadProc, "Thread 3")
ThreadPool.QueueUserWorkItem(AddressOf ThreadProc, "Thread 4")
```

```
// C#
ThreadPool.QueueUserWorkItem(ThreadProc, "Thread 1");
ThreadPool.QueueUserWorkItem(ThreadProc, "Thread 2");
ThreadPool.QueueUserWorkItem(ThreadProc, "Thread 3");
ThreadPool.QueueUserWorkItem(ThreadProc, "Thread 4");
```

By default, the thread pool has 250 worker threads per available processor. You can change this setting using the *ThreadPool.SetMaxThreads* method. Threads are recycled after the called method finishes, so you need to increase the maximum number of threads only if you will have more than 250 background threads active simultaneously.

You can check the number of available threads using *ThreadPool.GetAvailableThreads*, as the following code sample demonstrates:

```
' VB
Dim workerThreads As Integer
Dim completionPortThreads As Integer
ThreadPool.GetAvailableThreads(workerThreads, completionPortThreads)
Console.WriteLine("Available threads: " + workerThreads.ToString())
```

```
// C#
int workerThreads;
int completionPortThreads;
ThreadPool.GetAvailableThreads(out workerThreads,
    out completionPortThreads);
Console.WriteLine("Available threads: " + workerThreads.ToString());
```

Understanding Foreground and Background Threads

Your main application thread is considered the foreground thread. So long as the foreground thread is active, your application continues to run. Background threads are cancelled as soon as the foreground thread stops.

You can determine whether the current thread is foreground or background using the *Thread.CurrentThread.IsBackground* boolean property. This is useful in situations where a method might need to perform specific actions, such as locking a resource (discussed in Lesson 2), but only if it is running as a background thread. The following code sample demonstrates how to call the *ThreadProc* sample method as either a foreground or background thread. To call it as a foreground thread, call the method normally. To create a background thread, call *ThreadPool.QueueUserWorkItem*:

```
' VB
Sub Main()
    ThreadPool.QueueUserWorkItem(AddressOf ThreadProc, "Thread 1")
    ThreadPool.QueueUserWorkItem(AddressOf ThreadProc, "Thread 2")
    ThreadProc("Thread 3") ' Called as part of the foreground thread
    ThreadPool.QueueUserWorkItem(AddressOf ThreadProc, "Thread 4")

    Console.WriteLine("Main thread does some work, then sleeps.")
    Thread.Sleep(1000)

    Console.WriteLine("Main thread exits.")
    Console.ReadKey()
End Sub

Sub ThreadProc(ByVal stateInfo As Object)
    Dim state As String = DirectCast(stateInfo, String)

    If Thread.CurrentThread.IsBackground Then
        Console.WriteLine("Hello from backgroud thread: " + state)
    Else
        Console.WriteLine("Hello from foreground thread: " + state)
    End If
End Sub
```

```
// C#
static void Main(string[] args)
{
    ThreadPool.QueueUserWorkItem(ThreadProc, "Thread 1");
    ThreadPool.QueueUserWorkItem(ThreadProc, "Thread 2");
    ThreadProc("Thread 3"); // Called as part of the foreground thread
    ThreadPool.QueueUserWorkItem(ThreadProc, "Thread 4");

    Console.WriteLine("Main thread does some work, then sleeps.");
    Thread.Sleep(1000);
```

```
        Console.WriteLine("Main thread exits.");
        Console.ReadKey();
    }

    static void ThreadProc(Object stateInfo)
    {
        string state = (string)stateInfo;

        if (Thread.CurrentThread.IsBackground)
            Console.WriteLine("Hello from backgroud thread: " + state);
        else
            Console.WriteLine("Hello from foreground thread: " + state);
    }
```

Lab: Improve Performance Using Multiple Threads

In this lab, you update a Console application that downloads Web pages to be multi-threaded and observe the performance improvement. Because downloading files requires the client to wait for the server, you can download multiple pages simultaneously.

Exercise: Start Multiple Threads Using *ThreadPool*   In this exercise, you update a Console application to download multiple pages simultaneously.

1. Navigate to the \<*InstallHome*>\Chapter07\Lesson1\Exercise1\Partial folder and open either the C# version or the Visual Basic .NET version of the solution file.

2. Build and run the application. Notice that it requests five different Web pages, and then displays the size of the requested page. Run the program several times and make note of the approximate elapsed time as displayed by the application. You can greatly reduce this time by rewriting the program to run multithreaded.

3. Add the *System.Threading* namespace to the program.

4. In the *foreach* loop, replace the direct call to *GetPage* with a *ThreadPool.QueueUser-WorkItem* call. Provide the *url* as the second parameter, as follows:

```
' VB
For Each url As String In urls
    ThreadPool.QueueUserWorkItem(AddressOf GetPage, url)
Next
```

```
// C#
foreach (string url in urls)
    ThreadPool.QueueUserWorkItem(GetPage, url);
```

5. In Visual Basic, you can build and run the application as is. In C#, you can't build the application yet, because the *GetPage* method must accept an *object* parameter, and it currently accepts a *string* parameter. So, you need to update the *GetPage*

method to accept an *object* parameter and then cast it to a *string*. The following example demonstrates this (the Visual Basic version is optional and provided only for consistency):

```vb
' VB
Sub GetPage(ByVal data As Object)
    ' Cast the object to a string
    Dim url As String = DirectCast(data, String)

    ' Request the URL
    Dim wr As WebResponse = WebRequest.Create(url).GetResponse()

    ' Display the value for the Content-Length header
    Console.WriteLine(url + ": " + wr.Headers("Content-Length"))

    wr.Close()
End Sub
```

```csharp
// C#
static void GetPage(object data)
{
    // Cast the object to a string
    string url = (string)data;

    // Request the URL
    WebResponse wr = WebRequest.Create(url).GetResponse();

    // Display the value for the Content-Length header
    Console.WriteLine(url + ": " + wr.Headers["Content-Length"]);

    wr.Close();
}
```

6. Build and run the application. You will notice a couple of changes:

   ❑ The application runs much faster and should complete in less than half the time.

   ❑ The elapsed time isn't displayed correctly because it does not wait until all page requests have returned before calculating the time. You will fix this bug in Lesson 2.

Lesson Summary

■ Multithreading allows more than one method to run simultaneously. This can have several benefits, including performing processing while allowing the application to respond to user input, splitting processing between multiple processors, and improving performance by allowing multiple long-running methods (such as methods that must wait for a response from a server on the network) to run simultaneously.

- You can call *ThreadPool.QueueUserWorkItem* to run a method in a background thread. Optionally, you can provide a single object as a parameter to the method.

- When you start a new thread, it is created as a background thread. Your main application continues to run in a foreground thread. Once the foreground thread has completed processing, all background threads are immediately terminated.

Lesson Review

You can use the following questions to test your knowledge of the information in Lesson 1, "Starting Multiple Threads." The questions are also available on the companion CD if you prefer to review them in electronic form.

NOTE Answers

Answers to these questions and explanations of why each answer choice is right or wrong are located in the "Answers" section at the end of the book.

---

1. You need to run a method named *ThreadProc* in a background thread. Which code sample does this correctly?

   A.
   ```
   ' VB
   ThreadPool.QueueUserWorkItem(AddressOf ThreadProc)
   ```

   ```
   // C#
   ThreadPool.QueueUserWorkItem(ThreadProc);
   ```

   B.
   ```
   ' VB
   ThreadPool.QueueUserWorkItem(ThreadProc)
   ```

   ```
   // C#
   ThreadPool.QueueUserWorkItem(out ThreadProc);
   ```

   C.
   ```
   ' VB
   ThreadStart.CreateDelegate(AddressOf ThreadProc)
   ```

   ```
   // C#
   ThreadStart.CreateDelegate(ThreadProc);
   ```

   D.
   ```
   ' VB
   ThreadStart.CreateDelegate(ThreadProc)
   ```

   ```
   // C#
   ThreadStart.CreateDelegate(out ThreadProc);
   ```

2. You are creating an application that performs time-consuming calculations. You create a method named *Calc* that performs the calculations. You need to provide two integer values to *Calc*. What should you do? (Each answer forms part of the complete solution. Choose all that apply.)

   A. Call *ThreadPool.GetAvailableThreads* to retrieve a handle to the thread.

   B. Create a custom class that contains two integer members and create an instance of that class containing the values that you need to pass to the method.

   C. Create a custom class that contains two integer members and a delegate for the *Calc* method and create an instance of that class containing the values you need to pass to the method.

   D. Call *ThreadPool.QueueUserWorkItem* and pass the *Calc* method and the instance of the custom class.

   E. Call *ThreadPool.QueueUserWorkItem* and pass only the instance of the custom class.

Lesson 2: Managing Threads

Although starting multiple threads is simple, when you begin using multiple threads in real-world applications, you'll quickly discover that simply starting a method in a background thread isn't sufficient for most practical purposes. Typically, you need to be able to receive results once processing is complete. In addition, you might need to start, pause, resume, and abort threads manually. Perhaps the most complex element of working with multiple threads is avoiding resource conflicts, which requires you to lock resources so they can be used by only one thread at a time.

This lesson describes more advanced techniques for managing threads.

After this lesson, you will be able to:

- Start and stop threads
- Examine thread state
- Pass data to threads and receive data from threads
- Synchronize access to resources
- Wait for threads to complete

Estimated lesson time: 45 minutes

Starting and Stopping Threads

Calling *ThreadPool.QueueUserWorkItem* is sufficient when you need to start a thread and let it run until the specified method is finished. If you need more control, such as the ability to stop a thread after it has been started, you can create a *Thread* object and then call *Thread.Start*. You can then terminate the thread by calling *Thread.Abort*. To allow the thread to respond to being aborted, you can catch an exception of type *ThreadAbortException*. On any method that might be run within a background thread and subsequently aborted, you should catch *ThreadAbortException* and close all resources within the *finally* clause.

The following Console application creates a new *Thread* object (using an instance of *ThreadStart* that specifies the method to run), starts the thread, and then calls *Thread. Abort* before the *DoWork* method can finish running:

```vb
' VB
Sub Main()
    ' Create the thread object, passing in the
    ' DoWork method using a ThreadStart delegate.
    Dim DoWorkThread As New Thread(New ThreadStart(AddressOf DoWork))
```

```vb
    ' Start the thread.
    DoWorkThread.Start()

    ' Wait one second to allow the thread to begin to run
    Thread.Sleep(1000)

    ' Abort the thread
    DoWorkThread.Abort()

    Console.WriteLine("The Main() thread is ending.")
    Thread.Sleep(6000)
End Sub

Public Sub DoWork()
    Console.WriteLine("DoWork is running on another thread.")
    Try
        Thread.Sleep(5000)
    Catch ex As ThreadAbortException
        Console.WriteLine("DoWork was aborted.")
    Finally
        Console.WriteLine("Use finally to close all open resources.")
    End Try
    Console.WriteLine("DoWork has ended.")
End Sub
```

```csharp
// C#
static void Main(string[] args)
{
    // Create the thread object, passing in the
    // DoWork method using a ThreadStart delegate.
    Thread DoWorkThread = new Thread(new ThreadStart(DoWork));

    // Start the thread.
    DoWorkThread.Start();

    // Wait one second to allow the thread to begin to run
    Thread.Sleep(1000);

    // Abort the thread
    DoWorkThread.Abort();

    Console.WriteLine("The Main() thread is ending.");
    Thread.Sleep(6000);
}

public static void DoWork()
{
    Console.WriteLine("DoWork is running on another thread.");
    try
    {
        Thread.Sleep(5000);
    }
```

```
    catch (ThreadAbortException ex)
    {
        Console.WriteLine("DoWork was aborted.");
    }
    finally
    {
        Console.WriteLine("Use finally to close all open resources.");
    }
    Console.WriteLine("DoWork has ended.");
}
```

This program outputs the following:

```
DoWork is running on another thread.
DoWork was aborted.
Use finally to close all open resources.
The Main() thread is ending.
```

Notice that the *DoWork* method never outputs "DoWork has ended." because the thread was aborted while *DoWork* was executing *Thread.Sleep*. If you were to comment out the *DoWorkThread.Abort* call, *DoWork* would finish running.

IMPORTANT   Calling *Thread.Suspend*

You can call *Thread.Suspend* and *Thread.Resume* to pause and resume a thread's execution. However, those methods have been deprecated. Because *Thread.Suspend* and *Thread.Resume* do not rely on the cooperation of the thread being controlled, they are highly intrusive and can result in serious application problems like deadlocks (for example, if you suspend a thread that holds a resource that another thread needs). Instead, you should use an instance of *Monitor*, as described in the section "Synchronizing Access to Resources," later in this chapter.

After you create a thread, but before starting a thread, you can set the *Thread.Priority* property using the *ThreadPriority* enumeration. Thread priority controls how the operating system schedules time to a thread. Generally, threads with higher priorities run before threads with lower priorities. Therefore, if you create two threads that perform processor-intensive work—one with a priority of *Highest* and one with a priority of *Lowest*, the thread with the priority of *Highest* finishes first. From highest to lowest priority, your options are the following:

- *Highest*
- *AboveNormal*
- *Normal*
- *BelowNormal*
- *Lowest*

By default, threads and applications run with *Normal* priority.

Thread State

You can check a thread's state using the *Thread.ThreadState* property. Threads can be in any of the following states:

- **Unstarted**   The initial state before a thread is started.

- **Running**   The thread is active and executing, typically as a result of another thread calling *Thread.Start*.

- **Stopped**   The thread has stopped.

- **WaitSleepJoin**   The thread is waiting for another thread to complete. Typically this happens after calling *Thread.Join* on another thread.

- **SuspendRequested**   The thread is currently responding to a *Thread.Suspend* request. When you call *Thread.Suspend*, the Common Language Runtime (CLR) allows the thread to execute until it has reached a safe point before actually suspending the thread. A safe point for a thread is a point in its execution at which garbage collection can be performed.

- **Suspended**   The thread has been suspended because another thread called *Thread.Suspend*.

- **AbortRequested**   The thread is currently responding to a *Thread.Abort* request.

- **Aborted**   The thread has been suspended because another thread called *Thread.Abort*.

Threads are often in more than one state at any given time. For example, if a thread is blocked on a *Monitor.Wait* call and another thread calls *Abort* on that same thread, the thread is in both the *WaitSleepJoin* and the *AbortRequested* state at the same time. In that case, as soon as the thread returns from the call to *Wait* or is interrupted, it receives the *ThreadAbortException*.

Passing Data to and from Threads

Up to this point, the threading examples called a method without providing any parameters and without retrieving any data from the thread. In practice, you almost always need to provide data to a thread (such as providing a print job or data to process) and retrieve the results from the thread.

To provide data to a thread, create a class with a constructor that accepts one or more parameters and stores the data. You create an instance of this class and use that instance when you create your *ThreadStart* object.

To retrieve data from a thread, create a method that accepts the return results as a parameter. Then, create a delegate for the method. Pass the delegate and the method itself as an additional parameter to your class constructor.

The following code sample demonstrates this technique. The *Multiply* class constructor accepts the data that will be processed by the new thread. The *Multiply.ThreadProc* method performs the actual processing, which simply involves displaying a text message and multiplying an integer by 2. The *ResultCallback* method accepts the return value from *Multiply.ThreadProc*, and *ResultDelegate* is the delegate for the *ResultCallback* method:

```vb
' VB
Sub Main()
    ' Supply the state information required by the task.
    Dim m As New Multiply("Hello, world!", 13, New ResultDelegate( _
        AddressOf ResultCallback))

    Dim t As New Thread(New ThreadStart(AddressOf m.ThreadProc))
    t.Start()
    Console.WriteLine("Main thread does some work, then waits.")
    t.Join()
    Console.WriteLine("Thread completed.")
    Console.ReadKey()
End Sub

' The callback method must match the signature of the callback delegate.
Sub ResultCallback(ByVal retValue As Integer)
    Console.WriteLine("Returned value: {0}", retValue)
End Sub

Public Class Multiply
    ' State information used in the task.
    Private greeting As String
    Private value As Integer

    ' Delegate used to execute the callback method when the task is
    ' complete.
    Private callback As ResultDelegate

    ' The constructor obtains the state information and the callback
    ' delegate.
    Public Sub New(ByVal _greeting As String, ByVal _value As Integer, _
        ByVal _callback As ResultDelegate)
        greeting = _greeting
        value = _value
        callback = _callback
    End Sub
```

```
    ' The thread procedure performs the tasks (displaying
    ' the greeting and multiplying the value by 2).
    Public Sub ThreadProc()
        Console.WriteLine(greeting)
        If (callback <> Nothing) Then
            callback(value * 2)
        End If
    End Sub
End Class

' Delegate that defines the signature for the callback method.
Delegate Sub ResultDelegate(ByVal value As Integer)
```

```
// C#
class Program
{
    static void Main()
    {
        // Supply the state information required by the task.
        Multiply m = new Multiply("Hello, world!", 13,
            new ResultDelegate(ResultCallback));

        Thread t = new Thread(new ThreadStart(m.ThreadProc));
        t.Start();
        Console.WriteLine("Main thread does some work, then waits.");
        t.Join();
        Console.WriteLine("Thread completed.");
        Console.ReadKey();
    }

    // The callback method must match the signature of the callback delegate.
    public static void ResultCallback(int retValue)
    {
        Console.WriteLine("Returned value: {0}", retValue);
    }
}

public class Multiply
{
    // State information used in the task.
    private string greeting;
    private int value;

    // Delegate used to execute the callback method when the task is complete.
    private ResultDelegate callback;

    // The constructor obtains the state information and the callback delegate.
    public Multiply(string _greeting, int _value, ResultDelegate _callback)
    {
        greeting = _greeting;
        value = _value;
        callback = _callback;
    }
```

```
    // The thread procedure performs the tasks (displaying
    // the greeting and multiplying the value by 2).
    public void ThreadProc()
    {
        Console.WriteLine(greeting);
        if (callback != null)
            callback(value * 2);
    }
}

// Delegate that defines the signature for the callback method.
public delegate void ResultDelegate(int value);
```

The previous code sample outputs the following:

```
Main thread does some work, then waits.
Hello, world!
Returned value: 26
Thread completed.
```

Synchronizing Access to Resources

If an application needs to write to a file, it typically locks the file. Locking the file prevents other applications from accessing it. If another application needs to access the file, it either must wait for the lock to be released or cancel the action that requires the file.

Multithreaded applications have similar challenges when accessing shared resources. To reduce problems, the .NET Framework provides synchronization objects that you can use to coordinate resources shared among multiple threads. Resources that require synchronization include the following:

- System resources (such as communications ports)
- Resources shared by multiple processes (such as file handles)
- The resources of a single application domain (such as global, static, and instance fields) accessed by multiple threads
- Object instances that are accessed by multiple threads

To understand what can happen if you don't synchronize access to resources in a multithreaded application, consider the following Console application. The constructor for the *Math* class accepts two integer values and provides methods to perform calculations using those values. However, the calculations take a full second to complete—therefore, the private *result* variable might be overwritten by other threads between the time the calculation is performed and the time the result is displayed to the console:

```vb
' VB
Sub Main()
    Dim m As New Math(2, 3)

    Dim t1 As New Thread(New ThreadStart(AddressOf m.Add))
    Dim t2 As New Thread(New ThreadStart(AddressOf m.Subtract))
    Dim t3 As New Thread(New ThreadStart(AddressOf m.Multiply))

    t1.Start()
    t2.Start()
    t3.Start()

    ' Wait for the user to press a key
    Console.ReadKey()
End Sub

Class Math
    Public value1 As Integer
    Public value2 As Integer
    Private result As Integer

    Public Sub New(ByVal _value1 As Integer, ByVal _value2 As Integer)
        value1 = _value1
        value2 = _value2
    End Sub

    Public Sub Add()
        result = value1 + value2
        Thread.Sleep(1000)
        Console.WriteLine("Add: " + result.ToString)
    End Sub

    Public Sub Subtract()
        result = value1 - value2
        Thread.Sleep(1000)
        Console.WriteLine("Subtract: " + result.ToString)
    End Sub

    Public Sub Multiply()
        result = value1 * value2
        Thread.Sleep(1000)
        Console.WriteLine("Multiply: " + result.ToString)
    End Sub
End Class
```

```csharp
// C#
class Program
{
    static void Main()
    {
        Math m = new Math(2, 3);
```

```
        Thread t1 = new Thread(new ThreadStart(m.Add));
        Thread t2 = new Thread(new ThreadStart(m.Subtract));
        Thread t3 = new Thread(new ThreadStart(m.Multiply));

        t1.Start();
        t2.Start();
        t3.Start();

        // Wait for the user to press a key
        Console.ReadKey();
    }
}
class Math
{
    public int value1;
    public int value2;
    private int result;

    public Math(int _value1, int _value2)
    {
        value1 = _value1;
        value2 = _value2;
    }

    public void Add()
    {
        result = value1 + value2;
        Thread.Sleep(1000);
        Console.WriteLine("Add: " + result);
    }

    public void Subtract()
    {
        result = value1 - value2;
        Thread.Sleep(1000);
        Console.WriteLine("Subtract: " + result);
    }

    public void Multiply()
    {
        result = value1 * value2;
        Thread.Sleep(1000);
        Console.WriteLine("Multiply: " + result);
    }
}
```

At first glance, you might expect that this Console application should display the following output:

```
Add: 5
Subtract: -1
Multiply: 6
```

However, because the *Math.Multiply* method was called last and the first two threads were in a *Sleep* state, *Math.Multiply* overwrote the value of *result* before *Math.Add* and *Math.Subtract* could display the value. So, the actual output is as follows:

```
Add: 6
Subtract: 6
Multiply: 6
```

The sections that follow describe different techniques for synchronizing access to resources.

Monitor   Just as the file system uses file locks to prevent different applications from accessing the same file, you can use the *Monitor* class to lock objects and prevent a specific section of code from running until the object is unlocked. Although you can use the *Monitor* class correctly, it's much easier to use built-in keywords to call the *Monitor.Enter* and *Monitor.Exit* methods. In C#, use the keyword *lock* to specify the object to monitor. In Visual Basic, use the keyword *SynLock*.

You can fix the console application in the previous section by using the *Monitor* class and the *lock* or *SynLock* keywords. The following code sample updates the *Math* class from the previous code sample to use locking and allows the *Math* class to provide accurate results:

```vb
' VB
Class Math
    Public value1 As Integer
    Public value2 As Integer
    Private result As Integer

    Public Sub New(ByVal _value1 As Integer, ByVal _value2 As Integer)
        value1 = _value1
        value2 = _value2
    End Sub

    Public Sub Add()
        SyncLock Me
            result = value1 + value2
            Thread.Sleep(1000)
            Console.WriteLine("Add: " + result.ToString)
        End SyncLock
    End Sub

    Public Sub Subtract()
        SyncLock Me
            result = value1 - value2
            Thread.Sleep(1000)
            Console.WriteLine("Subtract: " + result.ToString)
        End SyncLock
    End Sub
```

```vbnet
    Public Sub Multiply()
        SyncLock Me
            result = value1 * value2
            Thread.Sleep(1000)
            Console.WriteLine("Multiply: " + result.ToString)
        End SyncLock
    End Sub
End Class
```

```csharp
// C#
class Math
{
    public int value1;
    public int value2;
    private int result;

    public Math(int _value1, int _value2)
    {
        value1 = _value1;
        value2 = _value2;
    }

    public void Add()
    {
        lock (this)
        {
            result = value1 + value2;
            Thread.Sleep(1000);
            Console.WriteLine("Add: " + result);
        }
    }

    public void Subtract()
    {
        lock (this)
        {
            result = value1 - value2;
            Thread.Sleep(1000);
            Console.WriteLine("Subtract: " + result);
        }
    }

    public void Multiply()
    {
        lock (this)
        {
            result = value1 * value2;
            Thread.Sleep(1000);
            Console.WriteLine("Multiply: " + result);
        }
    }
}
```

The *SynLock Me* and *lock (this)* calls allow the code to run only if no other section of code currently has the object locked. Therefore, the *t2* instance cannot run the *Subtract* method until the *t1* instance has completed running the *Add* method, preventing the *result* value from being overwritten.

Monitor locks reference types (also known as objects), not value types. Therefore, while the previous code sample could lock the current instance of the *Math* class, it couldn't lock the *result* integer because *result* is a value type.

ReaderWriterLock   Using the *Monitor* class and the *SynLock* or *lock* keyword is a straightforward way to prevent two threads from accessing a resource simultaneously. However, the *Monitor* class does not distinguish between read and write locks.

By providing separate logic for read and write locks, you can improve the efficiency of multithreaded applications in which multiple threads might need to read a value simultaneously. Typically, the methods reading the resource need to keep the resource open for an extended period of time for there to be a significant improvement.

For example, consider an application that used three threads, each of which spent several seconds reading a file from memory, and a fourth thread that occasionally updated the file. Using *Monitor*, only one thread could access the file at a time—if two threads wanted to read the file simultaneously, one would need to wait. Using *Reader-WriterLock*, you could allow the threads to all read the file simultaneously. The only time a thread could not read the file is when a thread was writing to the file.

For example, consider the following Console application, which uses the standard *Monitor* locks to protect access to the *file* resource. This application takes about nine seconds to run:

```vb
' VB
Sub Main()
    Dim m As New MemFile()

    Dim t1 As New Thread(New ThreadStart(AddressOf m.ReadFile))
    Dim t2 As New Thread(New ThreadStart(AddressOf m.WriteFile))
    Dim t3 As New Thread(New ThreadStart(AddressOf m.ReadFile))
    Dim t4 As New Thread(New ThreadStart(AddressOf m.ReadFile))

    t1.Start()
    t2.Start()
    t3.Start()
    t4.Start()
End Sub

Class MemFile
    Private file As String = "Hello, world!"
```

```vb
    Public Sub ReadFile()
        SyncLock Me
            For i As Integer = 1 To 3
                Console.WriteLine(file)
                Thread.Sleep(1000)
            Next
        End SyncLock
    End Sub

    Public Sub WriteFile()
        SyncLock Me
            file += " It's a nice day!"
        End SyncLock
    End Sub
End Class
```

```csharp
// C#
static void Main(string[] args)
{
    MemFile m = new MemFile();

    Thread t1 = new Thread(new ThreadStart(m.ReadFile));
    Thread t2 = new Thread(new ThreadStart(m.WriteFile));
    Thread t3 = new Thread(new ThreadStart(m.ReadFile));
    Thread t4 = new Thread(new ThreadStart(m.ReadFile));

    t1.Start();
    t2.Start();
    t3.Start();
    t4.Start();
}

class MemFile
{
    string file = "Hello, world!";
    public void ReadFile()
    {
        lock (this)
        {
            for (int i = 1; i <= 3; i++)
            {
                Console.WriteLine(file);
                Thread.Sleep(1000);
            }
        }
    }

    public void WriteFile()
    {
        lock (this)
        {
            file += " It's a nice day!";
        }
    }
}
```

If you update the *MemFile* class to use *ReaderWriterLock*, the total time to run the application is reduced from nine seconds to about six seconds. The improved efficiency occurs because after the write lock is completed, the remaining two reader threads can share simultaneous read access to the file:

```vb
' VB
Class MemFile
    Private file As String = "Hello, world!"
    Private rwl As ReaderWriterLock = New ReaderWriterLock()

    Public Sub ReadFile()
        ' Allow thread to continue only if no other thread
        ' has a write lock
        rwl.AcquireReaderLock(10000)
        For i As Integer = 1 To 3
            Console.WriteLine(file)
            Thread.Sleep(1000)
        Next
        rwl.ReleaseReaderLock()
    End Sub

    Public Sub WriteFile()
        ' Allow thread to continue only if no other thread
        ' has a read or write lock
        rwl.AcquireWriterLock(10000)
        file += " It's a nice day!"
        rwl.ReleaseWriterLock()
    End Sub
End Class
```

```csharp
// C#
class MemFile
{
    string file = "Hello, world!";
    ReaderWriterLock rwl = new ReaderWriterLock();

    public void ReadFile()
    {
        // Allow thread to continue only if no other thread
        // has a write lock
        rwl.AcquireReaderLock(10000);
        for (int i = 1; i <= 3; i++)
        {
            Console.WriteLine(file);
            Thread.Sleep(1000);
        }
        rwl.ReleaseReaderLock();
    }

    public void WriteFile()
    {
        // Allow thread to continue only if no other thread
        // has a read or write lock
```

```
        rwl.AcquireWriterLock(10000);
        file += " It's a nice day!";
        rwl.ReleaseWriterLock();
    }
}
```

Interlocked   As an alternative to locking access to a resource, you can use the *Interlocked* class to perform basic operations in a thread-safe way. *Interlocked* can perform atomic operations by calling the following static methods. An atomic operation cannot be interrupted by another thread:

- ***Increment***   Increments a specified variable and stores the result. This is equivalent to calling *val += 1*.

- ***Decrement***   Increments a specified variable and stores the result. This is equivalent to calling *val -= 1*.

- ***Exchange***   Sets the value of an object. This is equivalent to calling *val = val2*.

- ***CompareExchange***   Sets the value of an object if the object's original value matches a specified value. This is equivalent to the pseudocode *if val == val2 then val = val3*.

- ***Add***   Increments a specified variable and stores the result. This is equivalent to calling *val += val2*.

- ***Read***   Examines a specified variable and stores the result. This is equivalent to reading a variable.

The following code sample demonstrates how to use *Interlocked*:

```
' VB
Dim num As Integer = 0

Interlocked.Increment(num)
Console.WriteLine(num.ToString())

Interlocked.Add(num, 10)
Console.WriteLine(num.ToString())

Interlocked.Exchange(num, 35)
Console.WriteLine(num.ToString())

Interlocked.CompareExchange(num, 75, 35)
Console.WriteLine(num.ToString())

// C#
int num = 0;

Interlocked.Increment(ref num);
Console.WriteLine(num.ToString());
```

```
Interlocked.Add(ref num, 10);
Console.WriteLine(num.ToString());

Interlocked.Exchange(ref num, 35);
Console.WriteLine(num.ToString());

Interlocked.CompareExchange(ref num, 75, 35);
Console.WriteLine(num.ToString());
```

To understand the importance of using *Interlocked* in multithreaded applications, run the following Console application on a computer with multiple processors:

```vb
' VB
Sub Main()
    Dim n As New myNum()
    For a As Integer = 1 To 10
        For i As Integer = 1 To 1000
            Dim t As New Thread(New ThreadStart(AddressOf n.AddOne))
            t.Start()
        Next
        Thread.Sleep(3000)
        Console.WriteLine(n.number)
    Next
    Console.ReadKey()
End Sub

Public Class myNum
    Public number As Integer = 0

    Public Sub AddOne()
        number += 1
    End Sub
End Class
```

```csharp
// C#
static void Main(string[] args)
{
    myNum n = new myNum();
    for (int a = 0; a < 10; a++)
    {
        for (int i = 1; i <= 1000; Interlocked.Increment(ref i))
        {
            Thread t = new Thread(new ThreadStart(n.AddOne));
            t.Start();
        }
        Thread.Sleep(3000);
        Console.WriteLine(n.number);
    }
    Console.ReadKey();
}
```

```
public class myNum
{
    public int number = 0;

    public void AddOne()
    {
        number += 1;
    }
}
```

That application *should* display the following output:

```
1000
2000
3000
4000
5000
6000
7000
8000
9000
10000
```

However, on multiprocessor computers, you're likely to see output resembling the following:

```
1000
2000
2999
3999
4999
5998
6998
7998
8998
9997
```

Some of the increments are lost—which would be disastrous in any real-world application. This happens because *myNum.AddOne()* can be running multiple times in different threads.

Incrementing an integer requires two basic steps: read the original value and then replace the value with the newly incremented value. In a multithreaded environment, Thread1 can begin the increment process by reading the original value (for example, 20), and then get interrupted by Thread2. Thread2 can then read the original value (which would still be 20, because it has not yet been updated by Thread1) and then replace the value with 21. When Thread1 continues processing, it increments the value as it was before Thread2 updated it—thus completing the increment operation but rewriting the value with 21. In this scenario, two increment operations resulted in incrementing the value only one time. As the previous code sample demonstrates, this can and does happen in real-world programming environments, and mathematical errors such as this can be disastrous.

To correct the problem, replace the *number += 1* operation in *myNum.AddOne* with *Interlocked.Increment(ref number),* and then run the application again. This time, the results are perfect because *Interlocked.Increment* does not allow another thread to interrupt the increment operation.

IMPORTANT   Multithreading Best Practices

For more information about how to minimize problems when writing multithreaded applications, read "Managed Threading Best Practices" at the MSDN Library *(http://msdn.microsoft.com/en-us/ library/1c9txz50.aspx).*

Waiting for Threads to Complete

Often, your application's primary thread must wait for background threads to complete before continuing. If you are waiting on a single thread, you can simply call *Thread.Join,* which halts processing until the thread terminates.

If you need to wait for multiple threads to complete, use the *WaitHandle.WaitAll* static method with an *AutoResetEvent* array. The following code sample demonstrates this. In this example, the custom *ThreadInfo* class provides everything that the background thread needs to execute; namely, an integer that represents the number of milliseconds to wait and an *AutoResetEvent* instance that it can set (by calling *AutoResetEvent.Set*) when processing is complete:

```
' VB
' Define an array with three AutoResetEvent WaitHandles.
Dim waitHandles As AutoResetEvent() = New AutoResetEvent() _
    {New AutoResetEvent(False), _
     New AutoResetEvent(False), _
     New AutoResetEvent(False)}

<MTAThread()> Sub Main()
    ' Queue up tasks on different threads; wait until all tasks are
    ' completed.
    ThreadPool.QueueUserWorkItem(New WaitCallback(AddressOf DoTask), _
        New ThreadInfo(3000, waitHandles(0)))
    ThreadPool.QueueUserWorkItem(New WaitCallback(AddressOf DoTask), _
```

```
            New ThreadInfo(2000, waitHandles(1)))
        ThreadPool.QueueUserWorkItem(New WaitCallback(AddressOf DoTask), _
            New ThreadInfo(1000, waitHandles(2)))
        WaitHandle.WaitAll(waitHandles)
        Console.WriteLine("Main thread is complete.")
        Console.ReadKey()
    End Sub

    Sub DoTask(ByVal state As Object)
        Dim ti As ThreadInfo = DirectCast(state, ThreadInfo)
        Thread.Sleep(ti.ms)
        Console.WriteLine("Waited for " + ti.ms.ToString() + " ms.")
        ti.are.Set()
    End Sub

    Class ThreadInfo
        Public are As AutoResetEvent
        Public ms As Integer

        Public Sub New(ByVal _ms As Integer, ByVal _are As AutoResetEvent)
            ms = _ms
            are = _are
        End Sub
    End Class

    // C#
    // Define an array with three AutoResetEvent WaitHandles.
    static AutoResetEvent[] waitHandles = new AutoResetEvent[]
    {
        new AutoResetEvent(false),
        new AutoResetEvent(false),
        new AutoResetEvent(false)
    };

    static void Main()
    {
        // Queue up tasks on different threads; wait until all tasks are
        // completed.
        ThreadPool.QueueUserWorkItem(new WaitCallback(DoTask),
            new ThreadInfo(3000, waitHandles[0]));
        ThreadPool.QueueUserWorkItem(new WaitCallback(DoTask),
            new ThreadInfo(2000, waitHandles[1]));
        ThreadPool.QueueUserWorkItem(new WaitCallback(DoTask),
            new ThreadInfo(1000, waitHandles[2]));
        WaitHandle.WaitAll(waitHandles);
        Console.WriteLine("Main thread is complete.");
        Console.ReadKey();
    }

    static void DoTask(Object state)
    {
        ThreadInfo ti = (ThreadInfo)state;
        Thread.Sleep(ti.ms);
```

```
        Console.WriteLine("Waited for " + ti.ms.ToString() + " ms.");
        ti.are.Set();
}

class ThreadInfo
{
    public AutoResetEvent are;
    public int ms;

    public ThreadInfo(int _ms, AutoResetEvent _are)
    {
        ms = _ms;
        are = _are;
    }
}
```

If you run that code, you see the following output:

```
Waited for 1000 ms.
Waited for 2000 ms.
Waited for 3000 ms.
Main thread is complete.
```

Notice that the message "Main thread is complete" displays only after all three threads have completed, indicating that the *Main* thread waited for the threads before continuing. If you comment out the call to *WaitHandle.WaitAll*, you see the following output, which indicates that the *Main* thread continued to process without waiting for the background threads:

```
Main thread is complete.
Waited for 1000 ms.
Waited for 2000 ms.
Waited for 3000 ms.
```

You can also call *WaitHandle.WaitAny*, which waits for the first thread to return. In this example, replacing *WaitHandle.WaitAll* with *WaitHandle.WaitAny* produces the following output:

```
Waited for 1000 ms.
Main thread is complete.
Waited for 2000 ms.
Waited for 3000 ms.
```

In this example, notice that the *Main* method in Visual Basic has the *MTAThread* attribute. Without it, the *Main* method would be started as a single-threaded apartment (STA) thread. STA is designed to be used in single-threaded environments. Only multithreaded apartment (MTA) threads support calling *WaitHandle.WaitAll*. C# starts the main method as an MTA thread by default, and thus it does not require the *MTAThread* attribute (although you could add it if you wanted; it's just unnecessary because it's the default setting).

Lab: Manage Threads

In this lab, you will expand the application that you created in Lesson 1 so that it properly waits for threads to complete. Then, you convert it to use multiple *Thread* instances rather than calling *ThreadPool.QueueUserWorkItem*.

Exercise 1: Wait for Threads to Complete   In this exercise, you must update the application you created in Lesson 1 so that it waits for all threads to complete before displaying the results.

1. Navigate to the *<InstallHome>*\Chapter07\Lesson2\Exercise1\Partial folder and open either the C# version or the Visual Basic .NET version of the solution file. Alternatively, you can continue working from the project you created for Lesson 1.

2. Build and run the application. Notice that the program attempts to display the time elapsed while retrieving the five Web pages, but it displays an incorrect value because it does not wait for the *GetPage* threads to complete.

3. First, create an array of *AutoResetEvent* objects within the *Main* method, with one element for every Uniform Resource Locator (URL). The following declaration works, but it must be placed after the *urls* variable is declared:

```vb
' VB
Dim waitHandles As AutoResetEvent() = New AutoResetEvent( _
    urls.Length - 1) {}
```

```csharp
// C#
AutoResetEvent[] waitHandles = new AutoResetEvent[urls.Length];
```

4. To use the *waitHandles* array, you must pass one element of the array to each thread. To do that, you must pass a single object to the method being called, and that object must contain both the element of the *waitHandles* array and the string that will be used as the URL. Therefore, you must create a new class that contains two members: an instance of *AutoResetEvent* and a string for the URL. The following demonstrates how to create this class:

```vb
' VB
Class ThreadInfo
    Public url As String
    Public are As AutoResetEvent

    Public Sub New(ByVal _url As String, ByVal _are As AutoResetEvent)
        url = _url
        are = _are
    End Sub
End Class
```

```
// C#
class ThreadInfo
{
    public string url;
    public AutoResetEvent are;

    public ThreadInfo(string _url, AutoResetEvent _are)
    {
        url = _url;
        are = _are;
    }
}
```

5. Update the *GetPage* method to cast the data object to an instance of *ThreadInfo*, as shown here:

```
' VB
Sub GetPage(ByVal data As Object)
    ' Cast the object to a ThreadInfo
    Dim ti As ThreadInfo = DirectCast(data, ThreadInfo)

    ' Request the URL
    Dim wr As WebResponse = WebRequest.Create(ti.url).GetResponse()

    ' Display the value for the Content-Length header
    Console.WriteLine(ti.url + ": " + wr.Headers("Content-Length"))

    wr.Close()

    ' Let the parent thread know the process is done
    ti.are.Set()
End Sub
```

```
// C#
static void GetPage(object data)
{
    // Cast the object to a ThreadInfo
    ThreadInfo ti = (ThreadInfo)data;

    // Request the URL
    WebResponse wr = WebRequest.Create(ti.url).GetResponse();

    // Display the value for the Content-Length header
    Console.WriteLine(ti.url + ": " + wr.Headers["Content-Length"]);

    wr.Close();

    // Let the parent thread know the process is done
    ti.are.Set();
}
```

6. Next, update the *foreach* loop in the *Main* method to create an instance of the *ThreadInfo* class and pass it to the *GetPage* method, as demonstrated here:

```
' VB
Dim i As Integer = 0
For Each url As String In urls
    waitHandles(i) = New AutoResetEvent(False)
    Dim ti As New ThreadInfo(url, waitHandles(i))
    ThreadPool.QueueUserWorkItem(AddressOf GetPage, ti)
    i += 1
Next
```

```
// C#
int i = 0;
foreach (string url in urls)
{
    waitHandles[i] = new AutoResetEvent(false);
    ThreadInfo ti = new ThreadInfo(url, waitHandles[i]);
    ThreadPool.QueueUserWorkItem(GetPage, ti);
    i++;
}
```

7. Finally, call the static *WaitHandle.WaitAll* method before displaying the elapsed time, as demonstrated here:

```
' VB
WaitHandle.WaitAll(waitHandles)
```

```
// C#
WaitHandle.WaitAll(waitHandles);
```

8. If you are using Visual Basic, add the *MTAThread* attribute to the *Main* method. (This is not required in C#, because it is the default.)

```
' VB
<MTAThread()> Sub Main()
```

9. Build and run the application. Notice that it correctly waits until all threads have returned before displaying the elapsed time. Bug fixed!

Exercise 2: Pass Values Back from Threads   In this exercise, you will update the application that you created in Lesson 1 to create a *Thread* object and return results to a callback method rather than calling *ThreadPool.QueueUserWorkItem*.

1. Navigate to the \<*InstallHome*>\Chapter07\Lesson2\Exercise2\Partial folder and open either the C# version or the Visual Basic .NET version of the solution file. Alternatively, you can continue working from the project you created for Lesson 2, Exercise 1.

2. To pass data to a method when you create an instance of *Thread*, you need a non-static method. Therefore, you should replace the *GetPage* method and *ThreadInfo* class with a class containing both parameters and a method that the thread will run, as shown here:

```vb
' VB
Public Class PageSize
    Public url As String
    Public are As AutoResetEvent
    Public bytes As Integer

    Public Sub New(ByVal _url As String, ByVal _are As AutoResetEvent)
        url = _url
        are = _are
    End Sub

    Public Sub GetPageSize()
        ' Request the URL
        Dim wr As WebResponse = WebRequest.Create(url).GetResponse()

        bytes = Integer.Parse(wr.Headers("Content-Length"))

        ' Display the value for the Content-Length header
        Console.WriteLine(url + ": " + bytes.ToString())

        wr.Close()

        ' Let the parent thread know the process is done
        are.Set()
    End Sub
End Class
```

```csharp
// C#
public class PageSize
{
    public string url;
    public AutoResetEvent are;
    public int bytes;

    public PageSize(string _url, AutoResetEvent _are)
    {
        url = _url;
        are = _are;
    }

    public void GetPageSize()
    {
        // Request the URL
        WebResponse wr = WebRequest.Create(url).GetResponse();

        bytes = int.Parse(wr.Headers["Content-Length"]);
```

```
        // Display the value for the Content-Length header
        Console.WriteLine(url + ": " + bytes.ToString());

        wr.Close();

        // Let the parent thread know the process is done
        are.Set();
    }
}
```

3. Threads can return values by calling a callback method that you pass to the thread as a parameter. To create a callback method, write the method and create a matching delegate. In this case, we want the thread to return both the URL and the bytes in the Web page, so we can simply pass an instance of the *PageSize* class. For the purpose of this example, the callback method can simply display the output to the console. The following code creates the method and the callback:

```
' VB
' The callback method must match the signature of the callback delegate.
Sub ResultCallback(ByVal ps As PageSize)
    Console.WriteLine("{0}: {1}", ps.url, ps.bytes.ToString())
End Sub

' Delegate that defines the signature for the callback method.
Delegate Sub ResultDelegate(ByVal ps As PageSize)

// C#
// The callback method must match the signature of the callback delegate.
static void ResultCallback(PageSize ps)
{
    Console.WriteLine("{0}: {1}", ps.url, ps.bytes.ToString());
}

// Delegate that defines the signature for the callback method.
public delegate void ResultDelegate(PageSize ps);
```

4. Update the *PageSize* class to accept the callback method as a parameter in the constructor, and then store the callback value, as shown here (you should not delete the *GetPageSize* method):

```
' VB
Class PageSize
    Public url As String
    Public are As AutoResetEvent
    Public bytes As Integer

    ' Delegate used to execute the callback method when the task is
    ' complete.
    Private callback As ResultDelegate
```

```vb
        Public Sub New(ByVal _url As String, ByVal _are As AutoResetEvent, _
            ByVal _callback As ResultDelegate)
            url = _url
            are = _are
            callback = _callback
        End Sub
    End Class
End Class
```

```csharp
// C#

public class PageSize
{
    public string url;
    public AutoResetEvent are;
    public int bytes;

    // Delegate used to execute the callback method when the task is
    // complete.
    private ResultDelegate callback;

    public PageSize(string _url, AutoResetEvent _are,
        ResultDelegate _callback)
    {
        url = _url;
        are = _are;
        callback = _callback;
    }
}
```

5. Next, update the *PageSize* class to store the callback method, and accept the callback as a parameter for the constructor. In addition, comment out the line in the *GetPageSize* method that displays the URL and page size to the console and instead call the callback method, passing the current *PageSize* instance. The following code demonstrates how to update the *PageSize* class (changes are shown in bold):

```vb
' VB
Public Sub GetPageSize()
    ' Request the URL
    Dim wr As WebResponse = WebRequest.Create(url).GetResponse()

    bytes = Integer.Parse(wr.Headers("Content-Length"))

    ' Display the value for the Content-Length header
    '''''' Console.WriteLine(url + ": " + bytes.ToString());
    wr.Close()

    callback(Me)

    ' Let the parent thread know the process is done
    are.[Set]()
End Sub
```

```
// C#
public void GetPageSize()
{
    // Request the URL
    WebResponse wr = WebRequest.Create(url).GetResponse();

    bytes = int.Parse(wr.Headers["Content-Length"]);

    // Display the value for the Content-Length header
    ///// Console.WriteLine(url + ": " + bytes.ToString());

    wr.Close();

    callback(this);

    // Let the parent thread know the process is done
    are.Set();
}
```

6. Finally, update the *foreach* loop in the *Main* method to create and start a new *Thread* instance rather than calling *ThreadPool.QueueUserWorkItem*. Pass the callback method to the *PageSize* constructor, as shown here:

```
' VB
For Each url As String In urls
    waitHandles(i) = New AutoResetEvent(False)
    Dim ps As New PageSize(url, waitHandles(i), _
        New ResultDelegate(AddressOf ResultCallback))
    Dim t As New Thread(New ThreadStart(AddressOf ps.GetPageSize))
    t.Start()
    i += 1
Next
```

```
// C#
foreach (string url in urls)
{
    waitHandles[i] = new AutoResetEvent(false);
    PageSize ps = new PageSize(url, waitHandles[i],
        new ResultDelegate(ResultCallback));
    Thread t = new Thread(new ThreadStart(ps.GetPageSize));
    t.Start();
    i++;
}
```

7. Build and run the application. Although it functions exactly the same as it did in Lesson 2, Exercise 1, the results are now being processed by a callback method. In the real world, this is a much more useful scenario—background threads almost always need to return results to the foreground thread.

Lesson Summary

- You can create an instance of the *Thread* class to provide more control over background threads than is available using *ThreadPool.QueueUserWorkItem*. Define the *Thread.Priority* property if you want to run the thread using a priority other than *Normal*. When the thread is configured, call *Thread.Start* to begin processing. If you need to stop the background thread, call *Thread.Abort*. If you might abort a thread, you should catch *ThreadAbortException* in the method to allow the method to close any open resources.

- If your foreground thread needs to monitor background threads, you can check the *Thread.ThreadState* property.

- When using the *Thread* class, the easiest way to pass data to a method is to create an instance of the class containing the method, and define attributes of the class. To pass data from a thread, define a callback method.

- Often, multiple threads need access to the same resources. To minimize resource conflicts, use *Monitor* locks to allow only a single thread to access a resource. If you want to provide separate logic for read locks and write locks, create an instance of the *ReaderWriterLock* class. To prevent basic mathematical calculations from being corrupted in multithreaded environments, use the static methods of the *Interlocked* class.

- The simplest way to wait for a thread to complete is to call *Thread.Join*. To wait for multiple threads to complete, create an array of *AutoResetEvent* objects, pass one item to each thread, and then call *WaitHandle.WaitAll* or *WaitHandle.WaitAny* from the foreground thread.

Lesson Review

You can use the following questions to test your knowledge of the information in Lesson 2, "Managing Threads." The questions are also available on the companion CD if you prefer to review them in electronic form.

NOTE   Answers

Answers to these questions and explanations of why each answer choice is right or wrong are located in the "Answers" section at the end of the book.

---

1. You will create an application that starts a new *Thread* object to run a method. You want the *Thread* to run as quickly as possible, even if that means it receives more processor time than the foreground thread. Which code sample does this correctly?

A.

```vbnet
' VB
Dim DoWorkThread As New Thread(New ThreadStart(AddressOf DoWork))
DoWorkThread.ThreadState = ThreadState.Running
DoWorkThread.Start()
```

```csharp
// C#
Thread DoWorkThread = new Thread(new ThreadStart(DoWork));
DoWorkThread.ThreadState = ThreadState.Running;
DoWorkThread.Start();
```

B.

```vbnet
' VB
Dim DoWorkThread As New Thread(New ThreadStart(AddressOf DoWork))
DoWorkThread.Priority = ThreadPriority.Highest
DoWorkThread.Start()
```

```csharp
// C#
Thread DoWorkThread = new Thread(new ThreadStart(DoWork));
DoWorkThread.Priority = ThreadPriority.Highest;
DoWorkThread.Start();
```

C.

```vbnet
' VB
Dim DoWorkThread As New Thread(New ThreadStart(AddressOf DoWork))
DoWorkThread.Priority = ThreadPriority.Lowest
DoWorkThread.Start()
```

```csharp
// C#
Thread DoWorkThread = new Thread(new ThreadStart(DoWork));
DoWorkThread.Priority = ThreadPriority.Lowest;
DoWorkThread.Start();
```

D.

```vbnet
' VB
Dim DoWorkThread As New Thread(New ThreadStart(AddressOf DoWork))
DoWorkThread.ThreadState = ThreadState.WaitSleepJoin
DoWorkThread.Start()
```

```csharp
// C#
Thread DoWorkThread = new Thread(new ThreadStart(DoWork));
DoWorkThread.ThreadState = ThreadState.WaitSleepJoin;
DoWorkThread.Start();
```

2. You are creating a method that is part of a custom class. The method might be run simultaneously within multiple threads. You need to ensure that no thread writes to the file while any thread is reading from the file. You want to provide the highest level of efficiency when multiple threads are reading from the file simultaneously. Which code sample should you use?

A.

```vb
' VB
SyncLock file
    ' Read file
End SyncLock
```

```csharp
// C#
lock (file)
{
    // Read file
}
```

B.

```vb
SyncLock
    ' Read file
End SyncLock
```

```csharp
// C#
lock
{
    // Read file
}
```

C.

```vb
' VB
Dim rwl As New ReaderWriterLock()
rwl.AcquireReaderLock()
    ' Read file
rwl.ReleaseReaderLock()
```

```csharp
// C#
ReaderWriterLock rwl = new ReaderWriterLock();
rwl.AcquireReaderLock();
    // Read file
rwl.ReleaseReaderLock();
```

D.

```vb
' VB
Dim rwl As New ReaderWriterLock()
rwl.AcquireReaderLock(10000)
    ' Read file
rwl.ReleaseReaderLock()
```

```csharp
// C#
ReaderWriterLock rwl = new ReaderWriterLock();
rwl.AcquireReaderLock(10000);
    // Read file
rwl.ReleaseReaderLock();
```

3. You are writing a method that tracks the total number of orders in shopping carts on your Web site. Orders might come from different users, and the request to increment the counter might come from different threads. Which of the following code samples increments the *orders* integer and guarantees accurate results?

A.

```vb
' VB
orders += 1
```

```csharp
// C#
orders += 1;
```

B.

```vb
SyncLock orders
    orders += 1
End SyncLock
```

```csharp
// C#
lock (orders)
{
    orders += 1;
}
```

C.

```vb
' VB
Interlocked.Increment(orders)
```

```csharp
// C#
Interlocked.Increment(ref orders);
```

D.

```vb
' VB
Dim rwl As New ReaderWriterLock()
rwl.AcquireReaderLock(10000)
orders += 1
rwl.ReleaseReaderLock()
```

```csharp
// C#
ReaderWriterLock rwl = new ReaderWriterLock();
rwl.AcquireReaderLock(10000);
orders += 1;
rwl.ReleaseReaderLock();
```

Chapter Review

To practice and reinforce the skills you learned in this chapter further, you can do any of the following:

- Review the chapter summary.
- Review the list of key terms introduced in this chapter.
- Complete the case scenarios. These scenarios set up real-world situations involving the topics of this chapter and ask you to create a solution.
- Complete the suggested practices.
- Take a practice test.

Chapter Summary

- The *System.Threading* namespace provides classes for starting and managing multiple threads. The simplest way to start a background thread is to call the *ThreadPool.QueueUserWorkItem* method. By providing the address of a method, the method you specify runs in the background until completion.

- If you need more control over threads than *ThreadPool.QueueUserWorkItem* provides, you can create an instance of the *Thread* class. The *Thread* class allows you to configure the priority of a thread and manually start, suspend, resume, and abort a thread. Regardless of whether you call *ThreadPool.QueueUserWorkItem* or create an instance of the *Thread* class, you can pass data to and from the thread. If multiple threads need to access the same resources, you should lock the resource to prevent conflicts and inaccurate calculations.

Key Terms

Do you know what these key terms mean? You can check your answers by looking up the terms in the glossary at the end of the book.

- Multithreaded
- Thread
- Thread-safe

Case Scenarios

In the following case scenarios, you apply what you've learned about how to implement and apply multithreading. You can find answers to these questions in the "Answers" section at the end of this book.

Case Scenario 1: Print in the Background

You are an application developer for City Power & Light, and you are adding the ability to print reports to an existing application. Your manager provides you with some basic requirements:

- Write a method named *Print* that accepts a *PrintJob* object.
- Print in the background to allow the user to continue working with the application's user interface.
- Write the simplest code possible.

Questions

Answer the following questions for your manager:

1. What's the easiest way to print the report?
2. Within the *Print* method, how can you access the *PrintJob* object?
3. If you need to display whether the print job succeeded later, how can you do it?

Case Scenario 2: Ensuring Integrity in a Financial Application

You are an application developer working for Humongous Insurance, and you are creating an application that accepts financial transactions from thousands of cash registers. The application is multithreaded, and if two cash registers submit a transaction at the same time, multiple threads can be running simultaneously. Accuracy is critical.

Questions

Answer the following questions for your manager:

1. The application maintains an object instance that tracks the total number of transactions. For every transaction, you need to increment the value of the object. How should you do that?

2. Most transactions require that you debit one account and credit another account. While the debit and credit takes place, you must ensure no other transactions occur. How can you do this?

Suggested Practices

To master the "Implementing service processes, threading, and application domains in a .NET Framework application" exam objective, complete the following tasks.

Develop Multithreaded .NET Framework Applications

For this task, you should complete at least Practices 1, 2, and 3. If you want a better understanding of how thread priorities affect performance, complete Practice 4 as well.

- **Practice 1**   Add multithreaded capabilities to a real-world application that you've written. Look for methods that prevent the user from interacting with the user interface, long-running methods that the user might want to cancel, processor-intensive tasks that can be distributed between multiple threads (and thus run on multiple processors simultaneously), and methods that need to wait for network connections.

- **Practice 2**   Using a multithreaded real-world application, look for potential resource access conflicts. Add locking as required to ensure resources are never overwritten.

- **Practice 3**   Create a Windows Presentation Foundation (WPF) application. When the user clicks a Start button, begin a processor-intensive task in a background thread, such as calculating the value of pi. (You can find algorithms by searching the Internet.) Continue calculating until the user clicks a Stop button, and then display the results to the user.

- **Practice 4**   To understand how thread priority affects performance, write an application that includes a method to calculate the value of pi. Create two *Thread* instances: one that calls the pi calculation method using the *Highest* priority, and a second that calls the pi calculation method using *Normal* priority. Notice how much farther the *Highest* priority thread gets in the calculation in a given amount of time.

Take a Practice Test

The practice tests on this book's companion CD offer many options. For example, you can test yourself on just the content covered in this chapter, or you can test yourself on all the 70-536 certification exam content. You can set up the test so that it closely simulates the experience of taking a certification exam, or you can set it up in study mode so that you can look at the correct answers and explanations after you answer each question.

MORE INFO   Practice tests

For details about all the practice test options available, see the section "How to Use the Practice Tests," in the Introduction to this book.

Chapter 8
Application Domains and Services

This chapter covers two distinct topics: application domains and services. *Application domains* enable you to call external assemblies with optimal efficiency and security. *Services* are a special type of assembly that runs in the background, presents no user interface, and is controlled by using special tools. This chapter discusses how to create and configure application domains, and how to develop and install services.

Exam objectives in this chapter:
- Create a unit of isolation for Common Language Runtime (CLR) in a .NET Framework application by using application domains.
- Implement, install, and control a service.

Lessons in this chapter:

Before You Begin

To complete the lessons in this chapter, you should be familiar with Microsoft Visual Basic or C# and be comfortable with the following tasks:

- Creating a Console application in Microsoft Visual Studio using Visual Basic or C#
- Adding namespaces and system class library references to a project
- Creating text files
- Adding events to the event log

Lesson 1: Creating Application Domains

Developers often need to run an external assembly. However, running an external assembly can lead to inefficient resource usage and security vulnerabilities. The best way to manage these risks is to create an application domain and call the assembly from within the protected environment.

After this lesson, you will be able to:

- Describe the purpose of an application domain
- Write code that uses the *AppDomain* class
- Create an application domain
- Start an assembly within an application domain
- Unload the application domain

Estimated lesson time: 20 minutes

What Is an Application Domain?

An *application domain* is a logical container that allows multiple assemblies to run within a single process but prevents them from directly accessing memory that belongs to other assemblies. In addition, application domains provide isolation from faults because unhandled exceptions do not affect other application domains, which allows applications in other application domains to continue running undisturbed. Another benefit of using multiple application domains is that each application domain can be assigned a different security access level (even though it might run in the same process as other application domains).

Application domains offer many of the features of a process, such as separate memory spaces and separate access to resources. However, application domains are more efficient than processes, enabling multiple assemblies to be run in separate application domains without the overhead of starting separate processes. Figure 8-1 shows how a single process can contain multiple application domains.

If an application runs with full trust, the application domain is not a secure boundary. Applications with full trust can bypass .NET Framework security checks by calling native code, which in turn can gain unrestricted access to anything within the process (and thus within any application domain).

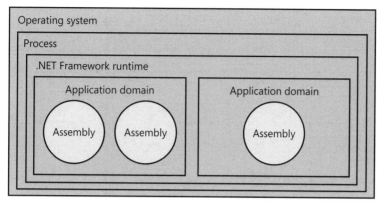

Figure 8-1 Application domains keep assemblies separate within a single process

---

IMPORTANT Contrasting Application Domains and Processes

The .NET Framework runtime manages application domains, whereas the operating system manages processes.

The best example of application domains in use today is the Microsoft Internet Information Services (IIS) ASP.NET worker process, implemented by w3wp.exe. If you have 10 ASP.NET applications on a single Web server, all applications can run within the same process. However, ASP.NET creates a separate application domain for each application, preventing each application from accessing another application's data. If two applications need to communicate, you need to use .NET remoting, Web services, or a similar technique.

Most of the time, you rely on the existing runtime hosts to create application domains for your assemblies automatically. Examples of runtime hosts built into Microsoft Windows are ASP.NET, Windows Internet Explorer (which creates a single application domain for all assemblies from a specific Web site), and the operating system. You can configure the behavior of these application domains by using friendly tools such as the Internet Information Services Manager and the .NET Framework Configuration tool.

However, just as w3wp.exe creates application domains to isolate multiple instances of an assembly, you can create your own application domains to call assemblies with little risk that the assembly will take any action or access any resources that you have not specifically permitted. Figure 8-2 shows how an assembly can host application domains.

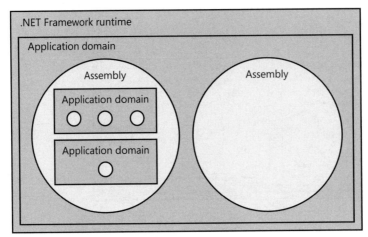

Figure 8-2 Assemblies can host child application domains

Besides isolating an assembly for security reasons, you can use application domains to improve reliability and efficiency.

Reliability

Use application domains to isolate tasks that might cause a process to terminate. If the state of the application domain that's executing a task becomes unstable, the application domain can be unloaded without affecting the process. This technique is important when a process must run for long periods without restarting. You can also use application domains to isolate tasks that should not share data. For example, if your application supports add-ins, you can load the add-ins into a separate application domain and unload it whenever necessary without affecting the parent application domain.

Efficiency

If an assembly is loaded into the default application domain, the assembly cannot be unloaded from memory while the process is running. However, if you open a second application domain to load and execute the assembly, the assembly is unloaded when that application domain is unloaded. Use this technique to minimize the working set of long-running processes that occasionally use large dynamic-link libraries (DLLs).

The *AppDomain* Class

Application domains are implemented in the .NET Framework using the *System .AppDomain* class. To use an application domain, create an instance of the *AppDomain* class and then execute an assembly within that domain. Table 8-1 shows the *AppDomain* properties.

Table 8-1 *AppDomain* Properties

Name	Description
ActivationContext	Gets the activation context for the current application domain.
ApplicationIdentity	Gets the identity of the application in the application domain.
ApplicationTrust	Gets information describing the permissions granted to an application and whether the application has a trust level that allows it to run.
BaseDirectory	Gets the base directory that the assembly resolver uses to probe for assemblies.
CurrentDomain	Gets the current application domain for the current thread. This property allows you to analyze the current domain to determine context or verify permissions.
DomainManager	Gets the domain manager that was provided by the host when the application domain was initialized.
DynamicDirectory	Gets the directory that the assembly resolver uses to probe for dynamically created assemblies.
Evidence	Gets the *Evidence* associated with this application domain that is used as input to the security policy. For more information about evidence, refer to Chapter 11, "Application Security."
FriendlyName	Gets the friendly name of this application domain. For domains created by the .NET Framework, this friendly name takes the form <*ProjectName*>.vshost.exe. You must specify the friendly name when you create application domains programmatically.
Id	Gets an integer that uniquely identifies the application domain within the process.
RelativeSearchPath	Gets the path relative to the base directory where the assembly resolver should probe for private assemblies.

Table 8-1 *AppDomain* Properties

Name	Description
SetupInformation	Gets the application domain configuration information for this instance.
ShadowCopyFiles	Gets an indication whether all assemblies loaded in the application domain are shadow copied.

Table 8-2 shows the most important *AppDomain* methods.

Table 8-2 *AppDomain* Methods

Name	Description
ApplyPolicy	Returns the assembly display name after a policy has been applied.
CreateComInstanceFrom	Creates a new instance of a specified COM type.
CreateDomain	Creates a new application domain. Use this method instead of an *AppDomain* constructor.
CreateInstance	Creates a new instance of a specified type defined in a specified assembly.
CreateInstanceAndUnwrap	Creates a new instance of a specified type.
CreateInstanceFrom	Creates a new instance of a specified type defined in the specified assembly file.
CreateInstanceFromAndWrap	Creates a new instance of a specified type defined in the specified assembly file.
DefineDynamicAssembly	Defines a dynamic assembly in the current application domain.
DoCallBack	Executes the code in another application domain that is identified by the specified delegate.
ExecuteAssembly	Executes the assembly contained in the specified file.
ExecuteAssemblyByName	Executes an assembly.

Table 8-2 *AppDomain* Methods

Name	Description
GetAssemblies	Gets the assemblies that have been loaded into the execution context of this application domain.
GetCurrentThreadId	Gets the current thread identifier.
GetData	Gets the value stored in the current application domain for the specified name.
InitializeLifetimeService	Gives the *AppDomain* an infinite lifetime by preventing a lease from being created.
IsDefaultAppDomain	Returns a value that indicates whether the application domain is the default application domain for the process.
IsFinalizingForUnload	Indicates whether this application domain is unloading and the objects it contains are being finalized by the CLR.
Load	Loads an *Assembly* into this application domain.
ReflectionOnlyGetAssemblies	Returns the assemblies that have been loaded into the reflection-only context of the application domain.
SetAppDomainPolicy	Establishes the security policy level for this application domain.
SetData	Assigns a value to an application domain property.
SetDynamicBase	Establishes the specified directory path as the location where dynamically generated files are stored and accessed.
SetPrincipalPolicy	Specifies how principal and identity objects should be attached to a thread if the thread attempts to bind to a principal while executing in this application domain.
SetShadowCopyFiles	Turns on shadow copying.

Table 8-2 *AppDomain* Methods

Name	Description
SetShadowCopyPath	Establishes the specified directory path as the location of assemblies to be shadow copied.
SetThreadPrincipal	Sets the default principal object to be attached to threads if they attempt to bind to a principal while executing in this application domain.
Unload	Unloads the specified application domain.

How to Create an Application Domain

To create an application domain, call one of the overloaded *AppDomain.CreateDomain* methods. At a minimum, you must provide a name for the new application domain. The following code demonstrates this process:

```
' VB
Dim d As AppDomain = AppDomain.CreateDomain("NewDomain")

Console.WriteLine("Host domain: " + AppDomain.CurrentDomain.FriendlyName)
Console.WriteLine("Child domain: " + d.FriendlyName)
```

```
// C#
AppDomain d = AppDomain.CreateDomain("NewDomain");

Console.WriteLine("Host domain: " + AppDomain.CurrentDomain.FriendlyName);
Console.WriteLine("Child domain: " + d.FriendlyName);
```

As the previous code sample demonstrated, you can access the application domain your assembly is currently running in (which was probably automatically created by the .NET Framework) by accessing *AppDomain.CurrentDomain*.

How to Load Assemblies in an Application Domain

Creating a new application domain and starting an assembly within that domain is as simple as creating an instance of the *System.AppDomain* class with a friendly name, and then calling the *ExecuteAssembly* method, as the following code demonstrates:

```
' VB
Dim d As AppDomain = AppDomain.CreateDomain("NewDomain")
d.ExecuteAssembly("Assembly.exe")
```

```
// C#
AppDomain d = AppDomain.CreateDomain("NewDomain");
d.ExecuteAssembly("Assembly.exe");
```

The *AppDomain.ExecuteAssembly* method has overloads that allow you to pass command-line arguments, too. As an alternative to providing the complete path to the assembly, you can add a reference to the assembly and then run it by name using the *AppDomain .ExecuteAssemblyByName* method, as the following code demonstrates:

```
' VB
Dim d As AppDomain = AppDomain.CreateDomain("NewDomain")
d.ExecuteAssemblyByName("Assembly")
```

```
// C#
AppDomain d = AppDomain.CreateDomain("NewDomain");
d.ExecuteAssemblyByName("Assembly");
```

Calling an assembly in this manner provides isolation for the assembly but does not take advantage of the huge power and flexibility built into application domains. Lesson 2, "Configuring Application Domains," discusses configuring application domains in more detail.

How to Unload an Application Domain

One of the advantages of loading assemblies in new application domains is that you can unload the application domain at any time, freeing up resources. To unload a domain and any assemblies within the domain, call the static *AppDomain.Unload* method as follows:

```
' VB
Dim d As AppDomain = AppDomain.CreateDomain("NewDomain")
AppDomain.Unload(d)
```

```
// C#
AppDomain d = AppDomain.CreateDomain("NewDomain");
AppDomain.Unload(d);
```

Individual assemblies or types cannot be unloaded.

Lab: Creating Domains and Loading Assemblies

In this lab, you will create an application domain and then load an assembly using two different techniques: by filename and by reference. If you encounter a problem completing an exercise, the completed projects are available along with the sample files.

▶ Exercise 1: Load an Assembly by Filename

In this exercise, you will create an application domain and use it to run an assembly that displays your %Windir%\Win.ini file.

1. Navigate to the \<*InstallHome*>\Chapter08\Lesson1\Exercise1\Partial folder and open either the C# version or the Visual Basic .NET version of the solution file.

2. Build and run the ShowWinIni Console application to verify that it works properly. If it does not properly display your Win.ini file, modify the application to display any text file.

3. Create a new Console Application solution named AppDomainDemo.

4. In your new Console application, write code to create an *AppDomain* object. For example, the following code works:

```
' VB
Dim d As AppDomain = AppDomain.CreateDomain("NewDomain")
```

```
// C#
AppDomain d = AppDomain.CreateDomain("New Domain");
```

5. Next, write code to run the *ShowWinIni* assembly within the newly created *AppDomain* by explicitly providing the full path to the file. For example, the following code works, but it needs to be adjusted to reflect where you saved the executable file:

```
' VB
d.ExecuteAssembly("ShowWinIni.exe")
```

```
// C#
d.ExecuteAssembly("ShowWinIni.exe");
```

6. Build the project and resolve any errors. Verify that the Console application successfully calls the ShowWinIni.exe assembly and that it displays the text file successfully.

▶ **Exercise 2: Load an Assembly by Assembly Name**

In this exercise, you will modify the Console application you created in Exercise 1 to run an assembly based on the assembly name rather than the filename.

1. Open the AppDomainDemo project that you created in Exercise 1. Alternatively, you can navigate to the \<*InstallHome*>\Chapter08\Lesson2\Exercise2\Partial folder and open either the C# version or the Visual Basic .NET version of the solution file.

2. Add a reference to the *ShowWinIni.exe* assembly.

3. Modify the call to the *AppDomain.ExecuteAssembly* method to call *AppDomain*
   .ExecuteAssemblyByName instead. For example, you might use the following code:

```
' VB
Dim d As AppDomain = AppDomain.CreateDomain("NewDomain")
d.ExecuteAssemblyByName("ShowWinIni")
```

```
// C#
AppDomain d = AppDomain.CreateDomain("New Domain");
d.ExecuteAssemblyByName("ShowWinIni");
```

4. Build the project and resolve any errors. Verify that the Console application successfully calls the ShowWinIni.exe assembly and that it displays the text file successfully.

Lesson Summary

- An application domain is a logical container that allows multiple assemblies to run within a single process but prevents them from directly accessing memory belonging to other assemblies. Create an application domain anytime you want to start an assembly.

- The *AppDomain* class contains methods for defining privileges, folders, and other properties for a new application domain, starting an assembly, and unloading an application domain.

- To create an instance of the *AppDomain* class, call the static *AppDomain.CreateDomain* method. *AppDomain* does not have any traditional constructors.

- To load an assembly in an application domain, create an instance of the *AppDomain* class and then call the *App.Domain.ExecuteAssembly* method.

- To unload an application domain, call the *AppDomain.Unload* static method.

Lesson Review

You can use the following questions to test your knowledge of the information in Lesson 1, "Creating Application Domains." The questions are also available on the companion CD if you prefer to review them in electronic form.

NOTE Answers

Answers to these questions and explanations of why each answer choice is right or wrong are located in the "Answers" section at the end of the book.

---

1. Which of the following are valid reasons to create an application domain? (Choose all that apply.)

   A. It is the only way to start a separate process.

   B. You can remove the application domain to free up resources.

   C. Application domains improve performance.

   D. Application domains provide a layer of separation and security.

2. Which of the following are valid ways to run an assembly within an application domain? (Choose all that apply.)

   A. *AppDomain.CreateDomain*

   B. *AppDomain.ExecuteAssembly*

   C. *AppDomain.ExecuteAssemblyByName*

   D. *AppDomain.ApplicationIdentity*

3. Which command would you use to close the application domain in the following code sample?

```vb
' VB
Dim d As AppDomain = AppDomain.CreateDomain("New Domain")
d.ExecuteAssemblyByName("MyAssembly")
```

```csharp
// C#
AppDomain d = AppDomain.CreateDomain("New Domain");
d.ExecuteAssemblyByName("MyAssembly");
```

   A. *d.DomainUnload()*

   B. *d = null*

   C. *d.Unload()*

   D. *AppDomain.Unload(d)*

Lesson 2: Configuring Application Domains

You can configure application domains to create customized environments for assemblies. The most important application of modifying the default settings for an application domain is restricting permissions to reduce the risks associated with security vulnerabilities. When configured ideally, an application domain not only provides a unit of isolation, but it limits the damage that attackers can do if they successfully exploit an assembly.

> **After this lesson, you will be able to:**
> - Start assemblies in an application domain with limited privileges.
> - Configure application domain properties to control folder locations and other settings.
>
> **Estimated lesson time: 25 minutes**

How to Use an Application Domain to Start Assemblies with Limited Privileges

Restricting the permissions of an application domain can greatly reduce the risk that an assembly you call will perform some malicious action. Consider the following scenario: You purchase an assembly from a third party and use the assembly to communicate with a database. An attacker discovers a security vulnerability in the third-party assembly and uses it to configure a spyware application to start automatically. To the user, the security vulnerability is your fault, because your application trusted the third-party assembly and ran it with privileges sufficient to install software.

Now consider the same scenario using an application domain with limited privileges: An attacker discovers a security vulnerability in the third-party assembly. However, when the attacker attempts to exploit the vulnerability to write files to the local hard disk, the file input/output (I/O) request is rejected because of insufficient privileges. Although the security vulnerability still exists, the limited privileges assigned to the application domain prevent it from being exploited.

In this example, starting assemblies with limited privileges is an example of *defense-in-depth*. Defense-in-depth is the security principle of providing multiple levels of protection so that you are still protected in the event of a vulnerability. Defense-in-depth is particularly important when calling external code because external code might have vulnerabilities that you are not aware of, cannot prevent, and cannot fix.

The following sections describe how to use evidence to configure application domains. There are several other ways to control the permissions granted to an assembly. For more information about code access security, refer to Chapter 11.

How to Provide Host Evidence for an Assembly

When you create an application domain and start assemblies, you have complete control over the host evidence. *Evidence* is the information that the runtime gathers about an assembly to determine to which code groups the assembly belongs. The code groups, in turn, determine the assembly's privileges. Common forms of evidence include the folder or Web site the assembly is running from and digital signatures.

By assigning evidence to an assembly, you can control the permissions that will be assigned to the assembly. To provide evidence for an assembly, first create a *System .Security.Policy.Evidence* object and then pass it as a parameter to the application domain's overloaded *ExecuteAssembly* method.

When you create an *Evidence* object with the constructor that requires two object arrays, you must provide one array that represents host evidence and a second array that provides assembly evidence. Either of the arrays can be null, and unless you have specifically created an assembly evidence object, you will probably assign only the host evidence array. It might seem odd that *Evidence* takes unspecified *object* arrays instead of strongly typed *Evidence* objects. However, evidence can be *anything*: a string, an integer, or a custom class. So even if you are using the evidence types built into the .NET Framework, you have to add them to an *object* array.

MORE INFO   Evidence

For more information about evidence, refer to Chapter 11.

The simplest way to control the permissions assigned to an assembly in an application domain is to pass zone evidence by using a *System.Security.Policy.Zone* object and the *System.Security.SecurityZone* enumeration. The following code demonstrates using the *Evidence* constructor that requires two object arrays by creating a *Zone* object, adding it to an *object* array named *hostEvidence*, and then using the *object* array to create an *Evidence* object named *internetEvidence*. Finally, that *Evidence* object is passed to the application domain's *ExecuteAssembly* method along with the filename of the assembly. The following code sample, which requires the *System.Security* and *System.Security .Policy* namespaces, demonstrates this process:

```vb
' VB
Dim hostEvidence As Object() = {New Zone (SecurityZone.Internet)}
Dim internetEvidence As Evidence = New Evidence (hostEvidence, Nothing)
```

```
Dim myDomain As AppDomain = AppDomain.CreateDomain("MyDomain")
myDomain.ExecuteAssembly("SecondAssembly.exe", internetEvidence)
```

```
// C#
object[] hostEvidence = {new Zone(SecurityZone.Internet)};
Evidence internetEvidence = new Evidence(hostEvidence, null);
AppDomain myDomain = AppDomain.CreateDomain("MyDomain");
myDomain.ExecuteAssembly("SecondAssembly.exe", internetEvidence);
```

The result is that the specified assembly runs in an isolated application domain with only the permission set granted to the Internet_Zone code group. When the application domain starts the assembly, the runtime analyzes the evidence provided. Because the evidence matches the Internet zone, the runtime assigns it to the Internet_Zone code group, which in turn assigns the Internet permission set, which is extremely restrictive by default. For more information about code groups, refer to Chapter 11, "Application Security."

IMPORTANT Controlling Evidence

Running an assembly using the Internet_Zone code group is useful for maximizing application security because the assembly has its permissions restricted as if it came from the Internet. But the assembly isn't necessarily coming from the Internet—it can be stored on the same folder as the running assembly. Essentially, you are providing false evidence to the runtime. Providing evidence to the runtime can also be used to grant an assembly *more* permissions than it would normally receive, which is a powerful capability. To control this capability, restrict the *SecurityPermission. ControlEvidence* permission, as discussed in Chapter 11.

How to Provide Host Evidence for an Application Domain

You can also provide evidence for entire application domains. The technique is similar to providing evidence for a new assembly, and it uses an overload of the *AppDomain.CreateDomain* method that accepts an *Evidence* object, as the following code sample (which requires the *System.Security* and *System.Security.Policy* namespaces) demonstrates:

```
' VB
Dim hostEvidence As Object() =  {New Zone (SecurityZone.Internet)}
Dim appDomainEvidence As Evidence = New Evidence (hostEvidence, Nothing)
Dim d As AppDomain = AppDomain.CreateDomain("MyDomain", appDomainEvidence)
d.ExecuteAssembly("SecondAssembly.exe")
```

```
// C#
object [] hostEvidence = {new Zone(SecurityZone.Internet)};
Evidence appDomainEvidence = new Evidence(hostEvidence, null);
AppDomain d = AppDomain.CreateDomain("MyDomain", appDomainEvidence);
d.ExecuteAssembly("SecondAssembly.exe");
```

You can also call the *Evidence.AddAssembly* and *Evidence.AddHost* methods to add evidence after creating the *Evidence* object.

How to Configure Application Domain Properties

You can provide the CLR with configuration information for a new application domain using the *AppDomainSetup* class. When creating your own application domains, the most important property is *ApplicationBase*. The other *AppDomainSetup* properties are used mainly by runtime hosts to configure a particular application domain. Changing the properties of an *AppDomainSetup* instance does not affect any existing *AppDomain*. It can affect only the creation of a new *AppDomain* when the *CreateDomain* method is called with the *AppDomainSetup* instance as a parameter.

Table 8-3 shows the most useful *AppDomainSetup* properties.

Table 8-3 *AppDomainSetup* Properties

Name	Description
ActivationArguments	Gets or sets data about the activation of an application domain.
ApplicationBase	Gets or sets the name of the root directory containing the application. By default, this is the folder containing the assembly (when an assembly is loaded from disk), or the parent that created the *AppDomain* (when an *AppDomain* is created by a running assembly). When the runtime needs to satisfy a type request, it probes for the assembly containing the type in the directory specified by the *ApplicationBase* property.
ApplicationName	Gets or sets the name of the application.
ApplicationTrust	Gets or sets an object containing security and trust information.
ConfigurationFile	Gets or sets the name of the configuration file for an application domain. The configuration file uses the same format as Machine.config, but specifies settings that apply only to the application domain. Typically, the file is named <*Assembly*>.config. For example, if your assembly is named MyApp.exe, the configuration file would be named MyApp.config.
DisallowApplication-BaseProbing	Specifies whether the application base path and private binary path are probed when searching for assemblies to load.

Table 8-3 *AppDomainSetup* Properties

Name	Description
DisallowBindingRedirects	Gets or sets a value indicating whether an application domain allows assembly binding redirection.
DisallowCodeDownload	Gets or sets a value indicating whether Hypertext Transfer Protocol (HTTP) download of assemblies is allowed for an application domain. The default value is *false,* which is not secure for services (discussed in Lesson 3, "Creating Windows Services," later in this chapter). To help prevent services from downloading partially trusted code, set this property to *true.*
DisallowPublisherPolicy	Gets or sets a value indicating whether the publisher policy section of the configuration file is applied to an application domain.
DynamicBase	Gets or sets the base directory where the directory for dynamically generated files is located.
LicenseFile	Gets or sets the location of the license file associated with this domain.
LoaderOptimization	Specifies the optimization policy used to load an executable.
PrivateBinPath	Gets or sets the list of directories under the application base directory that is probed for private assemblies.

To apply these properties to an application domain, create and configure an *AppDomainSetup* object and pass it (along with an *Evidence* object) to the *AppDomain.CreateDomain* method. The following code sample demonstrates this process:

```
' VB
' Construct and initialize settings for a second AppDomain
Dim ads As AppDomainSetup = New AppDomainSetup
ads.ApplicationBase = "file://" + System.Environment.CurrentDirectory
ads.DisallowBindingRedirects = False
ads.DisallowCodeDownload = True
ads.ConfigurationFile = AppDomain.CurrentDomain.SetupInformation.ConfigurationFile

' Create the second AppDomain
Dim d As AppDomain = AppDomain.CreateDomain("New Domain", Nothing, ads)
```

```
// C#
// Construct and initialize settings for a second AppDomain.
AppDomainSetup ads = new AppDomainSetup();
ads.ApplicationBase = "file://" + System.Environment.CurrentDirectory;
ads.DisallowBindingRedirects = false;
ads.DisallowCodeDownload = true;
ads.ConfigurationFile = AppDomain.CurrentDomain.SetupInformation.ConfigurationFile;

// Create the second AppDomain
AppDomain d = AppDomain.CreateDomain("New Domain", null, ads);
```

To examine the properties for the current application domain, use the *AppDomain
.CurrentDomain.SetupInformation* object, as the following code sample demonstrates:

```
' VB
Dim ads As AppDomainSetup = AppDomain.CurrentDomain.SetupInformation
Console.WriteLine(ads.ApplicationBase)
Console.WriteLine(ads.ApplicationName)
Console.WriteLine(ads.DisallowCodeDownload)
Console.WriteLine(ads.DisallowBindingRedirects)
```

```
// C#
AppDomainSetup ads = AppDomain.CurrentDomain.SetupInformation;
Console.WriteLine(ads.ApplicationBase);
Console.WriteLine(ads.ApplicationName);
Console.WriteLine(ads.DisallowCodeDownload);
Console.WriteLine(ads.DisallowBindingRedirects);
```

Lab: Control Application Domain Privileges

In this lab, you will create an application domain with reduced privileges to reduce
the security risks of running an external assembly. If you encounter a problem completing an exercise, the completed projects are available along with the sample files.

▶ Exercise: Load an Assembly with Restricted Privileges

In this exercise, you will load an assembly without granting it privileges to read system
files.

1. Navigate to the \<*InstallHome*>\Chapter08\Lesson2\Exercise1\Partial folder and
   open either the C# version or the Visual Basic .NET version of the solution file.

2. Add a reference to the ShowWinIni.exe file that you created in Lesson 1.

3. Add the *System.Security* and *System.Security.Policy* namespaces to your code file.

4. Prior to the creation of the *AppDomain* object, create an *Evidence* object containing the Intranet security zone. The following code works:

   ```
   ' VB
   ' Create an Evidence object for the Internet zone
   Dim hostEvidence As Object() = {New Zone(SecurityZone.Intranet)}
   Dim e As Evidence = New Evidence(hostEvidence, Nothing)
   ```

```csharp
// C#
// Create an Evidence object for the Internet zone
object[] hostEvidence = { new Zone(SecurityZone.Intranet) };
Evidence e = new Evidence(hostEvidence, null);
```

5. Modify the call to the *AppDomain.CreateDomain* method to provide the *Evidence* object you created. For example:

```vb
' VB
' Create an AppDomain
Dim d As AppDomain = AppDomain.CreateDomain("NewDomain", e)
```

```csharp
// C#
// Create an AppDomain.
AppDomain d = AppDomain.CreateDomain("New Domain", e);
```

6. Build and run the AppDomainDemo Console application. This time, when your assembly attempts to run ShowWinIni, the runtime will throw a *SecurityException*. The application domain you created is in the Intranet zone, which lacks privileges to read the Win.ini file. If the assembly contained a security vulnerability or deliberately malicious code, providing restrictive evidence for the application domain could have prevented a security compromise such as a virus or spyware infection.

7. In your code, change *SecurityZone.Intranet* to *SecurityZone.MyComputer*. Build and run the Console application again. This time, ShowWinIni successfully displays the Win.ini file because the MyComputer zone has privileges to read the Win.ini file.

Lesson Summary

-   The simplest way to use an application domain to start an assembly with limited privileges is to specify a restricted zone, such as the Internet zone, as evidence.

-   To configure an application domain's properties, create an instance of the *AppDomainSetup* class. Then use the instance when creating the application domain.

Lesson Review

You can use the following questions to test your knowledge of the information in Lesson 2, "Configuring Application Domains." The questions are also available on the companion CD if you prefer to review them in electronic form.

NOTE Answers

Answers to these questions and explanations of why each answer choice is right or wrong are located in the "Answers" section at the end of the book.

1. How does the runtime use evidence when creating an application domain?

    A. To determine the priority at which the process should run

    B. To identify the author of the assembly

    C. To determine which privileges the assembly should receive

    D. To track the actions of the assembly for audit purposes

2. Which of the following code samples runs an assembly as if it were located on the Internet? (Choose all that apply.)

    A.

```
' VB
Dim hostEvidence As Object() =  {New Zone (SecurityZone.Internet)}
Dim e As Evidence = New Evidence (hostEvidence, Nothing)
Dim d As AppDomain = AppDomain.CreateDomain("MyDomain", e)
d.ExecuteAssembly("Assembly.exe")
```

```
// C#
object[] hostEvidence = {new Zone(SecurityZone.Internet)};
Evidence e = new Evidence(hostEvidence, null);
AppDomain d = AppDomain.CreateDomain("MyDomain", e);
d.ExecuteAssembly("Assembly.exe");
```

    B.

```
' VB
Dim hostEvidence As Object() =  {New Zone (SecurityZone.Internet)}
Dim d As AppDomain = AppDomain.CreateDomain("MyDomain")
Dim e As Evidence = New Evidence (hostEvidence, Nothing)
d.Evidence = e
d.ExecuteAssembly("Assembly.exe")
```

```
// C#
object[] hostEvidence = {new Zone(SecurityZone.Internet)};
AppDomain d = AppDomain.CreateDomain("MyDomain");
Evidence e = new Evidence(hostEvidence, null);
d.Evidence = e;
d.ExecuteAssembly("Assembly.exe");
```

    C.

```
' VB
Dim myDomain As AppDomain = AppDomain.CreateDomain("MyDomain")
myDomain.ExecuteAssembly("Assembly.exe", New Zone (SecurityZone.Internet))
```

```
// C#
AppDomain myDomain = AppDomain.CreateDomain("MyDomain");
myDomain.ExecuteAssembly("Assembly.exe", new Zone(SecurityZone.Internet));
```

    D.

```
' VB
Dim e As Evidence = New Evidence
e.AddHost(New Zone (SecurityZone.Internet))
```

```
Dim myDomain As AppDomain = AppDomain.CreateDomain("MyDomain")
myDomain.ExecuteAssembly("Assembly.exe", e)

// C#
Evidence e = new Evidence();
e.AddHost(new Zone(SecurityZone.Internet));
AppDomain myDomain = AppDomain.CreateDomain("MyDomain");
myDomain.ExecuteAssembly("Assembly.exe", e);
```

3. How can you set the base directory for an application in an application domain?

   A. Create an instance of the *AppDomain* class and then set the *DynamicDirectory* property.

   B. Create an instance of the *AppDomain* class and then set the *BaseDirectory* property.

   C. Create an instance of the *AppDomainSetup* class and then set the *DynamicBase* property.

   D. Create an instance of the *AppDomainSetup* class and then set the *Application-Base* property.

4. You need to notify the user if your assembly is running without the ability to use HTTP to download assemblies. How can you determine whether you have that permission?

   A. Examine *AppDomain.CurrentDomain.SetupInformation.DisallowCodeDownload*

   B. Examine *AppDomain.CurrentDomain.DisallowCodeDownload*

   C. Examine *AppDomain.CurrentDomain.SetupInformation.DisallowPublisherPolicy*

   D. Examine *AppDomain.CurrentDomain.DisallowPublisherPolicy*

Lesson 3: Creating Windows Services

Creating services enables you to run an assembly in the background without any interaction from the user. Services are perfect when you want to monitor something continuously, when your assembly needs to listen for incoming network connections, or when you need to start your assembly before the user logs on. Because of their unique nature, services require special security and installation considerations.

After this lesson, you will be able to:

- Describe the purpose of a service.
- Create a service project in Visual Studio.
- Specify properties for a service.
- Install a service manually.
- Create a setup project for a service.
- Start and manage a service using tools built into Windows.

Estimated lesson time: 45 minutes

What Is a Windows Service?

A *Windows Service* is a process that runs in the background without a user interface and in its own user session. Services can be started automatically when the computer starts, even if a user does not log on. Therefore, services are an ideal way to implement an application that should be running constantly and does not need to interact with the user. Windows has dozens of services built in, including Server (which shares folders on the network), Workstation (which connects to shared folders), and World Wide Web Publishing (which serves Web pages).

NOTE **Creating Windows Services in Different Versions of Visual Studio**

The Windows Service template and associated functionality is not available in Visual Studio, Standard Edition.

Service applications function differently from other project types in several ways:

- The compiled executable file that a service application project creates must be installed before the project can function in a meaningful way. You cannot debug or run a service application by pressing F5 or F11; you cannot run a service or step into its code directly. Instead, you must install and start your service and then attach a debugger to the service's process. If you use Windows Communication Foundation (WCF), you can use the Visual Studio debugger for services. For more information, visit *http://msdn.microsoft.com/en-us/library/bb552361.aspx*.

MORE INFO Debugging Services

For more information about debugging services, see "How to: Debug Windows Service Applications" at *http://msdn.microsoft.com/library/7a50syb3.aspx*.

- Unlike some other types of projects, you must create installation components for service applications. The installation components install and register the service on the server and create an entry for your service with the Windows Services Control Manager.

- The *Main* method for your service application must issue the *Run* command for the services that your project contains. The *Run* method loads the services into the Services Control Manager on the appropriate server. If you use the Windows Services project template, this method is written for you automatically.

- Windows Service applications run in a different window station than the interactive station of the logged-on user. A *window station* is a secure object that contains a Clipboard, a set of global atoms, and a group of desktop objects. Because the station of the Windows Service is not interactive, dialog boxes raised from within a Windows Service application are not seen and might cause your program to stop responding. Similarly, error messages should be logged in the Windows event log rather than raised in the user interface.

- Windows Service applications run in their own security context and are started before the user logs into the Windows computer on which the service applications are installed. You should plan carefully what user account to run the service within; a service running under the system account has more permissions and privileges than a user account. The more privileges your service has, the more damage attackers can do if they successfully exploit a security vulnerability in your service. Therefore, you should run your service with the fewest privileges possible to minimize potential damage.

Real World

Tony Northrup

I started using the .NET Framework as soon as betas of the first version were available. However, earlier versions did not support creating services with the .NET Framework. I didn't want to revert to another development environment, so I relied on hacks to enable .NET assemblies to run in the background. Typically, I would create a Console application, and then use Scheduled Tasks to configure it to start automatically under a special user account. This technique enabled the process to run continuously in the background, but was difficult to manage because I couldn't use the services snap-in to start or stop the service.

How to Create a Service Project

At a high level, you follow these steps to create a service project:

1. Create a project using the Windows Service application template, as shown in Figure 8-3. This template creates a class for you that inherits from *ServiceBase* and writes much of the basic service code, such as the code to start the service.

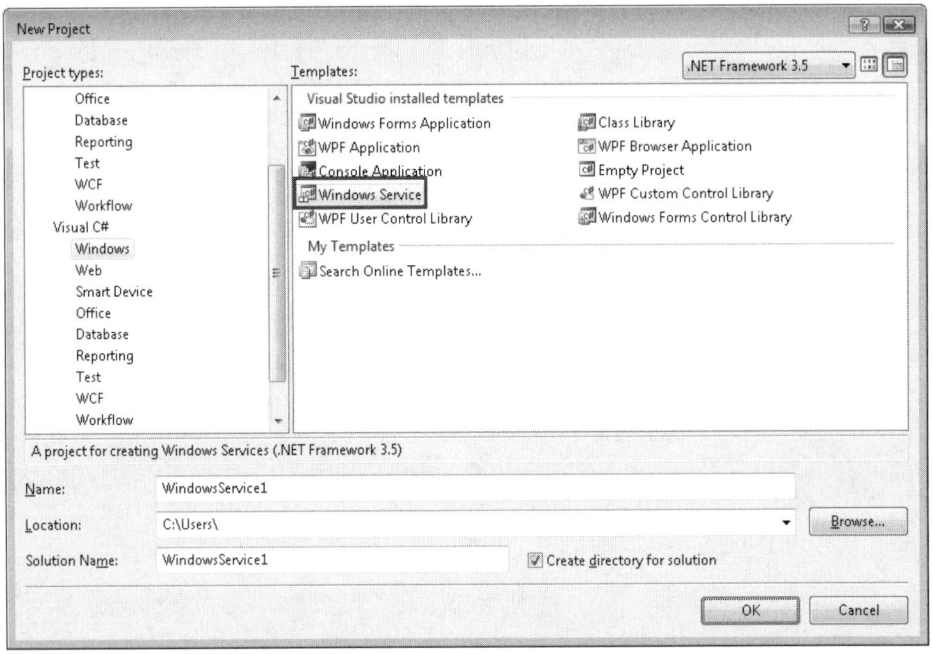

Figure 8-3   Visual Studio includes the Windows Service application template

2. Write the code for the *OnStart* and *OnStop* procedures and override any other methods that you want to redefine.

3. Add the necessary installers for your service application. By default, a class containing two or more installers is added to your application when you click the Add Installer link: one to install the process, and one for each of the associated services your project contains.

4. Build your project.

5. Create a setup project to install your service and then install it.

6. Use the Services snap-in to start your service.

The following sections describe how to implement these capabilities at the code level.

How to Implement a Service

After you create a new service project in Visual Studio, follow these steps to implement the service:

1. In the properties for your designer, modify the *ServiceBase.ServiceName* property. Every service must have a unique name; therefore, it is very important to change this setting. The ServiceName setting is not the friendly name you will see in the Services snap-in. Instead, the ServiceName setting is used by the operating system to identify the service and can be used to identify the service programmatically. For example, you can start a service from the command line by running *Net Start <ServiceName>*.

2. Add code to the *OnStart* method to set up whatever polling or monitoring your service requires. Note that *OnStart* does not actually do the monitoring. The *OnStart* method must return to the operating system once the service's operation has begun. It must not loop forever or block. To set up a simple polling mechanism, you can use the *System.Timers.Timer* component. In the *OnStart* method, you set parameters on the component and set the *Enabled* property to *true*. The timer then raises events in your code periodically, at which time your service could do its monitoring. Refer to Lab Exercise 1, later in this lesson, for an example.

3. Add code to the *OnStop* method to perform any actions required for your service to stop.

4. Optionally, override the *OnPause* and *OnContinue* methods. *OnPause* is called when a user pauses your service from the Services snap-in (a rare event). Typically,

a paused service should continue to service existing requests and user connections but stop accepting new requests and connections. For example, a paused Web service might allow users to continue browsing the site but block users who haven't previously connected. This would permit a systems administrator to allow connected users to finish their sessions in preparation for taking the server offline. *OnContinue* is called when a service resumes from a paused state. If you do override these methods, set *ServiceBase.CanPauseAndContinue* to *true*.

5. Optionally, override the *OnShutdown* method. *OnShutdown* is called when a computer shuts down. If you do override this method, set *ServiceBase.CanShutdown* to *true*.

6. Optionally, override the *OnPowerEvent* method. *OnPowerEvent* is called when a computer goes into suspend mode—a common occurance for mobile computers. If you do override this method, set *ServiceBase.CanHandlePowerEvent* to *true*.

How to Create an Install Project for a Service

Unlike with other applications, you cannot simply run a service executable file. This limitation prevents you from running and debugging the application directly from the Visual Studio development environment. Services must be installed prior to running. The .NET Framework provides the *ServiceInstaller* and *ServiceProcessInstaller* classes for this purpose. Use *ServiceInstaller* to define the service description, display name, service name, and start type. Use *ServiceProcessInstaller* to define the service account settings.

In practice, you do not need to write code that uses the *ServiceInstaller* and *Service-ProcessInstaller* classes because Visual Studio automatically generates the code. To create a service installer using Visual Studio, follow these steps:

1. In Visual Studio, open the design view for your service. Right-click the designer, and then click Add Installer. Visual Studio creates a ProjectInstaller component.

2. Set the *StartType* property for the ProjectInstaller ServiceInstaller component to one of the following values:
   - ❑ **Automatic** The service starts automatically after the computer starts, whether or not a user logs in.
   - ❑ **Manual** A user must start the service manually. This is the default.
   - ❑ **Disabled** The service does not start automatically, and users cannot start the service without first changing the start-up type.

3. Set the *Description* and *DisplayName* properties for the ServiceInstaller component.

4. Define the *ServicesDependedOn* property with a list of service names that must be running for your service to function. For example, if your service connects to a shared folder, you will need the Workstation service, which has a service name of LanmanWorkstation. To determine the service name, open the Services snap-in (available in the Computer Management console in Windows Vista). Then, double-click the service to view its properties and examine the Service Name value.

5. Specify the security context for your service by setting the *Account* property for the ProjectInstaller ServiceProcessInstaller component to one of the following values:

    ❑ **LocalService** Runs in the context of an account that acts as a nonprivileged user on the local computer, and presents anonymous credentials to any remote server. Use LocalService to minimize security risks.

    ❑ **NetworkService** Enables the service to authenticate to another computer on the network. This authentication is not required for anonymous connections, such as most connections to a Web server.

    ❑ **LocalSystem** The service runs with almost unlimited privileges and presents the computer's credentials to any remote server. Using this account type presents a severe security risk; any vulnerabilities in your application could be exploited to take complete control of the user's computer.

    ❑ **User** Causes the system to prompt for a valid user name and password when the service is installed (unless you set values for both the *Username* and *Password* properties of your *ServiceProcessInstaller* instance). This is the default.

6. Define your service project's start-up object. Right-click the project in Solution Explorer and then click Properties. In the Project Designer, on the Application tab, select your service project from the Startup Object list.

7. Now build your project.

At this point, you can install the service manually using the InstallUtil tool or create a setup project that will provide a wizard-based installation interface and a Windows Installer (MSI) package. The following sections discuss each of these options.

How to Install a Service Manually

After you implement and build your service, you can install it manually. To install a service manually, run InstallUtil.exe from the command line with your service's name as a parameter. To install your service, run *InstallUtil <yourservice.exe>*. To uninstall your service, run *InstallUtil /u <yourservice.exe>*. InstallUtil.exe is available in the %windir%\Microsoft.NET\Framework\v2.0.50727\ folder.

How to Build a Setup Project for a Service

To build a setup project for a service, perform the following steps:

1. Add a Setup Project to your current solution, as shown in Figure 8-4.

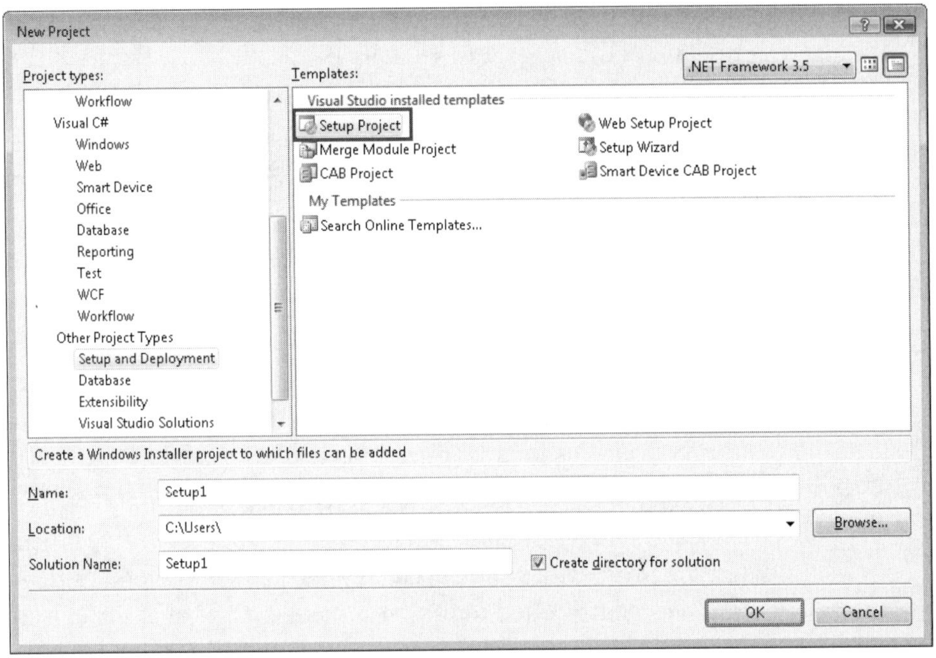

Figure 8-4   Adding a setup project simplifies deploying services

2. Add the output from your service project to your setup project by following these steps:

   a. Right-click your setup project in Solution Explorer, click Add, and then click Project Output.

   b. In the Add Project Output Group dialog box, select your service project from the Project list, select Primary Output, and then click OK.

3. Finally, add a custom action to install the service executable file by following these steps:

   a. Right-click your setup project in Solution Explorer, click View, and then click Custom Actions.

   b. In the Custom Actions editor, right-click Custom Actions and then click Add Custom Action.

c. In the Select Item In Project dialog box, double-click Application Folder. Click Add Output, and then select Primary Output. Click OK to add the primary output from your service project, as shown in Figure 8-5. Click OK again to add the primary output to all four nodes of the Custom Actions: Install, Commit, Rollback, and Uninstall.

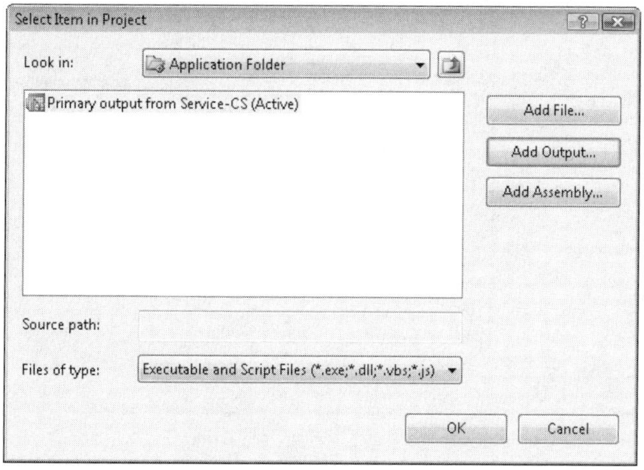

Figure 8-5   Creating a setup project for a service requires special considerations

d. In Solution Explorer, right-click your setup project and then click Build. The service setup build folder now includes a Setup.exe file to interactively install the service and an MSI file for automatic deployment of the service.

After installation, you can uninstall the service using the standard methods: manually, using the Control Panel, or automatically, using Windows Installer (MSI) tools.

How to Manage and Control a Service

After you install a service, you need to start it. If you set the service start-up type to Automatic, rebooting the computer causes the service to start. If the service start-up type is set to Manual, or you want to start the service without restarting the computer, you use the Services snap-in to start the service by performing the following steps:

1. While logged on as an administrator or another user account with privileges to manage services, click Start, right-click Computer, and then click Manage. Respond to any UAC prompts that appear.

2. Expand Services And Applications, and then click Services. The Services snap-in is also available in the Windows Server 2008 Server Manager.

3. In the right pane, right-click your service and then click Start, as shown in Figure 8-6.

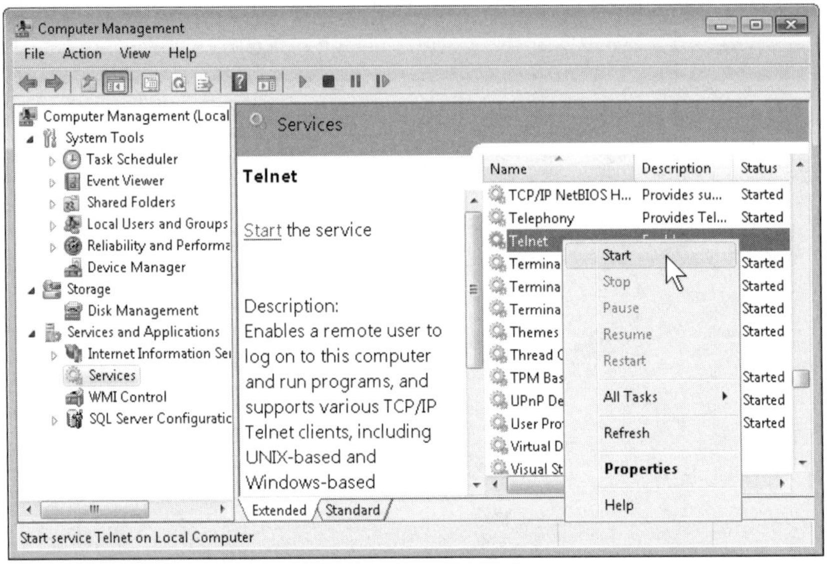

Figure 8-6   Start services from the Services snap-in

You can use the same process to stop, pause, resume, or restart your service. To change the service start-up type or user account, right-click the service and then click Properties, as shown in Figure 8-7.

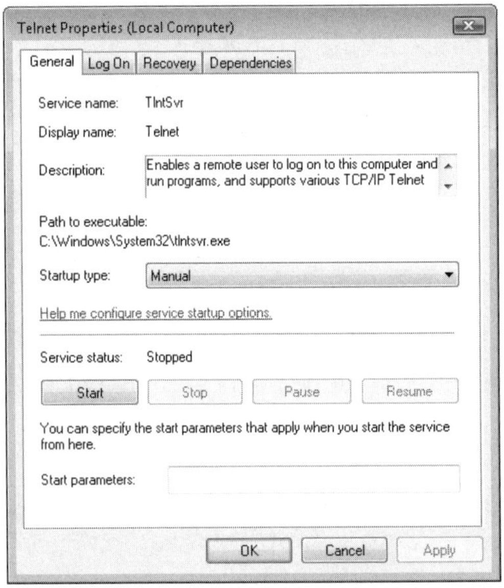

Figure 8-7   Configure service start-up type and user account after setup by viewing the service Properties dialog box

You can also control services from the command line by using the *Net* command with the format *Net Start <ServiceName>* or *Net Stop <ServiceName>*.

To control services from an assembly, use the *System.ServiceProcess.ServiceController* class. This class gives you the ability to connect to a service on the local computer or a remote computer; examine the service's capabilities; and start, stop, pause, or resume the service. The following code sample, which requires both the *System .ServiceProcess* namespace (for which you must add a reference manually in Visual Studio) and *System.Threading* namespace, demonstrates this process:

```vb
' VB
' Connect to the Server service
Dim sc As ServiceController = New ServiceController("Server")

' Stop the service
sc.Stop()

' Wait two seconds before starting the service
Thread.Sleep(2000)

' Start the service
sc.Start()
```

```csharp
// C#
// Connect to the Server service
ServiceController sc = new ServiceController("Server");

// Stop the service
sc.Stop();

// Wait two seconds before starting the service
Thread.Sleep(2000);

// Start the service
sc.Start();
```

Lab: Create, Install, and Start a Service to Monitor a Web Site

In this lab, you will create a service project using Visual Studio and write code to log the status of a Web site every 10 seconds. Then you will create a setup project for the service. Finally, you will install and start the service.

▶ Exercise 1: Create a Service to Monitor a Web Site

In this exercise, you will create and build a Windows Service that checks a Web site every 10 seconds and writes a message to a log file indicating whether the Web site returned a page successfully.

1. Using Visual Studio, create a project using the Windows Service application template. Name the project MonitorWebSite.

2. Using the service designer view, change the Name and the ServiceName to MonitorWebSite. Set the *CanPauseAndContinue* and *CanShutdown* properties to *true*.

3. Switch to code view and add the *System.Timers*, *System.IO*, and *System.Net* namespaces to the code file.

4. Within the *MonitorWebSite* class, create a *Timer* object. For example, the following code works:

```
' VB
Private t As Timer = Nothing
```

```
// C#
private Timer t = null;
```

5. Within the *MonitorWebSite* constructor (in Visual Basic, the *New* method is located in Service1.VB), configure the timer to call a method every 10 seconds, as the following code demonstrates:

```
' VB
t = New Timer(10000)
AddHandler t.Elapsed, New System.Timers.ElapsedEventHandler(AddressOf _
    Me.t_Elapsed)
```

```
// C#
t = new Timer(10000);
t.Elapsed += new ElapsedEventHandler(t_Elapsed);
```

Add code to the *OnStart* method to enable and start the timer, as demonstrated here:

```
' VB
t.Start()
```

```
// C#
t.Start();
```

6. Add code to the *OnStop* method to stop the timer, as the following sample demonstrates:

```
' VB
t.Stop()
```

```
// C#
t.Stop();
```

7. Override the *OnPause*, *OnContinue*, and *OnShutdown* methods and add code to start and stop the timer, as demonstrated here:

```vb
' VB
Protected Overrides Sub OnContinue()
    t.Start()
End Sub

Protected Overrides Sub OnPause()
    t.Stop()
End Sub

Protected Overrides Sub OnShutdown()
    t.Stop()
End Sub
```

```csharp
// C#
protected override void OnContinue()
{
    t.Start();
}

protected override void OnPause()
{
    t.Stop();
}

protected override void OnShutdown()
{
    t.Stop();
}
```

8. In the method that you specified for the *ElapsedEventHandler*, write the code to check the Web site and write the current time and status code to a text file. Add an event to the event log if you experience an exception, because services lack a user interface to communicate the exception information easily to the user. The following code demonstrates this:

```vb
' VB
Protected Sub t_Elapsed(ByVal sender As System.Object, _
    ByVal e As System.Timers.ElapsedEventArgs)

    Try
        ' Send the HTTP request
        Dim url As String = "http://www.microsoft.com"
        Dim g As HttpWebRequest = CType(WebRequest.Create(url), _
            HttpWebRequest)
        Dim r As HttpWebResponse = CType(g.GetResponse, HttpWebResponse)
```

```vb
            ' Log the response to a text file
            Dim path As String = _
                AppDomain.CurrentDomain.SetupInformation.ApplicationBase + _
                "log.txt"
            Dim tw As TextWriter = New StreamWriter(path, True)
            tw.WriteLine(DateTime.Now.ToString + " for " + url + ": " + _
                r.StatusCode.ToString)
            tw.Close()

            ' Close the HTTP response
            r.Close()
        Catch ex As Exception
            System.Diagnostics.EventLog.WriteEntry("Application", _
                "Exception: " + ex.Message.ToString)
        End Try
    End Sub
```

```csharp
// C#
void t_Elapsed(object sender, ElapsedEventArgs e)
{
    try
    {
        // Send the HTTP request
        string url = "http://www.microsoft.com";
        HttpWebRequest g = (HttpWebRequest)WebRequest.Create(url);
        HttpWebResponse r = (HttpWebResponse)g.GetResponse();

        // Log the response to a text file
        string path =
            AppDomain.CurrentDomain.SetupInformation.ApplicationBase +
            "log.txt";
        TextWriter tw = new StreamWriter(path, true);
        tw.WriteLine(DateTime.Now.ToString() + " for " + url +
            ": " + r.StatusCode.ToString());
        tw.Close();

        // Close the HTTP response
        r.Close();
    }
    catch (Exception ex)
    {
        System.Diagnostics.EventLog.WriteEntry("Application",
            "Exception: " + ex.Message.ToString());
    }
}
```

9. Build the project and resolve any problems that appear. Note that you cannot yet run the service because you have not created an installer. You will do that in the next exercise.

▶ **Exercise 2: Create a Service Installer**

In this exercise, you will create an installer for the project you created in Exercise 1.

1. Add an installer to your service project by right-clicking the service designer and selecting Add Installer.

2. Set the installer properties as follows:
   - ❏ *StartType* Automatic
   - ❏ *Description* Logs Responses From Microsoft.com
   - ❏ *DisplayName* Website Monitor
   - ❏ *Account* LocalSystem

NOTE Using *LocalSystem* is not typically recommended; however, this project requires access to write a text file to the file system, which *LocalSystem* provides. A more secure method would be to create a custom user account with only the necessary privileges; however, this would distract from the purpose of this exercise.

---

3. Define the service project as the start-up object if you have not yet done so. To do this, perform the following steps:
   a. Right-click the project in Solution Explorer and then click Properties.
   b. In the Project Designer, on the Application tab, select MonitorWebSite .Program from the Startup Object list (if you are using C#) or select Monitor-WebSite from the Startup Object list (if you are using Visual Basic .NET).

4. Add a Setup Project to your solution, and then add the output from your service project to your setup project. To do this, perform the following steps:
   a. From the File menu, select Add, and then click New Project.
   b. In the Project Types list, expand Other Project Types, and then select Setup And Deployment.
   c. In the Templates box, select Setup Project, and then click OK.

5. Add a custom action to install the service executable file in the application folder. To do this, perform the following steps:
   a. Right-click your setup project in Solution Explorer, click View, and then click Custom Actions.
   b. In the Custom Actions Editor, right-click Custom Actions, and then click Add Custom Action.
   c. In the Select Item In Project dialog box, double-click Application Folder. Click Add Output, select Primary Output, and then click OK twice.

6. Change the Title and Product Name properties of the Setup1 project to Monitor Web Site.

7. Change the Author and Manufacturer properties of the Setup1 project to Contoso.

8. Build your setup project by right-clicking the project in Solution Explorer and then clicking Build.

▶ **Exercise 3: Install, Start, and Manage the Service**

In this exercise, you will install and manage the project you created in Exercises 1 and 2.

1. Start the Setup.exe that you created in Exercise 2 and install the service with the default settings. If any User Account Control (UAC) prompts appear, allow the access. You might also have to respond to Windows Defender or another anti-malware application to allow the configuration settings.

2. Start Computer Management, expand Services And Applications, and select the Services node.

3. Right-click the Website Monitor service and then select Start. Even though the service is set to start automatically and will start the next time the computer is restarted, you need to start the service manually if you want it to run immediately after installation. Notice that the Services snap-in shows the Name and Description that you provided in Exercise 2.

4. Wait 30 seconds and then open the text file to which your service logs request responses (in the %Program Files%\Contoso\Monitor Web Site folder). Verify that it is successfully querying the Web server and writing the results to the text file.

5. Pause the service, wait 30 seconds, and verify that it no longer adds information to the log file.

6. Resume the service, wait 30 seconds, and verify that it continues adding information to the log file.

7. Stop the service by opening a command line with administrative privileges and running the command **net stop monitorwebsite**.

8. Finally, uninstall the service by rerunning Setup.exe. You always need to uninstall a service before you can reinstall it.

Lesson Summary

- A Windows Service is a process that runs in the background, without a user interface, in its own user session.

- To create a Windows Service, use Visual Studio to create a project using the Windows Service application template. Then write the code for the *OnStart* and

OnStop procedures and override any other methods that you want to redefine. Add the necessary installers for your service application. Finally, create a setup project to install your service.

■ To implement a service, specify the service name, description, and start-up type. Then override the *OnStart*, *OnStop*, *OnPause*, *OnContinue*, and *OnShutdown* procedures as necessary.

■ To create an install project for a service, first define the properties of a *Service-Installer* object to specify the service description, display name, service name, and start type. Then define the properties of a *ServiceProcessInstaller* to specify the service account settings. At this point, you can install the service manually or build a setup project for the service.

■ To control a service manually, you can use the Net command at a command prompt or the Services snap-in. Alternatively, you can use the *System.ServiceProcess .ServiceController* class to control a service from an assembly.

Lesson Review

You can use the following questions to test your knowledge of the information in Lesson 3, "Creating Windows Services." The questions are also available on the companion CD if you prefer to review them in electronic form.

NOTE Answers

Answers to these questions and explanations of why each answer choice is right or wrong are located in the "Answers" section at the end of the book.

---

1. Which account type should you choose to minimize security risks?

    A. *LocalService*

    B. *NetworkService*

    C. *LocalSystem*

    D. *User*

2. Which account type should you choose to minimize the possibility of problems caused by overly restrictive permissions on the local computer?

    A. *LocalService*

    B. *NetworkService*

    C. *LocalSystem*

    D. *User*

3. Which of the following are valid ways to install a service on a computer? (Choose all that apply.)

   A. Add a shortcut to your assembly to the user's Startup group

   B. Use InstallUtil to install your service

   C. Configure Scheduled Tasks to start your assembly upon startup

   D. Use Visual Studio to create an installer for your service

4. Which tools can you use to change the user account for a service after the service is installed?

   A. My Computer

   B. Computer Management

   C. The *Net* command

   D. NET Framework Configuration tool

5. You need to configure a service so that it runs in the context of a specific user account. Systems administrators already have created the user account and provided you with the username and password. What should you do?

   A. Define the *Account*, *Username*, and *Password* properties of the *ServiceProcessInstaller* class.

   B. Define the *ServiceInstaller.StartType* property.

   C. In the Services snap-in, set the Startup Type to Manual.

   D. On the Security tab of the project properties, use the Zone to define the account settings.

Chapter Review

To practice and reinforce the skills you learned in this chapter further, you can complete the following tasks:

- Review the chapter summary.
- Review the list of key terms introduced in this chapter.
- Complete the case scenarios. These scenarios set up real-world situations involving the topics of this chapter and ask you to create a solution.
- Complete the suggested practices.
- Take a practice test.

Chapter Summary

- Application domains are logical containers that allow multiple assemblies to run within a single process without being able to access memory belonging to each other directly. Application domains offer separate memory spaces and separate access to resources without the overhead of creating a second process.
- When you create a new application domain, you can control many aspects of that application domain's configuration. Most importantly, you can restrict the privileges of assemblies running within the application domain by providing evidence when creating the application domain or when starting the process.
- Services run in the background without providing an interface to the user. Creating a service is different from creating other types of applications because you cannot run a service executable file directly. Instead, you must install the service manually or create a setup project for the service. Other considerations unique to services include start-up type, account type, and management tools.

Key Terms

Do you know what these key terms mean? You can check your answers by looking up the terms in the glossary at the end of the book.

- Application domain
- Defense-in-depth
- Evidence

- *LocalService*
- *LocalSystem*
- *NetworkService*
- Service

Case Scenarios

In the following case scenarios, you apply what you've learned about how to use application domains and services. You can find answers to these questions in the "Answers" section at the end of this book.

Case Scenario 1: Creating a Testing Tool

You are a developer for the Baldwin Museum of Science. Your users run your application from various locations. Because the .NET Framework runtime assigns different permission sets based on the assembly's location, your assembly is often running in a partially trusted environment. This situation has caused problems for your users. Your manager asks you to interview key company personnel and to then come to her office to answer some questions. Your manager needs you to create an application that creates an application domain and starts an assembly in the new application domain using Internet zone permissions to enable more realistic testing procedures.

Interviews

The following is a list of company personnel interviewed and their statements.

- **Customer Support Manager** "We're getting a lot of calls from customers who want to deploy our app from a Web server. It seems like this doesn't work for some reason, though. Users end up getting different errors. From the way they describe the errors, it seems like the application crashes at different times depending on whether the application is started from the public Internet or the user's local intranet. Right now we just tell them to copy it to their local computers and run it, and that seems to solve the problem. The IT people don't like this workaround, though, and want to know why we can't make it work from a Web server."

- **Development Manager** "I talked to the Customer Support Manager, and it sounds like users are having problems because of code access security restrictions. We need to start testing our application in different zones so that we can identify problems when permissions are restricted. Do me a favor, and write an application that allows our Quality Assurance team to run our application in different zones."

Questions

Answer the following questions for your manager:

1. At a high level, how would you create the application?

2. How could you create an application that creates an application domain and starts an assembly named CASDemands in the new application domain using Internet zone permissions?

Case Scenario 2: Monitoring a File

You are an application developer working for the IT department of Humongous Insurance. You just released a project that you've been working on for months. The IT manager has decided to use your spare time by having you create a tool to help the systems administrators maintain the integrity of the desktop computers in your organization.

Interviews

The following is a list of company personnel interviewed and their statements.

- **IT Manager** "Thanks to the most recent round of application updates produced by your team, all of our applications support XML-based configuration files. This is great, because it allows our most advanced users to tweak configuration settings. However, we noticed that one of our users made a change that disabled the application's built-in security features. I want users to be able to make some changes, but I want to be notified if they change the configuration setting that controls the security features. File auditing isn't precise enough, because it notifies me when the user makes any change to the configuration file. I need to be able to deploy the service using our Systems Management Server (SMS) infrastructure, so please provide an MSI file."

- **Development Manager** "We don't need to prevent users from making changes, and I don't know how we could do that anyway without blocking all access to the configuration file. We just need to add an event to the event log if we detect that the user changes the security settings in the configuration file. After the event is added to the event log, the IT department's event management infrastructure will notify an administrator who can address the problem. We need to create the event immediately after the user saves the change, however, so running a process nightly will not be sufficient."

Questions

Answer the following questions for your manager:

1. What type of application will you create to address the IT department's need?

2. How will you address the need to deploy the application using an MSI file?

3. What start-up type will you specify?

4. What account type will you specify?

Suggested Practices

To help you master the objectives covered in this chapter, complete the following tasks.

Create a Unit of Isolation for the Common Language Runtime within a .NET Framework Application by Using Application Domains

For this task, you should complete both practices.

- **Practice 1**   Create an assembly that mimics malware by reading a file from the current user's Documents folder and then connecting to a Web server. Then create a second assembly that specifies evidence to create a restrictive application domain for the malware assembly and prevents it from reading the user's personal information.

- **Practice 2**   Create an assembly that allocates large amounts of memory. Run the assembly and use the Performance snap-in to monitor the assembly's memory usage. Then create a second assembly that starts the first assembly in an application domain and then unloads the application domain. Monitor the assembly's memory usage to verify that the resources are deallocated.

Implement, Install, and Control a Service

For this task, you should complete at least Practice 1. If you want a better understanding of the challenges involved with implementing services in the real world, complete Practices 2 and 3 as well.

- **Practice 1**   Create a service that listens for incoming network connections and use the InstallUtil tool to install the service. Once you have verified that it works properly, use the InstallUtil tool to uninstall the service.

- **Practice 2**   Create a service that performs the tasks described in Case Scenario 2 earlier in this chapter.

■ **Practice 3** Modify the service you created in Exercises 1 and 2 of Lesson 3 so that it runs using the LocalService account. Identify the privileges that the LocalService account requires to enable the service to function correctly. Create a new user account with only the necessary privileges, and configure the service to run under the new user account.

Take a Practice Test

The practice tests on this book's companion CD offer many options. For example, you can test yourself on just one exam objective, or you can test yourself on all the 70-536 certification exam content. You can set up the test so that it closely simulates the experience of taking a certification exam, or you can set it up in study mode so that you can look at the correct answers and explanations after you answer each question.

MORE INFO Practice tests

For details about all the practice test options available, see the section "How to Use the Practice Tests" in the Introduction of this book.

Chapter 9

Installing and Configuring Applications

Most of the sample applications in this book run without needing installation or configuration because they are designed to demonstrate a specific feature of the .NET Framework. In practice, however, most applications need to be installed on a client computer and then configured by either systems administrators or users. This chapter describes how to install applications, provide persistent configuration settings for applications, and configure different aspects of the .NET Framework.

Exam objectives in this chapter:

- Embed configuration management functionality into a .NET Framework application.
- Create a custom Microsoft Windows Installer for .NET components by using the *System.Configuration.Install* namespace, and configure .NET Framework applications by using configuration files, environment variables, and the .NET Framework Configuration tool (Mscorcfg.msc).

Lessons in this chapter:

Before You Begin

To complete the lessons in this chapter, you should be familiar with Microsoft Windows networking and be comfortable with the following tasks:

- Creating an application in Microsoft Visual Studio using Visual Basic or C#
- Adding namepaces and system class library references to a project
- Creating files programmatically

Lesson 1: Configuring Applications

Although the example applications in this book often rely on hard-coding configuration settings for simplicity, you should always store values such as user preferences and database connection strings in external files that systems administrators can edit. This lesson describes classes in the .NET Framework that simplify storing and retrieving that type of configuration setting.

> **After this lesson, you will be able to:**
> - Read and write application configuration settings and connection strings
> - Read machine configuration settings
> - Create custom classes to allow you to access configuration settings using strong types
>
> **Estimated lesson time: 30 minutes**

.NET Framework Application Configuration

.NET Framework applications are configured using multiple Extensible Markup Language (XML) configuration files. The XML format allows systems administrators to edit settings with a text editor while still allowing efficient programmatic access.

Applications typically pull settings from two files: the centralized Machine.config file, which is accessible to all .NET Framework applications, and an application-specific .config file located in the assembly's working folder. For versions 3.0 and 3.5 of the .NET Framework, the Machine.config file is located at %Windir%\Microsoft.NET\ Framework\v2.0.50727\Config\Machine.config. The Machine.config file contains settings for all .NET Framework applications, including Windows Presentation Foundation (WPF) applications, Windows console applications, and Web applications. These settings apply to the entire computer.

Some of the settings in the Machine.config file can be overridden by settings in an application configuration file, which is typically stored in the same folder as the application with the filename *<Application_Name>*.config. Settings in an application's configuration file can override Machine.config settings, or they can be application-specific (for example, storing a connection string for a database).

The Machine.config file defines which settings cannot be overridden. Settings with an *allowDefinition* property set to *MachineOnly* can be defined only in the Machine.config file. Settings with an *allowDefinition* property set to *MachineToApplication* can be defined in each application. For example, by default you can control authentication on an application-by-application basis because the default Machine.config file sets the *allowDefinition* property to *MachineToApplication*, as shown in bold in this excerpt:

```
<section name="authentication"
      type="System.Web.Configuration.AuthenticationConfigHandler,
      System.Web,
      Version=2.0.0.0,
      Culture=neutral,
      PublicKeyToken=b03f5f7f11d50a3a"
      allowDefinition="MachineToApplication" />
```

The following sections describe how to use the *System.Configuration* namespace to write and read application configuration settings and connection strings.

Using the *System.Configuration* Namespace

Often, applications need custom configuration settings that are saved between sessions. Although you could write custom code to read and write a file containing the configuration settings required by your application, the *System.Configuration* namespace includes classes for reading and writing configuration settings. This makes it simple to store and retrieve settings.

Prior to .NET Framework 2.0, the .NET Framework included a *System.Configuration* namespace, but that version of the namespace is now outdated. If you simply add the *System.Configuration* namespace to your project, your application references the outdated namespace. Instead, follow these steps to add a reference to the correct dynamic link library (DLL):

1. In Visual Studio, open the project that requires the *System.Configuration* namespace.

2. Click the Project menu and then click Add Reference.

3. On the .NET tab, select System.Configuration, as shown in Figure 9-1, and click OK.

4. Now you can add the *System.Configuration* namespace to your project normally, using *Imports* (in Visual Basic) or *using* (in C#), and your application will reference the correct version of the namespace.

Defining Application Configuration Settings

You can define configuration settings in an application's *<Application_Name>*.config file, located in the executable's folder. To define the configuration settings, either manually create the XML file or use an instance of the *Configuration* class.

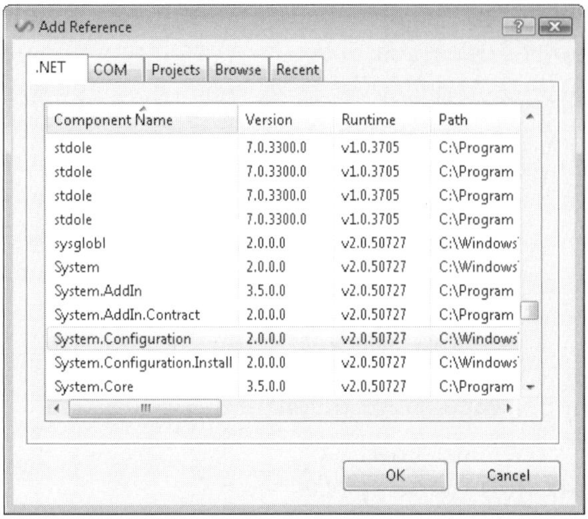

Figure 9-1   You must add a reference to System.configuration.dll

To define application configuration settings programmatically, create an instance of the *Configuration* class by calling *ConfigurationManager.OpenExeConfiguration*. Then, call *Configuration.Add* to add the name and value pair to the application configuration settings. Finally, call *Configuration.Save* to write the updated values to the configuration file.

The following example, which you must run manually from outside the Visual Studio Integrated Development Environment (IDE) after building it, demonstrates how to add a value:

```vb
' VB
Dim config As Configuration = _
    ConfigurationManager.OpenExeConfiguration(ConfigurationUserLevel.None)
config.AppSettings.Settings.Add("MyKey", "MyValue")

' Save the configuration file.
config.Save(ConfigurationSaveMode.Modified)
```

```csharp
// C#
Configuration config =
    ConfigurationManager.OpenExeConfiguration(ConfigurationUserLevel.None);
config.AppSettings.Settings.Add("MyKey", "MyValue");

// Save the configuration file.
config.Save(ConfigurationSaveMode.Modified);
```

You cannot simply run the application from Visual Studio; you must build the executable and then run it directly. When running from Visual Studio, applications run in a virtual host and do not use the standard .config file. After running the application, it generates the following file, which contains the name and value pair:

```xml
<?xml version="1.0" encoding="utf-8"?>
<configuration>
    <appSettings>
        <add key="MyKey" value="MyValue" />
    </appSettings>
</configuration>
```

This file also demonstrates how you would create an application configuration file manually. Using the XML format, create opening and closing tags for a *<configuration>* section. Within the *<configuration>* section, create opening and closing tags for an *<appSettings>* section. Then, create *<add>* elements that define key and value properties.

Reading Application Configuration Settings

You can read application configuration settings using the static *ConfigurationManager .AppSettings* name/value collection. For example, the following code sample displays all application configuration settings to the console:

```vb
' VB
For i As Integer = 0 To ConfigurationManager.AppSettings.Count - 1
    Console.WriteLine("{0}: {1}", _
        ConfigurationManager.AppSettings.AllKeys(i), _
        ConfigurationManager.AppSettings(i))
Next
```

```csharp
// C#
for (int i = 0; i < ConfigurationManager.AppSettings.Count; i++)
{
    Console.WriteLine("{0}: {1}",
        ConfigurationManager.AppSettings.AllKeys[i],
        ConfigurationManager.AppSettings[i]);
}
```

You can also access specific settings using the key name. For example, assume you have the following .config file:

```xml
<?xml version="1.0" encoding="utf-8"?>
<configuration>
    <appSettings>
        <add key="MyKey" value="MyValue" />
        <add key="Greeting" value="Hello, world!" />
    </appSettings>
</configuration>
```

The following code would display the value associated with the *Greeting* key ("Hello, world!"):

```
' VB
Console.WriteLine(ConfigurationManager.AppSettings("Greeting"))
```

```
// C#
Console.WriteLine(ConfigurationManager.AppSettings["Greeting"]);
```

Using Connection Strings

One of the most common uses of application settings is to define a database connection string. Connection strings define how a client application connects to a back-end database. By storing connection strings in a configuration file, systems administrators can define the connection string by editing the configuration file. It's important for systems administrators to be able to do this because database servers might change names, locations, or credentials.

To access connection strings, use the *ConfigurationManager.ConnectionStrings* static collection similar to the way you accessed *ConfigurationManager.AppSettings*. However, although *AppSettings* is a standard *NameValueCollection*, *ConnectionStrings* is a *ConnectionStringSettingsCollection*. The three most useful properties of the *ConnectionStringSettings* class are *Name* (which defines the name of the connection), *ProviderName* (which defines the type of database connection), and *ConnectionString* (which defines how the client connects to the server).

For example, consider the following connection string, which could be defined either in an application's .config file or in the Machine.config file. (The connection string has been formatted to fit on the printed page, but must appear on a single line in the file.)

```
<connectionStrings>
    <add name="LocalSqlServer"
        connectionString="data source=.\SQLEXPRESS;
            Integrated Security=SSPI;
            AttachDBFilename=|DataDirectory|aspnetdb.mdf;
            User Instance=true"
        providerName="System.Data.SqlClient" />
</connectionStrings>
```

The following code sample accesses that connection string by name (the most common real-world use) and then displays all connection strings:

```
' VB
' Display a specific connection string
Console.WriteLine(ConfigurationManager.ConnectionStrings( _
    "LocalSqlServer").ConnectionString)
```

```
' Display all connection strings
Dim connections As ConnectionStringSettingsCollection = _
    ConfigurationManager.ConnectionStrings
For Each connection As ConnectionStringSettings In connections
    Console.WriteLine("Name: {0}", connection.Name)
    Console.WriteLine("Connection string: {0}", _
        connection.ConnectionString)
    Console.WriteLine("Provider: {0}", connection.ProviderName)
    Console.WriteLine("Source: {0}", _
        connection.ElementInformation.Source)
Next

// C#
// Display a specific connection string
Console.WriteLine(ConfigurationManager.ConnectionStrings[
    "LocalSqlServer"].ConnectionString);

// Display all connection strings
ConnectionStringSettingsCollection connections =
    ConfigurationManager.ConnectionStrings;
foreach (ConnectionStringSettings connection in connections)
{
    Console.WriteLine("Name: {0}", connection.Name);
    Console.WriteLine("Connection string: {0}",
        connection.ConnectionString);
    Console.WriteLine("Provider: {0}", connection.ProviderName);
    Console.WriteLine("Source: {0}",
        connection.ElementInformation.Source);
}
```

Once you create a *ConnectionStringSettings* object, you can examine the *ProviderName* parameter to determine which type of database connection object to create. The following code sample demonstrates how to use *ProviderName* to create a database platform-specific *DbConnection* object using a *ConnectionStringsSettings* object named *connection*:

```
' VB
Dim db As DbConnection = Nothing
Select Case connection.ProviderName
    Case "System.Data.SqlClient"
        db = New SqlConnection(connection.ConnectionString)
        Exit Select
    Case "System.Data.OleDb"
        db = New OleDbConnection(connection.ConnectionString)
        Exit Select
    Case "System.Data.Odbc"
        db = New OdbcConnection(connection.ConnectionString)
        Exit Select
    Case "System.Data.OracleClient"
        db = New OracleConnection(connection.ConnectionString)
        Exit Select
End Select
```

```
// C#
DbConnection db = null;
switch (connection.ProviderName)
{
    case "System.Data.SqlClient":
        db = new SqlConnection(connection.ConnectionString);
        break;
    case "System.Data.OleDb":
        db = new OleDbConnection(connection.ConnectionString);
        break;
    case "System.Data.Odbc":
        db = new OdbcConnection(connection.ConnectionString );
        break;
    case "System.Data.OracleClient":
        db = new
        OracleConnection(connection.ConnectionString);
        break;
}
```

Reading Machine Configuration Settings

Typically, you do not need to read machine configuration settings directly. However, when you need to, you can call the *ConfigurationManager.OpenMachineConfiguration* method to create a *Configuration* object representing the Machine.config file.

For example, the Machine.config file contains a *<configProtectedData>* section that describes cryptographic technologies available for protecting configuration data. The following code shows a typical *<configProtectedData>* section in the Machine.config file:

```
<configProtectedData
    defaultProvider="RsaProtectedConfigurationProvider">
    <providers>
        <add name="RsaProtectedConfigurationProvider"
type="System.Configuration.RsaProtectedConfigurationProvider,
System.Configuration, Version=2.0.0.0, Culture=neutral,
PublicKeyToken=b03f5f7f11d50a3a"
description="Uses RsaCryptoServiceProvider to encrypt and decrypt"
keyContainerName="NetFrameworkConfigurationKey" cspProviderName=""
useMachineContainer="true" useOAEP="false" />
        <add name="DataProtectionConfigurationProvider"
type="System.Configuration.DpapiProtectedConfigurationProvider,
System.Configuration, Version=2.0.0.0, Culture=neutral,
PublicKeyToken=b03f5f7f11d50a3a"
description="Uses CryptProtectData and CryptUnProtectData Windows
APIs to encrypt and decrypt"
useMachineProtection="true" keyEntropy="" />
    </providers>
</configProtectedData>
```

As you can see, that section defines two providers (*RsaProtectedConfigurationProvider* and *DataProtectionConfigurationProvider*), and defines *RsaProtectionConfiguration-Provider* as the default provider. You can access the default provider, or any aspect of the configured providers, by following these steps:

1. Retrieve the machine configuration.

2. Call *Configuration.GetSection* to retrieve the *<configProtectedData>* section.

3. Cast the *ConfigurationSection* object returned by *Configuration.GetSection* to a class specific to the configuration section you are accessing. In the case of *<configProtectedData>*, you need to use the *ProtectedConfigurationSection* class.

4. Access the properties of the *ProtectedConfigurationSection* class, or whichever *ConfigurationSection* type you are using.

The following code sample displays the default protection configuration provider and then displays the description of *DataProtectionConfigurationProvider*:

```
' VB
' Open the Machine.config file
Dim machineSettings As Configuration = _
    ConfigurationManager.OpenMachineConfiguration()

' Retrieve the configProtectedData section
Dim pcs As ProtectedConfigurationSection = _
    DirectCast(machineSettings.GetSection("configProtectedData"), _
    ProtectedConfigurationSection)

' Display the default provider
Console.WriteLine(pcs.DefaultProvider)

' Display the description for the DataProtectionConfigurationProvider
Console.WriteLine(pcs.Providers( _
    "DataProtectionConfigurationProvider").Parameters("description"))

// C#
// Open the Machine.config file
Configuration machineSettings =
    ConfigurationManager.OpenMachineConfiguration();

// Retrieve the configProtectedData section
ProtectedConfigurationSection pcs =
    (ProtectedConfigurationSection)machineSettings.GetSection(
        "configProtectedData");

// Display the default provider
Console.WriteLine(pcs.DefaultProvider);

// Display the description for the DataProtectionConfigurationProvider
Console.WriteLine(pcs.Providers[
    "DataProtectionConfigurationProvider"].Parameters["description"]);
```

Each configuration section has a unique class. To determine which class a configuration section uses, call *ConfigurationManager.OpenMachineConfiguration().GetSection("<sectionName>").ElementInformation.Type.ToString*.

Creating Custom Sections

To allow you to access custom application configuration settings using strong types, you can create custom classes. There are two ways to do this: by implementing the *IConfigurationSectionHandler* interface and by deriving a class from *ConfigurationSection*.

Exam Tip   The *IConfigurationSectionHandler* interface is included in this book only because it might be covered on the 70-536 certification exam; it is deprecated in the .NET Framework version 2.0 and later.

Creating Custom Sections Using *IConfigurationSectionHandler*

Just as there are unique classes for different sections in the Machine.config file, you can create unique classes for custom sections in your application's .config file by creating a class that inherits from the *IConfigurationSectionHandler* interface.

When implementing the *IConfigurationSectionHandler* interface, you only need to create a constructor and implement the *Create* method. Of the three parameters required by the *Create* method, you typically need to access only the third parameter, an object of the type *System.Xml.XmlNode*. You can call *XmlNode.InnerText* to access the data stored within the element.

For example, consider the following simple Console application, which reads two parameters from a custom section in the application's .config file and outputs them to the console. Notice that within the *Main* method, custom settings are accessed using strong types, which is more elegant than parsing text from application settings. The *CustomConfigHandler* class implements the *IConfigurationSectionHandler* interface, and the *CustomConfigHandler.Create* method reads the settings from the appropriate section of the .config file and stores the values in a new instance of the custom *MySettings* class:

```
' VB
Public Class MySettings
    Public lastUser As String
    Public lastNumber As Integer

    Public Sub New()
    End Sub
End Class
```

```
Public Class CustomConfigHandler
    Implements IConfigurationSectionHandler
    Function Create(ByVal parent As Object, _
        ByVal configContext As Object, ByVal section As Xml.XmlNode) _
        As Object Implements IConfigurationSectionHandler.Create

        Dim settings As New MySettings()
        settings.lastUser = _
            section.SelectSingleNode("lastUser").InnerText
        settings.lastNumber = _
            Integer.Parse(section.SelectSingleNode("lastNumber").InnerText)
        Return settings
    End Function
End Class

Module Module1
    Sub Main()
        Dim settings As MySettings = _
            DirectCast(ConfigurationManager.GetSection( _
                "customSettings"), MySettings)
        Console.WriteLine(settings.lastUser)
        Console.WriteLine(settings.lastNumber)
    End Sub
End Module
```

// C#
```
namespace ConfigApp
{
    public class MySettings
    {
        public string lastUser;
        public int lastNumber;

        public MySettings()
        {
        }
    }

    public class CustomConfigHandler : IConfigurationSectionHandler
    {
        public CustomConfigHandler()
        {
        }

        public object Create(object parent,
            object configContext, System.Xml.XmlNode section)
        {
            MySettings settings = new MySettings();
            settings.lastUser =
                section.SelectSingleNode("lastUser").InnerText;
            settings.lastNumber =
                int.Parse(section.SelectSingleNode(
                    "lastNumber").InnerText);
            return settings;
        }
    }
```

```
class Program
{
    static void Main(string[] args)
    {
        MySettings settings =
            (MySettings)ConfigurationManager.GetSection(
                "customSettings");
        Console.WriteLine(settings.lastUser);
        Console.WriteLine(settings.lastNumber);
    }
}
}
```

The following .config file demonstrates how to structure a custom configuration section. Notice the *<configSections>* section, which declares the section name (in the *name* property) and the method that implements *IConfigurationSectionHandler* and the assembly name (in the *type* property). Then, notice the custom configuration section, with elements for each custom value. Examine this configuration file and how the *CustomConfigHandler.Create* method reads the values. (The *<appSettings>* section is included only to demonstrate that a .config file can contain both custom settings and standard application settings.)

```
<configuration>
  <configSections>
    <section name="customSettings"
      type="ConfigApp.CustomConfigHandler, ConfigApp"/>
  </configSections>

  <appSettings>
      <add key="Greeting" value="Hello, world!" />
      <add key="Another Key" value="Another value" />
  </appSettings>

  <customSettings>
    <lastUser>Tony</lastUser>
    <lastNumber>32</lastNumber>
  </customSettings>
</configuration>
```

Exam Tip   Although *IConfigurationSectionHandler* is covered on the 70-536 exam objectives, it is deprecated in .NET Framework version 2.0 and later. Instead, you should use *ConfigurationSection*, described in the next section.

Creating Custom Sections Using *ConfigurationSection*

Deriving a custom class from *ConfigurationSection* is the preferred way to implement custom configuration sections in .NET Framework version 2.0 and later. *Configuration-Section* allows you to declare properties that the Common Language Runtime (CLR) automatically populates based on the data in the .config file, saving you the trouble of manually parsing XML elements. You can also use attributes to configure default values, validators, and other requirements for properties. The following code sample provides similar functionality to the *IConfigurationSectionHandler* example:

```vb
' VB
Public Class MyHandler
    Inherits ConfigurationSection

    Public Sub New()
    End Sub

    <ConfigurationProperty("lastUser", DefaultValue:="User", _
        IsRequired:=True)> _
    <StringValidator(InvalidCharacters:="~!@#$%^&*()[]{}/;'\|\\", _
        MinLength:=1, MaxLength:=60)> _
    Public ReadOnly Property LastUser() As String
        Get
            Return CStr(Me("lastUser"))
        End Get
    End Property

    <ConfigurationProperty("lastNumber")> _
    Public Property LastNumber() As Integer
        Get
            Return CStr(Me("lastNumber"))
        End Get
        Set(ByVal value As Integer)
            Me("lastNumber") = value
        End Set
    End Property
End Class

Module Module1
    Sub Main()
        Dim settings As MyHandler = _
            DirectCast(ConfigurationManager.GetSection( _
                "customSettings"), MyHandler)
        Console.WriteLine(settings.LastUser)
        Console.WriteLine(settings.LastNumber.ToString())
    End Sub
End Module
```

```csharp
// C#
namespace ConfigApp
{
    public class MyHandler:ConfigurationSection
    {
        public MyHandler()
        {
        }
```

```
        [ConfigurationProperty("lastUser", DefaultValue = "User",
            IsRequired = true)]
        [StringValidator(InvalidCharacters =
            "~!@#$%^&*()[]{}/;'\"|\\",
            MinLength = 1, MaxLength = 60)]
        public string LastUser
        {
            get
            {
                return (string)this["lastUser"];
            }
            set
            {
                this["lastUser"] = value;
            }
        }

        [ConfigurationProperty("lastNumber")]
        public int LastNumber
        {
            get
            {
                return (int)this["lastNumber"];
            }
            set
            {
                this["lastNumber"] = value;
            }
        }

    }

    class Program
    {
        static void Main(string[] args)
        {
            MyHandler settings =
                (MyHandler)ConfigurationManager.GetSection(
                    "customSettings");
            Console.WriteLine(settings.LastUser);
            Console.WriteLine(settings.LastNumber);
        }
    }
}
```

This code sample requires a slightly modified .config file, which declares the custom values as attributes:

```
<?xml version="1.0" encoding="utf-8"?>

<configuration>
  <configSections>
```

```
   <section name="customSettings" type="ConfigApp2.MyHandler, ConfigApp2"/>
  </configSections>

  <customSettings lastUser="Tony" lastNumber="32" />
</configuration>
```

Real World

Tony Northrup

Windows Vista includes User Account Control (UAC), which limits the privileges of the currently logged-on user. Even if your account is a member of the Administrators group, programs run in the security context of a standard user by default. This can cause problems when updating a .config file after installing a .NET Framework application because most applications are installed into the %Program Files% folder, which standard users do not have permission to update. This is a problem only if users need to update the .config file after installation—setup typically has administrative privileges, and systems administrators will still be able to update the .config file manually.

To allow users to update settings, create a settings file in the user's application data folder. This folder is defined by the *%AppData%* environment variable. Although the 70-536 exam won't test your knowledge of standard user privileges, you'll definitely run into problems when developing applications in the real world.

Lab: Persistently Storing Configuration Settings

In this lab, you will store data to your application's .config file and read it when the application starts.

Exercise: Reading and Writing Application Configuration Settings

In this exercise, you will open an existing WPF application and add functionality to save and read settings.

1. Navigate to the *<InstallHome>*\Chapter09\Lesson1\Exercise1\Partial folder and open either the C# version or the Visual Basic .NET version of the solution file.

2. Add a project reference to the System.configuration.dll file.

3. Add the *System.Collections.Specialized* and *System.Configuration* namespaces to your Window1 code file.

4. Add a handler for the Save Settings button's *Click* event. Write code to open the application's configuration file, remove previous settings for the Title and Name settings, add settings based on the values in the *titleTextBox* and *numberSlider* controls, and then write the settings to the configuration file. The following code demonstrates how to do this:

```vb
' VB
Dim config As Configuration = _
    ConfigurationManager.OpenExeConfiguration( _
        ConfigurationUserLevel.None)
config.AppSettings.Settings.Remove("Title")
config.AppSettings.Settings.Add("Title", titleTextBox.Text)

config.AppSettings.Settings.Remove("Number")
config.AppSettings.Settings.Add("Number", _
    numberSlider.Value.ToString())
config.Save(ConfigurationSaveMode.Modified)
```

```csharp
// C#
Configuration config =
    ConfigurationManager.OpenExeConfiguration(
        ConfigurationUserLevel.None);
config.AppSettings.Settings.Remove("Title");
config.AppSettings.Settings.Add("Title", titleTextBox.Text);

config.AppSettings.Settings.Remove("Number");
config.AppSettings.Settings.Add("Number",
    numberSlider.Value.ToString());
config.Save(ConfigurationSaveMode.Modified);
```

5. In the Extensible Application Markup Language (XAML) file, create a handler for the window's *Loaded* event. For example, you could add the line shown here in bold to the <*Window*> XAML element:

```xml
<Window x:Class="RememberSettings.Window1"
    xmlns="http://schemas.microsoft.com/winfx/2006/xaml/presentation"
    xmlns:x="http://schemas.microsoft.com/winfx/2006/xaml"
    Loaded="Window_Loaded"
    Title="No title!" Height="154" Width="300">
```

6. In the *Window.Loaded* event handler, write code that determines whether the Title and Number application settings have been defined. If they have been, define the window's *Title* property and the *titleTextBox.Text* property using the *Title* application setting. Then, define the value of *numberSlider* using the *Number* application setting. The following code demonstrates this:

```vb
' VB
If ConfigurationManager.AppSettings("Title") IsNot Nothing Then
    Me.Title = ConfigurationManager.AppSettings("Title")
    titleTextBox.Text = ConfigurationManager.AppSettings("Title")
End If
```

```
If ConfigurationManager.AppSettings("Number") IsNot Nothing Then
    numberSlider.Value = _
        Double.Parse(ConfigurationManager.AppSettings("Number"))
End If

// C#
if (ConfigurationManager.AppSettings["Title"] != null)
{
    this.Title = ConfigurationManager.AppSettings["Title"];
    titleTextBox.Text = ConfigurationManager.AppSettings["Title"];
}

if (ConfigurationManager.AppSettings["Number"] != null)
    numberSlider.Value =
        double.Parse(ConfigurationManager.AppSettings["Number"]);
```

7. Build the application, and then manually run the executable file. You cannot run the application from the debugger and have the settings correctly stored in the .config file.

8. With the application running, type text into the Title box. Then, move the Number slider. Click Save Settings and then close the application.

9. Examine the RememberSettings.config file, which is located in the same folder as the executable file. Notice that two settings are defined in the *<appSettings>* section: *Title* and *Number*. Edit the values of both and save the RememberSettings.config file.

10. Rerun the executable file. Notice that the application automatically reads the settings that you defined and restores both the window title and the number value.

Lesson Summary

■ Use the *System.Configuration* namespace to read and write application settings. To write settings, create a *Configuration* object by calling *ConfigurationManager .OpenExeConfiguration*. Then call *Configuration.Add* to add the name and value pair to the application configuration settings. Finally, call *Configuration.Save* to write the updated values to the configuration file. To read settings, use the static *ConfigurationManager.AppSettings* collection. To access connection strings, use the *ConfigurationManager.ConnectionStrings* static collection.

■ To read systemwide configuration settings in the Machine.config file, create a *Configuration* object by calling the *ConfigurationManager.OpenMachineConfiguration* method.

■ To allow you to access custom application configuration settings using strong types, derive a custom class from *ConfigurationSection*. Although it's deprecated in .NET Framework version 2.0 and later, you can also implement the *IConfigurationSectionHandler* interface.

Lesson Review

You can use the following questions to test your knowledge of the information in Lesson 1, "Configuring Applications." The questions are also available on the companion CD if you prefer to review them in electronic form.

NOTE Answers

Answers to these questions and explanations of why each answer choice is right or wrong are located in the "Answers" section at the end of the book.

---

1. Systems administrators have configured a connection string in the Machine.config file on every computer. It is identified using the key *MySql*, and there are no other connection strings. How can you access the connection string value programmatically?

   A.
   ```
   ' VB
   ConfigurationManager.AppSettings("MySql")
   ```
   ```
   // C#
   ConfigurationManager.AppSettings["MySql"]
   ```

   B.
   ```
   ' VB
   ConfigurationManager.ConnectionStrings("MySql").ConnectionString
   ```
   ```
   // C#
   ConfigurationManager.ConnectionStrings["MySql"].ConnectionString
   ```

   C.
   ```
   ' VB
   ConfigurationManager.ConnectionStrings.ElementInformation.Source
   ```
   ```
   // C#
   ConfigurationManager.ConnectionStrings.ElementInformation.Source
   ```

   D.
   ```
   ' VB
   ConfigurationManager.AppSettings.GetKey("MySql")
   ```
   ```
   // C#
   ConfigurationManager.AppSettings.GetKey("MySql")
   ```

2. You are creating a WPF application and want to read settings from a custom section in the application's .config file. Which of the following should you do? (Choose all that apply.)

   A. Create a class that derives from *ConfigurationSection*.

   B. Create a class that implements *IConfigurationSectionHandler*.

    C. Define a *<configSections>* section in the application's .config file.

    D. Create a custom section within the *<configuration>* section in the application's .config file.

3. You write the following code to store application configuration settings:

```
' VB
ConfigurationManager.AppSettings.[Set]("Key1", "Value1")
Dim config As Configuration = _
    ConfigurationManager.OpenExeConfiguration( _
        ConfigurationUserLevel.None)
config.AppSettings.Settings.Add("Key2", "Value2")
config.Save((ConfigurationSaveMode.Modified))
config.AppSettings.Settings.Add("Key3", "Value3")

// C#
ConfigurationManager.AppSettings.Set("Key1", "Value1");
Configuration config =
    ConfigurationManager.OpenExeConfiguration(
        ConfigurationUserLevel.None);
config.AppSettings.Settings.Add("Key2", "Value2");
config.Save((ConfigurationSaveMode.Modified));
config.AppSettings.Settings.Add("Key3", "Value3");
```

Which setting is stored?

    A. Key1

    B. Key2

    C. Key3

    D. None of the above

Lesson 2: Configuring the .NET Framework

In many environments, you never have to modify the .NET Framework configuration. However, it does have hundreds of configuration options, and you might need to change a setting to enable applications to function correctly. In addition, installing shared libraries on a computer requires adding an assembly into the assembly cache. This lesson describes how to use configuration files and the Microsoft .NET Framework 2.0 Configuration tool to configure the .NET Framework.

> **After this lesson, you will be able to:**
> - Edit the Machine.config file to configure .NET Framework settings
> - Use the Microsoft .NET Framework 2.0 Configuration tool to manage the assembly cache, configure assembly version binding and codebases, configure remoting services, and manage applications
>
> **Estimated lesson time: 15 minutes**

Configuring .NET Framework Settings

Besides configuring connection strings and application settings, you can configure .NET Framework settings using your application's .config file. For example, by default, .NET Framework applications run using the version of .NET Framework with which they were built. To allow an application to run using a different version of .NET Framework, add a section to your .config file such as the following:

```
<configuration>
  <startup>
    <supportedRuntime version="v1.1.4322" />
  </startup>
</configuration>
```

You can use the *<assemblyBinding>* element in the *<runtime>* section of the Machine.config file to specify where the runtime can find an assembly. This is a common requirement when multiple applications must access a shared assembly. The following sample demonstrates how to redirect requests for an assembly named *myAssembly* (as defined in the *<assemblyIdentity>* element) to a fictional location on the http://www.contoso.com Web site (as defined in the *<codebase>* element):

```
<configuration>
   <runtime>
      <assemblyBinding xmlns="urn:schemas-microsoft-com:asm.v1">
         <dependentAssembly>
            <assemblyIdentity name="myAssembly"
```

```
                    publicKeyToken="32ab4ba45e0a69a1"
                    culture="neutral" />
         <codeBase version="2.0.0.0"
                   href="http://www.contoso.com/myAssembly.dll"/>
       </dependentAssembly>
     </assemblyBinding>
   </runtime>
</configuration>
```

Another way to configure the runtime to find a shared assembly is by using the DEV-PATH environment variable. The runtime automatically searches all folders specified in the DEVPATH environment variable for any referenced assemblies. DEVPATH is a standard environment variable, just like PATH, and can be set by following these steps in Windows Vista:

1. Click Start, right-click Computer, and then click Properties.

2. Click Advanced System Settings. Respond to the UAC prompt appropriately.

3. On the Advanced tab of the System Properties dialog box, click Environment Variables.

4. In the Environment Variables dialog box, click New.

5. In the New User Variable dialog box, specify DEVPATH for the Variable Name. In the Variable Value box, type the full path to the shared assembly (in a development environment, this is typically the build path defined in Visual Studio). You can specify multiple paths by separating them with semicolons.

6. Click OK three times.

You can also define environment variables using the *Set* command at a command prompt or in a script.

After defining the environment variable, set the *developerInstallation* value to *true* in the *<runtime>* section of the Machine.config file, as shown here:

```
<configuration>
  <runtime>
    <developmentMode developerInstallation="true"/>
  </runtime>
</configuration>
```

You can also configure either the Machine.config file or your application's .config file to specify the location of a remote object for the purposes of remoting. *Remoting* makes a call to a separate assembly (possibly located on another computer) and retrieves the results. The following configuration file declares a server-activated (well-known) remote type for consumption and specifies that the client application should use the HttpChannel (which allows remote calls using a Web server) but allow the .NET Framework remoting system to find an appropriate port on the client's behalf:

```
<configuration>
   <system.runtime.remoting>
      <application>
         <client>
            <wellknown
               type="RemoteType, RemoteAssembly"
               url="http://computername:8080/RemoteType.rem"
            />
         </client>
         <channels>
            <channel
               ref="http"
               port="0"
            />
         </channels>
      </application>
   </system.runtime.remoting>
</configuration>
```

Using the Microsoft .NET Framework 2.0 Configuration Tool

You can start the Microsoft .NET Framework 2.0 Configuration tool (Mscorcfg.msc) from the Administrative Tools folder on the Start menu or by opening the %WinDir%\ Microsoft.NET\Framework\v2.0.50727\Mscorcfg.msc snap-in. This tool is used for versions 2.0 to 3.5 of .NET Framework (and perhaps later versions that have not been released as of the time of this writing).

NOTE   The .NET Framework 2.0 Configuration Tool

There's no new configuration tool for .NET Framework versions 3.0 and 3.5. You should use the .NET Framework 2.0 Configuration tool to manage versions 2.0, 3.0, and 3.5 of the .NET Framework. To install the .NET Framework 2.0 Configuration tool, install the .NET Framework 2.0 Software Development Kit (SDK), available for download at *http://www.microsoft.com/downloads/ details.aspx?FamilyID=fe6f2099-b7b4-4f47-a244-c96d69c35dec*. Then you can start the tool from the Administrative Tools folder on your Start menu or by opening the %WinDir%\Microsoft.NET\ Framework\v2.0.50727\Mscorcfg.msc snap-in. The snap-in might also be located in \Program Files\Microsoft.NET\SDK\v2.0\Bin\.

The following sections describe how to perform common configuration tasks with the Microsoft .NET Framework 2.0 Configuration tool. For information about configuring code access security (CAS), refer to Chapter 11, "Application Security."

Managing the Assembly Cache

The *assembly cache* is a central location that contains shared assemblies that can be referenced by other assemblies. For example, if you have a class that is used by multiple applications, you could store the class in an assembly and add the assembly to the assembly cache. Then, regardless of where the assembly is located on the computer, other assemblies can reference it.

To add an assembly to the assembly cache, follow these steps:

1. Build the assembly and sign it with a strong name. For more information, visit *http://msdn.microsoft.com/library/xc31ft41.aspx.*

2. In the .NET Framework 2.0 Configuration tool, expand My Computer, right-click Assembly Cache, and then click Add.

3. In the Add An Assembly dialog box, select the assembly you want to add and then click Open.

You can also use the Global Assembly Cache tool (Gacutil.exe). For more information, visit *http://msdn.microsoft.com/library/ex0ss12c.aspx.*

Configuring Assembly Version Binding and Codebases

You can configure an assembly with an *assembly version binding policy* or a *codebase,* as follows:

- **Assembly version binding policy** Allows you to specify a new version of the assembly when an application requests a different version.

- **Codebase** Allows you to specify the location of an assembly for a particular version. Codebases are particularly useful if the computer does not already have the version of the assembly needed to run the application.

To configure either of these, follow these steps:

1. In the .NET Framework 2.0 Configuration tool, expand My Computer, right-click Configured Assemblies, and then click Add.

2. In the Configure An Assembly wizard, either select an assembly that has already been added to the assembly cache and click Choose Assembly, or manually enter the assembly information. Click Finish.

3. In the Properties dialog box that appears, select the Binding Policy tab to specify binding redirections from a requested version to a new version. Select the Codebases tab to specify codebases for specific versions of the assembly and then click OK.

Configuring Remoting Services

Remoting services allow assemblies to call methods in other assemblies, even if they're located on another computer across the network. If you use remoting, you might need to configure settings for a specific remoting channel. To configure remoting settings, follow these steps:

1. In the .NET Framework 2.0 Configuration tool, expand My Computer, right-click Remoting Services, and then click Properties.

2. Select a channel (assuming that a valid channel exists) and then add or edit any attributes and values. Click OK.

Managing Applications

To configure an application, follow these steps:

1. In the .NET Framework 2.0 Configuration tool, expand My Computer, right-click Applications, and then click Add.

2. In the list, click your assembly and then click OK. Alternatively, you can click Other and select your assembly.

3. Under My Computer\Applications, right-click your assembly and then click Properties.

4. Configure the Garbage Collection Mode (which only needs to be changed for server applications) and the search path for referenced assemblies. Click OK.

To view which external assemblies are required, select the Assembly Dependencies subnode. You can use the Configured Assemblies or Remoting Services subnodes to configure a specific application's settings, exactly as described earlier in this section for the .NET Framework.

Lab: Configure a Shared Assembly

In this lab, you will configure a shared assembly so that the classes contained within the assembly can be centrally accessed.

Exercise: Adding an Assembly to the Assembly Cache

In this exercise, you must create an installer for the program you created in Lesson 1.

1. Open the project you created in Lesson 1.

2. From the Project menu select RememberSettings Properties.

3. Select the Signing tab. Then, select the Sign The Assembly check box.

4. Click the Choose A Strong Name Key File drop-down list and then click New.

5. In the Create Strong Name Key dialog box, type a Key File Name of **Remember-Settings**. In the Enter Password and Confirm Password boxes, type a password. Click OK.

6. Verify that the Delay Sign Only check box is cleared. Then, build the assembly.

7. From the Administrative Tools folder on the Start menu, start the Microsoft .NET Framework 2.0 Configuration tool (or open the %WinDir%\Microsoft .NET\Framework\v2.0.50727\Mscorcfg.msc snap-in).

8. In the .NET Framework 2.0 Configuration tool, expand My Computer, right-click Assembly Cache, and then click Add.

9. In the Add An Assembly dialog box, select the signed RememberSettings.exe assembly and then click Open.

10. Under Tasks, click View List Of Assemblies In The Assembly Cache. Note that RememberSettings is now in the assembly cache. Classes within the assembly can now be referenced by any other assembly.

11. Right-click RememberSettings and then click Delete. Then confirm the removal by clicking Yes.

Lesson Summary

- You can use your application's .config file to change or override settings in the Machine.config file. In addition, you can define application-specific configuration settings such as identifying compatible versions of the .NET Framework or specifying the location of shared assemblies.

- The Microsoft .NET Framework 2.0 Configuration tool allows you to manage the assembly cache, configure assembly version binding and codebases, configure remoting services, and manage applications.

Lesson Review

You can use the following questions to test your knowledge of the information in Lesson 2, "Configuring the .NET Framework." The questions are also available on the companion CD if you prefer to review them in electronic form.

NOTE Answers

Answers to these questions and explanations of why each answer choice is right or wrong are located in the "Answers" section at the end of the book.

---

1. You are creating an assembly named MyClasses.dll. The classes in your assembly will be accessed by several different applications installed on your computer. You would like all the applications to access the same instance of the assembly. How can you allow other applications to reference the MyClasses.dll assembly centrally? (Choose all that apply.)

   A. Use the .NET Framework 2.0 Configuration tool to add MyClasses.dll to the list of configured assemblies.

   B. Use the .NET Framework 2.0 Configuration tool to add MyClasses.dll to the assembly cache.

   C. Use Visual Studio to enable delay signing on the assembly.

   D. Use Visual Studio to add a Setup project to the MyClasses solution.

2. You develop a Windows Forms application using version 3.5 of the .NET Framework. You test the assembly using .NET Framework version 1.1 and verify that it works correctly. Some computers in your organization do not have a more recent version of the .NET Framework. Which element can you add to your application's .config file to allow the assembly to run using .NET Framework version 1.1 if that is the only version installed on the computer?

   A. *codeBase*

   B. *assemblyIdentity*

   C. *supportedRuntime*

   D. DEVPATH

3. You currently have two instances of Visual Studio open. You are using one instance to develop a class library, and you are using the second instance to create a WPF application that references the class library. You would like the WPF application to be able to access the referenced class library in the build folder, but you don't want to add the class library to the assembly cache. Which environment variable should you add?

   A. DEVPATH

   B. PATH

   C. APPDATA

   D. PATHEXT

Lesson 3: Installing Applications

Typically, you can create an application installer by adding a Setup project to your solution. However, the .NET Framework also allows you to implement custom installers. Exercise 1 in this lesson walks you through the straightforward process of creating a standard Setup project. Creating a standard Setup project isn't covered by the 70-536 certification exam and doesn't require a conceptual overview. Therefore, the remainder of this lesson and Exercise 2 show you how to create a custom installer.

After this lesson, you will be able to:

- Create a custom installer

Estimated lesson time: 15 minutes

Creating Custom Installers

Visual Studio provides Setup projects that makes creating an installer for most applications very straightforward. For an example of how to create a standard Setup project, complete Exercise 1 at the end of this lesson.

Sometimes, however, you might need more complete control over application installation. In these circumstances, you can create a custom instance of the *Installer* class (part of the *System.Configuration.Install* namespace). *Installer* provides four methods that you can overwrite for different phases of installation and uninstallation:

- **Install**   The method primarily responsible for verifying prerequisites (including that the user has sufficient privileges), copying files, and configuring other resources required by the application.

- **Commit**   *Commit* is called after *Install* completes successfully. In the *Commit* phase, you should finalize the installation.

- **Rollback**   This phase is called only if installation fails or is cancelled. The *Rollback* phase should remove any files and settings configured during the *Install* phase so that *Install* either completely succeeds or leaves no trace of a failed attempt.

- **Uninstall**   The *Uninstall* phase occurs only after a successful installation, when the user requests the application be removed. It should remove all traces of an application.

In each of the four methods, call the base method to perform the standard installation tasks. Then, before and after the base method call, you can perform additional setup tasks programmatically. The following code shows the most basic implementation of a custom installer, which should always include the *RunInstaller* attribute:

```vb
' VB
<RunInstaller(True)> _
Public Class CustomInstaller
    Inherits Installer
    Public Sub New()
        MyBase.New()
    End Sub

    Public Overloads Overrides Sub Commit(ByVal mySavedState As IDictionary)
        MyBase.Commit(mySavedState)
    End Sub

    Public Overloads Overrides Sub Install(ByVal stateSaver As IDictionary)
        MyBase.Install(stateSaver)
    End Sub

    Public Overloads Overrides Sub Uninstall(ByVal savedState As IDictionary)
        MyBase.Uninstall(savedState)
    End Sub

    Public Overloads Overrides Sub Rollback(ByVal savedState As IDictionary)
        MyBase.Rollback(savedState)
    End Sub
End Class
```

```csharp
// C#
[RunInstaller(true)]
public class CustomInstaller : Installer
{
    public CustomInstaller()
        : base()
    {
    }

    public override void Commit(IDictionary mySavedState)
    {
        base.Commit(mySavedState);
    }

    public override void Install(IDictionary stateSaver)
    {
        base.Install(stateSaver);
    }

    public override void Uninstall(IDictionary savedState)
    {
        base.Uninstall(savedState);
    }
```

```
    public override void Rollback(IDictionary savedState)
    {
        base.Rollback(savedState);
    }
}
```

To perform an installation programmatically, call your custom *Installer.Install* method. If the installation is successful, call *Installer.Commit*. If the installation fails, call *Installer.Rollback*. If the user needs to uninstall the application, call *Installer.Uninstall*. All methods require a single instance of *IDictionary*, which is used to track the changes made during the installation. The following sample code demonstrates how to call the *Install* and *Commit* methods using the sample class shown in the previous code sample. In the real world, you typically have code to verify that the *Install* phase was successful before calling *Commit*:

```
' VB
Dim ci As New CustomInstaller()
Dim actions As IDictionary = New Hashtable()

ci.Install(actions)
ci.Commit(actions)

// C#
CustomInstaller ci = new CustomInstaller();
IDictionary actions = new Hashtable();

ci.Install(actions);
ci.Commit(actions);
```

You can also invoke an installer from the command line or a script using the Install-Util.exe tool, available in the %Windir%\Microsoft.NET\Framework\v2.0.50727\ folder. For example, assuming you've added an *Installer* class with the *RunInstaller* attribute to an assembly named MyAssembly, you could install it by running the following command:

```
InstallUtil myAssembly.exe
```

Similarly, you could uninstall it by running this command:

```
InstallUtil /u myAssembly.exe
```

InstallUtil.exe uses reflection to inspect the specified assembly and find all *Installer* types that have the *RunInstaller* attribute set to *true*. The tool then executes either the *Install* method or the *Uninstall* method on each such instance of the *Installer* type. InstallUtil.exe performs installation in a transactional manner; if one of the assemblies fails to install, it rolls back the installations of all other assemblies. *Uninstall* is not transactional.

Lab: Installing Applications

In this lab, you will create a standard and custom installer.

Exercise 1: Add a Setup Project

In this exercise, you will create an installer for the program you created in Lesson 1.

1. Open the project you created in Lesson 2. If you have a problem building the project, you can open the completed project from Lesson 1 included with this book's sample files.

2. From the File menu, select Add, and then click New Project.

3. In the Add New Project dialog box, in the Project Types list, expand Other Project Types, and then click Setup And Deployment. From the Templates pane, click Setup Project. In the Name box, type **SetupRememberSettings** and click OK.

4. In the properties for the deployment project, define the following values:

    ❑ **Author** Contoso, Inc.

    ❑ **Description** Allows user to customize the window title

    ❑ **Manufacturer** Contoso, Inc.

    ❑ **ManufacturerUrl** http://www.contoso.com

    ❑ **ProductName** Remember Settings

    ❑ **SupportUrl** http://support.contoso.com

    ❑ **Title** Remember Settings Installer

5. Right-click Application Folder in the left pane, click Add, and then click Project Output. In the Add Project Output Group dialog box, click Primary Output and then click OK.

6. Right-click Primary Output From RememberSettings and then click Create Shortcut. Type **Remember Settings** for the name and then drag the shortcut to User's Desktop.

7. Right-click User's Programs Menu, click Add, and then click Folder. Name the folder Contoso.

8. Click Application Folder. Again, right-click Primary Output From RememberSettings and then click Create Shortcut. Type **Remember Settings** for the name and then drag the shortcut to User's Programs Menu\Contoso.

9. Right-click File System On Target Machine, click Add Special Folder, and then click User's Send To Menu. Create another shortcut to the primary output, name it **Remember Settings**, and drag it to the User's Send To Menu folder.

10. In Solution Explorer, right-click SetupRememberSettings and then click Build.

11. From the build destination folder, double-click SetupRememberSettings.msi.

12. The Remember Settings wizard appears.

13. On the Welcome To The Remember Settings Setup Wizard page, click Next.

14. On the Select Installation Folder page, notice that the default folder uses both the company name and program name that you provided in the Setup project's Properties dialog box. Click Next.

15. On the Confirm Installation page, click Next.

16. Wait for the installation to complete. If prompted, allow any User Account Control (UAC) prompts.

17. On the Installation Complete page, click Close.

18. Run the Remember Settings program from the Start menu. Notice that it is located in a folder named Contoso under All Programs.

19. Click Save Settings. If you are using Windows Vista and have UAC enabled, the application experiences an unhandled exception because it does not have permission to update files in the Program Files folder. Close the programs.

20. Verify that the program also runs from your computer's desktop.

21. Uninstall the application. Open Control Panel and start the tool for uninstalling applications. Right-click Remember Settings, and then click Uninstall. Respond to any UAC prompts that appear.

Exercise 2: Create a Custom Installer

In this exercise, you will create a simple application with a custom installer.

1. Use Visual Studio to create a WPF application named Hello in either Visual Basic.NET or C#.

2. Add a project reference to the *System.Configuration.Install* DLL.

3. Add the *System.Collections*, *System.IO*, *System.Configuration.Install*, and *System .ComponentModel* namespaces to the project.

4. Create a class named *HelloInstaller* that derives from the *Installer* class. In the *Install* method, create a file named Install.txt. In the *Commit* method, create a file

named Commit.txt. In the *Uninstall* method, remove both of those files. In the *Rollback* method, remove just the Install.txt file. Then, add the *RunInstaller* attribute. The following code sample demonstrates how to do this:

```vb
' VB
<RunInstaller(True)> _
Public Class HelloInstaller
    Inherits Installer
    Public Sub New()
        MyBase.New()
    End Sub

    Public Overloads Overrides Sub Commit(ByVal mySavedState As IDictionary)
        MyBase.Commit(mySavedState)
        System.IO.File.CreateText("Commit.txt")
    End Sub

    Public Overloads Overrides Sub Install(ByVal stateSaver As IDictionary)
        MyBase.Install(stateSaver)
        System.IO.File.CreateText("Install.txt")
    End Sub

    Public Overloads Overrides Sub Uninstall(ByVal savedState As IDictionary)
        MyRase.Uninstall(savedState)
        File.Delete("Commit.txt")
        File.Delete("Install.txt")
    End Sub

    Public Overloads Overrides Sub Rollback(ByVal savedState As IDictionary)
        MyBase.Rollback(savedState)
        File.Delete("Install.txt")
    End Sub
End Class
```

```csharp
// C#
[RunInstaller(true)]
public class HelloInstaller : Installer
{
    public HelloInstaller()
        : base()
    {
    }

    public override void Commit(IDictionary mySavedState)
    {
        base.Commit(mySavedState);
        System.IO.File.CreateText("Commit.txt");
    }

    public override void Install(IDictionary stateSaver)
    {
        base.Install(stateSaver);
        System.IO.File.CreateText("Install.txt");
    }
}
```

```
public override void Uninstall(IDictionary savedState)
{
    base.Uninstall(savedState);
    File.Delete("Commit.txt");
    File.Delete("Install.txt");
}

public override void Rollback(IDictionary savedState)
{
    base.Rollback(savedState);
    File.Delete("Install.txt");
}
}
```

5. Build the project. You do not need to run the assembly.

6. Open a command prompt and switch to the folder containing the Hello.exe assembly. Run the following command, which you might need to edit to specify the correct folder to your InstallUtil.exe application:

```
%windir%\Microsoft.NET\Framework\v2.0.50727\installutil hello.exe
```

7. View the output from InstallUtil.exe and verify that the installation succeeded. Then view the folder's directory and verify that the Install.txt and Commit.txt files have been successfully created.

8. Now, uninstall the application by running the following command:

```
%windir%\Microsoft.NET\Framework\v2.0.50727\installutil /u hello.exe
```

9. View the directory again and verify that the *Uninstall* method removed the Install.txt and Commit.txt files.

10. Using Notepad, examine the Hello.InstallLog text file to familiarize yourself with the format.

Lesson Summary

You can create a custom installer by deriving a class from *Installer* and then overriding the *Install*, *Commit*, *Uninstall*, and *Rollback* methods. To use a custom installer, run the InstallUtil.exe tool.

Lesson Review

You can use the following questions to test your knowledge of the information in Lesson 3, "Installing Applications." The questions are also available on the companion CD if you prefer to review them in electronic form.

NOTE Answers

Answers to these questions and explanations of why each answer choice is right or wrong are located in the "Answers" section at the end of the book.

1. You create the following class:

```vb
' VB
Public Class CustomInstaller
    Inherits Installer
    Public Sub New()
        MyBase.New()
    End Sub

    Public Overloads Overrides Sub Commit(ByVal mySavedState As IDictionary)
        MyBase.Commit(mySavedState)
    End Sub

    Public Overloads Overrides Sub Install(ByVal stateSaver As IDictionary)
        MyBase.Install(stateSaver)
    End Sub

    Public Overloads Overrides Sub Uninstall(ByVal savedState As IDictionary)
        MyBase.Uninstall(savedState)
    End Sub

    Public Overloads Overrides Sub Rollback(ByVal savedState As IDictionary)
        MyBase.Rollback(savedState)
    End Sub
End Class
```

```csharp
// C#
public class CustomInstaller : Installer
{
    public CustomInstaller()
        : base()
    {
    }

    public override void Commit(IDictionary mySavedState)
    {
        base.Commit(mySavedState);
    }

    public override void Install(IDictionary stateSaver)
    {
        base.Install(stateSaver);
    }

    public override void Uninstall(IDictionary savedState)
    {
        base.Uninstall(savedState);
    }
```

```
    public override void Rollback(IDictionary savedState)
    {
        base.Rollback(savedState);
    }
}
```

What do you need to add to allow the installer to function when the assembly is called with the InstallUtil.exe tool?

  A. Add a Setup project to the solution.

  B. Add the *Installing* method.

  C. Add a constructor that accepts an *IDictionary* object.

  D. Add the *RunInstaller* attribute to the class.

2. You are implementing a custom *Installer* class. If the installation fails, you need to remove any files that were copied over during the installation attempt. In which method should you write the code to remove the files?

  A. *Install*

  B. *Commit*

  C. *Rollback*

  D. *Uninstall*

Chapter Review

To practice and reinforce the skills you learned in this chapter further, you can:

- Review the chapter summary.
- Review the list of key terms introduced in this chapter.
- Complete the case scenarios. These scenarios set up real-world situations involving the topics of this chapter and ask you to create a solution.
- Complete the suggested practices.
- Take a practice test.

Chapter Summary

- You can store configuration settings in an XML file, which can then be updated by systems administrators. By default, applications use a configuration file named *<Application_Name>*.config. In addition, all applications can read settings stored in the central Machine.config file. You can use the *ConfigurationManager* class to read and write these settings, including database connection strings. To create a strongly typed custom configuration section, derive a class from the *Configuration-Section* class.

- You configure the .NET Framework in two different ways: by updating the Machine.config file or by using the .NET Framework 2.0 Configuration tool. The most common configuration tasks are adding a shared assembly to the assembly cache and configuring assembly version binding and codebases.

- If your application has complex installation requirements, you can create a custom installer by deriving from the *Installer* class. The *Installer* class has four methods that you can override: *Install*, *Commit*, *Rollback*, and *Uninstall*. Use the InstallUtil.exe tool to call a custom installer.

Key Terms

Do you know what these key terms mean? You can check your answers by looking up the terms in the glossary at the end of the book.

- Assembly cache
- Assembly version binding policy
- Codebase
- Remoting

Case Scenarios

In the following case scenarios you apply what you've learned about how to configure and install .NET Framework applications. You can find answers to these questions in the "Answers" section at the end of this book.

Case Scenario 1: Configuring an Application

You are an applications developer for Fabrikam, Inc. You have developed an application that employees will use to enter reimbursable expenses into a central database. Your application will be distributed to about 2,000 computers throughout your organization. The application functions in several different modes, depending on the organization where the user belongs. In addition, your company's systems administrators have requested the ability to configure which database server the application connects to.

Your manager asks you to interview key people and then answer questions about your design choices.

Interviews

The following is a list of company personnel interviewed and their statements.

- **Information Technology (IT) Manager**   "Right now, your application connects to a Microsoft SQL Server 2005 database at db.fabrikam.com. Both the name and the database platform are going to change in the next couple of weeks, though. They might change after that, too. So, we'd like the ability to configure the database server. Preferably, the configuration settings would be in a text or XML file. Several other applications connect to the same server, and if possible, we'd like to configure database settings for all applications in a central location so we can change it in a single place."

- **Finance Manager**   "Depending on employees' levels and roles, your application needs to show them different options. I'd like the IT department to be able to configure those settings on individual computers, rather than having the settings stored in the database."

Questions

Answer the following questions for your manager:

1. How can you allow the IT department to configure which database server your application connects to?
2. How can you allow the IT department to configure an employee's level and role?
3. Should you store the settings in the application's .config file or the Machine.config file?

Case Scenario 2: Installing an Application

You are an application developer working for Humongous Insurance. At the request of your IT department, you have developed an assembly that performs automated network troubleshooting tasks.

To make the assembly easy to deploy, IT has requested that it be deployable as a single .exe file. However, IT would like the option of installing it with a shortcut on the desktop and the Start menu. They would like to be able to install it using a Windows Installer package or directly from the assembly's .exe file.

Questions

Answer the following questions for your manager:

1. How can you meet the requirements to install the application using a Windows Installer package?

2. How can you allow the assembly to install itself from within the .exe file?

Suggested Practices

To master the "Embedding Configuration, Diagnostic, Management, and Installation Features into a .NET Framework Application" exam objective, complete the following tasks.

Embed Configuration Management Functionality into a .NET Framework Application

For this task, you should complete all three practices.

- **Practice 1** Using the last real-world application you wrote, add customizable settings using a .config file stored in the assembly's installation folder.

- **Practice 2** Create an application that updates configuration data in a folder that standard users on Windows Vista have privileges to update.

- **Practice 3** Using the last real-world application you wrote that connects to a database, update it to read the connection string from either the Machine.config file or the application's .config file. Make the code flexible enough so that it can connect to a variety of different database platforms.

Create a Custom Microsoft Windows Installer for the .NET Framework Components by Using the *System.Configuration.Install* Namespace, and Configure the .NET Framework Applications by Using Configuration Files, Environment Variables, and the .NET Framework 2.0 Configuration Tool (Mscorcfg.Msc)

For this task, you should complete all three practices.

- **Practice 1** Using the last real-world application you wrote that included a Setup project, re-create the Setup project's functionality using a custom installer. Install and uninstall the application using InstallUtil.exe and verify that it works correctly.

- **Practice 2** Create a custom installer for an application. By restricting security settings so that a required file cannot be created or a required registry setting cannot be updated, cause the installation to fail midway. Verify that the *Rollback* method correctly removes any traces of the application installation.

- **Practice 3** Add a class library assembly to your computer's assembly cache. Then reference it from a different project.

Take a Practice Test

The practice tests on this book's companion CD offer many options. For example, you can test yourself on just the content covered in this chapter, or you can test yourself on all the 70-536 certification exam content. You can set up the test so that it closely simulates the experience of taking a certification exam, or you can set it up in study mode so that you can look at the correct answers and explanations after you answer each question.

MORE INFO   Practice tests

For details about all the practice test options available, see the section "How to Use the Practice Tests" in the Introduction of this book.

Chapter 10
Logging and Systems Management

Real-world applications, especially those deployed in IT environments, must be manageable. Making an application manageable involves allowing systems administrators to monitor and troubleshoot the application. The .NET Framework provides the *Systems.Diagnostics* namespace to allow you to write events to the event log, create debug and trace information, and provide performance counters.

IT departments also regularly need internal tools that analyze computer status or respond to changes in the operating system. Windows Management Instrumentation (WMI) provides these capabilities, and the .NET Framework provides a useful WMI interface.

Exam objectives in this chapter:
- Manage an event log by using the *System.Diagnostics* namespace.
- Manage system processes and monitor the performance of a .NET Framework application by using the diagnostics functionality of the .NET Framework.
- Debug and trace a .NET Framework application by using the *System.Diagnostics* namespace.
- Embed management information and events into a .NET Framework application.

Lessons in this chapter:

Before You Begin

This book assumes that you have at least two to three years of experience developing Web-based, Microsoft Windows–based, or distributed applications using the .NET Framework. Candidates should have a working knowledge of Microsoft Visual Studio.

Before you begin, you should be familiar with Microsoft Visual Basic or C# and be comfortable with the following tasks:

- Creating Console and Windows Presentation Foundation (WPF) applications in Visual Studio using Visual Basic or C#
- Adding namespaces and system class library references to a project
- Running a project in Visual Studio

Lesson 1: Logging Application State

Systems administrators rely heavily on the *Windows event log*, a central repository for information about operating system and application activities and errors. For example, Windows adds events each time the operating system starts or shuts down. Applications typically add events when users log on or off, when users change important settings, or when serious errors occur.

By taking advantage of the Windows event log (rather than creating a text-based log file), you allow systems administrators to use their existing event management infrastructure. Most enterprise IT departments have software in place to monitor event logs for important events and forward those events to a central help desk for further processing. Using the Windows event log saves you from writing custom code to support these capabilities.

This lesson describes how to add events, read the event log, and create custom event logs.

After this lesson, you will be able to:

- Read and write events
- Log debugging and trace information

Estimated lesson time: 45 minutes

Reading and Writing Events

Systems administrators use the Windows event log to monitor and troubleshoot the operating system. By adding events to the event log, you can provide systems administrators with useful details about the inner workings of your application without directly displaying the information to the user. Because many IT departments have an event management infrastructure that aggregates events, the simple act of adding events to the event log can allow your application to be monitored in enterprise environments.

How to View the Event Logs

Use the Event Viewer snap-in to view event logs. You can open the Event Viewer snap-in by following these steps in Windows Vista:

1. Click Start, right-click Computer, and then click Manage. Respond to the User Account Control (UAC) prompt if it appears.

2. Expand the Computer Management, System Tools, and Event Viewer nodes.

3. Browse the subfolders to select an event log.

Recent versions of Windows include the following three event logs (among other less frequently used event logs, depending on the version of Windows and the components installed), located within Event Viewer\Windows Logs in Windows Vista:

- **System**   Stores all non-security-related operating system events.

- **Security**   Stores auditing events, including user logons and logoffs. If nonstandard auditing is enabled, the Security event log can store events when users access specific files or registry values. Applications cannot write to the Security event log.

- **Application**   Originally intended to store all events from all applications that do not create an application-specific event log.

How to Register an Event Source

Events always include a source, which identifies the application that generated the event. Before you log events, you must register your application as a source.

Adding an event source requires administrative privileges. Because Windows Vista does not run programs with administrative privileges by default, adding an event source is best done during the setup process (which typically does have administrative privileges).

If your application is not running as an administrator, you can register an event source manually by following these steps:

1. Log on as an administrator to the application server.
2. Start the registry editor by running Regedit.exe.
3. Locate the following registry subkey:

    HKEY_LOCAL_MACHINE\SYSTEM\CurrentControlSet\Services\Eventlog\Application

4. Right-click the Application subkey, click New, and then click Key.
5. Type the name of your event source for the key name (for example, **My Application**), and then press Enter.
6. Close the registry editor.

To create an event log source programmatically, call the static *EventLog.CreateEventSource* method with administrative privileges. You can then create events with the registered source. The following code sample determines whether a source already exists and registers the event source with the Application event log if the source does not yet exist:

```vb
' VB
If Not EventLog.SourceExists("My Application") Then
    EventLog.CreateEventSource("My Application", "Application")
End If
```

```csharp
// C#
if (!EventLog.SourceExists("My Application"))
    EventLog.CreateEventSource("My Application", "Application");
```

You can also use *EventLog.CreateEventSource* to create a custom event log, simply by specifying the name. For example, the following code sample creates an event log named My Log and registers a source named My App:

```vb
' VB
If Not EventLog.Exists("My Log") Then
    EventLog.CreateEventSource("My App", "My Log")
End If
```

```csharp
// C#
if (!EventLog.Exists("My Log") )
    EventLog.CreateEventSource("My App", "My Log");
```

In the Windows Vista Event Viewer snap-in, the custom event log appears under Applications And Services Logs. Because calling *EventLog.CreateEventSource* requires administrative privileges, you should call it during your application's setup procedure.

How to Log Events

Once your application is registered as a source, you can add an event by using an instance of the *EventLog* class (in the *System.Diagnostics* namespace), defining the *EventLog.Source* property, and then calling the *EventLog.WriteEntry* method. *EventLog .WriteEntry* supports the following parameters:

- **message** A text message that should describe the condition as thoroughly as possible.

- **type** The *EventLogEntryType* enumeration, which can be *Information*, *Warning*, *Error*, *FailureAudit* (used when a user is denied access to a resource), or *Success-Audit* (used when a user is allowed access to a resource).

- **eventID** A number that uniquely identifies the event type. Administrators might use this to search for specific events. You can create your own application-specific event IDs.

- **category** A number that identifies the event category. Like the event ID, this is application-specific.

- **rawData** A byte array that you can provide if you want to give administrators more information about the event.

The following code sample adds an event to the Application event log, assuming that the source "My Application" has already been registered with the Application event log:

```vb
' VB
Dim myLog As New EventLog("Application")
myLog.Source = "My Application"
myLog.WriteEntry("Could not connect", EventLogEntryType.Error, 1001, 1S)
```

```csharp
// C#
EventLog myLog = new EventLog("Application");
myLog.Source = "My Application";
myLog.WriteEntry("Could not connect", EventLogEntryType.Error, 1001, 1);
```

How to Read Events

To read events, create an *EventLog* instance. Then, access the *EventLog.Entries* collection. The following application displays all Application events to the console:

```vb
' VB
Dim myLog As New EventLog("Application")
For Each entry As EventLogEntry In myLog.Entries
    Console.WriteLine(entry.Message)
Next
```

```csharp
// C#
EventLog myLog = new EventLog("Application");
foreach (EventLogEntry entry in myLog.Entries)
    Console.WriteLine(entry.Message);
```

Real World

Tony Northrup

Whether you're a developer, systems administrator, or user, you've been frustrated by ambiguous error messages at some point. For example, I have this error message in my Application event log: "Faulting application, version, faulting module, version 0.0.0.0, fault address 0x00000000". Good luck fixing the problem based on that!

> To avoid this frustration and to facilitate troubleshooting, good developers pro-
> vide very detailed error messages. Although this is a very user-friendly practice,
> it can also weaken the security of your application if you list confidential infor-
> mation like usernames, passwords, or connection strings.

Logging Debugging and Trace Information

Often, during the development process, developers write messages to the console or display dialog boxes to track the application's processes. Although this information can be
useful, you wouldn't want it to appear in a production application. To add debug-only
code that will not run in release builds, you can use the *System.Diagnostics .Debug* class.

Use the static *Debug.Indent* method to cause all subsequent debugging output to be
indented. Use the static *Debug.Unindent* method to remove an indent. Set the *Debug*
.IndentSize property to specify the number of spaces with each indent (the default is
four), and set the *Debug.IndentLevel* property to specify an indentation level.

The following code sample demonstrates how to use the *Debug* class to mark the
beginning and end of an application. If you build this code in Visual Studio with the
build type set to Debug, you will see the Starting Application and Ending Application
messages. If you build this code with the build type set to Release, you will not see
those messages. However, you will still see the "Hello, world!" message:

```vb
'VB
Debug.Listeners.Add(New ConsoleTraceListener())
Debug.AutoFlush = True
Debug.Indent()
Debug.WriteLine("Starting application")
Console.WriteLine("Hello, world!")
Debug.WriteLine("Ending application")
Debug.Unindent()
```

```csharp
//C#
Debug.Listeners.Add(new ConsoleTraceListener());
Debug.AutoFlush = true;
Debug.Indent();
Debug.WriteLine("Starting application");
Console.WriteLine("Hello, world!");
Debug.WriteLine("Ending application");
Debug.Unindent();
```

Debug.Write and *Debug.WriteLine* function exactly the same as *Console.Write* and
Console.WriteLine. To reduce the amount of code that you need to write, the *Debug*

class adds the *WriteIf* and *WriteLineIf* methods, each of which accepts a boolean value as the first parameter and writes the output only if the value is *True*.

Debug.Assert also accepts a boolean condition. In general, you should use assertions to verify something that you know should *always* be true. For example, in a financial application, you might use an assertion to verify that the due date of a bill is after the year 2000. If an assertion fails, the Common Language Runtime (CLR) stops program execution and displays a dialog box similar to that shown in Figure 10-1. You should not use asserts in production applications.

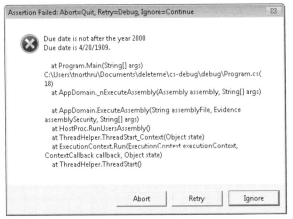

Figure 10-1 A failed call to *Debug.Assert*

Debug.AutoFlush determines whether debug output is written immediately. If you always want *Debug* output to be displayed immediately (the most common option), set *Debug.AutoFlush* to *True*. If you want to store *Debug* output and display it all at once (such as when an application exits), set *Debug.AutoFlush* to *False* and call *Debug.Flush* to write the output.

Using Trace

The *Trace* class functions almost identically to the *Debug* class. However, calls to *Trace* are executed in both Debug and Release builds. Therefore, use the *Debug* class to write messages only in the Debug build, and use the *Trace* class to write messages regardless of the build type. For example, consider the following code sample:

```
'VB
Debug.Listeners.Add(New ConsoleTraceListener())
Debug.AutoFlush = True
Debug.Indent()
```

```
Debug.WriteLine("Debug: Starting application")
Trace.WriteLine("Trace: Starting application")

Console.WriteLine("Hello, world!")

Debug.WriteLine("Debug: Ending application")
Trace.WriteLine("Trace: Ending application")

//C#
Debug.Listeners.Add(new ConsoleTraceListener());
Debug.AutoFlush = true;
Debug.Indent();

Debug.WriteLine("Debug: Starting application");
Trace.WriteLine("Trace: Starting application");

Console.WriteLine("Hello, world!");

Debug.WriteLine("Debug: Ending application");
Trace.WriteLine("Trace: Ending application");
```

This code sample generates the following output in a Debug build:

```
    Debug: Starting application
    Trace: Starting application
Hello, world!
    Debug: Ending application
    Trace: Ending application
```

The code sample generates the following, shorter output in a Release build. Notice that the output is not indented because the call to *Debug.Indent* was not executed:

```
Trace: Starting application
Hello, world!
Trace: Ending application
```

Properties that you configure for the *Debug* class also apply to the *Trace* class. For example, if you add a listener to the *Debug* class, you do not need to add the same listener to the *Trace* class.

Using Listeners

By default, *Debug* and *Trace* write to the Output window in Visual Studio (if you are running the application directly from Visual Studio) because they have a default listener: *DefaultTraceListener*. This allows you to view trace output without directly affecting the application's user interface.

If viewing debug and trace output in the Output window is not sufficient, you can also add the following listeners to the *Debug.Listeners* collection:

- **ConsoleTraceListener**   Sends output to the console or the standard error stream.

- **TextWriterTraceListener**   Sends output to a text file or a stream. Use *Console.Out* to write output to the console.

- **XmlWriterTraceListener**   Sends output to an Extensible Markup Language (XML) file using a *TextWriter* or *Stream* instance. This is useful for creating log files.

- **EventSchemaListener**   Sends output to an XML schema–compliant log file. This is useful only if you need output to comply to an existing schema.

- **DelimitedListTraceListener**   Sends output to a delimited text file. You can configure the delimiter using the *DelimitedListTraceLister.Delimiter* property.

- **EventLogTraceListener**   Writes output to the event log. Each time output is flushed, a separate event is generated. To avoid generating large numbers of events (and possibly affecting performance) set *Debug.AutoFlush* to *False*.

Configuring Debugging Using a .config File

Often, it's useful to allow users to view trace output. For example, they might be able to use the trace output to isolate a problem or to provide detailed information to you about the internal workings of the application in a production environment. To allow users to enable tracing, add the *<system.diagnostics>* section to your application's .config file.

The following .config file configures a console trace listener and provides instructions for users that allow them to enable tracing selectively:

```
<configuration>
 <system.diagnostics>
   <trace autoflush="false" indentsize="4">
       <listeners>
           <add name="configConsoleListener"
               type="System.Diagnostics.ConsoleTraceListener" />
       </listeners>
   </trace>
   <switches>
       <!-- This switch controls data messages. In order to receive
          data trace messages, change value="0" to value="1" -->
       <add name="DataMessagesSwitch" value="0" />
       <!-- This switch controls general messages. In order to
          receive general trace messages change the value to the
          appropriate level. "1" gives error messages, "2" gives
          errors and warnings, "3" gives more detailed error
          information, and "4" gives verbose trace information -->
```

```
            <add name="TraceLevelSwitch" value="0" />
        </switches>
    </system.diagnostics>
<configuration>
```

The following .config file directs tracing output to a text file and removes the default listener. Notice that you use the *initializeData* attribute when adding the listener to specify the output file—this is true for other listeners that require a filename as well:

```
<configuration>
 <system.diagnostics>
    <trace autoflush="false" indentsize="4">
        <listeners>
            <add name="TextTraceListener"
                type="System.Diagnostics.TextWriterTraceListener"
                initializeData="output.txt" />
            <remove name="Default" />
        </listeners>
    </trace>
 </system.diagnostics>
<configuration>
```

Lab: Working with Event Logs

In this lab, you will create a WPF application that adds events to a custom event log.

Exercise 1: Create an Event Log and Log an Event

In this exercise, you must create a solution that includes three projects: a WPF application, a class derived from *Installer*, and a Setup project. You must create a Setup project to add the custom event log during the setup process because the user typically has administrative credentials only during setup.

1. Use Visual Studio to create a new WPF Application project named LoggingApp in either Visual Basic.NET or C#.

2. In the Extensible Application Markup Language (XAML) for the LoggingApp window, add an event handler for the *Loaded* event. The XAML now resembles the following:

```
<Window x:Class="LoggingApp.Window1"
    xmlns="http://schemas.microsoft.com/winfx/2006/xaml/presentation"
    xmlns:x="http://schemas.microsoft.com/winfx/2006/xaml"
    Loaded="Window_Loaded"
    Title="Window1" Height="300" Width="300">
    <Grid>

    </Grid>
</Window>
```

3. In the code file, add the *System.Diagnostics* namespace. Then implement the *Loaded* event handler to add an event indicating that the application has started. Add the event to a custom event log named LoggingApp Log with a source of LoggingApp. The following code demonstrates how to do this:

```vb
' VB
Dim myLog As New EventLog("LoggingApp Log")
myLog.Source = "LoggingApp"
myLog.WriteEntry("LoggingApp started!", _
    EventLogEntryType.Information, 1001)
```

```csharp
// C#
EventLog myLog = new EventLog("LoggingApp Log");
myLog.Source = "LoggingApp";
myLog.WriteEntry("LoggingApp started!",
    EventLogEntryType.Information, 1001);
```

4. Add a new project to the solution using the Class Library template, and name it LoggingAppInstaller.

5. In the *LoggingAppInstaller* namespace, derive a custom class named *InstallLog* from the *Installer* class. As described in Lesson 3 of Chapter 9, "Installing and Configuring Applications," implement the *Install, Rollback,* and *Uninstall* methods to add and remove an event log named LoggingApp and a source named Logging AppSource. Note that you need to add a reference to the System.Configuration .Install dynamic-link library (DLL). The following code sample demonstrates how to write the code:

```vb
' VB
Imports System.Diagnostics
Imports System.Configuration.Install
Imports System.ComponentModel
Imports System.Collections

    <RunInstaller(True)> _
    Public Class InstallLog
        Inherits Installer
        Public Sub New()
            MyBase.New()
        End Sub

        Public Overrides Sub Commit( _
            ByVal mySavedState As IDictionary)
            MyBase.Commit(mySavedState)
        End Sub

        Public Overrides Sub Install( _
            ByVal stateSaver As IDictionary)
            MyBase.Install(stateSaver)
```

```vbnet
            If Not EventLog.Exists("LoggingApp Log") Then
                EventLog.CreateEventSource("LoggingApp", "LoggingApp Log")
            End If
        End Sub

        Public Overrides Sub Uninstall( _
            ByVal savedState As IDictionary)
            MyBase.Uninstall(savedState)
            RemoveLog()
        End Sub

        Public Overrides Sub Rollback( _
            ByVal savedState As IDictionary)
            MyBase.Rollback(savedState)
            RemoveLog()
        End Sub

        Public Sub RemoveLog()
            If EventLog.Exists("LoggingApp Log") Then
                EventLog.DeleteEventSource("LoggingApp")
                EventLog.Delete("LoggingApp Log")
            End If
        End Sub
    End Class
```

```csharp
// C#
using System;
using System.Collections.Generic;
using System.Linq;
using System.Text;

using System.Diagnostics;
using System.Configuration.Install;
using System.ComponentModel;
using System.Collections;

namespace LoggingAppInstaller
{
    [RunInstaller(true)]
    public class InstallLog : Installer
    {
        public InstallLog()
            : base()
        {
        }

        public override void Commit(IDictionary mySavedState)
        {
            base.Commit(mySavedState);
        }
```

```
public override void Install(IDictionary stateSaver)
{
    base.Install(stateSaver);
    if (!EventLog.Exists("LoggingApp Log"))
        EventLog.CreateEventSource(
            "LoggingApp", "LoggingApp Log"));
}

public override void Uninstall(IDictionary savedState)
{
    base.Uninstall(savedState);
    RemoveLog();
}

public override void Rollback(IDictionary savedState)
{
    base.Rollback(savedState);
    RemoveLog();
}

public void RemoveLog()
{
    if (EventLog.Exists("LoggingApp Log"))
    {
        EventLog.DeleteEventSource("LoggingApp"),
        EventLog.Delete("LoggingApp Log");
    }
}
    }
}
```

6. Add a Setup project to your solution named LoggingApp Setup.

7. Right-click Application Folder in the left pane, click Add, and then click Project Output. In the Add Project Output Group dialog box, click Primary Output for the LoggingApp project and then click OK.

8. Right-click Primary Output From LoggingApp, and then click Create Shortcut To Primary Output From LoggingApp. Name the shortcut LoggingApp and then drag it to the User's Programs Menu folder.

9. Add custom actions to the Setup Project to call the appropriate *InstallLog* methods. Right-click LoggingApp Setup in Solution Explorer, click View, and then click Custom Actions.

10. Right-click Install and then click Add Custom Action. In the Select Item In Project dialog box, double-click Application Folder and then click Add Output. In the Add Project Output Group dialog box, click the Project drop-down list, click LoggingAppInstaller, select Primary Output, and then click OK. Then, click OK again. Accept the default name, and notice that the *InstallerClass* property for the primary output is set to *True*.

11. Right-click Rollback and then click Add Custom Action. In the Select Item In Project dialog box, double-click Application Folder, click Primary Output From LoggingAppInstaller, and then click OK.

12. Repeat step 11 to add the LoggingAppInstaller DLL for the Uninstall custom action.

13. Build your solution. Right-click LoggingApp Setup in Solution Explorer, and then click Build.

14. Open the LoggingApp Setup build destination folder and double-click LoggingApp Setup.msi to start the installer. Accept the default settings to install the application. If you are running Windows Vista, respond appropriately when User Account Control (UAC) prompts you for administrative credentials.

15. Click Start, click All Programs, and then click LoggingApp to start the program. Then, close the window.

16. Open Event Viewer. In Windows Vista, you can do this by clicking Start, right-clicking Computer, and then clicking Manage. Respond to the UAC prompt, expand System Tools, and select Event Viewer.

17. Navigate to Event Viewer, Applications And Services Logs, and LoggingApp Log to verify that the new event log exists. Notice the single event in the event log, indicating that LoggingApp started.

18. Uninstall LoggingApp using the Programs And Features tool in Control Panel.

19. Close and reopen Event Viewer. Notice that LoggingApp Log has been removed.

Lesson Summary

■ Before you can add events, you must register an event source by calling *EventLog .CreateEventSource*. You can then call *EventLog.WriteEntry* to add events. Read events by creating an instance of the *EventLog* class and accessing the *EventLog .Entries* collection.

■ Use the *Debug* and *Trace* classes to log the internal workings of your application for troubleshooting purposes. *Debug* functions only in Debug releases. *Trace* can function with any release type. Users can configure listeners for *Debug* and *Trace* using the .config files.

Lesson Review

You can use the following questions to test your knowledge of the information in Lesson 1, "Logging Application State." The questions are also available on the companion CD if you prefer to review them in electronic form.

NOTE   Answers

Answers to these questions and explanations of why each answer choice is right or wrong are located in the "Answers" section at the end of the book.

---

1. You are creating a custom installer for an application that needs to add events to the Application event log. Which of the following do you need to do during the setup process?

    A. Call *EventLog.CreateEventSource*

    B. Call *EventLog.Create*

    C. Call *EventLog.GetEventLogs*

    D. Call *EventLog.WriteEntry*

2. You are creating a custom tool for your IT department that analyzes failure audits generated by the operating system. Which event log should you examine?

    A. Application

    B. System

    C. Security

    D. Setup

3. When running a Debug build of an application, you want to display a dialog box if the result of a calculation (stored in the *result* integer) is less than zero. Which of the following methods does this correctly?

    A. Debug.Assert(result >= 0, "Result error")

    B. Trace.Assert(result >= 0, "Result error")

    C. Debug.WriteIf(result >= 0, "Result error")

    D. Trace.WriteIf(result >= 0, "Result error")

4. You are creating a Console application, and you want *Debug* and *Trace* output displayed directly to the console. Which code sample does this correctly?

    A.

```
'VB
Debug.Listeners.Add(New DefaultTraceListener())
Debug.AutoFlush = True

//C#
Debug.Listeners.Add(new DefaultTraceListener ());
Debug.AutoFlush = true;
```

B.

```VB
'VB
Debug.Listeners.Add(New ConsoleTraceListener())
Debug.AutoFlush = True
```

```C#
//C#
Debug.Listeners.Add(new ConsoleTraceListener());
Debug.AutoFlush = true;
```

C.

```VB
'VB
Debug.Listeners.Add(New EventLogTraceListener())
Debug.AutoFlush = True
```

```C#
//C#
Debug.Listeners.Add(new EventLogTraceListener());
Debug.AutoFlush = true;
```

D.

```VB
'VB
Debug.Listeners.Add(New XmlWriterTraceListener())
Debug.AutoFlush = True
```

```C#
//C#
Debug.Listeners.Add(new XmlWriterTraceListener());
Debug.AutoFlush = true;
```

Lesson 2: Working with Performance Counters

For years, administrators have used performance counters to monitor the performance of computers, networks, and applications. Developers have also used performance counters to help identify bottlenecks in their application's performance.

With the *System.Diagnostics* namespace in the .NET Framework, you can add custom performance counters and update the performance data from within your application. Then, you or an administrator can monitor any aspect of your application's performance, which can be useful for performance tuning and troubleshooting.

This lesson describes how to monitor standard and custom performance counters and how to add and update custom performance counters.

After this lesson, you will be able to:

- Monitor performance counters
- Add custom performance counters
- Provide performance counter data

Estimated lesson time: 25 minutes

Monitoring Performance Counters

Windows includes hundreds of performance counters that allow you to monitor the operating system's activities in real time. You can view these counters using the Performance snap-in. In Windows Vista, you can access the Performance snap-in from within the Computer Management console by following these steps:

1. Click Start, right-click Computer, and then click Manage. Respond to the UAC prompt if it appears.

2. In the Computer Management console, expand System Tools, Reliability And Performance, and Monitoring Tools, and then select Performance Monitor.

3. On the Performance Monitor toolbar, click the button marked with a green plus sign to add a counter.

   The Add Counters dialog box appears, as shown in Figure 10-2.

4. In the Available Counters list, expand a category name and then click a counter. If required, select an instance and click Add.

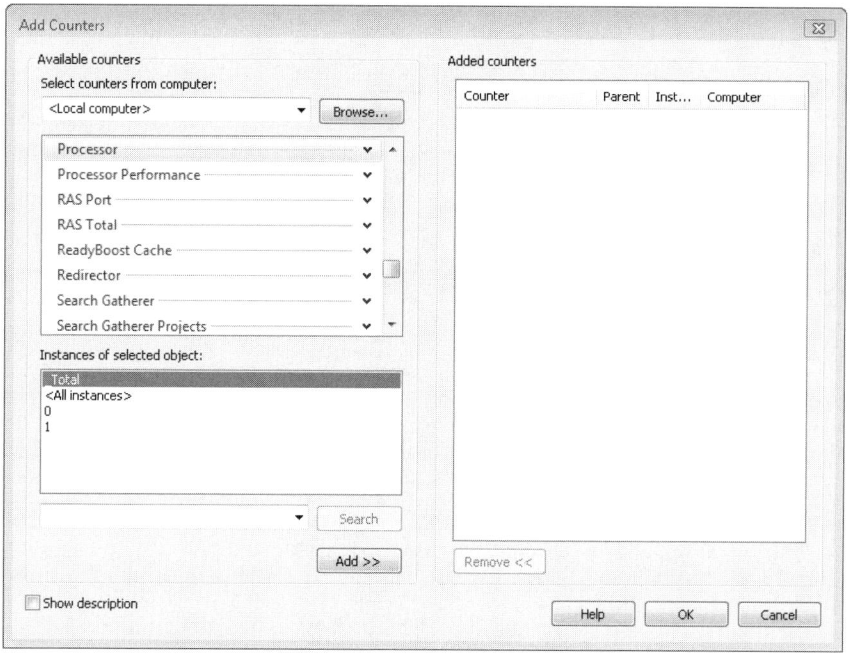

Figure 10-2   Adding a performance counter

5. Repeat step 4 to add more counters.

6. Click OK to begin monitoring the counters in real time.

   The Performance snap-in displays the values for the counters you selected.

To monitor performance counters within a program, create an instance of *Performance-Counter* by specifying the performance object, counter, and (if required) the instance. You can determine the names of these parameters, and whether an instance is required, by using the Performance snap-in. Then call the *PerformanceCounter.NextValue* method to reset the counter. Make a second call to *PerformanceCounter.NextValue* to retrieve the performance data. Depending on the counter, the performance data might be averaged over the time passed between calls to *PerformanceCounter.NextValue*.

The following code sample, which requires both the *System.Diagnostics* and *System .Threading* namespaces, displays the current processor utilization averaged over a period of 1 second:

'VB
```
' Create a PerformanceCounter object that measures processor time
Dim pc As New PerformanceCounter("Processor", "% Processor Time", "_Total")
```

```
' Reset the performance counter
pc.NextValue()

' Wait one second
Thread.Sleep(1000)

' Retrieve the processor usage over the past second
Console.WriteLine(pc.NextValue())

//C#
// Create a PerformanceCounter object that measures processor time
PerformanceCounter pc = new
    PerformanceCounter("Processor", "% Processor Time", "_Total");

// Reset the performance counter
pc.NextValue();

// Wait one second
Thread.Sleep(1000);

// Retrieve the processor usage over the past second
Console.WriteLine(pc.NextValue());
```

The first call to *PerformanceCounter.NextValue* always returns zero; therefore, it is always meaningless. Only subsequent calls contain useful data. The following code illustrates this by showing the datagrams sent per second:

```
'VB
Dim pc As New PerformanceCounter("IPv4", "Datagrams/sec")
For i As Integer = 0 To 9

    Console.WriteLine(pc.NextValue())
Next

//C#
PerformanceCounter pc = new PerformanceCounter("IPv4", "Datagrams/sec");

for (int i = 0; i < 10; i++)
{
    Console.WriteLine(pc.NextValue());
}
```

The output resembles the following, showing that the network interface was receiving 100 to 220 datagrams per second:

```
0
136.4877
213.3919
210.881
106.4458
186.9752
```

```
208.2334
172.8078
127.5594
219.6767
```

Because the IPv4\Datagrams/sec counter is averaged over 1 second, you can query it repeatedly and always retrieve the previous second's average. If you queried the Processor\% Processor Time_Total counter repeatedly, the results would resemble the following because repeatedly querying the value results in the instantaneous uti-lization. In the case of a computer processor, in any given instant, the processor is either idle or fully utilized—values between 0 and 100 occur only when examining the utilization over a period of time:

```
0
100
100
100
100
100
0
0
100
100
```

Adding Custom Performance Counters

If you want to provide performance data generated by your application, you should create a custom performance counter category and then add the counters to that cat-egory. You can't add performance counters to a built-in category.

To add a custom performance counter category and a single counter, call the static *PerformanceCounterCategory.Create* method. Provide the category name, a description of the category, a name for the counter, and a description of the counter. The follow-ing code sample demonstrates this:

```vb
'VB
PerformanceCounterCategory.Create("CategoryName", "CounterHelp", _
    PerformanceCounterCategoryType.MultiInstance, "CounterName", _
    "CounterHelp")
```

```csharp
//C#
PerformanceCounterCategory.Create("CategoryName", "CounterHelp",
    PerformanceCounterCategoryType.MultiInstance, "CounterName",
    "CounterHelp");
```

Note the third parameter: the *PerformanceCounterCategoryType* enumeration. You should specify *SingleInstance* if the counter definitely has only one instance. Specify

MultiInstance if the counter might have multiple instances. For example, because computers might have two or more processors, counters that display processor status are always *MultiInstance*.

If you want to add multiple counters to a single category, create an instance of *Counter-CreationDataCollection* and add multiple *CounterCreationData* objects to the collection. The following code sample demonstrates this:

```VB
'VB
Dim counters As CounterCreationDataCollection = New CounterCreationDataCollection
counters.Add(New CounterCreationData("Sales", _
    "Number of total sales", PerformanceCounterType.NumberOfItems64))
counters.Add(New CounterCreationData("Active Users", _
    "Number of active users", PerformanceCounterType.NumberOfItems64))
counters.Add(New CounterCreationData("Sales value", _
    "Total value of all sales", PerformanceCounterType.NumberOfItems64))
PerformanceCounterCategory.Create("MyApp Counters", _
    "Counters describing the performance of MyApp", _
    PerformanceCounterCategoryType.SingleInstance, counters)
```

```C#
//C#
CounterCreationDataCollection counters = new CounterCreationDataCollection();
counters.Add(new CounterCreationData("Sales",
    "Number of total sales", PerformanceCounterType.NumberOfItems64));
counters.Add(new CounterCreationData("Active Users",
    "Number of active users", PerformanceCounterType.NumberOfItems64));
counters.Add(new CounterCreationData ("Sales value",
    "Total value of all sales", PerformanceCounterType.NumberOfItems64));
PerformanceCounterCategory.Create("MyApp Counters",
    "Counters describing the performance of MyApp",
    PerformanceCounterCategoryType.SingleInstance, counters);
```

To check whether a category already exists, use the *PerformanceCounterCategory.Exists* method. To remove an existing category, call *PerformanceCounterCategory.Delete*.

You should add performance counters during an application's setup process for two reasons. First, adding performance counters requires administrative privileges. Second, the operating system requires a few moments to refresh the list of performance counters. Therefore, they might not be accessible the moment you add the counters. However, the typical delay between installing an application and running the application is generally sufficient.

Providing Performance Counter Data

After you create a custom performance counter, you can update the data as needed. You don't need to update it constantly—just when the value changes. Performance counter data is sampled only every 400 milliseconds, so if you update the value more frequently than that, it won't improve the accuracy significantly.

To update a performance counter, create a *PerformanceCounter* object just as you would for reading a performance counter value. However, you must set the *ReadOnly* property to *false*. You can do this using the overloaded *PerformanceCounter* constructor that takes a boolean parameter, as shown here, or you can set the *ReadOnly* property after creating the object:

```vb
'VB
Dim pc As PerformanceCounter = New PerformanceCounter( _
    "MyApp Counters", "Sales", False)
```

```csharp
//C#
PerformanceCounter pc = new PerformanceCounter(
    "MyApp Counters", "Sales", false);
```

After creating the *PerformanceCounter* object, you can set the value directly by defining the *RawValue* property. Alternatively, you can call the thread-safe *Decrement*, *Increment*, and *IncrementBy* methods to adjust the value relative to the current value. The following code sample demonstrates how to use each of these methods:

```vb
'VB
Dim pc As PerformanceCounter = New PerformanceCounter( _
    "MyApp Counters", "Sales", False)
pc.RawValue = 7
pc.Decrement
pc.Increment
pc.IncrementBy(3)
```

```csharp
//C#
PerformanceCounter pc = new PerformanceCounter(
    "MyApp Counters", "Sales", false);
pc.RawValue = 7;
pc.Decrement();
pc.Increment();
pc.IncrementBy(3);
```

PerformanceCounter.Increment and *PerformanceCounter.Decrement* are thread-safe, but they're much slower than simply updating *PerformanceCounter.RawValue*. Therefore, you should use *PerformanceCounter.Increment* and *PerformanceCounter.Decrement* only when multiple threads might update the performance counter simultaneously.

Lab: Providing Performance Data

In this lab, you will create an application that provides performance data that systems administrators can use to monitor the application's performance.

Exercise 1: Create and Update Performance Counters

In this exercise, you will create a solution that includes three projects: a WPF application, a class derived from *Installer*, and a Setup project. You must create a Setup project to add the custom performance counter during the setup process because the user typically has administrative credentials only during setup. The application that you create will record the number of times the user has clicked a button in a custom performance counter.

1. Use Visual Studio to create a new WPF Application project named PerfApp in either Visual Basic .NET or C#.

2. Add a single *Label* control named *counterLabel* and a single *Button* control named *counterButton* to the form. Double-click *counterButton* to edit the *Click* event handler.

3. In the code file, add the *System.Diagnostics* namespace. Then write code in the *counterButton.Click* event handler to increment the *PerfApp\Clicks* counter and display the current value in *counterLabel*. The following code demonstrates how to do this:

```vb
' VB
Dim pc As New PerformanceCounter("PerfApp", "Clicks", False)
pc.Increment()
counterLabel.Content = pc.NextValue().ToString()
```

```csharp
// C#
PerformanceCounter pc = new PerformanceCounter("PerfApp", "Clicks", false);
pc.Increment();
counterLabel.Content = pc.NextValue().ToString();
```

4. Add a new project to the solution using the Class Library template. Name the project PerfAppInstaller.

5. In the *PerfAppInstaller* namespace, derive a custom class named *InstallCounter* from the *Installer* class. As described in Lesson 3 of Chapter 9, implement the *Install, Rollback,* and *Uninstall* methods to add and remove a performance category named PerfApp and a counter named Clicks. You need to add a reference to the System.Configuration.Install DLL. The following code sample demonstrates how to write the code:

```vb
' VB
Imports System.Configuration.Install
Imports System.ComponentModel

<RunInstaller(True)> _
    Public Class InstallCounter
    Inherits Installer
    Public Sub New()
        MyBase.New()
    End Sub
```

```vb
    Public Overloads Overrides Sub Commit( _
        ByVal mySavedState As IDictionary)
        MyBase.Commit(mySavedState)
    End Sub

    Public Overloads Overrides Sub Install( _
        ByVal stateSaver As IDictionary)
        MyBase.Install(stateSaver)
        If Not PerformanceCounterCategory.Exists("PerfApp") Then
            PerformanceCounterCategory.Create("PerfApp", _
                "Counters for PerfApp", _
                PerformanceCounterCategoryType.SingleInstance, _
                "Clicks", "Times the user has clicked the button.")
        End If
    End Sub

    Public Overloads Overrides Sub Uninstall( _
        ByVal savedState As IDictionary)
        MyBase.Uninstall(savedState)
        If PerformanceCounterCategory.Exists("PerfApp") Then
            PerformanceCounterCategory.Delete("PerfApp")
        End If
    End Sub

    Public Overloads Overrides Sub Rollback( _
        ByVal savedState As IDictionary)
        MyBase.Rollback(savedState)
        If PerformanceCounterCategory.Exists("PerfApp") Then
            PerformanceCounterCategory.Delete("PerfApp")
        End If
    End Sub
End Class

// C#
using System;
using System.Collections.Generic;
using System.Linq;
using System.Text;

using System.Diagnostics;
using System.Configuration.Install;
using System.ComponentModel;
using System.Collections;

namespace PerfAppInstaller
{
    [RunInstaller(true)]
    public class InstallCounter : Installer
    {
        public InstallCounter()
            : base()
        {
        }
```

```csharp
public override void Commit(IDictionary mySavedState)
{
    base.Commit(mySavedState);
}

public override void Install(IDictionary stateSaver)
{
    base.Install(stateSaver);
    if (!PerformanceCounterCategory.Exists("PerfApp"))
        PerformanceCounterCategory.Create("PerfApp",
            "Counters for PerfApp",
            PerformanceCounterCategoryType.SingleInstance,
            "Clicks",
            "Times the user has clicked the button.");
}

public override void Uninstall(IDictionary savedState)
{
    base.Uninstall(savedState);
    if (PerformanceCounterCategory.Exists("PerfApp"))
        PerformanceCounterCategory.Delete("PerfApp");
}

public override void Rollback(IDictionary savedState)
{
    base.Rollback(savedState);
    if (PerformanceCounterCategory.Exists("PerfApp"))
        PerformanceCounterCategory.Delete("PerfApp");
}
}
}
```

6. Add a Setup project named PerfApp Setup to your solution.

7. Right-click Application Folder in the left pane, click Add, and then click Project Output. In the Add Project Output Group dialog box, click Primary Output for the PerfApp project and click OK.

8. Right-click Primary Output From PerfApp and then click Create Shortcut To Primary Output From PerfApp. Name the shortcut PerfApp and then drag it to the User's Programs Menu folder.

9. Add custom actions to the Setup project to call the appropriate *InstallLog* methods. Right-click PerfApp Setup in Solution Explorer, click View, and then click Custom Actions.

10. Right-click Install and then click Add Custom Action. In the Select Item In Project dialog box, double-click Application Folder and then click Add Output. In the Add Project Output Group dialog box, click the Project drop-down list

and then click PerfAppInstaller. Select Primary Output, click OK and then click OK again. Accept the default name, and notice that the InstallerClass property for the primary output is set to True.

11. Right-click Rollback and then click Add Custom Action. In the Select Item In Project dialog box, double-click Application Folder. Click Primary Output From PerfAppInstaller and then click OK.

12. Repeat step 11 to add the PerfAppInstaller DLL for the Uninstall custom action.

13. Build your solution. Right-click PerfApp Setup in Solution Explorer and then click Build.

14. Open the PerfApp Setup build destination folder and double-click PerfApp Setup.msi to start the installer. Accept the default settings to install the application. If you are running Windows Vista, respond appropriately when UAC prompts you for administrative credentials.

15. Open the Performance snap-in and add the *PerfApp\Clicks* counter to monitor it in real time.

16. Leave the Performance snap-in running. Click Start, click All Programs, and then click PerfApp to start the program. Click the button several times to increment the counter. Notice that *counterLabel* displays the number of clicks and the Performance snap-in shows the value in real time.

17. Uninstall PerfApp using the Programs And Features tool in Control Panel.

18. Close and reopen the Performance snap-in. Notice that the *PerfApp* counter category has been removed.

Lesson Summary

- To monitor performance counters programmatically, create an instance of *PerformanceCounter*. Then call the *PerformanceCounter.NextValue* method to reset the counter. Make subsequent calls to *PerformanceCounter.NextValue* to retrieve the performance data.

- To add custom performance counters, call the static *PerformanceCounterCategory .Create* method. Provide the category name, a description of the category, a name for the counter, and a description of the counter.

- To provide performance counter data, create a *PerformanceCounter* object and set the *ReadOnly* property to *false*. You can then set the value directly by defining the *RawValue* property or by calling the thread-safe *Decrement*, *Increment*, and *IncrementBy* methods.

Lesson Review

You can use the following questions to test your knowledge of the information in Lesson 2, "Working with Performance Counters." The questions are also available on the companion CD if you prefer to review them in electronic form.

NOTE   Answers

Answers to these questions and explanations of why each answer choice is right or wrong are located in the "Answers" section at the end of the book.

---

1. You are creating a multithreaded application. You create an instance of *PerformanceCounter* named *pc* that might be referenced from multiple threads simultaneously. Which of the following calls is thread-safe? (Choose all that apply.)

    A. *pc.RawValue = pc.RawValue + 32*

    B. *pc.Increment()*

    C. *pc.Decrement()*

    D. *pc.Increment(12)*

2. You want to add a performance counter category with multiple counters programmatically. Which class should you use to specify the counters?

    A. *PerformanceCounterCategory*

    B. *CounterSample*

    C. *CounterCreationDataCollection*

    D. *CounterCreationData*

Lesson 3: Managing Computers

Applications often need to examine aspects of a computer, such as currently running processes and locally attached storage devices. In addition, it's often useful to respond to changes in the system status, such as a new process starting or a newly attached storage device. You can use the *Process* class and Windows Management Instrumentation (WMI) to accomplish these tasks with the .NET Framework.

After this lesson, you will be able to:

■ Examine processes

■ Access WMI information and respond to WMI events

Estimated lesson time: 20 minutes

Examining Processes

You can use the *Process.GetProcesses* static method to retrieve a list of current processes. The following code sample lists the process ID (PID) and process name of all processes visible to the assembly. Processes run by other users might not be visible:

```
' VB
For Each p As Process In Process.GetProcesses()
   Console.WriteLine("{0}: {1}", p.Id.ToString(), p.ProcessName)
Next
```

```
// C#
foreach (Process p in Process.GetProcesses())
   Console.WriteLine("{0}: {1}", p.Id, p.ProcessName);
```

To retrieve a specific process by ID, call *Process.GetProcessById*. To retrieve a list of processes with a specific name, call *Process.GetProcessesByName*. To retrieve the current process, call *Process.GetCurrentProcess*.

Once you create a *Process* instance, you can access a list of the modules loaded by that process using *Process.Modules* (if you have sufficient privileges). If you lack sufficient privileges (which vary depending on the process), the CLR throws a *Win32Exception*. The following code sample demonstrates how to list all processes and modules when sufficient privileges are available:

```
' VB
For Each p As Process In Process.GetProcesses()
   Console.WriteLine("{0}: {1}", p.Id.ToString(), p.ProcessName)
   Try
      For Each pm As ProcessModule In p.Modules
```

```
        Console.WriteLine("    {0}: {1}", pm.ModuleName, _
            pm.ModuleMemorySize.ToString())
    Next
  Catch ex As System.ComponentModel.Win32Exception
      Console.WriteLine("    Unable to list modules")
  End Try
Next
```

```
// C#
foreach (Process p in Process.GetProcesses())
{
    Console.WriteLine("{0}: {1}", p.Id.ToString(), p.ProcessName);
    try
    {
        foreach (ProcessModule pm in p.Modules)
            Console.WriteLine("    {0}: {1}", pm.ModuleName,
                pm.ModuleMemorySize.ToString());
    }
    catch (System.ComponentModel.Win32Exception ex)
    {
        Console.WriteLine("    Unable to list modules");
    }
}
```

The first time you reference any *Process* property, the *Process* class retrieves and caches values for all *Process* properties. Therefore, property values might be outdated. To retrieve updated information, call the *Process.Refresh* method.

The following are some of the most useful *Process* properties:

- **BasePriority**   The priority of the process.

- **ExitCode**   After a process terminates, the instance of the *Process* class populates the *ExitCode* and *ExitTime* properties. The meaning of the *ExitCode* property is defined by the application, but typically zero indicates a nonerror ending, and any nonzero value indicates the application ended with an error.

- **ExitTime**   The time the process ended.

- **HasExited**   A boolean value that is *true* if the process has ended.

- **Id**   The PID.

- **MachineName**   The name of the computer on which the process is running.

- **Modules**   A list of modules loaded by the process.

- **NonpagedMemorySize64**   The amount of nonpaged memory allocated to the process. Nonpaged memory must be stored in RAM.

- **PagedMemorySize64**   The amount of paged memory allocated to the process. Paged memory can be moved to the paging file.

- **ProcessName**   The name of the process, which is typically the same as the executable file.

- **TotalProcessorTime**   The total amount of processing time the process has consumed.

To start a new process, call the *Process.Start* static method and specify the name of the executable file. If you want to pass the process parameters (such as command-line parameters), pass those as a second string. The following code sample shows how to start Notepad and have it open the C:\Windows\Win.ini file:

```
' VB
Process.Start("Notepad.exe", "C:\windows\win.ini")
```

```
// C#
Process.Start("Notepad.exe", @"C:\windows\win.ini");
```

Accessing Management Information

Windows exposes a great deal of information about the computer and operating system through WMI. WMI information is useful when you need to examine the computer to determine how to set up your application, or when creating tools for systems management or inventory.

First, define the management scope by creating a new *ManagementScope* object and calling *ManagementScope.Connect*. Typically, the management scope is \\<*computer_name*>\root\cimv2. The following code sample, which requires the *System.Management* namespace, demonstrates how to create the management scope:

```
' VB
Dim scope As New ManagementScope("\\localhost\root\cimv2")
scope.Connect()
```

```
// C#
ManagementScope scope =
   new ManagementScope(@"\\localhost\root\cimv2");
scope.Connect();
```

You also need to create a WMI Query Language (WQL) query using an instance of *ObjectQuery*, which will be executed within the scope you specified. WQL is a subset of Structured Query Language (SQL) with extensions to support WMI event notification and other WMI-specific features. The following code sample demonstrates how to query all objects in the *Win32_OperatingSystem* object. However, there are many different WMI objects. For a complete list, refer to WMI Classes at *http://msdn.microsoft.com/en-us/ library/aa394554.aspx.*

```vb
' VB
Dim query As New ObjectQuery( _
    "SELECT * FROM Win32_OperatingSystem")
```

```csharp
// C#
ObjectQuery query = new ObjectQuery(
    "SELECT * FROM Win32_OperatingSystem");
```

With the scope and query defined, you can execute your query by creating a *ManagementObjectSearcher* object and then calling the *ManagementObjectSearcher.Get* method to create a *ManagementObjectCollection* object.

```vb
' VB
Dim searcher As New ManagementObjectSearcher(scope, query)
Dim queryCollection As ManagementObjectCollection = searcher.Get()
```

```csharp
// C#
ManagementObjectSearcher searcher = new ManagementObjectSearcher(scope, query);
ManagementObjectCollection queryCollection = searcher.Get();
```

Alternatively, you can use the overloaded *ManagementObjectSearcher* constructor to specify the query without creating separate scope or query objects, as the following example demonstrates:

```vb
' VB
Dim searcher As New ManagementObjectSearcher( _
    "SELECT * FROM Win32_LogicalDisk")
Dim queryCollection As ManagementObjectCollection = searcher.Get()
```

```csharp
// C#
ManagementObjectSearcher searcher =
   new ManagementObjectSearcher(
       "SELECT * FROM Win32_LogicalDisk");
ManagementObjectCollection queryCollection = searcher.Get();
```

Finally, you can iterate through the *ManagementObject* objects in the *ManagementObjectCollection* and directly access the properties. The following loop lists several properties from the *ManagementObject* defined in the *Win32_OperatingSystem* example shown earlier:

```vb
' VB
For Each m As ManagementObject In queryCollection
    Console.WriteLine("Computer Name : {0}", m("csname"))
    Console.WriteLine("Windows Directory : {0}", m("WindowsDirectory"))
```

```
    Console.WriteLine("Operating System: {0}", m("Caption"))
    Console.WriteLine("Version: {0}", m("Version"))
    Console.WriteLine("Manufacturer : {0}", m("Manufacturer"))
Next
```

```
// C#
foreach (ManagementObject m in queryCollection)
{
    Console.WriteLine("Computer Name : {0}", m["csname"]);
    Console.WriteLine("Windows Directory : {0}", m["WindowsDirectory"]);
    Console.WriteLine("Operating System: {0}", m["Caption"]);
    Console.WriteLine("Version: {0}", m["Version"]);
    Console.WriteLine("Manufacturer : {0}", m["Manufacturer"]);
}
```

The following code sample demonstrates how to query the local computer for operating system details:

```
'VB
' Perform the query
Dim searcher As New ManagementObjectSearcher( _
    "SELECT * FROM Win32_OperatingSystem")
Dim queryCollection As ManagementObjectCollection = searcher.Get()

' Display the data from the query
For Each m As ManagementObject In queryCollection
    ' Display the remote computer information
    Console.WriteLine("Computer Name : {0}", m("csname"))
    Console.WriteLine("Windows Directory : {0}", m("WindowsDirectory"))
    Console.WriteLine("Operating System: {0}", m("Caption"))
    Console.WriteLine("Version: {0}", m("Version"))
    Console.WriteLine("Manufacturer : {0}", m("Manufacturer"))
Next
```

```
//C#
// Perform the query
ManagementObjectSearcher searcher =
    new ManagementObjectSearcher(
        "SELECT * FROM Win32_OperatingSystem");
ManagementObjectCollection queryCollection = searcher.Get();

// Display the data from the query
foreach (ManagementObject m in queryCollection)
{
    // Display the remote computer information
    Console.WriteLine("Computer Name : {0}", m["csname"]);
    Console.WriteLine("Windows Directory : {0}", m["WindowsDirectory"]);
    Console.WriteLine("Operating System: {0}", m["Caption"]);
    Console.WriteLine("Version: {0}", m["Version"]);
    Console.WriteLine("Manufacturer : {0}", m["Manufacturer"]);
}
```

Similarly, the following code lists all disks connected to the local computer:

```vb
'VB
' Create a scope to identify the computer to query
Dim scope As New ManagementScope("\\localhost\root\cimv2")
scope.Connect()

' Create a query for operating system details
Dim query As New ObjectQuery("SELECT * FROM Win32_LogicalDisk")

' Perform the query
Dim searcher As New ManagementObjectSearcher(scope, query)
Dim queryCollection As ManagementObjectCollection = searcher.Get()

' Display the data from the query
For Each m As ManagementObject In queryCollection
    ' Display the remote computer information
    Console.WriteLine("{0} {1}", m("Name").ToString(), _
        m("Description").ToString())
Next
```

```csharp
//C#
// Create a scope to identify the computer to query
ManagementScope scope = new ManagementScope(@"\\localhost\root\cimv2");
scope.Connect();

// Create a query for operating system details
ObjectQuery query =
    new ObjectQuery("SELECT * FROM Win32_LogicalDisk");

// Perform the query
ManagementObjectSearcher searcher =
    new ManagementObjectSearcher(scope, query);
ManagementObjectCollection queryCollection = searcher.Get();

// Display the data from the query
foreach (ManagementObject m in queryCollection)
{
    // Display the remote computer information
    Console.WriteLine("{0} {1}", m["Name"].ToString(),
        m["Description"].ToString());
}
```

Exam Tip   The number of WMI Classes is immense. Fortunately, you don't have to be able to list them for the 70-536 exam. Instead, familiarize yourself conceptually with how to write WMI queries and retrieve the results. For a complete reference, refer to WMI Classes at *http://msdn.microsoft.com/en-us/library/aa394554.aspx.*

Waiting for WMI Events

You can also respond to WMI events, which are triggered by changes to the operating system status by creating an instance of *WqlEventQuery*. To create an instance of *WqlEventQuery*, pass the constructor an event class name, a query interval, and a query condition. Then, use the *WqlEventQuery* to create an instance of *Management-EventWatcher*.

You can then use *ManagementEventWatcher* to either create an event handler that will be called (using *ManagementEventWatcher.EventArrived*) or wait for the next event (by calling *ManagementEventWatcher.WaitForNextEvent*). If you call *ManagementEvent-Watcher.WaitForNextEvent*, it returns an instance of *ManagementBaseObject*, which you can use to retrieve the query-specific results.

The following code creates a WQL event query to detect a new process, waits for a new process to start, and then displays the information about the process:

```vb
'VB
' Create event query to be notified within 1 second of a change
' in a service
Dim query As New WqlEventQuery("__InstanceCreationEvent", _
    New TimeSpan(0, 0, 1), "TargetInstance isa ""Win32_Process""")

' Initialize an event watcher and subscribe to events that match this query
Dim watcher As New ManagementEventWatcher(query)

' Block until the next event occurs
Dim e As ManagementBaseObject = watcher.WaitForNextEvent()

' Display information from the event
Console.WriteLine("Process {0} has been created, path is: {1}", _
    DirectCast(e("TargetInstance"), ManagementBaseObject)("Name"), _
    DirectCast(e("TargetInstance"), ManagementBaseObject)("ExecutablePath"))

' Cancel the subscription
watcher.Stop()
```

```csharp
//C#
// Create event query to be notified within 1 second of a change
// in a service
WqlEventQuery query = new WqlEventQuery("__InstanceCreationEvent",
      new TimeSpan(0, 0, 1),
      "TargetInstance isa \"Win32_Process\"");

// Initialize an event watcher and subscribe to events that match this query
ManagementEventWatcher watcher = new ManagementEventWatcher(query);

// Block until the next event occurs
ManagementBaseObject e = watcher.WaitForNextEvent();
```

```
// Display information from the event
Console.WriteLine("Process {0} has been created, path is: {1}",
    ((ManagementBaseObject)e["TargetInstance"])["Name"],
    ((ManagementBaseObject)e["TargetInstance"])["ExecutablePath"]);

// Cancel the subscription
watcher.Stop();
```

Responding to WMI Events with an Event Handler

You can respond to the *ManagementEventWatcher.EventArrived* event to call a method each time a WMI event occurs. Your event handler must accept two parameters: an *object* parameter and an *EventArrivedEventArgs* parameter. *EventArrivedEventArgs.NewEvent* is a *ManagementBaseObject* that describes the event.

The following Console application demonstrates how to handle WMI events asynchronously. It performs the exact same task as the previous code sample:

```vbnet
'VB
Sub Main()
    Dim watcher As ManagementEventWatcher = Nothing

    Dim receiver As New EventReceiver()

    ' Create the watcher and register the callback.
    watcher = GetWatcher(New EventArrivedEventHandler( _
        AddressOf receiver.OnEventArrived))

    ' Watcher starts to listen to the Management Events.
    watcher.Start()

    ' Run until the user presses a key
    Console.ReadKey()
    watcher.Stop()
End Sub

' Create a ManagementEventWatcher object.
Public Function GetWatcher(ByRef handler As EventArrivedEventHandler) _
    As ManagementEventWatcher
    ' Create event query to be notified within 1 second of a change
    ' in a service
    Dim query As New WqlEventQuery("__InstanceCreationEvent", _
        New TimeSpan(0, 0, 1), "TargetInstance isa ""Win32_Process""")

    ' Initialize an event watcher and subscribe to events that match
    ' this query
    Dim watcher As New ManagementEventWatcher(query)

    ' Attach the EventArrived property to EventArrivedEventHandler method with the required
    handler to allow watcher object communicate to the application.
```

```
        AddHandler watcher.EventArrived, handler
        Return watcher
End Function

Class EventReceiver
    ' Handle the event and display the ManagementBaseObject properties.
    Public Sub OnEventArrived(ByVal sender As Object, _
        ByVal e As EventArrivedEventArgs)
        ' EventArrivedEventArgs is a management event.
        Dim evt As ManagementBaseObject = e.NewEvent

        ' Display information from the event
        Console.WriteLine("Process {0} has been created, path is: {1}", _
            DirectCast(evt("TargetInstance"), _
                ManagementBaseObject)("Name"),  _
            DirectCast(evt("TargetInstance"), _
                ManagementBaseObject)("ExecutablePath"))
    End Sub
End Class

//C#
static void Main(string[] args)
{
    ManagementEventWatcher watcher = null;

    EventReceiver receiver = new EventReceiver();

    // Create the watcher and register the callback
    watcher = GetWatcher(
        new EventArrivedEventHandler(receiver.OnEventArrived));

    // Watcher starts to listen to the Management Events.
    watcher.Start();

    // Run until the user presses a key
    Console.ReadKey();
     watcher.Stop();
}

// Create a ManagementEventWatcher object.
public static ManagementEventWatcher GetWatcher(
    EventArrivedEventHandler handler)
{
    // Create event query to be notified within 1 second of a
    // change in a service
    WqlEventQuery query = new WqlEventQuery("__InstanceCreationEvent",
        new TimeSpan(0, 0, 1),
        "TargetInstance isa \"Win32_Process\"");

    // Initialize an event watcher and subscribe to events that
    // match this query
    ManagementEventWatcher watcher = new ManagementEventWatcher(query);
```

```
        // Attach the EventArrived property to
        // EventArrivedEventHandler method with the
        // required handler to allow watcher object communicate to
        // the application.
        watcher.EventArrived += new EventArrivedEventHandler(handler);
        return watcher;
    }

    // Handle the event and display the ManagementBaseObject
    // properties.
    class EventReceiver
    {
        public void OnEventArrived(object sender,
            EventArrivedEventArgs e)
        {

            // EventArrivedEventArgs is a management event.
            ManagementBaseObject evt = e.NewEvent;

            // Display information from the event
            Console.WriteLine("Process {0} has been created, path is: {1}",
                ((ManagementBaseObject)
                    evt["TargetInstance"])["Name"],
                ((ManagementBaseObject)
                    evt["TargetInstance"])["ExecutablePath"]);
        ]
    }
}
```

Lab: Create an Alarm Clock

In this lab, you create a WPF application that uses WMI events to trigger an alarm every minute.

Exercise 1: Respond to a WMI Event

In this exercise, you create a WPF application that displays a dialog box every minute by responding to WMI events when the value of the computer's clock equals zero seconds.

1. Use Visual Studio to create a new WPF Application project named Alarm, in either Visual Basic.NET or C#.

2. In the XAML, add handlers for the *Loaded* and *Closing* events, as shown in bold here:

```
<Window x:Class="Alarm.Window1"
    xmlns="http://schemas.microsoft.com/winfx/2006/xaml/presentation"
    xmlns:x="http://schemas.microsoft.com/winfx/2006/xaml"
    Loaded="Window_Loaded"
    Closing="Window_Closing"
    Title="Window1" Height="300" Width="300">
```

3. Add a reference to System.Management.dll to your project. Then add the *System .Management* namespace to the code file.

4. In the window's class, declare an instance of *ManagementEventWatcher* so that it can be accessible from all methods in the class. You need to use this instance to start and stop the *EventArrived* handler:

```vb
' VB
Class Window1
    Dim watcher As ManagementEventWatcher = Nothing
End Class
```

```csharp
// C#
public partial class Window1 : Window
{
    ManagementEventWatcher watcher = null;
}
```

5. Add a class and a method to handle the WMI query event by displaying the current time in a dialog box. The following code sample demonstrates this:

```vb
' VB
Class EventReceiver
    Public Sub OnEventArrived(ByVal sender As Object, _
        ByVal e As EventArrivedEventArgs)
        Dim evt As ManagementBaseObject = e.NewEvent

        ' Display information from the event
        Dim time As String = [String].Format("{0}:{1:00}", _
            DirectCast(evt("TargetInstance"), _
                ManagementBaseObject)("Hour"), _
            DirectCast(evt("TargetInstance"), _
                ManagementBaseObject)("Minute"))

        MessageBox.Show(time, "Current time")
    End Sub
End Class
```

```csharp
// C#
class EventReceiver
{
    public void OnEventArrived(object sender, EventArrivedEventArgs e)
    {
        ManagementBaseObject evt = e.NewEvent;

        // Display information from the event
        string time = String.Format("{0}:{1:00}",
            ((ManagementBaseObject)evt["TargetInstance"])["Hour"],
            ((ManagementBaseObject)evt["TargetInstance"])["Minute"]);

        MessageBox.Show(time, "Current time");
    }
}
```

6. Add a method to the *Window* class to create a WMI event query that is triggered when the number of seconds on the computer's clock is zero. This causes the event to be triggered every minute. Then register *OnEventArrived* as the event handler. The following code demonstrates this:

```vb
' VB
Public Shared Function GetWatcher(ByVal handler As _
    EventArrivedEventHandler) As ManagementEventWatcher
    ' Create event query to be notified within 1 second of a
    ' change in a service
    Dim query As New WqlEventQuery("__InstanceModificationEvent", _
        New TimeSpan(0, 0, 1), _
        "TargetInstance isa 'Win32_LocalTime' AND " + _
        "TargetInstance.Second = 0")

    ' Initialize an event watcher and subscribe to events that
    ' match this query
    Dim watcher As New ManagementEventWatcher(query)

    ' Attach the EventArrived property to EventArrivedEventHandler method
    ' with the required handler to allow watcher object communicate to the
    ' application.
    AddHandler watcher.EventArrived, handler
    Return watcher
End Function
```

```csharp
// C#
public static ManagementEventWatcher GetWatcher(
    EventArrivedEventHandler handler)
{
    // Create event query to be notified within 1 second of a change in a
    // service
    WqlEventQuery query = new WqlEventQuery("__InstanceModificationEvent",
        new TimeSpan(0, 0, 1),
        "TargetInstance isa 'Win32_LocalTime' AND " +
        "TargetInstance.Second = 0");

    // Initialize an event watcher and subscribe to events that
    // match this query
    ManagementEventWatcher watcher = new ManagementEventWatcher(query);

    // Attach the EventArrived property to EventArrivedEventHandler method
    // with the required handler to allow watcher object communicate to the
    // application.
    watcher.EventArrived += new EventArrivedEventHandler(handler);
    return watcher;
}
```

7. Finally, handle the window's *Loaded* and *Closing* events to start and stop the event handler, as follows:

```vb
' VB
Private Sub Window_Loaded(ByVal sender As Object, _
    ByVal e As RoutedEventArgs)
    ' Event Receiver is a user-defined class.
    Dim receiver As New EventReceiver()

    ' Here, we create the watcher and register the callback with it
    ' in one shot.
    watcher = GetWatcher(New EventArrivedEventHandler( _
        AddressOf receiver.OnEventArrived))

    ' Watcher starts to listen to the Management Events.
    watcher.Start()
End Sub

Private Sub Window_Closing(ByVal sender As Object, _
    ByVal e As System.ComponentModel.CancelEventArgs)
    watcher.Stop()
End Sub
```

```csharp
// C#
private void Window_Loaded(object sender, RoutedEventArgs e)
{
    // Event Receiver is a user-defined class.
    EventReceiver receiver = new EventReceiver();

    // Here, we create the watcher and register the callback with it
    // in one shot.
    watcher = GetWatcher(
        new EventArrivedEventHandler(receiver.OnEventArrived));

    // Watcher starts to listen to the Management Events.
    watcher.Start();
}

private void Window_Closing(object sender,
    System.ComponentModel.CancelEventArgs e)
{
    watcher.Stop();
}
```

8. Build and run the application. When the number of seconds on your computer's clock equals zero, the *OnEventArrived* method displays a dialog box showing the current time.

Lesson Summary

■ You can examine processes by calling the *Process.GetProcesses* method. To start a process, call *Process.Start*.

■ To read WMI data, first define the management scope by creating a new *ManagementScope* object and calling *ManagementScope.Connect*. Then create a query using an instance of *ObjectQuery*. With the scope and query defined, you can execute your query by creating a *ManagementObjectSearcher* object and then calling the *ManagementObjectSearcher.Get* method. You can also respond to WMI events by creating an instance of *WqlEventQuery*. Then, use the *WqlEventQuery* to create an instance of *ManagementEventWatcher*. You can then use *ManagementEventWatcher* to either create an event handler or wait for the next event.

Lesson Review

You can use the following questions to test your knowledge of the information in Lesson 3, "Managing Computers." The questions are also available on the companion CD if you prefer to review them in electronic form.

NOTE   Answers

Answers to these questions and explanations of why each answer choice is right or wrong are located in the "Answers" section at the end of the book.

---

1. You need to retrieve a list of all running processes. Which method should you call?

    A. *Process.GetProcessesByName*

    B. *Process.GetCurrentProcess*

    C. *Process.GetProcesses*

    D. *Process.GetProcessById*

2. You need to query WMI for a list of logical disks attached to the current computer. Which code sample correctly runs the WMI query?

    A.

    ```
    ' VB
    Dim searcher As New ObjectQuery("SELECT * FROM Win32_LogicalDisk")
    Dim query As ManagementObject = searcher.Get()

    // C#
    ObjectQuery searcher = new ObjectQuery("SELECT * FROM Win32_LogicalDisk");
    ManagementObject query = searcher.Get();
    ```

B.

```vb
' VB
Dim searcher As New ManagementObjectSearcher( _
    "SELECT * FROM Win32_LogicalDisk")
Dim queryCollection As ManagementObjectCollection = searcher.Get()
```

```csharp
// C#
ManagementObjectSearcher searcher =
    new ManagementObjectSearcher("SELECT * FROM Win32_LogicalDisk");
ManagementObject query = searcher.Get();
```

C.

```vb
' VB
Dim searcher As New ObjectQuery("SELECT * FROM Win32_LogicalDisk")
Dim queryCollection As ManagementObjectCollection = searcher.Get()
```

```csharp
// C#
ObjectQuery searcher = new ObjectQuery("SELECT * FROM Win32_LogicalDisk");
ManagementObjectCollection queryCollection = searcher.Get();
```

D.

```vb
' VB
Dim searcher As New ManagementObjectSearcher( _
    "SELECT * FROM Win32_LogicalDisk")
Dim queryCollection As ManagementObjectCollection = searcher.Get()
```

```csharp
// C#
ManagementObjectSearcher searcher =
    new ManagementObjectSearcher("SELECT * FROM Win32_LogicalDisk");
ManagementObjectCollection queryCollection = searcher.Get();
```

3. You are creating an application that responds to WMI events to process new event log entries. Which of the following do you need to do? (Choose all that apply.)

   A. Call the *ManagementEventWatcher.Query* method.

   B. Create a *ManagementEventWatcher* object.

   C. Create an event handler that accepts *object* and *ManagementBaseObject* parameters.

   D. Register the *ManagementEventWatcher.EventArrived* handler.

Chapter Review

To practice and reinforce the skills you learned in this chapter further, you can

- Review the chapter summary.
- Review the list of key terms introduced in this chapter.
- Complete the case scenarios. These scenarios set up real-world situations involving the topics of this chapter and ask you to create a solution.
- Complete the suggested practices.
- Take a practice test.

Chapter Summary

- Before you can add events, you must register an event source by calling *Event-Log.CreateEventSource*. You can then call *EventLog.WriteEntry* to add events. Read events by creating an instance of the *EventLog* class and accessing the *EventLog .Entries* collection. Use the *Debug* and *Trace* classes to log the internal workings of your application for troubleshooting purposes. *Debug* functions only in Debug releases. *Trace* can function with any release type. Users can configure listeners for *Debug* and *Trace* using the .config files.

- To monitor performance counters programmatically, create an instance of *PerformanceCounter*. To add custom performance counters, call the static *PerformanceCounterCategory.Create* method. To provide performance counter data, create a *PerformanceCounter* object and set the *ReadOnly* property to *false*.

- You can examine processes by calling the *Process.GetProcesses* method. To start a process, call *Process.Start*. To read WMI data, create a *ManagementScope* object and call *ManagementScope.Connect*. Then, create a query using an instance of *ObjectQuery*. You can also respond to WMI events by creating an instance of *WqlEventQuery*. Then use the *WqlEventQuery* to create an instance of *Management-EventWatcher*. At this point, you can use *ManagementEventWatcher* to either create an event handler or wait for the next event.

Key Terms

Do you know what these key terms mean? You can check your answers by looking up the terms in the glossary at the end of the book.

- Windows event log
- WMI Query Language (WQL)

Case Scenarios

In the following case scenarios, you apply what you've learned about how to log application data and manage computer systems. You can find answers to these questions in the "Answers" section at the end of this book.

Case Scenario 1: Improving the Manageability of an Application

You are an application developer for the Graphic Design Institute. For the last year, you and your team have been managing the first version of an internal application named Orders. You are now identifying requirements for the second version of the application. Your manager asks you to interview key people and then answer questions about your design choices.

Interviews

The following is a list of company personnel interviewed and their statements.

- **IT Manager** "Orders v1 usually worked great. However, it was difficult to manage. Sometimes, users would complain about poor performance, and we had no way to isolate the source of the problem. Also, it would have been helpful to identify degrading performance proactively so we could take measures to prevent it from being worse. Also, we have a new event management system, and we need user logon and logoff events in the event log that we can collect for security purposes."

- **Development Manager** "Occasionally, IT discovers what they think is a bug in the application. Unfortunately, the only way to isolate the problem is to have them document how to re-create it and then have one of my developers attempt to re-create the problem with a debugger running. It would be much more useful if we could enable a troubleshooting mode in the application to have it create a log file while running on the end-user computer. Then, we could analyze the log file and attempt to isolate the problem."

Questions

Answer the following questions for your manager:

1. How can you meet the requirements outlined by the IT manager?
2. How can you meet the requirements outlined by the development manager?

Case Scenario 2: Collecting Information About Computers

You are an application developer working for Trey Research. Recently, an employee took confidential data out of the organization on a USB flash drive. Now, the IT department is requesting custom development to help them assess the storage currently attached to their computers and new storage devices that employees might attach.

The IT manager provides you with the following requests:

- **Storage inventory**   Create a tool that IT can distribute to every computer. The tool should generate a list of all disks attached to the computer.

- **Storage change notification**   Create an application that runs in the background when users log on. If a user connects a new disk, including a USB flash drive, it should display a warning message that the user should not remove confidential documents from the network. Then it should log the device connection.

Questions

Answer the following questions for your manager:

1. How can you generate a list of all disks attached to the computer?

2. How can you detect when a USB flash drive is attached to the computer?

Suggested Practices

To master the "Embedding configuration, diagnostic, management, and installation features into a .NET Framework application" exam objective, complete the following tasks.

Manage an Event Log by Using the *System.Diagnostics* Namespace

For this task, you should complete at least Practice 1. If you want a better understanding of how events can be used in the real world and you have the resources, complete Practices 2 and 3 as well.

- **Practice 1**   Go through your Application event log, or other custom event logs, and examine the events. Notice which events are the most useful for troubleshooting and which characteristics make them useful.

- **Practice 2**   Configure event forwarding on computers running Windows Vista to forward events selectively from multiple computers to a single computer. Administrators often use event forwarding to assist in managing events.

- **Practice 3**   Using a real-world application that you wrote, create a custom event log in the application's setup. Then add events to the event log when users log on or off or perform other tasks that might be relevant for security auditing.

Manage System Processes and Monitor the Performance of a .NET Framework Application by Using the Diagnostics Functionality of the .NET Framework

For this task, you should complete at least Practices 1 and 2. If you want a better understanding of how events can be used in the real world and you have the resources, complete Practice 3 as well.

- **Practice 1**   Create an application that adds a custom performance counter category with both single-instance and multi-instance counters.

- **Practice 2**   Use the Performance snap-in to monitor the performance of a remote computer. Examine the Performance counters added by applications and think about how system administrators might use the counters in a real-world environment.

- **Practice 3**   Using a real-world application that you wrote, add code to the setup procedure to establish a custom performance counter category. Then add code to the application to populate several counters revealing internal application metrics.

Debug and Trace a .NET Framework Application by Using the *System.Diagnostics* Namespace

For this task, you should complete both practices.

- **Practice 1**   Using a real-world application that you developed, add debugging and trace commands to allow you to follow the application's execution. Use debugging commands for information that would be useful only in a development environment. Use trace commands when the output might be useful for troubleshooting problems in a real-world environment.

- **Practice 2**   Install the application you used in Practice 1. Then update the .config file to write trace output to a text file.

Embed Management Information and Events into a .NET Framework Application

For this task, you should complete all three practices.

- **Practice 1** Create a program that displays new event log entries to the console.

- **Practice 2** Create a program that displays a dialog box when a user connects a USB flash drive.

- **Practice 3** Create a program that examines all network adapters connected to a computer and identifies the network adapter with the highest bandwidth.

Take a Practice Test

The practice tests on this book's companion CD offer many options. For example, you can test yourself on just the content covered in this chapter, or you can test yourself on all the 70-536 certification exam content. You can set up the test so that it closely simulates the experience of taking a certification exam, or you can set it up in study mode so that you can look at the correct answers and explanations after you answer each question.

MORE INFO Practice tests

For details about all the practice test options available, see the section "How to Use the Practice Tests" in the Introduction of this book.

Chapter 11

Application Security

Everyone has heard that you shouldn't log on to your computer as an Administrator. The reason isn't because you don't trust yourself not to delete your hard drive; it's because you don't trust the applications you run. When you run an unmanaged application in Windows Server 2003, Windows XP, and earlier versions of Microsoft Windows, that code gets all the privileges your user account has. If you accidentally run a virus or a Trojan horse, the application can do anything your user account has permissions to do. So, you want to log on with minimal privileges to restrict application permissions.

Code access security (CAS), a concept that the .NET Framework introduced to Windows, enables you to control the permissions that individual applications have. If a friend sends you a new .NET Framework text editor, you can restrict it to opening a window and prompting you to open and save files—and nothing else. The text editor wouldn't be able to send e-mails, upload files to a Web site, or create files, even if you run it while logged on as an Administrator.

CAS enables users to restrict on a very granular level what managed code can do. As a developer, you must understand how to create applications that work even when some permissions are restricted. You can also use CAS to improve your application's security by restricting which callers can use your code and forcibly limiting your application to a restricted permission set.

Exam objectives in this chapter:

- Implement code access security to improve the security of a .NET Framework application
- Modify the Code Access Security Policy at the computer, user, and enterprise level by using the Code Access Security Policy tool (Caspol.exe)
- Control permissions for resources by using the *System.Security.Permissions* classes
- Control code privileges by using the *System.Security.Policy* classes

Lessons in this chapter:

Before You Begin

To complete the lessons in this chapter, you should be familiar with Microsoft Visual Basic or C# and be comfortable with the following tasks:

- Creating a Console application in Microsoft Visual Studio using Visual Basic or C#
- Adding namespaces and system class library references to a project
- Writing to files and streams

Lesson 1: Understanding CAS

If you have experience working with the .NET Framework, you might already be familiar with code access security (CAS) concepts. If you have been a Windows developer but haven't previously used the .NET Framework, using CAS requires you to understand completely novel security concepts. This lesson describes the concept behind CAS and each of the components that the .NET Framework uses to implement CAS.

After this lesson, you will be able to:

- Describe the purpose of CAS
- List the four most important elements of CAS and the significance of each
- Describe how security policy defines an assembly's permission set
- Explain how CAS works with operating system security
- Use the .NET Framework 2.0 Configuration tool to configure CAS
- Use Caspol to configure CAS

Estimated lesson time: 60 minutes

What Is CAS?

Code access security (CAS) is a security system that allows administrators and developers to control application authorization similar to the way they have always been able to authorize users. With CAS, you can allow one application to read and write to the registry while restricting registry access for a different application. You can control authorization for most of the same resources you've always been able to restrict using the operating system's role-based security (RBS), including the following:

- The file system
- The registry
- Printers
- The event logs

You can also restrict resources that you can't control using RBS. For example, you can control whether a particular application can send Web requests to the Internet or whether an application can make Domain Name System (DNS) requests. These are the types of requests that malicious applications are likely to make to abuse a user's privacy, so it makes sense that CAS allows you to restrict those permissions.

Unfortunately, CAS can be applied only to managed applications that use the .NET Framework runtime. Unmanaged applications run without any CAS restrictions and are limited only by the operating system's RBS. If CAS is used to restrict the permissions of an assembly, the assembly is considered *partially trusted*. Partially trusted assemblies must undergo CAS permission checks each time they access a protected resource. Some assemblies are exempt from CAS checks and are considered *fully trusted*. Fully trusted assemblies, like unmanaged code, can access any system resource that the user has permissions to access.

Elements of CAS

Every security system needs a way to identify users and determine what a user can and can't do, and CAS is no exception. However, because CAS identifies and assigns permissions to applications rather than to people, it can't use the usernames, passwords, and access control lists (ACLs) that you're accustomed to using.

Instead, CAS identifies assemblies using evidence. Each piece of evidence is a way that an assembly can be identified, such as the location where the assembly is stored, a hash of the assembly's code, or the assembly's signature. An assembly's evidence determines which code group it belongs to. Code groups, in turn, grant an assembly a permission set. The following sections describe each of these components in more detail.

What Is Evidence?

Evidence is the information that the runtime gathers about an assembly to determine to which code groups the assembly belongs. Common forms of evidence include the folder or Web site from which the assembly is running and digital signatures.

NOTE   Evidence: A Misnomer

Identification might be a better term than *evidence*. Evidence sounds like a set of clues you use to track down someone who didn't want to be identified. In CAS, evidence is used just like a person's passport, password, and personal identification number (PIN)—information that proves identity and describes an individual as deserving a certain level of trust.

Table 11-1 shows the common types of evidence that a host can present to the run-time. Each row corresponds to a member class of the *System.Security.Policy* namespace.

Table 11-1   Evidence Types

Evidence	Description
Application directory	The directory in which the assembly resides.
Hash	The cryptographic hash of the assembly, which uniquely identifies a specific version of an assembly. Any modifications to the assembly make the hash invalid.
Publisher	The assembly's publisher's digital signature, which uniquely identifies the software developer. Using Publisher evidence requires the assembly to be signed.
Site	The site from which the assembly was downloaded, such as *www.microsoft.com*.
Strong Name	The cryptographic strong name of the assembly, which uniquely identifies the assembly's namespace. The assembly must be signed to use Strong Name evidence.
URL	The URL from which the assembly was downloaded, such as *www.microsoft.com/assembly.exe*.
Zone	The zone in which the assembly is running, such as the Internet zone or the LocalIntranet zone.

There are two types of evidence: host evidence and assembly evidence. *Host evidence* describes the assembly's origin, such as the application directory, URL, or site. Host evidence can also describe the assembly's identity, such as the hash, publisher, or strong name. *Assembly evidence* is custom user- or developer-provided evidence.

What Is a Permission?

A *permission* is a CAS access control entry. For example, the File Dialog permission determines whether an assembly can prompt the user with the Open dialog box, the Save dialog box, both, or neither. Figure 11-1 shows the File Dialog permission being configured.

By default, 19 permissions are available for configuration in the .NET Framework 2.0 Configuration tool. Each corresponds to two members of the *System.Security.Permissions* namespace: one for imperative use and one for declarative use. Table 11-2 describes each of these permissions. In addition, you can add custom permissions.

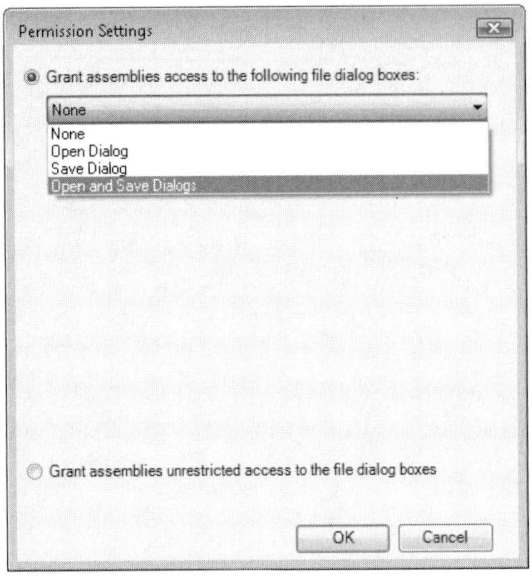

Figure 11-1   Permissions specify whether an assembly can or can't perform specific actions

Table 11-2   Default Permissions

Permission	Description
Directory Services	Grants an assembly access to Active Directory Domain Services (AD DS). You can specify paths and whether Browse or Write access is available.
DNS	Enables or restricts an assembly's access to submit DNS requests.
Environment Variables	Grants assemblies access to environment variables, such as *Path*, *Username*, and *Number_Of_Processors*. You can grant an assembly access to all environment variables or specify those that the assembly should be able to access. To view all environment variables, open a command prompt and run the Set command.
Event Log	Provides an assembly access to event logs. You can grant unlimited access or limit access to browsing or auditing.
File Dialog	Controls whether an assembly can prompt the user with the Open dialog box, the Save dialog box, or both.
File IO	Restricts access to files and folders. You can grant an assembly unrestricted access, or you can specify a list of paths and whether each path should grant Read, Write, Append, or Path Discovery access.

Table 11-2 Default Permissions

Permission	Description
Isolated Storage File	Grants assemblies access to isolated storage. You can configure the level of isolation and the size of the disk quota.
Message Queue	Allows an assembly to access message queues, which can be restricted by path and access type.
Performance Counter	Controls whether an assembly can read or write performance counters.
Printing	Limits an assembly's capability to print.
Reflection	Controls whether an assembly can discover member and type information in other assemblies.
Registry	Restricts access to registry keys. You can grant an assembly unrestricted access; or you can specify a list of keys and whether each key should grant Read, Write, or Delete access.
Security	Provides granular control over the assembly's access to various CAS features. All assemblies must have at least the Enable Assembly Execution setting to run. This permission also controls whether assemblies can call unmanaged code, assert permissions, and control threads, among other settings.
Service Controller	Specifies which services, if any, an assembly can browse or control.
Socket Access	Used to control whether an assembly can initiate TCP/IP connections. You can control the destination, port number, and protocol.
SQL Client	Controls whether an assembly can access Microsoft SQL Server and whether blank passwords are allowed.
User Interface	Determines whether an assembly can create new windows or access the Clipboard.
Web Access	Determines whether the assembly can access Web sites and which Web sites can be accessed.
X509 Store	Grants assemblies access to the X509 certificate store and controls whether they can add, remove, and open certificate stores.

What Is a Permission Set?

A *permission set* is a CAS ACL. For example, the Internet default permission set contains the following permissions:

- File Dialog
- Isolated Storage File
- Security
- User Interface
- Printing

The LocalIntranet zone contains more permissions, based on the theory that code running on your local network deserves more trust than code running from the Internet:

- Environment Variables
- File Dialog
- Isolated Storage File
- Reflection
- Security
- User Interface
- DNS
- Printing

The .NET Framework includes seven default permission sets, as described in Table 11-3.

Table 11-3   Default Permission Sets

Permission Set	Description
FullTrust	Exempts an assembly from CAS permission checks.
SkipVerification	Enables an assembly to bypass permission checks, which can improve performance, but it sacrifices security.
Execution	Enables an assembly to run and grants no other permissions.
Nothing	Grants no permissions to an assembly. The assembly is not even allowed to run.

Table 11-3   Default Permission Sets

Permission Set	Description
LocalIntranet	Grants a generous set of permissions to assemblies, including the capability to print and access the event log. Notably, it does not allow the assembly to access the file system except through the Open and Save dialog boxes.
Internet	Grants a restricted set of permissions to an assembly. Generally, you can run an assembly with this permission set with very little risk. Even malicious assemblies should not be able to cause any serious damage when run with this permission set.
Everything	Grants assemblies all permissions. This is different from FullTrust, which skips all CAS security checks. Assemblies with the Everything permission set will still be subject to CAS checks.

What Are Code Groups?

Code groups are authorization devices that associate assemblies with permission sets. Code groups provide a similar service to CAS as user groups provide to RBS. For example, if an administrator wants to grant a set of users access to a folder, the administrator creates a user group, adds the users to the group, and then assigns file permissions to the group. Code groups work similarly except that you don't have to add individual assemblies to a group manually. Instead, group membership is determined by the evidence that you specify as the code group's membership condition.

For example, any code running from the Internet should be a member of the Internet_Zone code group. As you can see from Figure 11-2, the Internet_Zone code group's default membership condition is that the host presents Zone evidence, and that piece of Zone evidence identifies the assembly as being in the Internet zone.

Whereas user groups control authorization based on distributed ACLs associated with each resource, code groups use centralized permission sets. For example, Figure 11-3 shows that the Internet_Zone code group assigns the Internet permission set. For convenience, the dialog box lists the permission set's individual permissions. However, you cannot specify individual permissions for a code group. A code group must be associated with a permission set.

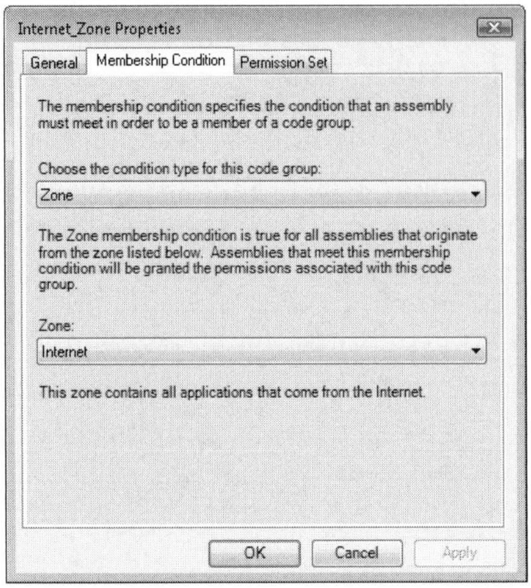

Figure 11-2   The Internet_Zone code group membership is restricted by using Zone evidence.

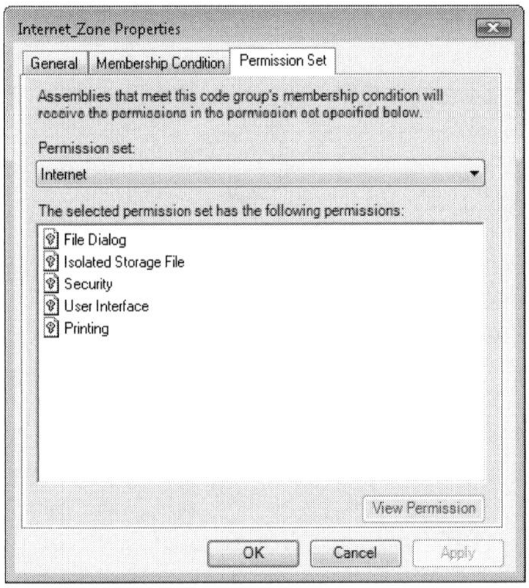

Figure 11-3   The Internet_Zone code group assigns the Internet permission set

---

BEST PRACTICES   Working with Files

Applications running in the Internet and LocalIntranet zones do not receive the *FileIOPermission*, and as such, they cannot directly access files. They do, however, have the *FileDialogPermission*. Therefore, assemblies in the Internet zone can open files by prompting the user to select the file using an *OpenFileDialog* object. Assemblies in the LocalIntranet zone can also save files by using the *SaveFileDialog* object. To access files without *FileIOPermission*, call the *ShowDialog* method of either *OpenFileDialog* or *SaveFileDialog*. If the user selects a file, you can use the file handle returned by the *OpenFile* method to access the file.

It might seem limiting that you can specify only a single type of evidence and a single permission set for a code group. However, just as a user account can be a member of multiple user groups, an assembly can be a member of multiple code groups. The assembly receives all the permissions assigned to each of the code groups (known as the union of the permission sets). In addition, you can nest code groups within each other and assign permissions only if the assembly meets all the evidence requirements of both the parent and child code groups. Nesting code groups allows you to assign permissions based on an assembly having more than one type of evidence. Figure 11-4 shows the Microsoft_Strong_Name code group nested within the My_Computer_Zone code group, which in turn is nested within the All_Code code group.

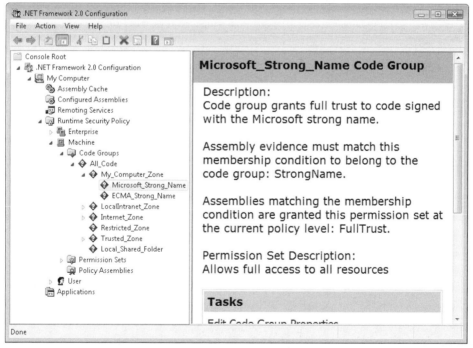

Figure 11-4 You can nest code groups to require multiple types of evidence

Table 11-4 lists the default machine code groups residing directly within the All_Code code group. In addition, some of these code groups contain nested code groups.

Table 11-4   Default Code Groups

Code Group	Evidence	Permission Set
My_Computer_Zone	Zone: My Computer	FullTrust
LocalIntranet_Zone	Zone: Local Intranet	LocalIntranet
Internet_Zone	Zone: Internet	Internet
Restricted_Zone	Zone: Untrusted sites	Nothing
Trusted_Zone	Zone: Trusted sites	Internet

What Is a Security Policy?

A *security policy* is a logical grouping of code groups and permission sets. In addition, a security policy can contain custom assemblies that define other types of policies. Security policies provide administrators with the flexibility to configure CAS settings at multiple levels. By default, there are four configurable policy levels: Enterprise, Machine, User, and Application Domain. Application domains were described in Chapter 8, "Application Domains and Services."

The Enterprise level is the highest security policy level, describing security policy for an entire enterprise. Enterprise security policy can be configured by using AD DS. Machine policy, the second security policy level, applies to all code run on a particular computer. User policy is the third level, and it defines permissions on a per-user basis. The runtime evaluates the Enterprise, Machine, and User levels separately, and it grants an assembly the minimum set of permissions granted by any of the levels (known as the intersection of the permission sets). By default, the Enterprise and User security policies grant all code full trust, which causes the Machine security policy alone to restrict CAS permissions.

Usefulness of Multiple Layers of Security Policy

To understand how security policies are used, consider an application developer who wants to play with an assembly she downloaded from the Internet. The developer has downloaded the assembly to her local computer so it will run within the My Computer Zone. The developer's computer is a member of an AD DS domain, and a domain administrator has created a code group in the Enterprise security policy that grants assemblies on the local computer the Everything

---

permission set. This is more restrictive than the FullTrust permission set that the Machine security policy grants assemblies in the My Computer zone, so the Everything permission set takes precedence.

The developer isn't sure that the assembly is safe to run, however, so she wants to apply the Internet permission set to prevent the assembly from writing to the disk or communicating across the network. She doesn't log on to her computer as an Administrator, but she can still start the .NET Framework 2.0 Configuration tool and modify the User security policy. (Standard users aren't allowed to modify the Machine security policy.) By modifying the User security policy, she can restrict assemblies in the My Computer zone to the Internet permission set. Assemblies that she runs will be restricted without affecting other users of the same computer.

The assembly is a member of three code groups: one in the Enterprise security policy, one in the Machine security policy, and one in the User security policy. The runtime determines the assembly's permissions by comparing each code group's permission sets and using the most restrictive set of permissions shared by all three permission sets (the intersection). Because the FullTrust and Everything permission sets contain all the Internet permission set's permissions (plus a few more permissions), the most restrictive set of permissions is exactly that defined by the Internet permission set.

How CAS Works with Operating System Security

CAS is completely independent of operating system security. In fact, you must use entirely different tools to administer CAS. Although you can control a user's or group's file permissions using Windows Explorer, you have to use the .NET Framework 2.0 Configuration tool to grant or restrict an assembly's permissions. Chapter 9, "Installing and Configuring Applications," explains where to download the tool and how to start it.

CAS works on top of existing operating system security. When determining whether an assembly can take a particular action, both CAS and the operating system security are evaluated. The most restrictive set of permissions is applied. For example, if CAS grants an assembly access to write to the C:\Windows folder but the user running the assembly does not have that permission, the assembly *cannot* write to the folder. Figure 11-5 shows how CAS relates to operating system security.

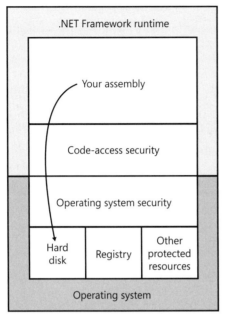

Figure 11-5   CAS complements, but does not replace, role-based security

---

Exam Tip   No assembly can have more permissions than the user running the assembly, regardless of how the assembly uses CAS.

How to Use the .NET Framework 2.0 Configuration Tool to Configure CAS

The .NET Framework 2.0 Configuration tool provides a graphical interface for managing .NET Framework security policy and applications that use remoting services. You can perform many different CAS-related tasks, including the following:

- Evaluating an assembly to determine the code groups of which it is a member
- Evaluating an assembly to determine which permissions it will be assigned
- Adding new permission sets
- Adding new code groups
- Increasing an assembly's trust
- Adjusting zone security
- Resetting policy levels

MORE INFO **.NET Framework 2.0 Configuration tool**

This chapter covers using the .NET Framework 2.0 Configuration tool only to manage CAS policy. For more information about the .NET Framework 2.0 Configuration tool, refer to Chapter 9.

The following sections provide procedures for performing these tasks.

How to Determine Which Code Groups Grant Permissions to an Assembly

When troubleshooting CAS permissions, you might need to determine which code groups grant permissions to your assembly. To do this, start the .NET Framework 2.0 Configuration tool from the Administrative Tools folder (or by opening the %WinDir%\Microsoft.NET\Framework\v2.0.50727\Mscorcfg.msc snap-in) and perform the following steps:

1. Expand the My Computer node and then click Runtime Security Policy.

2. Click Evaluate Assembly. The Evaluate An Assembly wizard appears.

3. On the What Would You Like To Evaluate? page, click Browse. Select your assembly and then click Open.

4. Select the View Code Groups That Grant Permissions To The Assembly option and then click Next.

5. Expand each policy level to determine which code groups grant permissions to your assembly. Figure 11-6 shows an assembly that receives permissions from the My_Computer_Zone code group.

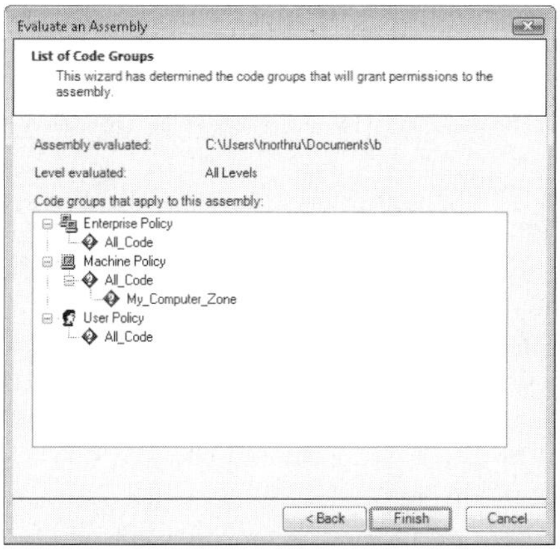

Figure 11-6 Use the Evaluate An Assembly wizard to determine which code groups apply permissions to your assembly

6. Click Finish.

How to Determine Total CAS Permissions Granted to an Assembly

When troubleshooting CAS permissions, you might need to determine which permissions the runtime will grant to your assembly. To do this, start the .NET Framework 2.0 Configuration tool and perform the following steps:

1. Expand the My Computer node and then click Runtime Security Policy.

2. Click Evaluate Assembly. The Evaluate An Assembly Wizard appears.

3. On the What Would You Like To Evaluate? page, click Browse. Select your assembly and then click Open.

4. Select the View Permissions Granted To The Assembly option and then click Next.

5. The wizard displays each permission assigned to your assembly. To view the detailed permission settings, select any permission, click View Permission and then click Finish.

How to Add a Permission Set

To create a new permission set, start the .NET Framework 2.0 Configuration tool and perform the following steps:

1. Expand the My Computer node and then expand Runtime Security Policy.

2. Expand Enterprise, Machine, or User, depending on the policy level in which you want to define the permission set.

3. Click Permission Sets. In the right pane, click Create New Permission Set.

4. On the Identify The New Permission Set page, specify a name and description, and click Next.

5. On the Assign Individual Permissions To Permission Set page, perform the following steps:

    a. Click the permission that you want to add to the permission set and click Add.

    b. For each permission, specify the permission settings that are unique to that permission and click OK.

    c. Repeat this process for each individual permission required by your permission set.

6. Click Finish.

How to Add a Code Group

To add a code group, start the .NET Framework 2.0 Configuration tool and perform the following steps:

1. Expand the My Computer node and then expand Runtime Security Policy.

2. Expand Enterprise, Machine, or User, depending on the policy level in which you want to define the code group.

3. Expand Code Groups, expand All_Code (if possible), and examine the existing child code groups. If the code group that you want to create defines a subset of permissions for an existing code group, click that code group. Otherwise, click All_Code.

4. Click Add A Child Code Group.

5. On the Identify The New Code Group page, type a name and a description, and then click Next.

6. On the Choose A Condition Type page, specify the condition type for the code group by choosing the evidence that the runtime will use to identify the code and then click Next.

7. On the Assign A Permission Set To The Code Group page, select the Use Existing Permission Set option if one of the current permission sets exactly meets your needs. Otherwise, select the Create A New Permission Set option and then click Next.

8. If you selected the Create A New Permission Set option, perform the following steps:

   a. On the Identify The New Permission Set page, specify a name and description and then click Next.

   b. On the Assign Individual Permissions To Permission Set page, click the permissions you want in the permission set and click Add. For each permission, specify the permission settings that are unique to that permission, click OK, and then click Next.

9. On the Completing The Wizard page, click Finish.

How to Increase an Assembly's Trust

If you have restricted the default CAS permissions on your computer, you might need to grant additional trust to specific assemblies to grant them the permissions they need to run correctly. To do this, start the .NET Framework 2.0 Configuration tool and perform the following steps:

1. Expand the My Computer node and then click Runtime Security Policy.

2. Click Increase Assembly Trust. The Trust An Assembly wizard appears.

3. On the What Would You Like To Modify? page, perform either or both of the following, as desired:

   ❑ Select the Make Changes To This Computer option to adjust the Machine policy level.

   ❑ Select the Make Changes For The Current User Only option to adjust the User policy level.

4. Click Next.

NOTE   You must be an administrator to adjust the Machine policy level.

---

5. On the What Assembly Do You Want To Trust? page, click Browse. Select the assembly that you want to trust and then click Open. You can trust only assemblies that have a strong name. Click Next.

6. On the Choose The Minimum Level Of Trust For The Assembly page, select the minimum trust level for the assembly and then click Next.

7. On the Completing The Wizard page, review your selections and then click Finish.

How to Adjust Zone Security

By default, the .NET Framework includes five zones, each with a unique set of CAS permissions. You should use these default zones whenever possible, but you might need to change the permission set that a zone uses. To do this, start the .NET Framework 2.0 Configuration tool and perform the following steps:

1. Expand the My Computer node and then expand Runtime Security Policy, expand Machine, expand Code Groups, and expand All_Code.

2. Click the zone that you want to adjust. In the right pane, click Edit Code Group Properties.

3. Click the Permission Set tab (shown in Figure 11-7), click an item in the Permission Set list to specify the desired permission set, and then click OK.

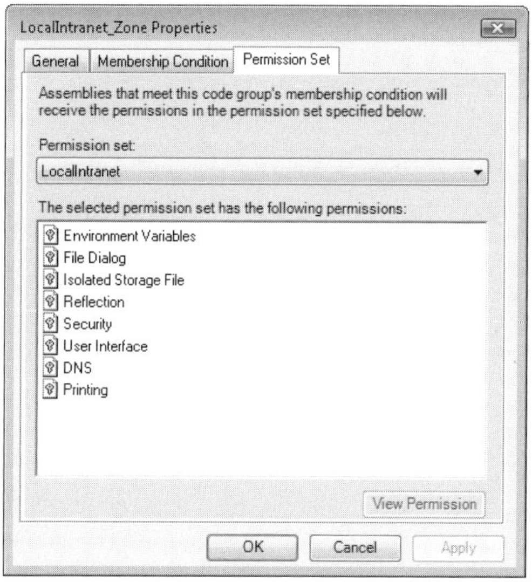

Figure 11-7   Adjust the permissions assigned to a zone by adjusting the associated code group's properties

As a developer, one of the first things you should do is adjust the permission set assigned to the My_Computer_Zone code group. By default, it's set to FullTrust, which means any CAS statements in your applications are completely ignored. Change this to the Everything permission set, which grants similar permissions but respects CAS statements in assemblies. Alternatively, you can restrict access to local assemblies further by choosing another permission set.

How to Reset Policy Levels

You might need to restore the default policy levels after making modifications. To do this, start the .NET Framework 2.0 Configuration tool and perform the following steps:

1. Expand the My Computer node and then click Runtime Security Policy. In the right pane, click Reset All Policy Levels.

2. Click Yes and then click OK.

The .NET Framework 2.0 Configuration tool restores the original policy level settings, including removing all custom code groups and permission sets that you created.

How to Use the Code Access Security Policy Tool

You can use the Code Access Security Policy tool (Caspol.exe, located in %Windir%\ Microsoft.NET\Framework\v2.0.50727\) to examine and modify Machine-, User-, and

Enterprise-level CAS policies. Although the .NET Framework 2.0 Configuration tool is the most convenient tool to use for manual configuration, Caspol provides similar functionality at the command line.

MORE INFO   Caspol

Caspol features a dizzying set of parameters, and this book covers only a handful of the most common ones. For complete instructions, at the command prompt, run this command:

```
Caspol -?
```

Caspol Parameters

Caspol uses an extremely complicated set of options. Table 11-5 lists the most commonly used options. The *–addgroup* and *–chggroup* options take additional parameters in the form of membership conditions and flags. Membership conditions, described in Table 11-6, are the evidence that the .NET Framework uses to determine to which code group to assign an assembly. Flags define the name, description, and other options and are listed in Table 11-7.

Table 11-5   Commonly Used Caspol Options

Option	Description
–addfulltrust assembly_file	Adds an assembly that implements a custom security object (such as a custom permission or a custom membership condition) to the full trust assembly list for a specific policy level. The *assembly_file* argument specifies the assembly to add. This file must be signed with a strong name.
–addgroup parent_name membership_condition permission_set_name [flags]	Adds a new code group. The *parent_name* argument specifies the name of the code group that will be the parent of the code group being added. The *membership_condition* argument specifies the membership condition for the new code group (described in Table 11-6).
	The *permission_set_name* argument is the name of the permission set to be associated with the new code group. You can also set one or more flags for the new group (described in Table 11-7).

Table 11-5   **Commonly Used Caspol Options**

Option	Description
–all	Indicates that all options following this one apply to the Enterprise, Machine, and the current User policy.
–chggroup name {membership_condition | permission_set_name | flags}	Changes a code group's membership condition, permission set, or the settings of the exclusive, levelfinal, name, or description flags. The *name* argument specifies the name of the code group to change. The *permission_set_name* argument specifies the name of the permission set to associate with the code group. See Tables 11-6 and 11-7 for information about the *membership_condition* and *flags* arguments.
–enterprise	Indicates that all options following this one apply to the Enterprise-level policy. Users who are not enterprise administrators do not have sufficient rights to modify the Enterprise policy, although they can view it.
–execution {on | off}	Turns on or off the mechanism that checks for the permission to run before code starts to run.
–help	Displays command syntax and options for Caspol.
–list	Lists the code group hierarchy and the permission sets for the specified Machine, User, or Enterprise policy level or all policy levels.
–listdescription	Lists all code group descriptions for the specified policy level.
–listfulltrust	Lists the contents of the full trust assembly list for the specified policy level.
–listgroups	Displays the code groups of the specified policy level or all policy levels. Caspol displays the code group's label first, followed by the name if it is not null.
–listpset	Displays the permission sets for the specified policy level or all policy levels.

Table 11-5   Commonly Used Caspol Options

Option	Description
–machine	Indicates that all options following this one apply to the Machine-level policy. Users who are not administrators do not have sufficient rights to modify the Machine policy, although they can view it. For administrators, *–machine* is the default.
–quiet	Temporarily disables the prompt that is normally displayed for an option that causes policy changes.
–recover	Recovers policy from a backup file. Whenever a policy change is made, Caspol stores the old policy in a backup file.
–remgroup name	Removes the specified code group. If the specified code group has child code groups, Caspol also removes all the child code groups.
–rempset permission_set_name	Removes the specified permission set from policy. The *permission_set_name* argument indicates which permission set to remove. Caspol removes the permission set only if it is not associated with any code group. The built-in permission sets cannot be removed.
–reset	Returns policy to its default state.
–resolvegroup assembly_file	Shows the code groups to which a specific assembly (*assembly_file*) belongs.
–resolveperm assembly_file	Displays all permissions that security policy would grant the assembly (*assembly_file*) if the assembly were allowed to run.
*–security {on	off}*	Turns code access security on or off. When code access security is disabled, all code access demands succeed.
–user	Indicates that all options following this one apply to the User-level policy for the user on whose behalf Caspol is running. For nonadministrative users, *-user* is the default.
–?	Displays command syntax and options for Caspol.

Table 11-6   Caspol Membership Conditions

This Membership Condition	Specifies
–all	All code.
–appdir	The application directory. If you specify *–appdir* as the membership condition, the URI evidence of code is compared with the application directory evidence of that code. If both evidence values are the same, this membership condition is satisfied.
–hash hash_algorithm {–hex hash_value | –file assembly_file }	Code that has the given assembly hash. To use a hash as a code group membership condition, you must specify either the hash value or the assembly file.
–pub { –cert cert_file_name | –file signed_file_name | –hex hex_string }	Code that has the given software publisher, as denoted by a certificate file, a signature on a file, or the hexadecimal representation of an X509 certificate.
–site website	Code that has the given site of origin. For example: `-site www.microsoft.com`

–strong –file file_name {name | –noname} {version | –noversion}	Code that has a specific strong name, as designated by the filename, the assembly name as a string, and the assembly version in the format *major.minor.build.revision*. For example:
	
	`-strong -file myAssembly.exe`
	`    myAssembly 1.2.3.4`
	
	(Enter the previous code as a single command. It is shown here on multiple lines so it can fit on the printed page.)

Table 11-6   Caspol Membership Conditions

This Membership Condition	Specifies
–url URL	Code that originates from the given URL. The URL must include a protocol, such as *http://* or *ftp://*. In addition, a wildcard character (*) can be used to specify multiple assemblies from a particular URL.
	To specify a file share on a network, use the following syntax:
	`-url \\servername\sharename\*`
	The trailing asterisk (*) is required to identify the share properly.
–zone zonename	Code with the given zone of origin. The *zonename* argument can be one of the following values: *MyComputer, Intranet, Trusted, Internet,* or *Untrusted.*

Table 11-7   Caspol Flags

Flag	Description
–description description	If used with the *–addgroup* option, specifies the description for a code group to add. If used with the *–chggroup* option, specifies the description for a code group to edit. You must add double quotes around the description, even if it does not include spaces.
–exclusive {on│off}	When set to *on*, indicates that only the permission set associated with the code group you are adding or modifying is considered when some code fits the membership condition of the code group. When this option is set to *off*, Caspol considers the permission sets of all matching code groups in the policy level.

Table 11-7   Caspol Flags

Flag	Description
–levelfinal {on|off}	When set to *on*, indicates that no policy level below the level in which the added or modified code group occurs is considered. This option is typically used at the Machine policy level. For example, if you set this flag for a code group at the Machine level, and some code matches this code group's membership condition, Caspol does not calculate or apply the User-level policy for this code.
–name "name"	If used with the *–addgroup* option, specifies the scripting name for a code group to add. If used with the *-chggroup* option, specifies the scripting name for a code group to edit. The name argument must be enclosed in double quotation marks, even though it cannot include spaces.

How to Perform Common Tasks with Caspol

The following list provides usage examples for common tasks that you might want to perform with Caspol:

NOTE The commands in this section have been formatted to fit on the printed page. They should be entered as a single command at the command prompt.

To grant an assembly full trust

```
Caspol –addfulltrust assemblyname.exe
```

For example, to grant the C:\Program Files\Mine\Mine.exe assembly full trust, you would run the following command:

```
Caspol –addfulltrust "C:\Program Files\Mine\Mine.exe"
```

To add a code group to the Machine policy

```
Caspol –machine –addgroup Parent_ Code_Group
    Membership_Conditions Permission_Set -name "Group_Name"
```

For example, to add a code group named My_Code_Group to the Machine policy level's All_Code code group, using a URL of *devserver**devshare*\, which grants LocalIntranet permissions, you would run the following command with administrative privileges:

```
Caspol -machine -addgroup All_Code -url \\devserver\devshare\* LocalIntranet
    -name "My_Code_Group"
```

To add a code group to the User policy

```
Caspol -user -addgroup Parent_Code_ Group Membership_Condition
    Permission_Set -name "Group_Name"
```

Similarly, to add a code group named User_Code_Group to the User policy level's All_Code group, using a site of *www.contoso.com*, which grants FullTrust permissions, you would run the following command:

```
Caspol -user -addgroup All_Code -site www.contoso.com FullTrust -name
    "User_Code_Group"
```

NOTE   **Refreshing the .NFT Framework 2.0 Configuration tool**

You must close and reopen the .NET Framework 2.0 Configuration tool to see changes caused by Caspol. But then again, if you have the .NET Framework 2.0 Configuration tool open, why are you using Caspol?

To adjust zone security for a Machine policy

```
Caspol -chggroup Code_Group Permission_Set
```

For example, to change the Machine My_Computer_Zone security policy to use the LocalIntranet permission set, run the following command with administrative privileges:

```
Caspol -chggroup My_Computer_Zone LocalIntranet
```

To reset policy levels for the Machine policy level

```
Caspol -recover
```

Lab: Configuring CAS

In this lab, you will configure CAS using both the graphical .NET Framework 2.0 Configuration tool and the command-line Caspol tool. Complete Exercises 1 through 3. The last step of Exercise 3 restores your original settings to ensure that future practices work correctly.

Exercise 1: Compile and Test the Permissions of a Sample Assembly

In this exercise, you will compile and test the permissions of a sample assembly in a restricted My_Computer_Zone.

1. Log on to your computer as an Administrator.

   NOTE **Logging on as an Administrator**

   For other practices in this chapter, and most tasks on your computer, you should be logged on as a standard user. This exercise is an exception because it uses the default C$ share, to which only administrators have access by default. You can log on as a standard user if you create a new share that can be accessed by standard users.

2. Navigate to the *<InstallHome>*\Chapter11\Lesson1\Exercise1\Partial folder and open either the C# version or the Visual Basic .NET version of the solution file.

3. From the Build menu select Build Solution. Visual Studio compiles the application.

4. Copy the ListPermissions.exe file to the root of your C: drive, and respond to any User Account Control (UAC) prompts that appear.

5. Open a command prompt and run the command **C:\ListPermissions.exe**. List-Permissions runs and displays several common permissions, and whether the assembly currently has that permission. Notice that you have all the listed permissions. Press Enter. Answer the following question:

   Why does the assembly have all the permissions?

   The assembly is currently running in the My_Computer_Zone because you started it from the C:\ drive. By default, that zone uses the FullTrust permission set.

6. Run the command **\\127.0.0.1\c$\ListPermissions.exe**. Notice that you are now missing several permissions; in particular, *IsolatedStorageFilePermission* is missing. Press Enter. Answer the following question:

   Why is the assembly now missing permissions, and what code group determined the permissions?

   The assembly is now being run from a shared folder, so it is running from the Internet zone. Because the IP address being used is the special loopback address, it is part of the Internet_Same_Site_Access code group.

Exercise 2: Create a Code Group and Permission Set with the .NET Framework 2.0 Configuration Tool

In this exercise, you will use the .NET Framework 2.0 Configuration tool to create a code group that uses a new permission set.

1. Start the .NET Framework 2.0 Configuration tool. Expand My Computer, Run-time Security Policy, Machine, Code Groups, and then All_Code.

2. Right-click All_Code and then click New. The Create Code Group wizard appears.

3. In the Name box, type **Local_Shared_Folder**. In the Description box, type **Code run from a network drive mapped to the local shared C: drive** an then click Next.

4. On the Choose A Condition Type page, select URL. In the URL box (as shown in Figure 11-8), type **file://127.0.0.1/c$/*** and then click Next.

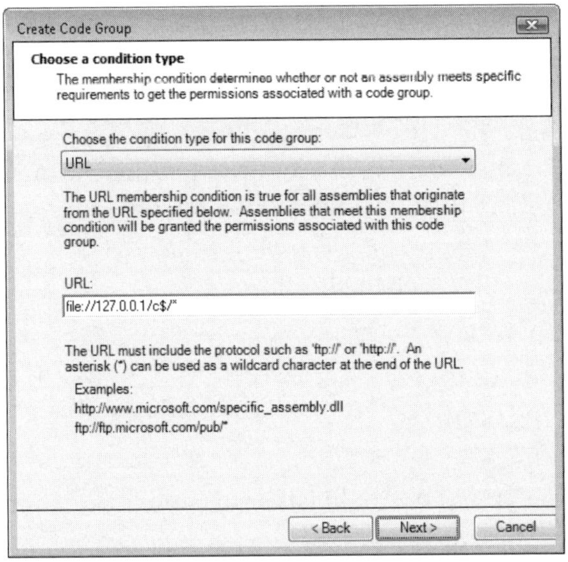

Figure 11-8   Use the URL condition to specify code groups for assemblies running from shared folders

5. On the Assign A Permission Set To The Code Group page, select the Create A New Permission Set option and then click Next.

6. On the Identify The New Permission Set page, type **GenerousPermissions** in the Name box. In the Description box, type **Permissions for the ListPermissions assembly** and then click Next.

7. On the Assign Individual Permissions To Permission Set page, double-click Isolated Storage File. In the Permission Settings dialog box, select the Grant Assemblies Unrestricted Access To File-Based Storage option. Click OK and then click Next.

8. On the Completing The Wizard page, click Finish.

9. Open a command prompt and run the command **\\127.0.0.1\c$\ListPermissions.exe**. Notice that ListPermission now has the *IsolatedStorageFilePermission*. Press Enter. Answer the following question:

   Why does the assembly now have the *IsolatedStorageFilePermission*?

   The assembly is currently running in both the Local_Shared_Folder code group and the Internet_Same_Site_Access code group. The permissions in the Generous-Permissions permission set have been added to the previously existing permissions.

Exercise 3: Modify a Code Group with the Caspol Tool and Restore Default Settings

In this exercise, you modify the newly created code group with the Caspol tool, test the change, and then restore the default settings.

1. Open the Visual Studio 2008 Command Prompt with Administrative privileges, and run the following command to change the Local_Shared_Folder code group permission set to Everything:

   ```
   Caspol -chggroup Local_Shared_Folder Everything
   ```

2. When prompted, press Y and then press Enter. If you receive an error message, manually rename the code group permission set to Local_Shared_Folder and repeat step 1.

3. Run **\\127.0.0.1\c$\Listpermissions**. Notice that the assembly now has all permissions, indicating that the Local_Shared_Folder code group now has the Everything permission set.

4. Restore the default CAS settings by running the command **Caspol -recover**.

Lesson Summary

- CAS is a security system that authorizes managed assemblies to access system resources.

- CAS is implemented by using the following four components:
  - Evidence, which identifies an assembly
  - Permissions, which describe which resources an assembly can access

❏   Permission sets, which collect multiple permissions

❏   Code groups, which assign permissions to an assembly based on evidence

■   A security policy is a logical grouping of code groups and permission sets. You can use multiple levels of security policy to simplify CAS administration. Assemblies receive the most restrictive set of permissions assigned by each of the policy levels.

■   CAS permissions can never override a user's operating system permissions. An assembly's effective permissions are the intersection of the permissions granted to the assembly by CAS and the permissions granted to the user by the operating system.

■   The .NET Framework 2.0 Configuration tool is a graphical tool for configuring any aspect of CAS. To use the tool, start the Microsoft .NET Framework 2.0 Configuration from the Administrative Tools group or by opening the %WinDir%\ Microsoft.NET\Framework\v2.0.50727\Mscorcfg.msc snap-in.

■   The Code Access Security Policy tool, Caspol, is a command-line tool with a large number of options for controlling almost every aspect of CAS behavior. To use Caspol, call it from the directory the .NET Framework 2.0 is installed into.

Lesson Review

You can use the following questions to test your knowledge of general CAS information. The questions are also available on the companion CD if you prefer to review them in electronic form.

NOTE   Answers

Answers to these questions and explanations of why each answer choice is right or wrong are located in the "Answers" section at the end of the book.

---

1. Which of the following evidence types require an assembly to be signed? (Choose all that apply.)

    A. Zone

    B. Strong Name

    C. Hash

    D. Publisher

2. Which permission must an assembly have to connect to a Web server?

    A. *SocketPermission*

    B. *WebPermission*

    C. *DnsPermission*

    D. *ServiceControllerPermission*

3. Which of the following code groups offers the most restrictive permission set?

    A. My_Computer_Zone

    B. LocalIntranet_Zone

    C. Internet_Zone

    D. Restricted_Zone

4. Your user account has Read access to a file named Text.txt. You run an assembly in the My_Computer_Zone code group, which grants it the FullTrust permission set. Which of the following actions can the assembly perform on the file?

    A. Read

    B. Write

    C. Change permissions

    D. Delete

Lesson 2: Using Declarative Security to Protect Assemblies

In Lesson 1, you learned that CAS can restrict permissions granted to an application. In some situations, CAS security is so restrictive that your application won't have the permissions required for even the most basic functionality, and the runtime should detect this problem and prevent your assembly from running. In other situations, your application has more permissions than necessary, which violates the principle of least privilege and makes your application unnecessarily vulnerable to abuse.

You can use declarative CAS demands to ensure that your assembly has all necessary permissions but none that it does not require. As an additional benefit, administrators deploying your application can examine the assembly's declarative CAS demands to identify the minimum permissions they need to grant to take advantage of all your application's functionality.

> **After this lesson, you will be able to:**
> - Describe why you should use CAS assembly declarations
> - List the classes built into the .NET Framework for CAS permissions
> - List the three types of CAS assembly declarations
> - Create CAS assembly declarations
> - Explain the guidelines for effectively implementing CAS assembly declarations
>
> **Estimated lesson time: 45 minutes**

Reasons to Use CAS Assembly Declarations

There are three main reasons to use CAS assembly declarations:

- **To ensure that the runtime never runs your application without granting access to required resources**   If you have not built exception handling into your application to respond to situations in which your assembly lacks the necessary CAS permissions, use *SecurityAction.RequestMinimum* to declare all CAS permissions required by your application. If a user attempts to run your application and CAS security policy does not grant a required permission, the runtime throws an exception. Users might not be able to identify the problem based on the exception information displayed by the runtime, but an administrator should understand the problem. Either way, using *SecurityAction.RequestMinimum* is better than having unexpected exceptions while your application is running.

- **To create a small sandbox for your application to ensure that an attacker does not manipulate your application to cause it to access unintended resources**   The principle of least privilege reduces the chances of an attacker abusing your assembly by causing it to take unintended actions, such as revealing the contents of private files, destroying data, or propagating malicious viruses and worms. By using assembly CAS declarations to restrict your assembly's CAS permissions to the bare minimum, you eliminate the risk of an attacker manipulating your application into accessing resources that it would not normally access. This reduces the risk of common attacks, such as canonicalization attacks in which the attacker tricks an application into processing an invalid file by providing a malformed path.

■ **To verify that your application can run with limited CAS permissions and therefore run in partially trusted zones** There is currently no way to identify the permissions required by an application easily. However, if you develop and test your application using *SecurityAction.RequestOptional* CAS declarations, the runtime grants your assembly only those permissions that you specify. If you add code that requires additional permissions, the runtime throws a *System.Security.Policy.Policy Exception*, indicating the required permission. You can then add another *Security-Action.RequestOptional* CAS declaration, ensuring that you maintain an accurate list of required permissions.

Classes for CAS Permissions

CAS can restrict access to many types of resources—from files and folders, to printers, to network access. For each type of resource that can be protected, the .NET Framework provides a class. Table 11-8 lists each class used for assembly CAS declarations and the rights that the class represents.

NOTE Using Attributes

The .NET Framework also provides attribute classes for each of the classes listed in Table 11-8. The attribute classes have *Attribute* appended to the name. You don't need to worry about this when writing code, however, because the .NET Framework automatically uses the attribute classes when you reference these classes declaratively.

Table 11-8 Classes and Interfaces Used for Assembly CAS Declarations

Class	Right Represented
AspNetHostingPermission	Access resources in ASP.NET-hosted environments.
DataProtectionPermission	Access encrypted data and memory.
DirectoryServicesPermission	Access to the *System.DirectoryServices* classes.
DnsPermission	Access to DNS.
EnvironmentPermission	Read or write environment variables.

Table 11-8   Classes and Interfaces Used for Assembly CAS Declarations

Class	Right Represented
EventLogPermission	Gives Read or Write access to event log services.
FileDialogPermission	Access files that have been selected by the user in an Open dialog box.
FileIOPermission	Read, append, or write files or directories.
GacIdentityPermission	Defines the identity permission for files originating in the global assembly cache (GAC).
IsolatedStorage File-Permission	Access isolated storage, which is storage that is associated with a specific user and with some aspect of the code's identity, such as its Web site, publisher, or signature.
IUnrestrictedPermission	An interface that allows a permission to expose an unrestricted state.
KeyContainerPermission	Access to public key encryption containers.
MessageQueuePermission	Access message queues through the managed Microsoft Message Queuing (MSMQ) interfaces.
OdbcPermission	Access an ODBC data source.
OleDbPermission	Access databases using OLE DB.
OraclePermission	Access an Oracle database.
Performance Counter-Permission	Access performance counters.
PrincipalPermission	Control access based on username and group memberships. This class is discussed in Chapter 12, "User and Data Security."
PrintingPermission	Access printers.
ReflectionPermission	Discover information about a type at runtime.
RegistryPermission	Read, write, create, or delete registry keys and values.
SecurityPermission	Execute, assert permissions, call into unmanaged code, skip verification, and other rights.

Table 11-8 Classes and Interfaces Used for Assembly CAS Declarations

Class	Right Represented
ServiceControllerPermission	Access running or stopped services.
SiteIdentityPermission	Defines the identity permission for the Web site from which the code originates.
SocketPermission	Make or accept connections on a transport address.
SqlClientPermission	Access SQL Server databases.
StorePermission	Access stores containing X.509 certificates.
StrongName Identity-Permission	Defines the identity permission for strong names.
UIPermission	Access user interface functionality. Required to debug an assembly.
UrlIdentityPermission	Defines the identity permission for the URL from which the code originates.
WebPermission	Make or accept connections on a Web address.
ZoneIdentityPermission	Defines the identity permission for the zone from which the code originates.

Each class has unique members that you can use to control permissions further. For example, you can set the *OleDbPermissionAttribute.AllowBlankPassword* property to control whether your assembly will be allowed to use a blank password. Similarly, the *DirectoryServicesPermissionAttribute.Path* property can be defined to limit your assembly's access to a specific branch of the AD DS. (Because of the large number of classes, this book does not describe the use of each class and property.)

Because the permission attribute classes are inherited from the *CodeAccessSecurity Attribute* class, they share some common properties and methods. However, you usually need to be familiar with only two standard properties:

- **Action** Specifies the security action to take. Set this using the *SecurityAction* enumeration.

- **Unrestricted** A *Boolean* value that specifies that the permission enables access to all the class's resources. Setting this value to true is equivalent to selecting the Grant Assemblies Unrestricted Access option when specifying permission settings with the .NET Framework 2.0 Configuration tool.

Types of Assembly Permission Declarations

All permission attribute classes define the *Action* property, which specifies how the runtime interprets the permission. When creating assembly CAS declarations, you must always set the *Action* property to one of three members of the *SecurityAction* enumeration. The following list describes each of these choices:

- **SecurityAction.RequestMinimum** Requires a permission for your assembly to run. If your assembly lacks the specified CAS permission, the runtime throws a *System.Security.Policy.PolicyException*.

- **SecurityAction.RequestOptional** Refuses all permissions not listed in a *Security Action.RequestOptional* or *SecurityAction.RequestMinimum* declaration. Defining permissions with this action ensures that your application will have no more permissions than those you have declared. If your assembly lacks the requested CAS permissions, the runtime does *not* throw an exception, unlike its behavior with *SecurityAction.RequestMinimum*. Therefore, use *SecurityAction.RequestMinimum* and *SecurityAction.RequestOptional* together when your application cannot adapt to a missing permission.

- **SecurityAction.RequestRefuse** Reduces the permissions assigned to your application. Use this type of declaration to ensure that your application does not have access to critical resources that could potentially be abused. Unlike *Security Action.RequestMinimum*, this declaration never causes the runtime to throw an exception at load time.

NOTE Confusing Names

If these security action names are confusing, the problem is not you. Why is a declaration called *RequestMinimum* if it's actually a requirement? The name *RequestMinimum* sounds like your code is politely asking for permissions. Given the way *RequestMinimum* behaves, it should be called *RequireMinimum* because the runtime doesn't respond nicely to a request for permissions that it can't provide—it throws an exception and refuses to run your assembly. Also, the runtime never grants your code permissions that the code wouldn't have had anyway. *RequestOptional* should actually be called *RefuseAllExcept* because the primary purpose is to list explicitly only those CAS permissions your application should have.

How to Create Assembly Declarations

The following code sample shows an assembly that requires CAS read access to the C:\Windows\Win.ini file. If security policy does not grant that permission to the assembly, the runtime throws an exception before running the assembly:

```vb
' VB
Imports System.Security.Permissions

<Assembly: FileIOPermissionAttribute(SecurityAction.RequestMinimum, _
    Read := "C:\windows\win.ini")>
Module Module1
    Sub Main()
        Console.WriteLine("Hello, World!")
    End Sub
End Module
```

```csharp
// C#
using System.Security.Permissions;

[assembly:FileIOPermissionAttribute(SecurityAction.RequestMinimum,
    Read=@"C:\windows\win.ini")]
namespace DeclarativeExample
{
    class Program
    {
        static void Main(string[] args)
        {
            Console.WriteLine("Hello, World!");
        }
    }
}
```

NOTE What You Say You Need vs. What You Really Need

The sample doesn't actually access the C:\Windows\Win.ini file. CAS declarations are completely arbitrary. It's up to you to make sure they're consistent with your application's requirements.

The preceding example uses *SecurityAction.RequestMinimum* to cause the .NET Framework runtime to throw an exception if the assembly does not have CAS permissions to read the C:\Windows\Win.ini file. This ensures that the assembly does not run unless the runtime provides the required permission, thereby preventing the application from experiencing problems while running. However, throwing the exception does not improve the security of the assembly because it does nothing to restrict the assembly's permissions.

Exam Tip For the exam, remember that CAS is significant only for partially trusted assemblies. The runtime completely ignores CAS declarations for fully trusted assemblies.

To improve the assembly's security, specify the *SecurityAction.RequestOptional* or *SecurityAction.RequestRefuse* enumerations for the permission's *Action* property. Optionally, you can combine multiple declarations in a single assembly. For example, if you want the runtime to throw an exception if you don't have access to the HKEY_ LOCAL_MACHINE\Software registry key, and you don't want any other CAS permissions (except, of course, the Enable Assembly Execution security permission), you would use the following declarations:

```vb
' VB
<Assembly: RegistryPermission(SecurityAction.RequestMinimum, _
    Read:="HKEY_LOCAL_MACHINE\Software")>
<Assembly: UIPermission(SecurityAction.RequestOptional, _
    Unrestricted:=True)>
<Assembly: RegistryPermission(SecurityAction.RequestOptional, _
    Read:="HKEY_LOCAL_MACHINE\Software")>
```

```csharp
// C#
[assembly:RegistryPermission(SecurityAction.RequestMinimum,
    Read=@"HKEY_LOCAL_MACHINE\Software")]
[assembly: UIPermission(SecurityAction.RequestMinimum, Unrestricted = true)]
[assembly: RegistryPermission(SecurityAction.RequestOptional,
    Read=@"HKEY_LOCAL_MACHINE\Software")]
```

If you use any *SecurityAction.RequestOptional* declarations and you want to debug your assembly, you must also declare the *UIPermission* attribute and set the *Unrestricted* parameter to *true*, as shown in the second statement of the previous example. You can specify either *SecurityAction.RequestOptional* or *SecurityAction.RequestMinimal* for the *UIPermission* attribute. Otherwise, your assembly does not have permission to interact with the debugger. You can run the assembly without a debugger, though.

You can combine *RequestMinimum*, *RequestOptional*, and *RequestRefuse*, but combining *RequestOptional* and *RequestRefuse* might accomplish nothing. After all, *Request Optional* refuses all permissions except those explicitly listed. The only case in which you would combine *RequestOptional* and *RequestRefuse* is to refuse a subset of the specified *RequestOptional* permissions.

For example, the following declarations (which require adding a reference for the *System.Drawing* namespace) cause the runtime to throw an exception if the assembly does not have CAS printing permissions. The runtime denies all CAS permissions except printing, opening windows, and file system access to the C:\ drive. Access to the C:\Windows directory also is denied:

```vb
' VB
<Assembly: PrintingPermission(SecurityAction.RequestMinimum)>
<Assembly: UIPermission(SecurityAction.RequestOptional, _
    Unrestricted:=True)>
<Assembly: FileIOPermissionAttribute(SecurityAction.RequestOptional, _
    Read:="C:\")>
<Assembly: FileIOPermissionAttribute(SecurityAction.RequestRefuse, _
    Read:="C:\Windows\")>
```

```
// C#
[assembly: PrintingPermission(SecurityAction.RequestMinimum)]
[assembly: UIPermission(SecurityAction.RequestMinimum,
    Unrestricted = true)]
[assembly: FileIOPermissionAttribute(SecurityAction.RequestOptional,
    Read = @"C:\")]
[assembly: FileIOPermissionAttribute(SecurityAction.RequestRefuse,
    Read = @"C:\Windows\")]
```

BEST PRACTICES   Use *SecurityAction.RequestOptional* Assembly Declarations

There are whole books about writing secure code, and you should always follow secure coding best practices. We're only human, though. Sometimes, you might simply forget to validate an input or to use strong typing. Other times, you might be rushing to finish a project and just get careless.

Using *SecurityAction.RequestOptional* assembly declarations is the one security best practice that you should always follow. These declarations take very little time to write because they consist of just a couple lines of code, they're easy to debug because the runtime throws an easily identifiable exception, and they offer protection for every line of code in your assembly. As an assembly grows in size, this protection decreases, so you should use method declarations, as discussed in Lesson 3, "Using Declarative and Imperative Security to Protect Methods."

Guidelines for Using Assembly Declarations

Follow these guidelines to choose which CAS assembly declarations to use:

- Use *SecurityAction.RequestMinimum* assembly declarations to require every permission needed by your assembly that your assembly does not imperatively check for.

- Use *SecurityAction.RequestOptional* assembly declarations to list every permission your assembly uses. Declare the most granular permissions possible, including specific files or registry keys that will be accessed.

- Use *SecurityAction.RequestRefuse* assembly declarations to refine permissions listed with *SecurityAction.RequestOptional* assembly declarations further.

Lab: Using Assembly Permission Requests

In this lab, you will work with CAS declarations to ensure that your assembly has sufficient privileges and to reduce security risks when your assembly runs.

▶ **Exercise: Declare Security Requirements**

In this exercise, you will modify an existing assembly to add CAS declarations.

1. Navigate to the \<*InstallHome*>\Chapter11\Lesson2\Exercise1\Partial folder and open either the C# version or the Visual Basic .NET version of the solution file.

2. Examine the code to determine what permissions are required. Add the *System .Security.Permissions* namespace to the assembly to allow you to declare the CAS permissions required.

3. Add CAS declarations to declare the minimum permissions required so that the runtime throws an exception if the assembly lacks the necessary permissions. The following code works:

```
' VB
<Assembly: UIPermission(SecurityAction.RequestMinimum, Unrestricted:=True)>
<Assembly: FileIOPermission(SecurityAction.RequestMinimum, _
    ViewAndModify:="C:\Hello.txt")>
```

```
// C#
[assembly: UIPermission(SecurityAction.RequestMinimum,
    Unrestricted = true)]
[assembly: FileIOPermission(SecurityAction.RequestMinimum,
    ViewAndModify = @"C:\Hello.txt")]
```

4. Run the assembly (you must have administrative privileges to do so) and verify that it works correctly.

5. Modify the CAS declarations to refuse permissions other than those required so that the assembly cannot be abused by an attacker and made to do something other than it was intended to do. The following code works:

```
' VB
<Assembly: UIPermission(SecurityAction.RequestOptional, _
    Unrestricted:=True)>
<Assembly: FileIOPermission(SecurityAction.RequestOptional, _
    ViewAndModify:="C:\Hello.txt")>
```

```
// C#
[assembly: UIPermission(SecurityAction.RequestOptional,
    Unrestricted = true)]
[assembly: FileIOPermission(SecurityAction.RequestOptional,
    ViewAndModify = @"C:\Hello.txt")]
```

6. Run the assembly and verify that it works correctly.

Note that you can use *SecurityAction.RequestOptional* to verify that you are declaring all the permissions required by your assembly, even if you ultimately plan to declare CAS permission requirements using *SecurityAction.RequestMinimum*. For example, in step 3 of this exercise, if you had declared the *FileIOPermission* attribute using *Read* instead of *ViewAndModify*, the runtime would not have thrown an exception even though the assembly writes to the file. However, when you change the declaration to *Security Action.RequestOptional*, the runtime does throw an exception, verifying that you did not declare all required permissions.

Lesson Summary

- Use CAS assembly declarations because they enable administrators to view the permissions required by your application, prevent your application from running without sufficient permissions, restrict the permissions granted to your application, and enable you to isolate your application to verify compatibility with partially trusted zones.

- The .NET Framework provides more than a dozen classes for CAS permissions, describing resources such as the file system, the registry, and printers.

- There are three types of CAS assembly declarations: *RequestMinimum*, *RequestOptional*, and *RequestRefuse*.

- To create assembly declarations, add assembly attributes by using permission classes.

- Use *RequestMinimum* declarations when your application doesn't handle missing permissions appropriately, use *RequestOptional* to list every permission required by your application, and use *RequestRefuse* to restrict your *Request Optional* permissions further.

Lesson Review

You can use the following questions to test your knowledge of declarative assembly security. The questions are also available on the companion CD if you prefer to review them in electronic form.

NOTE Answers

Answers to these questions and explanations of why each answer choice is right or wrong are located in the "Answers" section at the end of the book.

---

1. An administrator runs the following Console application on a computer running Windows XP with the Everything permission set. What is the output from the application?

```
' VB
<Assembly: UIPermission(SecurityAction.RequestOptional, _
    Unrestricted:=True)>
<Assembly: FileIOPermissionAttribute(SecurityAction.RequestOptional, _
    Read:="C:\")>
<Assembly: FileIOPermissionAttribute(SecurityAction.RequestRefuse, _
    Read:="C:\Windows\")>
Module Module1
    Sub Main()
        Console.WriteLine("Reading one line of the boot.ini file:")
```

```
                  Dim sr As StreamReader = New StreamReader("C:\boot.ini")
                  Console.WriteLine("First line of boot.ini: " + sr.ReadLine)
          End Sub
    End Module
```

```
// C#
[assembly: UIPermission(SecurityAction.RequestOptional,
    Unrestricted = true)]
[assembly: FileIOPermissionAttribute(SecurityAction.RequestOptional,
    Read = @"C:\")]
[assembly: FileIOPermissionAttribute(SecurityAction.RequestRefuse,
    Read = @"C:\Windows\")]
namespace console_cs2
{
    class Program
    {
        static void Main(string[] args)
        {
            Console.WriteLine("Reading one line of the boot.ini file:");
            StreamReader sr = new StreamReader(@"C:\boot.ini");
            Console.WriteLine("First line of boot.ini: " + sr.ReadLine());
        }
    }
}
```

A.

```
Unhandled Exception: System.Security.SecurityException: Request for the
permission of type 'System.Security.Permissions.
FileIOPermission, mscorlib, Version=2.0.0.0, Culture=neutral,
PublicKeyToken=b77a5c561934e089' failed.
```

B.

```
Reading one line of the boot.ini file:
Unhandled Exception: System.Security.SecurityException: Request for the
permission of type 'System.Security.Permissions.
FileIOPermission, mscorlib, Version=2.0.0.0, Culture=neutral,
PublicKeyToken=b77a5c561934e089' failed.
```

C.

```
Reading one line of the boot.ini file:
First line of boot.ini: [boot loader]
```

D. An unhandled *SecurityException* occurs before the application begins execution.

2. An administrator runs the following Console application on a computer running Windows XP with the Everything permission set. What is the output from the application?

```
' VB
<Assembly: UIPermission(SecurityAction.RequestOptional, _
    Unrestricted:=True)>
```

```
<Assembly: FileIOPermissionAttribute(SecurityAction.RequestOptional, _
    Read:="C:\Temp")>
<Assembly: FileIOPermissionAttribute(SecurityAction.RequestRefuse, _
    Read:="C:\Windows\")>
Module Module1
    Sub Main()
        Console.WriteLine("Reading one line of the boot.ini file:")
        Dim sr As StreamReader = New StreamReader("C:\boot.ini")
        Console.WriteLine("First line of boot.ini: " + sr.ReadLine)
    End Sub
End Module

// C#
[assembly: UIPermission(SecurityAction.RequestOptional,
    Unrestricted = true)]
[assembly: FileIOPermissionAttribute(SecurityAction.RequestOptional,
    Read = @"C:\Temp")]
[assembly: FileIOPermissionAttribute(SecurityAction.RequestRefuse,
    Read = @"C:\Windows\")]
namespace console_cs2
{
    class Program
    {
        static void Main(string[] args)
        {
            Console.WriteLine("Reading one line of the boot.ini file:");
            StreamReader sr = new StreamReader(@"C:\boot.ini");
            Console.WriteLine("First line of boot.ini: " + sr.ReadLine());
        }
    }
}
```

A.

```
Unhandled Exception: System.Security.SecurityException: Request for the
permission of type 'System.Security.Permissions.
FileIOPermission, mscorlib, Version=2.0.0.0, Culture=neutral,
PublicKeyToken=b77a5c561934e089' failed.
```

B.

```
Reading one line of the boot.ini file:
Unhandled Exception: System.Security.SecurityException: Request for the
permission of type 'System.Security.Permissions.
FileIOPermission, mscorlib, Version=2.0.0.0, Culture=neutral,
PublicKeyToken=b77a5c561934e089' failed.
```

C.

```
Reading one line of the boot.ini file:
First line of boot.ini: [boot loader]
```

D. An unhandled *SecurityException* occurs before the application begins execution.

3. An administrator runs the following Console application on a computer running Windows XP with the Everything permission set. What is the output from the application?

```
' VB
<Assembly: UIPermission(SecurityAction.RequestMinimum, Unrestricted:=True)>
<Assembly: FileIOPermissionAttribute(SecurityAction.RequestMinimum, _
    Read:="C:\Temp")>
<Assembly: FileIOPermissionAttribute(SecurityAction.RequestRefuse, _
    Read:="C:\Windows\")>
Module Module1
    Sub Main()
        Console.WriteLine("Reading one line of the boot.ini file:")
        Dim sr As StreamReader = New StreamReader("C:\boot.ini")
        Console.WriteLine("First line of boot.ini: " + sr.ReadLine)
    End Sub
End Module
```

```
// C#
[assembly: UIPermission(SecurityAction.RequestMinimum,
    Unrestricted = true)]
[assembly: FileIOPermissionAttribute(SecurityAction.RequestMinimum,
    Read = @"C:\Temp")]
[assembly: FileIOPermissionAttribute(SecurityAction.RequestRefuse,
    Read = @"C:\Windows\")]
namespace console_cs2
{
    class Program
    {
        static void Main(string[] args)
        {
            Console.WriteLine("Reading one line of the boot.ini file:");
            StreamReader sr = new StreamReader(@"C:\boot.ini");
            Console.WriteLine("First line of boot.ini: " + sr.ReadLine());
        }
    }
}
```

A.

```
Unhandled Exception: System.Security.SecurityException: Request for the
permission of type 'System.Security.Permissions.
FileIOPermission, mscorlib, Version=2.0.0.0, Culture=neutral,
PublicKeyToken=b77a5c561934e089' failed.
```

B.

```
Reading one line of the boot.ini file:
Unhandled Exception: System.Security.SecurityException: Request for the
permission of type 'System.Security.Permissions.
FileIOPermission, mscorlib, Version=2.0.0.0, Culture=neutral,
PublicKeyToken=b77a5c561934e089' failed.
```

C.

```
Reading one line of the boot.ini file:
First line of boot.ini: [boot loader]
```

D. An unhandled *SecurityException* occurs before the application begins execution.

4. Which of the following permissions is required for all Console applications running with a debugger?

A. *SocketPermission*

B. *WebPermission*

C. *UIPermission*

D. *FileIOPermission*

Lesson 3: Using Declarative and Imperative Security to Protect Methods

CAS can be used either declaratively, in which case the compiler performs security checks prior to running code, or imperatively, in which case the code itself performs security checks and controls what happens if the check fails. In Lesson 2, you learned how to use CAS declarations to protect an entire assembly. You can also use CAS to declaratively protect individual methods within an assembly or use CAS to imperatively protect sections of code within a method. In this lesson, you learn how and why to use both imperative and declarative CAS demands to protect code within an assembly.

After this lesson, you will be able to:

- List the types of method permission requests
- Describe how method permission requests should be used to maximize application security
- Use CAS to require specific permissions for individual methods
- Restrict permissions for a method to reduce the risk of the method being misused by an attacker
- Use the *Assert* method to relax permissions and improve performance
- Use permission sets to demand, restrict, or assert multiple permissions simultaneously

Estimated lesson time: 45 minutes

Types of Method Permission Requests

Although there are only three types of CAS assembly declarations (*RequestOptional*, *RequestMinimum*, and *RequestRefuse*), you have four options available for imperative and declarative permissions within a method. The following list describes each option:

- **Assert**   Instructs the runtime to ignore the fact that callers might not have the specified permission. Assemblies must have the Assert Any Permission That Has Been Granted security permission setting.

- **Demand**   Instructs the runtime to throw an exception if the caller and all callers higher in the stack lack the specified permission.

- **Deny**   Causes the runtime to reduce the method's access by removing the specified permission.

- **PermitOnly**   Instructs the runtime to reduce the method's access by removing all permissions except for the specified permission.

You have two additional options available for declarative demands that cannot be used imperatively:

- *LinkDemand*   Causes the runtime to throw an exception if the immediate caller, but not callers higher in the stack, lack the specified permission.

- *InheritanceDemand*   Instructs the runtime to throw an exception if the assembly inherited from the class lacks the specified permission.

To understand each of these methods, consider a group of four guests who want to enter an exclusive party. The host (your method) has hired a bouncer (the .NET Framework runtime) to make sure that only guests (calling assemblies) with an invitation (a CAS permission) are allowed to enter the party (call your method).

If the host calls *InvitedGuests.LinkDemand*, the bouncer checks the invitation of the first guest and then allows everyone else into the party. This is quick, but it might let unauthorized people sneak into the party. If the host calls *InvitedGuests.Demand*, the bouncer checks the invitation of every guest individually. This process takes more time, but it ensures that nobody can sneak in.

To speed up the process of checking invitations, the first invited guests might use *InvitedGuests.Assert* to assure the bouncer that all the guests in the group were invited—assuming that the bouncer trusted the first guest enough. This procedure also allows the first guest to bring guests who lacked invitations, which might be a good thing if the host wanted to have a lot of people at the party but didn't want to hand out too many invitations (which might fall into the wrong hands). However, it might be a bad thing if a thief discovered that he could sneak into the party that way.

If the host wanted to ensure that people danced at the party (and never did anything else), the host would use *Dancing.PermitOnly* to instruct the bouncer to make sure that guests stayed on the dance floor. If the host wanted people to do anything *but* dance, the host would use *Dancing.Deny* to prevent anyone from dancing.

Guidelines for Using Method Permission Requests

As a developer, you have many choices for implementing CAS in your applications. Choosing how to implement CAS for a particular situation can be complicated, however. Follow these guidelines to choose which CAS methods to use:

- Use *SecurityAction.PermitOnly* declarations to limit the permissions available to each method. List every permission the method requires.

- Use *SecurityAction.Deny* declarations to refine further the permissions available to each method.

- Use *CodeAccessPermission.PermitOnly* to imperatively reduce permissions when a section of a method requires fewer permissions than the rest of the method. This is particularly important when calling objects created by third parties. Use *CodeaccessPermission.RevertPermitOnly* to restore the permission.

- Use *CodeAccessPermission.Assert* when you want to allow partially trusted code to call a method that requires permissions the caller might lack. Review your code carefully for potential security vulnerabilities; *Assert* can be abused by an attacker to gain elevated privileges. After you perform the functions requiring elevated privileges, use *CodeAccessPermission.RevertAssert* to restore the original permissions.

- Use *CodeAccessPermission.Demand* only when your assembly implements customized functionality that does not rely on functionality built into the .NET Framework, such as calls to unmanaged code.

NOTE   **Security Risks of Declarative Demands**

There's a school of thought that says that declarative security demands are less secure than imperative security demands because declarative demands can reveal to attackers too much about the code's design and potential vulnerabilities. It's true that declarative security demands are a bit easier for an attacker to analyze, but a sophisticated attacker could also examine imperative demands by using a tool that analyzes your assembly's Intermediate Language (IL) code. It's a bit harder for the attacker to analyze IL than to analyze the declarative security demands, but it wouldn't make much of a difference to an attacker who was sophisticated enough to make use of security demand information. Also, declarative demands are faster than imperative demands.

Techniques for Demanding Permissions

Two of the *SecurityAction* enumerations cause the runtime to throw an exception if the specified CAS permission is missing: *Demand* and *LinkDemand*. The difference between the two enumerations is that *Demand* causes the permission check to verify the access of all callers, whereas *LinkDemand* verifies only the immediate caller.

To understand the difference, compare the *Demand* process demonstrated in Figure 11-9 with the *LinkDemand* process demonstrated in Figure 11-10. As you can see, *Demand* detects whether any caller lacks the demanded permission or permission set and throws an exception if so. This is more secure than using *LinkDemand*, which checks only the immediate caller. However, as with almost every security mechanism, there is a trade-off. *Demand* requires the runtime to do more checks, which requires more processing time and slows performance. Using *LinkDemand* improves performance but increases the risk of an attacker successfully bypassing the check.

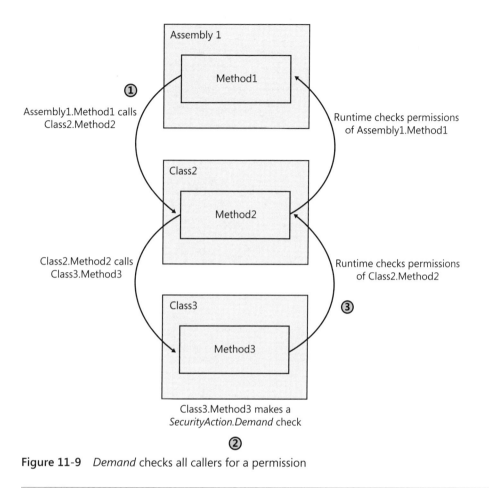

Figure 11-9   *Demand* checks all callers for a permission

IMPORTANT   *Demand* and *LinkDemand* Check the Caller

Demand and *LinkDemand* do *not* check the current method's permissions—they check the caller. However, if your assembly calls a private method that uses *Demand* or *LinkDemand*, the runtime checks your assembly's permission because in this case your assembly is the caller.

How to Demand CAS Permissions Declaratively

Creating CAS method declarations is very similar to creating CAS assembly declarations. However, you must create the declarations as attributes to the method instead of to the assembly and you must use different *SecurityAction* enumerations. To create a declarative request, use one of the classes discussed in Lesson 2 of this chapter with the *Security Action.Demand* or *SecurityAction.LinkDemand* enumerations. The following sample shows two methods that use *FileIOPermissionAttribute* (in *System.Security.Permissions*)

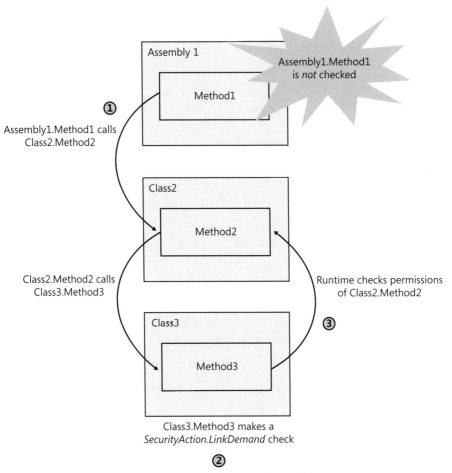

Figure 11-10 *LinkDemand* checks only the immediate caller

and *WebPermissionAttribute* (in *System.Net*) classes to declaratively verify that callers of particular methods have access to specific files and the *www.microsoft.com* Web site:

```vb
' VB
<FileIOPermissionAttribute(SecurityAction.Demand, _
    Write:="C:\Program Files\")> _
Public Sub createProgramFolder()
    ' Method logic
End Sub

<WebPermission(SecurityAction.Demand, _
    ConnectPattern:="http://www\.microsoft\.com/.*")> _
Public Sub requestWebPage()
    ' Method logic
End Sub
```

```
// C#
[FileIOPermission(SecurityAction.Demand, Write = @"C:\Program Files\")]
public static void createProgramFolder()
{
    // Method logic
}

[WebPermission(SecurityAction.Demand,
    ConnectPattern = @"http://www\.microsoft\.com/.*")]
public static void requestWebPage()
{
    // Method logic
}
```

If you write classes from which other developers will derive, you can restrict which assemblies can inherit from your classes using the *SecurityAction.InheritanceDemand* enumeration. For example, only assemblies signed with the C:\Certificates\ MyCertificate.cer certificate could inherit from the following class:

```
' VB
<PublisherIdentityPermission(SecurityAction.InheritanceDemand, _
    CertFile:="C:\Certificates\MyCertificate.cer")> _
Public Class ProtectedInheritance
    ' Class logic
End Class
```

```
// C#
[PublisherIdentityPermission(SecurityAction.InheritanceDemand,
    CertFile = @"C:\Certificates\MyCertificate.cer")]
public class ProtectedInheritance
{
    // Class logic
}
```

You can use the same declarative syntax to protect individual class members from being overridden by a derived class. This approach is necessary only when you want to provide levels of protection for individual members that are higher than the level of protection for the base class.

How to Demand CAS Permissions Imperatively

Four of the six *SecurityAction* enumerations used to specify CAS declarations, *Assert*, *Demand*, *Deny*, and *PermitOnly*, have corresponding *CodeAccessPermission* methods with the same name and function used for imperative permissions. You use the *SecurityAction* enumerations for declarative security and the *CodeAccessPermission* methods for imperative security. The following sample performs the same checks as the sample code that uses declarative CAS demands, but it performs the check imperatively:

```vb
' VB
Public Shared Sub createProgramFolder()
    Try
        Dim filePermissions As FileIOPermission = _
            New FileIOPermission(FileIOPermissionAccess.Write, "C:\Program Files\")
        filePermissions.Demand()
        ' Method logic
    Catch
        ' Error handling logic
    End Try
End Sub

Public Shared Sub requestWebPage()
    Try
        Dim connectPattern As Regex = New Regex("http://www\.microsoft\.com/.*")
        Dim webPermissions As WebPermission = _
            New WebPermission(NetworkAccess.Connect, connectPattern)
        webPermissions.Demand()
        ' Method logic
    Catch
        ' Error handling logic
    End Try
End Sub
```

```csharp
// C#
public static void createProgramFolder()
{
    try
    {
        FileIOPermission filePermissions =
            new FileIOPermission(FileIOPermissionAccess.Write, @"C:\Program Files\");
        filePermissions.Demand();
        // Method logic
    }
    catch
    {
        // Error-handling logic
    }
}

public static void requestWebPage()
{
    try
    {
        Regex connectPattern = new Regex(@"http://www\.microsoft\.com/.*");
        WebPermission webPermissions =
            new WebPermission(NetworkAccess.Connect, connectPattern);
        webPermissions.Demand();
```

```
        // Method logic
    }
    catch
    {
        // Error-handling logic
    }
}
```

The advantage of using imperative demands is that you can catch the security exception within your method and deal with it gracefully. If you just want to throw an exception back to the caller, use a declarative demand.

How to Analyze Granted Permissions

If you need to determine whether your assembly has a particular CAS permission, don't use *Demand*. *Demand* is designed to check an assembly's *caller* for permission, not the assembly itself. Instead, use the *System.Security.SecurityManager.IsGranted* method, as demonstrated by the following code sample:

```vb
' VB
Dim filePermissions As FileIOPermission =  New _
    FileIOPermission(FileIOPermissionAccess.Read, "C:\Windows\")
If SecurityManager.IsGranted(filePermissions) = True Then
    ' Assembly can read the C:\Windows directory
Else
    ' Assembly cannot read the C:\Windows directory
End If
```

```csharp
// C#
FileIOPermission filePermissions = new
    FileIOPermission(FileIOPermissionAccess.Read, @"C:\Windows\");
if ( SecurityManager.IsGranted(filePermissions) == true )
    // Assembly can read the C:\Windows directory
else
    // Assembly cannot read the C:\Windows directory
```

The *ListPermissions* sample application from the Lesson 1 lab uses this method; examine the source code on the companion CD for a working example.

BEST PRACTICES   Avoid Redundant Demands

Most classes in the .NET Framework use demands to ensure that callers have the permissions required to use them, so also calling *Demand* is redundant. For example, if you're reading a line from a text file using a *StreamWriter* object, the object itself will demand *FileIOPermission*. Generally, use demands to protect custom resources that require custom permissions.

Techniques for Limiting Permissions

Always use CAS assembly declarations to restrict the CAS permissions granted to your assembly so that your assembly has only the bare minimum required for all functionality. You can control permissions on a more granular level by restricting permissions for individual methods using method declarations or by restricting permissions within methods using imperative statements.

Two of the *SecurityAction* enumerations and permission methods cause the runtime to reduce CAS permissions: *Deny* and *PermitOnly*. The difference between the two enumerations is that *Deny* removes a single permission or permission set, whereas *PermitOnly* removes all permissions except the requested permission or permission set. Recall from Lesson 2 that *Deny* performs a similar function to *RequestRefuse*, whereas *PermitOnly* is similar to *RequestOptional*.

Exam Tip   For the exam, remember to use *RequestRefuse* and *RequestOptional* for assembly declarations, and use *Deny* and *PermitOnly* for methods.

How to Limit Method Permissions Declaratively

The following two declarations demonstrate how to prevent a method from accessing the C:\Windows directory and how to limit outgoing Web requests to only *www .microsoft.com:*

```vb
' VB
<FileIOPermissionAttribute(SecurityAction.Deny, _
    ViewAndModify := "C:\Windows\")> _
<WebPermission(SecurityAction.PermitOnly, _
    ConnectPattern:="http://www\.microsoft\.com/.*")> _
```

```csharp
// C#
[FileIOPermission(SecurityAction.Deny, ViewAndModify = @"C:\Windows\")]
[WebPermission(SecurityAction.PermitOnly,
    ConnectPattern = @"http://www\.microsoft\.com/.*")]
```

NOTE   **Limitations of Declarative Security**

Declarative security criteria must be static. If you need to generate file paths, Web addresses, or any other aspects of the security criteria dynamically, you must enforce the security limitations imperatively.

How to Limit Permissions Imperatively

The following sample forces the same limitations as the sample code that uses declarative CAS demands, but it limits the permissions imperatively:

```
' VB
' Deny access to the Windows directory
Dim filePermissions As FileIOPermission = New _
    FileIOPermission(FileIOPermissionAccess.AllAccess, "C:\Windows\")
filePermissions.Deny()
' Method logic

' Permit only Web access, and limit it to www.microsoft.com
Dim connectPattern As Regex = New Regex("http://www\.microsoft\.com/.*")
Dim webPermissions As WebPermission = _
    New WebPermission(NetworkAccess.Connect, connectPattern)
webPermissions.PermitOnly()
' Method logic
```

```
// C#
// Deny access to the Windows directory
FileIOPermission filePermissions =
    new FileIOPermission(FileIOPermissionAccess.AllAccess, @"C:\Windows\");
filePermissions.Deny();
// Method logic

// Permit only Web access, and limit it to www.microsoft.com
Regex connectPattern = new Regex(@"http://www\.microsoft\.com/.*");
WebPermission webPermissions = new WebPermission(NetworkAccess.Connect,
    connectPattern);
webPermissions.PermitOnly();
// Method logic
```

If part of your code needs to use a permission that you previously blocked with *Deny* or *PermitOnly*, use the *System.Security.CodeAccessPermission.RevertDeny* or *System .Security.CodeAccessPermission.RevertPermitOnly* static methods to reenable the permission.

Best Practice for Handling Errors

Use *PermitOnly* to limit permissions during error-handling routines. Attackers often initiate an error condition in an application and then abuse that error condition to perform tasks that would not be possible under normal circumstances. Using *PermitOnly* to limit CAS permissions to the bare minimum required to log the event and report an error to the user significantly reduces the risk that your error-handling routine can be abused. If your application continues running after the error, be sure to revert to your original permissions—otherwise, normal application functionality will not be available.

For example, the following code catches an exception, restricts CAS permissions to those required to add events, and then reverts to the previous permission set:

```
' VB
Try
    ' Assembly logic
Catch
    Dim errorPerms As EventLogPermission = _
        New EventLogPermission (PermissionState.Unrestricted)
    errorPerms.PermitOnly
    ' Log event
    CodeAccessPermission.RevertPermitOnly
End Try
```

```
// C#
try
{
    // Assembly logic
}
catch
{
    EventLogPermission errorPerms = new
        EventLogPermission(PermissionState.Unrestricted);
    errorPerms.PermitOnly();
    // Log event
    CodeAccessPermission.RevertPermitOnly();
}
```

Restricting permissions to those required for a specific block of code is an excellent example of following the principle of least privilege. Although it's particularly important during error-catching routines, you can use this technique to limit the permissions of any block of code.

How to Relax Permissions and Potentially Improve Performance

Using CAS demands improves the security of an assembly but can decrease performance. In particular, calling a permission's *Demand* method is costly because it forces the runtime to check the permission of every caller systematically. *LinkDemand*, discussed earlier, is one way to improve upon the performance of the *Demand* method, but it sacrifices some level of security. Another technique is the *Assert* method, which causes the runtime to bypass any security checks.

IMPORTANT   Compared with *Assert* in C++

CodeAccessPermission.Assert is nothing like the *assert* function in C or C++.

Permission objects include the *Assert* method to enable a method to vouch for all callers. Figure 11-11 shows how a call to *Assert* stops the runtime from checking the CAS permissions of assemblies higher in the stack. This has two effects: improving performance by reducing the number of permission checks and allowing underprivileged code to call methods with higher CAS permission requirements.

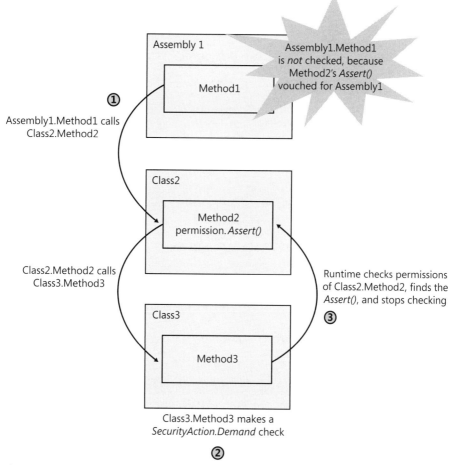

Figure 11-11   *Assert* blocks demand checks, increasing performance and allowing underprivileged code to call methods with CAS permission requirements

For example, if you create a *RegistryPermission* object and call the *Assert* method, your assembly must be granted *RegistryPermission*, but any code calling your assembly does not require the permission. If you call another method that uses *Demand* to require *RegistryPermission*, *Demand* succeeds whether or not your caller has been granted *RegistryPermission*.

You can use *Assert* either declaratively or imperatively, and the syntax is identical to other types of CAS declarations. The following example asserts permissions declaratively:

```
' VB
<FileIOPermissionAttribute(SecurityAction.Assert, _
    ViewAndModify := "C:\Program Files\")> _
<WebPermission(SecurityAction.Assert, _
    ConnectPattern:="http://www\.microsoft\.com/.*")> _
```

```
// C#
[FileIOPermission(SecurityAction.Assert, ViewAndModify = @"C:\Windows\")]
[WebPermission(SecurityAction.Assert,
    ConnectPattern = @"http://www\.microsoft\.com/.*")]
```

On the other hand, the following example asserts permissions imperatively:

```
' VB
' Block all CAS permission checks for file access to the Windows directory
Dim filePermissions As FileIOPermission = _
    New FileIOPermission(FileIOPermissionAccess.AllAccess, "C:\Windows\")
filePermissions.Assert()
' Method logic

' Block all CAS permission checks for Web access to www.microsoft.com
Dim connectPattern As Regex = New Regex("http://www\.microsoft\.com/.*")
Dim webPermissions As WebPermission = _
    New WebPermission(NetworkAccess.Connect, connectPattern)
webPermissions.Assert()
' Method logic
```

```
// C#
// Block all CAS permission checks for file access to the Windows directory
FileIOPermission filePermissions =
    new FileIOPermission(FileIOPermissionAccess.AllAccess, @"C:\Windows\");
filePermissions.Assert();
// Method logic

// Block all CAS permission checks for Web access to www.microsoft.com
Regex connectPattern = new Regex(@"http://www\.microsoft\.com/.*");
WebPermission webPermissions =
    new WebPermission(NetworkAccess.Connect, connectPattern);
webPermissions.Assert();
// Method logic
```

To use *Assert* successfully, the assembly must have the *SecurityPermissionFlag.Assertion* privilege as well as the privilege being asserted. In the .NET Framework 2.0 Configuration tool, *SecurityPermissionFlag.Assertion* is represented by the Assert Any Permission That Has Been Granted item in the Security Permission Properties dialog box. The FullTrust, LocalIntranet, and Everything permission sets have this permission.

Using *Assert* allows an assembly to vouch for the security of lesser privileged assemblies. This is an excellent way to grant additional functionality to assemblies that normally lack CAS permissions. For example, you can use an *Assert* to allow an assembly in the Internet zone to save a file to the user's disk. Simply create an assembly with the *AllowPartiallyTrustedCallersAttribute*. Then create a public method that writes the file, create a *FileIOPermission* object, and call the *Assert* method before writing the file. The assembly in the Internet zone can save a file to a user's disk without requiring the administrators to grant file permissions to the Internet zone.

To decrease the opportunity for an attacker to abuse asserted permissions, use the *CodeAccessPermission.RevertAssert* static method. As the name suggests, calling this method erases the assertion and returns CAS permission checking to the normal state. Use a *try/finally* block to ensure that you call *RevertAssert* after every *Assert*, even if a failure occurs. The following method demonstrates this and is also an excellent example of how to fail to a more secure permission set:

```vb
' VB
Dim filePermissions As FileIOPermission = _
    New FileIOPermission (FileIOPermissionAccess.Write, _
    "C:\Inetpub\NewFile.txt")
filePermissions.Assert
Try
    Dim newFile As StreamWriter = New StreamWriter _
        ("C:\Inetpub\NewFile.txt")
    newFile.WriteLine("Lesser privileged applications can save a file.")
    newFile.Close
Finally
    CodeAccessPermission.RevertAssert
End Try
```

```csharp
// C#
FileIOPermission filePermissions =
    new FileIOPermission(FileIOPermissionAccess.Write, @"C:\Inetpub\");
filePermissions.Assert();
try
{
    StreamWriter newFile = new StreamWriter(@"C:\Inetpub\NewFile.txt");
    newFile.WriteLine("Lesser privileged applications can save a file.");
    newFile.Close();
}
finally
{
    CodeAccessPermission.RevertAssert();
}
```

Assert does have a few limitations. You can use *Assert* only once in a method. If you have to assert multiple permissions, you need to create a custom permission set (as described later in this lesson). Second, *Assert* doesn't override the operating system's role-based security, regardless of the assembly's CAS permissions. If a user lacks permission to write to the D: drive and runs an assembly with full trust that asserts that file permission, the *Assert* succeeds, but the assembly still can't write to the D: drive. The assembly remains limited by the user's access restrictions.

How to Call Trusted Code from Partially Trusted Code

To prevent partially trusted code from bypassing security checks, partially trusted code can't call strong-named assemblies by default. You can control this on an assembly-by-assembly basis, however, by adding the *AllowPartiallyTrustedCallers Attribute* assembly-level custom attribute as follows:

```
' VB
<assembly:AllowPartiallyTrustedCallers>
```

```
// C#
[assembly:AllowPartiallyTrustedCallers]
```

If your assembly doesn't have a strong name, partially trusted code can access your public methods even when you don't add that attribute.

How to Use Permission Sets

Permission sets are a collection of permissions that can be used imperatively in the same ways you use individual permissions. Use the *System.Security.PermissionSet* class to create a permission set and then use the *AddPermission* method to specify the permissions that define the permission set. Then you can call any standard permission methods, including *Assert*, *Demand*, *Deny*, and *PermitOnly*.

For example, the following code creates a permission set consisting of Read access to the C:\Windows folder, write access to the C:\Inetpub folder, and Read access to the HKEY_LOCAL_MACHINE\Software registry key. Then it demands access to all those resources to cause the runtime to throw an exception if any of the specified permissions are not available:

```
' VB
Dim myPerms As PermissionSet = New PermissionSet(PermissionState.None)
myPerms.AddPermission(New FileIOPermission _
    (FileIOPermissionAccess.Read, "C:\Windows"))
myPerms.AddPermission(New FileIOPermission _
    (FileIOPermissionAccess.Write, "C:\Inetpub"))
myPerms.AddPermission(New _
    RegistryPermission (RegistryPermissionAccess.Write, _
    "HKEY_LOCAL_MACHINE"))
myPerms.Demand
```

```
// C#
PermissionSet myPerms = new PermissionSet(PermissionState.None);
myPerms.AddPermission(new FileIOPermission(
    FileIOPermissionAccess.Read, @"C:\Windows"));
myPerms.AddPermission(new FileIOPermission(
    FileIOPermissionAccess.Write, @"C:\Inetpub"));
myPerms.AddPermission(new
    RegistryPermission(RegistryPermissionAccess.Write,
    @"HKEY_LOCAL_MACHINE\Software"));
myPerms.Demand();
```

You can call *Assert* only once in a method, so if you need to assert multiple permissions, you *must* use a permission set.

Lab: Protecting Methods with CAS Demands

In this lab, you will work with *Deny* and *Assert* methods to validate your understanding of both declarative and imperative CAS demands. Complete Exercises 1 through 4. You will reset all policy levels at the end of Exercise 4.

Exercise 1: Experiment with the Default Permission Set

In this exercise, you experiment with declarative and imperative CAS demands and determine how each reacts when CAS is not restricted. To complete this exercise, you must have a folder named C:\Documents and Settings\Administrator (which might be hidden). If this folder is not present, create it prior to performing this exercise.

1. Navigate to the \<*InstallHome*>\Chapter11\Lesson3\Exercise1\Partial folder and open either the C# version or the Visual Basic .NET version of the solution file.

2. Build the project and copy the resulting executable file to a folder on your computer that standard users (users who are not a member of the Administrators group) can access.

3. Log on to your computer as a standard user account and run the CASDemands.exe file.

4. In the Code Access Security Demands application, click the Create File With No Demand button and then answer the following questions:

   ❏ In which zone is the assembly running?

   The assembly is using the My_Computer_Zone because it is being run from the computer's local file system.

   ❏ What permission set did the .NET Framework runtime grant the assembly?

By default, the My_Computer_Zone grants assemblies the FullTrust permission set.

❑ What type of exception was thrown, and why was that particular type of exception thrown?

The .NET Framework threw a *System.UnauthorizedAccessException* because a nonadministrative user does not have access to create new files within the C:\Documents and Settings\Administrator\ folder.

5. In the Code Access Security Demands application, click the Create File With Declarative Demand button and then answer the following questions:

❑ What type of exception was thrown, and why was that particular type of exception thrown?

The .NET Framework threw a *System.UnauthorizedAccessException* because standard users do not have access to create new files within the C:\Documents and Settings\Administrator\ folder.

❑ Notice that the error message reads Failed When Attempting To Create File, not Failed Before Attempting To Create File. Use Visual Studio .NET to examine the *declarativeDemandButton_Click* method. This method calls the *declarativeCreateFile* method, which requires Write access to a file that the user lacks permission to create. Why was the exception thrown within the *createFile* method and not thrown when the declarative security demand was processed before the *declarativeCreateFile* method was run?

Declarative CAS demands cause an exception to be thrown when the *code* itself lacks the required permission. In this case, the *user* lacks the required permission, but the code does have CAS permissions to create the file. Therefore, the declarative security demand is successful, but the more restricted role-based security requirement enforced by the operating system causes the .NET Framework runtime to throw an exception when the application attempts to create the file itself in the *createFile* method.

6. In the Code Access Security Demands application, click the Create File With Imperative Demand button and then answer the following questions:

❑ What type of exception was thrown, and why was that particular type of exception thrown?

The .NET Framework threw a *System.UnauthorizedAccessException*, just as it did for the other buttons, because CAS is not being taken into account because the assembly is running with the FullTrust permission set.

7. Close the Code Access Security Demands application.

Exercise 2: Restrict Permissions to the My_Computer_Zone

In this exercise, you will restrict permissions to the My_Computer_Zone.

1. Log on to your computer as an administrator.

2. Start the Microsoft .NET Framework 2.0 Configuration tool. In the .NET Framework 2.0 Configuration tool, expand My Computer, expand Runtime Security Policy, expand Machine, expand Code Groups, and then expand All_Code. Right-click My_Computer_ Zone and then click Properties.

3. Select the Permission Set tab, set Permission Set to Internet, and then click OK.

4. Log on to your computer as a standard user account.

5. Run the CASDemands.exe file. The assembly no longer has unrestricted permissions, and the .NET Framework displays a security warning. Close the warnng bubble.

6. In the Code Access Security Demands application, click the Create File With No Demand button and then answer the following questions:

    ❏ In which zone is the assembly running?

    The assembly is using the My_Computer_Zone because it is being run from the computer's local file system.

    ❏ What permission set did the .NET Framework runtime grant the assembly?

    Because you used the Administrator account to modify the default configuration, the My_Computer_Zone grants the Internet permission set to the assembly.

    ❏ What type of exception was thrown, and why was that particular type of exception thrown?

    The .NET Framework threw a *System.Security.SecurityException* because the application, running under the Internet permission set, did not have CAS permissions to use the file system.

7. In the Code Access Security Demands application, click the Create File With Declarative Demand button and then answer the following questions:

    ❏ What type of exception was thrown, and why was that particular type of exception thrown?

    The .NET Framework threw a *System.Security.SecurityException* for the same reasons that it threw the exception when you clicked the Create File With No Demand button.

    ❏ In which method was the exception caught?

The Failed Before Attempting To Create File error message indicates that the exception was caught in the *declarativeDemandButton_Click* method because the exception was thrown when the declarative demand associated with the *declarativeCreateFile* method was processed. The .NET Framework runtime never ran the *createFile* method because it was prevented by the security demand.

8. In the Code Access Security Demands application, click the Create File With Imperative Demand button and then answer the following questions:

   ❑ What type of exception was thrown, and what method caught the exception?

   As with the declarative security demand, the *System.Security.SecurityException* was caught before it reached the *createFile* method. In this case, the exception was caught in the *imperativeDemandButton_Click* method.

9. Close the Code Access Security Demands application.

10. Finally, use the .NET Framework 2.0 Configuration tool with administrative privileges to reset all policy levels, as described in Lesson 1 of this chapter.

Exercise 3: Grant Access to Partially Trusted Code

In this exercise, you will modify a class to enable code without *FileIOPermission* to write to the disk.

1. Log on to your computer as an administrator.

2. Navigate to the \<*InstallHome*>\Chapter11\Lesson3\Exercise3\Partial folder.

3. Open the TrustedClass.sln file and build the solution. While you have the solution open, examine the *Distrust* class. Note that it has one member: *WriteToFile*, which uses a *StreamWriter* class, which automatically demands *FileIOPermission*.

4. Copy the TrustedClass.dll file to the C:\TrustedClass folder.

5. At an administrative command prompt, run the following command to share the folder:

   ```
   net share trusted="C:\TrustedClass"
   ```

6. Open the PartiallyTrustedAssembly.sln file.

7. Select the Project menu and then click Add Reference. In the Add Reference dialog box, click the Browse tab. In the File Name box, type **\\127.0.0.1\Trusted\ TrustedClass.dll** and then click OK.

8. Build the solution and then copy both the PartiallyTrustedAssembly.exe file and the TrustedClass.dll file to the C:\PartiallyTrustedAssembly folder.

9. At a command prompt, run the following command to share the folder:

   ```
   net share untrusted="C:\PartiallyTrustedAssembly"
   ```

10. At a command prompt, issue the following command:

    ```
    \\127.0.0.1\untrusted\PartiallyTrustedAssembly
    ```

11. Answer the following question:

    ❑ PartiallyTrustedAssembly attempts to write to a file. Did it succeed?

    No, it failed and reported a *SecurityException* because a request for *FileIO Permission* failed.

    ❑ Examine the source code and explain the behavior.

    PartiallyTrustedAssembly calls the *TrustedClass.Distrust.WriteToFile* method. This method uses the .NET Framework's *StreamWriter* object, which contains a demand for *FileIOPermission*. After the *StreamWriter* object issues the demand, the runtime checks each caller for the CAS permission. Because PartiallyTrusted-Assembly lacks the permission, the runtime throws a *SecurityException*.

12. Replace the method in *TrustedClass.Distrust* named *WriteToFileWrapper* with a method that uses *Assert* to block the *FileIOPermission* check (as shown in the next step). Rebuild the assembly and copy it to C:\TrustedClass.

13. In the PartiallyTrustedAssembly solution, remove and re-add the TrustedClass reference. Then modify the PartiallyTrustedAssembly source code to call *WriteToFileWrapper* instead of *WriteToFile*. Answer the following question:

    ❑ What code did you write to create the assembly?

    The exact code will vary, but it should resemble the following:

    ```vb
    ' VB
    Public Shared Sub WriteToFileWrapper(ByVal fileName As String, _
        ByVal contents As String)
        ' Assert permission to allow caller to bypass security check
        Dim newFilePermission As FileIOPermission = _
            New FileIOPermission(FileIOPermissionAccess.Write, fileName)
        newFilePermission.Assert()
        Try
            WriteToFile(fileName, contents)
        Finally
            ' Clean up the assertion
            CodeAccessPermission.RevertAssert()
        End Try
    End Sub
    ```

    ```csharp
    // C#
    public static void WriteToFileWrapper(string fileName, string contents)
    {
        // Assert permission to allow caller to bypass security check
    ```

```
FileIOPermission newFilePermission =
    new FileIOPermission(FileIOPermissionAccess.Write, fileName);
newFilePermission.Assert();
try
{
    WriteToFile(fileName, contents);
}
finally
{
    // Clean up the assertion
    CodeAccessPermission.RevertAssert();
}
}
```

14. Rebuild the solution and then copy both the PartiallyTrustedAssembly.exe file and the TrustedClass.dll file to the C:\PartiallyTrustedAssembly folder.

15. At the command prompt, issue the following command:

    `\\127.0.0.1\Untrusted\PartiallyTrustedAssembly`

16. Answer the following questions:

    ❏ PartiallyTrustedAssembly attempts to write to a file. Did it succeed? Why or why not?

    No, it failed and reported a *SecurityException* because a request for *SecurityPermission* failed. The new method attempts to use an *Assert*, which is a security permission it lacks because of the permission set assigned to *TrustedClass*.

17. Now, you must increase the *TrustedClass* assembly's trust to enable it to use an *Assert*. However, before you can increase an assembly's trust, it must be signed. Therefore, in the TrustedClass solution, modify the project properties to sign the assembly. For detailed instructions, read "How to: Sign a Visual Basic or Visual C# Assembly" at *http://msdn.microsoft.com/en-us/library/ms180781.aspx*. Then rebuild the assembly, and copy it to C:\TrustedClass.

18. Start the .NET Framework 2.0 Configuration tool. Expand My Computer, click Runtime Security Policy, and then click Increase Assembly Trust in the right pane.

19. On the What Would You Like To Modify? page, select the Make Changes To This Computer option and then click Next.

20. On the Which Assembly Do You Want To Trust? page, type **\\127.0.0.1\ trusted\trustedclass.dll** and then click Next.

21. On the Trust This Assembly Or All Assemblies From This Publisher page, select the This One Assembly option and then click Next.

22. On the Choose The Minimum Level Of Trust For The Assembly page, move the slider to Full Trust. Click Next and then click Finish.

23. In the PartiallyTrustedAssembly solution, remove and re-add the TrustedClass reference. Rebuild the solution and then copy both the PartiallyTrustedAssembly.exe file and the TrustedClass.dll file to the C:\PartiallyTrustedAssembly folder.

24. At the command prompt, issue the following command:

```
\\127.0.0.1\Untrusted\PartiallyTrustedAssembly
```

25. Answer the following questions:

     ❑ A PartiallyTrustedAssembly attempts to write to a file. Did it succeed? Why or why not?

     Yes, it succeeded because the *WriteToFileWrapper* method includes an *Assert* that blocks the *StreamWriter*'s inherent *Demand* from checking the permissions of PartiallyTrustedAssembly. In addition, *TrustedClass* has sufficient trust to use the *Assert*.

26. Remove the shares you created by running the following commands at an Administrator command prompt:

```
net share trusted /delete
net share untrusted /delete
```

27. Finally, use the .NET Framework 2.0 Configuration tool with administrative privileges to reset all policy levels, as described in Lesson 1 of this chapter.

Lesson Summary

- You can use six different techniques to control permissions in an assembly: *Assert*, *Demand*, *Deny*, *InheritanceDemand*, *LinkDemand*, and *PermitOnly*.

- You should use *PermitOnly* and *Deny* within an assembly to reduce the likelihood of the assembly being misused by an attacker. Use *Demand* and *Link Demand* only when accessing custom resources or unmanaged code.

- You can use *LinkDemand* to protect methods declaratively, and *Demand* to protect methods either declaratively or imperatively. You can use *InheritanceDemand* declaratively to restrict which assemblies can derive new classes from your own.

- You can use *PermitOnly* and *Deny* both declaratively and imperatively to restrict the permissions assigned to a method.

- To bypass CAS demands and enable underprivileged assemblies to call privileged methods, use *Assert*.

■ Permission sets have the same capabilities as individual permissions, but apply a single action to multiple permissions simultaneously. To create a permission set, use the *System.Security.PermissionSet* class and then use the *Add Permission* method to specify the permissions that define the permission set. Then you can call any standard permission methods, including *Assert*, *Demand*, *Deny*, and *PermitOnly*.

Lesson Review

You can use the following questions to test your knowledge of declarative assembly security. The questions are also available on the companion CD if you prefer to review them in electronic form.

NOTE   Answers

Answers to these questions and explanations of why each answer choice is right or wrong are located in the "Answers" section at the end of the book.

---

1. Which of the following would you use to throw an exception before method execution begins if a caller lacked a specific privilege?

   A. *SecurityAction.Demand*

   B. *SecurityAction.Deny*

   C. *SecurityAction.Assert*

   D. *SecurityAction.RequestMinimum*

2. You have created a *FileIOPermission* object named *fp*. Which method would you use to determine whether the current assembly had a specific permission without throwing an exception?

   A. *fp.Deny*

   B. *fp.IsGranted*

   C. *SecurityManager.Deny(fp)*

   D. *SecurityManager.IsGranted(fp)*

3. Given the following code, which statement would reverse the security restriction? (Choose all that apply.)

```vb
' VB
Dim e As EventLogPermission = _
    New EventLogPermission (PermissionState.Unrestricted)
e.PermitOnly
```

```
// C#
EventLogPermission e =
    new EventLogPermission(PermissionState.Unrestricted);
e.PermitOnly();
```

    A. *e.RevertPermitOnly()*

    B. *CodeAccessPermission.RevertPermitOnly()*

    C. *e.RevertAll()*

    D. *CodeAccessPermission.RevertAll()*

    E. *e.RevertDeny()*

    F. *CodeAccessPermission.RevertDeny()*

4. You are creating a class library that connects to an intranet Web server. You plan to deploy the class library to the global assembly cache (GAC) with full trust. You add the following code:

```
' VB
Dim connectPattern As Regex = New Regex("http://intranet\.contoso\.com/.*")
Dim webPermissions As WebPermission = _
    New WebPermission(NetworkAccess.Connect, connectPattern)
webPermissions.Assert()
```

```
// C#
Regex connectPattern = new Regex(@"http://intranet\.contoso\.com/.*");
WebPermission webPermissions =
    new WebPermission(NetworkAccess.Connect, connectPattern);
webPermissions.Assert();
```

Which method should you call to cancel the assertion?

    A. *webPermissions.PermitOnly()*

    B. *webPermissions.Deny()*

    C. *CodeAccessPermission.RevertAssert()*

    D. *CodeAccessPermission.RevertDeny()*

Chapter Review

To practice and reinforce the skills you learned in this chapter further, you can perform the following tasks:

- Review the chapter summary.
- Review the list of key terms introduced in this chapter.
- Complete the case scenarios. These scenarios set up real-world situations involving the topics of this chapter and ask you to create a solution.
- Complete the suggested practices.
- Take a practice test.

Chapter Summary

- CAS controls managed code's access in a way similar to the way operating system security restricts a user's access to system resources. You can configure CAS by using either the .NET Framework 2.0 Configuration tool or the Caspol command-line tool.
- Assembly permission requests enable administrators to view the permission requirements of an assembly. They can also dramatically reduce the likelihood of an assembly being abused by ensuring that the assembly cannot access any system resources that it does not require.
- You can control CAS permissions within an assembly either imperatively or declaratively, allowing more granular control than can be accomplished with assembly declarations. This further increases the application's security.

Key Terms

Do you know what these key terms mean? You can check your answers by looking up the terms in the glossary at the end of the book.

- Assembly evidence
- Code access security (CAS)
- Code group
- Fully trusted

- Host evidence
- Partially trusted code
- Permission
- Permission set
- Security policy

Case Scenarios

In the following case scenarios, you apply what you've learned about how to implement and apply CAS. You can find answers to these questions in the "Answers" section at the end of this book.

Case Scenario 1: Explaining CAS

You are a developer at Blue Yonder Airlines. The CEO of your company read an article that quoted a security analyst who stated that the CAS in the .NET Framework could be used to prevent viruses from spreading. You run into him in the hallway and he says, "Hey, I just read this article in the paper. What's this about the .NET Framework? It's got some kind of new security that can stop programs from doing bad things, eh? Maybe you can install it on my computer so that I don't have to worry about viruses spreading or about other dangerous software sending my private files off to the Internet somewhere." He then asks you a series of questions.

Questions

Answer the following questions for your CEO:

1. Can .NET Framework CAS prevent viruses from spreading? Why or why not?

2. Will installing the .NET Framework on my computer improve its security? If not, what will it accomplish?

3. Could a .NET Framework–based virus running in the Internet zone with the default CAS permissions effectively replicate itself across our network? Why or why not?

4. Could a malicious .NET Framework–based assembly running in the Intranet zone with the default CAS permissions delete files on your hard drive? Why or why not?

Case Scenario 2: Customizing CAS

You are an application developer for Contoso, Inc. You and your coworkers have been creating applications for internal use using the .NET Framework since version 1.0. However, you have never used CAS. Now, managers are requesting that partners outside your organization install your client application. However, they are concerned that your application might have security vulnerabilities that could expose partners to security risks, potentially tarnishing Contoso's reputation. CAS might be able to limit your risk.

In a meeting, your manager tells you, "The people in charge of customer and partner relations are begging us to let outsiders install your app. I'm concerned about security, especially because some clients will be installing the app on public kiosk computers that people are constantly trying to hack into. I'd like some assurance that if someone installs our app, an attacker can't abuse it to gain elevated privileges, or write a virus to the disk of the local computer, etc."

Questions

Answer the following questions for your manager:

1. How can you let partners and customers install your application while virtually eliminating the possibility that the application could be misused to read or write to the file system?

2. What class would you use to restrict your application's access to the file system?

3. How will users be affected by implementing CAS security?

Suggested Practices

To help you master the "Improving the security of .NET Framework applications by using the .NET Framework 2.0 security features" exam objective, complete the following tasks.

Implement Code Access Security to Improve the Security of a .NET Framework Application

For this task, you should complete at least Practice 1. If you want a solid understanding of how to analyze permissions, complete Practices 2 and 3 as well.

- **Practice 1**   Use the Caspol tool to add a code group to the Machine policy level. Then use the .NET Framework 2.0 Configuration tool to remove the code group.

- **Practice 2**   Create an assembly that retrieves Web pages and saves them to a file on the local hard disk. Imperatively verify that the user has sufficient privileges by using *SecurityManager.IsGranted* to check the most granular permissions possible. Display an error message if the user lacks the necessary permissions.

- **Practice 3**   Create an assembly that retrieves Web pages and saves them to a file on the local hard disk. Verify that the user has sufficient privileges by creating an instance of *PermissionSet* with the most granular permissions possible and calling *PermissionSet.Demand*.

Control Permissions for Resources by Using the *System.Security.Permissions* Classes

For this task, you should complete all three practices to gain experience using *Permission* classes with a real-world application.

- **Practice 1**   Open the last assembly that you created as part of your job, and add the most granular assembly permission requests possible. Be very specific—if your assembly needs access to only a single file, limit your file system access to that file. If you use Web services, restrict the *WebPermission* object to allow your assembly access only to the server and path that the Web service uses. If your assembly does not explicitly check for the permissions, configure the assembly permission requests so that the runtime will throw an exception if the permissions are not present before the runtime runs the assembly.

- **Practice 2**   Using the same assembly as in Practice 1, add permission declarations to each method.

- **Practice 3**   Again using the same assembly, add imperative security where required.

Control Code Privileges by Using *System.Security.Policy* Classes

For this task, you should complete at least Practice 1. If you want a deeper understanding of how to analyze evidence, complete Practice 2 as well.

- **Practice 1**   Create a new code group that requires an assembly to be signed with your publisher certificate. Then verify that the .NET Framework correctly analyzes the evidence and places the assembly in the correct code group.

- **Practice 2**   Write a Console application that displays the current assembly's evidence.

Take a Practice Test

The practice tests on this book's companion CD offer many options. For example, you can test yourself on just one exam objective, or you can test yourself on all the 70-536 certification exam content. You can set up the test so that it closely simulates the experience of taking a certification exam, or you can set it up in study mode so that you can look at the correct answers and explanations after you answer each question.

MORE INFO   **Practice tests**

For details about all the practice test options available, see the section "How to Use the Practice Tests," in the Introduction of this book.

Chapter 12

User and Data Security

Businesses must be able to control who can access confidential data. For example, an expense-tracking application should show users their own expenses, but only managers should be able to view other people's expenses. Unauthorized users should not be able to view any of the data—even if they are able to bypass your application's built-in protection.

Protecting data requires coordinating several different technologies. *Role-based security (RBS)* allows you to control what users can access based on their username and group memberships. With the .NET Framework, you can make RBS decisions based on the local user database, an Active Directory Domain Services (AD DS) domain, or a custom user database. You can also use the .NET Framework to configure *access control lists* (ACLs). ACLs are the operating system's method for tracking who should have access to what and determining which actions require adding an event to the event log. Finally, to protect data if an attacker bypasses operating system security, the .NET Framework provides cryptography tools for encrypting, validating, and signing data.

Exam objectives in this chapter:

- Access and modify identity information by using the *System.Security.Principal* classes.

- Implement a custom authentication scheme by using the *System.Security .Authentication* classes.

- Implement access control by using the *System.Security.AccessControl* classes.

- Encrypt, decrypt, and hash data by using the *System.Security.Cryptography* classes.

Lessons in this chapter:

Before You Begin

To complete the lessons in this chapter, you should be familiar with Microsoft Visual Basic or C# and be comfortable with the following tasks:

- Creating a Console application in Microsoft Visual Studio using Visual Basic or C#
- Writing to files and streams
- Managing user accounts with the graphical tools built into Microsoft Windows
- Managing file permissions with the graphical tools built into Windows

Lesson 1: Authenticating and Authorizing Users

In this lesson, you learn the meaning of the term "authentication" and how it differs from authorization. You then learn how to implement and analyze both authentication (checking a user's identity) and authorization (verifying a user's right to access resources). You can use the techniques described in this lesson to protect portions of your code from unauthorized use, so that only specific users or members of specific groups can run an assembly, method, or code segment.

If your organization uses AD DS or local user databases, you can integrate your application's authorization controls into your existing directory service using the *WindowsIdentity* and *WindowsPrincipal* classes. You can also build your own authentication system or integrate into a non-Microsoft directory service. For straightforward user databases, you can use the *GenericIdentity* and *GenericPrincipal* classes. If you need complete control over users and roles, you can implement the *IIdentity* and *IPrincipal* interfaces.

After this lesson, you will be able to:

- Explain how authorization relates to authentication
- Use the *WindowsIdentity* class to examine a user's name and authentication type to make decisions within your application
- Explain the purpose of the *WindowsPrincipal* class
- Describe the purpose of the *PrincipalPermission* class
- Use declarative RBS demands to restrict access to methods
- Use imperative RBS demands to create applications that restrict access to portions of your application's logic
- Create custom identity classes by using the *IIdentity* interface, the *IPrincipal* interface, the *GenericIdentity* class, and the *GenericPrincipal* class
- Describe the different circumstances in which the runtime uses *Authentication-Exception* and *InvalidCredentialException*

Estimated lesson time: 90 minutes

Authentication and Authorization Overview

Authentication, the process of identifying a user, is the most visible and fundamental concept in security. From personal identification numbers (PINs) to driver's licenses to usernames and passwords, authentication is a part of everyone's daily life. Without authentication, restricting access to resources based on a person's identity is impossible.

Authorization is the process of verifying that a user is allowed to access a requested resource. Authorization generally happens only after authentication. After all, how can you determine whether someone is allowed to do something if you don't know who he or she is? Figure 12-1 shows how authentication and authorization together provide a user's identity and validate the user's permissions.

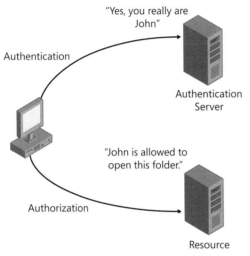

Figure 12-1   To access a resource, a user must be authenticated and then authorized

Whether you're withdrawing money from a bank, entering a restricted building, or boarding an airplane, gaining access to a restricted resource requires both authentication and authorization. The two processes are closely related and often confused. To understand the difference between authentication and authorization, consider an example in the physical world that most people are familiar with: boarding an airplane. Before you can board a plane, you must present both your identification and your ticket. Your identification, typically a driver's license or a passport, enables the airport staff to determine who you are. Validating your identity is the *authentication* part of the boarding process. The airport staff also checks your ticket to make sure that the flight you are boarding is the correct one. Verifying that you are allowed to board that particular plane is the *authorization* process.

On networks, authentication is often performed by providing a username and password. The username identifies you, and the password offers the computer system some assurance that you really are who you claim to be. After you are authenticated, the computer agrees that you are who you claim to be. However, it doesn't yet know whether you are allowed to access the resource that you are requesting. For example, managers should be allowed to view all expense reports, but regular users should be allowed to view only their own expense reports. To authorize the user, the computer system typically checks an ACL, which lists users and groups of users who are permitted to access a resource.

WindowsIdentity Class

The *System.Security.Principal.WindowsIdentity* class represents a Windows user account. This class provides access to the current user's name, authentication type, and account token. It does not allow you to authenticate a user; Windows has already taken care of the authentication. *WindowsIdentity* simply stores the results of the authentication, including the user's name and authentication token.

Generally, when you create an instance of the *WindowsIdentity* class, you call one of three methods to create the object:

- **GetAnonymous**   Returns a *WindowsIdentity* object that represents an anonymous, unauthenticated Windows user. You can use this method to impersonate an anonymous user to ensure that your code operates without credentials.

- **GetCurrent**   Returns a *WindowsIdentity* object that represents the current Windows user. You can use this method to examine the current user's username and group memberships.

- **Impersonate**   Returns a *WindowsImpersonationContext* object that represents a specified user on the system. You can use this method to impersonate a particular user account when your application has access to the user's credentials.

For example, the following code (which requires the *System.Security.Principal* namespace) creates a *WindowsIdentity* object named *currentIdentity* that represents the current user:

```vb
' VB
Dim currentIdentity As WindowsIdentity = WindowsIdentity.GetCurrent()
```

```csharp
// C#
WindowsIdentity currentIdentity = WindowsIdentity.GetCurrent();
```

After the variable is assigned, you can access several useful properties that provide information about the user:

- **AuthenticationType**   A string representing the authentication method. This is usually "NTLM".

- **IsAnonymous**   A boolean value set to *true* if the user is anonymous.

- **IsAuthenticated** A boolean value set to *true* if the user is authenticated.

- **IsGuest** A boolean value set to *true* if the user is a guest.

- **IsSystem** A boolean value set to *true* if the user is part of the system, such as the system account used by some services.

- **Name** A string representing the authentication domain and username of the user, separated by a backslash in the format, "*DOMAIN\Username*". If the user's account is in the local user database, the domain is the machine name. Otherwise, the domain represents the name of the AD DS domain.

- **Token** An integer representing the user's authentication token, assigned by the computer that authenticated the user.

Use the *WindowsIdentity* class to examine the current user's name and authentication type to determine whether the user is authorized to run privileged portions of your code. Examining objects of this class is useful if, for example, a section of your code displays information that should be available only to authenticated users

The following code (which requires the *System.Security.Principal* namespace) demonstrates the use of the *WindowsIdentity* class by displaying information about the current user:

```
' VB
' Grab the current user
Dim currentIdentity As WindowsIdentity = WindowsIdentity.GetCurrent()

' Display the name, token, and authentication type for the current user
Console.WriteLine("Name: " + currentIdentity.Name)
Console.WriteLine("Token: " + currentIdentity.Token.ToString())
Console.WriteLine("Authentication Type: " + _
    currentIdentity.AuthenticationType)

' Display information based on Boolean properties of the current user
If currentIdentity.IsAnonymous = True Then
    Console.WriteLine("Is an anonymous user")
End If
If currentIdentity.IsAuthenticated = True Then
    Console.WriteLine("Is an authenticated user")
End If
If currentIdentity.IsSystem = True Then
    Console.WriteLine("Is part of the system")
End If
If currentIdentity.IsGuest = True Then
    Console.WriteLine("Is a guest")
End If
```

```
// C#
// Grab the current user
WindowsIdentity currentIdentity = WindowsIdentity.GetCurrent();

// Display the name, token, and authentication type for the current user
Console.WriteLine("Name: " + currentIdentity.Name);
Console.WriteLine("Token: " + currentIdentity.Token.ToString());
Console.WriteLine("Authentication Type: " +
    currentIdentity.AuthenticationType);

// Display information based on Boolean properties of
// the current user
if (currentIdentity.IsAnonymous)
    Console.WriteLine("Is an anonymous user");
if (currentIdentity.IsAuthenticated)
    Console.WriteLine("Is an authenticated user");
if (currentIdentity.IsGuest)
    Console.WriteLine("Is a guest");
if (currentIdentity.IsSystem)
    Console.WriteLine("Is part of the system");
```

WindowsPrincipal Class

The *System.Security.Principal.WindowsPrincipal* class provides access to a user's group memberships. This class must be created by using an instance of the *WindowsIdentity* class. For example, the following code creates a *WindowsIdentity* object named *currentIdentity* that represents the current user, and then it creates a *WindowsPrincipal* object named *currentPrincipal* that represents the current user:

```
' VB
Dim currentIdentity As WindowsIdentity = WindowsIdentity.GetCurrent()
Dim currentPrincipal As WindowsPrincipal = _
    New WindowsPrincipal(currentIdentity)
```

```
// C#
WindowsIdentity currentIdentity = WindowsIdentity.GetCurrent();
WindowsPrincipal currentPrincipal = new WindowsPrincipal(currentIdentity);
```

As an alternative to creating a *WindowsIdentity* object using the *WindowsIdentity.GetCurrent* method, you can extract the current *WindowsPrincipal* object by querying the current thread directly. To do this, first set the current principal policy to use Windows security, and then create a new *WindowsPrincipal* object by casting *System.Threading.Thread.CurrentPrincipal* as a *WindowsPrincipal* object. The following code (which requires both the *System.Security.Principal* and *System.Threading* namespaces) demonstrates this:

```
' VB
' Specify that WindowsPrincipal should be used
AppDomain.CurrentDomain.SetPrincipalPolicy(PrincipalPolicy.WindowsPrincipal)
```

```
' Cast the current principal as a WindowsPrincipal object
Dim currentPrincipal As WindowsPrincipal = _
    CType(Thread.CurrentPrincipal, WindowsPrincipal)
```

```
// C#
// Specify that WindowsPrincipal should be used
AppDomain.CurrentDomain.SetPrincipalPolicy(PrincipalPolicy.WindowsPrincipal);

// Cast the current principal as a WindowsPrincipal object
WindowsPrincipal currentPrincipal = (WindowsPrincipal)Thread.CurrentPrincipal;
```

You can use the *WindowsPrincipal* class to determine which groups a user is a member of. To query for built-in groups, pass to the *WindowsPrincipal.IsInRole* method a member of the *System.Security.Principal.WindowsBuiltInRole* class. Each member of the *WindowsBuiltInRole* class represents a built-in group that exists either within the computer's local user database or within an AD DS domain. For example, the following portion of a Console application checks three separate members of the *WindowsBuiltInRole* class and displays whether the current local user is a member:

```
' VB
' Create a WindowsIdentity object representing the current user
Dim currentIdentity As WindowsIdentity =  WindowsIdentity.GetCurrent()

' Create a WindowsPrincipal object representing the current user
Dim currentPrincipal As WindowsPrincipal = _
    New WindowsPrincipal(currentIdentity)

Console.WriteLine("The current user is a member of the following roles: ")

' Check for three common group memberships
If currentPrincipal.IsInRole(WindowsBuiltInRole.Administrator) Then
    Console.WriteLine(WindowsBuiltInRole.Administrator.ToString())
End If
If currentPrincipal.IsInRole(WindowsBuiltInRole.PowerUser) Then
    Console.WriteLine(WindowsBuiltInRole.PowerUser.ToString())
End If
If currentPrincipal.IsInRole(WindowsBuiltInRole.User) Then
    Console.WriteLine(WindowsBuiltInRole.User.ToString())
End If
```

```
// C#
// Create a WindowsIdentity object representing the current user
WindowsIdentity currentIdentity = WindowsIdentity.GetCurrent();

// Create a WindowsPrincipal object representing the current user
WindowsPrincipal currentPrincipal = new WindowsPrincipal(currentIdentity);

Console.WriteLine("The current user is a member of the following roles: ");
```

```
// Check for three common group memberships
if (currentPrincipal.IsInRole(WindowsBuiltInRole.Administrator))
    Console.WriteLine(WindowsBuiltInRole.Administrator.ToString());
if (currentPrincipal.IsInRole(WindowsBuiltInRole.PowerUser))
    Console.WriteLine(WindowsBuiltInRole.PowerUser.ToString());
if (currentPrincipal.IsInRole(WindowsBuiltInRole.User))
    Console.WriteLine(WindowsBuiltInRole.User.ToString());
```

The presence of built-in groups varies depending on the operating system and whether the computer is a domain controller, so always be prepared to catch an exception when checking user roles.

To query for custom groups or groups in a domain rather than for the local user database, pass a string value to the overloaded *IsInRole* method in the format "*DOMAIN\Group Name*". For example, if you have code that should execute only if the user is a member of the CONTOSO\Accountants group, you could use the following *if* statement:

```
' VB
If currentPrincipal.IsInRole("CONTOSO\Accounting") Then
    Console.WriteLine("User is in Accounting")
End If
```

```
// C#
if (currentPrincipal.IsInRole(@"CONTOSO\Accounting"))
    Console.WriteLine("User is in Accounting");
```

In most circumstances, however, you will not know the computer name or domain name ahead of time to insert it into the string you pass the *IsInRole* method. Instead, construct it using the *System.Environment.MachineName* string property or the *System.Environment.UserDomainName* string property. *System.Environment.MachineName* can be used to specify group names only on the local computer. Use *System.Environment.UserDomainName* to specify group names that exist on the local computer or in the AD DS domain, depending on how the user logged on.

PrincipalPermission Class

The *System.Security.Permissions.PrincipalPermission* class and the related *PrincipalPermissionAttribute* class enable you to check the active principal for both declarative and imperative security actions. They (collectively referred to as *PrincipalPermission*) are typically used to demand declaratively that users running your code have been authenticated or belong to a specified role. By passing identity information (username, role, or both) to the constructor, *PrincipalPermission* can be used to demand that the identity of the active principal match this information.

You can set any combination of three properties for *PrincipalPermission*:

- **Authenticated**   A boolean value. If set to *true*, the permission requires the user to be authenticated.

- **Name**   A string that must match the identity's username.

- **Role**   A string that must match one of the principal's roles.

Exam Tip   Memorize these three properties. Remember, *PrincipalPermission* doesn't expose any other properties—not a user's full name, phone number, password, or any other attribute.

PrincipalPermission has several methods; however, only the *PrincipalPermission .Demand* method is used with the RBS techniques described in this chapter. The *Demand* method verifies that the active principal meets the requirements specified in the *Authenticated*, *Name*, and *Role* properties. If the principal does not match any non-null properties, the principal throws an exception.

How to Use Declarative RBS Demands to Restrict Access to Methods

Declarative RBS demands instruct the runtime to perform an RBS check before running a method. This is the most secure way to use RBS to restrict access to code because security is enforced by the runtime before it runs your code. There are two primary disadvantages to declarative RBS demands:

- They can be used only to restrict access to entire methods.

- They might result in the runtime throwing an exception. If the method was called by a Windows event, Windows catches the exception, and your application might stop running.

To use declarative RBS demands, you must have three elements in your code:

- The *System.AppDomain.CurrentDomain.SetPrincipalPolicy* method to specify the principal security policy

- A *try/catch* block to catch underprivileged access attempts and to report the error appropriately

- A *PrincipalPermission* attribute to declare the method's access requirements

First, specify the principal policy for the thread from within your application using the *System.AppDomain.CurrentDomain.SetPrincipalPolicy* method, as described earlier in this lesson. Next, create a *try/catch* block to catch the *System.Security.SecurityException* exceptions that the runtime will throw when it attempts to run the method but lacks the permission demanded. It's important to catch this type of exception and provide a useful error message to the user because without the error message, the user could quickly become frustrated and might spend a significant amount of time attempting to troubleshoot the access problem. In addition, log failed access attempts so that administrators can analyze the events to detect potential compromises.

For example, the following code calls a method named *AdministratorsOnlyMethod* (not shown) that is protected with a declarative RBS demand and displays a message box if the user lacks the necessary permission:

```
' VB
Try
    AdministratorsOnlyMethod()
Catch ex As System.Security.SecurityException
    MessageBox.Show("Your account lacks permission to that function.")
End Try
```

```
// C#
try
    { AdministratorsOnlyMethod(); }
catch (System.Security.SecurityException ex)
    { MessageBox.Show("Your account lacks permission to that function."); }
```

Finally, add declarative permission statements using the *PrincipalPermission* class before each method to which you need to restrict access. You must define two things for *PrincipalPermission*:

- The action that *PrincipalPermission* will take using the *System.Security.Permissions.SecurityAction* enumeration. Typically, you use *SecurityAction.Demand* for declarative RBS.

- One or more *PrincipalPermission* properties. Use *Authenticated* to restrict access to authenticated users, *Role* to restrict access by group memberships, and *User* to restrict access to a specific username.

For example, the following code (which requires the *System.Security.Permissions* namespace) causes the runtime to throw a *System.Security.SecurityException* when the user is not a member of the local Administrators group:

```
' VB
<PrincipalPermission(SecurityAction.Demand, Role:="BUILTIN\Administrators")> _
Private Sub AdministratorsOnlyMethod ()
    ' Code that can only be run by Administrators
End Sub
```

```
// C#
[PrincipalPermission(SecurityAction.Demand, Role = @"BUILTIN\Administrators")]
static void AdministratorsOnlyMethod()
{
    // Code that can only be run by Administrators
}
```

You can also use multiple declarative demands to enable users who meet any of the demands to execute the code. The following code enables any of the following to run the method:

- An account named Administrator

- A user named CONTOSO\User1 who is also a member of the CONTOSO\Managers group

- Any user who is authenticated

```
' VB
<PrincipalPermission(SecurityAction.Demand, _
    Name:="CONTOSO\Administrator")> _
<PrincipalPermission(SecurityAction.Demand, _
    Name:="CONTOSO\User1", Role:="CONTOSO\Managers")> _
<PrincipalPermission(SecurityAction.Demand, Authenticated:=True)> _
Private Sub AdministratorsOnlyMethod ()
    ' Code that can only be run by specified users
End Sub
```

```
// C#
[PrincipalPermission(SecurityAction.Demand,
    Name = @"CONTOSO\Administrator")]
[PrincipalPermission(SecurityAction.Demand,
    Name = @"CONTOSO\User1", Role = @"CONTOSO\Managers")]
[PrincipalPermission(SecurityAction.Demand, Authenticated = true)]
static void AdministratorsOnlyMethod()
{
    // Code that can only be run by specified users
}
```

Before demanding permissions using Windows security, you must set the application domain's principal policy to *WindowsPrincipal*. Otherwise, demands for principal permissions fail.

How to Use Imperative RBS Demands to Create Applications That Restrict Access to Portions of Their Logic

Imperative RBS demands are declared within your code and can be used to restrict access to portions of code on a more specific basis than declarative RBS demands. In other words, imperative RBS demands allow you to restrict portions of a method, whereas declarative RBS demands require you to restrict entire methods. To use imperative RBS demands, you must have four elements in your code:

- The *System.AppDomain.CurrentDomain.SetPrincipalPolicy* method to specify the principal security policy
- A *try/catch* block to catch underprivileged access attempts and report the error appropriately
- A *PrincipalPermission* object, with properties set according to the restrictions you want to impose
- A call to the *PrincipalPermission.Demand* method to declare the method's access requirements

The first two elements are exactly the same as those required by declarative RBS demands and should be implemented in exactly the same way. The use of the *PrincipalPermission* class is different, however. First, you must create a new *Principal-Permission* object. *PrincipalPermission* has three overloaded constructors:

- **PrincipalPermission(PermissionState)**   Enables you to specify the *PrincipalPermisson* object's properties by using a *System.Security.Permissions.PermissionState* object.

- **PrincipalPermission(Name, Role)**   Specifies values for the new object's *Name* and *Role* properties. If you want to specify only a username or a role, simply specify *null* for the other value.

- **PrincipalPermission(Name, Role, Authenticated)**   Specifies values for the new object's *Name*, *Role*, and *Authenticated* properties. Specify *null* for any properties that you do not want to use to restrict access.

The following two lines of code throw an exception when the user is not a member of the local Administrators group. Note that the first argument to the *PrincipalPermission* constructor is *null*, which indicates that no particular username is required. The last argument, set to *true*, requires that the user be authenticated (which is redundant and could effectively be left out because no unauthenticated user would be a member of the Administrators group):

```vb
' VB
Dim p As PrincipalPermission= New PrincipalPermission (Nothing, _
    "BUILTIN\Administrators", True)
p.Demand
```

```csharp
// C#
PrincipalPermission p = new PrincipalPermission(null,
    @"BUILTIN\Administrators", true);
p.Demand();
```

To tie the imperative use of the *PrincipalPermission* object into a larger application, consider the following code. This code displays "Access allowed" if the current user is a member of the local VS Developers group. Otherwise, it catches the exception thrown by the *PrincipalPermission.Demand* method and displays "Access denied":

```vb
' VB
' Define the security policy in use as Windows security
System.AppDomain.CurrentDomain.SetPrincipalPolicy( _
    PrincipalPolicy.WindowsPrincipal)

' Concatenate the group name as "MachineName\VS Developers"
Dim r As String = System.Environment.MachineName + "\VS Developers"

' Catch any security denied exceptions so that they can be logged
Try
    ' Create and demand the PrincipalPermission object
    Dim p As PrincipalPermission = New PrincipalPermission( _
        Nothing, r, True)
    p.Demand()
    Console.WriteLine("Access allowed.")
    ' TODO: Main application
Catch ex As System.Security.SecurityException
    Console.WriteLine("Access denied: " + ex.Message)
    ' TODO: Log error
End Try
```

```csharp
// C#
// Define the security policy in use as Windows security
System.AppDomain.CurrentDomain.SetPrincipalPolicy(
    PrincipalPolicy.WindowsPrincipal);

// Concatenate the group name as "MachineName\VS Developers"
string r = System.Environment.MachineName + @"\VS Developers";

// Catch any security denied exceptions so that they can be logged
try
{
    // Create and demand the PrincipalPermission object
    PrincipalPermission p = new PrincipalPermission(null, r, true);
    p.Demand();

    Console.WriteLine("Access allowed.");
    // TODO: Main application
}
catch(System.Security.SecurityException ex)
{
    Console.WriteLine("Access denied: " + ex.Message);
    // TODO: Log error
}
```

How to Implement Custom Users and Roles

If you need to authenticate users against a custom database, you can use the *System.Security.Principal.IIdentity* and *System.Security.Principal.IPrincipal* interfaces. You can extend these interfaces by implementing your own classes with additional properties and functionalities. For example, you could create your own *IIdentity*-based class that includes custom user attributes such as name and address, or you could create your own *IPrincipal*-based class that implements hierarchical roles.

How to Create a Custom Identity Class

The *IIdentity* interface is a template for creating identity classes. The *WindowsIdentity* class is an implementation of *IIdentity*, and the bulk of *WindowsIdentity*'s properties and methods are inherited directly from *IIdentity*. Similarly, *FormsIdentity* and *PassportIdentity* implement *IIdentity* for working with Web authentication, and the *GenericIdentity* class provides a very flexible implementation of *IIdentity*.

If none of the existing implementations of *IIdentity* suits your needs, you can extend *IIdentity*'s functionality by creating your own class based on it. By doing this, you can add any properties you see fit. After creating the class, you can use the new class in the same ways you used *WindowsIdentity*.

To implement *IIdentity*, you must implement the following properties:

- **AuthenticationType**   A string used to store a description of the user's authentication mechanism. Applications can use this property to determine whether the authentication mechanism can be trusted. For example, one application might determine that Passport authentication meets the security requirements but Basic authentication does not. If you create a custom authentication mechanism, specify a unique *AuthenticationType*.

- **IsAuthenticated**   A boolean value that should be set to *true* if the user has been authenticated. If you create your own custom authentication mechanism, set this value when the user is authenticated.

- **Name**   A string that stores the user's username. This property must exist, even when your authentication mechanism does not use a username. It must uniquely identify the user; only one account should have any given name.

In addition, you need to implement a constructor that defines each of the object's properties.

The following class implements *IIdentity* and adds properties for the user's first and last name, address, city, state, and postal code. This class provides two constructors: one that takes no parameters and initializes all properties to a default state, and a second one that initializes every property.

```vb
' VB
Public Class CustomIdentity
    Implements IIdentity
    Private _isAuthenticated As Boolean
    Private _name As String
    Private _authenticationType As String
    Private _firstName As String
    Private _lastName As String
    Private _address As String
    Private _city As String
    Private _state As String
    Private _zip As String

    Public Sub New()
        Me._name = String.Empty
        Me._isAuthenticated = False
        Me._authenticationType = "None"
        Me._firstName = String.Empty
        Me._lastName = String.Empty
        Me._address = String.Empty
        Me._city = String.Empty
        Me._state = String.Empty
        Me._zip = String.Empty
    End Sub

    Public Sub New(ByVal isLogin As Boolean, _
        ByVal newAuthenticationType As String, _
        ByVal newFirstName As String, ByVal newLastName As String, _
        ByVal newAddress As String, _
        ByVal newCity As String, ByVal newState As String, _
        ByVal newZip As String)

        Me._name = newFirstName + newLastName
        Me._isAuthenticated = isLogin
        Me._authenticationType = newAuthenticationType
        Me._firstName = newFirstName
        Me._lastName = newLastName
        Me._address = newAddress
        Me._city = newCity
        Me._state = newState
        Me._zip = newZip
    End Sub

    Public ReadOnly Property IsAuthenticated() As Boolean _
        Implements IIdentity.IsAuthenticated
```

```vb
        Get
            Return Me._isAuthenticated
        End Get
    End Property

    Public ReadOnly Property Name() As String Implements IIdentity.Name
        Get
            Return Me._name
        End Get
    End Property

    Public ReadOnly Property AuthenticationType() As String _
        Implements IIdentity.AuthenticationType

        Get
            Return Me._authenticationType
        End Get
    End Property

    Public ReadOnly Property FirstName() As String
        Get
            Return Me._firstName
        End Get
    End Property

    Public ReadOnly Property LastName() As String
        Get
            Return Me._lastName
        End Get
    End Property

    Public ReadOnly Property Address() As String
        Get
            Return Me._address
        End Get
    End Property

    Public ReadOnly Property City() As String
        Get
            Return Me._city
        End Get
    End Property

    Public ReadOnly Property State() As String
        Get
            Return Me._state
        End Get
    End Property

    Public ReadOnly Property Zip() As String
        Get
            Return Me._zip
        End Get
    End Property
End Class
```

```csharp
// C#
class CustomIdentity : IIdentity
{
    // Implement private variables for standard properties
    private bool isAuthenticated;
    private string name, authenticationType;

    // Implement private variables for custom properties
    private string firstName, lastName, address, city, state, zip;

    // Allow the creation of an empty object
    public CustomIdentity()
    {
        this.name = String.Empty;
        this.isAuthenticated = false;
        this.authenticationType = "None";

        this.firstName = String.Empty;
        this.lastName = String.Empty;
        this.address = String.Empty;
        this.city = String.Empty;
        this.state = String.Empty;
        this.zip = String.Empty;
    }

    // Allow caller to create the object and specify all properties
    public CustomIdentity(bool isLogin, string newAuthenticationType,
        string newFirstName,
        string newLastName, string newAddress, string newCity,
        string newState, string newZip)
    {
        // Create a unique username by concatenating first and last name
        this.name = newFirstName + newLastName;
        this.isAuthenticated = isLogin;
        this.authenticationType = newAuthenticationType;

        this.firstName = newFirstName;
        this.lastName = newLastName;
        this.address = newAddress;
        this.city = newCity;
        this.state = newState;
        this.zip = newZip;
    }

    // Implement public read-only interfaces for standard properties
    public bool IsAuthenticated
    { get { return this.isAuthenticated; } }

    public string Name
    { get { return this.name; } }

    public string AuthenticationType
    { get { return this.authenticationType; } }
```

```
// Implement public, read-only interfaces for custom properties
public string FirstName
{ get { return this.firstName; } }

public string LastName
{ get { return this.lastName; } }

public string Address
{ get { return this.address; } }

public string City
{ get { return this.city; } }

public string State
{ get { return this.state; } }

public string Zip
{ get { return this.zip; } }
}
```

BEST PRACTICES   When Not to Implement *IIdentity*

This code shows how to implement a custom identity based on *IIdentity*. However, if you want to add properties to a Windows logon while still using the Windows token or other Windows security properties, base your custom identity on the *WindowsIdentity* class instead. The same applies for *IPrincipal* and *WindowsPrincipal*.

How to Create a Custom Principal Class

Just as *WindowsIdentity* is based on *IIdentity*, the *WindowsPrincipal* and *GenericPrincipal* classes are based on the *IPrincipal* interface. Objects based on the *IPrincipal* interface represent the security context of a user, including that user's identity and any roles or groups to which they belong.

To implement *IPrincipal*, you must implement at least one constructor, one property, and one method. The constructor must accept an *IIdentity* object and an array of strings containing the identity's roles, although you can add overloaded constructors. The property that you must implement is *IPrincipal.Identity*, which should return the principal's identity object (which must be defined when the object is constructed). The method is the boolean *IPrincipal.IsInRole*, which takes a single string indicating the role being queried, and returns *true* when the principal's identity is a member of that role. Otherwise, it returns *false*.

You can add the following interesting functionalities by overriding *IPrincipal*:

- Add a *Roles* property that returns an array of strings containing the roles the user is a member of.

- Add *IsInAllRoles* and *IsInAnyRole* methods that determine whether the user is a member of multiple roles.

- Add *IsHigherThanRole* and *IsLowerThanRole* methods to enable hierarchical group memberships. For example, a principal who is a member of the Presidents role would evaluate *IPrincipal.IsHigherThanRole("Vice-Presidents")* as *true*.

To create a custom principal class, implement it based on *IPrincipal*; and at a minimum override the constructor, the *Identity* property, and the *IsInRole* method. For example, the following class implements the *IPrincipal* interface without extending the functionality:

```vb
' VB
Public Class CustomPrincipal
    Implements IPrincipal

    ' Implement private variables for standard properties
    Private _identity As IIdentity
    Private _roles As String()

    ' Allow caller to create the object and specify all properties
    Public Sub New(ByVal identity As IIdentity, ByVal roles As String())
        _identity = identity
        roles.CopyTo(_roles, 0)
        Array.Sort(_roles)
    End Sub

    ' Implement public read-only interfaces for standard properties
    Public Function IsInRole(ByVal role As String) As Boolean _
        Implements IPrincipal.IsInRole

        If Array.BinarySearch(_roles, role) >= 0 Then
            Return True
        Else
            Return False
        End If
    End Function

    Public ReadOnly Property Identity() As IIdentity _
        Implements IPrincipal.Identity

        Get
            Return _identity
        End Get
    End Property
End Class
```

```csharp
// C#
class CustomPrincipal : IPrincipal
{
    private IIdentity _identity;
    private string[] _roles;
```

```
    // Allow caller to create the object and specify all properties
    public CustomPrincipal(IIdentity identity, string[] roles)
    {
        _identity = identity;
        _roles = new string[roles.Length];
        roles.CopyTo(_roles, 0);
        Array.Sort(_roles);
    }

    public IIdentity Identity
    { get { return _identity; } }

    public bool IsInRole(string role)
    { return Array.BinarySearch(_roles, role) >= 0 ? true : false; }
}
```

How to Create Simple Custom User Privilege Models

If you don't want to use any of the classes based on *IIdentity* and *IPrincipal* that are built into the runtime, and you need only the basic functionality provided by the *IIdentity* and *IPrincipal* interfaces, use *System.Security.Principal.GenericIdentity* and *System.Security.Principal.GenericPrincipal*. These classes, provided by the runtime, implement only the properties and methods required by the interfaces. They each provide constructors that your application must use to specify each class's properties.

GenericIdentity has two overloaded constructors. To create a new *GenericIdentity* object, you can use just a username, or you can use both a username and an authentication type. You can't change these values later; you must specify them when the object is created. The following code sample demonstrates both usages:

```
' VB
Dim myUser1 As GenericIdentity = New GenericIdentity("JHealy")
Dim myUser2 As GenericIdentity = New GenericIdentity("TAdams", "SmartCard")
```

```
// C#
GenericIdentity myUser1 = new GenericIdentity("JHealy");
GenericIdentity myUser2 = new GenericIdentity("TAdams", "SmartCard");
```

GenericPrincipal has only a single constructor that requires both a *GenericIdentity* object and an array of strings containing the identity's roles. The following code sample extends the previous code sample to demonstrate how to create a *GenericPrincipal* object where *myUser1* is a *GenericIdentity* object that was previously created:

```
' VB
Dim myUser1Roles() As String = New String() {"IT", "Users", "Administrators"}
Dim myPrincipal1 As GenericPrincipal = _New GenericPrincipal(myUser1, myUser1Roles)
```

```
// C#
String[] myUser1Roles = new String[]{"IT", "Users", "Administrators"};
GenericPrincipal myPrincipal1 =
    new GenericPrincipal(myUser1, myUser1Roles);
```

After creating the principal object in the previous code sample, *myPrincipal1.IsIn-Role("Users")* method would return *true*.

How to Use RBS Demands with Custom Identities and Principals

Whether you define custom *IIdentity* and *IPrincipal* interfaces or use *GenericIdentity* and *GenericPrincipal*, you can take advantage of the same declarative and imperative RBS techniques used for *WindowsIdentity* and *WindowsPrincipal*. To do this, perform the following steps in your application:

1. Create an *IIdentity* or *GenericIdentity* object representing the current user.
2. Create an *IPrincipal* or *GenericPrincipal* object based on your *IIdentity* object.
3. Set the *Thread.CurrentPrincipal* property to your *IPrincipal* object.
4. Add any declarative or imperative RBS demands required.

The following Console application (which requires the *System.Security.Permissions*, *System.Security.Principal*, and *System.Threading* namespaces) performs all these steps to demonstrate how to use declarative RBS demands with the *GenericIdentity* and *Generic-Principal* classes. In this example, only members of the IT role can run the *TestSecurity* method. Two identities and principals are created. The object *myUser1*, with the username JHealy, is a member of the IT role and should be able to run the method. The object *myUser2*, with the username TAdams, is not a member of that role:

```
' VB
Sub Main()
    Dim myUser1 As GenericIdentity = New GenericIdentity("JHealy")
    Dim myUser1Roles As String() = _
        New String() {"IT", "Users", "Administrators"}
    Dim myPrincipal1 As GenericPrincipal = _
        New GenericPrincipal(myUser1, myUser1Roles)

    Dim myUser2 As GenericIdentity = New GenericIdentity("TAdams")
    Dim myUser2Roles As String() = New String() {"Users"}
    Dim myPrincipal2 As GenericPrincipal = _
        New GenericPrincipal(myUser2, myUser2Roles)

    Try
        Thread.CurrentPrincipal = myPrincipal1
        TestSecurity()

        Thread.CurrentPrincipal = myPrincipal2
        TestSecurity()
```

```
        Catch ex As Exception
            Console.WriteLine(ex.GetType.ToString + " caused by " + _
                Thread.CurrentPrincipal.Identity.Name)
        End Try
    End Sub


    <PrincipalPermissionAttribute(SecurityAction.Demand, Role:="IT")> _
    Private Sub TestSecurity()
        Console.WriteLine(Thread.CurrentPrincipal.Identity.Name + " is in IT.")
    End Sub
```

```
// C#
static void Main(string[] args)
{
    GenericIdentity myUser1 = new GenericIdentity("JHealy");
    String[] myUser1Roles = new String[]{"IT", "Users", "Administrators"};
    GenericPrincipal myPrincipal1 =
        new GenericPrincipal(myUser1, myUser1Roles);

    GenericIdentity myUser2 = new GenericIdentity("TAdams");
    String[] myUser2Roles = new String[]{"Users"};
    GenericPrincipal myPrincipal2 =
        new GenericPrincipal(myUser2, myUser2Roles);

    try
    {
        Thread.CurrentPrincipal = myPrincipal1;
        TestSecurity();

        Thread.CurrentPrincipal = myPrincipal2;
        TestSecurity();
    }
    catch(Exception ex)
    { Console.WriteLine(ex.GetType().ToString() + " caused by " +
            Thread.CurrentPrincipal.Identity.Name); }
}

[PrincipalPermission(SecurityAction.Demand, Role = "IT")]
private static void TestSecurity()
{ Console.WriteLine(Thread.CurrentPrincipal.Identity.Name + " is in IT."); }
```

This application produces the following output, which verifies that the declarative RBS demand does protect the *TestSecurity* method from users who are not in the IT role:

```
JHealy is in IT.
System.Security.SecurityException caused by TAdams
```

Handling Authentication Exceptions in Streams

When authenticating to remote computers using the *System.Net.Security.Negotiate-Stream* or *System.Net.Security.SslStream* classes, the .NET Framework throws an exception if either the client or server cannot be properly authenticated. Therefore, you should always be prepared to catch one of the following exceptions when using *NegotiateStream* or *SslStream*:

- **System.Security.Authentication.AuthenticationException** An exception of this type indicates that you should prompt the user to provide different credentials and then retry authentication.

- **System.Security.Authentication.InvalidCredentialException** An exception of this type indicates that the underlying stream is not in a valid state, and the user cannot retry authentication.

Lab: Adding RBS to an Application

In this lab, you will add RBS security to an application so that features are limited based on the user's name and group membership. If you encounter a problem completing an exercise, the completed projects are available along with the sample files.

Exercise: Protect an Application with RBS

In this exercise, you will update a Windows Forms calculator application to include RBS. You will use the most secure techniques possible to meet the following requirements:

- Only members of the Users group can run the method linked to the Add button.
- Only members of the Administrators group can run the *multiply* method.
- Only the CPhilips user can run the method linked to the Divide button.
- You must hide buttons to which users do not have access.

    1. Navigate to the <*InstallHome*>\Chapter12\Lesson1\Exercise1\Partial folder and open either the C# version or the Visual Basic .NET version of the solution file.

    2. Add the *System.Security.Permissions* and *System.Security.Principal* namespaces to your code.

    3. To enable you to check Windows group memberships, set the principal policy to Windows Policy. You should do this in a method that will run when the form opens, such as the form constructor (which might be hidden in a collapsed region titled Windows Forms Designer Generated Code). The following code works:

```
' VB
Public Sub New()
    MyBase.New()
    InitializeComponent()
```

```
    ' Set the security policy context to Windows security
    System.AppDomain.CurrentDomain.SetPrincipalPolicy( _
        PrincipalPolicy.WindowsPrincipal)
End Sub
```

```
// C#
public Form1()
{
    InitializeComponent();

    // Set the security policy context to Windows security
    System.AppDomain.CurrentDomain.SetPrincipalPolicy(
        PrincipalPolicy.WindowsPrincipal);
}
```

4. Address the first requirement, "Only members of the Users group can run the method linked to the Add button." The following code works for the *addButton_Click* method:

```
' VB
Try
    ' Demand that user is member of the built-in Users group.
    ' Because this method is called by a Windows event, protect it
    ' with an imperative RBS demand.
    Dim userPermission As PrincipalPermission = _
        New PrincipalPermission(Nothing, "BUILTIN\Users")
    userPermission.Demand()

    ' Perform calculations
    Dim answer As Integer = (Integer.Parse(integer1.Text) + _
        Integer.Parse(integer2.Text))
    answerLabel.Text = answer.ToString()
Catch ex As System.Security.SecurityException
    ' Display message box explaining access denial
    MessageBox.Show("You have been denied access: " + ex.Message)
    ' TODO: Log error
End Try
```

```
// C#
try
{
    // Demand that user is member of the built-in Users group.
    // Because this method is called by a Windows event, protect it
    // with an imperative RBS demand.
    PrincipalPermission userPermission =
        new PrincipalPermission(null, @"BUILTIN\Users");
    userPermission.Demand();

    // Perform the calculation
    int answer = (int.Parse(integer1.Text) + int.Parse(integer2.Text));
    answerLabel.Text = answer.ToString();
}
```

```
catch (System.Security.SecurityException ex)
{
    // Display message box explaining access denial
    MessageBox.Show("You have been denied access: " + ex.Message);
    // TODO: Log error
}
```

5. Address the second requirement, "Only members of the Administrators group can run the *multiply* method." Because the *multiply* method is not called directly by a Windows event, you can use declarative security. The following code declaration protects the *multiply* method:

```
' VB
<PrincipalPermission(SecurityAction.Demand, _
    Role:="BUILTIN\Administrators")> _
```

```
// C#
[PrincipalPermission(SecurityAction.Demand,
    Role = @"BUILTIN\Administrators")]
```

6. Address the third requirement, "Only the CPhilips user can run the method linked to the Divide button." The following code works for the *divideButton_Click* method:

```
' VB
' Concatenate the computer and username
Dim allowUser As String = System.Environment.MachineName + "\cphilips"
Try
    ' Demand that user has the username "cphilips" on the local
    ' computer. Because this method is called by a Windows event,
    ' protect it with an imperative RBS demand.
    Dim p As PrincipalPermission = _
        New PrincipalPermission(allowUser, Nothing)
    p.Demand()

    ' Perform super-secret mathematical calculations
    Dim answer As Decimal = (Decimal.Parse(integer1.Text) _
        / Decimal.Parse(integer2.Text))
    answerLabel.Text = Decimal.Round(answer, 2).ToString()
Catch ex As System.Security.SecurityException
    ' Display message box explaining access denial
    MessageBox.Show("You have been denied access: " + ex.Message)
    ' TODO: Log error
End Try
```

```
// C#
// Concatenate the computer and username
string allowUser = System.Environment.MachineName + @"\cphilips";
try
{
    // Demand that user has the username "cphilips" on the local
    // computer. Because this method is called by a Windows event,
```

```
    // protect it with an imperative RBS demand.
    PrincipalPermission p = new PrincipalPermission(allowUser, null);
    p.Demand();

    // Perform super-secret mathematical calculations
    Decimal answer = (Decimal.Parse(integer1.Text)
        / Decimal.Parse(integer2.Text));
    answerLabel.Text = Decimal.Round(answer, 2).ToString();
}
catch (System.Security.SecurityException ex)
{
    // Display message box explaining access denial
    MessageBox.Show("You have been denied access: " + ex.Message);
    // TODO: Log error
}
```

7. Address the fourth requirement, "You must hide buttons to which users do not have access." You should do this in a method that runs when the form opens, such as the form constructor. The following code works:

```
' VB
Public Sub New()
    MyBase.New()
    InitializeComponent()

    ' Create a WindowsIdentity object representing the current user
    Dim currentIdentity As WindowsIdentity = WindowsIdentity.GetCurrent()

    ' Create a WindowsPrincipal object representing the current user
    Dim currentPrincipal As WindowsPrincipal = _
        New WindowsPrincipal(currentIdentity)

    ' Set the security policy context to Windows security
    System.AppDomain.CurrentDomain.SetPrincipalPolicy( _
        PrincipalPolicy.WindowsPrincipal)

    ' Hide the subtract and multiply buttons if the user
    ' is not an Administrator
    If Not currentPrincipal.IsInRole(WindowsBuiltInRole.Administrator) Then
        subtractButton.Visible = False
        multiplyButton.Visible = False
    End If

    ' Hide the Add button if the user is not in the Users group
    If Not currentPrincipal.IsInRole(WindowsBuiltInRole.User) Then
        addButton.Visible = False
    End If

    ' Hide the Divide button if the user is not named CPhilips
    If Not (currentIdentity.Name.ToLower() = _
        System.Environment.MachineName.ToLower() + "\cphilips") Then
        divideButton.Visible = False
    End If
End Sub
```

```
// C#
public Form1()
{
    InitializeComponent();

    // Create a WindowsIdentity object representing the current user
    WindowsIdentity currentIdentity = WindowsIdentity.GetCurrent();

    // Create a WindowsPrincipal object representing the current user
    WindowsPrincipal currentPrincipal =
        new WindowsPrincipal(currentIdentity);

    // Set the security policy context to Windows security
    System.AppDomain.CurrentDomain.SetPrincipalPolicy(
        PrincipalPolicy.WindowsPrincipal);

    // Hide the subtract and multiply buttons if the user
    // is not an Administrator
    if (!currentPrincipal.IsInRole(WindowsBuiltInRole.Administrator))
    {
        subtractButton.Visible = false;
        multiplyButton.Visible = false;
    }

    // Hide the Add button if the user is not in the Users group
    if (!currentPrincipal.IsInRole(WindowsBuiltInRole.User))
        addButton.Visible = false;

    // Hide the Divide button if the user is not named CPhilips
    if (!(currentIdentity.Name.ToLower() ==
        System.Environment.MachineName.ToLower() + @"\cphilips"))
        divideButton.Visible = false;
}
```

8. Build and run your project. Test it when running with different user accounts, including a user account named Cphilips, a user account that is a member of the Administrators group, and a user account that is only a member of the Users group.

Lesson Summary

- Authentication, such as checking your photo identification, verifies your identity by requiring you to provide unique credentials that are not easily impersonated. Authorization, such as checking your plane ticket, verifies that you have permission to perform the action you are attempting. Authentication, which determines who you are, must happen before authorization, which determines whether you are allowed to access a resource.

- The *WindowsIdentity* class provides .NET Framework applications access to a Windows user's account properties. You can examine the current user's username and authentication type by creating a new *WindowsIdentity* object using the *WindowsIdentity.GetCurrent* method.

- The *WindowsPrincipal* class enables assemblies to query the Windows security database to determine whether a user is a member of a particular group. To examine the current user's group memberships, create a *WindowsPrincipal* object by using the current user's identity and then call the *WindowsPrincipal.IsInRole* method.

- You use the *PrincipalPermission* class to specify username, role, and authentication requirements.

- Declarative RBS demands restrict access to an entire method by throwing an exception if the current principal does not meet the specified access requirements. Use declarative RBS demands by setting the principal policy, creating a *try/catch* block to handle users with insufficient privileges, and declaring a *PrincipalPermission* attribute to declare the method's access requirements.

- Use imperative RBS demands by setting the principal policy, creating a *try/catch* block to handle users with insufficient privileges, creating a *PrincipalPermission* object to declare the method's access requirements, and then calling the *Principal-Permission.Demand* method. Use the *WindowsPrincipal.IsInRole* method to make decisions based on group memberships. Declarative RBS demands are perfect for situations in which your application calls a method directly, and access to the entire method must be restricted. Use imperative RBS demands when you need to protect only a portion of a method or when you are protecting a method that can be called by a Windows event.

- To create custom identity and principal classes, extend the *IIdentity* and *IPrincipal* interfaces by overriding the existing properties and adding your custom methods and properties. To create simple custom user models, use the *GenericIdentity* and *GenericPrincipal* classes instead of the *IIdentity* and *IPrincipal* interfaces. To create declarative and imperative RBS demands with custom identities and principals, set the *Thread.CurrentPrincipal* property to your custom principal.

- If you are establishing an *SslStream* connection, you should catch two different types of exceptions. If you catch an *AuthenticationException*, you should prompt the user for different credentials. If you catch an *InvalidCredentialException*, some aspect of the stream is corrupted, and you cannot retry authentication.

Lesson Review

You can use the following questions to test your knowledge of the information in Lesson 1, "Authenticating and Authorizing Users." The questions are also available on the companion CD if you prefer to review them in electronic form.

NOTE Answers

Answers to these questions and explanations of why each answer choice is right or wrong are located in the "Answers" section at the end of the book.

---

1. You must restrict access to a method based on a user's group memberships in the local user database. You want to use the most secure method possible. Which technique will you use?

    A. *WindowsPrincipal.IsInRole*

    B. *WindowsIdentity.IsInRole*

    C. Imperative RBS demands

    D. Declarative RBS demands

2. You must restrict access to a method that is called by a Windows event based on a user's group memberships in the local user database. If the user lacks sufficient access, you want to log an event and display a message to the user. You want to use the most secure method possible. Which technique will you use?

    A. *WindowsPrincipal.IsInRole*

    B. *WindowsIdentity.IsInRole*

    C. Imperative RBS demands

    D. Declarative RBS demands

3. You are writing a method for a Console application that lists options available to a user based on the user's group memberships. Which technique should you use?

    A. *WindowsPrincipal.IsInRole*

    B. *WindowsIdentity.IsInRole*

    C. Imperative RBS demands

    D. Declarative RBS demands

4. You are creating a front-end interface to a back-end database that stores usernames and groups within the database itself. The user database is very simple, storing only usernames and group memberships. You want to be able to use

imperative and declarative RBS demands within your application based on the custom user database. Which of the following classes meets your requirements and would be most efficient to implement? (Choose all that apply.)

A. *GenericIdentity*

B. *GenericPrincipal*

C. *IIdentity*

D. *IPrincipal*

Lesson 2: Using Access Control Lists

In Lesson 1, you learned how to use permission demands to restrict access to portions of your code to specific users. Operating systems use access control lists (ACLs) to provide similar functionality. ACLs are the most common technique for restricting access to files, folders, printers, services, registry values, and just about every other operating system resource. As a developer, you must understand ACLs for two important reasons:

- You can configure them to restrict access to sensitive files, folders, and other objects used by your application.

- You can configure them to allow users to access files and other objects that the users are not typically allowed to access but that the application needs to access.

In this lesson, you learn the fundamentals of ACLs and how to analyze and configure them from within your application.

> **After this lesson, you will be able to:**
> - Explain the purpose of a discretionary ACL and describe how Windows calculates effective permissions
> - Explain the purpose of a security ACL
> - View and configure ACLs using the *System.Security.AccessControl* namespace
>
> **Estimated lesson time: 30 minutes**

What Is a Discretionary Access Control List?

A *discretionary access control list (DACL)* is an authorization restriction mechanism that identifies the users and groups that are allowed or denied access to an object. Windows Vista and Windows Server 2008, like all recent members of the Windows family, keep track of the privileges that users have for accessing resources by using a DACL. If a DACL does not identify explicitly a user or any groups that a user is a member of, the user is denied access to that object. By default, a DACL is controlled by the owner of an object or the person who created the object, and it contains access control entries (ACEs) that determine user access to the object. An ACE is an entry in an object's DACL that grants permissions to a user or group.

Explicit and Inherited Permissions

When you assign a DACL directly to an object, you create an explicit permission. Assigning explicit permissions to every individual folder, file, registry value, and AD DS object would be a ponderous task. In fact, managing the massive number of

ACLs that would be required would have a significant negative impact on the performance of Windows.

To make managing permissions more efficient, Windows includes the concept of inheritance. When Windows is initially installed, most objects have only inherited permissions. *Inherited permissions* propagate to an object from its parent object. For example, the file system uses inherited permissions. Therefore, each new folder you create in the root C:\ folder inherits the exact permissions assigned to the C:\ folder. Similarly, each subkey you create in the HKEY_LOCAL_MACHINE\Software key inherits the exact permissions assigned to the parent key.

Because of inheritance, you typically do not need to specify permissions explicitly when creating a file, folder, registry key, or other object. The new object inherits its parent's permissions. Systems administrators often put a great deal of time and energy into choosing permissions and configuring inheritance, and in most circumstances, you should trust the system administrator's judgment. However, it is important to use care to create objects in the proper place. For example, you should create temporary files in the temporary folder and save user files in user directories.

How Windows Calculates Effective Permissions

Calculating a user's effective permissions requires Windows to do more than simply look up that user's name in the ACL. ACEs can assign rights directly to the user, or they can assign rights to a group. In addition, users can be members of multiple groups, and groups can be nested within each other. Therefore, a single user can have several different ACEs in a single ACL. To understand what a user's effective permissions will be, you must understand how permissions are calculated when multiple ACEs apply to the user.

Permissions that are granted to a user or the groups to which the user belongs are cumulative. If Mary is a member of both the Accounting group and the Managers group, and the ACL for a file grants Read privileges to Mary's user account, Modify privileges to the Accounting group, and Full Control privileges to the Managers group, Mary will have Full Control privileges. There's a catch, though. ACEs that deny access always override ACEs that grant access. Therefore, if the Accounting group is denied access to the file explicitly, Mary cannot open the file. Even though Mary is a member of the Managers group, and the Managers group has Full Control privileges, the Deny ACE means that all members of the Managers group are denied access to the file.

If no ACEs in an ACL apply to a user, that user is denied access to the object. In other words, not explicitly having privileges to an object is exactly the same as being explicitly denied access.

ACEs in the .NET Framework

Different resources have unique permissions that are used to define an ACE. Although both files and the registry have Full Control and Delete permissions, the Read & Execute permission is unique to files and folders, and the Query Values permission is unique to the registry. Therefore, each resource has its own set of classes in the .NET Framework. Fortunately, permissions for different resources function similarly, and all classes inherit from common base classes.

In the .NET Framework, you use the *FileSystemRights* enumeration to specify file and folder permissions. This enumeration has 24 members that correspond to the standard and special permissions you can view and edit using the Properties dialog box from Windows Explorer. Table 12-1 lists the members that correspond to the standard file and folder permissions.

Table 12-1 Standard File and Folder Permissions

FileSystemRights Member	Standard Permission	Description
FullControl	Full Control	Users can perform any action on the file or folder, including creating and deleting it, and modifying its permissions.
Modify	Modify	Users can read, edit, and delete files and folders.
ReadAndExecute	Read & Execute	Users can view files and run applications.
ListDirectory	List Folder Contents	Users can browse a folder.
Read	Read	Users can view a file or the contents of a folder. If an executable file has Read permission but not Read & Execute permission, the user cannot start the executable.

Table 12-1   Standard File and Folder Permissions

FileSystemRights Member	Standard Permission	Description
Write	Write	Users can create files in a directory, but they cannot necessarily read them. This permission is useful for creating a folder in which multiple users can copy files but not access each other's files or even see what other files exist.
Other members	Special permissions	Special permissions are permissions that are more specific and that make up the standard permissions you work with most often.

What Is a Security Access Control List?

A *security access control list* (SACL) is a usage event logging mechanism that determines how file or folder access is audited. Unlike a DACL, an SACL cannot restrict access to a file or folder. However, an SACL can cause an event to be recorded in the security event log when a user accesses a file or folder. This auditing can be used to troubleshoot access problems or to identify intrusions.

To a security professional, an SACL is a critical tool for intrusion detection. A systems administrator is more likely to use SACLs to identify permissions that need to be granted to a user to allow an application to run correctly. A developer uses SACLs to track resources to which her application is denied access so that she can customize the application to allow it to run without problems under a less privileged account.

Exam Tip   It's important to understand the difference between SACLs and DACLs for the exam. The difference between the two is also a common question in technical interviews. Fortunately, it's simple: DACLs restrict access, whereas SACLs audit access. Realistically, though, you're not going to spend much time thinking about SACLs when you write an application, but you might dedicate many hours to troubleshooting problems relating to DACLs. For that reason, this book uses the term *ACL* to refer to DACLs.

By default, Windows does not log auditing events, even if you add an SACL. First, you must enable the Audit Object Access security policy on a computer by following these steps:

1. Open the Local Security Policy console from within Administrative Tools, or by running Secpol.msc.

2. Expand Local Policies and click Audit Policy.

3. In the right pane, double-click Audit Object Access. Select Failure to enable failure auditing, and select Success to enable success auditing.

In an AD DS domain, domain administrators can enable object auditing for all member computers using Group Policy settings.

How to View and Configure ACLs from within an Assembly

The *System.Security.AccessControl* namespace contains a variety of classes for viewing and configuring ACLs for different types of objects. The following sections give an overview of this namespace and describe how to analyze and change ACLs.

Overview of the *System.Security.AccessControl* Namespace

You can use the classes in the *System.Security.AccessControl* namespace to access DACLs, SACLs, and ACEs programmatically for files, folders, registry keys, cryptographic keys, Event Wait handles, mutexes, and semaphores.

For each resource type, the *System.Security.AccessControl* namespace provides three ACL classes:

- *<Type>Security* The most commonly used class, these classes provide methods for retrieving a collection of DACLs (*GetAccessRules*) or SACLs (*GetAuditRules*) and adding and removing ACLs (*AddAccessRule*, *RemoveAccessRule*, *AddAuditRule*, and *RemoveAuditRule*). These classes all inherit from *NativeObjectSecurity*.

- *<Type>AccessRule* Represents a set of access rights allowed or denied for a user or group. These classes all inherit from *AccessRule*, which in turn inherits from *AuthorizationRule*.

- *<Type>AuditRule* Represents a set of access rights to be audited for a user or group. These classes all inherit from *AuditRule*, which in turn inherits from *AuthorizationRule*.

In addition, you can retrieve an instance of the *AuthorizationRuleCollection* class by calling *<Type>Security.GetAccessRules*. This class contains a collection of *<Type>AccessRule* or *<Type>AuditRule* instances that you can iterate through to analyze an object's ACLs.

How to Analyze ACLs

To analyze ACLs, follow these steps:

1. Create an instance of a class that inherits from *NativeObjectSecurity*, such as *DirectorySecurity*, *FileSecurity*, *RegistrySecurity*, or *MutexSecurity*. Several classes in the *Microsoft.Win32* namespace include a *GetAccessControl* method for creating these objects.

2. Call the *GetAccessRules* method to retrieve an instance of *AuthorizationRuleCollection*.

3. Iterate through items in the *AuthorizationRuleCollection* instance to retrieve and analyze individual ACLs.

The following code sample (which requires both the *System.Security.AccessControl* and *System.Security.Principal* namespaces) demonstrates how to display DACLs for a folder; however, the same technique could be used to analyze a file, registry value, or other object:

```vb
' VB
' You could also call Directory.GetAccessControl for the following line
Dim ds As DirectorySecurity = New DirectorySecurity("C:\Program Files", _
    AccessControlSections.Access)
Dim arc As AuthorizationRuleCollection = ds.GetAccessRules(True, _
    True, GetType(NTAccount))
For Each ar As FileSystemAccessRule In arc
    Console.WriteLine(ar.IdentityReference.ToString + ": " + _
        ar.AccessControlType.ToString + " " + ar.FileSystemRights.ToString)
Next
```

```csharp
// C#
// You could also call Directory.GetAccessControl for the following line
DirectorySecurity ds = new DirectorySecurity(@"C:\Program Files",
    AccessControlSections.Access);
AuthorizationRuleCollection arc = ds.GetAccessRules(true, true,
    typeof(NTAccount));
foreach (FileSystemAccessRule ar in arc)
    Console.WriteLine(ar.IdentityReference + ": " + ar.AccessControlType +
        " " + ar.FileSystemRights);
```

You can follow the same general procedure for other object types, although the specific classes you use to retrieve the object vary. For example, the following code sample (which requires the *System.Security.AccessControl*, *System.Security.Principal*, and

Microsoft.Win32 namespaces) displays access rules for the HKEY_LOCAL_MACHINE
registry key:

```vb
' VB
Dim rs As RegistrySecurity = Registry.LocalMachine.GetAccessControl
Dim arc As AuthorizationRuleCollection = rs.GetAccessRules(True, _
    True, GetType(NTAccount))
For Each ar As RegistryAccessRule In arc
    Console.WriteLine(ar.IdentityReference.ToString + ": " _
        + ar.AccessControlType.ToString + " " + ar.RegistryRights.ToString)
Next
```

```csharp
// C#
RegistrySecurity rs = Registry.LocalMachine.GetAccessControl();
AuthorizationRuleCollection arc = rs.GetAccessRules(true,
    true, typeof(NTAccount));
foreach (RegistryAccessRule ar in arc)
    Console.WriteLine(ar.IdentityReference + ": "
        + ar.AccessControlType + " " + ar.RegistryRights);
```

To analyze SACLs, follow the same steps, but call *GetAuditRules* instead of *GetAccess-Rules* and substitute audit classes where necessary.

How to Configure ACLs

To configure ACLs, follow these steps:

1. Call the *GetAccessControl* method to get an instance of a class that inherits from *NativeObjectSecurity*, such as *DirectorySecurity*, *FileSecurity*, *RegistrySecurity*, or *MutexSecurity*.

2. Add or remove ACL entries from the object. Typically, you provide a username or group name, an enumeration describing the rights (such as *FileSystemRights* or *RegistryRights*), and an *AccessControlType* enumeration specifying whether to allow or deny the rights.

3. Call the *SetAccessControl* method to apply the changes.

The following code sample (which requires both the *System.Security.AccessControl* and *System.IO* namespaces) demonstrates how to add an access rule to a folder by granting the Guest user Read access to the "C:\Test" folder. The same general technique could be used to add an ACL to a file, registry value, or other object:

```vb
' VB
Dim dir As String = "C:\test"
Dim ds As DirectorySecurity = Directory.GetAccessControl(dir)
ds.AddAccessRule(New FileSystemAccessRule("Guest", _
    FileSystemRights.Read, AccessControlType.Allow))
Directory.SetAccessControl(dir, ds)
```

```
// C#
string dir = @"C:\test";
DirectorySecurity ds = Directory.GetAccessControl(dir);
ds.AddAccessRule(new FileSystemAccessRule("Guest",
    FileSystemRights.Read, AccessControlType.Allow));
Directory.SetAccessControl(dir, ds);
```

To remove an access rule, simply replace *AddAccessRule* with *RemoveAccessRule*.

Lab: Working with DACLs and Inheritance

In this lab, you will work with file and folder DACLs, and you will learn how to rescue folders created with permissions that make them inaccessible. If you encounter a problem completing an exercise, the completed projects are available along with the sample files.

Exercise: Create a Folder with Explicit Permissions

In this exercise, you will write an application that creates a folder named C:\Guest and grants the Guest user Read access to the folder. Then you create a file within that folder and display the permissions assigned to both the folder and the file to verify that your application functioned correctly.

1. Create a new Console application in either Visual Basic or C#.

2. Add the *System.Security.AccessControl*, *System.Security.Policy*, *System.Security.Principal*, and *System.IO* namespaces to your project.

3. In the *Main* method, write code to create a *DirectorySecurity* object that grants the Guest user Read access to a new folder, Guest, within the current user's Documents folder. Create the folder by specifying the *DirectorySecurity* object. Do not create the folder before creating the *DirectorySecurity* object. For example, the following code works:

```
' VB
Dim ds As New DirectorySecurity()
ds.AddAccessRule(New FileSystemAccessRule("Guest", FileSystemRights.Read,
AccessControlType.Allow))
Dim newFolder As String = System.IO.Path.Combine( _
Environment.GetFolderPath(Environment.SpecialFolder.Personal), "Guest")
Directory.CreateDirectory(newFolder, ds)
```

```
// C#
DirectorySecurity ds = new DirectorySecurity();
ds.AddAccessRule(new FileSystemAccessRule("Guest",
    FileSystemRights.Read, AccessControlType.Allow));
string newFolder = System.IO.Path.Combine(
    Environment.GetFolderPath(Environment.SpecialFolder.Personal), "Guest");
Directory.CreateDirectory(newFolder, ds);
```

4. Now, create a file within the folder named Data.dat, as the following code demonstrates:

```vb
' VB
Dim newFile As String = System.IO.Path.Combine(newFolder, "Data.dat")
File.Create(newFile)
```

```csharp
// C#
string newFile = System.IO.Path.Combine(newFolder, "Data.dat");
File.Create(newFile);
```

5. Build and run your application. The runtime should throw an exception when you attempt to create the file because you did not grant yourself permissions to modify the folder. The folder did not inherit the parent's permissions because you explicitly provided access controls when creating the folder. If you had first created the folder without specifying access permissions and then modified the permissions, the parent's permissions would have been inherited.

6. Use Windows Explorer to view the permissions assigned to the C:\Guest folder. If your application worked properly, the Guest account should have Read permissions, and no other account should have access.

MORE INFO   **File Permissions in Windows XP**

For detailed instructions on how to view and edit file permissions in Windows XP, read *http://technet.microsoft.com/library/bb456988.aspx*. Windows Vista uses a similar procedure.

---

7. Before you can delete the C:\Guest folder, you must take ownership of it. Do so by performing the following steps:

   A. While logged on as a member of the Administrators group, open the C:\Guest Properties dialog box.

   B. On the Security tab of the Guest Properties dialog box, click Advanced.

   C. Click the Owner tab, select the Replace Owner On Subcontainers And Objects check box, and click OK.

   D. Click Yes, and then click OK again.

8. Now use Windows Explorer to delete the C:\Guest folder.

Lesson Summary

- DACLs are used to restrict access to files, folders, and other operating system objects. By default, child objects (such as a subfolder) inherit ACLs from their parent object (such as a root folder).

- SACLs determine the conditions under which object access is audited.

- You can use the members of the *System.Security.AccessControl* namespace to view and configure ACLs for a variety of objects, including files, folders, registry keys, cryptographic keys, Event Wait handlers, semaphores, and mutexes. Each object type has three classes: an object derived from *NativeObjectSecurity*, an object derived from *AccessRule*, and an object derived from *AuditRule*.

Lesson Review

You can use the following questions to test your knowledge of the information in Lesson 2, "Using Access Control Lists." The questions are also available on the companion CD if you prefer to review them in electronic form.

NOTE Answers

Answers to these questions and explanations of why each answer choice is right or wrong are located in the "Answers" section at the end of the book.

1. Which of the following resources can you control access to using the .NET Framework? (Choose all that apply.)

   A. Files

   B. Registry keys

   C. Printers

   D. Network shares

2. Given the following code sample, which line correctly finalizes the ACL changes?

```vb
' VB
Dim dir As String = "C:\MyApp"
Dim ds As DirectorySecurity = Directory.GetAccessControl(dir)
ds.AddAccessRule(New FileSystemAccessRule("Administrator", _
    FileSystemRights.FullControl, AccessControlType.Allow))
Directory.SetAccessControl(dir, ds)
```

```csharp
// C#
string dir = @"C:\myApp";
DirectorySecurity ds = Directory.GetAccessControl(dir);
ds.AddAccessRule(new FileSystemAccessRule("Guest",
    FileSystemRights.FullControl, AccessControlType.Allow));
Directory.SetAccessControl(dir, ds);
```

A.

```
' VB
Directory.SetAccessControl(dir, ds)
```

```
// C#
Directory.SetAccessControl(dir, ds);
```

B.

```
' VB
Directory.CreateDirectory(dir, ds)
```

```
// C#
Directory.CreateDirectory(dir, ds);
```

C.

```
' VB
Directory.SetAccessControl(ds)
```

```
// C#
Directory.SetAccessControl(ds);
```

D.

```
' VB
Directory.CreateDirectory(ds)
```

```
// C#
Directory.CreateDirectory(ds);
```

3. Which of the following classes describes an SACL for a registry key?

   A. *RegistryAccessRule*

   B. *RegistryAuditRule*

   C. *AccessRule*

   D. *AuditRule*

4. Which of the following is returned by the *DirectorySecurity.GetAccessRules* method?

   A. A generic *Collection* object containing *AccessRule* objects

   B. A generic *Collection* object containing *FileSystemAccessRule* objects

   C. An instance of *AuthorizationRuleCollection* containing *FileSystemAccessRule* objects

   D. An instance of *AuthorizationRuleCollection* containing *AuthorizationRule* objects

Lesson 3: Encrypting and Decrypting Data

Data is most vulnerable when it is stored persistently or transferred across a network. Although you can use permission demands to control access to your application and ACLs to protect data, an attacker with access to the hard disk or network infrastructure can bypass software security and either extract private information from the data or modify the data. However, you are not defenseless. You can use cryptography to protect the privacy and integrity of the data that your application stores or transfers. The .NET Framework provides classes for several different types of cryptography, including symmetric and asymmetric encryption, hashing, and digital signatures. In this lesson, you learn when and how to use each type of cryptography.

After this lesson, you will be able to:

- Encrypt and decrypt data using secret-key encryption, known as *symmetric encryption*
- Encrypt and decrypt data using public-key encryption, known as *asymmetric encryption*
- Use hashing to validate the integrity of data
- Sign files with digital signatures to verify that the file is authentic and has not been modified

Estimated lesson time: 90 minutes

Encrypting and Decrypting Data with Symmetric Keys

Many people are introduced to encryption at an early age. Children protect even the most mundane communications from imaginary spies with a secret decoder ring—a toy with two rings that translates encrypted characters to unencrypted characters. The rings on a decoder ring rotate, and a message can be decrypted only when the two rings are lined up correctly. To exchange an encrypted message, the children first must agree on how the rings will line up. After they have exchanged this secret piece of information, they can pass encrypted messages freely, without worrying that someone will be able to decrypt them. Even if an imaginary spy had a decoder ring, the spy would need to know how to position the rings to decrypt the message.

Because both the sender and the recipient of the message must know the same secret to encrypt and decrypt a message, secret decoder rings are an example of symmetric key encryption. Symmetric key encryption is a game for children, but it is also the foundation for most encrypted communications today. As children know, encryption is a fun topic. You should enjoy building it into your application, and you'll greatly reduce the chance of private data being compromised.

What Is Symmetric Key Encryption?

Symmetric key encryption, also known as secret-key encryption, is a cryptography technique that uses a single secret key to both encrypt and decrypt data. Symmetric encryption algorithms (also called *ciphers*) process plain text with the secret *encryption key* to create encrypted data called *cipher text*. The cipher text cannot easily be decrypted into the plain text without possession of the secret key. Figure 12-2 shows symmetric key encryption and decryption.

Encryption

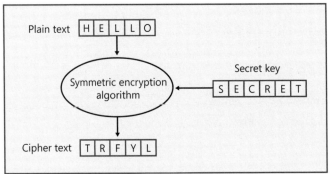

Decryption

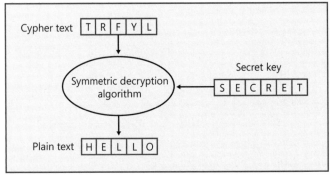

Figure 12-2   Symmetric encryption uses the same key for both encryption and decryption

Symmetric algorithms are extremely fast and are well suited for encrypting large quantities of data. Even though symmetric encryption is very secure, an attacker can identify the plain text, given the cipher text and enough time. To identify the plain text, the attacker needs to use only a brute force attack to generate symmetric keys sequentially until the attacker has tried every single possibility. Typically, the time required to try all the possible keys is hundreds of years, if not longer.

The disadvantage of secret-key encryption is that it presumes that two parties have already agreed on a key. Agreeing on a symmetric key is a challenge because the key itself cannot be encrypted. If you've decided to use encryption, it must be because you don't trust your system to prevent an attacker from gaining access to your data. Therefore, users must find a secure way to exchange secret keys. After the secret keys are exchanged, encrypted data can be exchanged freely between the parties. However, keys should be changed on a regular basis for the same reasons that passwords should be changed regularly. Each time the key must be changed, users must resort to the secure communication mechanism.

Figure 12-3 shows how users must transfer both the encrypted message and the key using different communication mechanisms to enable the recipient to decrypt the message, while preventing an attacker who can capture your communications across only a single network from decrypting the message. Keys are often transferred by voice across the phone network, sent physically through the mail system, or carried to the recipient. After the *shared secret* has been established, the two peers can use it to encrypt and decrypt any number of messages.

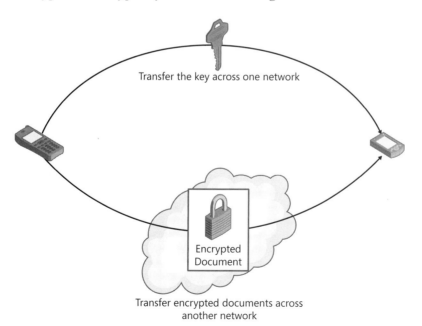

Transfer the key across one network

Encrypted
Document

Transfer encrypted documents across
another network

Figure 12-3 Symmetric key encryption requires separately exchanging both the key and the encrypted document

The need to establish a shared secret key rules out relying solely on symmetric encryption for encrypting spontaneous network communications. For example, symmetric key encryption is not initially used between a Web client and Web server because users on the Internet aren't typically willing to wait several days while the Web site physically mails them a secret key. Instead, Web sessions are initially established by using asymmetric keys.

Symmetric Algorithm Classes in the .NET Framework

Most of the .NET Framework's cryptography functionality is built into the *System.Security.Cryptography* namespace, including the four implementations of symmetric encryption algorithms. Table 12-2 shows symmetric encryption algorithm classes.

Table 12-2   Symmetric Cryptography Classes

Class	Key Length	Description
RijndaelManaged	128 through 256 bits, in 32-bit increments	The .NET Framework implementation of the Rijndael symmetric encryption algorithm. Because this and *AesManaged* are fully managed implementations, they can be used in partially trusted environments.
AesManaged	128 bits	The .NET Framework implementation of the Rijndael symmetric encryption algorithm. As a government encryption standard, this algorithm is also known as *Advanced Encryption Standard*, or *AES*. The AES algorithm is essentially the Rijndael symmetric algorithm with a fixed block size and iteration count. This class functions the same way as the *RijndaelManaged* class, but it limits blocks to 128 bits.
DES	56 bits	The *Data Encryption Standard (DES)* is a symmetric encryption algorithm that uses relatively short key lengths that are vulnerable to cracking attacks. As a result, it should be avoided. However, it remains commonly used because it is compatible with a wide range of legacy platforms.

Table 12-2 Symmetric Cryptography Classes

Class	Key Length	Description
TripleDES	156 bits, of which only 112 bits are effectively used for encryption	The .NET Framework implementation of the *Triple DES* symmetric encryption algorithm; it essentially applies the DES algorithm three times.
RC2	Variable	An encryption standard designed to replace DES that uses variable key sizes.

All symmetric algorithm classes are derived from the *System.Security.Cryptography .SymmetricAlgorithm* base class and share the following properties:

- **BlockSize** Gets or sets the block size of the cryptographic operation in bits. The block size is the number of bits that the algorithm processes at a single time and can usually be ignored when creating applications that use encryption.

- **FeedbackSize** Gets or sets the feedback size of the cryptographic operation in bits. The feedback size determines one aspect of the algorithm's encryption technique; however, as a developer, you can ignore this property safely.

- **IV** Gets or sets the initialization vector (IV) for the symmetric algorithm. Like the *Key* property, both the encryptor and decryptor must specify the same value. To avoid the overhead of transferring the IV securely between the encryptor and decryptor, you might choose to define the IV in your application statically or to derive this from the *Key* property.

> **NOTE Understanding Initialization Vectors**
>
> An *initialization vector (IV)* is data that symmetric encryption algorithms use to obscure further the first block of data being encrypted, which makes unauthorized decrypting more difficult. You don't need to understand what IVs do to use encryption so long as you know that you must synchronize the IV values for both the encryptor and decryptor.

- **Key** Gets or sets the secret key for the symmetric algorithm. Keys are generated automatically if you have not defined them specifically. After encryption, you must store this value and transfer it to the decryptor. During decryption, you must specify the same key used during encryption.

- *KeySize*   Gets or sets the size of the secret key used by the symmetric algorithm in bits. When you create a symmetric algorithm object, the runtime chooses the largest key size supported by the platform. As a result, you usually can ignore this property. However, if the message's recipient does not support the same key sizes as the sender, you must set this property to the highest value supported by both the encryptor and the decryptor.

- *LegalBlockSizes*   A *KeySizes* array that gets the block sizes that are supported by the symmetric algorithm. Each array member contains *MinSize* and *MaxSize* properties, which define the valid key ranges in bits; and a *SkipSize* property that specifies in bits the interval between valid key sizes.

- *LegalKeySizes*   A *KeySizes* array that gets the key sizes that are supported by the symmetric algorithm. Each array member contains *MinSize* and *MaxSize* properties that define the valid key ranges in bits, and a *SkipSize* property that specifies the interval between valid key sizes in bits.

- *Mode*   A property set to one of the *CipherMode* enumeration values that determines one aspect of the encryption algorithm's behavior. This property is usually set to Cipher Block Chaining (CBC), the default. You usually should leave this set to CBC. If you do change this value, you must change it at both the encryptor and decryptor.

- *Padding*   A *PaddingMode* enumeration value, this property determines how the encryption algorithm fills out any difference between the algorithm's block size and the length of the plain text. You generally should not change this property.

In addition, the symmetric algorithm classes share the following methods (standard object methods have been omitted):

- *CreateDecryptor*   To decrypt messages, you must create a symmetric algorithm object and call this method to create an *ICryptoTransform* object that a *CryptoStream* object can use to decrypt the stream.

- *CreateEncryptor*   Creates a symmetric encryptor object used by *CryptoStream* objects to encrypt a stream.

- *GenerateIV*   Generates a random IV to be used for the algorithm. Generally, there is no need to call this method because IVs are randomly generated automatically unless you specifically define them. You call this method only if you have defined an IV and later need to use a different random IV.

- ***GenerateKey***   Generates a random key to be used for the algorithm. Like *GenerateIV*, you need to call this method only if you already have defined the *Key* property and later need to use a random key.

- ***ValidKeySize***   Determines whether the specified key size is valid for the current algorithm and returns a boolean value. Use this method when you are working with an unknown symmetric algorithm class to verify that your key is valid for the given algorithm.

BEST PRACTICES   Choosing a Symmetric Key Algorithm

Use the Rijndael algorithm whenever both the encryptor and decryptor are running on Windows XP or later operating systems; otherwise, use Triple DES. Of all symmetric key algorithms supported by the .NET Framework, the U.S. government–approved Rijndael algorithm is considered the most secure. This algorithm supports 128-, 192-, and 256-bit keys. Another reason to choose Rijndael is that it is natively supported by the .NET Framework. Other than the less flexible *AesManaged* class, the other algorithms must make calls to unmanaged code.

How to Establish a Symmetric Key

Before you can encrypt and decrypt messages by using symmetric encryption, both the encryptor and decryptor must have the same key. You can't use just any piece of data as a key, however. Symmetric encryption algorithms must use keys of a specific length, so you cannot simply set the *Key* property to a user-provided password. To generate a random key, simply create and use a symmetric algorithm object. If you specify a value for the *Key* property and later want to use a random key, call the *GenerateKey* method.

You can also generate a valid key based on a user-provided password if you can rely on users to transfer the password between the encryptor and decryptor. You cannot use passwords directly as encryption keys, but you can use the *System.Security.Cryptography .Rfc2898DeriveBytes* class to turn a password into a key. This is particularly useful when a shared secret has already been established between an encryptor and a decryptor. For example, if you create a custom authentication mechanism and your application is privy to the user's username and password, you could concatenate the user's own username and password to derive the same key at both the encryptor and decryptor.

Rfc2898DeriveBytes requires three values in addition to the user's password: a salt value, an IV, and the number of iterations used to generate the key. Ideally, all these values are generated randomly. Changing any of these values produces a different key, so you are required to use the same values at both the encryptor and decryptor. There-fore, when random values are used, the values must be exchanged in the same way the password is exchanged. For this reason, it usually is not possible to securely exchange these values in addition to the password. Instead, you can specify static values that both the encryptor and decryptor applications have stored within their source code, but it is more secure to generate the values based on other shared secret information, such as the password.

Creating symmetric keys based on a password requires several different values to be synchronized between the encryptor and decryptor:

- The password
- The salt value
- The IV
- The number of iterations used to generate the key (or you can accept the default)

The simplest way to specify these values is to pass them to the *Rfc2898DeriveBytes* con-structor. After initialization, you can retrieve a key by calling the *Rfc2898DeriveBytes* *.GetBytes* method. *GetBytes* accepts the number of bytes to return as an integer. When deriving a key, determine the length based on the number of bits required by the algo-rithm object's *KeySize* property. Note that *KeySize* is defined as a number of bits, whereas the *Rfc2898DeriveBytes.GetBytes* method requires a number of bytes. You must divide the number of bits required for the key by 8 to determine the number of bytes required.

Besides the key, the encryption algorithm must also have the same IV specified at both the encryptor and decryptor. For optimal security, when only a password is shared between the encryptor and decryptor, you should also generate the IV based on the password. Whereas the length of the key being generated must be based on the *KeySize* property, the length of the IV must be based on the encryption algorithm's *BlockSize* property. Like *KeySize*, *BlockSize* is defined as a number of bits, so you need to divide the number of bits by 8 to determine the number of bytes required.

The following sample code generates a key and IV for the *SymmetricAlgorithm* object named *myAlg* using a static password, but in real-world use, the password should be provided by the user:

```vb
' VB
' In practice, the user would provide the password
Dim password As String = "P@S5w0r]>"

' Create an algorithm object
```

```
Dim myAlg As RijndaelManaged = New RijndaelManaged()

' Derive the key and use it to define the algorithm
Dim salt As Byte() = System.Text.Encoding.ASCII.GetBytes("This is my salt")
Dim key As Rfc2898DeriveBytes = New Rfc2898DeriveBytes(password, salt)
myAlg.Key = key.GetBytes(myAlg.KeySize / 8)
myAlg.IV = key.GetBytes(myAlg.BlockSize / 8)
```

```
// C#
// In practice, the user would provide the password
string password = "P@S5wOr]>";

// Create an algorithm object
RijndaelManaged myAlg = new RijndaelManaged();

// Derive the key and use it to define the algorithm
byte[] salt = Encoding.ASCII.GetBytes("This is my salt");
Rfc2898DeriveBytes key = new Rfc2898DeriveBytes(password, salt);
myAlg.Key = key.GetBytes(myAlg.KeySize / 8);
myAlg.IV = key.GetBytes(myAlg.BlockSize / 8);
```

How to Encrypt and Decrypt Messages Using Symmetric Keys

After both the encryptor and decryptor have the same key, they can begin exchanging encrypted messages. The .NET Framework makes this process easy. In fact, using encryption is similar to reading and writing to standard files and streams, and it requires only a few additional lines of code. To encrypt or decrypt messages in your application, perform the following tasks:

1. Create a *Stream* object to interface with the memory or file that you will be reading from or writing to.

2. Create a *SymmetricAlgorithm* object.

3. Specify the algorithm's key, the IV, or both.

4. Call *SymmetricAlgorithm.CreateEncryptor()* or *SymmetricAlgorithm.CreateDecryptor()* to create an *ICryptoTransform* object.

5. Create a *CryptoStream* object using the *Stream* object and the *ICryptoTransform* object.

6. Read from or write to the *CryptoStream* object just as you would any other *Stream* object.

The following code demonstrates these steps by reading an unencrypted file (the C:\Windows\Win.ini file), encrypting it with the Rijndael algorithm, and saving the encrypted results as a new file. The code requires the *System.IO* and *System.Security.Cryptography* namespaces:

```vb
' VB
Dim inFileName As String = "C:\Windows\win.ini"
Dim outFileName As String = "C:\Windows\win.ini.enc"

' Step 1: Create the Stream objects
Dim inFile As FileStream = New FileStream(inFileName, _
    FileMode.Open, FileAccess.Read)
Dim outFile As FileStream = New FileStream(outFileName, _
    FileMode.OpenOrCreate, FileAccess.Write)

' Step 2: Create the SymmetricAlgorithm object
Dim myAlg As SymmetricAlgorithm = New RijndaelManaged

' Step 3: Specify a key (optional)
myAlg.GenerateKey()

' Read the unencrypted file into fileData
Dim fileData(inFile.Length - 1) As Byte
inFile.Read(fileData, 0, CType(inFile.Length, Integer))

' Step 4: Create the ICryptoTransform object
Dim encryptor As ICryptoTransform = myAlg.CreateEncryptor

' Step 5: Create the CryptoStream object
Dim encryptStream As CryptoStream = _
    New CryptoStream(outFile, encryptor, _
    CryptoStreamMode.Write)

' Step 6: Write the contents to the CryptoStream
encryptStream.Write(fileData, 0, fileData.Length)

' Close the file handles
encryptStream.Close()
inFile.Close()
outFile.Close()

// C#
string inFileName = @"C:\Windows\win.ini";
string outFileName = @"C:\Windows\win.ini.enc";

// Step 1: Create the Stream objects
FileStream inFile = new FileStream(inFileName,
    FileMode.Open, FileAccess.Read);
FileStream outFile = new FileStream(outFileName,
    FileMode.OpenOrCreate, FileAccess.Write);

// Step 2: Create the SymmetricAlgorithm object
SymmetricAlgorithm myAlg = new RijndaelManaged();
```

```
// Step 3: Specify a key (optional)
myAlg.GenerateKey();

// Read the unencrypted file into fileData
byte[] fileData = new byte[inFile.Length];
inFile.Read(fileData, 0, (int)inFile.Length);

// Step 4: Create the ICryptoTransform object
ICryptoTransform encryptor = myAlg.CreateEncryptor();

// Step 5: Create the CryptoStream object
CryptoStream encryptStream =
    new CryptoStream(outFile, encryptor, CryptoStreamMode.Write);

// Step 6: Write the contents to the CryptoStream
encryptStream.Write(fileData, 0, fileData.Length);

// Close the file handles
encryptStream.Close();
inFile.Close();
outFile.Close();
```

Because the key is randomly generated, running the application repeatedly generates different results each time. Because the key is not stored, the file never can be decrypted. The key is simply an array of bytes and can be stored by using the *Binary-Writer* object or by transferring the key across a network.

The code for decrypting a file is almost identical to the code for encrypting a file, except that it must read the encryption key that was used to encrypt the data rather than randomly generating it, and it must call decryption methods instead of encryption methods. To reverse the process to decrypt a file, simply make the following changes to an application:

- Change the code for step 3 to read the key and IV that were used to encrypt the data.

- Change the code for step 4 to use the *CreateDecryptor* method instead of *CreateEncryptor*.

- Change the code for step 5 to use the *CryptoStreamMode.Read* enumeration instead of *CryptoStreamMode.Write*.

- Change the code for step 6 to read from the *CryptoStream* object.

Encrypting and Decrypting Data with Asymmetric Keys

Asymmetric encryption, also known as public-key encryption, overcomes symmetric encryption's most significant disadvantage: that it requires both the encryptor and decryptor to know a shared secret. Asymmetric encryption relies on key pairs. In a key pair, there is one public key and one private key. The public key can be shared freely because it cannot be easily abused, even by an attacker. Messages encrypted with the public key can be decrypted only with the private key, allowing anyone to send encrypted messages that can be decrypted only by a single individual.

The asymmetric encryption process begins with public keys being exchanged. Generally, both the client and server exchange public keys. However, if only one side of the communication needs to be encrypted, only the peer receiving encrypted communications must provide a public key. After the public keys are exchanged, communications are encrypted using the recipient's public key. Such communications can be decrypted only by the recipient because only the recipient holds the private key that matches the public key. Figure 12-4 shows a simple asymmetric encryption arrangement in which only one side of the communications provides a public key.

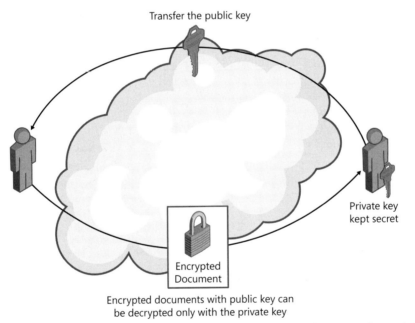

Transfer the public key

Private key
kept secret

Encrypted
Document

Encrypted documents with public key can
be decrypted only with the private key

Figure 12-4 Asymmetric cryptography uses separate keys for encryption and decryption

Asymmetric algorithms are not as fast as symmetric algorithms, but they are much more secure. Asymmetric algorithms are not well suited to encrypting large amounts of data because of the performance overhead. One common use of asymmetric algorithms is to encrypt and transfer a symmetric key and IV. The symmetric encryption algorithm is then used for all messages being sent back and forth. This is the technique used by Hypertext Transfer Protocol Secure (HTTPS) and Secure Sockets Layer (SSL) to encrypt Web communications—asymmetric encryption is used only during session establishment. This common combination of asymmetric and symmetric encryption is shown in Figure 12-5.

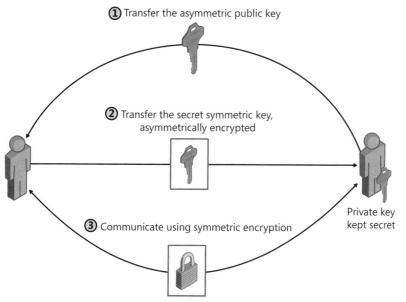

Figure 12-5   Combine asymmetric and symmetric algorithms to optimize both security and performance

The other significant challenge of asymmetric encryption is key management. To manage keys, organizations typically implement a public key infrastructure (PKI), such as Certificate Services included with Windows Server 2003 and Windows Server 2008. A *PKI* is an infrastructure for distributing, managing, and revoking certificates in an organization. As a developer, you generally are not responsible for configuring a PKI.

Asymmetric Algorithm Classes in the .NET Framework

The .NET Framework provides two classes for working with asymmetric encryption, and they are both based on the *System.Security.Cryptography.AsymmetricAlgorithm* class. This base class has the following properties, several of which are identical to the *SymmetricAlgorithm* counterparts:

- **KeyExchangeAlgorithm**   Gets the name of the key exchange algorithm. Generally, you do not need to access this property directly.

- *KeySize* Gets or sets the size in bits of the secret key used by the symmetric algorithm. Asymmetric keys are much larger than symmetric keys. For example, although a typical symmetric key is 182 bits, the .NET Framework implementation of the RSA algorithm supports key lengths from 384 through 16,384 bits.

- *LegalKeySizes* A *KeySizes* array that gets the key sizes that are supported by the symmetric algorithm. Each array member contains *MinSize* and *MaxSize* properties that define the valid key ranges in bits, and a *SkipSize* property that specifies the interval between valid key sizes in bits.

- *SignatureAlgorithm* Gets the URL of an Extensible Markup Language (XML) document describing the signature algorithm. Generally, you do not need to access this property directly.

Unlike the *SymmetricAlgorithm* base class, the *AsymmetricAlgorithm* base class has no useful methods. Instead, the encryption functionality is built into the objects that implement the *AsymmetricAlgorithm* class. The .NET Framework provides two implementations of this class:

- *RSACryptoServiceProvider* Used for all asymmetric encryption and decryption. *RSACryptoServiceProvider* is the .NET Framework implementation of the RSA algorithm. RSA is named for the last initial of its three creators—Ronald Rivest, Adi Shamir, and Leonard Adleman—who developed the algorithm in 1977. The *RSACryptoServiceProvider* class is a managed wrapper around the unmanaged RSA implementation provided by the Cryptography API.

- *DSACryptoServiceProvider* Used for digitally signing messages, it is also a managed wrapper around unmanaged code.

In addition to the properties provided by *AsymmetricAlgorithm*, *RSACryptoServiceProvider* provides the following properties:

- *PersistKeyInCsp* Gets or sets a value indicating whether the key should be persisted in the Crypto Service Provider (CSP). Set this to *true* when you want to reuse the key without exporting it.

- *UseMachineKeyStore* Gets or sets a value indicating whether the key should be persisted in the computer's key store instead of the user profile store.

The default constructors always populate the algorithm parameters with the strongest defaults available to the run-time environment, giving you the strongest algorithm possible without changing any settings. The *RSACryptoServiceProvider* class also includes methods for encrypting and decrypting, as well as for importing and exporting keys. The following list describes each of these methods:

- **Decrypt**   Decrypts data with the RSA algorithm.

- **Encrypt**   Encrypts data with the RSA algorithm.

- **ExportParameters**   Exports an *RSAParameters* structure, which defines the algorithm's key pair. Pass *true* to this method to export both the private and public key, or pass *false* to export only the public key.

- **FromXmlString**   Imports a key pair from an XML string.

- **ImportParameters**   Imports to a public key or key pair the specified *RSAParameters* object.

- **SignData**   Computes the hash value of the specified data and stores the signature in a byte array.

- **SignHash**   Computes the signature for the specified hash value by encrypting it with the private key and stores the signature in a byte array.

- **VerifyData**   Verifies the specified signature data by comparing it with the signature computed for the specified data.

- **VerifyHash**   Verifies the specified signature data by comparing it with the signature computed for the specified hash value.

How to Export and Import Asymmetric Keys and Key Pairs

RSA keys are much more complex than symmetric encryption keys. In fact, RSA keys are called *parameters* and are represented by an *RSAParameters* structure. Table 12-3 lists the significant members of this structure and their purpose. The structure includes several parameters that are not listed, but you will not need to access these directly: *DP*, *DQ*, *InverseQ*, *P*, and *Q*.

Table 12-3   *RSAParameters* Structure Members

Parameter	Description
D	The private key.
Exponent	Also known as *e*, this is the short part of the public key.
Modulus	Also known as *n*, this is the long part of the public key.

You almost always need to export your public key because without the public key, nobody can send encrypted messages to you. To export your public key to an instance of the *RSAParamaters* structure, use the *RSACryptoServiceProvider.ExportParameters* method, and pass it a boolean parameter of *false*. The *false* parameter value causes the method to export only the public key. If it were set to *true*, *ExportParameters* would export both the public and private key.

IMPORTANT   **Exporting the Private Key**

Export your private key only if you need to reuse it later. If you do store it, your application must protect the privacy of the private key.

The following code sample demonstrates how to create a new instance of an RSA algorithm and export its automatically generated public key to an *RSAParameters* object named *publicKey*:

```
' VB
' Create an instance of the RSA algorithm object
Dim myRSA As RSACryptoServiceProvider = New RSACryptoServiceProvider

' Create a new RSAParameters object with only the public key
Dim publicKey As RSAParameters = myRSA.ExportParameters(False)

// C#
// Create an instance of the RSA algorithm object
RSACryptoServiceProvider myRSA = new RSACryptoServiceProvider();

// Create a new RSAParameters object with only the public key
RSAParameters publicKey = myRSA.ExportParameters(false);
```

After you create an *RSAParameters* object, you can freely access any of the byte array parameters described in Table 12-3. If you need to store or transmit the export key or keys, you should use the *RSACryptoServiceProvider.ToXmlString* method instead. Like *ExportParameters*, this method takes a boolean value that indicates whether the private key should be exported. However, *ToXmlString* stores the data in an XML format that can be easily stored, transferred, and imported with the *FromXmlString* method. The following example shows an abbreviated version of an exported RSA key pair created by calling *RSACryptoServiceProvider.ToXmlString(true)*:

```
<RSAKeyValue>
    <Modulus>vilaR5C3XtmH5…IGZNTs=</Modulus>
    <Exponent>AQAB</Exponent>
    <P>699j5bpT04JlVkjz…66sYYxLG6VQ==</P>
    <Q>zmNovTJlGUamUlVk…EMtEJqhZgzhTw==</Q>
    <DP>OWBf5p7qB6JzB7xek…tkQGoiMBK+Q==</DP>
```

```
    <DQ>NLbZUrGjduA/99K…scf2pOzQTvKw==</DQ>
    <InverseQ>BYZ3vVwb/N+…HjPcGz7Yg==</InverseQ>
    <D>Jz81qMuPbP4MdEaF/…hYZ5WmrzeRRE=</D>
</RSAKeyValue>
```

How to Store Key Pairs for Later Reuse

You can also export keys to the CSP by using *CryptoAPI* key storage. To store your private keys persistently, add the following elements to your code:

1. Create a *CspParameters* object.

2. Specify the *CspParameters.KeyContainerName* property.

3. Create an *RSACryptoServiceProvider* object using the overloaded constructor that accepts a *CspParameters* object.

4. Set the *RSACryptoServiceProvider.PersistKeyInCsp* property to *true.*

The .NET Framework handles creating and retrieving keys automatically. The first time you specify a *CspParameters* object and set the *PersistKeyInCsp* property to *true,* the .NET Framework creates the key container and stores your key. If you run the same application again, the .NET Framework detects that a key container with that name already exists and retrieves the stored private key. For example, if you run this application repeatedly, it displays the same private key every time:

```
' VB
' Create a CspParameters object
Dim persistantCsp As CspParameters = New CspParameters
persistantCsp.KeyContainerName = "AsymmetricExample"

' Create an instance of the RSA algorithm object
Dim myRSA As RSACryptoServiceProvider = _
    New RSACryptoServiceProvider (persistantCsp)

' Specify that the private key should be stored in the CSP
myRSA.PersistKeyInCsp = True

' Create a new RSAParameters object with the private key
Dim privateKey As RSAParameters = myRSA.ExportParameters(True)

' Display the private key
For Each thisByte As Byte In privateKey.D
    Console.Write(thisByte.ToString("X2") + " ")
Next

// C#
// Create a CspParameters object
CspParameters persistantCsp = new CspParameters();
persistantCsp.KeyContainerName = "AsymmetricExample";
```

```
// Create an instance of the RSA algorithm object
RSACryptoServiceProvider myRSA = new RSACryptoServiceProvider(persistantCsp);

// Specify that the private key should be stored in the CSP
myRSA.PersistKeyInCsp = true;

// Create a new RSAParameters object with the private key
RSAParameters privateKey = myRSA.ExportParameters(true);

// Display the private key
foreach (byte thisByte in privateKey.D)
    Console.Write(thisByte.ToString("X2") + " ");
```

However, if you change the *KeyContainerName* value and rerun the application, the application displays a new private key because the .NET Framework will not find an existing key container.

How to Encrypt and Decrypt Messages Using Asymmetric Encryption

To encrypt and decrypt messages using asymmetric encryption, call the *RSACrypto-ServiceProvider.Encrypt* and *RSACryptoServiceProvider.Decrypt* methods. Both take two parameters:

- **byte[] rgb**   An array of bytes containing the message to be encrypted or decrypted.

- **bool fOAEP**   A boolean value. When set to *true*, encryption and encryption use Optimal Asymmetric Encryption Padding (OAEP) data padding, which is supported only on Windows XP and later operating systems. When set to *false*, Public Key Cryptography Standard (PKCS) #1 v1.5 data padding is used. Both the encryption and decryption methods *must* use the same data padding.

The most challenging aspect of encryption is converting data into the byte array format. To convert strings to byte arrays, use the *System.Text.Encoding.Unicode.GetBytes* and *System.Text.Encoding.Unicode.GetString* methods. For example, the following code encrypts a string using PKCS#1 v1.5 data padding and then immediately decrypts and displays the string:

```vb
' VB
Dim messageString As String = "Hello, World!"
Dim myRsa As RSACryptoServiceProvider = New RSACryptoServiceProvider

Dim messageBytes As Byte() = Encoding.Unicode.GetBytes(messageString)
Dim encryptedMessage As Byte() = myRsa.Encrypt(messageBytes, False)

Dim decryptedBytes As Byte() = myRsa.Decrypt(encryptedMessage, False)
Console.WriteLine(Encoding.Unicode.GetString(decryptedBytes))
```

```
// C#
string messageString = "Hello, World!";
RSACryptoServiceProvider myRsa = new RSACryptoServiceProvider();

byte[] messageBytes = Encoding.Unicode.GetBytes(messageString);
byte[] encryptedMessage = myRsa.Encrypt(messageBytes, false);

byte[] decryptedBytes = myRsa.Decrypt(encryptedMessage, false);
Console.WriteLine(Encoding.Unicode.GetString(decryptedBytes));
```

Whichever encoding method you use to convert the data into a byte array, be sure you use a matching decoding method after decrypting the data.

Validating Data Integrity with Hashes

Another important use of cryptography is protecting data integrity by using hashes. A *hash* is a checksum that is unique to a specific file or piece of data. You can use a hash value to verify that a file has not been modified after the hash was generated.

Unlike encryption, you cannot derive the original data from the hash, even if the original data is very small. In other words, creating a hash is a one-way operation. Hashes are often used to enable passwords to be verified without storing the password itself. After the hash of the password has been stored, the application can verify the password by calculating the hash of the provided password and comparing it with the stored hash. The two hash values match if the user has provided the same password; however, an attacker cannot determine the original password, even if the attacker gains access to the password's hash value.

Hash Algorithms in the .NET Framework

The .NET Framework includes six nonkeyed hash algorithms and two keyed hash algorithms. Table 12-4 lists each of the nonkeyed hash algorithms included with the .NET Framework. Each is a member of the *System.Security.Cryptography* class and is derived from *System.Security.Cryptography.HashAlgorithm*.

Table 12-4   Nonkeyed Hashing Algorithms

Abstract Class	Implementation Class	Description
MD5	MD5CryptoServiceProvider	The Message Digest 5 (MD5) algorithm. The hash size is 128 bits.
RIPEMD160	RIPEMD160Managed	The Message Digest 160 (MD160) hash algorithm. The hash size is 160 bits.

Table 12-4   **Nonkeyed Hashing Algorithms**

Abstract Class	Implementation Class	Description
SHA1	*SHA1CryptoServiceProvider*	The Secure Hash Algorithm 1 (SHA1). The hash size is 160 bits.
SHA256	*SHA256Managed*	The Secure Hash Algorithm 256 (SHA256). The hash size is 256 bits.
SHA384	*SHA384Managed*	The Secure Hash Algorithm 384 (SHA384). The hash size is 384 bits.
SHA512	*SHA512Managed*	The Secure Hash Algorithm 512 (SHA512). The hash size is 512 bits.

You have to take care to prevent attackers from modifying a hash value. If an attacker can modify a hash, he or she can effectively defeat the purpose of the hash. *Keyed hash algorithms* are algorithms that protect against modification of the hash by encrypting it by using a secret key that both the sender and receiver must have. Table 12-5 lists the two keyed hash algorithms included with the .NET Framework, both derived from *System.Security.Cryptography.KeyedHashAlgorithm.*

Table 12-5   **Keyed Hashing Algorithms**

Class	Description
HMACSHA1	Hash-based Message Authentication Code (HMAC) using SHA1. Used to determine whether a message sent over an insecure channel has been tampered with, provided that the sender and receiver share a secret key. HMACSHA1 accepts keys of any size and produces a hash sequence with a length of 20 bytes.
MACTripleDES	Message Authentication Code (MAC) using TripleDES. Like *HMACSHA1, MACTripleDES* is used to determine whether a message sent over an insecure channel has been tampered with, provided that the sender and receiver share a secret key. *MACTripleDES* uses a key with a length of 8, 16, or 24 bytes, and produces a hash sequence with a length of 8 bytes.

Real World

Tony Northrup

Many years ago, I was a developer creating a database that indexed thousands of files for one of the first major Internet download services. A single file was often submitted using multiple filenames, so avoiding duplicate files required more than simply checking to see whether the filename already existed. Initially, I sorted through the files to verify that each was unique by examining the size and contents of the files. However, this was an extremely slow process.

I decided to create an index of files by using an MD5 hash of each file. Then my application could check whether a file already existed simply by looking up the MD5 hash. I was surprised when my application found a duplicate file. After checking into it further, I discovered that it had found two unique files that produced the same hash! This was supposed to be almost impossible; however, because the size of the MD5 was a reasonably small 128 bits and the size of the files was much larger, the possibility existed that multiple files would produce the same hash. In my case, I had stumbled across such an unlikely occurrence. Using a longer hash, such as SHA512, reduces the likelihood of such an occurrence.

How to Compute a Nonkeyed Hash

To compute a nonkeyed hash, perform the following steps in your code:

1. Create the hash algorithm object.
2. Store the data to be hashed in a byte array.
3. Call the *HashAlgorithm.ComputeHash* method.
4. Retrieve the *HashAlgorithm.Hash* byte array, which contains the hash value.

The following code demonstrates how to create a hash by calculating the hash of the file specified in *args[0]*, and displaying the hash using Base64 text encoding:

```vb
' VB
' Step 1: Create the hash algorithm object
Dim myHash As MD5 = New MD5CryptoServiceProvider

' Step 2: Store the data to be hashed in a byte array
Dim file As FileStream = New FileStream (args(0), _
    FileMode.Open, FileAccess.Read)
Dim reader As BinaryReader = New BinaryReader (file)
```

```
' Step 3: Call the HashAlgorithm.ComputeHash method
myHash.ComputeHash(reader.ReadBytes(CType(file.Length, Integer)))

' Step 4: Retrieve the HashAlgorithm.Hash byte array
Console.WriteLine(Convert.ToBase64String(myHash.Hash))

// C#
// Step 1: Create the hash algorithm object
MD5 myHash = new MD5CryptoServiceProvider();

// Step 2: Store the data to be hashed in a byte array
FileStream file = new FileStream(args[0], FileMode.Open, FileAccess.Read);
BinaryReader reader = new BinaryReader(file);

// Step 3: Call the HashAlgorithm.ComputeHash method
myHash.ComputeHash(reader.ReadBytes((int)file.Length));

// Step 4: Retrieve the HashAlgorithm.Hash byte array
Console.WriteLine(Convert.ToBase64String(myHash.Hash));
```

Repeatedly running that application to calculate the hash of a single file always produces the same hash result until the file is modified. After the file is modified, the hash result also changes. Consider the following sequence of commands and their output. The sequence creates a new text file, computes the hash repeatedly, and then modifies the file. After the file is modified, the hash also changes:

```
C:\>echo Hello, World! > HashThis.txt

C:\>HashExample HashThis.txt
h7GTmgvuZdNOSGROA6qdBA==

C:\>HashExample HashThis.txt
h7GTmgvuZdNOSGROA6qdBA==

C:\>echo Hello, again. >> HashThis.txt

C:\>HashExample HashThis.txt
F1QQWOeK/Yc2EwNR2BxCuw==
```

Because all nonkeyed hash algorithms are derived from a single class, you can change the hash algorithm used just by changing the algorithm declaration. The more bits used in the hash, the longer the hash that is displayed. To verify later that the data has not been modified, simply recalculate the hash using the same algorithm and compare the two values.

How to Compute a Keyed Hash

To compute a keyed hash, perform the following steps in your code:

1. Create a secret key that is shared among all parties who will compute or verify the hash.

2. Create the hash algorithm object using the secret key. If you do not provide a secret key, one is generated automatically for you.

3. Store the data to be hashed in a byte array.

4. Call the *KeyedHashAlgorithm.ComputeHash* method.

5. Retrieve the *KeyedHashAlgorithm.Hash* byte array, which contains the hash value.

The following code demonstrates how to create a HMACSHA1 hash by calculating the hash of the file specified in *args[1]* by using a password specified in *args[0]* to generate a secret key:

```vb
' VB
' Step 1: Create a secret key
Dim saltValueBytes As Byte() = _
    System.Text.Encoding.ASCII.GetBytes("This is my salt")
Dim key As Rfc2898DeriveBytes = _
    New Rfc2898DeriveBytes(args(0), saltValueBytes)
Dim secretKey As Byte() = key.GetBytes(16)

' Step 2: Create the hash algorithm object
Dim myHash As HMACSHA1 = New HMACSHA1(secretKey)

' Step 3: Store the data to be hashed in a byte array
Dim file As FileStream = _
    New FileStream(args(1), FileMode.Open, FileAccess.Read)
Dim reader As BinaryReader = New BinaryReader(file)

' Step 4: Call the HashAlgorithm.ComputeHash method
myHash.ComputeHash(reader.ReadBytes(CType(file.Length, Integer)))

' Step 5: Retrieve the HashAlgorithm.Hash byte array
Console.WriteLine(System.Convert.ToBase64String(myHash.Hash))

// C#
byte[] saltValueBytes  = Encoding.ASCII.GetBytes("This is my salt");
Rfc2898DeriveBytes passwordKey =
    new Rfc2898DeriveBytes(args[0], saltValueBytes);
byte[] secretKey = passwordKey.GetBytes(16);

// Step 2: Create the hash algorithm object
HMACSHA1 myHash = new HMACSHA1(secretKey);

// Step 3: Store the data to be hashed in a byte array
FileStream file = new FileStream(args[1], FileMode.Open, FileAccess.Read);
BinaryReader reader = new BinaryReader(file);
```

```
// Step 4: Call the HashAlgorithm.ComputeHash method
myHash.ComputeHash(reader.ReadBytes((int)file.Length));

// Step 5: Retrieve the HashAlgorithm.Hash byte array
Console.WriteLine(Convert.ToBase64String(myHash.Hash));
```

If either the file contents or the password changes, the computed hash also changes. This ensures that both the sender and recipient used the same password to generate the hash, which prevents an attacker from modifying the hash. Consider the following sequence of commands and their output. The sequence creates a new text file, computes the hash repeatedly, and then modifies the file. After either the file or the password (and key) are modified, the hash also changes:

```
C:\>echo Hello, World! > HashThis.txt

C:\>KeyedHashExample SomePassword HashThis.txt
tO4kYA9Z2ki+JbzUqe7llE6EjN4=

C:\>KeyedHashExample SomePassword HashThis.txt
tO4kYA9Z2ki+JbzUqe7llE6EjN4=

C:\>KeyedHashExample NotSomePassword HashThis.txt
TFNPh9TspBobOvixylyJOfX/+vo=

C:\>echo Hello, again. >> HashThis.txt

C:\>KeyedHashExample SomePassword HashThis.txt
yW6K6G7diJEV3bV2nNttgtcCMOo=
```

Either HMACSHA1 or MACTripleDES can be used for the previous example. However, whereas HMACSHA1 accepts a secret key of any length, MACTripleDES accepts only secret keys of 8, 16, or 24 bytes.

Signing Files

A *digital signature* is a value that can be appended to electronic data to prove that it was created by someone who possesses a specific private key. Public-key algorithms can also be used to form digital signatures. Digital signatures authenticate the identity of a sender (if you trust the sender's public key) and help protect the integrity of data. A signature can be verified by anyone because the sender's public key can be publicly accessible and is typically included in the digital signature format.

IMPORTANT   **The Difference Between Digital Signatures and Encryption**

Digital signatures do not protect the secrecy of the data being signed. To protect the secrecy of the file, you must encrypt it.

Digital Signature Classes in the .NET Framework

The .NET Framework provides two classes for generating and verifying digital signatures: *DSACryptoServiceProvider* and *RSACryptoServiceProvider*. These classes use different algorithms but provide similar functionality. Each implements the following four methods for use with digital signatures:

- **SignHash**   Generates a digital signature based on the hash of a file

- **SignData**   Generates a digital signature by first generating the hash for a file and then generating a signature based on the hash

- **VerifyHash**   Verifies a digital signature based on the hash of a file

- **VerifyData**   Verifies a digital signature given the entire file's contents

Digital signatures provide separate methods for signing and verifying data, whereas hashes do not provide separate methods for verification. The reason that hash algorithms do not need a separate method for signing and verifying is that the recipient can easily re-create the hash and then compare the hash she generated with the hash the sender provided. However, digital signatures use asymmetric encryption. Therefore, the recipient cannot regenerate the signature without the sender's private key, although the signature can be verified by using the sender's public key. The *VerifyData* and *VerifyHash* methods use the public sender's public key; the *SignData* and *SignHash* methods use the sender's private key.

How to Generate and Verify a Digital Signature for a File

To generate a digital signature for a file, perform the following steps in your code:

1. Create the digital signature algorithm object.
2. Store the data to be signed in a byte array.
3. Call the *SignData* method and store the signature.
4. Export the public key.

To verify the digital signature, perform the following steps:

1. Create the digital signature algorithm object.
2. Import the signature and public key.
3. Store the data to be verified in a byte array.
4. Call the *VerifyData* method.

The following code sample is the *Main* method of a Console application that accepts a filename as a command-line argument and displays a Base64-encoded digital signature for the file based on a dynamically generated key pair. The public key and digital signature are stored in variables. Then the application verifies the signature with the public key by creating new objects:

```vb
' VB
' Signing Step 1: Create the digital signature algorithm object
Dim signer As DSACryptoServiceProvider = New DSACryptoServiceProvider

' Signing Step 2: Store the data to be signed in a byte array.
Dim file As FileStream = New FileStream(args(0), FileMode.Open, FileAccess.Read)
Dim reader As BinaryReader = New BinaryReader(file)
Dim data As Byte() = reader.ReadBytes(CType(file.Length, Integer))

' Signing Step 3: Call the SignData method and store the signature
Dim signature As Byte() = signer.SignData(data)

' Signing Step 4: Export the public key
Dim publicKey As String = signer.ToXmlString(False)
Console.WriteLine("Signature: " + Convert.ToBase64String(signature))
reader.Close()
file.Close()

' Verifying Step 1: Create the digital signature algorithm object
Dim verifier As DSACryptoServiceProvider = New DSACryptoServiceProvider

' Verifying Step 2: Import the signature and public key.
verifier.FromXmlString(publicKey)

' Verifying Step 3: Store the data to be verified in a byte array
Dim file2 As FileStream = New FileStream(args(0), FileMode.Open, FileAccess.Read)
Dim reader2 As BinaryReader = New BinaryReader(file2)
Dim data2 As Byte() = reader2.ReadBytes(CType(file2.Length, Integer))

' Verifying Step 4: Call the VerifyData method
If verifier.VerifyData(data2, signature) Then
    Console.WriteLine("Signature verified")
Else
    Console.WriteLine("Signature NOT verified")
End If
reader2.Close()
file2.Close()

// C#
// Signing Step 1: Create the digital signature algorithm object
DSACryptoServiceProvider signer = new DSACryptoServiceProvider();

// Signing Step 2: Store the data to be signed in a byte array.
FileStream file = new FileStream(args[0], FileMode.Open, FileAccess.Read);
BinaryReader reader = new BinaryReader(file);
byte[] data = reader.ReadBytes((int)file.Length);
```

```
// Signing Step 3: Call the SignData method and store the signature
byte[] signature = signer.SignData(data);

// Signing Step 4: Export the public key
string publicKey = signer.ToXmlString(false);

Console.WriteLine("Signature: " + Convert.ToBase64String(signature));
reader.Close();
file.Close();

// Verifying Step 1: Create the digital signature algorithm object
DSACryptoServiceProvider verifier = new DSACryptoServiceProvider();

// Verifying Step 2: Import the signature and public key.
verifier.FromXmlString(publicKey);

// Verifying Step 3: Store the data to be verified in a byte array
FileStream file2 = new FileStream(args[0], FileMode.Open, FileAccess.Read);
BinaryReader reader2 = new BinaryReader(file2);
byte[] data2 = reader2.ReadBytes((int)file2.Length);

// Verifying Step 4: Call the VerifyData method
if (verifier.VerifyData(data2, signature))
    Console.WriteLine("Signature verified");
else
    Console.WriteLine("Signature NOT verified");
reader2.Close();
file2.Close();
```

The previous example uses the *DSACryptoServiceProvider* class, but you can also use *RSACryptoServiceProvider* for digital signatures. *RSACryptoServiceProvider* usage is similar, but it requires providing a hash algorithm object for both the *SignData* and *Verify-Data* methods. The following code sample shows only the lines that would need to change from the previous example to use *RSACryptoServiceProvider* with the *SHA1CryptoServiceProvider* hash algorithm:

```
' VB
' Signing Step 1: Create the digital signature algorithm object
Dim signer As RSACryptoServiceProvider = New RSACryptoServiceProvider

' Signing Step 3: Call the SignData method and store the signature
Dim signature As Byte() = _
    signer.SignData(data, New SHA1CryptoServiceProvider)

' Verifying Step 1: Create the digital signature algorithm object
Dim verifier As RSACryptoServiceProvider = New RSACryptoServiceProvider

' Verifying Step 4: Call the VerifyData method
If verifier.VerifyData(data2, New SHA1CryptoServiceProvider, signature) Then

// C#
// Signing Step 1: Create the digital signature algorithm object
RSACryptoServiceProvider signer = new RSACryptoServiceProvider();
```

```
// Signing Step 3: Call the SignData method and store the signature
byte[] signature = signer.SignData(data, new SHA1CryptoServiceProvider());

// Verifying Step 1: Create the digital signature algorithm object
RSACryptoServiceProvider verifier = new RSACryptoServiceProvider();

// Verifying Step 4: Call the VerifyData method
if (verifier.VerifyData(data2, new SHA1CryptoServiceProvider(), signature))
```

Although this simplified example creates and verifies a signature within a single application, you typically would transfer the public key and digital signature across a network. The most convenient way to transfer digital signatures is to create a binary file that contains the public key, the digital signature, and the file data itself. However, you can also transmit them as separate files or separate network communications.

Lab: Encrypting and Decrypting Files

In this lab, you will write Console applications that encrypt and decrypt files using a password. The Console applications should take three parameters: the filename of the unencrypted file to read, the filename of the encrypted file to write, and the password. If you encounter a problem completing an exercise, the completed projects are available along with the sample files.

Exercise 1: Write a Console Application to Encrypt Files

In this exercise, you will create a Console application that encrypts files using a password.

1. Create a new Console application in either Visual Basic or C#.

2. Add the *System.Security.Cryptography* and *System.IO* namespaces to your project.

3. Add code to read the command-line parameters into strings. If you are using Visual Basic, you have to change the *Main* parameter declaration to accept an array of strings—for example, *Sub Main(ByVal args As String())*. The following code works, although you should add error handling that displays usage information if the user does not provide the correct parameters:

```
' VB
Dim inFileName As String = args(0)
Dim outFileName As String = args(1)
Dim password As String = args(2)

// C#
string inFileName = args[0];
string outFileName = args[1];
string password = args[2];
```

4. Write code to create the encryption object and specify the key and IV based on the provided password. The following code works:

```vb
' VB
' Create the password key
Dim saltValueBytes As Byte() = _
    System.Text.Encoding.ASCII.GetBytes("This is my salt")
Dim passwordKey As Rfc2898DeriveBytes = _
    New Rfc2898DeriveBytes(password, saltValueBytes)

' Create the algorithm and specify the key and IV
Dim alg As RijndaelManaged = New RijndaelManaged
alg.Key = passwordKey.GetBytes(alg.KeySize / 8)
alg.IV = passwordKey.GetBytes(alg.BlockSize / 8)
```

```csharp
// C#
// Create the password key
byte[] saltValueBytes  = Encoding.ASCII.GetBytes("This is my salt");
Rfc2898DeriveBytes passwordKey =
    new Rfc2898DeriveBytes(password, saltValueBytes);

// Create the algorithm and specify the key and IV
RijndaelManaged alg = new RijndaelManaged();
alg.Key = passwordKey.GetBytes(alg.KeySize/8);
alg.IV = passwordKey.GetBytes(alg.BlockSize/8);
```

5. Read the unencrypted file into a byte array, as the following code demonstrates:

```vb
' VB
' Read the unencrypted file into fileData
Dim inFile As FileStream = New FileStream(inFileName, _
    FileMode.Open, FileAccess.Read)
Dim fileData(inFile.Length) As Byte
inFile.Read(fileData, 0, CType(inFile.Length, Integer))
```

```csharp
// C#
// Read the unencrypted file into fileData
FileStream inFile = new FileStream(inFileName,
    FileMode.Open, FileAccess.Read);
byte[] fileData = new byte[inFile.Length];
inFile.Read(fileData, 0, (int)inFile.Length);
```

6. Create the *ICryptoTransform* object based on your cryptography algorithm. Then create a *FileStream* object to write the encrypted file. Create a *CryptoStream* object based on the *ICryptoTransform* object and the *FileStream* object, and then write the contents of the unencrypted file to the *CryptoStream*. The code to do this is as follows:

```vb
' VB
' Create the ICryptoTransform and CryptoStream object
Dim encryptor As ICryptoTransform = alg.CreateEncryptor
Dim outFile As FileStream = _
    New FileStream(outFileName, FileMode.OpenOrCreate, _
    FileAccess.Write)
```

```
Dim encryptStream As CryptoStream = _
    New CryptoStream(outFile, encryptor, CryptoStreamMode.Write)

' Write the contents to the CryptoStream
encryptStream.Write(fileData, 0, fileData.Length)

// C#
// Create the ICryptoTransform and CryptoStream object
ICryptoTransform encryptor = alg.CreateEncryptor();
FileStream outFile =
    new FileStream(outFileName, FileMode.OpenOrCreate, FileAccess.Write);
CryptoStream encryptStream = new CryptoStream(outFile, encryptor,
CryptoStreamMode.Write);

// Write the contents to the CryptoStream
encryptStream.Write(fileData, 0, fileData.Length);
```

7. Finally, close the files, as shown here:

```
' VB
' Close the file handles
encryptStream.Close()
inFile.Close()
outFile.Close()

// C#
// Close the file handles
encryptStream.Close();
inFile.Close();
outFile.Close();
```

8. Open a command prompt and use your application to encrypt a text file and an image file. Verify that the size of the encrypted files is approximately the same as the size of the unencrypted files. (It might be slightly larger due to padding added during encryption.) Attempt to open the encrypted files and verify that they are unreadable.

Exercise 2: Write a Console Application to Decrypt Files

In this exercise, you will create a Console application that decrypts files using a password.

1. Create a new Console application in either Visual Basic or C#.

2. Add the *System.Security.Cryptography* and *System.IO* namespaces to your project.

3. Similar to the application you wrote for Exercise 1, add code that creates an encryption algorithm object based on a password, reads an encrypted file, and writes a decrypted file. (If you are using Visual Basic, you have to change the *Main* parameter declaration to accept an array of strings.) For example, the

following code works, although you should add error handling that displays usage information if the user does not provide the correct parameters:

```vb
' VB
Sub Main(ByVal args As String())
    ' Read the command-line parameters
    Dim inFileName As String = args(0)
    Dim outFileName As String = args(1)
    Dim password As String = args(2)

    ' Create the password key
    Dim saltValueBytes As Byte() = _
        System.Text.Encoding.ASCII.GetBytes("This is my salt")
    Dim passwordKey As Rfc2898DeriveBytes = _
        New Rfc2898DeriveBytes(password, _
            saltValueBytes)

    ' Create the algorithm and specify the key and IV
    Dim alg As RijndaelManaged = New RijndaelManaged
    alg.Key = passwordKey.GetBytes(alg.KeySize / 8)
    alg.IV = passwordKey.GetBytes(alg.BlockSize / 8)

    ' Read the encrypted file into fileData
    Dim decryptor As ICryptoTransform = alg.CreateDecryptor
    Dim inFile As FileStream = _
        New FileStream(inFileName, FileMode.Open, FileAccess.Read)
    Dim decryptStream As CryptoStream = _
        New CryptoStream(inFile, decryptor, CryptoStreamMode.Read)
    Dim fileData(inFile.Length) As Byte
    decryptStream.Read(fileData, 0, CType(inFile.Length, Integer))

    ' Write the contents of the unencrypted file
    Dim outFile As FileStream = _
        New FileStream(outFileName, FileMode.OpenOrCreate, _
        FileAccess.Write)
    outFile.Write(fileData, 0, fileData.Length)

    ' Close the file handles
    decryptStream.Close()
    inFile.Close()
    outFile.Close()
End Sub

// C#
// Read the command-line parameters
string inFileName = args[0];
string outFileName = args[1];
string password = args[2];

// Create the password key
byte[] saltValueBytes = Encoding.ASCII.GetBytes("This is my salt");
Rfc2898DeriveBytes passwordKey =
    new Rfc2898DeriveBytes(password, saltValueBytes);
```

```
// Create the algorithm and specify the key and IV
RijndaelManaged alg = new RijndaelManaged();
alg.Key = passwordKey.GetBytes(alg.KeySize / 8);
alg.IV = passwordKey.GetBytes(alg.BlockSize / 8);

// Read the encrypted file into fileData
ICryptoTransform decryptor = alg.CreateDecryptor();
FileStream inFile =
    new FileStream(inFileName, FileMode.Open, FileAccess.Read);
CryptoStream decryptStream =
    new CryptoStream(inFile, decryptor, CryptoStreamMode.Read);
byte[] fileData = new byte[inFile.Length];
decryptStream.Read(fileData, 0, (int)inFile.Length);

// Write the contents of the unencrypted file
FileStream outFile =
    new FileStream(outFileName, FileMode.OpenOrCreate, FileAccess.Write);
outFile.Write(fileData, 0, fileData.Length);

// Close the file handles
decryptStream.Close();
inFile.Close();
outFile.Close();
```

4. Open a command prompt and use your application to decrypt the text file and image files that you encrypted earlier. Attempt to open the decrypted files, and verify that they are readable. Attempt to decrypt the files with the incorrect password and note that the application throws a *System.Security.Cryptography.CryptographicException*. You should catch this exception and display a friendly error message to the user indicating that they probably mistyped the password.

Lesson Summary

■ Symmetric key encryption is a cryptographic technique for protecting the privacy of data in situations where both the encryptor and decryptor have access to the same secret key. There are four symmetric algorithm classes in the .NET Framework: *RijndaelManaged*, *DES*, *TripleDES*, and *RC2*. The primary disadvantage of symmetric key encryption is that you have to transfer the key between the sender and receiver, and the key can be very complex. Alternatively, you can generate a key based on a user password by using the *Rfc2898DeriveBytes* class.

■ Asymmetric key encryption is a cryptographic technique for encrypting data using key pairs, in which one key performs the encryption, and the other key must be used to perform decryption. There are two asymmetric algorithm classes in the .NET Framework: *RSACryptoServiceProvider* and *DSACryptoService-Provider* (used only for creating digital signatures).

■ Hashes process a file and produce a unique key that can be used to validate the integrity of the file. If the file is modified in any way, a different hash results. Therefore, hashing is useful when you want to ensure that a file has not been changed.

■ Digital signatures enable you to use a public key to verify that a file is signed with a private key. In environments with a public-key infrastructure, you can use digital signatures to verify that a specific user created a file.

Lesson Review

You can use the following questions to test your knowledge of the information in Lesson 3, "Encrypting and Decrypting Data." The questions are also available on the companion CD if you prefer to review them in electronic form.

NOTE Answers

Answers to these questions and explanations of why each answer choice is right or wrong are located in the "Answers" section at the end of the book.

---

1. Which of the following classes requires both the encryptor and decryptor to have the same key? (Choose all that apply.)

   A. *RSACryptoServiceProvider*

   B. *RijndaelManaged*

   C. *TripleDES*

   D. *DSACryptoServiceProvider*

   E. *DES*

   F. *RC2*

2. Which of the following must be synchronized between the encryptor and decryptor when using symmetric encryption? (Choose all that apply.)

   A. *SymmetricAlgorithm.Key*

   B. *SymmetricAlgorithm.Salt*

   C. *SymmetricAlgorithm.IV*

   D. *SymmetricAlgorithm.Mode*

3. Under which circumstances should you export the private key from an asymmetric encryption algorithm?

   A. When transferring data across a network for a single session

   B. When a remote computer will be sending you a private file that you must be able to decrypt

   C. When you are encrypting a file that needs to be read later

   D. When you are sending a remote computer a private file that the remote computer must be able to decrypt

4. Which of the following are keyed hashing algorithms? (Choose all that apply.)

   A. *RIPEMD160*

   B. *HMACSHA1*

   C. *SHA512*

   D. *MACTripleDES*

   E. *MD5*

Chapter Review

To practice and reinforce the skills you learned in this chapter further, you can perform the following tasks:

- Review the chapter summary.
- Review the list of key terms introduced in this chapter.
- Complete the case scenarios. These scenarios set up real-world situations involving the topics of this chapter and ask you to create a solution.
- Complete the suggested practices.
- Take a practice test.

Chapter Summary

- Use role-based security (RBS) to control which users can access which aspects of your application. You can base RBS on the local Windows user database, an AD DS domain, or a custom user database.
- Discretionary access control lists (DACLs) define which users can access which objects, whereas security access control lists (SACLs) define what logging is performed when users attempt to access a file. You can use classes in the *System.Security.AccessControl* namespace to view and manipulate both types of ACLs.
- The cryptography classes in the *System.Security.Cryptography* namespace enable you to encrypt and decrypt data (using either symmetric or asymmetric algorithms), validate data (using hashing), and sign data (using digital signatures).

Key Terms

Do you know what these key terms mean? You can check your answers by looking up the terms in the glossary at the end of the book.

- Access control list (ACL)
- Advanced Encryption Standard (AES)
- Asymmetric encryption
- Authentication
- Authorization

- Cipher text
- Data Encryption Standard (DES)
- Declarative RBS demands
- Digital signature
- Discretionary access control list (DACL)
- Encryption key
- Hash
- Imperative RBS demands
- Inherited permissions
- Initialization vector (IV)
- Keyed hash algorithms
- *MD5* class
- Public Key Infrastructure (PKI)
- *RC2* class
- Role-based security (RBS)
- Security access control list (SACL)
- *SHA1* class
- Shared secret
- Symmetric encryption
- Triple DES

Case Scenarios

In the following case scenarios, you apply what you've learned about user and application security. You can find answers to these questions in the "Answers" section at the end of this book.

Case Scenario 1: Creating Custom Authentication Methods

You are a developer in the IT department of Litware, Inc., a company that manages electronic distribution for software companies. Your manager asks you to develop a Windows Forms application for the Accounting department. The application needs to work with the existing database to enable the Accounting team to keep track of accounts payable and to issue payments (to authorized users only). You interview key personnel and review the technical requirements before coming up with your solution.

Interviews

The following is a list of company personnel interviewed and their statements.

- **IT Manager** "The accounting team wanted to upgrade their commercial accounting package, but it costs, like, a zillion dollars and I said we could write our own program to add the new functionality they needed for, like, half that cost. They just need to enter payments when a bill comes in and then click a button to make the payment. Oh, they're concerned about security because apparently they don't trust some of their people. I'm not sure how they want to control things, but I will tell you that the user accounts and groups they use to access the application are stored in the database, not in our Active Directory."

- **Accountant** "Our needs, actually, are pretty simple. We have three different types of employees: temps, accountants, and managers. The temps do data entry and create new accounts payable entries. The accountants pay bills, but only if these bills are less than $1,500. Any bill $1,500 or higher must be paid by a manager."

- **Database Administrator** "This accounting database is a nightmare, but we're stuck with it. There's one big table, called Users, that has a row for each user containing the username and password *in cleartext*. Yeah, I told you it was bad, but at least you won't have to fool with encryption. There's another table named Groups that contains a row for every group membership. So, for example, John the temp has a row in the Users table containing his username and password, and another row in the Groups table that indicates that he is a member of the Temps group. Lori, the IT manager, happens to be in both the Accountants and Managers groups, so she has one row in the Users table and two rows in the Groups table. Make sense?"

Technical Requirements

Create a Windows Forms application that implements a customized authentication mechanism that queries the accounting database. Assume that you have two methods: *AddBill* and *PayBill*. Use each user's group memberships to determine whether the user can run a particular method.

Questions

Your manager asks you the following questions:

1. Which classes or interfaces will you use to implement the custom authentication mechanism?
2. How will you restrict access to the *AddBill* method?
3. How will you restrict access to the *PayBill* method?

Case Scenario 2: Protecting Data by Using Cryptography

You are a developer for Blue Yonder Airlines. Blue Yonder Airlines is a national airline that has been growing rapidly in the past two years and has more than quadrupled the number of flights in that time period. Blue Yonder Airlines has only a handful of developers, however. Your manager recently sent you to security training, and now she plans to use your skills to provide recommendations for different security problems throughout the organization.

Questions

Answer the following questions for your manager:

1. We keep the master records of all flights and passengers in a centralized database. An application that our team created then transfers that data to remote offices. What's the best way to encrypt this data?
2. Our application stores usernames and passwords in a database. How should we protect those passwords?
3. Occasionally, we distribute bonuses to employees and customers in the form of frequent flier miles and upgrades. These bonuses are always distributed from the central office. We want the application that runs at the remote offices to be able to verify that the bonus originated from the central office. How can we do this?

Suggested Practices

To help you master the "Improving the security of .NET Framework applications by using the .NET Framework security features" exam objective, complete the following tasks.

Implement a Custom Authentication Scheme by Using the *System.Security.Authentication* Classes

To master this objective, you should complete Practices 1 and 2.

- **Practice 1**   Create a client/server application that establishes an *SslStream* connection between the two hosts.

- **Practice 2**   Add authentication error handling to the application created in Practice 1 by catching multiple types of exceptions based on classes in the *System.Security.Authentication* namespace.

Access and Modify Identity Information by Using the *System.Security.Principal* Classes

For this task, you should complete at least Practices 1 and 2. If you want a better understanding of how you can implement custom authentication, complete Practice 3. If you have written an application that uses other authentication techniques, complete Practice 4 as well.

- **Practice 1**   List every time you have been authenticated in the past week.

- **Practice 2**   Write an application that implements a custom authentication scheme by implementing the *GenericIdentity* and *GenericPrincipal* classes.

- **Practice 3**   Write an application that implements a custom authentication scheme by implementing the *IIdentity* and *IPrincipal* interfaces.

- **Practice 4**   If you have written an application that authenticates users to a database, update the application to make use of the *System.Security.Authentication* classes.

Implement Access Control by Using the *System.Security.AccessControl* Classes

For this task, you should complete all three practices to gain a good understanding of how to view and control ACLs.

- **Practice 1**   Write an application that analyzes every folder on your hard drive and displays folders for which the Everyone group has access.

- **Practice 2**   Write a Console application named CopyACLs that functions exactly like the Copy command-line tool but copies both files and ACLs.

■ **Practice 3** Write an application that enables auditing for successfully adding values to the *Run* and *RunOnce* registry keys located in HKEY_LOCAL_MACHINE\Software\Microsoft\Windows\CurrentVersion\ and HKEY_CURRENT_USER\Software\Microsoft\Windows\CurrentVersion\.

Encrypt, Decrypt, and Hash Data by Using the *System.Security.Cryptography* Classes

For this task, you should complete at least Practices 1 and 2 to understand how to use digital signatures and hashing in the real world. Complete Practice 3 to gain a better understanding of how to use asymmetric encryption.

■ **Practice 1** Write an application to sign files and then verify the digital signature.

■ **Practice 2** Write an application that stores hashes of every .dll and .exe file on your computer and that later analyzes the files for changes and shows you which files have been modified.

■ **Practice 3** Write a client/server application that encrypts files on the client using a public key provided by the server, transfers them across a network, and then decrypts them on the server using the private key.

Take a Practice Test

The practice tests on this book's companion CD offer many options. For example, you can test yourself on just one exam objective or you can test yourself on all the 70-536 certification exam content. You can set up the test so that it closely simulates the experience of taking a certification exam or you can set it up in study mode so that you can look at the correct answers and explanations after you answer each question.

MORE INFO **Practice tests**

For details about all the practice test options available, see the section "How to Use the Practice Tests" in the Introduction of this book.

Chapter 13
Interoperating with COM

Although managed applications have many advantages over unmanaged applications, the vast amount of existing unmanaged applications means that .NET Framework developers must know how to interoperate with Component Object Model (COM) objects. Fortunately, it's usually very straightforward. At times, however, you need to control the marshaling process carefully to ensure that data is passed in correct formats.

This chapter describes how to access COM objects from .NET Framework applications and how to allow COM clients to use managed classes.

Exam objectives in this chapter:
- Expose COM components to the .NET Framework and the .NET Framework components to COM.
- Call unmanaged DLL functions in a .NET Framework application, and control the marshaling of data in a .NET Framework application.

Lessons in this chapter:

Before You Begin

To complete the lessons in this chapter, you should be familiar with Microsoft Visual Basic or C# and be comfortable with the following tasks:

- Creating a Console application in Microsoft Visual Studio using Visual Basic or C#
- Adding namespaces and system class library references to a project

Lesson 1: Using COM Components from the .NET Framework

Although the .NET Framework contains managed implementations of most Microsoft Windows application programming interfaces (APIs), several important APIs are still available only as COM objects. In addition, developers regularly need to access custom COM objects from .NET Framework applications. This lesson describes how to access COM components from managed assemblies.

After this lesson, you will be able to:

- Add a reference to a COM library or type library
- Import a type library using the Type Library Importer (Tlbimp.exe)
- Call unmanaged dynamic-link libraries (DLLs) using the *DllImport* attribute
- Use the *Marshal* class
- Pass structures to COM functions
- Implement callback functions
- Create a wrapper class

Estimated lesson time: 25 minutes

How to Add a Reference to a COM Library or Type Library

COM types are defined in a *type library. Component Object Model (COM)* is an unmanaged object-oriented programming model, and COM libraries contain classes, methods, and types. Type libraries can be stand-alone .tlb files that define only types, or they can be embedded in a .dll, .exe, .ocx, or .olb file.

The easiest way to access a COM library or type library from a .NET Framework application is to add a reference to it in Visual Studio. To add a reference to a COM library or type library, follow these steps:

1. In Visual Studio, from the Project menu, select Add Reference.

2. In the Add Reference dialog, click the COM tab.

3. Select the DLL you want to import and then click OK. If the DLL is not listed, or you want to add a reference to a .tlb file, click the Browse tab, select the file, and then click OK.

Now, you can reference the methods in the COM library just like a .NET Framework namespace. For example, if you add a reference to the Microsoft Speech Object Library (%Windir%\System32\Speech\Common\Sapi.dll), and import the *SpeechLib* namespace that it uses, you can write the following code in a .NET Framework application, which does exactly what it appears to do:

```vb
' VB
Dim voice As New SpVoice()
voice.Speak("Hello, world!", SpeechVoiceSpeakFlags.SVSFDefault)
```

```csharp
// C#
SpVoice voice = new SpVoice();
voice.Speak("Hello, world!", SpeechVoiceSpeakFlags.SVSFDefault);
```

As you can see, COM interop allows you to reference COM types and functions directly.

Deploying Applications That Use Interop

When deploying the application, be sure to distribute the appropriate COM DLL as well (if it is not included with Windows).

How to Import a Type Library Using the Type Library Importer

The Type Library Importer (Tlbimp.exe, available in the Visual Studio Command Prompt) creates an interop assembly that allows a .NET Framework to use a type defined in a type library. To use Tlbimp.exe, run it with administrative privileges and specify the path to the file containing the type library. The following sample illustrates this:

```
tlbimp %windir%\system32\speech\common\sapi.dll
```

The preceding command generates a new assembly. In this example, the assembly is named SpeechLib.dll, based on the name of the type library contained within Sapi.dll. (Use the */out* parameter to specify a filename for the new assembly.) You can then add a reference to the new assembly and use the types just as you would use a native .NET Framework type. If you simply add a reference to the type library in Visual Studio, the .NET Framework imports it automatically.

The namespace of the imported library by default uses the same name as that of the library from which it was created. To change the namespace, use the */namespace* parameter.

If you want the interop assembly to have a strong name, use the */keyfile* parameter to specify a key. With a strong name, you can install signed assemblies into the global assembly cache (GAC). For more information about the GAC, read Lesson 2 of Chapter 9, "Installing and Configuring Applications."

MORE INFO   For more information about Tlbimp.exe, visit *http://msdn.microsoft.com/en-us/library/ tt0cf3sx.aspx*. To export a type library programmatically, use the *TypeLibConverter.ConvertType LibToAssembly* method.

How to Call Unmanaged DLLs Using DllImport

Although the most straightforward way to call unmanaged DLLs is to add a reference to them in Visual Studio, you can also use the *System.Runtime.InteropServices* namespace and the *DllImport* attribute to import an unmanaged DLL. Then, you can declare a managed prototype that you will use to access the Win32 function.

The following Console application shows how to call the unmanaged *MessageBox* function in User32.dll:

```vb
' VB
Imports System.Runtime.InteropServices

Module Module1
    <DllImport("user32.dll")> _
    Public Function MessageBox(ByVal hWnd As Integer, _
        ByVal txt As String, ByVal caption As String, _
        ByVal Typ As Integer) As IntPtr
    End Function

    Sub Main()
        MessageBox(New IntPtr(0), "Hello, world!", "My box", 0)
    End Sub
End Module
```

```csharp
// C#
using System;
using System.Runtime.InteropServices;

namespace com_example
{
    class Program
    {
        [DllImport("user32.dll")]
        private static extern int MessageBox(IntPtr hWnd, String
            text, String caption, uint type);
```

```
    static void Main(string[] args)
    {
        MessageBox(
            new IntPtr(0), "Hello, world!", "My box", 0);
    }
  }
}
```

The .NET Framework uses interop marshaling to pass data between the .NET Framework and COM. *Marshaling* is the process of formatting parameters for use by COM, and it is required because COM types and classes in the .NET Framework can use slightly different formats. For example, if you pass a .NET string instance to a COM object, COM interop automatically converts it to the COM type *BStr*.

Although the default settings work for most scenarios, you can use the following properties with the *DllImport* attribute to control aspects of the external function call:

- **BestFitMapping** Enables or disables best-fit mapping when converting Unicode characters (used by the .NET Framework) to American National Standards Institute (ANSI) characters (used by COM). Setting this property to *true* enables Interop Marshaling to provide a similar character when no exact match exists. For example, it will convert the Unicode copyright character to *c* for unmanaged methods that accept ANSI characters. If no similar character exists, it is usually converted to the default *?* ANSI character (which causes an exception to be thrown if *ThrowOnUnmappableChar* is *true*).

- **CallingConvention** Specifies the calling convention to use in passing method arguments. The default, *WinAPI*, is typically sufficient.

- **CharSet** Controls how string parameters are marshaled. The default is *CharSet .Ansi*, which is sufficient unless you know the target function requires a different character set.

- **EntryPoint** Specifies the name of the function to be called. You need to specify this only if you want your managed prototype to have a different name from the COM function.

- **ExactSpelling** Controls whether an entry point should be modified to correspond to the character set. Typically, the default setting is sufficient.

- **PreserveSig** Controls whether unmanaged methods that have return values are translated directly or whether *HRESULT* or *retval* return values are converted to exceptions automatically. The default is *true*, which directly translates the return values. Set this to *false* only if you would rather perform exception handling in your application than examine the return value.

- **SetLastError**   Enables the caller to use the *Marshal.GetLastWin32Error* API function to determine whether an error occurred while executing the method. In Visual Basic, the default is *true* (which adds some overhead); in C# and C++, the default is *false*.

- **ThrowOnUnmappableChar**   Set this to *true* to throw an exception if marshaling encounters an unmappable Unicode character that is converted to an ANSI ? character.

For example, if you want to call the *MessageBox* function using the method name *ShowBox*, you need to specify the function name using the *EntryPoint* property, as the following example demonstrates:

```
' VB
Imports System.Runtime.InteropServices

Module Module1
    <DllImport("user32.dll", EntryPoint := "MessageBox")> _
    Public Function ShowBox(ByVal hWnd As Integer, _
        ByVal txt As String, ByVal caption As String, _
        ByVal Typ As Integer) As IntPtr
    End Function

    Sub Main()
        ShowBox(New IntPtr(0), "Hello, world!", "My box", 0)
    End Sub
End Module
```

```
// C#
using System;
using System.Runtime.InteropServices;

namespace com_example
{
    class Program
    {
        [DllImport("user32.dll", EntryPoint="MessageBox")]
        private static extern int ShowBox(IntPtr hWnd, String text,
            String caption, uint type);

        static void Main(string[] args)
        {
            ShowBox(new IntPtr(0), "Hello, world!", "My box", 0);
        }
    }
}
```

How to Use the *Marshal* Class

The *Marshal* class provides a set of static methods that are useful for interoperability. Perhaps most useful is the *Marshal.GetLastWin32Error* method, which returns an integer representing the last error that occurred. Typically, if an error occurs, Win32 functions return a *Boolean* value of *false* to indicate that an error occurred—you must then call *Marshal.GetLastWin32Error* to retrieve the error code. The following code sample demonstrates this:

```vb
' VB
Dim f As Boolean = Win32Call()
If Not f Then
    Console.WriteLine("Error: {0}", Marshal.GetLastWin32Error())
End If
```

```csharp
// C#
Boolean f = Win32Call();
if (!f)
{
    Console.WriteLine("Error: {0}", Marshal.GetLastWin32Error());
}
```

Another useful method is *Marshal.SizeOf*, which returns the number of bytes required for a class or object after it is marshaled to an unmanaged class. The following code sample demonstrates how to check the size both of a class and of an object. In this example, the size is 8 bytes for each because the class and the object are the same type:

```vb
' VB
Console.WriteLine(Marshal.SizeOf(GetType(Point)))
Dim p As New Point()
Console.WriteLine(Marshal.SizeOf(p))
```

```csharp
// C#
Console.WriteLine(Marshal.SizeOf(typeof(Point)));
Point p = new Point();
Console.WriteLine(Marshal.SizeOf(p));
```

Other useful methods include the following:

- **Copy** Copies data between a managed array and an unmanaged memory pointer

- **GenerateGuidForType** Returns the globally unique identifier (GUID) for the specified type or generates a new GUID

- **GenerateProgIdForType** Returns the programmatic identifier (ProgID) for the specified type

- **GetExceptionForHR** and **GetHRForException** Converts an *HRESULT* error code to a corresponding *Exception*, or vice versa

- **ReadByte, ReadInt16, ReadInt32, ReadInt64,** and **ReadIntPtr** Reads values from unmanaged memory

- ■ *WriteByte, WriteInt16, WriteInt32, WriteInt64,* and *WriteIntPtr*   Writes values to unmanaged memory

- ■ *ThrowExceptionForHR*   Throws an exception with the specified *HRESULT* value

In addition, *Marshal* provides two useful read-only properties:

- ■ *SystemDefaultCharSize*   The default character size on the system; the default is 2 for Unicode systems and 1 for ANSI systems.

- ■ *SystemMaxDBCSCharSize*   The maximum size of a double byte character set (DBCS), in bytes.

How to Pass Structures

Unmanaged functions often accept structures as parameters. Passing a structure to an unmanaged function might require you to specify the layout of the structure. You can specify the layout of a structure by using the *StructLayout* and *FieldOffset* attributes.

For example, consider the *PtInRect* function in User32.dll. The function has the following signature:

```
BOOL PtInRect(const RECT *lprc, POINT pt);
```

Notice that the first parameter must be passed by reference (as indicated by the asterisk preceding the parameter name). The following example demonstrates how to specify the layouts of the structures that are required to call the function:

```
' VB
Imports System.Runtime.InteropServices

<StructLayout(LayoutKind.Sequential)> Public Structure Point
    Public x As Integer
    Public y As Integer
End Structure

<StructLayout(LayoutKind.Explicit)> Public Structure Rect
    <FieldOffset(0)> Public left As Integer
    <FieldOffset(4)> Public top As Integer
    <FieldOffset(8)> Public right As Integer
    <FieldOffset(12)> Public bottom As Integer
End Structure

Class Win32API
    Declare Auto Function PtInRect Lib "user32.dll" _
    (ByRef r As Rect, p As Point) As Boolean
End Class
```

```csharp
// C#
using System.Runtime.InteropServices;

[StructLayout(LayoutKind.Sequential)]
public struct Point {
    public int x;
    public int y;
}

[StructLayout(LayoutKind.Explicit)]
public struct Rect {
    [FieldOffset(0)] public int left;
    [FieldOffset(4)] public int top;
    [FieldOffset(8)] public int right;
    [FieldOffset(12)] public int bottom;
}

class Win32API {
    [DllImport("User32.dll")]
    public static extern bool PtInRect(ref Rect r, Point p);
}
```

Notice the use of the *LayoutKind* enumeration with the *StructLayout* attribute. *Layout-Kind.Auto* gives full control to the CLR over the layout, including the sequence of the fields. *LayoutKind.Sequential* allows the CLR to define the layout of the structure using the sequence you specify. *LayoutKind.Explicit* requires you, the developer, to specify the number of bytes for every field in the structure (using the *FieldOffset* attribute).

How to Implement Callback Functions

Similar to handling events in a .NET Framework application, some COM functions will want to call into a method that you provide in order to return results. This is often indicated by arguments that begin with the *lp-* (long pointer) prefix and end with the *-Func* (function) suffix. For example, the *EnumWindows* function in User32.dll requires a callback for the first argument, as indicated by its signature:

```
BOOL EnumWindows(WNDENUMPROC lpEnumFunc, LPARAM lParam)
```

To call a function that requires a callback, follow these steps:

1. Create a method to handle the callback.

2. Create a delegate for the method.

3. Create a prototype for the function, specifying the delegate for the callback argument.

4. Call the function.

The following code sample demonstrates how to fulfill these requirements and call the *EnumWindows* function:

```vb
' VB
' Create a delegate for the method
Public Delegate Function CallBack(ByVal hwnd As Integer, _
    ByVal lParam As Integer) As Boolean

' Create a prototype for the function
Declare Function EnumWindows Lib "user32" ( _
    ByVal x As CallBack, ByVal y As Integer) As Integer

Sub Main()
    ' Call the function
    EnumWindows(AddressOf Report, 0)
End Sub

' Declare the method to handle the callback
Public Function Report(ByVal hwnd As Integer, _
    ByVal lParam As Integer) _
    As Boolean
    Console.WriteLine("Window handle is " & hwnd)
    Return True
End Function 'Report
```

```csharp
// C#
// Create a delegate for the method
public delegate bool CallBack(int hwnd, int lParam);

public class EnumReportApp {

    // Create a prototype for the function
    [DllImport("user32")]
    public static extern int EnumWindows(CallBack x, int y);

    public static void Main()
    {
        // Create an instance of the delegate
        CallBack myCallBack = new CallBack(EnumReportApp.Report);

        // Call the function
        EnumWindows(myCallBack, 0);
    }

    // Declare the method to handle the callback
    public static bool Report(int hwnd, int lParam) {
        Console.WriteLine("Window handle is " + hwnd);
        return true;
    }
}
```

In the preceding example, note that the *Report* method always returns *true*. Callback functions often require a nonzero return value to indicate success. Therefore, returning anything but zero indicates that the callback succeeded.

How to Create a Wrapper Class

To allow assemblies to call unmanaged code through a managed class, you can create a managed class with methods that, in turn, call unmanaged code. This layer of abstraction isn't necessary, but it can be convenient.

To create a wrapper class, declare DLL functions within a class. Then define a static method for each DLL function you want to call. For example, the following code sample creates a wrapper class named *Win32MessageBox* that calls the *MessageBox* function in User32.dll each time a .NET Framework application calls the *Win32MessageBox.Show* method. Notice that the *Main* method doesn't need to be aware that it's actually calling a function in an unmanaged DLL. This code sample requires the *System.Runtime .InteropServices* namespace:

```vb
' VB
Imports System.Runtime.InteropServices

Module Module1

    Public Class Win32MessageBox
        <DllImport("user32.dll")> _
        Private Shared Function MessageBox(ByVal hWnd As Integer, _
            ByVal txt As String, ByVal caption As String, _
            ByVal Typ As Integer) As IntPtr
        End Function

        Public Shared Sub Show(ByVal message As String, _
            ByVal caption As String)
            MessageBox(New IntPtr(0), message, caption, 0)
        End Sub
    End Class

    Sub Main()
        Win32MessageBox.Show("Hello, world!", "My box")
    End Sub

End Module
```

```csharp
// C#
using System;
using System.Runtime.InteropServices;

class Win32MessageBox
{
    [DllImport("user32.dll")]
    private static extern int MessageBox(IntPtr hWnd, String text,
        String caption, uint type);

    public static void Show(string message, string caption)
    {
        MessageBox(new IntPtr(0), message, caption, 0);
    }
}
```

```
class Program
{
    static void Main(string[] args)
    {
        Win32MessageBox.Show("Hello, world!", "My box");
    }
}
```

Real World

Tony Northrup

The .NET Framework provides managed equivalents to almost every Win32 function that you might need to call. In the real world, you'll use interoperability primarily to connect to internally developed COM objects that haven't been migrated to the .NET Framework. Typically, the most efficient way to handle interoperability is to create a wrapper class that exposes all useful functionality in the underlying COM object. Then you can make managed calls to the wrapper class. If you later migrate the COM object to the .NET Framework, simply add the functionality to your wrapper class, and you won't have to update any assemblies that use the wrapper class.

Lab: Create an Instance of a COM Object

Although the .NET Framework provides managed interfaces for most useful Windows features, the .NET Framework does not provide managed speech synthesis capabilities. Therefore, to generate speech, you must make calls into an unmanaged COM object. In this lab, you will do just that.

Exercise: Use the *SpeechLib* COM object

In this exercise, you will add a reference to the *SpeechLib* COM object and then pass it parameters from a WPF application.

1. Using Visual Studio, create a project using the WPF Application template in either Visual Basic .NET or C#. Name the project Speaker.

2. Add a textbox control and a button control to the WPF application.

3. Add a reference to the *SpeechLib* library. Click Project and then click Add Reference. Click the COM tab, click Microsoft Speech Object Library, and then click OK.

4. Create the *Button.Click* event handler by double-clicking the button control.

5. Add the *SpeechLib* namespace to the code file.

6. In the *Button.Click* event handler, write code to create an instance of *SpVoice*, and then call *SpVoice.Speak* with the contents of the textbox control. The following code sample demonstrates how to do this:

```VB
' VB
Dim voice As New SpVoice()
voice.Speak(textBox1.Text, SpeechVoiceSpeakFlags.SVSFDefault)
```

```C#
// C#
SpVoice voice = new SpVoice();
voice.Speak(textBox1.Text, SpeechVoiceSpeakFlags.SVSFDefault);
```

7. Build and run the application. Make sure the volume on your computer is turned up. Type a sentence into the text box and then click the button. The assembly calls the method in the COM object, which runs successfully.

Lesson Summary

- The easiest way to make calls into a COM library is to add a reference to the COM library to your Visual Studio project.

- You can use the Tlbimp.exe command-line tool to import a type library into an assembly.

- You can create prototype methods for functions in a COM library by using the *DllImport* attribute. If your prototype method uses a different name than the function, specify the function name using the *EntryPoint* property.

- Use the *Marshal.GetLastWin32Error* static method to retrieve the last Win32 error code. You can also use *Marshal.SizeOf* to determine the size of an object after it is marshaled.

- You might need to specify the layout of structures by using the *StructLayout* attribute. If you specify *LayoutKind.Explicit*, you must also use the *FieldOffset* attribute to specify exactly how the fields are laid out.

- To implement a callback function, create a method to handle the callback. Then create a delegate for the method. Next, create a prototype for the function, specifying the delegate for the callback argument. Finally, call the function.

- Wrapper classes are useful to provide a managed interface for unmanaged objects. To create a wrapper class, simply create a class that passes all calls to the unmanaged object.

Lesson Review

You can use the following questions to test your knowledge of the information in Lesson 1, "Using COM Components from the .NET Framework." The questions are also available on the companion CD if you prefer to review them in electronic form.

NOTE Answers

Answers to these questions and explanations of why each answer choice is right or wrong are located in the "Answers" section at the end of the book.

---

1. You are creating a new .NET Framework application that will replace an existing unmanaged application. Although you have long-term plans to replace all unmanaged code, in the interim you need to call an unmanaged method in a COM object. How can you do this? (Choose two; each correct answer is part of a complete solution.)

    A. Create an instance of the *Marshal* class

    B. Create a prototype method for the COM function

    C. Add *DllImportAttribute*

    D. Call the *Marshal.Copy* method

2. You need to call a static function in a COM object. The function is named *MyFunc* and is located in the MyApp.dll library. In your .NET Framework application, you want to call it using the name *MyMethod*. Which code sample allows you to do this?

    A.

    ```
    ' VB
    <DllImport("MyApp.dll", EntryPoint := "MyFunc")> _
    Public Sub MyMethod(ByVal text As String)
    End Sub

    // C#
    [DllImport("MyApp.dll", EntryPoint="MyFunc")]
    public static extern void MyMethod(String text);
    ```

    B.

    ```
    ' VB
    <DllImport("MyApp.dll", EntryPoint := "MyMethod")> _
    Public Sub MyFunc(ByVal text As String)
    End Sub

    // C#
    [DllImport("MyApp.dll", EntryPoint="MyMethod")]
    public static extern void MyFunc(String text);
    ```

C.

```vb
' VB
<DllImport("MyApp.dll", BestFitMapping := "MyFunc")> _
Public Sub MyMethod(ByVal text As String)
End Sub
```

```csharp
// C#
[DllImport("MyApp.dll", BestFitMapping="MyFunc")]
public static extern void MyMethod(String text);
```

D.

```vb
<DllImport("MyApp.dll", BestFitMapping := "MyMethod")> _
Public Sub MyFunc(ByVal text As String)
End Sub
```

```csharp
// C#
[DllImport("MyApp.dll", BestFitMapping="MyMethod")]
public static extern void MyFunc(String text);
```

Lesson 2: Using .NET Types from COM Applications

COM applications can create instances of .NET Framework classes and call .NET Framework methods. However, for your assembly to be accessible, you must export it to a type library and register it. In addition, to ensure compatibility, you might have to update your code to map exceptions and *HRESULT* error codes or to override the default marshaling settings.

After this lesson, you will be able to:

- Design .NET types to be accessed by COM applications
- Use interoperability attributes to adjust the default behavior when exposing .NET types to COM applications
- Export a type library using the Type Library Exporter
- Register an assembly
- Map *HRESULT* error codes and exceptions
- Control marshaling manually

Estimated lesson time: 25 minutes

Guidelines for Exposing .NET Types to COM Applications

Follow these guidelines when planning to expose a .NET type to a COM application:

- Types, methods, properties, fields, and events must be public. Use *ComVisible-Attribute* to prevent COM applications from accessing a member.

- Classes should implement interfaces explicitly. Although you can allow the COM interop to generate a class interface automatically, changes to your class might alter the layout of the automatically generated class interface.

- Types must have a default constructor with no parameters. You should avoid using parameterized constructors.

- Types cannot be abstract.

- You should avoid using static methods. Instead, design classes so that the consumer creates an instance of them.

- Define event-source interfaces in managed code.

- Include *HRESULT* error codes in custom exception classes.

- Supply GUIDs for types that require them.

Interoperability Attributes

The *System.Runtime.InteropServices* namespace provides several attributes that you can use to adjust the default behavior when exposing .NET types to COM applications. Although the most important attributes have already been discussed, the following attributes are also useful:

- **AutomationProxyAttribute** Specifies whether the type should be marshaled using the Automation marshaler or a custom proxy.

- **ClassInterfaceAttribute** Controls whether Tlbexp.exe automatically generates a class interface. Generally, you should avoid using the automatically generated interface.

- **ComRegisterFunctionAttribute and ComUnregisterFunctionAttribute** Specifies a method that should be called when the assembly is registered or unregistered for use from COM so that you can run custom code.

- **ComSourceInterfacesAttribute** Identifies COM event sources. The class event name and the interface method name must be the same.

- **ComVisibleAttribute** When set to *false*, prevents COM from viewing a type or an entire assembly. By default, all managed public types are visible.

- **InAttribute** Indicates that data should be marshaled into the caller. This is often combined with *OutAttribute* to allow the caller to see the changes made by the callee.

- **OutAttribute** Indicates that the data in a field or parameter must be marshaled from a called object back to its caller. This is equivalent to using the *out* keyword in C#.

- **ProgIdAttribute** Specifies the ProgID of a class manually. If you don't specify this, it is automatically generated by combining the namespace with the type name.

The following code sample demonstrates how to use *ComVisibleAttribute* to hide a method and a property in a custom class:

```vb
' VB
Imports System.Runtime.InteropServices

Class MySecretClass
    Public Sub New()
    End Sub

    <ComVisible(False)> _
    Public Function Method1(param As String) As Integer
        Return 0
    End Function
```

```
    Public Function Method2() As Boolean
        Return True
    End Function

    <ComVisible(False)> _
    Public ReadOnly Property Property1() As Integer
        Get
            Return Property1
        End Get
    End Property

End Class

// C#
using System.Runtime.InteropServices;

class MySecretClass
{
    public MySecretClass()
    {
    }

    [ComVisible(false)]
    public int Method1(string param)
    {
        return 0;
    }

    public bool Method2()
    {
        return true;
    }

    [ComVisible(false)]
    public int Property1
    {
        get
        {
            return Property1;
        }
    }
}
```

How to Export a Type Library Using the Type Library Exporter

The Type Library Exporter (Tlbexp.exe, available in the Visual Studio Command Prompt) creates a COM type library from an assembly. To use Tlbexp.exe, simply specify the path to the file containing the type library, as the following sample illustrates:

```
tlbexp MyAssembly.dll
```

The previous command generates a new type library with a .tlb extension. To specify a different filename, use the /out parameter. COM clients can use the type library to create an instance of the .NET Framework class and call the methods of the instance, just as if it were a COM object.

For more information about Tlbexp.exe, visit *http://msdn.microsoft.com/en-us/ library/hfzzah2c.aspx*. To export a type library programmatically, use the *TypeLib Converter.ConvertAssemblyToTypeLib* method.

How to Register an Assembly

To allow COM clients to create .NET Framework classes without explicitly loading the exported type library, register the assembly or type library. You can do this using Visual Studio or by using the Assembly Registration Tool (Regasm.exe). Regasm.exe is available in the %Windir%\Microsoft.NET\Framework\v2.0.50727\ folder and works with all versions of the .NET Framework, or you can run it from the Visual Studio 2008 Command Prompt (provided that you open the command prompt with administrative privileges).

How to Register an Assembly Using Visual Studio

To register an assembly during the build process using Visual Studio, follow these steps:

1. Create the .NET Framework class library.
2. From the Project menu select *<classname>* Properties.
3. Click the Build tab. Select the Register For COM Interop check box in the Output section.
4. Build the project.

When you build the project, Visual Studio creates the type library and registers it so that it can be accessed from COM.

How to Register an Assembly Manually

Use Regasm.exe to register an assembly manually. The following command, which requires administrative privileges, registers all public classes contained in myAssembly.dll:

```
regasm myAssembly.dll
```

The following command generates a file called MyAssembly.reg, which you can open to install the necessary registry entries. Regasm.exe does not update the registry when you use the */regfile* parameter, though:

```
regasm myAssembly.dll /regfile:myAssembly.reg
```

The following command registers all public classes contained in MyAssembly.dll and generates and registers a type library called MyAssembly.tlb, which contains definitions of all the public types defined in myAssembly.dll:

```
regasm myAssembly.dll /tlb:myAssembly.tlb
```

MORE INFO   For more information about Regasm.exe, visit *http://msdn.microsoft.com/en-us/library/ tzat5yw6.aspx*. To export a type library programmatically, use the *RegistrationServices* class.

How to Map HRESULT Error Codes and Exceptions

The .NET Framework uses exceptions to indicate errors, whereas COM methods return *HRESULT* values. .NET Framework interoperability automatically maps *HRESULT* error codes and exceptions, so you don't need to specify an *HRESULT* value for standard managed exceptions. For example, the *COR_E_IO HRESULT* maps to *IOException*, and the *COR_E_THREADABORTED HRESULT* maps to *ThreadAbortException*.

If you create a custom exception class, you can specify your own *HRESULT* by providing a value for the *Exception.HResult* integer, as the following code sample demonstrates:

```vb
' VB
Public Class NoAccessException
    Inherits ApplicationException
    Public Sub New()
        HResult = 12
    End Sub
End Class
```

```csharp
// C#
public class NoAccessException : ApplicationException
{
    public NoAccessException()
    {
        HResult = 12;
    }
}
```

When handling exceptions from COM objects, these *Exception* properties provide access to details from the COM *HRESULT*:

- **ErrorCode**   *HRESULT* returned from call

- **Message**   String returned from *IErrorInfo->GetDescription*

- **Source**   String returned from *IErrorInfo->GetSource*

- **StackTrace**   The stack trace

- **TargetSite**   The name of the method that returned the failing *HRESULT*

How to Control Marshaling

COM interop automatically marshals data types for you, so manual conversion isn't necessary. However, if the COM function expects a different format than marshaling would provide by default, you can control marshaling manually to override the automatic behavior. The runtime has a default marshaling behavior for every type. However, if you want a parameter, field, or return value to be converted to a nondefault COM type, you can specify the *MarshalAs* attribute. The following code sample demonstrates how to marshal a string parameter to the *LPStr* COM type:

```
' VB
Private Sub MyMethod(<MarshalAs(LPStr)> ByVal s As String)
End Sub

// C#
void MyMethod([MarshalAs(LPStr)] String s);
```

The following code sample demonstrates how to use the *MarshalAs* attribute to control the marshaling of a return value:

```
' VB
Public Function SayHi() As <MarshalAs(UnmanagedType.LPWStr)> String
    Return "Hello World"
End Function

// C#
[return: MarshalAs(UnmanagedType.LPWStr)]
public String SayHi()
{
    return "Hello World";
}
```

The following code sample demonstrates how to use the *MarshalAs* attribute to control the marshaling of a property:

```VB
' VB
Class SimpleClass
    <MarshalAs(UnmanagedType.LPWStr)> Public txt As String
End Class
```

```C#
// C#
class SimpleClass
{
    [MarshalAs(UnmanagedType.LPWStr)]
    public String txt;
}
```

You need to configure marshaling manually only when the COM caller requires a data format other than what the default marshaling would use.

Lab: Expose a .NET Framework Class to COM

In this lab, you will prepare a .NET Framework class to be accessed from COM applications.

Exercise: Prepare and Register a .NET Framework Class

In this exercise, you will update a .NET Framework class so that it follows guidelines for being accessed from a COM application. Then you register the library with COM.

1. Navigate to the \<*InstallHome*>\Chapter13\Lesson2\Exercise1\Partial folder and open either the C# version or the Visual Basic .NET version of the solution file.

2. Add the *System.Runtime.InteropServices* namespace to your code file.

3. Types, methods, properties, fields, and events must be public. Although the *_value* property shouldn't be accessed directly, you still must change it to public. To prevent COM applications from accessing it, use the *ComVisible* attribute to hide it.

    ```VB
    ' VB
    <ComVisible(False)> _
    Public _value As Integer = 0
    ```

    ```C#
    // C#
    [ComVisible(false)]
    public int _value = 0;
    ```

4. Build the assembly. Note the folder that the assembly is stored in.

5. Run the Visual Studio Command Prompt with administrative credentials. In Windows Vista, you need to right-click the prompt, click Run As Administrator, and then respond to the User Account Control (UAC) prompt.

6. Use Tlbexp.exe to create a type library from the assembly by running the following command, replacing *<path>* appropriately:

```
Tlbexp "<path>\MathLibrary.dll"
```

7. The type library is ready to use. Now, register the assembly using Regasm. Run the following command:

```
Regasm /tlb "<path>\MathLibrary.dll"
```

Now, your .NET Framework class is ready to be accessed from a COM application.

Lesson Summary

- When creating a .NET type to be used by COM applications, mark all types, methods, properties, fields, and events as public, and use *ComVisibleAttribute* to hide members. Provide only a default constructor. Avoid using abstract types and static methods. Include HRESULT error codes in custom exception classes and provide GUIDs for types that require them.

- Use *InAttribute* and *OutAttribute* to allow callers to see changes made to parameters by the callee.

- Use Tlbexp.exe to export an assembly to a type library.

- You can register an assembly during the build process using Visual Studio. Alternatively, you can use Regasm.exe to register an assembly manually.

- Set the *Exception.HResult* property to define an *HRESULT* value for a custom exception class.

- Use the *MarshalAs* attribute to override the default marshaling behavior. This is required only when the caller requires the data in a format other than the format that marshaling provides by default.

Lesson Review

You can use the following questions to test your knowledge of the information in Lesson 2, "Using .NET Types from COM Applications." The questions are also available on the companion CD if you prefer to review them in electronic form.

NOTE Answers

Answers to these questions and explanations of why each answer choice is right or wrong are located in the "Answers" section at the end of the book.

---

1. You are creating a class that will be accessed by COM applications. Which of the following should you do? (Choose all that apply.)

    A. Make the class abstract

    B. Create all methods as public

    C. Create all methods as static

    D. Provide a default constructor

2. You are creating a class that will be accessed from COM applications. You want changes made to parameters to be available to the calling application. Which of the following attributes should you apply to the parameters? (Choose all that apply.)

    A. *ClassInterfaceAttribute*

    B. *InAttribute*

    C. *OutAttribute*

    D. *AutomationProxyAttribute*

3. You are creating a .NET Framework application that needs to call methods located in a COM object. You want to create a .NET Framework assembly using the COM object so that you can reference it more easily in your project. Which tool should you use?

    A. Tlbimp.exe

    B. Tlbexp.exe

    C. Regasm.exe

    D. Regedit.exe

Chapter Review

To practice and reinforce the skills you learned in this chapter further, you can perform the following tasks:

- Review the chapter summary.
- Review the list of key terms introduced in this chapter.
- Complete the case scenarios. These scenarios set up real-world situations involving the topics of this chapter and ask you to create a solution.
- Complete the suggested practices.
- Take a practice test.

Chapter Summary

- You can access a COM library by adding a reference in Visual Studio, by using the Tlbimp.exe command-line tool, or by creating prototype methods using the *DllImport* attribute. Use the *Marshal.GetLastWin32Error* static method to retrieve the last Win32 error code. If a function requires a nonstandard structure layout, specify the layout using the *StructLayout* attribute. To implement a callback function, create a method to handle the callback, a delegate, and a prototype. Create a wrapper class to provide a managed interface for unmanaged objects.

- For .NET types to be accessible to COM applications, they must follow specific guidelines, including having public members, providing a default constructor, and avoiding static methods. Use Tlbexp.exe to export an assembly to a type library. You can register an assembly during the build process using Visual Studio or with the Regasm.exe tool. Set the *Exception.HResult* property to define an *HRESULT* value for a custom exception class. Use the *MarshalAs* attribute to override the default marshaling behavior.

Key Terms

Do you know what these key terms mean? You can check your answers by looking up the terms in the glossary at the end of the book.

- Component Object Model (COM)
- Marshaling
- Type library

Case Scenarios

In the following case scenarios, you apply what you've learned about how to interoperate with COM. You can find answers to these questions in the "Answers" section at the end of this book.

Case Scenario 1: Creating a .NET Framework User Interface with COM Libraries

You are an application developer for Alpine Ski House. You and your team are updating the application that employees use to sell lift tickets, book rooms, and rent equipment.

The previous version of the application was written in C++ using Win32. It uses several COM libraries for application logic, such as communicating with the back-end database.

As you begin to migrate the application to the .NET Framework, you plan to start by rewriting the user interface. Once the user interface is in place, you will rewrite the application logic. Therefore, you need the user interface (written using the .NET Framework) to call methods in the COM libraries.

Questions

Answer the following questions for your manager:

1. How can you call methods in COM libraries from a .NET Framework application?

2. Several of the COM functions require you to pass structures to them. How can you ensure that the structures are passed in the correct format?

3. I'd rather have the other developers accessing a .NET Framework class. Can you create a managed class that simply forwards all requests to the unmanaged types?

Case Scenario 2: Creating a .NET Library That Can Be Accessed from COM

You are an application developer working for Proseware, Inc. You are in the process of updating a three-tiered application. Currently, the user interface is a Win32 application. The application logic is implemented in COM objects. The third layer is a SQL Server database. Although you plan to replace both the user interface and the application logic with the .NET Framework, you plan to replace the application logic first.

To replace COM objects, you must allow the Win32 user interface to create instances of managed classes. Although you can update the Win32 user interface to access different libraries, you want to minimize the scope of the changes.

Questions

Answer the following questions for your manager:

1. How can you replace the COM objects with a .NET Framework library?

2. Given that COM applications don't support exceptions, how will you pass error information back to COM?

3. How can you ensure that strings are passed back in the correct format?

Suggested Practices

To master the "Implementing Interoperability, Reflection, and Mailing Functionality in a .NET Framework Application" exam objective, complete the following tasks.

Expose COM Components to the .NET Framework and the .NET Framework Components to COM

For this task, you should complete at least Practices 1 and 2. If you have the resources and knowledge to create Win32 applications, complete Practices 3 and 4 as well.

- **Practice 1** Create a .NET Framework application that accesses a COM object. Handle any exceptions that might arise.

- **Practice 2** Create a wrapper class for a COM object so that you can access it directly from managed code.

- **Practice 3** Create a Win32 application that accesses a .NET Framework class that you created for a real-world application. Troubleshoot any problems that arise.

- **Practice 4** Create a Win32 application that accesses the *Math* class that you created in the Lesson 2 lab.

Call Unmanaged DLL Functions within a .NET Framework Application, and Control the Marshaling of Data in a .NET Framework Application

For this task, you should complete both practices.

- **Practice 1** Using a real-world class that you created, manually configure marshaling for all properties and methods.

- **Practice 2** Create a custom exception class (or use a real-world exception class that you created) and define a specific *HRESULT* value.

Take a Practice Test

The practice tests on this book's companion CD offer many options. For example, you can test yourself on just the content covered in this chapter, or you can test yourself on all the 70-536 certification exam content. You can set up the test so that it closely simulates the experience of taking a certification exam, or you can set it up in study mode so that you can look at the correct answers and explanations after you answer each question.

MORE INFO   Practice tests

For details about all the practice test options available, see the section "How to Use the Practice Tests," in the Introduction of this book.

Chapter 14
Reflection

Using *reflection*, the .NET Framework gives you the ability to open, run, and even generate assemblies and the types contained within dynamically. Reflection is useful anytime you need to examine or run code that isn't available at runtime, such as when you need to load add-ons. This chapter provides an overview of how to use reflection.

Exam objective in this chapter:
- Implement reflection functionality in a .NET Framework application, and create metadata, Microsoft intermediate language (MSIL), and a PE file by using the *System.Reflection.Emit* namespace.

Lesson in this chapter:

Before You Begin

To complete the lesson in this chapter, you should be familiar with Microsoft Visual Basic or C# and be comfortable with the following tasks:

- Creating a Console application in Microsoft Visual Studio using Visual Basic or C#

- Adding namespaces and system class library references to a project

Lesson 1: Using Reflection

In most development scenarios, you have access to all the assemblies and code that your application requires during the development process. However, some applications require extensibility that can be achieved only by writing code that can dynamically add features contained in external assemblies. Depending on your requirements, you might even need to generate an assembly dynamically. This lesson provides an overview of reflection and describes how to create instances of types and call methods in a dynamically loaded assembly, how to load assemblies, how to define and examine assembly attributes, and how to generate assemblies and types dynamically.

After this lesson, you will be able to:

- Describe how reflection works
- Load assemblies dynamically
- Create instances of types and call methods in a dynamically loaded assembly
- Edit and read assembly attributes
- Generate assemblies, types, constructors, and methods dynamically

Estimated lesson time: 30 minutes

Reflection Overview

Most of the time, you have direct access to types during development. However, there are times when you might want to load an assembly, and the types and methods contained within, dynamically at runtime. For example, an application that supports plug-ins should be written to run a plug-in dynamically even though the plug-in is not accessible when the application is being developed.

Reflection allows you to load assemblies at runtime, dynamically create an instance of a type, and bind the type to an existing object. Then you can invoke the type's methods and access its properties.

How to Load Assemblies

You can load an assembly at runtime. Once you load the assembly, you can examine its attributes and, depending on the method you used to load it, create instances of types and run methods. The methods you can use to load an assembly are the following:

- *Assembly.Load*   Loads an assembly by name, usually from the Global Assembly Cache (GAC)

- *Assembly.LoadFile*   Loads an assembly by specifying the filename

- *Assembly.LoadFrom* Loads an assembly given its filename or path

- *Assembly.ReflectionOnlyLoad* Loads an assembly, usually from the GAC, in a reflection-only context (described next)

- *Assembly.ReflectionOnlyLoadFrom* Loads an assembly, in a reflection-only context, by specifying the filename

Loading an assembly in a reflection-only context allows you to examine the assembly but not create instances of types or run methods. Therefore, it's useful only when you need to examine an assembly or the code contained within it. Often, developers use the reflection-only context to examine assemblies compiled for other platforms or for other versions of the .NET Framework.

To load an assembly in a reflection-only context, use the *Assembly.ReflectionOnlyLoad* or *Assembly.ReflectionOnlyLoadFrom* method. Although you can't create objects, you can examine the assembly's attributes, as described later in this lesson.

How to Create Instances and Call Methods

You can use reflection to create an instance of a type that isn't available until runtime by creating an instance of the *Type* class. Although you can simply specify an existing type, typically you would create the *Type* by calling *Assembly.GetType* and specifying the name of the type to load from the assembly.

Once you create an instance of *Type*, you can access the members of the type. Call *Type.GetMethod* to create an instance of *MethodInfo*. *GetMethod* requires you to specify the method name (as a string) and the parameters required by the method (as a *Type* array).

Once you create an instance of *MethodInfo*, you can call the method using *MethodInfo.Invoke*. The first parameter of *Invoke* is the object instance that contains the method. The second parameter of *Invoke* is an object array representing the parameters required by the method. *Invoke* always returns an *Object* instance, which you can cast to the type returned by the method you called.

The following code sample demonstrates how to create a *StringBuilder* instance and call *StringBuilder.Append* using reflection. In the real world, you wouldn't create a *Type* instance for a class built into the .NET Framework. Instead, you would load a type from an external assembly:

```
' VB
' Create a Type instance.
' Typically, this would be done by loading an external assembly,
' and then calling Assembly.GetType()
Dim t As Type = GetType(StringBuilder)
```

```
' Create a ConstructorInfo instance that will allow us to create an
' instance of the Type we just loaded.
' GetConstructor requires a list of parameters in a Type array
' that match those required by the constructor.
' This example represents the StringBuilder constructor that
' requires a single parameter.
Dim ci As ConstructorInfo = t.GetConstructor(New Type() {GetType(String)})

' Create an instance of the type by calling ConstructorInfo.Invoke.
' Provide the parameters required by the constructor: a single string.
' This creates a StringBuilder instance.
Dim sb As Object = ci.Invoke(New Object() {"Hello, "})

' Create a MethodInfo instance representing the StringBuilder.Append method.
' GetMethod requires the first parameter to be the name of the method.
' The second parameter is a Type array representing the parameters required
' by the method. We're using the Append overload that requires a single string.
Dim sbAppend As MethodInfo = t.GetMethod("Append", New Type() {GetType(String)})

' Call StringBuilder.Append and provide a single parameter: the string "world!".
Dim result As Object = sbAppend.Invoke(sb, New Object() {"world!"})

' Write the StringBuilder instance to the console.
Console.WriteLine(result)

// C#
// Create a Type instance.
// Typically, this would be done by loading an external assembly,
// and then calling Assembly.GetType()
Type t = typeof(StringBuilder);

// Create a ConstructorInfo instance that will allow us to create an
// instance of the Type we just loaded.
// GetConstructor requires a list of parameters in a Type array
// that match those required by the constructor.
// This example represents the StringBuilder constructor that
// requires a single parameter.
ConstructorInfo ci = t.GetConstructor(new Type[] { typeof(string) });

// Create an instance of the type by calling ConstructorInfo.Invoke.
// Provide the parameters required by the constructor: a single string.
// This creates a StringBuilder instance.
Object sb = ci.Invoke(new Object[] { "Hello, " });

// Create a MethodInfo instance representing the StringBuilder.Append method.
// GetMethod requires the first parameter to be the name of the method.
// The second parameter is a Type array representing the parameters required
// by the method. We're using the Append overload that requires a single string.
MethodInfo sbAppend = t.GetMethod("Append", new Type[] { typeof(string) });

// Call StringBuilder.Append and provide a single parameter: the string "world!".
Object result = sbAppend.Invoke(sb, new Object[] { "world!" });
```

```
// Write the StringBuilder instance to the console.
Console.WriteLine(result);
```

Once you create an instance of *MethodInfo*, you can call *MethodInfo.GetMethodBase* to retrieve an instance of *MethodBody*. You then can call *MethodBody.GetILAsByteArray* to retrieve a byte array containing the actual intermediate language (IL) code used to run the method; information that is primarily useful for analyzing another developer's code. *Intermediate language (IL)* is the language to which managed applications are compiled. *MethodBody.LocalVariables* is a collection of local variables (although you cannot retrieve the values or names of the variables). *MethodBody.ExceptionHandlingClauses* is a collection of exception handling clauses in the method body.

Exam Tip   Although developers rarely use this class in practice, *MethodBody* is listed on the official 70-536 exam objectives, and for that reason, you should be familiar with it.

You can access properties, fields, and constructors using the *Type.GetProperty*, *Type.GetField*, and *Type.GetConstructors* methods, which return *PropertyInfo*, *FieldInfo*, and *ConstructorInfo* instances, respectively. These work in almost the identical way as *Type.GetMethod*.

The *MethodBase* Class

MethodBase is the base class for both *MethodInfo* and *ConstructorInfo*. Although you won't have to directly use the class, it is listed on the 70-536 exam objectives.

The following example demonstrates how to use reflection to access the *StringBuilder.Length* read-only property and display the value to the console:

```
' VB
Dim t As Type = GetType(StringBuilder)
Dim ci As ConstructorInfo = t.GetConstructor(New Type() {GetType(String)})
Dim sb As Object = ci.Invoke(New Object() {"Hello, world!"})

' Create a PropertyInfo instance representing the StringBuilder.Length property.
Dim lengthProperty As PropertyInfo = t.GetProperty("Length")

' Retrieve the Length property and cast it to the native type.
Dim length As Integer = CInt(lengthProperty.GetValue(sb, Nothing))
Console.WriteLine(length.ToString())

// C#
Type t = typeof(StringBuilder);
ConstructorInfo ci = t.GetConstructor(new Type[] { typeof(string) });
Object sb = ci.Invoke(new Object[] { "Hello, world!" });

// Create a PropertyInfo instance representing the StringBuilder.Length property.
PropertyInfo lengthProperty = t.GetProperty("Length");
```

636   Chapter 14   Reflection

```
// Retrieve the Length property and cast it to the native type.
int length = (int)lengthProperty.GetValue(sb, null);
Console.WriteLine(length.ToString());
```

To browse events, fields, properties, and methods at once, call *Type.GetMembers*. If you don't provide any parameters to the method, it returns a *MemberInfo* array containing all public members. To retrieve a different set of members, such as including private members or only static members, use the *BindingFlags* enumeration. The following code sample demonstrates how to show all static, private members of the *Console* type:

```
' VB
Dim t As Type = GetType(Console)

Dim mi As MemberInfo() = t.GetMembers( _
    BindingFlags.NonPublic Or BindingFlags.Static)
For Each m As MemberInfo In mi
    Console.WriteLine("{0}: {1}", m.Name, m.MemberType)
Next
```

```
// C#
Type t = typeof(Console);

MemberInfo[] mi = t.GetMembers(
    BindingFlags.NonPublic | BindingFlags.Static);
foreach (MemberInfo m in mi)
{
    Console.WriteLine("{0}: {1}", m.Name, m.MemberType);
}
```

BindingFlag provides the following options, which you can combine with boolean operators:

- **DeclaredOnly**   Ignores inherited members.

- **Default**   Equivalent to not specifying a *BindingFlag*.

- **FlattenHierarchy**   Returns declared, inherited, and protected members.

- **IgnoreCase**   Allows you to use a case-insensitive matching of the member name.

- **Instance**   Members that are part of an instance of type are included.

- **NonPublic**   Protected and internal members are included.

- **Public**   Public members are included.

- **Static**   Static members are included.

Assembly Attributes

Assembly attributes describe your assembly (including information such as the name, version, and year of copyright). Typically, you add attributes to the AssemblyInfo file in your project, which initially contains default settings for many of the attributes. Visual Studio allows you to edit assembly attributes from the Project Properties page by clicking the Assembly Information button on the Assembly tab.

The AssemblyInfo file includes these attributes by default (among others):

```
' VB
<assembly: AssemblyCompany("Contoso, Inc.")>
<assembly: AssemblyCopyright("Copyright ©  2008")>
<assembly: AssemblyVersion("1.0.0.0")>
```

```
// C#
[assembly: AssemblyCompany("Contoso, Inc.")]
[assembly: AssemblyCopyright("Copyright ©  2008")]
[assembly: AssemblyVersion("1.0.0.0")]
```

You can apply the following attributes to an assembly:

- **AssemblyAlgorithmId**   Specifies a hash algorithm to use for reading file hashes in the assembly. You shouldn't need to change the default.

- **AssemblyCompany**   Defines the company name that developed the assembly.

- **AssemblyConfiguration**   Specifies whether an assembly is retail, debug, or a custom setting.

- **AssemblyCopyright**   Defines a copyright.

- **AssemblyCulture**   Specifies a culture for the assembly, such as *en* for English or *de* for German. Most assemblies are culture-neutral, so typically you don't need to specify this.

- **AssemblyDefaultAlias**   Defines a friendly default alias for an assembly manifest. You need to specify this only if the name of the assembly is particularly long (and thus would be a nuisance to type).

- **AssemblyDelaySign**   Specifies that the assembly is not fully signed when created. Delayed signing typically is used in environments where a manager must sign assemblies before they are released to production.

- **AssemblyDescription**   Provides a description for an assembly.

- **AssemblyFileVersion**   Specifies the version number that will be displayed when viewing the file's properties in Windows Explorer. If you don't supply this, *AssemblyVersion* is used instead.

- ***AssemblyFlags*** Specifies *AssemblyNameFlags* flags for an assembly, describing just-in-time (JIT) compiler options, whether the assembly is retargetable, and whether it has a full or tokenized public key.

- ***AssemblyInformationalVersion*** Defines additional version information for an assembly manifest that is never used by the runtime. In other words, although you might read this attribute programmatically, the runtime doesn't use it for versioning purposes.

- ***AssemblyKeyFile*** Specifies the name of a file containing the key pair used to generate a strong name.

- ***AssemblyKeyName*** Specifies the name of a key container within the CryptoServiceProvider (CSP) containing the key pair used to generate a strong name.

- ***AssemblyProduct*** Defines a product name custom for an assembly manifest.

- ***AssemblyTitle*** Defines an assembly title.

- ***AssemblyTrademark*** Defines a trademark for an assembly manifest.

- ***AssemblyVersion*** Specifies the version of the assembly. Assembly versions takes the form *<Major_version>.<Minor_version>.<build_number>.<revision>*, such as 2.0.243.2. You can specify an asterisk for the build number and revision, in which case, Visual Studio automatically updates them. For example, if you specify "2.0.*.*", Visual Studio automatically updates the build number daily and replaces the revision number with a randomly generated number.

You can read attributes by calling *Assembly.GetCustomAttributes*, which returns an array of *Attribute* objects. Then iterate through the objects to identify the attribute you need to access and cast it to the correct type. The following code sample demonstrates this by displaying the values for the *AssemblyCopyright*, *AssemblyCompany*, and *AssemblyDescription* attributes:

```
' VB
Dim asm As Assembly = Assembly.GetExecutingAssembly()

For Each attr As Attribute In asm.GetCustomAttributes(False)
    If attr.GetType() Is GetType(AssemblyCopyrightAttribute) Then
        Console.WriteLine("Copyright: {0}", _
            DirectCast(attr, AssemblyCopyrightAttribute).Copyright)
    End If

    If attr.GetType() Is GetType(AssemblyCompanyAttribute) Then
        Console.WriteLine("Company: {0}", _
            DirectCast(attr, AssemblyCompanyAttribute).Company)
    End If
```

```
        If attr.GetType() Is GetType(AssemblyDescriptionAttribute) Then
            Console.WriteLine("Description: {0}", _
                DirectCast(attr, AssemblyDescriptionAttribute).Description)
        End If
Next
```

```
// C#
Assembly asm = Assembly.GetExecutingAssembly();

foreach (Attribute attr in asm.GetCustomAttributes(false))
{
    if (attr.GetType() == typeof(AssemblyCopyrightAttribute))
        Console.WriteLine("Copyright: {0}",
            ((AssemblyCopyrightAttribute)attr).Copyright);

    if (attr.GetType() == typeof(AssemblyCompanyAttribute))
        Console.WriteLine("Company: {0}",
            ((AssemblyCompanyAttribute)attr).Company);

    if (attr.GetType() == typeof(AssemblyDescriptionAttribute))
        Console.WriteLine("Description: {0}",
            ((AssemblyDescriptionAttribute)attr).Description);
}
```

Alternatively, you can use the overloaded *GetCustomAttributes* method to retrieve attributes of a specific type. Because there should only be one attribute for any given type, this code sample simply accesses the first element in the array:

```
' VB
Dim asm As Assembly = Assembly.GetExecutingAssembly()

Dim descs As Object() = _
    asm.GetCustomAttributes(GetType(AssemblyDescriptionAttribute), False)
Dim desc As AssemblyDescriptionAttribute = _
    DirectCast(descs(0), AssemblyDescriptionAttribute)
Console.WriteLine(desc.Description)
```

```
// C#
Assembly asm = Assembly.GetExecutingAssembly();

object[] descs =
    asm.GetCustomAttributes(typeof(AssemblyDescriptionAttribute), false);
AssemblyDescriptionAttribute desc = (AssemblyDescriptionAttribute)descs[0];
Console.WriteLine(desc.Description);
```

Generating Types Dynamically

You can use the classes in the *System.Reflection.Emit* namespace to build classes dynamically at runtime. For example, you can create a new type, complete with constructors, methods, properties, events, and fields. The *Builder* classes are logically named as follows:

- *AssemblyBuilder*
- *ConstructorBuilder*
- *EnumBuilder*
- *EventBuilder*
- *FieldBuilder*
- *LocalBuilder*
- *MethodBuilder*
- *ModuleBuilder*
- *ParameterBuilder*
- *PropertyBuilder*
- *TypeBuilder*

To create types dynamically, first create an assembly and module. Then you can create the type within the module and add any members that you require. At that point, you can create an instance of the dynamically generated type and call any constructors or methods.

The following code creates an assembly, module, and type. It then adds a static method named *Greeter* to the type, and adds code to the dynamically generated method to write "Hello, world!" to the console. It then uses reflection to call the *Greeter* method:

```vb
' VB
' Create an AssemblyBuilder instance
Dim ab As AssemblyBuilder = _
    AppDomain.CurrentDomain.DefineDynamicAssembly( _
        New AssemblyName("dynAssembly"), AssemblyBuilderAccess.RunAndSave)

' Create a ModuleBuilder
Dim mb As ModuleBuilder = ab.DefineDynamicModule("dynMod")

' Create a TypeBuilder public class
Dim tb As TypeBuilder = mb.DefineType("dynType", _
    TypeAttributes.Class Or TypeAttributes.Public)

' Create a default constructor (this isn't necessary for this example)
Dim cb As ConstructorBuilder = _
    tb.DefineDefaultConstructor(MethodAttributes.Public)

' Create a public, static method named Greet that doesn't accept parameters
' or return a value
```

```vb
Dim method As MethodBuilder = tb.DefineMethod("Greet", _
    MethodAttributes.Public Or MethodAttributes.Static)

' Create an ILGenerator for the method, which allows us to write code for it
Dim dynCode As ILGenerator = method.GetILGenerator()

' Add a line of code to the method, equivalent to Console.WriteLine
dynCode.EmitWriteLine("Hello, world!")

' Add a line of code to return from the method
dynCode.Emit(OpCodes.Ret)

' Create an instance of the dynamic type
Dim myDynType As Type = tb.CreateType()

' Call the static method we dynamically generated
myDynType.GetMethod("Greet").Invoke(Nothing, Nothing)
```

```csharp
// C#
// Create an AssemblyBuilder instance
AssemblyBuilder ab = AppDomain.CurrentDomain.DefineDynamicAssembly(
    new AssemblyName("dynAssembly"), AssemblyBuilderAccess.RunAndSave);

// Create a ModuleBuilder
ModuleBuilder mb = ab.DefineDynamicModule("dynMod");

// Create a TypeBuilder public class
TypeBuilder tb = mb.DefineType("dynType",
    TypeAttributes.Class | TypeAttributes.Public);

// Create a default constructor (this isn't necessary for this example)
ConstructorBuilder cb =
    tb.DefineDefaultConstructor(MethodAttributes.Public);

// Create a public, static method named Greet that doesn't accept
// parameters or return a value
MethodBuilder method = tb.DefineMethod("Greet",
    MethodAttributes.Public | MethodAttributes.Static);

// Create an ILGenerator for the method, which allows us to write code for it
ILGenerator dynCode = method.GetILGenerator();

// Add a line of code to the method, equivalent to Console.WriteLine
dynCode.EmitWriteLine("Hello, world!");

// Add a line of code to return from the method
dynCode.Emit(OpCodes.Ret);

// Create an instance of the dynamic type
Type myDynType = tb.CreateType();

// Call the static method we dynamically generated
myDynType.GetMethod("Greet").Invoke(null, null);
```

MORE INFO Writing code that in turn writes code is complicated because you must write the generated code in IL. You don't need to know how to write IL for the 70-536 exam, and it's rarely required in real-world development scenarios, either. Therefore, it is not discussed in detail here. For more information, read "Emitting Dynamic Methods and Assemblies" at *http://msdn.microsoft.com/en-us/library/8ffc3x75.aspx*, and "Generating Code at Run Time With *Reflection.Emit*" at *http://www.ddj.com/windows/184416570*.

After creating an assembly, call *AssemblyBuilder.Save* to write it to the disk. When creating the dynamic assembly, be sure to specify either *AssemblyBuilderAccess.Save* (if you just want to write the assembly to disk) or *AssemblyBuilderAccess.RunAndSave* (if you need to execute the code and then write the assembly to the disk).

Real World

Tony Northrup

In practice, it's generally easier to generate C# or Visual Basic .NET code and then use a compiler to generate an assembly. Writing IL directly is slow, error-prone, and extremely difficult to troubleshoot. Be familiar with writing IL directly for the exam, but avoid it in the real world.

Lab: Load and Run Add-Ons Dynamically

In this lab, you will create an application that searches the current folder for add-ons and runs code within every add-on it finds.

Exercise 1: Run a Method Using Reflection

In this exercise, you will create a Console application that loads two assemblies, reads an attribute from the assembly, identifies a class and method contained in each assembly, and then runs the method.

1. Using Visual Studio, create a project using the Console Application template. Name the project Greeter.

2. In the code file, add the *System.Reflection* and *System.IO* namespaces.

3. In the *Main* method, create a *foreach* loop that searches the current folder for dynamic link libraries (DLLs) with filenames that start with "Addon-". If it finds a suitable DLL, load it into an assembly. Then, display the *AssemblyDescription* attribute. This code sample demonstrates how to do this:

```
' VB
For Each f As String In _
    Directory.GetFiles(System.Environment.CurrentDirectory, "addon-*.dll")
```

```vb
        Dim asm As Assembly = Assembly.LoadFile(f)

        Dim descs As Object() = _
            asm.GetCustomAttributes(GetType(AssemblyDescriptionAttribute), False)
        Dim desc As AssemblyDescriptionAttribute = _
            DirectCast(descs(0), AssemblyDescriptionAttribute)
        Console.WriteLine(desc.Description)
    Next
```

```csharp
// C#
foreach (string f in
    Directory.GetFiles(System.Environment.CurrentDirectory, "addon-*.dll"))
{
    Assembly asm = Assembly.LoadFile(f);

    object[] descs =
        asm.GetCustomAttributes(typeof(AssemblyDescriptionAttribute), false);
    AssemblyDescriptionAttribute desc =
        (AssemblyDescriptionAttribute)descs[0];
    Console.WriteLine(desc.Description);
}
```

4. Within the *foreach* loop, load the type named *Greeting*. Then call the *Greeting.Greet* method. There are several different approaches to this. This technique allows for each class to have a different namespace by searching for a method name that ends in Greeting:

```vb
' VB
For Each t As Type In asm.GetTypes()
    If t.Name.EndsWith("Greeting") Then
        Dim greet As MethodInfo = t.GetMethod("Greet")
        greet.Invoke(Nothing, Nothing)
        Exit For
    End If
Next
```

```csharp
// C#
foreach (Type t in asm.GetTypes())
{
    if (t.Name.EndsWith("Greeting"))
    {
        MethodInfo greet = t.GetMethod("Greet");
        greet.Invoke(null, null);
        break;
    }
}
```

5. Navigate to the \<*InstallHome*>\Chapter14\Lesson1\Exercise1\Partial folder and open both the Addon-console and Addon-dialog solution files. To demonstrate that the development language does not matter when calling an external assembly, Addon-console is written in C#, and Addon-dialog is written in Visual Basic.

6. Add a description to both solutions by editing the *AssemblyDescription* attribute in the AssemblyInfo file or by clicking the Assembly Information button on the Assembly tab of the Project Properties dialog box. For Addon-console, set the description to "Displays a greeting to the console." For Addon-dialog, set the description to "Displays a greeting in a dialog box."

7. Build both solutions. Then, copy the DLL files to the Greeter build folder.

8. Build and run the Greeter solution. It should find both assemblies, display the *AssemblyDescription* value, and then call the *Greet* method.

   Developers could create any number of assemblies and copy them to the application folder, and the Greeter application would run them all, provided that they meet the file, type, and method naming requirements.

Lesson Summary

- Reflection allows you to load assemblies at runtime, create instances of types defined within a dynamically loaded assembly, and call methods defined within a dynamically loaded assembly. You can use reflection to make your application extensible by allowing developers to create their own assemblies that offer custom functionality.

- The *Assembly* class includes several methods you can use to load an assembly dynamically: *Load*, *LoadFrom*, *LoadFile*, *ReflectionOnlyLoad*, and *ReflectionOnly-LoadFrom*.

- After loading an assembly, call *Assembly.GetType* to load a type from the assembly, and call *Type.GetConstructor* to create an instance of *ConstructorInfo*. Then you can create an instance of the type by calling *ConstructorInfo.Invoke*. To call a method, call *Type.GetMethod* to create an instance of *MethodInfo*. Once you create an instance of *MethodInfo*, you can call the method using *MethodInfo.Invoke*.

- Assembly attributes describe the assembly and are defined in the AssemblyInfo file. You can read attributes by calling *Assembly.GetCustomAttributes*.

- Use the *Builder* classes to create assemblies, modules, types, constructors, methods, and other members dynamically. You can create an instance of *ILGenerator* to write code for methods or constructors.

Lesson Review

You can use the following questions to test your knowledge of the information in Lesson 1, "Using Reflection." The questions are also available on the companion CD if you prefer to review them in electronic form.

NOTE Answers

Answers to these questions and explanations of why each answer choice is right or wrong are located in the "Answers" section at the end of the book.

---

1. You need to load an assembly and run a method contained within a type dynamically. Which class should you use to run the method?

   A. *MethodBase*

   B. *MethodInfo*

   C. *MethodBuilder*

   D. *ConstructorInfo*

2. You need to write code equivalent to the following, but using reflection:

```
' VB
Dim d As New DateTime(2008, 5, 1)
Console.WriteLine(d.ToShortDateString())
```

```
// C#
DateTime d = new DateTime(2008, 5, 1);
Console.WriteLine(d.ToShortDateString());
```

   Which code sample does this correctly?

   A.

```
' VB
Dim t As Type = GetType(DateTime)
Dim mi As MethodInfo = t.GetConstructor( _
    New Type() {GetType(Integer), GetType(Integer), GetType(Integer)})
Dim d As Object = mi.Invoke(New Object() {2008, 5, 1})
Dim dToShortDateString As ConstructorInfo = t.GetMethod("ToShortDateString")
Console.WriteLine(DirectCast(dToShortDateString.Invoke(d, Nothing), String))
```

```
// C#
Type t = typeof(DateTime);
MethodInfo mi = t.GetConstructor(
    new Type[] { typeof(int), typeof(int), typeof(int) });
Object d = mi.Invoke(new Object[] { 2008, 5, 1 });
ConstructorInfo dToShortDateString = t.GetMethod("ToShortDateString");
Console.WriteLine((string)dToShortDateString.Invoke(d, null));
```

   B.

```
' VB
Dim t As Type = GetType(DateTime)
Dim ci As ConstructorInfo = t.GetConstructor(New Object() {2008, 5, 1})
Dim d As Object = ci.Invoke( _
    New Type() {GetType(Integer), GetType(Integer), GetType(Integer)})
Dim dToShortDateString As MethodInfo = t.GetMethod("ToShortDateString")
Console.WriteLine(DirectCast(dToShortDateString.Invoke(d, Nothing), String))
```

```csharp
// C#
Type t = typeof(DateTime);
ConstructorInfo ci = t.GetConstructor(new Object[] { 2008, 5, 1 });
Object d = ci.Invoke(
    new Object[] { new Type[] { typeof(int), typeof(int), typeof(int) });
MethodInfo dToShortDateString = t.GetMethod("ToShortDateString");
Console.WriteLine((string)dToShortDateString.Invoke(d, null));
```

C.

```vbnet
' VB
Dim t As Type = GetType(DateTime)
Dim dToShortDateString As MethodInfo = t.GetMethod("ToShortDateString")
Console.WriteLine(DirectCast(dToShortDateString.Invoke(t, Nothing), String))
```

```csharp
// C#
Type t = typeof(DateTime);
MethodInfo dToShortDateString = t.GetMethod("ToShortDateString");
Console.WriteLine((string)dToShortDateString.Invoke(t, null));
```

D.

```vbnet
' VB
Dim t As Type = GetType(DateTime)
Dim ci As ConstructorInfo = _
    t.GetConstructor(New Type() {GetType(Integer), GetType(Integer),
GetType(Integer)})
Dim d As Object = ci.Invoke(New Object() {2008, 5, 1})
Dim dToShortDateString As MethodInfo = t.GetMethod("ToShortDateString")
Console.WriteLine(DirectCast(dToShortDateString.Invoke(d, Nothing), String))
```

```csharp
// C#
Type t = typeof(DateTime);
ConstructorInfo ci = t.GetConstructor(new Type[] { typeof(int), typeof(int),
typeof(int) });
Object d = ci.Invoke(new Object[] { 2008, 5, 1 });
MethodInfo dToShortDateString = t.GetMethod("ToShortDateString");
Console.WriteLine((string)dToShortDateString.Invoke(d, null));
```

3. You need to examine an assembly's metadata from an application. The assembly is located in the GAC. However, the assembly was developed for a different platform, and you cannot run the code contained within the assembly. Which method should you call?

   A. *Assembly.ReflectionOnlyLoad*

   B. *Assembly.LoadFrom*

   C. *Assembly.LoadFile*

   D. *Assembly.ReflectionOnlyLoadFrom*

Chapter Review

To practice and reinforce the skills you learned in this chapter further, you can perform the following tasks:

- Review the chapter summary.
- Review the list of key terms introduced in this chapter.
- Complete the case scenarios. These scenarios set up real-world situations involving the topics of this chapter and ask you to create a solution.
- Complete the suggested practices.
- Take a practice test.

Chapter Summary

- Reflection allows you to make your application extensible. Use the static *Assembly* methods to load an assembly dynamically. After loading an assembly, call *Assembly.GetType* to load a type, call *Type.GetConstructor* to create an instance of *ConstructorInfo*, and call *Type.GetMethod* to create an instance of *MethodInfo*. You can then call the *Invoke* method to run a constructor or method.

- Define assembly attributes in the *AssemblyInfo* file and read them by calling *Assembly.GetCustomAttributes*. Use the *Builder* classes to dynamically create assemblies, modules, types, constructors, methods, and other members. You can create an instance of *ILGenerator* to write code for methods or constructors.

Key Terms

Do you know what these key terms mean? You can check your answers by looking up the terms in the glossary at the end of the book.

- Intermediate language (IL)
- Reflection

Case Scenarios

In the following case scenarios, you apply what you've learned about reflection and dynamically generating assemblies. You can find answers to these questions in the "Answers" section at the end of this book.

Case Scenario 1: Supporting Add-ons

You are an application developer for Litware, Inc., a commercial software company. Your company currently is planning to release media player software. The Strategy group has requested several extensibility features. Specifically, they want users with development experience to be able to create plug-ins that do the following:

- Read different media formats
- Control playback (like a remote control)
- Display or play back the media in different ways

The application will be developed using the .NET Framework.

Questions

Answer the following questions for your manager:

1. How can you allow users to create their own plug-ins?
2. How can you ensure that user-developed classes implement the methods required to provide the necessary functionality?
3. Because you are developing this in C#, do users also have to develop in C#, or can they use Visual Basic?
4. We would like to extend the About dialog box to display the developer's name and copyright information for every loaded plug-in. How can you do this?

Case Scenario 2: Code-writing Code

You are an application developer working for Proseware, Inc. You have recently been assigned to create a new application for young computer science students. During a planning meeting, the Marketing manager describes her requirements for the application:

"We're creating software to pique children's interest in development. Before introducing them to the full .NET Framework, we'd like to have them write simple code using our custom user interface. Then the application would create an assembly from the code that they write."

Questions

Answer the following questions for your manager:

1. Is it even possible to write an application that generates other applications?
2. How can you generate code dynamically?
3. When using *GetILGenerator*, do you just dynamically generate C# or VB code?

Suggested Practices

To master the "Implementing Interoperability, Reflection, and Mailing Functionality in a .NET Framework Application" exam objective, complete the following tasks.

Implement Reflection Functionality in a .NET Framework Application, and Create Metadata, Microsoft Intermediate Language (MSIL), and a PE File by Using the System.Reflection.Emit Namespace

For this task, you should complete as many practices as possible. Each practice is more complex than the last, but they all give you important real-world experience with reflection.

- **Practice 1**   Using the last real-world application you created, specify valid values for all standard assembly attributes. Then read these attributes at runtime to populate the application's About dialog box.

- **Practice 2**   Using a real-world application, identify functionality that users might want to replace. Update the application to load an assembly containing the functionality at runtime and give users a method to replace the functionality with a custom assembly.

- **Practice 3**   Derive a class from the *Binder* class to control type conversions for dynamic code. For more information about this class, read "Binder Class" at *http://msdn.microsoft.com/en-us/library/system.reflection.binder.aspx*.

Take a Practice Test

The practice tests on this book's companion CD offer many options. For example, you can test yourself on just the content covered in this chapter, or you can test yourself on all the 70-536 certification exam content. You can set up the test so that it closely simulates the experience of taking a certification exam, or you can set it up in study mode so that you can look at the correct answers and explanations after you answer each question.

MORE INFO   **Practice tests**

For details about all the practice test options available, see the section "How to Use the Practice Tests," in the Introduction of this book.

Chapter 15

Mail

E-mail is an extremely popular communication mechanism. Unlike the telephone and most other ways of communicating, e-mail is easy for applications to use. For a developer, e-mail is an effective way to allow an application to send files or reports to users and to notify users of problems or events.

The .NET Framework includes the *System.Net.Mail* namespace, which provides classes that enable you to easily create and transmit e-mail messages. Messages can include plain text, Hypertext Markup Language (HTML), and file attachments. At a high level, sending e-mail has two steps: creating the mail message and then sending the message to a Simple Mail Transfer Protocol (SMTP) server. Lesson 1, "Creating an E-mail Message," covers how to create a message, and Lesson 2, "Sending E-mail," covers how to send the message.

Exam objective in this chapter:
- Send electronic mail to a Simple Mail Transfer Protocol (SMTP) server for delivery from a .NET Framework application.

Lessons in this chapter:

Before You Begin

To complete the lessons in this chapter, you should be familiar with Microsoft Visual Basic or C# and be comfortable with the following tasks:

- Creating a console application in Microsoft Visual Studio using Visual Basic or C#
- Adding references to system class libraries to a project

Lesson 1: Creating an E-mail Message

Creating an e-mail message can be simple or complex. At its simplest, an e-mail message has a sender, recipient, subject, and body. These simple messages can be created with a single line of code using the .NET Framework. At their most complex, e-mail messages can have custom encoding types, multiple views for plain text and HTML, attachments, and images embedded within HTML.

> **After this lesson, you will be able to:**
> - Describe the process of creating and sending an e-mail
> - Create a *MailMessage* object
> - Attach one or more files to an e-mail message
> - Create HTML e-mails with or without pictures
> - Catch and respond to different exceptions that might be thrown while creating a message
>
> **Estimated lesson time: 30 minutes**

The Process of Creating and Sending an E-mail Message

To create and send an e-mail message, follow these steps:

1. Create a *MailMessage* object. *MailMessage* and other mail-related classes are in the *System.Net.Mail* namespace.

2. If you did not specify the recipients in the *MailMessage* constructor, add them to the *MailMessage* object.

3. If you need to provide multiple views (such as plain text and HTML), create *AlternateView* objects and add them to the *MailMessage* object.

4. If necessary, create one or more *Attachment* objects and add them to the *MailMessage* object.

5. Create an *SmtpClient* object and specify the SMTP server.

6. If the SMTP server requires clients to authenticate, add credentials to the *SmtpClient* object.

7. Pass your *MailMessage* object to the *SmtpClient.Send* method. Alternatively, you can use *SmtpClient.SendAsync* to send the message asynchronously.

Steps 5 through 7 are described in detail in Lesson 2.

How to Create a *MailMessage* Object

The *MailMessage* object has four different constructors that allow you to create a blank *MailMessage,* specify both the sender and recipient, or specify the sender, recipient, subject, and message body. If you are creating a simple message with a single recipient, you can do the bulk of the work in the *MailMessage* constructor, as follows:

```
' VB
Dim m As MailMessage = New MailMessage _
    ("jane@contoso.com", _
     "ben@contoso.com", _
     "Quarterly data report.", _
     "See the attached spreadsheet.")
```

```
// C#
MailMessage m = new MailMessage
   ("jane@contoso.com",
    "ben@contoso.com",
    "Quarterly data report.",
    "See the attached spreadsheet.");
```

NOTE Sending Quick Messages

You can also use an overload of the *SmtpClient.Send* method to send an e-mail without creating a *MailMessage* object. *SmtpClient* is described in Lesson 2.

You can specify the sender and the recipient as either a string or *MailAddress* object. The *MailAddress* object allows you to specify an e-mail address, a display name, and an encoding type, as the following code sample demonstrates:

```
' VB
Dim m As MailMessage = New MailMessage _
    (New MailAddress("lance@contoso.com", "Lance Tucker"), _
     New MailAddress("ben@contoso.com", "Ben Miller"))
```

```
// C#
MailMessage m = new MailMessage
   (new MailAddress("lance@contoso.com", "Lance Tucker"),
    new MailAddress("ben@contoso.com", "Ben Miller"));
```

NOTE Encoding Types

Specifying the encoding type for e-mail addresses is rarely necessary.

If you need to specify multiple recipients, use the blank *MailMessage* constructor. Then add *MailAddress* objects to the *MailMessage.To* property (which is of the

MailAddressCollection type) and specify *MailMessage.From*, *MailMessage.Subject*, and *MailMessage.Body,* as follows:

```vb
' VB
Dim m As MailMessage = New MailMessage()
m.From = New MailAddress("lance@contoso.com", "Lance Tucker")
m.To.Add(New MailAddress("james@contoso.com", "James van Eaton"))
m.To.Add(New MailAddress("ben@contoso.com", "Ben Miller"))
m.To.Add(New MailAddress("burke@contoso.com", "Burke Fewel"))
m.Subject = "Quarterly data report."
m.Body = "See the attached spreadsheet."
```

```csharp
// C#
MailMessage m = new MailMessage();
m.From = new MailAddress("lance@contoso.com", "Lance Tucker");
m.To.Add(new MailAddress("james@contoso.com", "James van Eaton"));
m.To.Add(new MailAddress("ben@contoso.com", "Ben Miller"));
m.To.Add(new MailAddress("burke@contoso.com", "Burke Fewel"));
m.Subject = "Quarterly data report.";
m.Body = "See the attached spreadsheet.";
```

In addition, you can add recipients to the *MailMessage.Cc* and *MailMessage.Bcc* properties in exactly the same way as you would add recipients to *MailMessage.From*. Recipients specified with *MailMessage.Cc* receive the message, and their names show up on the CC: line of the e-mail, which is visible to all recipients. Recipients specified with *MailMessage.Bcc* receive the message, but their names are not visible to other recipients. BCC stands for "blind carbon copy," a term that originated when people made duplicates of typed paper memos using carbon paper.

NOTE   The Risk of Using BCC

Instead of using BCC, you should send a separate copy of your message to each recipient that you want to receive a blind copy. The problem with BCC is that spam filters frequently block messages that do not have the recipient's e-mail address in the To header. Therefore, if you use BCC, the message is more likely to be filtered.

MailMessage has the following less frequently used properties:

- **DeliveryNotificationOptions**   Instructs the SMTP server to send a message to the address specified in *MailMessage.From* if a message is delayed, fails, or is successfully delivered or relayed to another server. The enumeration is of type *DeliveryNotificationOptions*, and the values are *OnSuccess*, *OnFailure*, *Delay*, *None*, and *Never*.

- **ReplyTo**   The e-mail address to which replies will be sent. Because the .NET Framework does not act as an e-mail client, and therefore your application will not typically be receiving e-mail, in most cases you should simply set *MailMessage .From* to the address that should receive replies instead of using *ReplyTo*.

■ *Priority*   The priority of the message. This does not in any way affect how the .NET Framework or the mail server handles the message. However, the priority might be visible in the recipient's e-mail client. The priority is also useful for filtering automatically generated e-mail based on the priority of the event that initiated the e-mail. This enumeration is of type *MailPriority* and can have values of *Normal*, *High*, and *Low*.

How to Attach Files

To attach a file, add it to the *MailMessage.Attachments AttachmentCollection* by calling the *MailMessage.Attachments.Add* method. The simplest way to add a file is to specify the filename as follows:

```vb
' VB
Dim m As MailMessage = New MailMessage()
m.Attachments.Add(New Attachment("C:\windows\win.ini"))
```

```csharp
// C#
MailMessage m = new MailMessage();
m.Attachments.Add(new Attachment(@"C:\windows\win.ini"));
```

You can also specify a *Multipurpose Internet Mail Extensions (MIME)* content type using the *System.Net.Mime.MediaTypeNames* enumeration. There are special MIME types for text and images, but you typically specify *MediaTypeNames.Application.Octet*. The following code sample (which requires *System.IO* and *System.Net.Mime* in addition to *System.Net.Mail*) demonstrates how to use a *Stream* as a file attachment and how to specify the MIME type:

```vb
' VB
Dim m As MailMessage = New MailMessage()
Dim sr As Stream = New FileStream( _
    "C:\Attachment.txt", FileMode.Open, FileAccess.Read)
m.Attachments.Add(New Attachment( _
    sr, "myfile.txt", MediaTypeNames.Application.Octet))
```

```csharp
// C#
MailMessage m = new MailMessage();
Stream sr = new FileStream(
    @"C:\Attachment.txt", FileMode.Open, FileAccess.Read);
m.Attachments.Add(new Attachment(
    sr, "myfile.txt", MediaTypeNames.Application.Octet));
```

As the previous example demonstrates, you should specify a filename when adding an attachment using a *Stream* object. Otherwise, the attachment will be labeled with a generic name such as "application_octect-stream.dat." Because the file extension would be incorrect in that case, users would not be able to easily open the attachment in the correct application.

How to Create HTML E-mails

To create an HTML e-mail message, supply HTML-tagged content for *MailMessage .Body* and set the *MailMessage.IsBodyHtml* attribute to *true*, as the following code sample demonstrates:

```vb
' VB
Dim m As MailMessage = New MailMessage
m.From = New MailAddress("lance@contoso.com", "Lance Tucker")
m.To.Add(New MailAddress("burke@contoso.com", "Burke Fewel"))
m.Subject = "Testing HTML"

' Specify an HTML message body
m.Body = _
    "<html><body><h1>My Message</h1><br>This is an HTML message.</body></html>"
m.IsBodyHtml = True

' Send the message
Dim client As SmtpClient = New SmtpClient("smtp.contoso.com")
client.Send(m)
```

```csharp
// C#
MailMessage m = new MailMessage();
m.From = new MailAddress("lance@contoso.com", "Lance Tucker");
m.To.Add(new MailAddress("burke@contoso.com", "Burke Fewel"));
m.Subject = "Testing HTML";

// Specify an HTML message body
m.Body =
    "<html><body><h1>My Message</h1><br>This is an HTML message.</body></html>";
m.IsBodyHtml = true;

// Send the message
SmtpClient client = new SmtpClient("smtp.contoso.com");
client.Send(m);
```

MailMessage.Subject is always plain text. You can define *MailMessage.Body* just like any HTML Web page. However, most e-mail clients ignore the *<head>* section, ignore any client-side scripts, and do not download images automatically from Web sites.

To embed images into an HTML message so that they appear when the user clicks the message (without requiring the user to choose explicitly to download images), use the *AlternateView* and *LinkedResource* classes. First, create an HTML message using *AlternateView* and then add images using *LinkedResource*, as the following sample code demonstrates:

```vb
' VB
' Create the HTML message body
' Reference embedded images using the content ID
Dim htmlBody As String = "<html><body><h1>Picture</h1><br>" + _
    "<img src=""cid:Pic1""></body></html>"
```

```vb
Dim avHtml As AlternateView = AlternateView.CreateAlternateViewFromString( _
    htmlBody, Nothing, MediaTypeNames.Text.Html)

' Create a LinkedResource object for each embedded image
Dim pic1 As LinkedResource = New LinkedResource( _
    "pic.jpg", MediaTypeNames.Image.Jpeg)
pic1.ContentId = "Pic1"
avHtml.LinkedResources.Add(pic1)

' Create an alternate view for unsupported clients
Dim textBody As String = _
    "You must use an e-mail client that supports HTML messages"
Dim avText As AlternateView = AlternateView.CreateAlternateViewFromString( _
    textBody, Nothing, MediaTypeNames.Text.Plain)

' Add the alternate views instead of using MailMessage.Body
Dim m As MailMessage = New MailMessage
m.AlternateViews.Add(avHtml)
m.AlternateViews.Add(avText)

' Address and send the message
m.From = New MailAddress("lance@contoso.com", "Lance Tucker")
m.To.Add(New MailAddress("james@contoso.com", "James van Eaton"))
m.Subject = "A picture using alternate views"
Dim client As SmtpClient = New SmtpClient("smtp.contoso.com")
client.Send(m)
```

```csharp
// C#
// Create the HTML message body
// Reference embedded images using the content ID
string htmlBody =
    "<html><body><h1>Picture</h1><br><img src=\"cid:Pic1\"></body></html>";
AlternateView avHtml = AlternateView.CreateAlternateViewFromString(
    htmlBody, null, MediaTypeNames.Text.Html);

// Create a LinkedResource object for each embedded image
LinkedResource pic1 =
    new LinkedResource("pic.jpg", MediaTypeNames.Image.Jpeg);
pic1.ContentId = "Pic1";
avHtml.LinkedResources.Add(pic1);

// Create an alternate view for unsupported clients
string textBody =
    "You must use an e-mail client that supports HTML messages";
AlternateView avText = AlternateView.CreateAlternateViewFromString(
    textBody, null, MediaTypeNames.Text.Plain);

// Add the alternate views instead of using MailMessage.Body
MailMessage m = new MailMessage();
m.AlternateViews.Add(avHtml);
m.AlternateViews.Add(avText);
```

```
// Address and send the message
m.From = new MailAddress("lance@contoso.com", "Lance Tucker");
m.To.Add(new MailAddress("james@contoso.com", "James van Eaton"));
m.Subject = "A picture using alternate views";
SmtpClient client = new SmtpClient("smtp.contoso.com");
client.Send(m);
```

This code produces the HTML message shown in Figure 15-1 (assuming that Pic.jpg was a picture of a cute puppy stored in the same folder as the assembly).

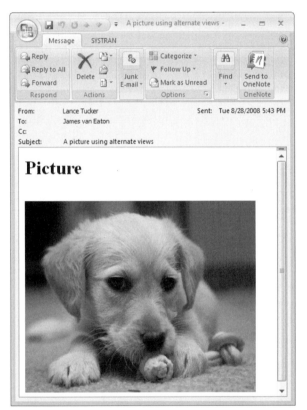

Figure 15-1 Using *AlternateView* and *LinkedResource* to embed images in an e-mail

To reference images attached as linked resources from your HTML message body, use "cid:*contentID*" in the <img> tag. Then specify the same name for the *LinkedResource .ContentID* property. In the previous example, the body of the HTML message contained the tag <img src=\"cid:Pic1\">, and *LinkedResource.ContentID* was set to "Pic1". Each *LinkedResource* should have a unique *ContentID*.

Lab: Generate an E-mail Message

In this lab, you will generate an e-mail message. In the next lab, you will send the e-mail message.

Exercise: Create a *MailMessage* Object

In this exercise, you will create a *MailMessage* object based on user input into a Microsoft Windows Forms application that is provided for you. If you encounter a problem completing an exercise, the completed projects are available along with the sample files.

1. Navigate to the \<*InstallHome*>\Chapter15\Lesson1\Exercise1\Partial folder and open either the C# version or the Visual Basic .NET version of the solution file.

2. Add the *System.Net.Mail* namespace to your code for Form1.

3. The runtime calls the *sendButton_Click* method when you click the Send button in the form. You now need to add logic to create a *MailMessage* object using user input. The following code demonstrates the first step:

   ```
   ' VB
   ' Create a MailMessage object
   Dim mm As MailMessage = New MailMessage
   ```

   ```
   // C#
   // Create a MailMessage object
   MailMessage mm = new MailMessage();
   ```

4. Now, specify the sender and recipient. Note that it's okay if the user hasn't typed display names for the To and From addresses, because the *MailAddress* constructor can accept *null* for the second string. This code demonstrates how to do this:

   ```
   ' VB
   ' Define the sender and recipient
   mm.From = New MailAddress(fromEmailAddress.Text, fromDisplayName.Text)
   mm.To.Add(New MailAddress(toEmailAddress.Text, toDisplayName.Text))
   ```

   ```
   // C#
   // Define the sender and recipient
   mm.From = new MailAddress(fromEmailAddress.Text, fromDisplayName.Text);
   mm.To.Add(new MailAddress(toEmailAddress.Text, toDisplayName.Text));
   ```

5. Next, define the subject and body, as the following code demonstrates:

   ```
   ' VB
   ' Define the subject and body
   mm.Subject = subjectTextBox.Text
   mm.Body = bodyTextBox.Text
   mm.IsBodyHtml = htmlRadioButton.Checked
   ```

   ```
   // C#
   // Define the subject and body
   mm.Subject = subjectTextBox.Text;
   mm.Body = bodyTextBox.Text;
   mm.IsBodyHtml = htmlRadioButton.Checked;
   ```

6. Build and run your project in Debug mode. Without typing anything, click the Send button. Notice that the runtime throws an *ArgumentException*. Create a

try/catch block around your code to catch an *ArgumentException* and display a message to the user, as the following code demonstrates:

```
' VB
Try
    ' Method logic omitted
Catch ex As ArgumentException
    MessageBox.Show("You must type from and to e-mail addresses", _
        "Invalid input", MessageBoxButtons.OK, MessageBoxIcon.Error)
End Try

// C#
try
{
    // Method logic omitted
}
catch (ArgumentException)
{
    MessageBox.Show("You must type from and to e-mail addresses",
        "Invalid input", MessageBoxButtons.OK, MessageBoxIcon.Error);
}
```

NOTE **Why not Validate Input Manually?**

In Chapter 3, "Searching, Modifying, and Encoding Text," you learned how to use regular expressions to validate user input. There are even specific examples in Chapter 3 of validating e-mail addresses. Although you could use regular expressions to validate input in this example, it would be redundant. The *MailMessage* object includes logic for validating input, as step 7 demonstrates. In some circumstances, security might be important enough to justify having two levels of validation. In this example, the additional complexity and increased chance of introducing a bug are not justified.

---

7. Build and run your project in Debug mode again. This time, type **hello** into the To and From e-mail address boxes and then click the Send button. Notice that the runtime throws a *FormatException* if the user provides an e-mail address in an invalid format. Add a *catch* block to catch a *FormatException* and display a message to the user, as the following code demonstrates:

```
' VB
Catch ex As FormatException
    MessageBox.Show( _
        "You must provide valid from and to e-mail addresses", _
        "Invalid input", MessageBoxButtons.OK, MessageBoxIcon.Error)

// C#
catch (FormatException)
{
    MessageBox.Show(
        "You must provide valid from and to e-mail addresses",
        "Invalid input", MessageBoxButtons.OK, MessageBoxIcon.Error);
}
```

8. Build and run your project. Populate the form's text boxes with valid data and click Send. Nothing will happen because you haven't written code yet to send the message. You will complete this application in Lesson 2.

Lesson Summary

■ To send an e-mail message, create a *MailMessage* object, specify the sender, subject, and body; and add recipients, alternate views, and file attachments. Then create an instance of the *SmtpClient* class, and call *SmtpClient.Send* or *SmtpClient .SendAsync* (covered in Lesson 2).

■ The *MailMessage* object includes constructors that allow you to create simple messages with a single line of code. More complex messages and messages with multiple recipients require adding more code.

■ To attach a file, create an instance of the *Attachment* class and add it to the *MailMessage.Attachments* collection.

■ Creating an HTML message without images is as simple as specifying HTML in the body and setting *MailMessage.IsBodyHtml* to *true*. If you need to include images in the message, create an *AlternateView* object and a *LinkedResource* object for each image.

Lesson Review

You can use the following questions to test your knowledge of the information in Lesson 1, "Creating an E-mail Message." The questions are also available on the companion CD if you prefer to review them in electronic form.

NOTE Answers

Answers to these questions and explanations of why each answer choice is right or wrong are located in the "Answers" section at the end of the book.

---

1. From which of the following sources can you attach a file to an e-mail message? (Choose all that apply.)

    A. Local file system

    B. *Stream*

    C. Web site

    D. An incoming e-mail message

2. Which of the following are required to send an HTML e-mail message? (Choose all that apply.)

   A. Set *MailMessage.Body* to an HTML message.

   B. Set *MailMessage.Head* to an HTML header.

   C. Set *MailMessage.IsBodyHtml* to *true*.

   D. Set *MailMessage.Subject* to HTML content.

3. Which of the following HTML tags correctly references the following linked resource as an image?

```vb
' VB
' Create a LinkedResource object for each embedded image
Dim lr As LinkedResource = New LinkedResource( _
    "myPic.jpg", MediaTypeNames.Image.Jpeg)
lr.ContentId = "myPic"
```

```csharp
// C#
// Create a LinkedResource object for each embedded image
LinkedResource lr = new LinkedResource(
    "myPic.jpg", MediaTypeNames.Image.Jpeg);
lr.ContentId = "myPic";
```

   A. `<img src="cid:myPic">`

   B. `<img src="cid:myPic.jpg">`

   C. `<img src="myPic">`

   D. `<img src="myPic.jpg">`

4. You want to send an HTML message that is also viewable in clients that do not support HTML. Which class should you use?

   A. *LinkedResource*

   B. *Attachment*

   C. *AlternateView*

   D. *SmtpClient*

Lesson 2: Sending E-mail

Often, sending an e-mail message is simple and requires only two lines of code. However, as with any network communication, it can become much more complex. If the server is unresponsive, you need to allow users to decide whether to wait for the message transfer or cancel it. Some servers require valid user credentials, so you might need to provide a username and password. When possible, you should enable *Secure Sockets Layer (SSL)* to encrypt the message in transit and reduce your security risks.

After this lesson, you will be able to:

- Configure an SMTP server and send an e-mail message
- Provide a username and password when required to authenticate to an SMTP server
- Enable SSL to encrypt SMTP communications
- Send a message asynchronously to allow your application to respond to the user or perform other tasks while an e-mail is being sent
- Catch and respond to different exceptions that might be thrown while sending a message

Estimated lesson time: 30 minutes

How to Send a Message

Once you create a message, you need to send it through an SMTP server, which in turn forwards it to the recipient. In the .NET Framework, the *SmtpClient* class represents the SMTP server. To send a message, call *SmtpClient.Send*. Most of the time, sending a message is as simple as this sample code (where "smtp.contoso.com" is the name of the local SMTP server):

```vb
' VB
Dim m As MailMessage = New MailMessage _
    ("jane@contoso.com", _
     "ben@contoso.com", _
     "Quarterly data report.", _
     "Hello, world.")
Dim client As SmtpClient = New SmtpClient("smtp.contoso.com")
client.Send(m)
```

```csharp
// C#
MailMessage m = new MailMessage
    ("jane@northrup.org",
     "ben@northrup.org",
     "Quarterly data report.",
     "Hello, world.");
SmtpClient client = new SmtpClient("smtp.contoso.com");
client.Send(m);
```

NOTE The *SmtpClient.PickupDirectoryLocation* Property

The *SmtpClient.PickupDirectoryLocation* property is intended for Web applications. To send messages through a Microsoft Internet Information Services (IIS)–based SMTP server, specify the hostname of the IIS server just as you would for any other SMTP server. To specify the local computer, use "localhost" or "127.0.0.1".

Real World

Tony Northrup

Years ago, I used to recommend that everyone install IIS, enable the SMTP service on the computer that would be running their application, and send messages through the local SMTP server. This process is much more efficient than using a remote SMTP server because the local IIS SMTP server directly contacts each recipient's SMTP server to send the message. In addition, you don't have to deal with network connections.

However, this approach became unreliable as organizations battled against spam. Organizations now block incoming messages from large groups of Internet Protocol (IP) addresses. Even if you are not a spammer, messages sent from a local SMTP server might be rejected if your IP address appears on one of these lists. To make it more complicated, you might be able to send messages to most domains but be rejected by others.

Ultimately, the job of managing SMTP servers is now too complex to have every user running his or her own mail server. As a result, I now recommend that people use the mail server of their Internet Service Provider (ISP) or of their organization for outgoing messages.

How to Handle E-mail Exceptions

Many things can go wrong when sending e-mail. For example, the mail server might not be available, the server might reject your user credentials, or the server might determine that one of your recipients is invalid. In each of these circumstances, the runtime throws an exception, and your application must be prepared to catch the exception.

When you send a message, you should always be prepared to catch an *SmtpException*. Messages frequently are rejected because the SMTP server cannot be found, the server identified the message as spam, or the server requires a username and password.

You should also catch *SmtpFailedRecipientException*, which the runtime throws if the SMTP server rejects a recipient e-mail address. SMTP servers reject only local recipients. In other words, if you are sending a message to tony@contoso.com using Contoso's SMTP server, the server is likely to reject the message if tony@contoso.com is not a valid address (causing the runtime to throw an *SmtpFailedRecipientException*). However, if you are sending a message to the same invalid address using Fabrikam's SMTP server, the SMTP server can't identify that the e-mail address is invalid. Therefore, the runtime does not throw an exception.

Table 15-1 summarizes these and other exceptions that the runtime might throw.

Table 15-1   Exceptions That Can Occur When Sending E-mail

Situation	Exception	Synchronous or Asynchronous
You did not define the server hostname.	*InvalidOperationException*	Both
The server hostname could not be found.	*SmtpException* with an inner *WebException*	Both
You are sending a message to a recipient at your local mail server, but the recipient does not have a mailbox.	*SmtpFailedRecipientException*	Synchronous
You are not a valid user, or there are other message transmission problems not covered by a more specific exception.	*SmtpException*	Both

When using *SmtpClient.SendAsync*, invalid recipients and several other events do not result in an exception. Instead, the runtime calls the *SmtpClient.SendCompleted* event. If *AsyncCompletedEventArgs.Error* is not *null*, an error occurred.

How to Configure Credentials

To reduce spam, all SMTP servers should reject messages from unauthorized users when the message recipients are not hosted by the SMTP server. SMTP servers provided by ISPs typically determine whether a user is authorized based on the user's IP address; if you are part of the ISP's network, you are allowed to use the SMTP server.

Other SMTP servers (and some ISP SMTP servers) require users to provide a valid username and password. To use the default network credentials, set *SmtpClient .UseDefaultCredentials* to *true*. Alternatively, you can set *SmtpClient.Credentials* to *CredentialCache.DefaultNetworkCredentials* (in the *System.Net* namespace), as the following code demonstrates:

```
' VB
Dim client As SmtpClient = New SmtpClient("smtp.contoso.com")
client.Credentials = CredentialCache.DefaultNetworkCredentials
```

```
// C#
SmtpClient client = new SmtpClient("smtp.contoso.com");
client.Credentials = CredentialCache.DefaultNetworkCredentials;
```

To specify the username and password, create an instance of the *System.Net.NetworkCredential* class and use it to define *SmtpClient.Credentials*. The following example shows hard-coded credentials; however, you should always prompt the user for credentials:

```
' VB
Dim client As SmtpClient = New SmtpClient("smtp.contoso.com")
client.Credentials = New NetworkCredential("user", "password")
```

```
// C#
SmtpClient client = new SmtpClient("smtp.contoso.com");
client.Credentials = new NetworkCredential("user", "password");
```

How to Configure SSL

Another important security-related property is *SmtpClient.EnableSsl*. When you set this value to *true*, the runtime encrypts the SMTP communications using SSL. Not all SMTP servers support SSL, but you should always enable this property if support is available.

How to Send a Message Asynchronously

Sending an e-mail message often takes less than a second. Other times, however, the SMTP server might be slow or completely unresponsive, causing your application to wait for the value specified by *SmtpClient.Timeout*. While your application waits for the SMTP server (up to 100 seconds by default), your application is unresponsive and the cursor changes to an hourglass. Users don't have much patience for unresponsive applications, and there is a good chance they will terminate your application if you make them wait too long.

Fortunately, you can send e-mails asynchronously to enable your application to respond to the user while you wait for the message to be sent. You can even give the user the opportunity to cancel the e-mail transmission. To send a message asynchronously, perform these tasks:

1. Create a method to respond to the *SmtpClient.SendCompleted* event. This method needs to determine whether the transmission was successful, unsuccessful, or cancelled.

2. Add your event handler to *SmtpClient.SendCompleted*.

3. Call *SmtpClient.SendAsync*.

4. If you wish, provide the user the opportunity to cancel the e-mail by calling the *SmtpClient.SendAsyncCancel* method.

For example, the following method responds to an *SmtpClient.SendCompleted* event (it requires the *System.ComponentModel* namespace):

```vb
' VB
Sub sc_SendCompleted(ByVal sender As Object, _
    ByVal e As AsyncCompletedEventArgs)
    If e.Cancelled Then
        Console.WriteLine("Message cancelled")
    Else
        If Not (e.Error Is Nothing) Then
            Console.WriteLine("Error: " + e.Error.ToString)
        Else
            Console.WriteLine("Message sent")
        End If
    End If
End Sub
```

```csharp
// C#
static void sc_SendCompleted(object sender, AsyncCompletedEventArgs e)
{
    if (e.Cancelled)
        Console.WriteLine("Message cancelled");
    else if (e.Error != null)
        Console.WriteLine("Error: " + e.Error.ToString());
    else
        Console.WriteLine("Message sent");
}
```

The following code creates the *SmtpClient* object, adds the event handler, calls the asynchronous send, and then immediately cancels the send. Naturally, in real code, you would wait for the user to initiate a cancellation. This code assumes a *MailMessage* object named *mm* already exists:

```vb
' VB
Dim sc As SmtpClient = new SmtpClient("server_name")

' Add the event handler
AddHandler sc.SendCompleted, AddressOf sc_SendCompleted
```

```
' Send the message asynchronously
sc.SendAsync(mm, Nothing)

' Cancel the send
sc.SendAsyncCancel()

// C#
SmtpClient sc = new SmtpClient("server_name");

// Add the event handler
sc.SendCompleted += new SendCompletedEventHandler(sc_SendCompleted);

// Send the message asynchronously
sc.SendAsync(mm, null);

// Cancel the send
sc.SendAsyncCancel();
```

SmtpClient.SendAsync accepts two parameters: the *MailMessage* object to be sent and a generic *Object.* You can specify *null* or any other object for the second parameter; it is strictly for your own use. The .NET Framework simply passes it to the event handler. If you were sending multiple messages asynchronously, you could use the second parameter to keep track of which message generated the event.

Lab: Send an E-mail Message

In this lab, you will complete the application you created in Lesson 1 by sending the e-mail message. If you encounter a problem completing an exercise, the completed projects are available along with the sample files.

Exercise 1: Create an *SmtpClient* Object to Send a *MailMessage* Object

In this exercise, you will extend an existing application to create an *SmtpClient* object and send an e-mail message.

1. Navigate to the \<*InstallHome*>\Chapter15\Lesson2\Exercise1\Partial folder and open either the C# version or the Visual Basic .NET version of the solution file. Alternatively, you can continue working with the application you created in Lesson 1, Exercise 1, adding new code right after the mail message definitions.

2. Add the *System.Net* namespace to your code for Form1. (You will need the *System .Net.NetworkCredential* class.)

3. Write code within the *try/catch* block to create an instance of *SmtpClient*, enable SSL if required, and configure credentials if required. The following code demonstrates this:

    ```
    ' VB
    ' Configure the mail server
    Dim sc As SmtpClient = New SmtpClient(serverTextBox.Text)
    ```

```
sc.EnableSsl = sslCheckBox.Checked
If Not String.IsNullOrEmpty(usernameTextBox.Text) Then
    sc.Credentials = _
        New NetworkCredential(usernameTextBox.Text, passwordTextBox.Text)
End If

// C#
// Configure the mail server
SmtpClient sc = new SmtpClient(serverTextBox.Text);
sc.EnableSsl = sslCheckBox.Checked;
if (!String.IsNullOrEmpty(usernameTextBox.Text))
    sc.Credentials =
        new NetworkCredential(usernameTextBox.Text, passwordTextBox.Text);
```

4. Write code to send the e-mail message and notify the user that the message was sent successfully. The following code demonstrates this:

```
' VB
' Send the message and notify the user of success
sc.Send(mm)
MessageBox.Show("Message sent successfully. ", _
    "Success", MessageBoxButtons.OK, MessageBoxIcon.Information)

// C#
// Send the message and notify the user of success
sc.Send(mm);
MessageBox.Show("Message sent successfully.",
    "Success", MessageBoxButtons.OK, MessageBoxIcon.Information);
```

5. Build and run your project in Debug mode. Type e-mail addresses in the From and To boxes, and then click the Send button without typing the server name. Notice that the runtime throws an *InvalidOperationException*. Create a *catch* block to catch an *InvalidOperationException* and display a message to the user, as the following code demonstrates:

```
' VB
Catch ex As InvalidOperationException
    MessageBox.Show("Please provide a server name.", _
        "No SMTP server provided", _
        MessageBoxButtons.OK, MessageBoxIcon.Error)

// C#
catch (InvalidOperationException)
{
    MessageBox.Show("Please provide a server name.",
        "No SMTP server provided",
        MessageBoxButtons.OK, MessageBoxIcon.Error);
}
```

6. Rerun your project. This time, provide an invalid server name and then click Send. Notice that the runtime throws an *SmtpException*. Using the debugger, examine the exception. The *SmtpException* object doesn't provide a useful description of

the problem. However, the inner exception object is a *WebException* instance, which describes the problem accurately as an invalid Domain Name System (DNS) name. Write code to catch an *SmtpException* and display the message from the base exception type, as the following sample demonstrates:

```VB
' VB
Catch ex As SmtpException
    ' Invalid hostnames result in a WebException InnerException that
    ' provides a more descriptive error, so get the base exception
    Dim inner As Exception = ex.GetBaseException
    MessageBox.Show("Could not send message: " + inner.Message, _
        "Problem sending message", MessageBoxButtons.OK, _
        MessageBoxIcon.Error)
```

```C#
// C#
catch (SmtpException ex)
{
    // Invalid hostnames result in a WebException InnerException that
    // provides a more descriptive error, so get the base exception
    Exception inner = ex.GetBaseException();
    MessageBox.Show("Could not send message: " + inner.Message,
        "Problem sending message", MessageBoxButtons.OK,
        MessageBoxIcon.Error);
}
```

7. Rerun your project. This time, type your SMTP server's hostname and, if necessary, user credentials. In the To box, provide an invalid e-mail address in your local domain. Then click Send. The runtime should throw an *SmtpFailed-RecipientException* (although SMTP server behavior can vary). Write code to catch an *SmtpFailedRecipientException* and display a message to the user:

```VB
' VB
Catch ex As SmtpFailedRecipientException
    MessageBox.Show("The mail server says that there is no mailbox for " + _
        toEmailAddress.Text + ".", "Invalid recipient", _
        MessageBoxButtons.OK, MessageBoxIcon.Error)
```

```C#
// C#
catch (SmtpFailedRecipientException)
{
    MessageBox.Show("The mail server says that there is no mailbox for " +
        toEmailAddress.Text + ".", "Invalid recipient",
        MessageBoxButtons.OK, MessageBoxIcon.Error);
}
```

8. Finally, rerun your project and send yourself an e-mail message to verify that your application works properly.

Exercise 2: Send an E-mail Asynchronously

In this exercise, you will modify the application you created earlier to allow the user to cancel the message before the transaction is completed. To do this, you will change the

SmtpClient.Send method to *SmtpClient.SendAsync*, change the Send button to Cancel while a message is being sent, and respond to a user clicking the Cancel button.

1. Navigate to the \<*InstallHome*>\Chapter15\Lesson2\Exercise2\Partial folder and open either the C# version or the Visual Basic .NET version of the solution file. Alternatively, you can continue working with the application you created in the previous exercise.

2. Comment out the existing *SmtpClient.Send* line.

3. You need to respond after the message is sent, so add an event handler to the *SmtpClient.SendCompleted* event. Then call *SmtpClient.SendAsync* and pass the *MailMessage* object. Remove the code that displays a message box indicating that the message was transmitted successfully because the runtime will continue processing immediately and will not wait for the message to be transmitted successfully. The following code demonstrates this:

```vb
' VB
' Send the message and notify the user of success
' sc.Send(mm)
AddHandler sc.SendCompleted, AddressOf sc_SendCompleted
sc.SendAsync(mm, Nothing)
```

```csharp
// C#
// Send the message and notify the user of success
// sc.Send(mm);
sc.SendCompleted += new SendCompletedEventHandler(sc_SendCompleted);
sc.SendAsync(mm, null);
```

4. To allow access to the *SmtpClient* variable from more than one method, move the variable declaration to the class level. However, you still need to define the variable by setting the value equal to *serverTextBox.Text* in the *sendButton_Click* method.

5. After you start sending the message, you need to give the user an opportunity to cancel the transmission. You could do this by adding a second button labeled Cancel or changing the Send button to Cancel. Either way, if the user clicks Cancel, you need to call *SmtpClient.SendAsyncCancel*. The following code demonstrates how to do this by adding an *If* statement to the *sendButton_Click* method, which determines whether the user has clicked the button while in a Send or Cancel state (the new code is shown in bold):

```vb
' VB
If sendButton.Text = "Send" Then
    ' ... code omitted for simplicity ...

    ' Send the message and notify the user of success
    ' sc.Send(mm)
    AddHandler sc.SendCompleted, AddressOf sc_SendCompleted
    sc.SendAsync(mm, Nothing)
    sendButton.Text = "Cancel"
```

```
Else
    sc.SendAsyncCancel()
End If

// C#
if (sendButton.Text == "Send")
{
    // ... code omitted for simplicity ...

    // Send the message and notify the user of success
    // sc.Send(mm);
    sc.SendCompleted += new SendCompletedEventHandler(sc_SendCompleted);
    sc.SendAsync(mm, null);
    sendButton.Text = "Cancel";
}
else
{
    sc.SendAsyncCancel();
}
```

6. Next, write a method to respond to the *SmtpClient.SendCompleted* event. The previous code sample specified the name of this as *sc_SendCompleted*. Within the method, you need to perform the following tasks:

   ❑ If the *SendAsync* was cancelled, display a message confirming the cancellation.

   ❑ If there was an error, display the error message to the user.

   ❑ If the transmission was successful, inform the user.

   The following code demonstrates this. If you are using Visual Basic, you need to add the *System.ComponentModel* namespace:

```
' VB
Sub sc_SendCompleted(ByVal sender As Object, ByVal e As AsyncCompletedEventArgs)
    If e.Cancelled Then
        MessageBox.Show("Message cancelled.", "Cancelled", _
            MessageBoxButtons.OK, MessageBoxIcon.Error)
    Else
        If Not (e.Error Is Nothing) Then
            MessageBox.Show("Error: " + e.Error.ToString, "Error", _
                MessageBoxButtons.OK, MessageBoxIcon.Error)
        Else
            MessageBox.Show("Message sent successfully.", "Success", _
                MessageBoxButtons.OK, MessageBoxIcon.Information)
        End If
    End If
    sendButton.Text = "Send"
End Sub

// C#
void sc_SendCompleted(object sender, AsyncCompletedEventArgs e)
{
    if (e.Cancelled)
        MessageBox.Show("Message cancelled.",
            "Cancelled", MessageBoxButtons.OK, MessageBoxIcon.Error);
```

```
        else if(e.Error != null)
            MessageBox.Show("Error: " + e.Error.ToString(),
                "Error", MessageBoxButtons.OK, MessageBoxIcon.Error);
        else
            MessageBox.Show("Message sent successfully.",
                "Success", MessageBoxButtons.OK, MessageBoxIcon.Information);
        sendButton.Text = "Send";
    }
```

7. Build and run your code. Verify that you can transmit a message successfully.

8. Send a message, but immediately click Cancel. If your SMTP server is extremely responsive, the Cancel button might disappear very quickly. Verify that your application correctly handles the cancellation and informs the user.

9. Finally, verify that your application correctly responds to incorrect server names, invalid users, and invalid credentials. Note whether an invalid server name is handled by the *SmtpClient.SendCompleted* event or the *sendButton_Click* exception handling.

Lesson Summary

- To send a message, create an instance of *SmtpClient*. Configure the SMTP server hostname and then call *SmtpClient.Send*.

- If you call *SmtpClient.Send* without defining the server hostname, the runtime throws an *InvalidOperationException*. If the hostname is defined but the server cannot be found, the runtime throws an *SmtpException* with an inner *WebException*. If the SMTP server reports that the recipient is invalid, the runtime throws an *SmtpFailedRecipientException*. All other problems sending e-mail result in an *SmtpException*.

- To use the default network credentials, set *SmtpClient.UseDefaultCredentials* to *true*. To specify the username and password, create an instance of the *System .Net.NetworkCredential* class, and use it to define *SmtpClient.Credentials*.

- To enable SSL encryption for the SMTP connection, set *SmtpClient.EnableSsl* to *true*. Not all SMTP servers support SSL.

- To send a message asynchronously, first create a method to respond to the *Smtp Client.SendCompleted* event. Then add your event handler to *SmtpClient.Send-Completed* and call *SmtpClient.SendAsync*. You can call *SmtpClien.SendAsync-Cancel* to cancel an asynchronous message transmission before it has completed.

Lesson Review

You can use the following questions to test your knowledge of the information in Lesson 2, "Sending E-mail." The questions are also available on the companion CD if you prefer to review them in electronic form.

NOTE Answers

Answers to these questions and explanations of why each answer choice is right or wrong are located in the "Answers" section at the end of the book.

---

1. Which method would you call to send an e-mail message and wait for the transmission to complete before proceeding?

   A. *MailMessage.Send*

   B. *SmtpClient.Send*

   C. *SmtpClient.SendAsync*

   D. *MailMessage.SendAsync*

2. You need to send e-mail messages from your assembly. The computer that will run your assembly also hosts an SMTP server. Which of the following are valid values for *SmtpClient.Host*? (Choose all that apply.)

   A. self

   B. 10.1.1.1

   C. localhost

   D. 127.0.0.1

3. What type of exception does the runtime throw if the SMTP server rejects a recipient e-mail address?

   A. *SmtpFailedRecipientException*

   B. *SmtpFailedRecipientsException*

   C. *SmtpException*

   D. *SmtpClientException*

4. You want to send an e-mail message to an SMTP server while encrypting the network communications. Which property do you need to modify from its default settings?

   A. *SmtpClient.Credentials*

   B. *SmtpClient.DeliveryMethod*

   C. *SmtpClient.Port*

   D. *SmtpClient.EnableSsl*

Chapter Review

To practice and reinforce the skills you learned in this chapter further, you can perform the following tasks:

- Review the chapter summary.
- Review the list of key terms introduced in this chapter.
- Complete the case scenarios. These scenarios set up real-world situations involving the topics of this chapter and ask you to create a solution.
- Complete the suggested practices.
- Take a practice test.

Chapter Summary

- To create an e-mail message, use the *System.Net.MailMessage* class. This class supports simple text e-mails, HTML e-mails, e-mails with multiple views and different encoding standards, and attachments.
- To send an e-mail message, use the *System.Net.SmtpClient* class. This class supports SMTP servers that accept anonymous connections, servers that require authentication, and servers that support SSL encryption. Additionally, you can send messages asynchronously to allow users to cancel a message before the transmission has completed.

Key Terms

Do you know what these key terms mean? You can check your answers by looking up the terms in the glossary at the end of the book.

- Multipurpose Internet Mail Extensions (MIME)
- Secure Sockets Layer (SSL)
- Simple Mail Transfer Protocol (SMTP)

Case Scenario

In the following case scenario, you apply what you've learned about how to send e-mails. You can find answers to these questions in the "Answers" section at the end of this book.

Case Scenario: Add E-mail Capabilities to an Existing Application

You are an application developer for Contoso, Inc. For the last two years, you have been developing and maintaining an internal customer relationship management system. Recently, the Contoso Sales group has asked for a way to send confirmation e-mails to customers before making changes to their account information. Your manager asks you to interview key people and then answer questions about your design choices.

Interviews

The following is a list of company personnel interviewed and their statements.

- **Sales Manager** "It's critical to customer satisfaction that our client database is accurate. We've had several situations where someone mistyped an address or a phone number, and this resulted in missed deliveries, unsatisfied customers, and lost sales. What we'd like is to send a confirmation e-mail to customers automatically when we make a change to their contact information. If the change is incorrect, the customer should be able to reject the change. I suppose they could either reply to the e-mail, click a link, or call us, based on how hard it is for you to develop the solution. The rejections shouldn't be that common."

- **Chief Security Officer** "I understand the desire to confirm changes to contact information; however, we need to manage our risk. Sending confidential information through e-mail is never good. You can, and should, encrypt the connection to the SMTP server, but you lose any control over the security of the data after you hand it off. Messages often bounce through several different servers, and most connections are not encrypted. Seeing as this is just contact information, I'm okay with sending the messages, but please do use security when possible."

Questions

Answer the following questions for your manager:

1. What .NET Framework classes will you use to send the e-mails?
2. How can you process e-mail responses from customers?
3. How can you protect the data in the e-mail messages?

Suggested Practices

To help you master the "Implementing interoperability, reflection, and mailing functionality in a .NET Framework application" exam objective, complete the following tasks.

Send Electronic Mail to a Simple Mail Transfer Protocol (SMTP) Server for Delivery from a .NET Framework Application

For this task, you should complete at least Practices 1 and 2. If you want a better understanding of how to work with file attachments, complete Practices 3 through 5. For a detailed understanding of the importance of using SSL, complete Practice 6 as well.

- **Practice 1** Using the application that you created in the labs in this chapter, attempt to send messages through different SMTP servers. Note how different servers respond. To look up the SMTP server for any domain, open a command prompt and run the command **nslookup -type=mx <*domain*>** (for example, *nslookup –type=mx contoso.com*).

- **Practice 2** Expand the application that you created in the labs in this chapter to enable the user to attach files.

- **Practice 3** Attempt to send increasingly larger file attachments until the SMTP server rejects your message. Test several different SMTP servers, and note the maximum file sizes.

- **Practice 4** Using a text file as an attachment, change the file extension to .txt, .jpg, .bat, .cmd, .dll, and .exe. Note which file extensions different mail servers allow, and which of the attachments can be viewed using e-mail clients such as Microsoft Office Outlook.

- **Practice 5** In Chapter 6, "Graphics," you created an application that generates a chart. Add a button to the application that sends the chart as an e-mail attachment.

- **Practice 6** Using a protocol analyzer (also known as a *sniffer*) such as Microsoft Network Monitor, capture the network communications created when sending a message using standard SMTP, standard SMTP with user credentials, and SMTP that is protected by SSL. Use the protocol analyzer to view the raw packets and determine whether an attacker with access to the network could view your message and user credentials.

Take a Practice Test

The practice tests on this book's companion CD offer many options. For example, you can test yourself on just one exam objective, or you can test yourself on all the 70-536 certification exam content. You can set up the test so that it closely simulates the experience of taking a certification exam, or you can set it up in study mode so that you can look at the correct answers and explanations after you answer each question.

MORE INFO   **Practice tests**

For details about all the practice test options available, see the section "How to Use the Practice Tests," in the Introduction of this book.

Chapter 16
Globalization

Globalization is the process of creating an application that supports localized user interfaces. To globalize your application properly, you must understand the different ways that cultures might display numbers, dates, and other information. Although the .NET Framework is capable of doing the bulk of the work for you, you still must understand how to properly use the tools provided.

This chapter doesn't cover all globalization issues. For example, it doesn't cover *localization*, which is the process of translating an application into different languages. Instead, it focuses on the globalization topics covered on the 70-536 exam: formatting and comparing data based on different cultures.

Exam objective in this chapter:
- Format data based on culture information.

Lesson in this chapter:

Before You Begin

This book assumes that you have at least two to three years of experience developing Web-based, Microsoft Windows–based, or distributed applications using the .NET Framework. Candidates also should have a working knowledge of Microsoft Visual Studio, be familiar with Microsoft Visual Basic or C#, and be comfortable with the following tasks:

- Creating Console applications and Windows Presentation Foundation (WPF) applications in Visual Studio using Visual Basic or C#

- Adding namespaces and system class library references to a project

- Running a project in Visual Studio, setting breakpoints, stepping through code, and watching the values of variables

Lesson 1: Formatting Data for Globalization

This lesson focuses on formatting data for different cultures. A *culture* defines how data is displayed to users in different regions. For example, in the United States (specifically, the *en-US* culture), people typically use a period to separate decimals (such as 123.45). However, in Spain (specifically, the *es-ES* culture), people typically use a comma to separate decimals (such as 123,45).

This lesson shows you how to create a culturally sensitive application that automatically formats data according to the user's culture.

After this lesson, you will be able to:

- Set the user's current culture
- Format the output of numbers and strings for different cultures
- Format data manually
- Sort and compare objects in a culture-sensitive way
- Perform culture-insensitive comparisons
- Build a custom culture

Estimated lesson time: 25 minutes

Setting the Culture

Generally, administrators configure a computer's culture. For example, a computer deployed to France would be configured for the French culture, and a computer deployed to China would be configured for the appropriate Chinese culture. However, you can also override the current culture settings. Your changes affect only the current application, however.

You use two different properties to set the culture (both are in the *System.Threading* namespace):

- ***Thread.CurrentThread.CurrentCulture***   Determines the results of culture-dependent functions, such as date, number, and currency formatting. You can define the *CurrentCulture* object only with specific cultures that define both language and regional formatting requirements, such as *es-MX* or *fr-FR*. You cannot define the *CurrentCulture* object with neutral cultures that define only a language, such as *es* or *fr*.

- ***Thread.CurrentThread.CurrentUICulture***   Determines which resources are loaded by the Resource Manager, if you have provided resources in multiple languages. Because this controls only which language is used, you can define *CurrentUICulture* with either neutral or specific cultures.

To change either of these settings, set them using an instance of *CultureInfo*. You can create a *CultureInfo* instance by specifying the culture abbreviation. For example, consider the following code sample:

```
' VB
' Change the current culture
Thread.CurrentThread.CurrentCulture = New CultureInfo("es-ES")
Thread.CurrentThread.CurrentUICulture = New CultureInfo("es-ES")
MessageBox.Show(Thread.CurrentThread.CurrentCulture.ToString())

Dim d As Double = 1234567.89

' Show the figure as currency using the current culture
MessageBox.Show(d.ToString("C"))

' Show the current time using the current culture
MessageBox.Show(DateTime.Now.ToString())

//C#
// Change the current culture
Thread.CurrentThread.CurrentCulture = new CultureInfo("es-ES");
Thread.CurrentThread.CurrentUICulture = new CultureInfo("es-ES");
MessageBox.Show(Thread.CurrentThread.CurrentCulture.ToString());

double d = 1234567.89;

// Show the figure as currency using the current culture
MessageBox.Show(d.ToString("C"));

// Show the current time using the current culture
MessageBox.Show(DateTime.Now.ToString());
```

This code sample produces the following output. Notice that both the currency and time information are displayed using the formatting settings for the *es-ES* culture:

```
es-ES
1.234.567,89 €
17/08/2008 11:07:46
```

Although the previous code sample hard-coded a culture abbreviation for the sake of the example, normally, you provide users with a list of cultures and languages for which you have configured resources. For example, if you have translated your application into English, Spanish, and French, you should allow users to choose from only one of those three options. However, you can also retrieve an array of all available cultures by calling the *System.Globalization.CultureInfo.GetCultures* method. Pass to this method a *CultureTypes* enumeration that specifies which subset of available cultures you want to list. The most useful *CultureTypes* values are:

- **AllCultures**   All cultures included with the .NET Framework, including both neutral and specific cultures. If you use *AllCultures* in your code, be sure to verify that a selected culture is a specific culture before assigning it to the *Culture* object.

- **NeutralCultures**   Neutral cultures that provide only a language, and not regional formatting definitions. Neutral cultures are identified with only two letters, such as *en* (for English) or *es* (for Spanish).

- **SpecificCultures**   Specific cultures that provide both a language and regional formatting definitions. Specific cultures are identified with four letters, such as *en-US* (for English in the United States) or *es-ES* (for Spanish in Spain).

The exercise at the end of this lesson demonstrates the *GetCultures* method to allow the user to select any specific culture.

How to Format Output for Different Cultures

Although the previous section demonstrated changing the current culture and allowing output to be formatted automatically, you can also specify a culture manually to format the output of some types. For example, the following code sample formats an instance of *DateTime* using different cultures (without changing the current culture):

```vb
' VB
' Display the current time using the default culture
Console.WriteLine(DateTime.Now.ToString())

' Display the current time using the English-Great Britain culture
Console.WriteLine(DateTime.Now.ToString(New CultureInfo("en-GB")))

' Display the current time using the Russian culture
Console.WriteLine(DateTime.Now.ToString(New CultureInfo("ru-RU")))
```

```csharp
// C#
// Display the current time using the default culture
Console.WriteLine(DateTime.Now.ToString());

// Display the current time using the English-Great Britain culture
Console.WriteLine(DateTime.Now.ToString(new CultureInfo("en-GB")));

// Display the current time using the Russian culture
Console.WriteLine(DateTime.Now.ToString(new CultureInfo("ru-RU")));
```

Assuming that your computer's default culture is set to *en-US*, the previous code produces the following output:

```
8/17/2008 10:06:31 PM
17/08/2008 20:06:31
17.08.2008 20:06:31
```

Notice the differences, as follows:

- In the *en-US* culture, dates are formatted *mm/dd/yyyy*, and times use a 12-hour format.

- In the *en-GB* culture, dates are formatted *dd/mm/yyyy*, and times use a 24-hour format.

- In the *ru-RU* culture, dates are formatted *dd.mm.yyyy*, and times use a 24-hour format.

Different cultures format numbers differently, too. For example, the United States uses a period (".") to separate decimals, whereas Russia uses a comma (",") to separate decimals. Currency has even more distinctions, including the currency symbol used. Consider the following code sample:

```
' VB
Dim d As Double = 1234567.89

' Show the figure as currency using the default culture
Console.WriteLine(d.ToString("C"))

' Show the figure as currency using the English-Great Britain culture
Console.WriteLine(d.ToString("C", New CultureInfo("en-GB")))

' Show the figure as currency using the Russian culture
Console.WriteLine(d.ToString("C", New CultureInfo("ru-RU")))

// C#
double d = 1234567.89;

// Show the figure as currency using the default culture
Console.WriteLine(d.ToString("C"));

// Show the figure as currency using the English-Great Britain culture
Console.WriteLine(d.ToString("C", new CultureInfo("en-GB")));

// Show the figure as currency using the Russian culture
Console.WriteLine(d.ToString("C", new CultureInfo("ru-RU")));
```

Assuming that your computer's default culture is set to *en-US*, the previous code produces the following output:

```
$1,234,567.89
£1,234,567.89
1 234 567,89p.
```

Notice the differences, as follows:

- In the *en-US* culture, the dollar sign precedes the number, commas separate groups of three digits, and a period separates the decimals.

- In the *en-GB* culture, the pound sign precedes the number, commas separate groups of three digits, and a period separates the decimals.

- In the *ru-RU* culture, the ruble symbol follows the number, spaces separate groups of three digits, and a comma separates the decimals. Notice that the console can't display the ruble symbol (it displays a question mark instead), but the sample output shows it as it would be displayed in a message box.

Real World

Tony Northrup

The most important guideline for globalization is a good guideline for programming in general: use strong types. For example, if you need to display the date to a user, don't simply generate a string with the month, date, and year. Instead, create a *DateTime* object and call *ToString* or another method to display the date. The built-in methods are culturally sensitive. Similarly, if you need to display currency, don't simply prefix a number with a dollar sign. Instead, format the number as currency, so that it is displayed using the current culture's currency settings.

How to Format Data Manually

When you need to format data manually, you can access culture-specific formatting information using *CultureInfo.NumberFormat* and *CultureInfo.DateTimeFormat*. These properties provide access to culture-specific numeric grouping separators (such as a comma or a space), date formatting information and separators, and other elements.

For example, the following Console application (which requires the *System.Globalization* and *System.Threading* namespaces) demonstrates how to use *NumberFormat.NumberDecimalSeparator, NumberFormat.NumberGroupSizes*, and *NumberFormat.NumberGroupSeparator* to format a long number manually for display:

```vb
' VB
Sub Main()
    FormatData(New CultureInfo("es-ES"))
    FormatData(New CultureInfo("ru-RU"))
    FormatData(New CultureInfo("en-US"))

    Console.ReadKey()
End Sub
```

```vb
Private Sub FormatData(ByVal ci As CultureInfo)
    ' Display the selected culture
    Console.WriteLine(ci.ToString() + ":")

    ' Identify the number and copy it to a string
    Dim d As Double = 1234567.89
    Dim formattedNumber As String = d.ToString()

    ' Identify the location of the culture-sensitive decimal point in the number
    Dim decimalIndex As Integer = formattedNumber.IndexOf( _
        Thread.CurrentThread.CurrentCulture.NumberFormat.NumberDecimalSeparator) + 1

    ' Extract only the decimal portion of the number
    formattedNumber = formattedNumber.Substring(decimalIndex, _
        formattedNumber.Length - decimalIndex)

    ' Add the culture-specific decimal point before the number
    formattedNumber = ci.NumberFormat.NumberDecimalSeparator + _
        formattedNumber

    ' Extract only the whole portion of the number
    Dim wholeDigits As String = Math.Floor(d).ToString()
    For a As Integer = 0 To wholeDigits.Length - 1

        ' Add each whole digit to formattedNumber, with grouping separators
        ' Examine CultureInfo.NumberFormat.NumberGroupSizes to determine
        ' whether the current location requires a separator
        Dim requiresSeparator As Boolean = False
        For Each sep As Integer In ci.NumberFormat.NumberGroupSizes
            If (a > 0) AndAlso ((a Mod sep) = 0) Then
                requiresSeparator = True
            End If
        Next

        ' Add a separator if required
        If requiresSeparator Then
            formattedNumber = ci.NumberFormat.NumberGroupSeparator + formattedNumber
        End If

        ' Add the number to the final string
        formattedNumber = _
            wholeDigits.ToCharArray()(wholeDigits.Length - a - 1) + formattedNumber
    Next

    ' Display the manual results and the automatically formatted version
    Console.WriteLine("  Manual:    {0}", formattedNumber)
    Console.WriteLine("  Automatic: {0}", d.ToString("N", ci))
End Sub

// C#
public static void Main()
{
    FormatData(new CultureInfo("es-ES"));
    FormatData(new CultureInfo("ru-RU"));
```

```csharp
        FormatData(new CultureInfo("en-US"));

        Console.ReadKey();
}

private static void FormatData(CultureInfo ci)
{
    // Display the selected culture
    Console.WriteLine(ci.ToString() + ":");

    // Identify the number and copy it to a string
    double d = 1234567.89;
    string formattedNumber = d.ToString();

    // Identify the location of the culture-sensitive decimal point in the number
    int decimalIndex = formattedNumber.IndexOf(
        Thread.CurrentThread.CurrentCulture.NumberFormat.NumberDecimalSeparator) + 1;

    // Extract only the decimal portion of the number
    formattedNumber = formattedNumber.Substring(
        decimalIndex, formattedNumber.Length - decimalIndex);

    // Add the culture-specific decimal point before the number
    formattedNumber = ci.NumberFormat.NumberDecimalSeparator + formattedNumber;

    // Extract only the whole portion of the number
    string wholeDigits = Math.Floor(d).ToString();

    // Add each whole digit to formattedNumber, with grouping separators
    for (int a = 0; a < wholeDigits.Length; a++)
    {
        // Examine CultureInfo.NumberFormat.NumberGroupSizes to determine
        // whether the current location requires a separator
        bool requiresSeparator = false;
        foreach (int sep in ci.NumberFormat.NumberGroupSizes)
        {
            if ( (a > 0) && ((a % sep) == 0) )
            {
                requiresSeparator = true;
            }
        }

        // Add a separator if required
        if (requiresSeparator)
        {
            formattedNumber = ci.NumberFormat.NumberGroupSeparator + formattedNumber;
        }

        // Add the number to the final string
        formattedNumber =
        wholeDigits.ToCharArray()[wholeDigits.Length - a - 1] + formattedNumber;
    }
```

```
    // Display the manual results and the automatically formatted version
    Console.WriteLine(" Manual:    {0}", formattedNumber);
    Console.WriteLine(" Automatic: {0}", d.ToString("N", ci));
}
```

This code sample produces the following output:

```
es-ES:
  Manual:    1.234.567,89
  Automatic: 1.234.567,89
ru-RU:
  Manual:    1 234 567,89
  Automatic: 1 234 567,89
en-US:
  Manual:    1,234,567.89
  Automatic: 1,234,567.89
```

CultureInfo.NumberFormat provides the following properties (among others):

- *CurrencyDecimalDigits*   Indicates the number of decimal places to use in currency values

- *CurrencyDecimalSeparator*   The decimal separator in currency values

- *CurrencyGroupSeparator*   The string that separates groups of digits to the left of the decimal in currency values

- *CurrencyGroupSizes*   The number of digits in each group to the left of the decimal in currency values

- *CurrencyNegativePattern*   The pattern for negative currency values

- *CurrencyPositivePattern*   The pattern for positive currency values

- *CurrencySymbol*   The currency symbol

- *CurrentInfo*   A *NumberFormatInfo* object that you can use to format values based on the current culture

- *DigitSubstitution*   A value that specifies how the graphical user interface displays the shape of a digit

- *NativeDigits*   A string array of native digits equivalent to the Western digits 0 through 9

- *NegativeSign*   The string that denotes that the associated number is negative

- *NumberDecimalSeparator*   The string to use as the decimal separator in numeric values

- **NumberGroupSeparator**   The string that separates groups of digits to the left of the decimal in numeric values

- **NumberGroupSizes**   The number of digits in each group to the left of the decimal in numeric values

- **PercentPositivePattern**   The format pattern for positive percent values

- **PercentSymbol**   The string to use as the percent symbol

- **PerMilleSymbol**   The string to use as the per mille symbol

- **PositiveInfinitySymbol**   The string that represents positive infinity

- **PositiveSign**   The string that denotes that the associated number is positive

CultureInfo.DateTimeFormat provides the following methods (among others):

- **GetAbbreviatedDayName**   Returns the culture-specific abbreviated name of the specified day of the week based on the culture associated with the current *DateTimeFormatInfo* object

- **GetAbbreviatedEraName**   Returns the string containing the abbreviated name of the specified era, if an abbreviation exists

- **GetAbbreviatedMonthName**   Returns the culture-specific abbreviated name of the specified month based on the culture associated with the current *DateTimeFormatInfo* object

- **GetAllDateTimePatterns**   Returns the standard patterns in which *DateTime* values can be formatted

- **GetDayName**   Returns the culture-specific full name of the specified day of the week based on the culture associated with the current *DateTimeFormatInfo* object

- **GetEra**   Returns the integer representing the specified era

- **GetEraName**   Returns the string containing the name of the specified era

- **GetInstance**   Returns the *DateTimeFormatInfo* associated with the specified *IFormatProvider*

- **GetMonthName**   Returns the culture-specific full name of the specified month based on the culture associated with the current *DateTimeFormatInfo* object

- **GetShortestDayName**   Obtains the shortest abbreviated day name for a specified day of the week associated with the current *DateTimeFormatInfo* object

- **SetAllDateTimePatterns**   Sets all the standard patterns in which a *DateTime* value can be formatted

CultureInfo.DateTimeFormat provides the following properties (among others):

- **AbbreviatedDayNames**   A one-dimensional array of type *String* containing the culture-specific abbreviated names of the days of the week

- **AbbreviatedMonthGenitiveNames**   A string array of abbreviated month names associated with the current *DateTimeFormatInfo* object. Genitive names in inflected languages are equivalent to the name with the preposition "of".

- **AbbreviatedMonthNames**   A one-dimensional array of type *String* containing the culture-specific abbreviated names of the months

- **AMDesignator**   The string designator for hours that are *ante meridiem* (before noon)

- **Calendar**   The calendar to use for the current culture

- **CalendarWeekRule**   A value that specifies which rule is used to determine the first calendar week of the year

- **CurrentInfo**   A read-only *DateTimeFormatInfo* object that formats values based on the current culture

- **DateSeparator**   The string that separates the components of a date–that is, the year, month, and day

- **DayNames**   A one-dimensional array of type *String* containing the culture-specific full names of the days of the week

- **FirstDayOfWeek**   The first day of the week

- **FullDateTimePattern**   The format pattern for a long date and long time value, which is associated with the *F* format pattern

- **LongDatePattern**   The format pattern for a long date value, which is associated with the *D* format pattern

- **LongTimePattern**   The format pattern for a long time value, which is associated with the *T* format pattern

- **MonthDayPattern**   The format pattern for a month and day value, which is associated with the *m* and *M* format patterns

- **MonthGenitiveNames** A string array of month names associated with the current *DateTimeFormatInfo* object

- **MonthNames** A one-dimensional array of type *String* containing the culture-specific full names of the months

- **NativeCalendarName** The native name of the calendar associated with the current *DateTimeFormatInfo* object

- **PMDesignator** Gets or sets the string designator for hours that are *post meridiem* (after noon)

- **RFC1123Pattern** Gets the format pattern for a time value, which is based on the Internet Engineering Task Force (IETF) Request for Comments (RFC) 1123 specification and is associated with the *r* and *R* format patterns

- **ShortDatePattern** The format pattern for a short date value, which is associated with the *d* format pattern

- **ShortestDayNames** A string array of the shortest unique abbreviated day names associated with the current *DateTimeFormatInfo* object

- **ShortTimePattern** The format pattern for a short time value, which is associated with the *t* format pattern

- **SortableDateTimePattern** The format pattern for a sortable date and time value, which is associated with the *s* format pattern

- **TimeSeparator** The string that separates the components of time—that is, the hour, minutes, and seconds

- **UniversalSortableDateTimePattern** The format pattern for a universal sortable date and time value, which is associated with the *u* format pattern

- **YearMonthPattern** The format pattern for a year and month value, which is associated with the *y* and *Y* format patterns

Sorting and Comparing Objects

Different cultures sort using different rules by default. For example, sort order can be case-sensitive or case-insensitive, or can also depend on the fundamental order that the language and culture use for the alphabet. For example, the Swedish language has an Æ character that it sorts after *Z* in the alphabet. The German language also has this character, but it sorts it right after *A* in the alphabet. In English, the Æ character is treated as a special symbol and is sorted before A in the standard English alphabet.

Consider the following code sample:

```vb
' VB
Public Sub Main()
    Dim words As String() = New String() {"Apple", "Æble"}

    Thread.CurrentThread.CurrentCulture = New CultureInfo("en-US")
    SortWords(words)

    Thread.CurrentThread.CurrentCulture = New CultureInfo("da-DK")
    SortWords(words)
End Sub

Private Sub SortWords(ByVal words As String())
    Console.WriteLine(Thread.CurrentThread.CurrentCulture)
    Array.Sort(words)
    For Each s As String In words
        Console.WriteLine(s)
    Next
End Sub
```

```csharp
// C#
public static void Main()
{
        string[] words = new string[] { "Apple", "Æble" };

        Thread.CurrentThread.CurrentCulture = new CultureInfo("en-US");
        SortWords(words);

        Thread.CurrentThread.CurrentCulture = new CultureInfo("da-DK");
        SortWords(words);
}

private static void SortWords(string[] words)
{
    Console.WriteLine(Thread.CurrentThread.CurrentCulture);
    Array.Sort(words);
    foreach (string s in words)
    {
        Console.WriteLine(s);
    }
}
```

This Console application produces the following output, demonstrating that changing the culture also changes the sort order:

```
en-US
Æble
Apple

da-DK
Apple
Æble
```

Some cultures support more than one sort order. For example, the *zh-CN* culture (Chinese in China) supports sorting either by pronunciation (the default) or by stroke count (the alternate). To specify the alternate sort order, create a new *CultureInfo* object (as described in the section "How to Build a Custom Culture Class," later in this lesson) using the locale identifier (LCID) for the alternate sort order. Table 16-1 lists the cultures that support multiple sort orders and the number that identifies each sort order.

Table 16-1   Cultures That Support Multiple Sort Orders

Culture Name	Culture	Default Sort Name and LCID	Alternate Sort Name and LCID
es-ES	Spanish (Spain)	International: 0x00000C0A	Traditional: 0x0000040A
zh-TW	Chinese (Taiwan)	Stroke Count: 0x00000404	Bopomofo: 0x00030404
zh-CN	Chinese (China)	Pronunciation: 0x00000804	Stroke Count: 0x00020804
zh-HK	Chinese (Hong Kong SAR)	Stroke Count: 0x00000c04	Stroke Count: 0x00020c04
zh-SG	Chinese (Singapore)	Pronunciation: 0x00001004	Stroke Count: 0x00021004
zh-MO	Chinese (Macao SAR)	Pronunciation: 0x00001404	Stroke Count: 0x00021404
ja-JP	Japanese (Japan)	Default: 0x00000411	Unicode: 0x00010411
ko-KR	Korean (Korea)	Default: 0x00000412	Korean Xwansung– Unicode: 0x00010412
de-DE	German (Germany)	Dictionary: 0x00000407	Phone Book Sort: 0x00010407
hu-HU	Hungarian (Hungary)	Default: 0x0000040e	Technical Sort: 0x0001040e
ka-GE	Georgian (Georgia)	Traditional: 0x00000437	Modern Sort: 0x00010437

The commonly used *String.IndexOf* method can return different results depending on the culture. For example, in the *en-US* culture, *Æ* matches *AE*, and vice versa. In the *da-DK* culture, *Æ* is considered a distinct letter and matches only *Æ*. Consider the following code sample, which identifies the index of *AE* and *Æ* in two different strings:

```vb
' VB
Public Sub Main()
    Dim words As String() = New String() {"AEble", "Æble"}

    Thread.CurrentThread.CurrentCulture = New CultureInfo("en-US")
    FindAE(words)

    Thread.CurrentThread.CurrentCulture = New CultureInfo("da-DK")
    FindAE(words)

    Console.ReadKey()
End Sub

Private Sub FindAE(ByVal words As String())
    Console.WriteLine(Thread.CurrentThread.CurrentCulture.ToString() + ":")
    Array.Sort(words)
    For Each s As String In words
        Console.WriteLine("   AE in {0}: {1}", s, s.IndexOf("AE"))
        Console.WriteLine("   Æ in {0}: {1}", s, s.IndexOf("Æ"))
    Next
    Console.WriteLine()
End Sub
```

```csharp
// C#
public static void Main()
{
    string[] words = new string[] { "AEble", "Æble" };

    Thread.CurrentThread.CurrentCulture = new CultureInfo("en-US");
    FindAE(words);

    Thread.CurrentThread.CurrentCulture = new CultureInfo("da-DK");
    FindAE(words);
}

private static void FindAE(string[] words)
{
    Console.WriteLine(Thread.CurrentThread.CurrentCulture + ":");
    Array.Sort(words);
    foreach (string s in words)
    {
        Console.WriteLine("   AE in {0}: {1}", s, s.IndexOf("AE"));
        Console.WriteLine("   Æ in {0}: {1}", s, s.IndexOf("Æ"));
    }
    Console.WriteLine();
}
```

String.IndexOf returns 0 if the value matches the first position of the string and −1 if the value cannot be found in the string. The previous code sample produces these results, demonstrating the differences between the *en-US* and *da-DK* cultures:

```
en-US:
    AE in Æble: 0
    Æ in Æble: 0
    AE in AEble: 0
    Æ in AEble: 0

da-DK:
    AE in AEble: 0
    Æ in AEble: -1
    AE in Æble: -1
    Æ in Æble: 0
```

Although you should be aware of possible sorting and comparison differences, typically, the differences do not require specific programming techniques. If, however, you plan to exchange data between computers with different cultures, you might need to specify culture-insensitive comparisons, as described in the next section.

Performing Culture-Insensitive Comparisons

Culture-specific sorting is important when displaying information to the user. However, it can cause very confusing inconsistencies when applied to internal sorting. For example, imagine comparing two instances of a sorted database for consistency using a computer in the United States and a computer in Denmark: If the sort order differed, the databases might appear to be inconsistent, even though they are identical.

To avoid such a problem, perform culture-insensitive comparisons by specifying *CultureInfo.InvariantCulture* as the culture or using *StringComparison.InvariantCulture* in overloaded string comparison methods. For example, suppose that you replace the *FindAE* method in the previous code sample with the following code shown in bold:

```vb
' VB
Private Sub FindAE(ByVal words As String())
    Console.WriteLine(Thread.CurrentThread.CurrentCulture.ToString() + ":")
    Array.Sort(words)
    For Each s As String In words
        Console.WriteLine("    AE in {0}: {1}", s, _
            s.IndexOf("AE", StringComparison.InvariantCulture))
        Console.WriteLine("    Æ in {0}: {1}", s, _
            s.IndexOf("Æ", StringComparison.InvariantCulture))
    Next
    Console.WriteLine()
End Sub
```

```csharp
// C#
private static void FindAE(string[] words)
{
    Console.WriteLine(Thread.CurrentThread.CurrentCulture + ":");
    Array.Sort(words);
    foreach (string s in words)
    {
        Console.WriteLine("   AE in {0}: {1}", s,
            s.IndexOf("AE", StringComparison.InvariantCulture));
        Console.WriteLine("   Æ in {0}: {1}", s,
            s.IndexOf("Æ", StringComparison.InvariantCulture));
    }
    Console.WriteLine();
}
```

This code produces the following results, which are consistent regardless of the current culture:

```
en-US:
    AE in Æble: 0
    Æ in Æble: 0
    AE in AEble: 0
    Æ in AEble: 0

da-DK:
    AE in AEble: 0
    Æ in AEble: 0
    AE in Æble: 0
    Æ in Æble: 0
```

Alternatively, specifying the current culture using the following line of code would cause all subsequent comparisons to be culture-insensitive, regardless of whether you specified it for each method call:

```vbnet
' VB
Thread.CurrentThread.CurrentCulture = CultureInfo.InvariantCulture
```

```csharp
//C#
Thread.CurrentThread.CurrentCulture = CultureInfo.InvariantCulture;
```

How to Build a Custom Culture

You can use the *System.Globalization.CultureAndRegionInfoBuilder* class to build a new culture based on an existing one by following these steps:

1. Create an instance of *CultureAndRegionInfoBuilder*, specifying the name of the new culture. This instantiates the *CultureName* property. Although *CultureAndRegion-InfoBuilder* is in the *System.Globalization* namespace, you must add a reference to *Sysglobl* on the .NET tab of the Add Reference dialog box. The dynamic-link library (DLL) is located in the %Windir%\Microsoft.NET\Framework\v2.0.50727 folder.

2. Call the *CultureAndRegionInfoBuilder.LoadDataFromCultureInfo* method to copy the settings from an existing *CultureInfo* object.

3. Call the *CultureAndRegionInfoBuilder.LoadDataFromRegionInfo* method.

4. Use administrative privileges to call the *CultureAndRegionInfoBuilder.Register* method to save the culture.

With the culture registered, you can create new *CultureInfo* instances using the name of your new culture. The following code sample demonstrates this by creating a culture named *en-PL*, registering it, and then creating an instance of the culture. To run this code sample, you need administrative privileges:

```
' VB
' Create a CultureAndRegionInfoBuilder object for the new culture.
Dim cib As CultureAndRegionInfoBuilder = _
    New CultureAndRegionInfoBuilder("en-PL", CultureAndRegionModifiers.None)

' Populate the new CultureAndRegionInfoBuilder object with culture information.
cib.LoadDataFromCultureInfo(New CultureInfo("en-US"))

' Populate the new CultureAndRegionInfoBuilder object with region information.
cib.LoadDataFromRegionInfo(New RegionInfo("US"))

' Define culture-specific settings.
cib.CultureEnglishName = "Pig Latin"
cib.CultureNativeName = "Igpay Atinlay"
cib.IsMetric = True
cib.ISOCurrencySymbol = "PLD"
cib.RegionEnglishName = "Pig Latin Region"
cib.RegionNativeName = "Igpay Atinlay Egionray"

' Register the custom culture (requires administrative privileges).
cib.Register()

' Display some of the properties of the custom culture.
Dim ci As CultureInfo = New CultureInfo("en-PL")

Console.WriteLine("Name: . . . . . . . . . . . . . {0}", ci.Name)
Console.WriteLine("EnglishName:. . . . . . . . . . {0}", ci.EnglishName)
Console.WriteLine("NativeName: . . . . . . . . . . {0}", ci.NativeName)
Console.WriteLine("TwoLetterISOLanguageName: . . . {0}", ci.TwoLetterISOLanguageName)
Console.WriteLine("ThreeLetterISOLanguageName: . . {0}", ci.ThreeLetterISOLanguageName)
Console.WriteLine("ThreeLetterWindowsLanguageName: {0}", ci.ThreeLetterWindowsLanguageName)
```

```
// C#
// Create a CultureAndRegionInfoBuilder object for the new culture.
CultureAndRegionInfoBuilder cib =
    new CultureAndRegionInfoBuilder("en-PL", CultureAndRegionModifiers.None);

// Populate the new CultureAndRegionInfoBuilder object with culture information.
cib.LoadDataFromCultureInfo(new CultureInfo("en-US"));
```

```
// Populate the new CultureAndRegionInfoBuilder object with region information.
cib.LoadDataFromRegionInfo(new RegionInfo("US"));

// Define culture-specific settings.
cib.CultureEnglishName = "Pig Latin";
cib.CultureNativeName = "Igpay Atinlay";
cib.IsMetric = true;
cib.ISOCurrencySymbol = "PLD";
cib.RegionEnglishName = "Pig Latin Region";
cib.RegionNativeName = "Igpay Atinlay Egionray";

// Register the custom culture (requires administrative privileges).
cib.Register();

// Display some of the properties of the custom culture.
CultureInfo ci = new CultureInfo("en-PL");

Console.WriteLine("Name: . . . . . . . . . . . . . {0}", ci.Name);
Console.WriteLine("EnglishName:. . . . . . . . . . {0}", ci.EnglishName);
Console.WriteLine("NativeName: . . . . . . . . . . {0}", ci.NativeName);
Console.WriteLine("TwoLetterISOLanguageName: . . . {0}", ci.TwoLetterISOLanguageName);
Console.WriteLine("ThreeLetterISOLanguageName: . . {0}", ci.ThreeLetterISOLanguageName);
Console.WriteLine("ThreeLetterWindowsLanguageName: {0}", ci.ThreeLetterWindowsLanguageName);
```

Because you require administrative privileges to register a culture, it should be done as part of the application's setup process. Once registered, you can create an instance of *CultureInfo* using your culture abbreviation with standard user privileges.

Lab: Browse Cultures

In this lab, you will create an application that allows you to browse different cultures and examine how they display data differently.

Exercise: Create a WPF Application That Works with Cultures

In this exercise, you will create a new WPF application that allows you to select a specific culture. Then the application formats data for that culture and displays it to the user.

1. In Visual Studio, create a new project named ShowCultures using the WPF Application template.

2. Add a combobox control to the form named *cultureComboBox*. This combobox will contain a list of specific cultures available to the .NET Framework.

3. Add four label controls to the form: *codeLabel, nativeLabel, currencyLabel,* and *dateLabel.* These labels will display information about the currently selected culture.

4. In your code file, add the *System.Globalization* namespace.

5. Edit the *Window.Loaded* event handler, which you can create by double-clicking the window in the designer. In the event handler, populate the *cultureComboBox* with a list of specific cultures, as the following code sample demonstrates:

```
' VB
For Each ci As CultureInfo In _
    CultureInfo.GetCultures(CultureTypes.SpecificCultures)
    cultureComboBox.Items.Add(ci)
Next
```

```
//C#
foreach (CultureInfo ci in
    CultureInfo.GetCultures(CultureTypes.SpecificCultures))
{
    cultureComboBox.Items.Add(ci);
}
```

6. Next, edit the *ComboBox.SelectionChanged* event handler, which you can create by double-clicking the *ComboBox* in the designer. In the event handler, populate the *Label* controls with information based on the currently selected culture. The following code sample demonstrates this:

```
' VB
Dim selectedCulture As CultureInfo = DirectCast(e.AddedItems(0), CultureInfo)
codeLabel.Content = selectedCulture.IetfLanguageTag
nativeLabel.Content = selectedCulture.NativeName

Dim d As Double = 1234567.89
currencyLabel.Content = d.ToString("C", selectedCulture)
dateLabel.Content = DateTime.Now.ToString(selectedCulture)
```

```
//C#
CultureInfo selectedCulture = (CultureInfo)e.AddedItems[0];
codeLabel.Content = selectedCulture.IetfLanguageTag;
nativeLabel.Content = selectedCulture.NativeName;

double d = 1234567.89;
currencyLabel.Content = d.ToString("C", selectedCulture);
dateLabel.Content = DateTime.Now.ToString(selectedCulture);
```

7. Build and run the application. Select different cultures and examine how they display currency and date values.

Lesson Summary

- You can set the user's current culture by setting *Thread.CurrentThread.Current-Culture* to an instance of *CultureInfo*.

- Overloads of *ToString* for numbers and the *DateTime* class support formatting output for a specific culture. Although *ToString* overloads will format output for the current culture by default, you can use different formatting rules simply by providing an instance of *CultureInfo* as a parameter.

- The *CultureInfo.NumberFormat* and *CultureInfo.DateTimeFormat* properties provide detailed information about how a culture formats numbers and dates.

- Different cultures have different sorting and comparison rules. To ensure consistent sorting and comparison rules, specify *CultureInfo.InvariantCulture* as the culture or use *StringComparison.InvariantCulture* in overloaded string comparison methods.

- To create a new culture, create an instance of *CultureAndRegionInfoBuilder* by specifying the name of the new culture. Then call the *CultureAndRegionInfoBuilder.LoadDataFromCultureInfo* and *CultureAndRegionInfoBuilder.LoadDataFromRegionInfo* methods to copy settings from an existing culture.

Lesson Review

You can use the following questions to test your knowledge of the information in Lesson 1, "Formatting Data for Globalization." The questions are also available on the companion CD if you prefer to review them in electronic form.

NOTE Answers

Answers to these questions and explanations of why each answer choice is right or wrong are located in the "Answers" section at the end of the book.

---

1. You are deploying a worldwide application. One of your offices is located in a region of China that does not have an existing culture code that exactly meets their needs. Although the *zh-CN* culture code is very close, this region uses slightly different number formatting. Which class should you use to build a custom culture that meets your requirements?

    A. *CultureInfo*

    B. *CultureAndRegionBuilderInfo*

    C. *RegionInfo*

    D. *CompareInfo*

2. You need to compare two strings, *s1* and *s2*, in such a way that the comparison is made in exactly the same way regardless of culture settings. Which code sample does this correctly?

    A. String.Compare(s1, s2, true)

    B. String.Compare(s1, s2, StringComparison.InvariantCulture)

    C. String.Compare(s1, s2, StringComparison.CurrentCulture)

    D. String.Compare(s1, s2, CultureTypes.NeutralCultures)

3. You need to display a number as currency according to the guidelines for the *es-ES* culture (which might not be the user's current culture). Which class should you use?

    A. *DateTimeFormat*

    B. *CurrentUICulture*

    C. *CultureInfo*

    D. *RegionInfo*

Chapter Review

To practice and reinforce the skills you learned in this chapter further, you can perform the following tasks:

- Review the chapter summary.
- Review the list of key terms introduced in this chapter.
- Complete the case scenario. This scenario sets up a real-world situation involving the topics of this chapter and asks you to create a solution.
- Complete the suggested practices.
- Take a practice test.

Chapter Summary

- You can set the user's current culture by setting *Thread.CurrentThread.Current-Culture* to an instance of *CultureInfo*. You can also use *CultureInfo* objects with the *ToString* method for numbers and for the *DateTime* class to format output for a specific culture. The *CultureInfo.NumberFormat* and *CultureInfo.DateTimeFormat* properties provide detailed information about how a culture formats numbers and dates.

- To avoid inconsistencies when sorting or comparing strings on computers with different cultures, specify *CultureInfo.InvariantCulture* as the culture or use *StringComparison.InvariantCulture* in overloaded string comparison methods.

- To create a new culture, create an instance of *CultureAndRegionInfoBuilder* by specifying the name of the new culture. Then call the *CultureAndRegionInfo-Builder.LoadDataFromCultureInfo* and *CultureAndRegionInfoBuilder.LoadData-FromRegionInfo* methods to copy settings from an existing culture.

Key Terms

Do you know what these key terms mean? You can check your answers by looking up the terms in the glossary at the end of the book.

- Culture
- Globalization
- Localization

Case Scenario

In the following case scenario, you apply what you've learned about how to implement and apply globalization technologies. You can find answers to these questions in the "Answers" section at the end of this book.

Case Scenario: Supporting a New Culture

You are an application developer for Contoso, Inc. Recently, your organization opened an office in a small town in Spain. After deploying one of your internal applications, you began to receive complaints from confused users indicating that the formatting of numbers is wrong. In the small town where your office is, they use commas to separate groups of numbers, and periods to separate decimals, exactly as people in the United States do. However, in most of Spain, periods are used to separate groups of numbers, whereas commas separate decimals.

Your application formats data correctly for different cultures. However, no existing culture exactly meets the needs of these new users.

Questions

Answer the following questions for your manager:

1. How can you create a new culture for the users?

2. Which properties of *CultureInfo* will you need to define to meet the requirements of the users?

3. At Contoso, users do not have administrative privileges. What privileges are required to register the new culture? If users lack the necessary privileges, how can you work around that?

Suggested Practices

To master the "Implementing globalization, drawing, and text manipulation functionality in a .NET Framework application" exam objective, complete the following tasks.

Format Data Based on Culture Information

For this task, you should complete at least Practices 1 and 2. If you want a better understanding of how to create a custom culture, complete Practice 3 as well.

- **Practice 1**   To understand another important difference between cultures, read "Custom Case Mappings and Sorting Rules" at *http://msdn.microsoft.com/ library/xk2wykcz.aspx*, and then run the code sample.

- **Practice 2**   Examine applications that you have written previously for globalization problems and correct them.

- **Practice 3**   Create a custom culture and implement a custom date format. Then implement methods to allow the custom date format to be parsed from a string to a *DateTime* instance.

Take a Practice Test

The practice tests on this book's companion CD offer many options. For example, you can test yourself on just the content covered in this chapter or you can test yourself on all the 70-536 certification exam content. You can set up the test so that it closely simulates the experience of taking a certification exam or you can set it up in study mode so that you can look at the correct answers and explanations after you answer each question.

MORE INFO   **Practice tests**

For details about all the practice test options available, see the section "How to Use the Practice Tests," in the Introduction of this book.

Answers

Chapter 1: Lesson Review Answers

Lesson 1

1. Correct Answers: A, C, and D

    A. **Correct:** *Decimal* is a value type.

    B. **Incorrect:** *String* is a reference type, though the *String* type is an exception and behaves in some ways like a value type.

    C. **Correct:** *System.Drawing.Point* is a value type.

    D. **Correct:** *Integer* is a value type.

2. Correct Answer: B

    A. **Incorrect:** The Visual Basic sample uses angle brackets rather than parentheses. The C# sample uses parentheses rather than angle brackets.

    B. **Correct:** This is the proper way to declare and assign a nullable integer. In C#, you could also use the following: *int? i = null;*.

    C. **Incorrect:** You must use the *nullable* generic to declare an integer as nullable. By default, integers are not nullable.

    D. **Incorrect:** This is not the correct syntax for using the *nullable* generic.

Lesson 2

1. Correct Answers: B and C

    A. **Incorrect:** Types declared as *Nullable* can only be value types.

    B. **Correct:** Strings are reference types.

    C. **Correct:** Exceptions are reference types.

    D. **Incorrect:** Value types derive from *System.Object*, so not all derived types are reference types.

2. **Correct Answer: C**

   A. **Incorrect:** You should order *catch* clauses from most specific to most general.

   B. **Incorrect:** The first type that matches is caught and subsequent *catch* clauses are skipped.

   C. **Correct:** The first type that matches is caught, and subsequent *catch* clauses are skipped. Therefore, you should order *catch* clauses from most specific to most general to enable you to catch errors that you have specific error-handling for, while still catching other exceptions with the more general *catch* clauses.

   D. **Incorrect:** The first type that matches is caught and subsequent *catch* clauses are skipped.

3. **Correct Answer: A**

   A. **Correct:** Using the *String* type to construct a dynamic string can result in a lot of temporary strings in memory because the *String* type is immutable. Therefore, using the *StringBuilder* class is preferable.

   B. **Incorrect:** Strings are limited to 32,767 bytes, not 256 bytes.

   C. **Incorrect:** You can search and replace with a standard *String* class.

   D. **Incorrect:** Strings are never value types; they are reference types.

4. **Correct Answer: B**

   A. **Incorrect:** Although this statement is true, the real advantage of using a *finally* block is that code is executed even if the runtime does not throw an exception. Code in a *catch* block is executed only if an exception occurs.

   B. **Correct:** Use *finally* blocks for code that should run whether or not an exception occurs.

   C. **Incorrect:** The compiler will not throw an error if you do not include a *finally* block. *finally* blocks are optional.

   D. **Incorrect:** You can dispose of resources in a *catch* block. However, the code will run only if an exception occurs. Typically, you need to dispose of resources whether or not an exception occurs.

5. **Correct Answer: B**

   A. **Incorrect:** The *Exception.Message* property provides a description of the exception, but it does not specify the line of code that caused the exception.

B. **Correct:** The *Exception.StackTrace* property provides a full dump of the call stack at the time the exception was thrown, including the file and line of code that caused the exception.

C. **Incorrect:** The *Exception.Source* property lists the library that the exception occurred in. However, this is rarely useful for troubleshooting.

D. **Incorrect:** The *Exception.Data* property is a collection of key/value pairs with user-defined information. It does not include the line of code that threw the exception.

6. **Correct Answer: B**

A. **Incorrect:** First, value types must be initialized before being passed to a procedure unless they are specifically declared as *nullable*. Second, passing a *null* value would not affect the behavior of a value type.

B. **Correct:** Procedures work with a copy of variables when you pass a value type by default. Therefore, any modifications that were made to the copy would not affect the original value.

C. **Incorrect:** The variable might have been redeclared, but it would not affect the value of the variable.

D. **Incorrect:** If the variable had been passed by reference, the original value would have been modified.

Lesson 3

1. **Correct Answers: B and C**

A. **Incorrect:** Interfaces define a contract between types; inheritance derives a type from a base type.

B. **Correct:** Interfaces define a contract between types, ensuring that a class implements specific members.

C. **Correct:** Inheritance derives a type from a base type, automatically implementing all members of the base class, while allowing the derived class to extend or override the existing functionality.

D. **Incorrect:** Interfaces define a contract between types; inheritance derives a type from a base type.

2. **Correct Answers: A and C**

A. **Correct:** *Nullable* is a generic type.

B. **Incorrect:** *Boolean* is a nongeneric value type.

   C. **Correct:** *EventHandler* is a generic type.

   D. **Incorrect:** *System.Drawing.Point* is a structure and is not generic.

3. **Correct Answer: D**

   A. **Incorrect:** The *object* class does not have a *Dispose* member method. Additionally, you would need to use a constraint to mandate types implementing the *IDisposable* interface to call the *Dispose* method.

   B. **Incorrect:** Implementing an interface does not enable generic types to use interface methods.

   C. **Incorrect:** Deriving the generic class from an interface does not enable generic types to use interface methods.

   D. **Correct:** If you use constraints to require types to implement a specific interface, you can call any methods used in the interface.

4. **Correct Answer: A**

   A. **Correct:** Delegates define the signature (arguments and return type) for the entry point.

   B. **Incorrect:** Event procedures can be *Shared/static* or instance members.

   C. **Incorrect:** If you mistyped the event procedure name, you would receive a different compiler error.

   D. **Incorrect:** Events work equally well, regardless of the language used.

5. **Correct Answer: D**

   A. **Incorrect:** *IEquatable* allows two instances of a class to be compared for equality but not sorted.

   B. **Incorrect:** *IFormattable* enables you to convert the value of an object into a specially formatted string.

   C. **Incorrect:** *IDisposable* defines a method to release allocated resources and is not related to sorting objects.

   D. **Correct:** *IComparable* requires the *CompareTo* method, which is necessary for instances of a class to be sorted.

Lesson 4

1. **Correct Answer: A**

   A. **Correct:** The primary reason to avoid boxing is because it adds overhead.

    B. **Incorrect:** Boxing requires no special privileges.

    C. **Incorrect:** Boxing does not make code less readable.

2. **Correct Answers: A and B**

    A. **Correct:** Value types are boxed when an abstract method inherited from *System.Object* is called. Overriding the method avoids boxing.

    B. **Correct:** By default, the *ToString* method simply returns the type name, which is typically not useful for a consuming application.

    C. **Incorrect:** The compiler does not require structures to override the *ToString* method.

    D. **Incorrect:** *ToString* never causes a run-time error; it simply returns the type name unless overridden.

3. **Correct Answer: B**

    A. **Incorrect:** You can't omit a member of an interface and still conform to that interface.

    B. **Correct:** *InvalidCastException* is the recommended exception to throw.

    C. **Incorrect:** While you could throw a custom exception, using standard exception types makes it easier for developers writing code to consume your type to catch specific exceptions.

    D. **Incorrect:** You must return a value for each conversion member.

4. **Correct Answers: A and C**

    A. **Correct:** You can convert from *Int16* to *Int32* because that is considered a widening conversion. Because *Int32* can store any value of *Int16*, implicit conversion is allowed.

    B. **Incorrect:** You cannot convert from *Int32* to *Int16* because that is considered a narrowing conversion. Because *Int16* cannot store any value of *Int32*, implicit conversion is not allowed.

    C. **Correct:** You can convert from *Int16* to *double* because that is considered a widening conversion. Because *double* can store any value of *Int16*, implicit conversion is allowed.

    D. **Incorrect:** You cannot convert from *Double* to *Int16* because that is considered a narrowing conversion. Because *Int16* cannot store any value of *Double*, implicit conversion is not allowed.

Chapter 1: Case Scenario Answers

Case Scenario: Designing an Application

1. Both subscribers and doctors have a lot of information in common, including names, phone numbers, and addresses. However, subscribers and doctors have unique categories of information as well. For example, you need to track the subscription plan and payment information for subscribers. For doctors, you need to track contract details, medical certifications, and specialties. Therefore, you should create separate classes for subscribers and doctors but derive them from a single class that contains all members shared by both classes. To do this, you could create a base class named *Person* and derive both the *Subscriber* and *Doctor* classes from *Person*.

2. You can use an array to store a group of subscribers.

3. Yes, you can use generics to create a method that can accept both subscribers and doctors. To access the information in the base class that both classes share, you need to make the base class a constraint for the generic method.

4. The security error would generate an exception. Therefore, to respond to the exception, you should wrap the code in a *try/catch* block. Within the *catch* block, you should inform users that they should contact their manager.

Chapter 2: Lesson Review Answers

Lesson 1

1. **Correct Answer: D**

    A. **Incorrect:** The *FileInfo* class provides information about individual files and cannot retrieve a directory listing.

    B. **Incorrect:** Use the *DriveInfo* class to retrieve a list of disks connected to the computer. It cannot be used to retrieve a directory listing.

    C. **Incorrect:** You can use the *FileSystemWatcher* class to trigger events when files are added or updated. You cannot use it to retrieve a directory listing, however.

    D. **Correct:** You can create a *DirectoryInfo* instance by providing the path of the parent directory and then call *DirectoryInfo.GetDirectories* to retrieve a list of sub-directories.

2. **Correct Answer: B**

   A. **Incorrect:** The *FileSystemWatcher* class can detect changes to files.

   B. **Correct:** You cannot use *FileSystemWatcher* to detect new drives that are connected to the computer. You would need to query manually by calling the *DriveInfo.GetDrives* method.

   C. **Incorrect:** The *FileSystemWatcher* class can detect new directories.

   D. **Incorrect:** The *FileSystemWatcher* class can detect renamed files.

3. **Correct Answers: B and D**

   A. **Incorrect:** The *File* type is static; you cannot create an instance of it.

   B. **Correct:** The easiest way to copy a file is to call the static *File.Copy* method.

   C. **Incorrect:** This code sample calls the *FileInfo.CreateText* method, which creates a new file that overwrites the existing File1.txt file.

   D. **Correct:** This code sample creates a *FileInfo* object that represents the existing File1.txt file and then copies it to File2.txt.

Lesson 2

1. **Correct Answer: A**

   A. **Correct:** When you write to a *MemoryStream*, the data is stored in memory instead of being stored to the file system. You can then call *MemoryStream.WriteTo* to store the data on the file system permanently.

   B. **Incorrect:** The *BufferedStream* class is useful for configuring how custom stream classes buffer data. However, you typically do not need to use it when working with standard stream classes.

   C. **Incorrect:** The *GZipStream* class compresses and decompresses data written to streams. You cannot use it alone to store streamed data temporarily in memory.

   D. **Incorrect:** While you would need to use the *FileStream* class to store data permanently on the file system, you should use *MemoryStream* to store the data temporarily.

2. **Correct Answers: B and C**

   A. **Incorrect:** You should use *GZipStream* only if you need to read or write a compressed file. While you can compress text, it would cease to be a standard text file if the data were compressed.

B. **Correct:** The *TextReader* class is ideal for processing text files.

C. **Correct:** *StreamReader* derives from *TextReader* and can also be used to read text files.

D. **Incorrect:** Use *BinaryReader* for processing binary data on a byte-by-byte basis. You cannot use *BinaryReader* to process data as strings without performing additional conversion.

3. **Correct Answer: A**

A. **Correct:** The *GetUserStoreForAssembly* method returns an instance of *IsolatedStorageFile* that is private to the user and assembly.

B. **Incorrect:** The *GetMachineStoreForAssembly* method returns an instance of *IsolatedStorageFile* that is private to the assembly but could be accessed by other users running the same assembly.

C. **Incorrect:** The *GetUserStoreForDomain* method returns an instance of *IsolatedStorageFile* that is private to the user but could be accessed by other assemblies running in the same application domain.

D. **Incorrect:** The *GetMachineStoreForDomain* method returns an instance of *IsolatedStorageFile* that could be accessed by other users or other assemblies running in the same application domain.

Chapter 2: Case Scenario Answers

Case Scenario 1: Creating a Log File

1. The *TextWriter* class is ideal for generating text files, including log files.

2. You could use the static *File.Copy* method. Alternatively, you could create an instance of the *FileIO* class and call the *CopyTo* method.

3. No. In this scenario, members of the accounting department need to have direct access to the files. You cannot access files directly in isolated storage from other processes.

Case Scenario 2: Compressing Files

1. Instead of writing directly to the *BinaryWriter* class, you could use the *GZipStream* class. *GZipStream* can compress or decompress data automatically, reducing the storage requirements.

2. Yes, if the application uses the same compression algorithm to access the files.

3. Yes, there's nothing to prevent you from using *GZipStream* with isolated storage.

Chapter 3: Lesson Review Answers

Lesson 1

1. **Correct Answer: C**

    A. **Incorrect:** This code sample would work correctly; however, it performs a case-sensitive replacement. Therefore, it would not replace "HTTP://" correctly.

    B. **Incorrect:** This code sample has the parameters reversed and would replace "https://" with "http://".

    C. **Correct:** This code sample correctly replaces "http://" with "https://" regardless of case.

    D. **Incorrect:** This code sample has the parameters reversed and would replace "https://" with "http://".

2. **Correct Answer: A**

    A. **Correct:** This code sample correctly specifies the *RegexOptions.Multiline* option and does not use angle brackets to name regular expression groups.

    B. **Incorrect:** You must specify the *RegexOptions.Multiline* option to process multiline input.

    C. **Incorrect:** When naming a group, you should not include the angle brackets.

    D. **Incorrect:** When naming a group, you should not include the angle brackets. In addition, you must specify the *RegexOptions.Multiline* option to process multiline input.

3. **Correct Answer: B**

    A. **Incorrect:** This regular expression would match "zoot", but it does not match "zot".

    B. **Correct:** This regular expression matches both strings.

    C. **Incorrect:** This regular expression does not match either string because it begins with the "$" symbol, which matches the end of the string.

    D. **Incorrect:** This regular expression does match "zot", but it does not match "zoot".

4. **Correct Answers: A, C, and E**

    A. **Correct:** This string matches the regular expression.

    B. **Incorrect:** This string does not match the regular expression because the fourth character does not match.

    C. **Correct:** This string matches the regular expression.

    D. **Incorrect:** This string does not match the regular expression because the second and third characters must be "mo".

    E. **Correct:** This string matches the regular expression.

Lesson 2

1. **Correct Answer: A**

    A. **Correct:** UTF-32 has the largest byte size and yields the largest file size.

    B. **Incorrect:** UTF-16 has a smaller byte size than UTF-32.

    C. **Incorrect:** UTF-8 has a smaller byte size than UTF-32.

    D. **Incorrect:** ASCII has a smaller byte size than UTF-32.

2. **Correct Answers: A, B, and C**

    A. **Correct:** UTF-32 provides large enough bytes to support Chinese Unicode characters.

    B. **Correct:** UTF-16 provides large enough bytes to support Chinese Unicode characters.

    C. **Correct:** UTF-8 provides large enough bytes to support Chinese Unicode characters.

    D. **Incorrect:** ASCII supports only English-language characters.

3. **Correct Answers: C and D**

    A. **Incorrect:** ASCII uses 8-bit bytes, whereas UTF-32 uses larger bytes.

    B. **Incorrect:** ASCII uses 8-bit bytes, whereas UTF-16 uses larger bytes.

    C. **Correct:** UTF-8 uses 8-bit bytes for characters in the ASCII range and is backward-compatible with ASCII.

    D. **Correct:** UTF-7 correctly decodes ASCII files.

4. **Correct Answer: D**

   A. **Incorrect:** iso-2022-kr provides support for Korean characters. However, Unicode also provides support for the Korean language, as well as other languages in the same file, and it provides the widest-ranging compatibility.

   B. **Incorrect:** x-EBCDIC-KoreanExtended provides support for Korean characters. However, Unicode also provides support for the Korean language, as well as other languages in the same file, and it provides the widest-ranging compatibility.

   C. **Incorrect:** x-mac-korean provides support for Korean characters. However, Unicode also provides support for the Korean language, as well as other languages in the same file, and it provides the widest-ranging compatibility.

   D. **Correct:** Though you could use one of several different Korean code pages, Unicode provides support for the Korean language and is the best choice for creating new documents.

Chapter 3: Case Scenario Answers

Case Scenario 1: Validating Input

1. You can use separate ASP.NET *RegularExpressionValidator* controls to restrict the input for each of the three boxes. For the company name validator, set the *ValidationExpression* property to *[a-zA-Z'`-Ã,Â´\s]{1,40}*. For the contact name validator, you can use the regular expression, *[a-zA-Z'`-Ã,Â´\s]{1,30}*. Finally, for the phone number validator, you can use the built-in regular expression built into ASP.NET, "((\(\(\d{3}\) ?)|(\d{3}-))?\d{3}-\d{4}".

2. You can write code to constrain, reject, and sanitize the input further. In particular, if the database developer provides further restrictions such as not allowing apostrophes or percent symbols, you can remove those symbols from the input by using the *String.Replace* method.

Case Scenario 2: Processing Data from a Legacy Computer

1. Yes, you can extract data from text reports using regular expressions. You could use the *Regex.Match* method and the *Match.Groups* collection to extract the important data.

2. Yes, you can read ASCII files. You do not need to specify a certain type of encoding to read ASCII files because the standard settings for file streams will process ASCII correctly.

Chapter 4: Lesson Review Answers

Lesson 1

1. **Correct Answer: C**

    A. **Incorrect:** *Stack.Pop* removes an item from the stack.

    B. **Incorrect:** *Stack.Push* adds an item to the stack.

    C. **Correct:** Calling *Stack.Clear* removes all items from the stack. When using an instance of the *Queue* class, you can call *Queue.Clear* to perform the same function.

    D. **Incorrect:** *Stack.Peek* accesses an item on the stack without removing it.

2. **Correct Answer: B**

    A. **Incorrect:** The *Queue* class does not allow sorting.

    B. **Correct:** *ArrayList* allows any type to be added to it and supports sorting. You could provide multiple classes implementing *IComparable* to allow for different sorting techniques.

    C. **Incorrect:** The *Stack* class does not allow sorting.

    D. **Incorrect:** The *StringCollection* class allows you to add only strings; you could not add your custom *ShoppingCartItem* class to a *StringCollection*.

3. **Correct Answers: A and B**

    A. **Correct:** You must implement the *IComparable* interface to allow items in a collection to be sorted.

    B. **Correct:** Implementing the *IComparable* interface requires the *CompareTo* method.

    C. **Incorrect:** The *IEnumerable* interface is required when a class is used within a *foreach* loop. It is not required for sorting.

    D. **Incorrect:** The *GetEnumerator* method is required only for the *IEnumerable* interface.

Lesson 2

1. **Correct Answer: C**

    A. **Incorrect:** *HashTable* can be used generically. However, you need to be able to retrieve the most recently added transactions easily, and the *Stack* class better suits your needs.

B. **Incorrect:** *SortedList* can be used generically. However, you do not need to sort your transactions.

C. **Correct:** Stacks provide a LIFO collection, which exactly meets your requirements. You can declare the *Stack* class generically, using your custom *DBTransaction* class.

D. **Incorrect:** While *Queue* can be used generically, it provides a FIFO collection. In this scenario, you need a LIFO collection.

2. **Correct Answer: B**

A. **Incorrect:** *StringDictionary* is strongly typed. However, you cannot use your custom class as the value. The value must always be a string.

B. **Correct:** By inheriting from a generic class, such as *Dictionary<T,U>*, you can create strongly typed collections.

C. **Incorrect:** *StringDictionary* cannot be used as a generic class.

D. **Incorrect:** *Dictionary* can be used only as a generic class.

3. **Correct Answer: A**

A. **Correct:** To be used as a key in a generic *SortedList<T,U>* collection, the class must implement the *IComparable* interface.

B. **Incorrect:** This class declaration does not implement the *IComparable* interface.

C. **Incorrect:** The *IEquatable* interface is used to allow instances of a class to be compared for equality. It does not allow a class to be sorted.

D. **Incorrect:** The *Equals* method is not sufficient to allow a class to be sorted.

Chapter 4: Case Scenario Answers

Case Scenario 1: Using Collections

1. You can create collection properties for *Crime* and *Convict* to store collections that contain multiple *Evidence* and *Behavior* instances.

2. There's no particular requirement that would cause you to use a dictionary, so your best choice is the generic *List<T>* class. You will be able to create strongly typed collections and provide as many different sorting algorithms as required. *ArrayList* would also work, but *List<T>* is more efficient because it is strongly typed.

3. You can write different methods for each sorting algorithm and pass the method as a parameter to the *List.Sort* method.

Case Scenario 2: Using Collections for Transactions

1. A *Queue* collection would meet your needs perfectly because it provides a FIFO sequence to hold pending transactions.

2. You need a LIFO sequence, and a *Stack* collection would work to hold completed transactions.

3. Yes. Both *Queue* and *Stack* can be used generically.

Chapter 5: Lesson Review Answers

Lesson 1

1. **Correct Answers: A and D**

    A. **Correct:** You must call the *BinaryFormatter.Serialize* or *SoapFormatter.Serialize* method to serialize an object.

    B. **Incorrect:** You do not necessarily need file permissions to serialize an object. You can also serialize an object to a network stream.

    C. **Incorrect:** Microsoft Internet Information Services (IIS) is not required for serialization; however, serialized objects are often transferred to Web services.

    D. **Correct:** The *BinaryFormatter.Serialize* method requires a stream object to act as the destination for the serialization.

2. **Correct Answer: B**

    A. **Incorrect:** *ISerializable* is an interface that you can implement to perform custom serialization. It is not an attribute.

    B. **Correct:** Classes must have the *Serializable* attribute to be serialized.

    C. **Incorrect:** *SoapInclude* is used when generating schemas for SOAP serialization. It is not required to enable serialization.

    D. **Incorrect:** *OnDeserialization* is an *ISerializable* method that you can implement to control serialization behavior. It is not an attribute.

3. **Correct Answer: A**

    A. **Correct:** The *NonSerialized* attribute prevents a member from being serialized.

    B. **Incorrect:** *Serializable* is an attribute that specifies a class should be serialized. It does not apply to members.

C. **Incorrect:** *SerializationException* is an exception class called when a serialization error occurs. It is not an attribute.

D. **Incorrect:** The *SoapIgnore* attribute prevents a member from being serialized only by *SoapFormatter*. It does not apply to *BinaryFormatter*.

4. **Correct Answer: C**

A. **Incorrect:** *IFormatter* provides functionality for formatting serialized objects.

B. **Incorrect:** *ISerializable* allows an object to control its own serialization and deserialization.

C. **Correct:** Implement the *IDeserializationCallback* interface and the *IDeserializationCallback.OnDeserialization* method to run code after an object is serialized.

D. **Incorrect:** *IObjectReferences* indicates that the current interface implementer is a reference to another object.

Lesson 2

1. **Correct Answers: A and C**

A. **Correct:** Classes serialized with XML serialization must be public.

B. **Incorrect:** You cannot use XML serialization on private classes.

C. **Correct:** For XML serialization to work, the class must have a parameterless constructor.

4. **Incorrect:** XML serialization does not require the *SerializationInfo* parameter.

2. **Correct Answer: D**

A. **Incorrect:** *XmlAnyAttribute* causes an array to be filled with *XmlAttribute* objects that represent all XML attributes unknown to the schema. It is used during deserialization, and it is not used during serialization.

B. **Incorrect:** Use the *XMLType* attribute to specify the name and namespace of the XML type.

C. **Incorrect:** *XMLElement* causes the field or property to be serialized as an XML element.

D. **Correct:** By default, members are serialized as elements. Add *XMLAttribute* to serialize a member as an attribute.

3. **Correct Answer: A**

   A. **Correct:** You can use the Xsd.exe tool to create classes based on an XML schema.

   B. **Incorrect:** Xdcmake.exe is a tool for compiling .xdc files into an .xml file. It cannot be used to create a class that conforms to an XML schema.

   C. **Incorrect:** XPadsi90.exe is used to register a SQL Server computer in Active Directory Domain Services. It cannot be used to create a class that conforms to an XML schema.

   D. **Incorrect:** Xcacls.exe is used to configure access control lists (ACLs) on files. It cannot be used to create a class that conforms to an XML schema.

4. **Correct Answer: B**

   A. **Incorrect:** Use the *XMLType* attribute to specify the name and namespace of the XML type.

   B. **Correct:** Use the *XMLIgnore* attribute to prevent a member from being serialized during XML serialization.

   C. **Incorrect:** *XMLElement* causes the field or property to be serialized as an XML element.

   D. **Incorrect:** *XMLAttribute* causes the field or property to be serialized as an XML attribute.

Lesson 3

1. **Correct Answers: A and C**

   A. **Correct:** The deserialization constructor must accept two objects, of types *SerializationInfo* and *StreamingContext*.

   B. **Incorrect:** Although the *Formatter* class is used during serialization, it is not passed to the deserialization constructor.

   C. **Correct:** The deserialization constructor must accept two objects, of types *SerializationInfo* and *StreamingContext*.

   D. **Incorrect:** Although the *ObjectManager* class is used during serialization, it is not passed to the deserialization constructor.

2. **Correct Answer: B**

   A. **Incorrect:** *OnSerializing* occurs before serialization, not before deserialization.

   B. **Correct:** *OnDeserializing* occurs immediately before deserialization.

    C. **Incorrect:** *OnSerialized* occurs after serialization, not immediately before deserialization.

    D. **Incorrect:** *OnDeserialized* occurs after deserialization, not before deserialization.

3. **Correct Answer: C**

    A. **Incorrect:** *OnSerializing* occurs before serialization, not after serialization.

    B. **Incorrect:** *OnDeserializing* occurs before deserialization, not immediately after serializing.

    C. **Correct:** *OnSerialized* occurs immediately after serialization.

    D. **Incorrect:** *OnDeserialized* occurs after deserialization, not immediately after serialization.

4. **Correct Answers: A and C**

    A. **Correct:** Methods that are called in response to a serialization event must accept a *StreamingContext* object as a parameter.

    B. **Incorrect:** Methods that are called in response to a serialization event must accept a *StreamingContext* object as a parameter and are not required to accept a *SerializationInfo* parameter.

    C. **Correct:** Methods that are called in response to a serialization event must return *void*.

    D. **Incorrect:** Methods that are called in response to a serialization event must return *void* and cannot return a *StreamingContext* object.

Chapter 5: Case Scenario Answers

Case Scenario 1: Choosing a Serialization Technique

1. You should use *BinaryFormatter* serialization. In this case, you will be communicating only with other .NET Framework–based applications. In addition, the network manager asked you to conserve bandwidth.

2. In all likelihood, you will need to add only the *Serializable* attribute to enable serialization.

3. It depends on how you establish the network connection, but the serialization itself should require only two or three lines of code.

Case Scenario 2: Serializing Between Versions

1. Yes, *BinaryFormatter* can deserialize objects serialized with the .NET Framework 1.0.

2. Yes, you can deserialize the *Preferences* class, even if the serialized class is missing members. However, you need to add the *OptionalField* attribute to any new members to prevent the runtime from throwing a serialization exception. Then you need to initialize the new members with default values after deserialization either by implementing *IDeserializationCallback* or by creating a method for the *OnDeserialized* event.

3. There's nothing to prevent the same class from being serialized by either *Binary-Formatter* or *XmlSerializer*. Your application should first check for the preferences of a serialized XML file. If the file does not exist, it should then attempt to deserialize the binary file.

Chapter 6: Lesson Review Answers

Lesson 1

1. **Correct Answer: E**

   A. **Incorrect:** *Graphics.DrawLines* draws multiple, connected lines. This method can be used to draw a square, but it cannot be used to draw a filled square.

   B. **Incorrect:** *Graphics.DrawRectangle* would be the most efficient way to draw an empty square. However, it cannot be used to draw a filled square.

   C. **Incorrect:** *Graphics.DrawPolygon* could be used to draw an empty square. However, it cannot be used to draw a filled square.

   D. **Incorrect:** *Graphics.DrawEllipse* is used to draw oval shapes and cannot be used to draw a filled square.

   E. **Correct:** *Graphics.FillRectangle* is used to draw filled squares or rectangles.

   F. **Incorrect:** *Graphics.FillPolygon* could be used to draw a filled square. However, it is not as efficient as using *FillRectangle*.

   G. **Incorrect:** *Graphics.FillEllipse* is used to draw oval shapes and cannot be used to draw a square.

2. **Correct Answer: C**

   A. **Incorrect:** *Graphics.DrawLines* draws multiple, connected lines. This method can be used to draw an empty triangle, but it is not the most efficient way.

   B. **Incorrect:** *Graphics.DrawRectangle* draws empty squares or rectangles. However, it cannot be used to draw a triangle.

   C. **Correct:** *Graphics.DrawPolygon* is the most efficient way to draw an empty triangle.

   D. **Incorrect:** *Graphics.DrawEllipse* is used to draw oval shapes and cannot be used to draw an empty triangle.

   E. **Incorrect:** *Graphics.FillRectangle* is used to draw filled squares or rectangles and cannot be used to draw an empty triangle.

   F. **Incorrect:** *Graphics.FillPolygon* could be used to draw a filled triangle. However, it cannot be used to draw an empty triangle.

   G. **Incorrect:** *Graphics.FillEllipse* is used to draw oval shapes and cannot be used to draw an empty triangle.

3. **Correct Answers: A and B**

   A. **Correct:** To draw a circle, call the *Graphics.DrawEllipse* method using an instance of the *Graphics* class.

   B. **Correct:** To call the *Graphics.DrawEllipse* method, you must provide an instance of the *Pen* class.

   C. **Incorrect:** *System.Drawing.Brush* is used to draw filled shapes, not empty shapes.

   D. **Incorrect:** You can create a *Graphics* object from *System.Drawing.Bitmap*; however, there are many better ways to create a *Graphics* class.

4. **Correct Answer: B**

   A. **Incorrect:** *HatchBrush* defines a rectangular brush with a hatch style, foreground color, and background color.

   B. **Correct:** *LinearGradientBrush* can be used to fill objects with a color that gradually fades to a second color.

   C. **Incorrect:** *PathGradientBrush* can be used to fill objects with a color that gradually fades to a second color; however, *LinearGradientBrush* is more efficient.

   D. **Incorrect:** *SolidBrush* fills objects with only a single color.

   E. **Incorrect:** *TextureBrush* is used to fill objects with an image.

5. **Correct Answer: D**

   A. **Incorrect:** The arrow points to the right.

   B. **Incorrect:** The arrow points to the right.

   C. **Incorrect:** The arrow points to the right.

   D. **Correct:** The arrow points to the right.

Lesson 2

1. **Correct Answers: A and B**

   A. **Correct:** You can load a picture from a file using the *Image* constructor and then call *Graphics.DrawImage* to display the picture in the form.

   B. **Correct:** The *Bitmap* class inherits from the *Image* class and can be used in most places where the *Image* class is used.

   C. **Incorrect:** You cannot use the *MetaFile* class to load a JPEG image.

   D. **Incorrect:** The *PictureBox* class is used to display pictures in a form, but it does not include a method to load a picture from a file.

2. **Correct Answer: C**

   A. **Incorrect:** You cannot create a *Graphics* object directly from a picture saved to the disk.

   B. **Incorrect:** The *Bitmap* class does not have methods for drawing graphics.

   C. **Correct:** You must first create a *Bitmap* object and then create a *Graphics* object from the *Bitmap* before saving it.

   D. **Incorrect:** There is no *Bitmap.CreateGraphics* method. Instead, you must call *Graphics.FromImage* to create a *Graphics* object.

3. **Correct Answer: C**

   A. **Incorrect:** You can use the BMP format to store photographs; however, the JPEG format uses much less space.

   B. **Incorrect:** The GIF format is not ideal for storing photographs.

   C. **Correct:** The JPEG format offers excellent quality and compression for photographs with almost universal application support.

   D. **Incorrect:** The PNG format is very efficient; however, it is not as universally compatible as the GIF and JPEG formats.

4. **Correct Answer: B**

   A. **Incorrect:** You can use the BMP format to store charts; however, the GIF format uses much less space.

   B. **Correct:** The GIF format is ideal for storing charts.

   C. **Incorrect:** You can use the JPEG format to store charts; however, the results may not be as clear as the GIF format.

   D. **Incorrect:** The PNG format is very efficient; however, it is not as universally compatible as GIF and JPEG.

Lesson 3

1. **Correct Answer: B**

   A. **Incorrect:** The *string* class does not have a *Draw* method.

   B. **Correct:** You add text by calling *Graphics.DrawString*, which requires a *Graphics* object, a *Font* object, and a *Brush* object.

   C. **Incorrect:** *Graphics.DrawString* requires a *Brush* object, not a *Pen* object.

   D. **Incorrect:** The *Bitmap* class does not have a *DrawString* method.

2. **Correct Answer: A**

   A. **Correct:** Create an instance of the *StringFormat* class and pass it to *Graphics.DrawString* to control the alignment of a string.

   B. **Incorrect:** *StringAlignment* can be used when specifying the formatting of a string; however, it is an enumeration and you cannot create an instance of it.

   C. **Incorrect:** *FormatFlags* can be used when specifying the formatting of a string; however, it is a property of *StringFormat* and you cannot create an instance of it.

   D. **Incorrect:** *LineAlignment* can be used when specifying the formatting of a string; however, it is a property of *StringFormat* and you cannot create an instance of it.

3. **Correct Answer: C**

   A. **Incorrect:** This statement would cause the line to be drawn at the top of the bounding rectangle.

   B. **Incorrect:** This statement would cause the line to be drawn at the bottom of the bounding rectangle.

C. **Correct:** This statement would cause the line to be drawn at the left of the bounding rectangle.

D. **Incorrect:** This statement would cause the line to be drawn at the right of the bounding rectangle.

4. **Correct Answer: C**

A. **Incorrect:** The *Metafile* class allows you to manipulate a sequence of graphics, but it cannot be used to manipulate all the required image formats directly.

B. **Incorrect:** The *Icon* class can only be used to manipulate icons, which are very small bitmaps.

C. **Correct:** You can use the *Bitmap* class to manipulate BMP, GIF, EXIF, JPEG, PNG and TIFF files.

D. **Incorrect:** The *Image* class is an abstract base class and should not be used directly.

Chapter 6: Case Scenario Answers

Case Scenario 1: Choosing Graphics Techniques

1. You can specify the size of an image as part of the *Bitmap* constructor, and the .NET Framework automatically resizes the image. Note, however, that to ensure the image is scaled proportionately (and not squeezed vertically or horizontally), you should open the image, check the size, and calculate a new size for the image that uses the same proportions as the original.

2. First, open the image file in a *Bitmap* object. Then create a *Graphics* object from the *Bitmap* object, and call *Graphics.DrawImage* to draw the corporate logo. The logo background needs to be transparent.

3. Determine a percentage of the horizontal and vertical area that the logo will consume as a maximum, calculate the maximum number of pixels as a percentage of the size of the splash screen, and then resize the logo.

4. This will not require using graphics at all—simply specify a different font and fontsize for labels and text boxes by editing the properties of the controls.

Case Scenario 2: Creating Simple Charts

1. You should use a *PictureBox* control.

2. *Graphics.DrawLines*

3. *Graphics.DrawRectangles*

4. You can call the *PictureBox.Image.Save* method.

Chapter 7: Lesson Review Answers

Lesson 1

1. **Correct Answer: A**

    A. **Correct:** You can run a method in a background thread by calling *Thread-Pool.QueueUserWorkItem*. In Visual Basic, specify the name of the method with the *AddressOf* keyword. In C#, simply specify the method name.

    B. **Incorrect:** In Visual Basic, you must provide the address of the method to run when you call *ThreadPool.QueueUserWorkItem*. Therefore, you must add the *AddressOf* keyword. In C#, you cannot use the *out* keyword; simply provide the name of the method.

    C. **Incorrect:** *ThreadStart* is a delegate and cannot be called directly to start a new thread.

    D. **Incorrect:** *ThreadStart* is a delegate and cannot be called directly to start a new thread.

2. **Correct Answers: B and D**

    A. **Incorrect:** *ThreadPool.GetAvailableThreads* retrieves the difference between the maximum number of thread pool threads returned by the *GetMax-Threads* method and the number currently active.

    B. **Correct:** You can pass a single object to *ThreadPool.QueueUserWorkItem*. Therefore, to pass multiple values, create a single class that contains all the values you need to pass.

    C. **Incorrect:** There is no need to add the delegate for the method. Instead, you specify the method when you call *ThreadPool.QueueUserWorkItem*.

    D. **Correct:** *ThreadPoolQueueUserWorkItem* can accept two parameters: a method to run using the new background thread and an instance of an object that will be passed to the method. Use this overload to pass parameters to the method.

E. **Incorrect:** You must pass the *Calc* method to *ThreadPoolQueueUserWork-Item* in addition to the instance of the custom class.

Lesson 2

1. **Correct Answer: B**

   A. **Incorrect:** *ThreadState* is a read-only property that you can check to determine whether a thread is running. You cannot set it to control a thread's priority.

   B. **Correct:** Define the *Thread.Priority* property to control how the processor schedules processing time. *ThreadPriority.Highest*, the highest priority available, causes the operating system to provide that thread with more processing time than threads with lower priorities.

   C. **Incorrect:** *ThreadPriority.Lowest*, the lowest priority available, causes the operating system to provide the thread with less processing time than other threads.

   D. **Incorrect:** *ThreadState* is a read-only property that you can check to determine whether a thread is running. You cannot set it to control a thread's priority.

2. **Correct Answer: D**

   A. **Incorrect:** While you could use the *SyncLock* or *lock* keyword to lock the file resource, this would not allow multiple threads to read from the file simultaneously. When using *SyncLock* or *lock*, all locks are exclusive.

   B. **Incorrect:** When using *SyncLock* or *lock*, you must specify a resource to be locked.

   C. **Incorrect:** When calling *ReaderWriterLock.AcquireReaderLock*, you must provide a timeout in milliseconds.

   D. **Correct:** *ReaderWriterLock* provides separate logic for read and write locks. Multiple read locks can be held simultaneously, allowing threads to read from a resource without waiting for other read locks to be released. However, write locks are still exclusive—if one thread holds a write lock, no other thread can read from or write to the resource.

3. **Correct Answer: C**

   A. **Incorrect:** This code sample attempts to increment the *orders* value, but it is not thread-safe. If two threads call the method simultaneously, one of the operations could be overwritten.

   B. **Incorrect:** *SyncLock* or *lock* cannot be used on value types such as *integer*. *SyncLock* or *lock* can be used only on reference types.

   C. **Correct:** Use the *Interlocked* class to add 1 to a value while guaranteeing the operation is thread-safe.

   D. **Incorrect:** *ReaderWriterLock* provides separate logic for read and write locks. Multiple read locks can be held simultaneously, allowing threads to read from a resource without waiting for other read locks to be released. This code sample creates a read lock, which does not prevent the section of code from running multiple times. This code sample would work if a write lock were used instead.

Chapter 7: Case Scenario Answers

Case Scenario 1: Print in the Background

1. Call *ThreadPool.QueueUserWorkItem* and pass the print job object.

2. When you use the overloaded *ThreadPool.QueueUserWorkItem* method and pass the print job as the second parameter, the *Print* method receives the print job as an argument. In C#, you need to cast this to the *PrintJob* type.

3. You need to create a callback method that displays the results and a delegate for the method. Then, add the delegate to the *PrintJob* class and call the method at the conclusion of the *Print* method.

Case Scenario 2: Ensuring Integrity in a Financial Application

1. You should use the *Interlocked.Increment* method. Simply adding 1 to the value could cause an increment operation to be lost in a multithreaded environment.

2. To allow multiple parts of a transaction to complete before other transactions take place, use the *SyncLock* or *lock* keyword. Alternatively, to allow multiple threads to read financial data simultaneously while preventing an update transaction from occurring, you could use the *ReaderWriterLock* class.

Chapter 8: Lesson Review Answers

Lesson 1

1. **Correct Answers: B and D**

    A. **Incorrect:** There are other ways to start separate processes.

    B. **Correct:** You can call *AppDomain.Unload* to close the application domain and free up resources.

    C. **Incorrect:** Creating a separate application domain does not improve performance.

    D. **Correct:** Application domains provide a layer of separation. In addition, you can limit the application domain's privileges, reducing the risk of a security vulnerability being exploited in an assembly.

2. **Correct Answers: B and C**

    A. **Incorrect:** *AppDomain.CreateDomain* creates a new application domain, but it does not run an assembly.

    B. **Correct:** You can use *AppDomain.ExecuteAssembly* to run an assembly if you have the path to the executable file.

    C. **Correct:** You can use *AppDomain.ExecuteAssemblyByName* to run an assembly if you have the name of the assembly and a reference to the assembly.

    D. **Incorrect:** *AppDomain.ApplicationIdentity* is a property and cannot be used to run an assembly.

3. **Correct Answer: D**

    A. **Incorrect:** *AppDomain.DomainUnload* is an event that is called when an application domain is unloaded.

    B. **Incorrect:** Setting an application domain to *null* does not cause it to be unloaded.

    C. **Incorrect:** Instances of the *AppDomain* class do not contain an *Unload* method.

    D. **Correct:** To unload an *AppDomain* object, pass it to the static *AppDomain.Unload* method.

Lesson 2

1. **Correct Answer: C**

    A. **Incorrect:** Evidence cannot be used to affect a process's priority.

    B. **Incorrect:** While evidence can identify the author of an assembly, the runtime uses this information only if security settings have been specifically configured for a given author.

    C. **Correct:** The primary purpose of providing evidence for an application domain is to modify the privileges that the runtime assigns to the application domain.

    D. **Incorrect:** Evidence is not related to auditing.

2. **Correct Answers: A and D**

    A. **Correct:** You can pass evidence to the *AppDomain.CreateDomain* method to apply the evidence to any assemblies run within that application domain.

    B. **Incorrect:** You can read *AppDomain.Evidence*, but you cannot set it. To specify evidence for an *AppDomain*, you must pass the *Evidence* as part of the constructor.

    C. **Incorrect:** *AppDomain.ExecuteAssembly* does not accept a zone as a parameter. You must add the zone to an *Evidence* object to pass it to the *ExecuteAssembly* method.

    D. **Correct:** You can pass evidence to the *AppDomain.ExecuteAssembly* method to associate the evidence with the specified assembly.

3. **Correct Answer: D**

    A. **Incorrect:** *DynamicDirectory* is read-only. In addition, it specifies the location in which dynamically generated files are located. It does not specify the base directory for an application.

    B. **Incorrect:** *BaseDirectory* is read-only.

    C. **Incorrect:** The *DynamicBase* property specifies the location in which dynamically generated files are located. It does not specify the base directory for an application.

    D. **Correct:** Use an instance of the *AppDomainSetup* class to configure an application domain and set the *AppDomainSetup.ApplicationBase* property to set the name of the directory containing the application.

4. **Correct Answer: A**

   A. **Correct:** The *DisallowCodeDownload* boolean property indicates whether the current application domain is allowed to download assemblies.

   B. **Incorrect:** The *DisallowCodeDownload* property is located within *App-Domain.CurrentDomain.SetupInformation.*

   C. **Incorrect:** The *DisallowPublisherPolicy* property gets or sets a value indicating whether the publisher policy section of the configuration file is applied to an application domain. You need to examine *DisallowCodeDownload* instead.

   D. **Incorrect:** First, the *DisallowPublisherPolicy* property is located within *App-Domain.CurrentDomain.SetupInformation.* Second, you need to examine *DisallowCodeDownload* instead.

Lesson 3

1. **Correct Answer: A**

   A. **Correct:** *LocalService* causes your service to run in the context of an account that acts as a nonprivileged user on the local computer, and it presents anonymous credentials to any remote server. Using *LocalService* is the best way to minimize security risks because it limits the damage a service can do if the service is successfully exploited.

   B. **Incorrect:** *NetworkService* can present authentication credentials to remote computers, which could be a security risk, though if so, it would be minimal.

   C. **Incorrect:** *LocalSystem* has almost unlimited privileges on the local computer, which enables a successful exploitation of the service to perform almost any action on the computer.

   D. **Incorrect:** *User* causes the system to prompt for a valid username and password when the service is installed. While this user account could have restricted privileges, the risk is likely to be greater than using *LocalService*.

2. **Correct Answer: C**

   A. **Incorrect:** *LocalService* causes your service to run in the context of an account that acts as a nonprivileged user on the local computer. Using *LocalService* is the best way to minimize security risks, but it can cause security problems when performing common tasks such as writing to the file system.

B. **Incorrect:** *NetworkService* should be used when the service needs to authenticate to remote computers. It is not recommended for services that need access only to the local computer.

C. **Correct:** *LocalSystem* has almost unlimited privileges on the local computer, which enables a service to take almost any action. You should use *LocalSystem* only when security is not a concern.

D. **Incorrect:** *User* causes the system to prompt for a valid user name and password when the service is installed. While this user account could have sufficient privileges, *LocalSystem* guarantees that you have unlimited privileges on the local computer.

3. **Correct Answers: B and D**

A. **Incorrect:** While you could start an assembly automatically by adding it to the Startup group, you cannot start a service this way.

B. **Correct:** You can use the InstallUtil command-line tool to install a service manually.

C. **Incorrect:** While you could start an assembly automatically by adding it to Scheduled Tasks, you cannot start a service this way.

D. **Correct:** The most user-friendly way to install a service is to use Visual Studio to create an installer for your service.

4. **Correct Answer: B**

A. **Incorrect:** My Computer does not contain a tool to configure user accounts for services.

B. **Correct:** Computer Management contains the Services snap-in, which you can use to configure user accounts for services.

C. **Incorrect:** While you can use the *Net* command to start, stop, pause, and continue a service, you cannot use *Net* to configure user accounts for services.

D. **Incorrect:** The .NET Framework Configuration tool does not contain a tool to configure user accounts for services.

5. **Correct Answer: A**

A. **Correct:** You must define the *ServiceProcessInstaller.Account* property as *User*, and then set the *ServiceProcessInstaller.Username* and *ServiceProcessInstaller.Password* properties.

B. **Incorrect:** The *StartType* property only defines whether a service starts automatically, manually, or is disabled. It does not define the account in which a service runs.

C. **Incorrect:** The Startup Type only defines whether a service starts automatically, manually, or is disabled. It does not define the account in which a service runs.

D. **Incorrect:** You can define the Zone to limit an assembly's permissions. However, you cannot use the Zone to configure an assembly to run in the context of a specific user account.

Chapter 8: Case Scenario Answers

Case Scenario 1: Creating a Testing Tool

1. You should create an application that prompts the user to select a zone and an assembly. Based on their selections, you should start the assembly in an application domain with evidence that would cause it to be assigned to the code group corresponding to the selected zone.

2. Although several techniques would work, the simplest way to do this is to assign Internet zone evidence to the assembly, as the following code demonstrates:

```
' VB
Dim hostEvidence As Object() = {New Zone (SecurityZone.Internet)}
Dim internetEvidence As Evidence = New Evidence (hostEvidence, Nothing)

Dim myDomain As AppDomain = AppDomain.CreateDomain("QADomain")
myDomain.ExecuteAssembly("C:\path\CASDemands.exe", internetEvidence)

// C#
object [] hostEvidence = {new Zone(SecurityZone.Internet)};
Evidence internetEvidence = new Evidence(hostEvidence, null);

AppDomain myDomain = AppDomain.CreateDomain("QADomain");
myDomain.ExecuteAssembly(@"C:\path\CASDemands.exe", internetEvidence);
```

When the CASDemands application runs, the runtime should warn you that the application is running in a partially trusted context. If you do not receive this warning, you have not successfully restricted the assembly's permissions.

Case Scenario 2: Monitoring a File

1. You should create a Windows service.

2. You will need to create a setup project for the service. The setup project will generate an MSI file that IT can distribute by using Systems Management Server (SMS).

3. You should set the startup type to Automatic.

4. You should specify the User account type and ask the IT department to create a user account that has only privileges to read the configuration file and add events. *LocalService* would not have sufficient privileges, and *LocalSystem* would have excessive privileges.

Chapter 9: Lesson Review Answers

Lesson 1

1. **Correct Answer: B**

    A. **Incorrect:** Application settings (accessible through *ConfigurationManager.AppSettings*) are separate from connection strings. Instead, you should access *ConfigurationManager.ConnectionStrings*.

    B. **Correct:** Access the *ConfigurationManager.ConnectionStrings* collection and specify the key to retrieve the connection string. If it has been configured correctly, the *ConnectionString* property can be used to connect to a database server.

    C. **Incorrect:** *ConfigurationManager.ConnectionStrings.ElementInformation.Source* returns the file that a connection string is defined in. Instead, you should access *ConfigurationManager.ConnectionStrings*.

    D. **Incorrect:** Application settings (accessible through *ConfigurationManager.AppSettings*) are separate from connection strings. Instead, you should access *ConfigurationManager.ConnectionStrings*.

2. **Correct Answers: A, C, and D**

    A. **Correct:** Because you are creating a WPF application, you are using a recent version of .NET Framework. Starting with .NET Framework version 2.0, you should derive from *ConfigurationSection* rather than inheriting from *IConfigurationSectionHandler*.

    B. **Incorrect:** While you can inherit from *IConfigurationSectionHandler* and accomplish the goals outlined in this scenario, *IConfigurationSectionHandler* is deprecated in .NET Framework version 2.0.

    C. **Correct:** Custom sections must be declared with a name and the type in the *<configSections>* section.

D. **Correct:** Within the *<configuration>* section of your application's .config file, create a custom section using the name declared in the *<configSections>* section. Then, either add XML attributes or elements to declare the settings.

3. **Correct Answer: B**

    A. **Incorrect:** Calling *ConfigurationManager.AppSettings.Set* does not save the setting to permanent storage.

    B. **Correct:** Key2 is written to the application's .config file because *config.Save* is called afterwards.

    C. **Incorrect:** Key3 is not written to the application's .config file because *config.Save* is not called after the key is added.

    D. **Incorrect:** Key2 is written successfully.

Lesson 2

1. **Correct Answer: B**

    A. **Incorrect:** Configured assemblies are not necessarily part of the assembly cache.

    B. **Correct:** By adding an assembly to the assembly cache, it can be managed and referenced centrally from any other assembly without copying the assembly to every referencing assembly's folder.

    C. **Incorrect:** While an assembly must be signed to add it to the assembly cache, delay signing does not accomplish this.

    D. **Incorrect:** Setup projects do not necessarily add an assembly to the assembly cache.

2. **Correct Answer: C**

    A. **Incorrect:** The *codebase* element is used to configure the location and version of an assembly when configuring an assembly binding.

    B. **Incorrect:** The *assemblyIdentity* element is used to identify an assembly when configuring an assembly binding.

    C. **Correct:** The *supportedRuntime* element allows you to configure an assembly to run in a version of the .NET Framework other than that which was used to build it.

    D. **Incorrect:** The DEVPATH environment variable lists folders that the CLR will search for a referenced assembly.

3. **Correct Answer: A**

   A. **Correct:** The DEVPATH environment variable stores a list of folders that the CLR will use to search for a referenced assembly.

   B. **Incorrect:** The PATH environment variable stores a list of folders that the operating system will use to search for an executable file. However, PATH is not used by the CLR to find assemblies.

   C. **Incorrect:** The APPDATA environment variable identifies the folder used by applications to store application data.

   D. **Incorrect:** The PATHHEXT environment variable identifies file extensions that the operating system will add to a command.

Lesson 3

1. **Correct Answer: D**

   A. **Incorrect:** A Setup project is not required for a custom installer called using InstallUtil.exe.

   B. **Incorrect:** While you can handle the *Installing* event in the *Installer*-derived class, you cannot add a method with the same name.

   C. **Incorrect:** While the *Commit, Install, Uninstall*, and *Rollback* methods accept an *IDictionary* parameter, the constructor does not require it.

   D. **Correct:** The InstallUtil.exe tool identifies the installation class using the *RunInstaller* attribute. Therefore, you must add it to your installation class.

2. **Correct Answer: C**

   A. **Incorrect:** The *Install* method performs the file copies.

   B. **Incorrect:** The *Commit* method finalizes an installation after the Install method has run successfully.

   C. **Correct:** The *Rollback* method is called instead of *Commit* if the *Install* method fails. Therefore, the *Rollback* implementation should remove any files left over from the failed install attempt.

   D. **Incorrect:** The *Uninstall* method is called only after the installation succeeds.

Chapter 9: Case Scenario Answers

Case Scenario 1: Configuring an Application

1. You can configure a *<connectionStrings>* section in either the Machine.config file or the application's .config file.

2. You can configure an *<appSettings>* section in either the Machine.config file or the application's .config file.

3. The *<connectionStrings>* setting should be stored in the Machine.config file because it will be shared by multiple applications. The application-specific settings should be stored in the application's .config file.

Case Scenario 2: Installing an Application

1. You can add a standard Setup project to your solution to build an .MSI Windows Installer package.

2. The most straightforward way would be to implement a custom *Installer* class, which systems administrators could then install using InstallUtil.exe.

Chapter 10: Lesson Review Answers

Lesson 1

1. **Correct Answer: A**

   A. **Correct:** Before adding events, you must register an event source for your application. This is best done during setup because it requires administrative privileges. To register an event source, call the static *EventLog.CreateEventSource* method.

   B. **Incorrect:** Use *EventLog.Create* to create a new event log. This is not required for this scenario because you are using the built-in Application event log.

   C. **Incorrect:** *EventLog.GetEventLogs* retrieves a collection of existing event logs.

   D. **Incorrect:** *EventLog.WriteEntry* is used to add an entry to the event log after creating an instance of *EventLog*.

2. **Correct Answer: C**

   A. **Incorrect:** Applications can store events in the Application event log. However, the operating system never stores events in this log.

   B. **Incorrect:** The System event log stores operating system events, but it does not store security or auditing events.

   C. **Correct:** The Security event log stores both success and failure audits as they are generated by the operating system.

   D. **Incorrect:** The Setup log is used only when installing the operating system or updates to the operating system.

3. **Correct Answer: A**

   A. **Correct:** Calls to the *Debug* class execute only when running a Debug build of an application. Calls to the *Assert* method display a message only if the boolean value is False.

   B. **Incorrect:** Calls to the *Trace* class execute regardless of whether the build is Debug or Release.

   C. **Incorrect:** The *WriteIf* method displays a message if the value is True, which would yield incorrect results in this example. In addition, *WriteIf* does not display a dialog box.

   D. **Incorrect:** Calls to the *Trace* class execute regardless of whether the build is Debug or Release. The *WriteIf* method displays a message if the value is True, which would yield incorrect results in this example. In addition, *WriteIf* does not display a dialog box.

4. **Correct Answer: B**

   A. **Incorrect:** The *DefaultTraceListener* writes output to the Visual Studio output window, not to the console.

   B. **Correct:** *ConsoleTraceListener* writes output to the console.

   C. **Incorrect:** The *EventLogTraceListener* writes output to event log events, not to the console. In addition, the constructor requires you to specify an event log.

   D. **Incorrect:** The *XmlWriterTraceListener* writes output to a stream in XML format, not to the console. In addition, the constructor requires a stream.

Lesson 2

1. **Correct Answers: B, C, and D**

    A. **Incorrect:** Updating the *RawValue* property directly is not thread-safe. If you update it and reference its own value, it's possible that the calculation will be corrupted by a different thread.

    B. **Correct:** The *Increment* method is thread-safe. However, because it's slow, you should use it only in multithreaded applications.

    C. **Correct:** The *Decrement* method is thread-safe. However, because it's slow, you should use it only in multithreaded applications.

    D. **Correct:** The *Increment* method is thread-safe regardless of whether you pass a parameter.

2. **Correct Answer: C**

    A. **Incorrect:** Use the *PerformanceCounterCategory* class to call the static *Create* method. However, you must pass a parameter of type *PerformanceCounter-Category* to specify the counters.

    B. **Incorrect:** *CounterSample* is a structure.

    C. **Correct:** The *CounterCreationDataCollection* class stores an array of performance counters and can be used by the *PerformanceCounterCategory.Create* method to create multiple counters.

    D. **Incorrect:** You can use *CounterCreationData* to create a single performance counter. However, you must use *CounterCreationDataCollection* to create multiple performance counters.

Lesson 3

1. **Correct Answer: C**

    A. **Incorrect:** *Process.GetProcessesByName* returns a collection of *Process* objects, but only those objects that match the name provided.

    B. **Incorrect:** *Process.GetCurrentProcess* returns only a single *Process* object representing the current process.

    C. **Correct:** *Process.GetProcesses* returns a collection of *Process* objects representing all processes visible to the current thread.

D. **Incorrect:** *Process.GetProcessById* returns only a single *Process* object with the process ID you specify.

2. **Correct Answer: D**

A. **Incorrect:** You cannot run a query directly with an instance of *ObjectQuery*.

B. **Incorrect:** The *ManagementObjectSearcher.Get* method returns an instance of *ManagementObjectCollection*. It does not return a *ManagementObject* instance.

C. **Incorrect:** You cannot run a query directly with an instance of *ObjectQuery*.

D. **Correct:** To run a WMI query, create an instance of *ManagementObject-Searcher*. Then call the *ManagementObjectSearcher.Get* method, which returns an instance of *ManagementObjectCollection*.

3. **Correct Answers: B and D**

A. **Incorrect:** *ManagementEventWatcher.Query* is a property, not a method.

B. **Correct:** You must create a *ManagementEventWatcher* object and specify the WMI query.

C. **Incorrect:** The event handler must accept *object* and *EventArrivedEventArgs* parameters. To retrieve the *ManagementBaseObject*, access *EventArrived-EventArgs.NewEvent*.

D. **Correct:** To handle WMI events, you must register a *ManagementEvent-Watcher.EventArrived* handler.

Chapter 10: Case Scenario Answers

Case Scenario 1: Improving the Manageability of an Application

1. To provide real-time performance data, create a custom performance counter category and publish performance information from your application. Systems administrators can then monitor the performance data either locally or across the network. To provide logging information compatible with their event management system, simply add events to the Application event log or a custom event log.

2. You can use the Trace class to write tracing data. Users could then edit the .config file to enable tracing to a log file or the event log.

Case Scenario 2: Collecting Information About Computers

1. You can create a WMI query, such as "SELECT * FROM Win32_LogicalDisk". The results describe every disk attached to the computer.

2. You can create a WMI event handler that detects a modification to the list of logical disks attached to the computer. In the event handler, log the details of the newly attached disk and display the warning dialog box.

Chapter 11: Lesson Review Answers

Lesson 1

1. **Correct Answers: B and D**

    A. **Incorrect:** Zone evidence is based on the location from which the assembly runs. It does not require a strong name.

    B. **Correct:** To provide the Strong Name evidence type, an assembly must be signed.

    C. **Incorrect:** Hash evidence is based on a unique signature generated using the assembly's binary. It does not require a strong name.

    D. **Correct:** To provide the Publisher evidence type, an assembly must be signed.

2. **Correct Answer: B**

    A. **Incorrect:** *SocketPermission* is related to networking; however, it is required for initiating raw Transmission Control Protocol/Internet Protocol (TCP/IP) connections rather than Hypertext Transfer Protocol (HTTP) Web connections.

    B. **Correct:** You must have *WebPermission* to initiate HTTP requests to a Web server.

    C. **Incorrect:** You need *DnsPermission* to look up DNS addresses, which is often part of sending a Web request. However, it is not a requirement.

    D. **Incorrect:** *ServiceControllerPermission* controls the ability to start, stop, and pause services.

3. **Correct Answer: D**

    A. **Incorrect:** My_Computer_Zone uses the FullTrust permission set and offers the highest level of privileges.

    B. **Incorrect:** LocalIntranet_Zone uses the LocalIntranet permission set, which provides a moderately high level of privileges.

C. **Incorrect:** Internet_Zone uses the Internet permission set, which provides a very restrictive level of privileges. However, it is not as restrictive as Restricted_Zone.

D. **Correct:** Restricted_Zone uses the Nothing permission set, which grants no privileges.

4. **Correct Answer: A**

A. **Correct:** You can read the file because both your user account and the assembly's CAS allow reading the file.

B. **Incorrect:** Although the assembly's CAS allows writing to the file, your user permissions restrict you to Read access.

C. **Incorrect:** Although the assembly's CAS allows changing the permissions of the file, your user permissions restrict you to Read access.

D. **Incorrect:** Although the assembly's CAS allows you to delete the file, your user permissions restrict you to Read access.

Lesson 2

1. **Correct Answer: C**

A. **Incorrect:** The Everything permission set is sufficient for the application to run.

B. **Incorrect:** The Everything permission set is sufficient for the application to run.

C. **Correct:** The declarative permissions do not stop the assembly from reading the first line of the C:\Boot.ini file.

D. **Incorrect:** A security exception prior to execution occurs only if the administrator were running the assembly with a debugger and the request for *UIPermission* was removed.

2. **Correct Answer: B**

A. **Incorrect:** The permissions are sufficient for the first line to be displayed, but the runtime throws an exception when the assembly attempts to access a file in the root of the C:\ drive.

B. **Correct:** The runtime throws an exception when the assembly attempts to access a file in the root of the C:\ drive because the *SecurityAction.Request-Optional FileIOPermissionAttribute* declaration refuses access to everything except for the C:\Temp folder.

C. **Incorrect:** The *SecurityAction.RequestOptional* declarative permission refuses permission to the root of the C:\ drive.

D. **Incorrect:** A security exception prior to execution would occur only if the administrator were running the assembly with a debugger and the request for *UIPermission* was removed.

3. **Correct Answer: C**

A. **Incorrect:** There are no *SecurityAction.RequestOptional* requests. Therefore, the only permissions denied to the assembly are those listed with *Security-Action.RequestRefuse*.

B. **Incorrect:** There are no *SecurityAction.RequestOptional* requests. Therefore, the only permissions denied to the assembly are those listed with *Security-Action.RequestRefuse*.

C. **Correct:** The assembly has permission to read a file in the root of the C:\ drive because it has the Everything permission set and the permission is not explicitly refused.

D. **Incorrect:** A security exception prior to execution would occur only if the administrator were running the assembly with a debugger and the request for UIPermission was removed.

4. **Correct Answer: C**

A. **Incorrect:** *SocketPermission* controls access to networking. This is not required for Console applications.

B. **Incorrect:** *WebPermission* controls access to HTTP requests. This is not required for Console applications.

C. **Correct:** *UIPermission* is required for Console applications running with a debugger to enable the application to communicate with the debugger.

D. **Incorrect:** *FileIOPermission* controls access to the file system. This is not required for Console applications.

Lesson 3

1. **Correct Answer: A**

A. **Correct:** *SecurityAction.Demand* instructs the runtime to throw an exception if the caller and all callers higher in the stack lack the specified permission.

B. **Incorrect:** *SecurityAction.Deny* causes the runtime to reduce the method's access by removing the specified permission.

C. **Incorrect:** *SecurityAction.Assert* instructs the runtime to ignore the fact that callers might not have the specified permission. Assemblies must have the Assert Any Permission That Has Been Granted security permission setting.

D. **Incorrect:** *SecurityAction.RequestMinimum* is used for checking permissions declaratively.

2. **Correct Answer: D**

A. **Incorrect:** *SecurityAction.Demand* instructs the runtime to throw an exception if the caller and all callers higher in the stack lack the specified permission. However, *SecurityAction.Demand* must be used imperatively, and the question describes a need for declarative security.

B. **Incorrect:** *SecurityAction.Deny* causes the runtime to reduce the method's access by removing the specified permission.

C. **Incorrect:** *SecurityAction.Assert* instructs the runtime to ignore the fact that callers might not have the specified permission.

D. **Correct:** *SecurityAction.RequestMinimum* is used for checking permissions declaratively. If the caller lacks the privilege, the runtime throws an exception.

3. **Correct Answer: D**

A. **Incorrect:** Calling *IPermission.Deny* throws an exception if the permission is missing.

B. **Incorrect:** The *IsGranted* method is a member of the *SecurityManager* class, not *IPermission*.

C. **Incorrect:** The *Deny* method is a member of the *IPermission* interface, not the *SecurityManager* class.

D. **Correct:** Use the *Boolean SecurityManager.IsGranted* method to determine whether the assembly has a specific permission.

4. **Correct Answers: B and D**

A. **Incorrect:** There is no *EventLogPermission.RevertPermitOnly* method.

B. **Correct:** Call *CodeAccessPermission.RevertPermitOnly* to remove a previous *EventLogPermission.PermitOnly* call.

C. **Incorrect:** The *RevertAll* method is a member of the *CodeAccessPermission* class, not *EventLogPermission*.

D. **Correct:** Call *CodeAccessPermission.RevertAll* to remove a previous *EventLogPermission.PermitOnly* or *EventLogPermission.Deny* call.

     E. **Incorrect:** The *RevertDeny* method is a member of the *CodeAccessPermission* class, not *EventLogPermission*.

     F. **Incorrect:** You should call *CodeAccessPermission.RevertDeny* to remove a previous *EventLogPermission.Deny* call. However, it cannot remove an *Event-LogPermission.PermitOnly* call.

5. **Correct Answer: C**

     A. **Incorrect:** Calling the *PermitOnly* method causes an exception if your method uses any permissions other than those permissions specified by the *CodeAccessPermission* instance. It does not cancel an assertion.

     B. **Incorrect:** Calling the *Deny* method removes the permissions specified by the *CodeAccessPermission* instance. It does not cancel an assertion.

     C. **Correct:** Call the static *CodeAccessPermission.RevertAssert* to remove any previous assertions.

     D. **Incorrect:** The static *CodeAccessPermission.RevertDeny* method removes any previous *Deny* calls; it does not cancel an assertion.

Chapter 11: Case Scenario Answers

Case Scenario 1: Explaining CAS

1. No. So long as operating systems enable unmanaged code to run, viruses can bypass CAS simply by not leveraging the .NET Framework. Unmanaged code is exempt from CAS permission checks.

2. No. However, it will let the CEO run applications that use the .NET Framework.

3. No, a virus based on the .NET Framework would be restricted by the Internet permission set, which restricts assemblies from communicating across the network except to contact the site from which the assembly originated.

4. No. The Intranet zone does not allow assemblies to access the file system directly. The most the assembly could do is prompt you to open or save files.

Case Scenario 2: Customizing CAS

1. You can build CAS functionality into your application to limit the permissions available and specifically restrict access to the file system. Use assembly declarations to limit the permissions that your assembly receives to the bare minimum. Protect methods using method declarations. Finally, you can use CAS imperatively

to control permissions within a method. If a method does need to write to the file system, you can ensure that the window of opportunity is as small as possible.

2. You would use *FileIOPermission*.

3. They shouldn't be affected at all.

Chapter 12: Lesson Review Answers

Lesson 1

1. **Correct Answer: D**

   A. **Incorrect:** You could use *WindowsPrincipal.IsInRole* to check imperatively for a group membership; however, declarative RBS demands offer greater security by performing the security check before running a method.

   B. **Incorrect:** The *IsInRole* method is a member of *WindowsPrincipal*, not *WindowsIdentity*.

   C. **Incorrect:** You could use imperative RBS demands to check for a group membership; however, declarative RBS demands offer greater security by performing the security check before running a method.

   D. **Correct:** Declarative RBS demands restrict access to an entire method while offering the highest level of resistance to security vulnerabilities.

2. **Correct Answer: C**

   A. **Incorrect:** You could use *WindowsPrincipal.IsInRole* to check imperatively for a group membership; however, imperative RBS demands are more secure because they throw an exception that prevents further processing.

   B. **Incorrect:** The *IsInRole* method is a member of *WindowsPrincipal*, not *WindowsIdentity*.

   C. **Correct:** Imperative RBS demands restrict access to code by throwing an exception. You can easily catch this exception and display an error message to the user.

   D. **Incorrect:** Although declarative RBS demands are more secure than imperative RBS demands, declarative RBS demands are defined as an attribute to a method, and it is difficult to catch security exceptions thrown by a declarative RBS demand when the method is called by a Windows event.

3. **Correct Answer: A**

   A. **Correct:** *WindowsPrincipal.IsInRole* is perfect when you simply need to branch your code based on user memberships and the code is not performing security-sensitive tasks.

   B. **Incorrect:** The *IsInRole* method is a member of *WindowsPrincipal*, not *WindowsIdentity*.

   C. **Incorrect:** Imperative RBS demands restrict access to code by throwing an exception. Exceptions interrupt processing; therefore, you should use an imperative RBS demand only when you need to completely prevent a user from running code.

   D. **Incorrect:** Declarative RBS demands completely prevent a user from running a method. In this scenario, the method should simply make a decision based on the group membership, and *WindowsPrincipal.IsInRole* allows that without blocking access to the entire method.

4. **Correct Answers: A and B**

   A. **Correct:** *GenericIdentity* represents individual users, supports imperative and declarative RBS demands, and meets the simple requirements.

   B. **Correct:** *GenericPrincipal* represents user groups, supports imperative and declarative RBS demands, and meets the simple requirements.

   C. **Incorrect:** You could implement *IIdentity* to represent users; however, *GenericIdentity* meets your requirements and would be more efficient to implement.

   D. **Incorrect:** You could implement *IPrincipal* to represent users; however, *GenericPrincipal* meets your requirements and would be more efficient to implement.

Lesson 2

1. **Correct Answers: A and B**

   A. **Correct:** You can control access to files using the *FileSecurity* class.

   B. **Correct:** You can control access to registry keys using the *RegistrySecurity* class.

   C. **Incorrect:** The .NET Framework does not provide libraries for configuring printer permissions.

   D. **Incorrect:** The .NET Framework does not provide libraries for configuring share permissions.

2. **Correct Answer: A**

   A. **Correct:** To apply ACL changes to a folder, call *Directory.SetAccessControl.* This method requires two parameters: the directory and the *DirectorySecurity* object containing the ACLs.

   B. **Incorrect:** Although you can create a new directory by specifying a *DirectorySecurity* object, in this example, the directory must exist already for the code to work properly.

   C. **Incorrect:** You must provide both a path and a *DirectorySecurity* object to *Directory.SetAccessControl.*

   D. **Incorrect:** Although you can create a new directory by specifying a *DirectorySecurity* object, in this example, the directory must exist already for the code to work properly. In addition, you cannot create a directory by specifying only a *DirectorySecurity* object.

3. **Correct Answer: B**

   A. **Incorrect:** *RegistryAccessRule* describes a DACL for a registry key.

   B. **Correct:** *RegistryAuditRule* describes an SACL for a registry key.

   C. **Incorrect:** *AccessRule* is the base class for all DACLs.

   D. **Incorrect:** *AuditRule* is the base class for all SACLs. However, it is not specific to registry keys. *RegistryAuditRule* inherits from *AuditRule* and specifically describes registry key SACLs.

4. **Correct Answer: C**

   A. **Incorrect:** *DirectorySecurity.GetAccessRules* returns an instance of *AuthorizationRuleCollection* containing *FileSystemAccessRule* objects.

   B. **Incorrect:** *DirectorySecurity.GetAccessRules* returns an instance of *AuthorizationRuleCollection* containing *FileSystemAccessRule* objects.

   C. **Correct:** *DirectorySecurity.GetAccessRules* returns an instance of *AuthorizationRuleCollection* containing *FileSystemAccessRule* objects.

   D. **Incorrect:** Although you could iterate through an instance of *AuthorizationRuleCollection* using *AuthorizationRule* objects, you would not have access to important elements of file system ACLs. Instead, you should use *FileSystemAccessRule*, which derives from *AuthorizationRule*.

Lesson 3

1. **Correct Answers: B, C, E, and F**

   A. **Incorrect:** The *RSACryptoServiceProvider* class provides asymmetric encryption, which requires the encryptor and decryptor to have related, but different, keys.

   B. **Correct:** The *RijndaelManaged* class provides symmetric encryption, which requires the encryptor and decryptor to have the same key.

   C. **Correct:** The *TripleDES* class provides symmetric encryption, which requires the encryptor and decryptor to have the same key.

   D. **Incorrect:** The *DSACryptoServiceProvider* class provides asymmetric digital signing, which requires the encryptor and decryptor to have related, but different, keys.

   E. **Correct:** The *DES* class provides symmetric encryption, which requires the encryptor and decryptor to have the same key.

   F. **Correct:** The *RC2* class provides symmetric encryption, which requires the encryptor and decryptor to have the same key.

2. **Correct Answers: A, C, and D**

   A. **Correct:** *SymmetricAlgorithm.Key* must be the same on both the encryptor and decryptor.

   B. **Incorrect:** Symmetric encryption algorithms do not use a salt. Salts are used when creating keys from passwords using the *Rfc2898DeriveBytes* class.

   C. **Correct:** *SymmetricAlgorithm.IV* must be the same on both the encryptor and decryptor.

   D. **Correct:** *SymmetricAlgorithm.Mode* must be the same on both the encryptor and decryptor.

3. **Correct Answer: C**

   A. **Incorrect:** When transferring data across a network, you need to export only the public key. Because you can create new keys for future network sessions, there is no need to save the private key.

   B. **Incorrect:** If you are decrypting a file encrypted by a remote computer, you should provide the remote computer your public key. You do not need to export your private key.

    C. **Correct:** If you need to decrypt a file at a later time, you must export the private key.

    D. **Incorrect:** If you are sending a file to a remote computer, you should encrypt it with the remote computer's private key. You do not need to generate or export encryption keys at all.

4. **Correct Answers: B and D**

    A. **Incorrect:** *RIPEMD160* is a nonkeyed hashing algorithm.

    B. **Correct:** *HMACSHA1* is a keyed hashing algorithm.

    C. **Incorrect:** *SHA512* is a nonkeyed hashing algorithm.

    D. **Correct:** *MACTripleDES* is a keyed hashing algorithm.

    E. **Incorrect:** *MD5* is a nonkeyed hashing algorithm.

Chapter 12: Case Scenario Answers

Case Scenario 1: Creating Custom Authentication Methods

1. Use *GenericIdentity* and *GenericPrincipal* because the simple relationship between users and groups used by the accounting application does not require you to create custom classes based on *IIdentity* and *IPrincipal*.

2. Use declarative RBS demands to restrict access to *AddBill*. So long as a user is authenticated and is a member of the Temps, Accountants, or Managers group, the user can use that method.

3. Use declarative RBS demands to restrict access to authenticated members of the Accountants or Managers group. Within the method, use the *GenericPrincipal .IsInRole* method to verify that the user is a member of the Managers role if the value of the bill being paid is $1,500 or higher.

Case Scenario 2: Protecting Data by Using Cryptography

1. Both symmetric and asymmetric encryption can meet the requirements, but symmetric encryption is the best choice because it minimizes administrative overhead. You can use symmetric key encryption because the data will be transferred between relatively stable computers in remote offices and because configuring each with a secret key would be easy. Alternatively, you can use asymmetric encryption, configure a key pair at the centralized database, and distribute the public key to each of the remote offices. The application then could use

asymmetric encryption to establish session keys to enable symmetric key encryption during the data transfers.

2. At the very least, you should store hashes of the password. A keyed hashing algorithm would be more secure than a nonkeyed algorithm. Your primary deterrence must be preventing attackers from gaining access to the password database, however.

3. You should use digital signatures. Store a key pair at the central office, and distribute the public key to each of the remote offices. Sign all bonus communications with the private key and then verify the signature at the remote offices.

Chapter 13: Lesson Review Answers

Lesson 1

1. **Correct Answers: B and C**

    A. **Incorrect:** The *Marshal* class provides many useful methods related to interoperability. However, it is not required to call a function in a COM object.

    B. **Correct:** To call a function in a COM object, you need to create a prototype method with matching parameters.

    C. **Correct:** *DllImportAttribute* specifies the DLL containing the COM function. You should add the attribute to the prototype method.

    D. **Incorrect:** *Marshal.Copy* copies data between a managed array and an unmanaged memory pointer. However, it is not required for this scenario.

2. **Correct Answer: A**

    A. **Correct:** Use the *DllImport* attribute to specify the name of the DLL. Add the *EntryPoint* property to specify the name of the function that you want to call. *EntryPoint* is required only if you want to call the function using a name other than its standard name.

    B. **Incorrect:** The *EntryPoint* property must be used to specify the name of the function that you are calling in the COM object. Specify the name of the method that you want to call when you declare the method.

    C. **Incorrect:** The *BestFitMapping* property is used to control how marshaling converts between Unicode and ANSI. It does not specify the name of the function that you are calling.

D. **Incorrect:** The *EntryPoint* property must be used to specify the name of the function that you are calling in the COM object. Specify the name of the method that you want to call when you declare the method. In addition, the *BestFitMapping* property is used to control how marshaling converts between Unicode and ANSI. It does not specify the name of the function that you are calling.

Lesson 2

1. **Correct Answers: B and D**

   A. **Incorrect:** You should avoid making classes abstract if they will be accessed from COM applications.

   B. **Correct:** All properties, fields, and methods must be public for the class to function correctly when accessed from a COM application.

   C. **Incorrect:** You should avoid using static methods.

   D. **Correct:** Classes exported to COM require a default constructor.

2. **Correct Answers: B and C**

   A. **Incorrect:** *ClassInterfaceAttribute* controls whether Tlbexp.exe automatically generates a class interface.

   B. **Correct:** *InAttribute* indicates that data should be marshaled in to the caller.

   C. **Incorrect:** *OutAttribute* indicates that the data in a field or parameter must be marshaled from a called object back to its caller. When combined with *InAttribute*, this allows the caller to retrieve changes made by the method.

   D. **Incorrect:** *AutomationProxyAttribute* specifies whether the type should be marshaled using the Automation marshaler or a custom proxy and stub.

3. **Correct Answer: A**

   A. **Correct:** Tlbimp.exe imports COM objects into an assembly.

   B. **Incorrect:** Tlbexp.exe exports assemblies into type libraries so they can be accessed from a COM object.

   C. **Incorrect:** Regasm.exe registers assemblies so they can be accessed from a COM object.

   D. **Incorrect:** Regedit.exe is a graphical tool for editing the registry.

Chapter 13: Case Scenario Answers

Case Scenario 1: Creating a .NET Framework User Interface with COM Libraries

1. It's very easy, and there are several different ways to do it. The simplest is to add a reference to the COM library to your project and then add the namespace to your code file. You can also use the *DllImport* attribute to create method prototypes for any COM functions you need to call. Alternatively, you could use TlbImp.exe to create an assembly from the library.

2. You can specify the layout of a structure by using the *StructLayout* and *FieldOffset* attributes. While this isn't always required, it sometimes might be, depending on whether the COM functions expect the structure in the same format that marshaling will use by default.

3. Yes, you can create a wrapper class that allows you to call a managed class which, in turn, passes all calls to the underlying unmanaged type.

Case Scenario 2: Creating a .NET Library that can be Accessed from COM

1. Create the .NET Framework library and replace all existing methods. Then export and register the library using Regasm.exe.

2. You can still throw exceptions. However, you should set the *HResult* property, which the Win32 interface uses to identify errors.

3. You can use *MarshalAsAttribute* to specify the format used for strings when they are passed back to the unmanaged caller.

Chapter 14: Lesson Review Answers

Lesson 1

1. **Correct Answer: B**

   A. **Incorrect:** *MethodBase* is the base class for *MethodInfo* and *ConstructorInfo*. While it does have an *Invoke* method, it's better to use *MethodInfo* directly.

   B. **Correct:** The *MethodInfo* class represents a dynamic method. Call *MethodInfo.Invoke* to run a method.

C.   **Incorrect:** *MethodBuilder* is used to create a method dynamically. You would use *MethodBuilder* if you were writing code dynamically. If you want to run an existing method, create an instance of *MethodInfo*.

D.   **Incorrect:** *ConstructorInfo* is used to represent a class constructor, not a method.

2.   **Correct Answer: D**

A.   **Incorrect:** *Type.GetConstructor* returns a *ConstructorInfo* object, not a *MethodInfo* object.

B.   **Incorrect:** *Type.GetConstructor* requires a *Type* array, while *ConstructorInfo.Invoke* requires an *Object* array.

C.   **Incorrect:** You must create an instance of *DateTime* before calling *DateTime.ToShortDateString*. This code sample attempts to call the method as if it were static.

D.   **Correct:** First, you must create an instance of the *DateTime* object, which requires you to create an instance of *ConstructorInfo* and then call the *ConstructorInfo.Invoke* method. Next, to call *DateTime.ToShortDateString*, you must create an instance of *MethodInfo* representing the method and then call *MethodInfo.Invoke*.

3.   **Correct Answer: A**

A.   **Correct:** The *ReflectionOnlyLoadFrom* method allows you to examine an assembly without running code.

B.   **Incorrect:** The *LoadFrom* method would allow you to run the code. You should call *ReflectionOnlyLoadFrom* instead.

C.   **Incorrect:** The *LoadFile* method would allow you to run the code. You should call *ReflectionOnlyLoadFrom* instead.

D.   **Incorrect:** You would use the *ReflectionOnlyLoadFrom* method if you needed to specify the full path to the assembly. Use *ReflectionOnlyLoad* to load an assembly from the GAC.

Chapter 14: Case Scenario Answers

Case Scenario 1: Supporting Add-ons

1. You can allow users to specify external assemblies that implement specific functionality. Then you can load these assemblies dynamically.

2. You can create an interface for each of the different types of plug-ins and have developers implement the interface.

3. Because you are loading the compiled assembly, it doesn't matter in which programming language users develop.

4. You can read that information from the assembly's attributes.

Case Scenario 2: Code-writing Code

1. Yes, you can use the .NET Framework to generate IL dynamically.

2. Create instances of *AssemblyBuilder*, *ModuleBuilder*, *TypeBuilder*, *ConstructorBuilder*, and *MethodBuilder*. Then call the *GetILGenerator* method to generate the code dynamically.

3. No. *GetILGenerator*, and the instance of *ILGenerator* that it creates, require you to generate IL code. IL is significantly more difficult to write than C# or VB.

Chapter 15: Lesson Review Answers

Lesson 1

1. Correct Answers: A and B

   A. **Correct:** You can attach a file from the local file system by specifying the filename.

   B. **Correct:** You can attach a file using a *Stream* object, which allows a great deal of flexibility for the source of the attachment.

   C. **Incorrect:** You cannot attach a file directly from a Web site. You need to download and save the file first.

   D. **Incorrect:** The .NET Framework does not provide support for receiving incoming e-mail messages.

2. **Correct Answers: A and C**

    A. **Correct:** To send an HTML message, you should set *MailMessage.Body* to HTML content.

    B. **Incorrect:** There is no *MailMessage.Head* property. Instead, you should include any headers in the body of the message (though e-mail clients typically do not process the header).

    C. **Correct:** To send an HTML message, you must set *MailMessage.IsBodyHtml* to *true*.

    D. **Incorrect:** *MailMessage.Subject* should always be plain text, not HTML.

3. **Correct Answer: A**

    A. **Correct:** To reference a linked resource as an image, use <*img src="cid:ContentID"*>

    B. **Incorrect:** You should not provide the image's filename.

    C. **Incorrect:** You must preface the content ID with*cid:*

    D. **Incorrect:** You should not provide the image's filename.

4. **Correct Answer: C**

    A. **Incorrect:** Use *LinkedResource* for embedded images.

    B. **Incorrect:** Use *Attachment* to attach files to a message.

    C. **Correct:** You can provide multiple versions of an e-mail message by using *AlternateView*. The e-mail client then can display the appropriate version.

    D. **Incorrect:** Use *SmtpClient* to send e-mail messages.

Lesson 2

1. **Correct Answer: B**

    A. **Incorrect:** The *MailMessage* class does not have a *Send* method.

    B. **Correct:** To send a message, create an instance of *SmtpClient* and call the *Send* method.

    C. **Incorrect:** There is no *SmtpServer* class.

    D. **Incorrect:** There is no *MailClient* class.

2. **Correct Answers: C and D**

    A. **Incorrect:** The keyword *self* is not special. The runtime would attempt to resolve the name as a DNS address.

    B. **Incorrect:** 10.1.1.1 is a private IP address, but it does not describe the local computer. The runtime would attempt to deliver the message to a computer at that IP address.

    C. **Correct:** The keyword *localhost* is special; it always describes the local computer.

    D. **Correct:** The IP address 127.0.0.1 is special; it always describes the local computer.

3. **Correct Answer: A**

    A. **Correct:** The runtime throws *SmtpFailedReceipientException* if the SMTP server rejects an e-mail address.

    B. **Incorrect:** *SmtpFailedReceipientsException* is used internally by the runtime. Your application will never catch an exception of this type.

    C. **Incorrect:** The runtime throws *SmtpException* for problems related to contacting the SMTP server.

    D. **Incorrect:** There is no *SmtpClientException* class.

4. **Correct Answer: D**

    A. **Incorrect:** You do not need to specify credentials to use SSL.

    B. **Incorrect:** You do not need to change the delivery method. The default value of *SmtpDeliveryMethod.Network* is correct.

    C. **Incorrect:** You do not need to change the port. SMTP uses the same port for both encrypted and nonencrypted communications (TCP 25).

    D. **Correct:** The only property you need to set is *EnableSsl*. It should be set to *true*.

Chapter 15: Case Scenario Answers

Case Scenario: Add E-mail Capabilities to an Existing Application

1. You can use the *System.Net.MailMessage* and *System.Net.SmtpClient* classes to send the e-mails.

2. The .NET Framework doesn't include classes to process incoming e-mail, and it would be very time-consuming to create those classes. Instead, you could set the From address to an e-mail address that someone in Sales manages so that person can correct any errors manually. Alternatively, you could set up an ASP.NET Web site and include a link to that Web site to allow customers to manage their own contact information.

3. You can enable SSL when sending the messages to the SMTP server. However, as the chief security officer mentioned, this does not protect the messages after the server receives them.

Chapter 16: Lesson Review Answers

Lesson 1

1. **Correct Answer: B**

   A. **Incorrect:** You cannot update a *CultureInfo* instance directly. Instead, create an instance of *CultureInfoRegionBuilderInfo* and then register it. After registering it, you can create a new *CultureInfo* for your custom culture.

   B. **Correct:** You can create an instance of *CultureAndRegionBuilderInfo* and then copy settings from the *zh-CN* culture. After making the changes you need, you can call *CultureAndRegionBuilderInfo.Register* to add the culture.

   C. **Incorrect:** You cannot update a *RegionInfo* instance directly. Instead, create an instance of *CultureInfoRegionBuilderInfo* and then register it. After registering it, you can create a new *RegionInfo* for your custom region.

   D. **Incorrect:** The *CompareInfo* class provides methods for culture-sensitive string comparisons. You cannot use it to create a custom culture.

2. **Correct Answer: B**

   A. **Incorrect:** Specifying *true* for the third parameter performs a case-insensitive comparison. However, that is not equivalent to a culture-insensitive comparison.

   B. **Correct:** To perform a culture-insensitive comparison, either change the current culture to *CultureInfo.InvariantCulture* or specify *StringComparison .InvariantCulture*.

   C. **Incorrect:** Specifying *StringComparison.CurrentCulture* would respect the current culture's comparison guidelines.

    D. **Incorrect:** *NeutralCultures* specifies a language without formatting and comparison guidelines. However, the *CultureTypes* enumeration is not a valid parameter for the *String.Compare* method.

3. **Correct Answer: C**

    A. **Incorrect:** The *DateTimeFormat* class can be used only to format *DateTime* objects, not number objects.

    B. **Incorrect:** The *CurrentUICulture* object reflects only the user's current language. It does not define regional settings such as number formatting.

    C. **Correct:** You should create a new *CultureInfo* object by specifying the *es-ES* culture and then use that new *CultureInfo* object when displaying the number as a string.

    D. **Incorrect:** You cannot use an instance of *RegionInfo* to format a number.

Chapter 16: Case Scenario Answers

Case Scenario: Supporting a New Culture

1. You can use the *System.Globalization.CultureAndRegionInfoBuilder* class to build a new culture based on an existing one. Then copy the settings from existing *CultureInfo* and *RegionInfo* objects. Finally, make any changes required for the new culture (such as changing the number grouping and decimal separators).

2. Use the *NumberFormat.NumberDecimalSeparator* and *NumberFormatNumberGroupSeparator* properties.

3. Administrative privileges are required to register a culture. To work around that, register the culture during the application's setup routine.

Glossary

Access control list (ACL)   A term most commonly used to refer to a discretionary access control list (DACL), which is an authorization restriction mechanism that identifies the users and groups that are assigned or denied access permissions on an object.

Advanced Encryption Standard (AES)   A synonym for Rijndael, which is a symmetric encryption algorithm that uses key sizes of 128 through 256 bits.

Application domain   A logical container that allows multiple assemblies to run within a single process, while preventing them from directly accessing another assembly's memory.

Assembly cache   A central location that contains shared assemblies that can be referenced by other assemblies.

Assembly evidence   Evidence that an assembly presents that describes the assembly's identity, such as the hash, the publisher, or the strong name.

Assembly version binding policy   A rule that allows you to specify a new version of the assembly when an application requests a different version.

Asymmetric encryption   A cryptography technique that uses separate private and public keys to encrypt and decrypt data. Also known as public-key encryption.

Authentication   The process of identifying a user.

Authorization   The process of verifying that a user is allowed to access a requested resource.

BinaryFormatter   Located in the *System.Runtime.Serialization.Formatters.Binary* namespace, this formatter is the most efficient way to serialize objects that will be read only by .NET Framework–based applications.

Bitmap   Located in the *System.Drawing* namespace, this class provides methods for loading and saving images, and editing individual pixels.

Boxing   Converting from a value type to a reference type, which often occurs implicitly.

Brush   Located in the *System.Drawing* namespace, classes derived from the *Brush* class are required for drawing text and filling in shapes.

CAS (code access security)   A security system that enables administrators and developers to authorize applications, similar to the way they have always been able to authorize users.

Cast   A conversion from one type to another.

Cipher text   Encrypted text generated by an encryption algorithm that cannot be converted to plain text without a secret key.

Codebase   A rule that allows you to specify the location of an assembly for a particular version. Codebases are particularly useful if the computer does not already have the version of the assembly needed to run the application.

Code group   Authorization device that associates assemblies with permission sets.

Code page   A list of selected character codes (with characters represented as code points) in a certain order. Code pages are usually defined to support specific languages or groups of languages that share common writing systems. Windows code pages contain 256 code points and are zero-based.

Collection   Any class that allows for gathering items into lists and for iterating through those items.

Component Object Model (COM)   An unmanaged object-oriented programming model.

Constraint   A condition on a type parameter that restricts the type argument you can supply for it. A constraint can require that the type argument implement a particular interface, be or inherit from a particular class, have an accessible parameterless constructor, or be a reference type or a value type. You can combine these constraints, but you can specify at most one class.

Contract   *See* interface.

Culture   A definition of how data is displayed to users in different regions.

Data Encryption Standard (DES)   A symmetric encryption algorithm that uses relatively short key lengths that are vulnerable to cracking attacks.

Declarative RBS demands   Access restrictions that are declared as an attribute to a method and that instruct the runtime to perform an access check before running the method.

Defense-in-depth   The security principle of providing multiple levels of protection so that your system is still protected in the event of a vulnerability.

Deflate An industry standard for compressing data that is efficient, commonly used, and patent-free.

Deserialization The process of converting a previously serialized sequence of bytes into an object.

Digital signature A value that can be appended to electronic data to prove that it was created by someone who possesses a specific private key.

Discretionary access control list (DACL) An authorization restriction mechanism that identifies the users and groups that are assigned or denied access permissions on an object.

Encryption key A value that can be used to encrypt and decrypt data. When used with symmetric encryption, this is also known as a shared secret.

Evidence The way an assembly is identified, such as the location where the assembly is stored, a hash of the assembly's code, or the assembly's signature.

Exception Unexpected events that interrupt normal execution of an assembly.

Extensible Markup Language (XML) A standardized, text-based document format for storing application-readable information.

Filtering exceptions The process of ordering Catch clauses so that specific exception types are caught before general exception types.

Fully trusted An assembly that is exempt from code access security (CAS) permission checks.

Garbage collection Recovery of memory in the heap through removal of dereferenced items.

Generic A class that can be strongly typed for a variety of different classes.

Generic type A single programming element that adapts to perform the same functionality for a variety of data types.

Globalization The process of creating an application that supports localized user interfaces.

Graphics Located in the *System.Drawing* namespace, this class provides methods for drawing lines, shapes, and text.

Gzip An industry standard extension to the deflate compression algorithm that allows for a header to carry additional information.

Hash   A value that summarizes a larger piece of data and can be used to verify that the data has not been modified since the hash was generated.

Heap   Area of memory where reference types are stored.

Host evidence   Evidence that an assembly's host presents describing the assembly's origin, such as the application directory, URL, or site.

Imperative RBS demands   Access restrictions that are declared within your code and can be used to restrict access to portions of code on a very granular basis.

Inherited permission   Permissions that propagate to an object from its parent object.

Initialization vector (IV)   Data that symmetric encryption algorithms use to further obscure the first block of data being encrypted, which makes unauthorized decrypting more difficult.

Interface   Defines a common set of members that all classes that implement the interface must provide.

Intermediate language (IL)   The language to which managed applications are compiled. The Common Language Runtime (CLR) is a virtual machine that executes IL code.

Isolated storage   A protected place in the file system to store data without requiring high-level rights to an application and that is scoped by user, assembly, or application.

Keyed hash algorithms   Algorithms that protect against modification of the hash by encrypting it by using a secret key that both the sender and receiver must have.

Localization   The process of translating an application into different languages.

LocalService   A service account that runs with very limited privileges.

LocalSystem   A service account that runs with almost unlimited privileges.

Marshaling   The process of formatting parameters for use by COM.

MD5 **class**   The Message Digest hashing algorithm. The hash size for the *MD5* algorithm is 128 bits.

Multipurpose Internet Mail Extensions (MIME)   A standard that enables binary data to be published and read on the Internet. The header of a file with binary data contains the MIME type of the data. This informs client programs (such as Web browsers and e-mail clients) that they cannot process the data as straight text.

Multithreaded   An application that uses multiple threads.

Narrowing   Converting a value from one type to another when the destination type can't accommodate all possible values from the source type. These conversions must be explicit in C# and in Visual Basic if Option Strict is on.

NetworkService   A service account that is capable of authenticating to remote computers.

Nullable type   A value type that can be set to *Nothing/null*.

Partially trusted code   An assembly that must undergo code access security (CAS) permission checks each time it accesses a protected resource.

Pen   Located in the *System.Drawing* namespace, this class is used to specify the color and width of drawings.

Permission   A code access security (CAS) access control entry (ACL).

Permission set   A CAS ACL consisting of multiple permissions.

Public Key Infrastructure (PKI)   A PKI is an infrastructure for distributing, managing, and revoking certificates in an organization.

RC2 **class**   A symmetric encryption standard designed to replace Data Encryption Standard (DES) that uses variable key sizes.

Reflection   The ability to open, run, and even generate assemblies and the types contained within assemblies dynamically.

Regular expression   A set of characters that can be compared to a string to determine whether the string meets specified format requirements so that it can be used to extract portions of the text or to replace text.

Remoting   A call to a method in a separate assembly, possibly located on another computer.

Role-based security (RBS)   Authenticating users and then authorizing them based on the permissions assigned to their user accounts and group memberships.

Secure Sockets Layer (SSL)   A standard that uses public-key encryption to protect network communications.

Security access control list (SACL)   A usage event logging mechanism that determines how file or folder access is audited.

Security policy   A logical grouping of code groups, permission sets, and custom policy assemblies.

Serialization   The process of serializing and deserializing objects so that they can be stored or transferred and then later re-created.

Service   A process that runs in the background, without a user interface, in its own user session.

SHA1 class   The Secure Hash Algorithm 1. The hash size for the SHA1 algorithm is 160 bits.

Shared secret   A symmetric encryption key.

Signature   The return type, parameter count, and parameter types of a member.

Simple Mail Transfer Protocol (SMTP)   The standard clients use to transmit e-mail messages to mail servers and mail servers use to transmit messages between themselves.

SoapFormatter   Located in the *System.Runtime.Serialization.Formatters.Soap* namespace, this XML-based formatter is the most reliable way to serialize objects that will be transmitted across a network or read by non–.NET Framework applications. *SoapFormatter* is more likely to successfully traverse firewalls than *BinaryFormatter*.

Stack   An area of memory where value types are stored.

Structure   A user-defined value type made up of other types.

Symmetric encryption   A cryptography technique that uses a single secret key to encrypt and decrypt data. Also known as secret-key encryption.

Thread   A thread is a unit of execution within a process.

Thread-safe   Able to be called by multiple threads without risk of conflict.

Triple DES   A symmetric encryption standard that uses 156-bit keys. Essentially, Triple DES repeats the (Data Encryption Standard) DES algorithm three times.

Type library   A container for COM classes. Type libraries can be stand-alone .tlb files that only define types, or they can be embedded in a .dll, .exe, .ocx, or .olb Type library.

Unboxing   Converting back from a reference type to a value type after boxing has occurred.

Unicode   A massive code page with tens of thousands of characters that support most languages and scripts, including Latin, Greek, Cyrillic, Hebrew, Arabic, Chinese, and Japanese (and many other scripts).

Widening   Converting a value from one type to another when the destination type can accommodate all possible values from the source type. These conversions can be implicit.

Windows event log   A central repository for information about operating system and application activities and errors.

WMI Query Language (WQL)   A subset of Structured Query Language (SQL) with extensions to support Windows Management Instrumentation (WMI) event notification and other WMI-specific features.

Index

Symbols and Numbers

For C# Developers

Microsoft® Visual C#® 2008 Express Edition: Build a Program Now!

Patrice Pelland

ISBN 9780735625426

Build your own Web browser or other cool application—no programming experience required! Featuring learn-by-doing projects and plenty of examples, this full-color guide is your quick start to creating your first applications for Windows®. DVD includes Express Edition software plus code samples.

Learn Programming Now! Microsoft XNA® Game Studio 2.0

Rob Miles

ISBN 9780735625228

Now you can create your own games for Xbox 360® and Windows—as you learn the underlying skills and concepts for computer programming. Dive right into your first project, adding new tools and tricks to your arsenal as you go. Master the fundamentals of XNA Game Studio and Visual C#—no experience required!

Windows via C/C++, Fifth Edition

Jeffrey Richter, Christophe Nasarre

ISBN 9780735624245

Jeffrey Richter's classic guide to C++ programming—now fully revised for Windows XP, Windows Vista®, and Windows Server® 2008. Learn to develop more-robust applications with unmanaged C++ code—and apply advanced techniques—with comprehensive guidance and code samples from the experts.

Microsoft Visual C# 2008 Step by Step

John Sharp

ISBN 9780735624306

Teach yourself Visual C# 2008—one step at a time. Ideal for developers with fundamental programming skills, this practical tutorial delivers hands-on guidance for creating C# components and Windows–based applications. CD features practice exercises, code samples, and a fully searchable eBook.

Programming Microsoft Visual C# 2008: The Language

Donis Marshall

ISBN 9780735625402

Get the in-depth reference, best practices, and code you need to master the core language capabilities in Visual C# 2008. Fully updated for Microsoft .NET Framework 3.5, including a detailed exploration of LINQ, this book examines language features in detail—and across the product life cycle.

CLR via C#, Second Edition

Jeffrey Richter

ISBN 9780735621633

Dig deep and master the intricacies of the common language runtime (CLR) and the .NET Framework. Written by programming expert Jeffrey Richter, this guide is ideal for developers building any kind of application—ASP.NET, Windows Forms, Microsoft SQL Server®, Web services, console apps—and features extensive C# code samples.

ALSO SEE

Microsoft Visual C# 2005 Step by Step
ISBN 9780735621299

Programming Microsoft Visual C# 2005: The Language
ISBN 9780735621817

Debugging Microsoft .NET 2.0 Applications
ISBN 9780735622029

System Requirements

It is possible to perform all of the practices in this training kit if you decide to use a virtual machine instead of standard computer hardware.

Hardware Requirements

The following hardware is required to complete the practice exercises:

- A computer with a 1.6 GHz or faster processor (2.2 GHz recommended)
- 512 megabytes (MB) of RAM or more (1 GB recommended)
- 2 gigabytes (GB) of available hard disk space
- A DVD-ROM drive
- 1,024 x 768 or higher resolution display with 256 or higher colors (1280 x 1024 recommended)
- A keyboard and Microsoft mouse, or compatible pointing device

Software Requirements

The following software is required to complete the practice exercises:

- One of the following operating systems, using either a 32-bit or 64-bit architecture:
  - Windows XP
  - Windows Server 2003
  - Windows Vista
- Visual Studio 2008 (A 90-day evaluation edition of Visual Studio 2008 Professional Edition is included on DVD with this book.)

What do you think of this book?

We want to hear from you!

Your feedback will help us continually improve our books and learning resources for you. To participate in a brief online survey, please visit:

microsoft.com/learning/booksurvey

...and enter this book's ISBN-10 or ISBN-13 number (appears above barcode on back cover). As a thank-you to survey participants in the U.S. and Canada, each month we'll randomly select five respondents to win one of five $100 gift certificates from a leading online merchant. At the conclusion of the survey, you can enter the drawing by providing your e-mail address, which will be used for prize notification only.*

Thank you in advance for your input!

Where to find the ISBN on back cover

ISBN-13: 000-0-0000-0000-0
ISBN-10: 0-0000-0000-0

9 0 0 0 0

0 000000 000000

Example only. Each book has unique ISBN.

Microsoft® Press

* No purchase necessary. Void where prohibited. Open only to residents of the 50 United States (includes District of Columbia) and Canada (void in Quebec). For official rules and entry dates see: **microsoft.com/learning/booksurvey**

Stay in touch!

To subscribe to the *Microsoft Press® Book Connection Newsletter*—for news on upcoming books, events, and special offers—please visit:

microsoft.com/learning/books/newsletter

Save 15%
on your Microsoft® Certification exam fee

Present this discount voucher to any participating test center worldwide, or use the discount code to register online or via telephone at participating Microsoft Certified Exam Delivery Providers. See microsoft.com/mcp/exams for locations.

Microsoft®

Microsoft® | Learning

Good for 15% off one exam fee in the Microsoft Certified Professional Program
Offer expires 12/31/2013

Your voucher discount code

exam voucher

Redeemable at Microsoft Certified Exam Delivery Providers worldwide. For locations, visit: www.microsoft.com/mcp/exams

Promotion Terms and Conditions

- Offer good for 15% off one exam fee in the Microsoft Certified Professional Program.
- Voucher code can be redeemed online or at Microsoft Certified Exam Delivery Providers worldwide.
- Exam purchased using this voucher code must be taken on or before December 31, 2013.
- Inform your Microsoft Certified Exam Delivery Provider that you want to use the voucher discount code at the time you register for the exam.

Voucher Terms and Conditions

- Expired vouchers will not be replaced.
- Each voucher code may only be used for one exam and must be presented at time of registration.
- This voucher may not be combined with other vouchers or discounts.
- This voucher is nontransferable and is void if altered or revised in any way.
- This voucher may not be sold or redeemed for cash, credit, or refund.

Part No. X15-02750

Microsoft®